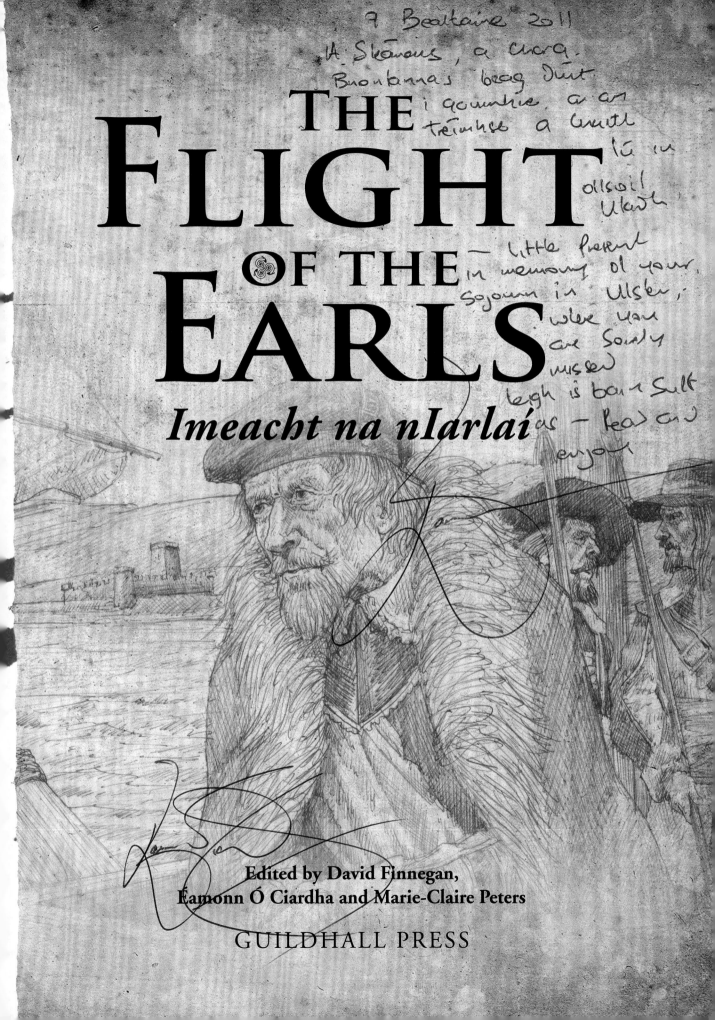

THE
FLIGHT
OF THE
EARLS

Imeacht na nIarlaí

**Edited by David Finnegan,
Éamonn Ó Ciardha and Marie-Claire Peters**

GUILDHALL PRESS

*7 Bealtaine 2011
A Shéamais, a chara.
Bronntanas beag duit
i gcuimhne a an
tréimhse a chaith
tú in
Ollscoil
Uladh
— little present
in memory of your
sojourn in Ulster,
where you
are sorely
missed
léigh is bain sult
as — read and
enjoy*

Do Bhreandán Bradshaw agus i ndilchuimhne
ar Bhreandán Ó Buachalla.

Dr Brendan Bradshaw
© Bridgid Fitzgerald and
History Ireland

Breandán Ó Buachalla
© Keough-Naughton
Institute for Irish Studies

Editors' Notes:
The editors have endeavoured to trace the copyright holders of all illustrations used in this publication. If we have unwittingly infringed copyright, we will be pleased, on being satisfied as to the owner's title, to pay an appropriate fee.

Ireland and Britain used the old (Julian) calendar until 1752 which put their date ten days behind continental Europe in the seventeenth century.

Published in December 2010 by
Guildhall Press
Ráth Mór Centre
Bligh's Lane
Derry BT48 0LZ
Ireland
T: (00 44 28) 7136 4413
info@ghpress.com www.ghpress.com

Copyright © the various contributors
Front cover/back cover: Seoirse Ó Dochartaigh

ISBN 978 1 906271 32 9

A CIP record for this book is available from the British Library.
The authors assert their moral rights in this work in accordance with the Copyright, Designs and Patents Act 1998.

ABBREVIATIONS

AFM   *Annála Ríoghachta Éireann: Annals of the kingdom of Ireland by the Four Masters from the earliest times to the year 1616,* (ed. and trans.) J. O'Donovan (7 vols, Dublin, 1851-56)

AGS   Archivo General de Simancas

AHN   Archivo Histórico Nacional

ARÉ   *Annála Ríoghachta Éireann* (see *AFM*)

BL   British Library, London

Bodl.   Bodleian Library, Oxford

CSPI   *Calendar of State Papers, Ireland*, (eds) H. C. Hamilton *et al* (24 vols, London, 1860-1912)

Cal. Carew MSS *Calendar of the Carew Manuscripts preserved in the archiepiscopal library at Lambeth, 1515-1624*, (eds) J. S. Brewer and W. Bullen (6 vols, London, 1867-73)

HMC   Historical Manuscripts Commission
                 Collections cited:
                 Downshire (1940)
                 Franciscan (1906)
                 Hastings (1947)
                 Salisbury (1872-1918)

IHS   *Irish Historical Studies*

NHI   *New History of Ireland*

NLI   National Library of Ireland, Dublin

NUI   National University of Ireland

RPCS   *Register of the Privy Council of Scotland* (Edinburgh, 1877-)

SPI   State Papers Irish (in TNA)

TNA   *The National Archives, London*

Turas   *Turas na dTaoíseach nUltach as Éirinn: from Ráth Maoláin to Rome: Tadhg Ó Cianáin's contemporary narrative of the journey into exile of the Ulster chieftains and their followers, 1607-08 (the so-called 'Flight of the Earls'),* (ed.) N. Ó Muraíle, incorporating work by P. Walsh and T. Ó Fiaich (Rome, 2007)

Mayor's Note

As Mayor of County Donegal it gives me great pleasure to welcome this publication, which portrays a key and integral part of our history. During 2007, Donegal County Council commemorated this event, working in close association with groups and individuals throughout Donegal and further afield. We were delighted to have the opportunity to work with Letterkenny Institute of Technology and the University of Ulster in relation to the International Conference held in the county in August of 2007. This publication, a major output from that conference, will be a key resource in furthering awareness and understanding of this important time in early modern Irish history.

Cuirim fáilte mhór roimh an fhoilseachán seo agus tá mé ag súil go mbainfear úsáid as go ceann i bhfad.

Cllr. Cora Harvey
Méara Chontae
Dhún na nGall

COMHAIRLE CHONTAE
Dhún na nGall
DONEGAL COUNTY COUNCIL

Brollach

The year 2007 marked the 400th anniversary of the flight of the earls, a landmark event in the histories of Donegal, Ireland and indeed Europe. During the course of that year people in all parts of Donegal and further afield became involved in a wide range of commemorative events and projects to mark the quatercentenary. A decision was taken by Donegal County Council and Donegal County Development Board to lead out on and to co-operate with various stakeholders in related projects, publications, exhibitions, drama, creative writing, public art, music, art, seminars and community festivals. Local authorities, community groups, special interest groups, schools and individuals took part across Donegal, in Northern Ireland and further afield. An example of this co-operation was the international conference which took place in Letterkenny in August of 2007 of which this publication is the major output. This conference was organised by Donegal County Council, Letterkenny Institute of Technology and the University of Ulster working in partnership.

Financial support for the 2007 programme of commemorative events was provided by Donegal County Council, the Department of Art, Sports & Tourism, the Department of An Taoiseach, the International Fund for Ireland, Fáilte Ireland and the European Union (Interreg IIIA).

The commemoration raised awareness and provided an understanding of this important time in our history which has had such an impact on the place in which we live in today. It also enabled Donegal to reach out to people with a connection to or interest in the county, wherever they may be living. It is said that this event marked the start of the Irish Diaspora. The flight of the earls will continue to be a theme which will be used to reach out to our Diaspora over the coming years.

Ba bhliain fíor-thábhactach í 1607 agus rinneadh iarracht mhór é a chomóradh ar an chaoi a b'fhearr a d'fhéadfaí i rith na bliana 2007. Bhí réimse leathan d'imeachtaí agus tionscnaimh a reachtáil i gCo. Dhún na nGall agus áiteanna eile in Éirinn agus thar lear i rith an ama. Bhí réimse leathan de pháirtnéirí i gceist agus d'éirigh leis an chomóradh daoine a chuir ar an eolas agus a theacht ar thuiscint maidir leis an tréimhse chinniúna seo inár stair. Tá an leabhar seo atá ag éirí as an Chomhdháil Idirnáisiúnta a reachtáileadh i Leitir Ceanainn i mí Lúnasa 2007 mar shampla den chineál obair a cuireadh i gcrích.

Michael Heaney/Micheál Ó hÉanaigh
Director of Community, Culture & Enterprise
Donegal County Council

FOREWORD

On 17-19 August 2007, a major international conference was held at Letterkenny Institute of Technology in County Donegal to mark the 400th anniversary of a pivotal event in Irish history – 'The flight of the earls'. It was fitting that the conference was jointly organised by Letterkenny Institute of Technology and the University of Ulster, a precursor of the North-West Gateway Strategic Alliance which is designed to enhance cross-border cooperation in higher education. It was also fitting that two higher education organisations from the north-west of Ireland came together to commemorate a historic event which has such a regional resonance.

For 'The Four Masters', the quartet of Franciscan friars writing their annals between 1632 and 1636 in Donegal Abbey, this flight was an unparalleled disaster and the following passage translated from the original Gaelic was once well known to Irish school children: 'Woe to the heart that meditated, woe to the mind that conceived, woe to the council that decided on, the project of their setting out on this voyage, without knowing whether they should ever return to their native principalities or patrimonies to the end of the world … it is indeed certain that the sea had not supported, and the winds had not wafted from Ireland, in modern times, a party of one ship who would have been more illustrious or noble, in point of genealogy, or more renowned for deeds, valour, prowess, or high achievements than they.'

The conference, attended by over 300 historians and academics, reassessed the political, cultural and religious history of the flight. There were three broad strands – the effects on Ireland, Britain and mainland Europe with Prof John McGurk setting the tone at the outset in questioning the very title by which the event has become known and suggesting another interpretation – 'Strategic Regrouping'.

A highlight was the launch by Prof John Morrill (Cambridge University) of the special commemorative volume of *History Ireland*, the Irish history magazine, which was commissioned and edited by Dr Billy Kelly and Dr Éamonn Ó Ciardha, to mark the flight's anniversary.

Conference delegates also had the opportunity to see a variety of exhibitions and online resources from the Community, Culture and Enterprise Division of Donegal County Council, Derry City Council archives, Donegal Historical Society, The Ó Fiaich Library and Rathmullan Historical Society.

The conference received generous support from Donegal County Council; Donegal Development Board; the Department of Arts, Sport and Tourism; Fáilte Ireland; and the School of Business, Letterkenny Institute of Technology.

It is difficult to overstate the importance of what happened in Rathmullan on 4 September 1607. Dr Ó Ciardha sums it up: 'It marked the effective collapse of an independent Gaelic Ulster and Ireland's full incorporation into the new tripartite Stuart monarchy. Furthermore, it precipitated the emergence of a military, religious and intellectual diaspora on continental Europe which made an enormous contribution to the martial, academic, political and diplomatic life of seventeenth-century Ireland, Britain and Europe.'

It is hoped that this volume will do full justice to these themes and reflect the importance of an event whose legacy still endures.

Mr Dermot Cavanagh
Letterkenny Institute of Technology

lyit

Institiúid Teicneolaíochta
Leitir Ceanainn
**Letterkenny Institute
of Technology**

BROLLACH

Gabhsad go Ráith Mealtain, an lá ag soilsiughadh orra an tan sin. Éirghid go Ráith Maoláin, áit i mbuí an long adubhramar ar angcairibh. Fuaradar Rudhraighe Ó Domhnaill, Iarla Thíre Chonaill, gus na daoinibh uaisle réamhráidhte maille re mórán d'oireacht agus do lucht leanamhna an iarla ag cur bhidh agus dighe isteach 'san luing. Tiaghaid isteach ar bord luinge timcheall mheadhóin lae dia hAoine do shonnradh. Tógbhaid a seólta annsin.

Mar sin a thug Tadhg Ó Cianáin cuntas ar an lá ciniúnach ar chruinnigh taoisigh na nUltach ar bhruach Loch Súilí, thug cúl ar Éireann agus aghaidh ar an mhór-roinn. Tháinig den imirce sin gur fágadh Cúige Uladh gan fir chinn riain; buille marfach a bhí ansin do sheanréimeas Ghael Éireann agus, as a dheireadh, thiocfadh athrach iomlán saoil: réim nua pholaitiúil, córas úr dlíthe agus ord nua béascnaíochta agus saíochta.

Ceithre céad bliain cothrom ina dhiaidh sin, tháinig Éigse Cholm Cille i gcionn a chéile ar bhruach na Feabhaile, ar Ollscoil Uladh i nDoire, chun oidhreacht liteartha na himeachta sin a spíonadh agus a chíoradh. De bhrí de, ar imirce do na hIarlaí, ní raibh siad gan chabhair lucht an léinn. Ar bord na loinge bhí Eoghan Rua Mac an Bhaird, file, maraon lena phríomhéarlamh Nuala, deirfiúr Iarla Thír Chonaill. Bhí Tadhg Ó Cianain ann a raibh a shinsir, le cian d'aimsir, ina lucht éigse ag Mag Uidir Fear Manach. Fir léinn, lena chois sin, a thug dídeán dóibh i bhFlondrais: Flaithrí Ó Maoil Chonaire a bhunaigh Coláiste San Antoine i Lobháin an bhliain roimhe sin; Aodh Mac Aingil, file, a bhí seal ina oide múinte ag clann mhac Iarla Thír Eoghain agus a insealbhaíodh ina léachtóir le diagacht i Lobháin an bhliain chéanna sin; agus Giolla Bríde Ó hEodhasa, file, fear gramadaí agus diagaire.

Léargas comhleanúnach, de réir a dtuisceana féin, a thug na léachtóirí dúinn ar shnáithe áimhréiteacha na tréimhse sin: Brian Lacey ar an dóigh ar tháinig na taoisigh i dtír ar a sinsearacht Ultach; Nollaig Ó Muraíle ar chúlra agus ar chúinsí Uí Chianáin; Breandán Ó Buachalla ar mhanadh na bhfilí léannta; Micheál Mac Craith ar litríocht chráifeach na Lobháine, agus Diarmaid Ó Doibhlin ar fhás na litríochta i lorg na himeachta. Fuarthas, mar thoradh, tuilleadh feasa ar mheon lucht an léinn agus ar chuid de na smaointe nua a bhí ag faibhriú ina n-intinn: coinsiasacht úr náisiúntachta a bheadh bunaithe ar chomhréiteach idir Gael agus Sean-Ghall faoin mhanadh nua *Éireannach*; stair na hÉireann a thiomsú leis an áit a ba dual di a thabhairt di i measc na náisiún Eorpach; bunfhorais an Fhrithreifirméisin a léiriú in ábhar dhiagachta a dhéanfadh náisiún na hÉireann a dhaingniú san chreideamh Chaitliceach; agus, as a chéile, tuiscint don *realpolitik* nach bhféadfaí gan comhréiteach intleachtúil a dhéanamh le rítheaghlach na Stiúbhartach mar rithe ar na trí ríochta.

Is mór an pléisiúr dom, thar cheann na hOllscoile agus thar cheann Éigse Cholm Cille, mo bhuíochas a ghabháil leis na cainteoirí a roinn a smaointe linn, agus leis an lucht éisteachta a choinnigh comhluadar linn. Ba mhaith liom buíochas a thabhairt do choiste na hÉigse agus do Fhoras na Gaeilge, a thug deontas fial airgid dúinn. Agus lena chois sin, an meall is mó ar deireadh, is mian liom buíochas ó chroí a thabhairt don Dr Éamonn Ó Ciardha a thug stiúradh eolach don Chomhdháil agus a chuir an leabhar álainn seo le chéile.

An tOllamh Ailbhe Ó Corráin
Ollscoil Uladh, Doire

FOREWORD

The flight of the earls is one of the great watershed events in the history of these islands. Those who drove the earls into flight, and the hopes and aspirations of the earls as they embarked at Rathmullan in September 1607, both envisaged a transformed future Irish and British socio-economic, political, confessional and cultural life. The flight proved to be a tipping point in both its intended and in its unintended consequences. It deserves (and in this book finally receives) a vivid and comprehensive scholarly discussion that is multi-disciplinary and indeed one written in the languages of both the Gaedhil and of the Gaill.

It is fitting that the volume should be dedicated to Brendan Bradshaw, an uncompromising exponent of Irish History in its British context and a powerful advocate of persistent and inter-disciplinary interrogation of Irish-language sources. I had the privilege of teaching with Brendan, generations of students (including a future English cricket captain!) the final-year option on 'The British Problem c. 1534-1707' at a key moment in my own career. We learnt much from one another and our co-teachers, Jim Smyth and David L. Smith, not least how it is possible both to seek to understand the past in its own terms and evaluate how that past informs our present. As the founding father of Cambridge's Irish Studies seminar, Brendan ensured that this period of Irish History also received special attention as indeed a tipping point (or was it that most elusive of historical phenomena, a turning point) merits.

John Morrill FBA
Professor of British and Irish History
University of Cambridge

Anyone who has engaged with Brendan Bradshaw's work will be aware that he has been gifted as an historian with three salient qualities rare enough in themselves and rarer still in combination.

The first is his extraordinary power of imagination. Whether he is dealing with the mind of English administrators as they sought to feel their way through the sober drifts and politic ways of Henrician policy toward Ireland, or the struggle of Gaelic Irish lords to come to terms with the world changing before them, or the zealous convictions of reforming monks, or the agonised efforts of Erasmian reformers who sought to preserve what was best in the world they sought to improve, Bradshaw's has invested the meagre and fragmentary sources with which he must deal with entirely unexpected depth and vitality.

Allied to this is Bradshaw's second gift without which imagination would be of little value. This is his extraordinary intellectual courage. From the beginning of his career as an historian Bradshaw has challenged old orthodoxies, championed unfashionable causes, and above all asked the (sometimes simple) questions which his colleagues have been unable (sometimes unwilling to pose). And as a consequence he has suffered the unpleasant consequences of one who strays beyond the pack.

He has borne the professional brickbats with admirable equanimity and calm. For his intellectual audacity is underpinned by no vanity or arrogance; but by his third and most natural gift. Those of us who have had the pleasure of knowing Brendan personally will be aware of his extraordinary generosity in all his dealings. But what may be less obvious is that this personal quality is just a facet of his essential empathy with humanity in all its forms – the quick and the dead, the good and the bad – and above all the merely mediocre. It is the sum of all these gifts – for which he himself will claim no credit – that has made him such a marvellous figure to know. He is now, and will long be remembered as, the most inspiring historian of his generation.

Professor Ciaran Brady
Trinity College Dublin

BROLLACH

Ní bréag a rá go dtagann stair nua-aimseartha na hÉireann amach as an 17ú haois. Is cuma nó fonóta formhór dar tharla don tír san 19ú agus san 20ú haois leis an gcorraíl mhór arbh í 'Imeacht na nIarlaí' a tús. Ar feadh i bhfad dob fhéidir staraithe a rangú go polaiticiúil de réir an tseasaimh a ghlac siad ar scéalta móra na haimsire caite, agus is áirithe gur féidir staraithe a rangú go polaiticiúil i gcónaí. Na téarmaí a ghlac tráchtairí na haoise sin chucu féin maidir le 'sibhialú' agus le 'nua-aoisiú' ní mór ná gurb iad sin féin na téarmaí céanna a ghlac an t-aos staire chucu féin chomh maith céanna. Ba dhóigh leat san allagar sin, ar uairibh, gurb ionann an dá aois, gurb ionann inné agus inniu.

Tá de dhifríocht ann, gan amhras, gurb eolaisí ar fad sinn anois ná na daoine a bhí thuas le linn na n-eachtraí seo a bheith ar siúl. Ní fheiceann an aimsir láithreach ach an chuid is caoile den aimsir láithreach a bhíonn ina haice. Tá de bhua ag an staraí gur féidir leis seasamh siar agus an t-ábhar a mheá leis an bhfianaise ar fad atá tagaithe chun solais. Agus is é is iontaí ná go bhfuil raidhse fianaise tagaithe chugainn maidir leis an tréimhse seo atá faoi chaibidil seachas mar a bhí scór bliain féin ar ais féin. Is toradh é an leabhar seo ar an gcuid is fearr de 'athscríobh na staire'. Is ann don athscríobh sin ar chúiseanna polaiticiúla go rómhinic, agus is gátarach an t-athscríobh de réir na fianaise i gcónaí.

Cuid mhór de luach an tsaothair seo go ngabhann sé lasmuigh de na foinsí a rabhthas i dtaobh leo go dtí seo. Foinsí stáit ba ea a bhformhór sin, foinsí stáit a dhein neamhaird de na foinsí Gaeilge agus Eorpacha araon. Den chéad uair, nach mór, faighimid cuntas níos fairsinge agus níos uileghabhálaí, agus dá réir sin, níos cruinne, ar na himeachtaí sin a dhealbhaigh is a mhúnlaigh ní hea amháin dioscúrsa na staire, ach an stair féin, le ceithre chéad bliain anuas. Mar fhreagra na ceiste 'Cáit ar ghabhadar Gaoidhil?' is é an freagra gonta ná nár imíodar áit ar bith. Is anseo atáid fós agus iad ag machnamh agus ag maranadh. Ní hé go bhfuil freagra gach ceiste i lúib an leabhair seo laistigh, ach is tuisceanaí agus is gaoismhire go mór sinn na mar a bhíomar riamh roimhe seo.

D'athraigh Breandán Ó Buachalla an tuiscint a bhí againn ar stair na hÉireann. Ní beag an méid sin a rá i dtaobh scoláire ar bith. D'athraigh sé go háirithe an tuiscint a bhí againn ar an náisiún Gaelach sa tseachtú agus san ochtú haois déag. Níorbh aon athrú beag é sin, ach athrú mór ó bhonn. D'fhocal gearra, b'í tuiscint a bhí forleathan i measc an aosa staire ná gur tháinig deireadh le réim na nGael Éireannach le Cath Chionn tSáile i dtús na bliana 1602. Níor thuiscint í sin a bhí bunaithe ar na foinsí a shíolraigh ón náisiún Gaelach féin. Léirigh agus chruthaigh Breandán Ó Buachalla thar amhras anonn go raibh dóchas riamh ag cine Gael go mbeadh an lá leo, ar a laghad chomh fada ar aghaidh le lár an ochtú céad déag. Níor theactaireachtaí baotha a bhí san aisling fhileata, ach réaladh fírinneach ar a gcuid dóchaistí féin. Níorbh fhoirm filíochta amháin a bhí san aisling ach ráiteas tairngreachta a raibh gearradh na fírinne inti, go fiú is gur dóchas gan dealramh as ríthe lofa a bhí ann i ndeireadh thiar thall.

Fág go raibh toisí éagsúla ag baint lena shaothar, mar theangeolaí, mar staraí, mar fhear gramadaí agus mar eagarthóir, fós féin is féidir a áiteamh go raibh aontacht áirithe ag baint leis. B'í aontacht í sin ná guth a thabhairt don tuiscint a bhí ag na Gaeil orthu féin, bíodh sin ceart nó cearr. Ghairm sé chuige filíocht agus léann na Gaeilge chun é sin a dhéanamh. Bíodh gurb é a thaighdigh, a scag is a scríobh a mhórshaothar *Aisling Ghéar* is é pobal na Gaeilge, is é sin le rá, pobal na hÉireann atá ag caint ann. Chuaigh sé síos i measc na ndaoine agus i measc an aosa léinn agus thóg sé aníos a raibh ina meon agus ina gcroí istigh. Ionann sin is gur chuaigh sé faoin gcraiceann agus chuardaigh sé an tsamhlaíocht dhúchais ar chuma níos cuimsithí ná mar a dhein aon duine roimhe, agus ar deacair a shamhlú go ndéanfaidh duine ar bith eile ina dhiaidh é go ceann i bhfad.

Ní bréag a rá gurb é coinsias agus fear cosanta an náisiúin Ghaelaigh é mar a tuigeadh an téarma sin idir dhá chéad agus trí chéad bliain ó shin. Is é oighear diachrach an scéil é ná gurbh 'athscríbhneoir' siar amach é san aighneas buile a bhíodh ann idir 'réiviseanóirí' agus a mhalairt ar ais. Ach 'athscríbhneoir' ar shlí eile ar fad ba ea é, seachas mar a shamhlaítear an téarma sin de ghnáth. D'athscríobh sé na hathscríbhneoirí a chuaigh roimhe, mar cad eile a dhéanfadh duine a raghadh go bun na dúide siar maidir le foinsí agus le cáipéisí bunaidh de? B'í an Ghaeilge féin an bhunfhoinse a bhí aige, agus níorbh uirlis í a bhféadfaí 'leas' a bhaint aisti anois is arís d'fhonn beagán risíní a chur sa chíste d'fhonn leathanaigeantachta a léiriú.

Thug sé ár ndúshlán go léir, dúshlán arb ionann é agus a fhógairt go gcaithfeadh gach duine eile a raghadh i ngleic leis an ábhar stairiúil seo a bheith ar a laghad chomh hoilte leis féin.

An tOllamh Alan Titley
Ollamh na Nua-Ghaeilge, Corcaigh

Tá an chomaoin a bhfuil scoláirí staire agus litríochta, agus pobail an oileánra seo i gcoitinne, faoi ag scoláirí ar nós Brendan Bradshaw agus Breandán Ó Buachalla le haithint ar chlár cuimsitheach na Féilscríbhinne seo ina n-onóir. Is fada an t-achar ó fhreagra Daniel Corkery ar Lecky go dtí géarchúis na nidirdhealuithe ar cheist na féiniúlachta ag scoláirí an lae inniu. Más í Cecile O'Rahilly a chéadmhúscail suim na staraithe i dtábhacht na bhfoinsí dúchasacha, baineann Bradshaw leis an nglúin sin a rinne an bheart. Cur chuige oibiachtúil, tomhaiste, uileghabhálach a spreag glúin óg eile scoláirí, idir scoláirí staire agus scoláirí Gaeilge, faoi mar is léir ó chlár na soláthraithe anseo istigh.

Brendan Bradshaw agus a chomhghleacaithe a bhain áit amach do staireografaíocht na hÉireann i lár an aonaigh; a rinne cíoradh agus slámadh ar thréimhse chasta na dTúdarach agus na Stíobhartach; agus a léirigh na ceangail chasta idir Gael, Gall, is Sean-Ghall i dtimpeallachtaí uirbeacha Chorcaí, Luimnigh agus na Gaillimhe. Samplaí ionadaíocha ar an athléamh seo is ea *Representing Ireland* (Bradshaw, Hadfield agus Maley, 1993); *The British Problem, c. 1534-1707, State Formation in the Atlantic Archipelago* (Bradshaw agus Morrill, 1996); agus *British Consciousness and Identity* (Bradshaw agus Roberts, 1998).

Chuir Bradshaw agus a chomhscoláirí bús faoi dhisciplín na staire agus na litríochta Gaeilge. D'fhágadar ar ár gcumas an scéal a insint ina cheart, ina bheacht agus ina fhírinne, faoi mar atá ag Breandán Ó Buachalla ina shárshaothar critice *Aisling Ghéar* (1996). Bheadh an Cairdinéal Newman sásta leis an bhfuadar idirdhisiplíneach seo go léir. Ní hí fírinne na litríochta fírinne na staire, ach ar scáth a chéile a mhaireann siad, agus is i bpáirt le chéile is fearr iad, faoi mar a déarfadh Seathrún Céitinn, idir Ghaeil agus Shean-Ghaill.

Cailleadh Breandán Ó Buachalla go tobann ó shin, faraoir. Ba é buachaill bán an léinn ag scata againn é, a d'adhain an tine bheo agus a shéid lasair an athuair i mbarrach na héigse. Scoláire pointeáilte, múinteoir prionsapálta, ceannródaí corráistiúil, ceannasaí spreagúil, téisclímí gortghlantach, fionnachtaí friochnamhach, a chuaigh ar an doimhin nuair a d'fhan scata eile le cladach. B'é Breandán an *navagatio* é a scaoil faoin nduibheagán ó aimsir *I mBéal Feirste Cois Cuain* (1968); ag cur seoda na hoidhreachta in uachtar in Oiri-alla; ag seoladh slán ar choire guairneáin Uí Chorcora; ag tabhairt cluas bhodhar do lucht an olagóin, gur nocht iomas forosna Mháire Bhuí Ní Laoire; gan an *Backward Look* a bhac ach a aghaidh ar an ród roimhe amach, *Nua-Dhuanaire* ina ghlac; nó gur sheol go Tír Tairngire sinn is gur nocht áille na háille ina *Aisling Ghéar,* dlaoi mhullaigh agus curadh mhír na scoláireachta Gaeilge ó aimsir an Chéitinnigh, a aithnítear mar mhíosúr agus mar thomhas na hacadúlachta Gaeilge ó shin i leith.

'Folamh anocht Éire dá éagmais'; 'anocht scaoilid na sgola'. Chuaigh le flosc na laoch don gcill. Dó is dlite maíomh Hóráis: *exegi monumentum aere perennius*. Dó féin agus ní do Ching Séamus is córa an gaisce a leanas a thagairt: 'Is é a rinne na heilimintí difriúla a tháthú le chéile go háititheach éifeachtach in aon teoiric chomhlántach amháin agus, níos tábhachtaí fós, an táthú a dhaingniú le gné den teoiric nár cuireadh an-bhéim uirthi roimhe sin.' Ní beag san. Go maire aisling ghéar (chúiseach) an Bhuachallaigh slán mar lón intinne agus anamúlachta dúinn. *Tolle lege.*

An Dr Tadhg Ó Dúshláine
Ollscoil na hÉireann, Má Nuad

Acknowledgements / Buíochas

Tá mo bhuíochas tuillte ag cuid mhór daoine a chabhraigh liom agus an leabhar seo idir lámha agam. I dtús, tháinig David Finnegan agus Marie-Claire Peters i mbun comhoibrithe liom mar eagarthóirí agus is fearr an leabhar dá bharr. Ó tháinig mé go hOllscoil Uladh is é a chuir muid romhainn (Billy Kelly, John Wilson agus mé féin) mór-eachtraí staire an Cúige is na Tíre (Plandáil Hamilton-Montgomery, Imeacht na nIarlaí, Éirí Amach Chathair Uí Dhochartaigh is Plandáil Uladh) a chomóradh san áit inar tharla siad. Is é atá san imleabhar seo ná cuid d'ábhar na gcomhdhálaí sin agus tá mé faoi chomaoin acu seo as a gcuidiú is a gcomhairle. Níorbh ann don leabhar seo, dár ndóigh, ach ab é go raibh ár scríbhneóirí sásta a gcuid altanna a thabhairt dúinn. Tá mé an-bhuíoch fosta de Choiste Éigse Cholm Cille a cheap mé i mo reachtaire ar Éigse 2007. Phléigh muid 'Imeacht na nIarlaí: An Oidhreacht Liteartha' mar théama na hÉigse. Bhí siad sásta ligint dom na torthaí á fhoilsiú sa chnuasach seo is tá ábhar an leabhair níos leithne agus níos iomláine dá bharr. Chan amháin sin, ach chuir An Coiste airgead ar fáil fá choinne pictiúir agus íomhánna, scríobh Máire Nic Cathmhaoil agus Malachy Ó Néill (baill den Choiste) ailt, chum Ailbhe Ó Corráin (Cathaoirleach na hÉigse) brollach agus chuidigh Peadar Mac Gabhann (Cisteoir na hÉigse) go mór leis an eagarthóireacht Ghaeilge nuair a bhí an leabhar faoi chamán. Shíl an Coiste go dtiocfadh na hIarlaí ar ais sula bhfeicfí an cnuasach seo i gcló, tá súil agam gur mór an taitneamh a bhainfidh siad as an tsaothar seo.

Tá mé faoi chomaoin ag Institúid Teicneolaíochta, Leitir Ceannain, ag Comhairle Chathair Dhoire, ag Comhairle Chontae Dhún na nGall, ag Oifig an Taoisigh agus ag Ollscoil Uladh a chuir airgead agus áiseanna ar fáil dúinn don trí chomhdháil seo. Gabhaim buíochas fosta le foirne na leabharlanna, na gcartlann is úinéirí na gcnuasach príobhláideach óna bhfuarthas léaráidí, pictiúir is léarscáileanna; Acadamh Ríoga na hÉireann; le Leabharlann na Breataine, le Leabharlann Ollscoil Cambridge, le Caisleán Dùn Bheagain, An t-Eilean Sgitheanach, Hatfield House, Ionad an Léinn Éireannaigh i dTeach na hInse, Institúid Mhíchíl Uí Chléirigh, Coláiste Ollscoile, Bhaile Átha Cliath, Leabharlann Náisiúnta na hÉireann, Leabharlann Choláiste na Trionóide, Cartlann Náisiúnta na Breataine, agus Túr Londain. Bhí an t-ádh orainn fosta go raibh mór-ealaíontóirí agus dealbhóirí na tíre (John Behan, John Conway, Maurice Harron, Seoirse Ó Dochartaigh, Seán Ó Brógáin agus Brian Vallely) toilteanach a gcuid dealbhóireachta agus a gcuid péintéireachta a chur ar fáil dúinn. Ba mhaith liom mo bhuíochas a ghabháil le Tomás Ó Brógáin as na léarscáileanna galánta a sholáthar go mór leis an leabhar.

Ba mhian liom an leabhar seo a bhronnadh ar Bhreandán Bradshaw agus a thíolacadh i gcuimhne ar Bhreandán Ó Buachalla, beirt cheannródaithe a raibh tionchar nach bheag acu orm féin agus ar stair, ar staireolaíocht agus ar litríocht na hÉireann. Theagasc an tOllamh Ó Buachalla Gaeilge agus mé i mo fhó-chéimí i gColáiste Ollscoile Bhaile Átha Cliath agus thug sé cuidiú, comhairle, spreagadh is tacaíocht dom nuair a bhí an tráchtas dochtúireachta ar bun agam. Lena chois sin, bhí sé mar phribhléid agam a bheith mar bhall den fhoireann chéanna teagaisc nuair a d'oibrigh muid le chéile i Notre Dame. Stiúraigh Breandán Bradshaw mé agus mé i mo mhac-léinn dochtúireachta aige. Ba fhial flaithiúil é i gcónaí i mbun a chuid comhairle. Is tráthúil agus is mithid go mbronnfaí leabhar ar Chonchas na dTúdarach, ar thabhacht na bhfoinsí Gaeilge i stair na hÉireann, ar thionchar an Leasú Creidimh agus ar an Fhrith-Reifirméiseain ar Éirinn ar scólairí a shaothraigh go dúthrachtach agus go héifeachtach sa réimse sin thar thréimhse dhá scór bliain.

This book comprises the proceedings of three conferences which took place in 2007-08 to mark the four hundred anniversary of the flight of the earls and the rebellion of Sir Cathair O'Doherty. I would like to thank my co-editors David Finnegan and Marie-Claire Peters for their enormous contribution to the commissioning and editorial process. There is no question that the volume is significantly better and considerably more attractive as a consequence of their joint efforts. I am truly grateful to Derry City Council (particularly Margaret Edwards, Craig McGuicken and Bernadette Walsh of the Museum Service); Donegal County Council (specifically Richard Gibson, Aidan Haughey, Garry Martin, Sally Murphy, Mícheál Ó hÉanaigh and Angela McLaughlin); Éigse Cholmcille (ach go h-áirithe Mary Delargy, Marius Harkin, Peadar Mac Gabhann, Máire Nic Cathmhaoil Aodh Ó Cannáin, Ailbhe Ó Corráin, Malachy Ó Néill and Caoimhín Ó Peatain) Letterkenny Institute of Technology (especially Paul Hannigan and Dermot Kavanagh), The Department of the Taoiseach and the University of Ulster (particularly Billy Kelly, John

Wilson and Ian Thatcher) for their advice, assistance and support (academic, financial, moral and otherwise) in organising these events and supporting the publishing process. I would also like to thank the Universität des Saarlandes, Saarbrücken, Germany, for appointing me Gastprofessor Europaicum for 2010-11, enabling me to visit many of the towns and villages through which the earls passed en route to Rome. A word of thanks is also due to Don MacRaild and James McConnel, my former colleagues in the old School of History and International Affairs of the University of Ulster. Councillor Gerard Diver (former Mayor of Derry), Professor James Allen, Provost of the Magee Campus, University of Ulster, and Mr Paul Hannigan, President of Letterkenny Institute of Technology, made the Guildhall (Derry), the Great Hall (Magee) and LYIT's excellent state-of-the-art facilities available to the speakers and delegates at the three conferences. A particular word of thanks is due to my friend and colleague Billy Kelly who played a key role in co-organising these events. In Dermot Cavanagh, Billy and I had a first-rate collaborator and the success of the Letterkenny/Ulster conference and the resulting academic outputs provide a model for future co-operation between our institutions. It is no exaggeration to say that this book would never have materialised without their support and organisational and fund-raising skills.

The publication itself was made possible by a generous subvention from Donegal County Council and we are particularly grateful to Garry Martin (Senior Executive Officer), Donna McGroarty (Assistant Social Inclusion Coordinator), Micheál Ó hEanaigh (Director of Service, Community, Culture and Planning) and Cáitlín Uí Chochláin (Comhordaitheoir Gaeilge, Rannóg Pobal, Cultúr agus Fiontar) for their energy, enthusiasm and patience, particularly at the final stages of the process. In addition to his hospitality during the conference itself, Mr Paul Hannigan kindly agreed to provide timely financial assistance for this publication while Dermot Cavanagh penned a short brollach on behalf of LYIT. Sincere thanks is also due for timely financial support from An Coiste, Éigse Cholmcille, as well as Professors Ian Thatcher and John Wilson (University of Ulster). It was a singular pleasure to work with Kevin and Paul Hippsley, Joe McAllister and the dedicated staff at Guildhall Press. My co-editors and I are truly grateful to them for their professionalism which has done much to enhance the finished product.

Finally, the volume is dedicated to Dr Brendan I. Bradshaw and to the memory of Professor Breandán Ó Buachalla, whose untimely death has cast a pall over the latter stages of the proceedings. The three editors of this volume have all been inspired in different ways by their paradigm-shifting research and writing in early modern Irish history, historiography and literature. I had the singular honour of knowing Professor Ó Buachalla as a teacher, mentor and colleague. The leading authority on the literature and ideology of early modern Ireland, he authored numerous books and articles on the impact of the Counter-Reformation on Irish political thought, early modern Irish historiography, morphology, linguistics, Gaelic poetry and the cult of the Stuarts in Irish literature. *Aisling Ghéar: na Stíobhartaigh agus an tAos Léinn* (1996), his magnum opus, is without question the most important book published in the broad field of Irish Studies. A cursory perusal of its one hundred page bibliography bears testimony to a staggering range of manuscript, newspaper, printed primary and secondary sources in Irish, Scots-Gaelic, English, French, Spanish, German, Welsh, Italian and Latin. He also contributed numerous other influential books articles, articles and reviews in leading journals (*Zeitschrift fur Celtische Phiologie, Ériu Celtica, Éigse, Studia Hibernica, Eighteenth-Century Ireland*), as well as periodicals such as *Comhar* and *Feasta*. On finishing my MA in 1991, he kindly furnished me with letters of recommendation for Cambridge University. This gave me the opportunity to study history under the expert supervision of Dr Brendan I. Bradshaw, another of the doyens of Irish scholarship. It was both an honour and a pleasure to work under the direction of a scholar of Dr Bradshaw's calibre. It is also most fitting that a book which covers all aspects of the flight of the earls should be dedicated to two scholars whose ground-breaking work on the Reformation and Counter-Reformation, early modern Irish historiography and literary criticism would inspire the editors and many of the contributors to this volume.

My co-editors and I hope that this volume will be worthy of two inspiring scholars and teachers whose interdisciplinary, pan-European approach to early modern Ireland has set the standard for Irish history and literary studies.

An Dr Éamonn Ó Ciardha
Ollscoil Uladh
Lúnasa 2010

Contents

Contents

'The flight of the earls'. © John Behan

INTRODUCTION

'Cáit ar ghabhadar Gaoidhil?' 'Where have the Gaels gone?'

David Finnegan and Éamonn Ó Ciardha

By the end of the sixteenth century, Hugh O'Neill, second earl of Tyrone, had emerged as the greatest single threat to English rule in Ireland. He took advantage of initial royal favour, exploited those elements in Ulster dissatisfied with the advance of government 'reform', and forged strategic political and marital alliances with the O'Donnells, O'Cahans, Maguire, MacMahons and O'Reillys to construct a powerful confederacy which proved a serious threat to English authority in Ireland. After a number of stunning successes against Elizabeth I's forces, an untimely Spanish descent on Kinsale forced O'Neill to march to its aid from his fastnesses in Ulster in the depths of winter. Decisively defeated in a pitched battle by Lord Deputy Mountjoy, he retraced his steps to Dungannon and waited in vain for further Spanish support. Assailed on all sides by land and sea, he held out until favourable terms were offered and concluded the Treaty of Mellifont, six days after the death of the last Tudor monarch.

Elizabeth's Irish wars have received little attention in David Starkey's historical documentaries on the Tudors and did not even merit a mention in the latest Hollywood blockbuster (*Elizabeth: The Golden Age*, in which Cate Blanchett delivered an Oscar-nominated performance as the 'Virgin Queen'). However, the Nine Years War (1594-1603) cost the parsimonious Elizabeth nearly £2 million sterling, eight times more than any previous Elizabethan campaign and as much as was spent on all continental wars waged during her reign. Furthermore, O'Neill gained enormous prestige among European Catholic princes, potentates and the greater Catholic populace. Henry IV of France described O'Neill as the 'third soldier of his age' after himself and the duke of Parma. His numerous victories over Protestant foes were not forgotten by aristocrats and artisans as he later made his way to Rome.

Pardoned and received at court in 1603 by the new king James I, O'Neill and Rory O'Donnell, newly ennobled as the first earl of Tyrconnell, nevertheless felt besieged by a coterie of English officials, servitors and settlers who decried their lenient treatment and coveted their lordships. The political and legal machinations of Lord Deputy Chichester and Attorney General Davies, rumours of the earls' traffic with Spain and an ominous royal summons to London ultimately precipitated the flight. O'Neill, O'Donnell and Cúchonnacht Maguire, lord of Fermanagh, departed Ulster on 4 September 1607 with their wives, families and followers in one of the most iconic and significant events in Irish history.

The historical importance of this exodus is difficult to overstate. In effect, it marked the effective collapse of an independent Gaelic Ulster and prepared the way for its subsequent plantation and full incorporation into the new tripartite Stuart monarchy. The servitors, soldiers and settlers who flooded into Ulster in the earls' wake, continually denounced as usurpers and interlopers in contemporary Gaelic literature, saw themselves less as planters but more as social engineers, harbingers of King James's policy to 'civilise these rude partes'. They would make an indelible mark on the politics, economics and material culture of Ulster and in turn found a multifaceted, transatlantic Diaspora to rival that constructed by their Catholic counterparts.

The flight remains one of the most poignant and intriguing episodes in Irish history,[1] its poignancy sharpened by its confirmation of Irish defeat in the Nine Years War and the re-opening of the great psychic scar inflicted upon Gaelic Ulster in the final stages of that conflict. It confirmed that there would be no reprieve for Gaelic Irish civilisation; in particular, the defeat at Kinsale ensured that the native Irish system in Ulster would undergo profound changes. O'Neill's surrender at Mellifont ensured that, thereafter, the sons of Milesius were to be directly ruled by the English Crown. In spite of his impeccable, fabricated Gaelic credentials, King James VI & I would exercise his sovereign power to transform Gaelic society, as revealed in the essays below by Breandán Ó Buachalla and Alison Cathcart.

Defeat in the Nine Years War exposed Ulster's lordships to external forces of change as evidenced in the essays of David Finnegan, Annaleigh Margey, Áine Ní Dhuibhne, Darren McGettigan and John McGurk. It is important to stress, however, that they were already in the process of modernisation.[2] The

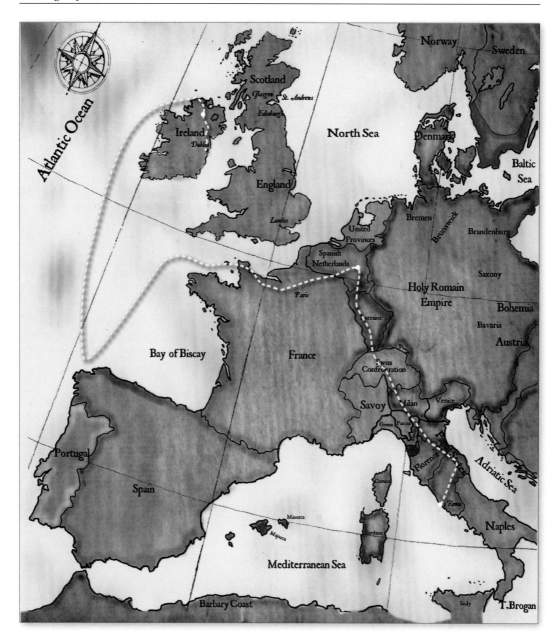

The route to Rome taken by the earls. © Tomás Ó Brógáin after Nollaig Ó Muraíle

earls returned home in late 1603, well aware that although their new king had received them 'into his good opinion and favour', he nevertheless expected them to prepare their earldoms and their people for the introduction of the English common law and local government structures.[3] In short, they had acknowledged that the Irish state would govern Ulster, a prospect guaranteed by the permanent presence of English garrisons within their earldoms.[4]

As with much of Gaelic Ireland's history, the flight has been remembered differently by Ireland's various political and confessional communities. This divergence of interpretation began almost as soon as their ship had weighed anchor. For the English and Scottish reformers who soon sought to erect a model 'British' society upon the ruins of Gaelic Ulster, it proved a providential occurrence. A divine punishment for the unnatural rebellion of the Ulster lords against Elizabeth, it also furnished clear evidence that they had again been plotting to plunge Ireland into rebellion, a point suggested by Valerie McGowan-Doyle's contribution. Breandán

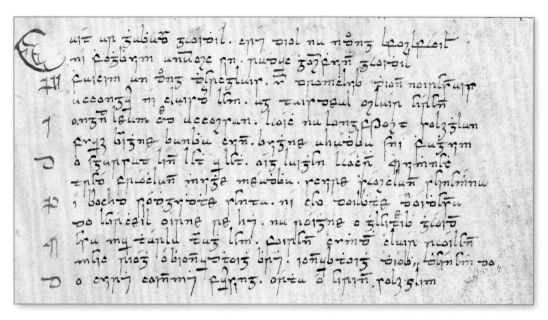

'Cáit ar ghabhadar Gaoidhil?' © Meamram Páipéar Ríomhaire le caoinchead Clonalis House / Teach Cluain Mhalais

Ó Buachalla's essay demonstrates that the earliest Irish commentators also offered a providential interpretation of the earls' departure. Ireland's spiritual and moral transgressions had dire political consequences; although the escape of Ireland's noblest lords from their foes – the enemies of Catholic Ireland – offered the possibility of restitution. Indeed, Ó Buachalla shows that the traditional conservatism often attributed to this mandarin literary caste masks their appreciation of, and reaction to, contemporary events. The doom-laden reaction to the flight, their heartrending laments at Ireland's sorry plight and despair at the continual scattering of her native aristocracy, co-existed with an emerging cult of the House of Stuart.[5]

These contrasting interpretations sustained two communities through the fluctuating fortunes of seventeenth- and eighteenth-century Ireland. At times of external threat or intestine rebellion Ireland's Protestant communities were united by a common fear of Catholic treachery and a fervent belief in their right to occupy land that an 'inferior' people had failed to develop.[6] Ireland's Catholics explained their misfortunes as punishments that must be endured, but they also made this providential model more bearable with the possibility of the 'wheel' taking 'a turn unforeseen'.[7]

The providentialist certainty underpinning these earliest interpretations partially evaporated under the fierce glare of the professionalised history which commenced in Ireland in the 1930s.[8]

Nevertheless, these increasingly sophisticated interpretations and the utilisation of new source material by scholars such as Nicholas Canny, Micheline Kerney Walsh, John McCavitt among others, have failed to produce a consensus on the reasons for the flight. This volume does not claim to provide a full explanation, although many of its contributions offer new perspectives on its causes, course, contexts and its commemorations.

Those seeking to explain the flight can readily draw on a rich, if occasionally problematic, corpus of source material. Unusually for a specific event in early modern Gaelic Ireland, it is well documented in the Irish sources. Tadhg Ó Cianáin's narrative traces the trials and tribulations of 'that noble cargo' from Rathmullan to Rome, and his unique account has been revisited here by Clare Carroll, Mícheál Mac Craith and Nollaig Ó Muraíle. At home, the Gaelic literati infused the episode with a romantic significance that brilliantly captured an awful sense of finality. Its longer-term resonance in the Irish historical consciousness owes much to its evocation of the mournful, tragic and enigmatic nature of Irish history, or more accurately Irish remembrance. It provided perfect material for the romantic nationalists, who, as Vincent Morley argues below, rediscovered the episode in the nineteenth century.[9]

There are other official accounts on the continent, those of ambassadors, agents and papal nuncios. Benjamin Hazard's and Óscar Recio Morales' essays throw further light on the Spanish context.

Queen Elizabeth I (1533-1603). Despite her glorious reputation, the last decade of her reign proved extremely difficult. At war with Spain, facing mounting debt and factionalism in her council, her crown began to slip. She displayed remarkable inflexibility in dealing with O'Neill and obsessed about destroying him before finally giving Mountjoy permission to negotiate terms. She died before his eventual surrender. © NPG

Political wall mural, Falls Road, Belfast. © Bill Rolston

The former's contribution reveals that the straitening financial circumstances of the Spanish state dictated strategic concerns and overrode its obligations to the Irish, while the latter's counterfactual essay shows that the earls had discussed leaving Ulster for Spain at least a year earlier than their actual flight. It also supports the former's argument that Philip III's moral commitment to support his Irish allies would be measured against the Iberian superpower's straitened economic circumstances and new priority of the *monarquía* to preserve the *Pax Hispanica*. These essays also explain why the Spanish king refused to grant the earls refuge in his dominions.

The most abundant sources are those of the Irish and English governments: letters to the king notifying him of the earls' departure, rumours of their plans for a return to Ireland, and the reports of ambassadors, informers and spies who tracked the fugitives throughout their journey. Accounts by key members of the Dublin administration provide a skewed picture of the events of the autumn of 1607, concerned as they were with confiscating their lands and securing their extradition from the continent. These also tended to stress the impropriety of the fugitives' treasonable behaviour, thoroughly undeserving of the succour of any foreign prince.

History is written by the winner, and Gaelic Ireland has been too often viewed through a distorting, Anglo-centric and teleological lens. So strong has been the influence of those writers who denigrated Gaelic Irish society that even those who viewed Irish history from the 'nationalist' perspective in the eighteenth and nineteenth centuries tended to see the end of Gaelic civilisation in romantic terms. While celebrating its atavistic militarism and independent tendencies, they also recognised its impotency against a centralising Renaissance state.[10] Until recently this romanticised version of Gaelic Irish history has exercised a persistent hold on the popular historical imagination.[11]

The Tudor, and later the Cromwellian conquests, as destructive of Ireland's Gaelic civilisation as the Spanish conquests of Mexico and Peru were of the Aztec and Inca civilisations, muffled but did not silence her voice. English Protestant abhorrence of 'papist superstition' and Gaelic 'backwardness' led to the widespread destruction of manuscripts – both Latin and Irish, monastic records, and much of the material inheritance of medieval Christianity in Ireland.[12] However, enough evidence survives

J. D. Reigh's stylized image of the encounter between O'Neill and Seagrave at Clontibret – shades of Richard the Lionheart and Saladin at Acre – hides the fact that O'Neill's life was saved by his subsequently estranged son-in-law Donal Ballagh O'Cahan. © NLI

to redress the imbalance, and Irish historians and literary scholars have painstakingly reconstructed the contours of Gaelic Irish society before its partial 'eclipse' at Kinsale.[13]

Ireland before the Elizabethan conquest was a society of considerable sophistication, well connected to European intellectual currents. It had created the earliest and one of the most original and extensive vernacular traditions in Western Europe. Irish monks and scholars played a key role in preserving Christian culture during the so-called 'Dark Ages', those seemingly apocalyptic times when the four horsemen wrought havoc on post-imperial Europe.[14] Irish missionaries evangelised more than half of England, large tracts of north-eastern France, and a great deal of Germany, Switzerland and northern Italy. They also made a fundamental contribution to the restoration of Latin learning and the creation of medieval European culture and literature, while visiting scholars from all over Europe attended Irish schools.[15] Significantly, Peter Lombard, David Rothe, Luke Wadding and other members of the Old English clerical diaspora forcefully made this point when protesting against the Anglicising efforts of the Irish state.

This durable civilisation survived the shock of the twelfth century Anglo-Norman invasion. Indeed, the cumulative pressures of the Hundred Years War, the Scottish Wars of Independence and the onset of the Black Death precipitated a Gaelic revival which significantly reversed the English conquest after the late thirteenth and early fourteenth centuries. Concurrently a cultural renaissance in Gaelic Ireland saw many Norman lords adopt the Irish language, culture, customs and, in some cases, the brehon law.[16] Ireland's material culture also flourished. Many of the great manuscript collections of Irish literature such as the Books of Uí Mhaine, Ballymote, Lecan, Lismore and the Leabhar Breac belong to this period, as do most important annalistic collections and translations of well-known Latin, French and English works. Legal studies flourished under the auspices of the church schools. Irish monks brought the eighth-century Hibernensis, one of the great European collections of canon law, to mainland Europe, where it had considerable influence.[17] Between the late seventh and twelfth centuries the brehons, Ireland's legal caste, developed a complex and sophisticated legal system which functioned right down to the destruction of the Gaelic military and political order in the early seventeenth century.[18]

Those settlers who sought to preserve English institutions and mores found themselves corralled into an increasingly small enclave centred on Dublin as a relatively integrated society emerged across the rest of the island. It is important to stress this balance, as an over-concentration on the confused politics of the age can only give an impression of near-anarchy and disorder throughout the island. The remains of the many churches, castles, monasteries and tower-houses from this period that still dot the Irish landscape give testimony to greater political stability and also increased prosperity.[19]

By 1500 the annals suggest that bards, brehons, doctors and churchmen (especially the Franciscans) prospered and held a high social position in most lordships outside the Pale. Bardic schools emerged for the study of literature and poetry; legal schools trained brehons and transmitted legal tracts and texts; huge numbers of medical treatises emerged from numerous Irish medical schools; while church schools transcribed and studies Latin, theology and philosophy. Although lacking university status and the reputation of the

Philip II (1527-98), King of Spain, sought to exploit the Ulster rebellion and turn Ireland into an English Netherlands. He concluded a formal pact with the Ulster confederates in June 1596 and subsequently dispatched two further Armadas – also scattered by seasonal storms – against England. On his death-bed, he dictated a letter of congratulation to O'Neill for his victory at the Yellow Ford. © NPG

great early Christian monastic schools, these studia produced scholars of international reputation such as Maurice O'Fihely [*Flos Mundi*] and later still Florence Conry and Hugh MacCaughwell. Alumni from Irish grammar schools, such as Peter Lombard and Luke Wadding, were given a firm grounding in the *studia humanitas* which allowed them to slot easily into European university life.

Such social stability also regulated the use of genealogy as a legitimating mechanism for Ulster's ruling elites, as outlined in the contributions of Brian Lacey and Malachy Ó Néill. Read alongside those of Brendan Kane, David Finnegan and Henry A. Jefferies, they reveal a Gaelic conception of nobility and honour which would prove a critical factor in the events that unfolded in early modern Ireland as the Irish state rubbed against the last bastion of Gaelic political power in Ulster. Áine Ní Dhuibhne's contribution testifies to the regulation of power in Gaelic society through the written and spoken record and the importance of tradition as a bulwark of authority, reinforcing the claims of lords and dynasties to particular

patrimonies, rights and duties. Her essay also describes the traumatic effects upon the natives that the social changes wrought by the influx of British settlers into Ulster in the seventeenth century.

Until recently, the focus on the flight has been very much centred upon the records of the Dublin administration, but the essays in this volume offer far greater analysis of the native Irish, English, Scottish and European contexts. Mary Ann Lyons's examination of the earls' stay in the Duchy of Lorraine reveals their importance in early seventeenth-century geopolitics. It also casts light on the diplomatic relations that lubricated relationships between polities in the period. The fugitives' lukewarm welcome in Flanders suggests archducal surprise at the flight which further erodes Micheline Kerney Walsh's 'tactical withdrawal' thesis. The reception received in Lorraine both underpins geopolitical concerns and dynastic ties (James I and Charles of Lorraine were cousins), thereby showing that religious solidarity often trumped dynastic considerations. Patricia Palmer's essay focuses upon Miguel de Cervantes's *Persiles y Sigismunda*, the story of a party of exiled northerners making a slow and perilous journey to Rome. If not directly influenced by the flight, it nonetheless reveals the continuing emotional hold that exiles had on the popular European imagination. It testifies also to the European reputation that the earls enjoyed, a point endorsed by Morales's essay. Similarly, Kevin De Ornellas's appraisal of *Captain Thomas Stukeley* (London, 1605) shows that the spectral figure of Hugh O'Neill haunted Tudor and Jacobean English drama. Clare Carroll's contribution on the lengthy treatment of the Loreto pilgrimage in Ó Cianáin's flight narrative demonstrates its careful construction and his utilisation of written sources. He aimed to represent the earls as exemplary practitioners of post-Tridentine Catholicism, thereby facilitating their acceptance as religious refugees. It may also have been a tactic to minimise the embarrassment caused by the anxiety of the Spaniards to move the fugitives from their territory. Rome had never, of course, been their original destination. Mícheál Mac Craith's contribution on 'Aspects of Tadhg Ó Cianáin's Rome' underlines this point, as well as wonderfully evoking the culture of contemporary European Catholicism. It also shows that Spanish influence remained strong at the heart of Catholic Europe, along with the genuine belief that the earls had 'lost all for conscience and religion'. His essay, combined with that of Noel O'Regan, reveals that the earls and their entourage were orthodox Catholics who clearly understood the mores of Tridentine observance.

The flight also led to the emergence of the first Irish diaspora, as outlined in Patrick Fitzgerald's and Éamon Ó Ciosáin's contributions. The collapse of the Gaelic political system in the early seventeenth century saw Irishmen dispersed as far afield as the Netherlands, Spain, Italy, Newfoundland, Barbados, Florida and even the Amazon.[20] Irish soldiers, the original 'wild geese', saw service in Sweden, Denmark, Poland and Russia, many of them having been transported by Chichester's government. The flight has assumed a very powerful place in the collective consciousness of a nation with a strong tradition of emigration. Forced or reluctant departures before an unfeeling state apparatus became a major feature of Irish life, often in the wake of political convulsion.

It was in Ireland, however, that the flight's profoundest consequences occurred, and perhaps its best-known and most significant sequel was the plantation of Ulster. This, the most enduring and pervasively colonial of the plantation schemes in the early modern period, was also the most evangelically charged plantation settlement, partly because of the king's provision of vast swathes of land for the Church of Ireland, and partly because of the involvement of Lowland Scottish Protestants. Alison Cathcart's essay on the Scottish context supports the view that although eager to advance reform, James sought to do so with the co-operation of his nobles, regardless of their faith, as long as they accepted his sovereignty. She also provides a detailed examination of what the Britannic context of James's rule over his three kingdoms meant in Ulster. The province lay open to penetration in the early Jacobean period, and Annaleigh Margey's contribution illustrates how the new monarchy used the plantation to promote the Britannicisation of Gaelic Ulster.

Pope Clement VIII (1536-1605) refused to force Catholics to chose between their faith and civil allegiance. His desire to pursue a more pro-French policy to free the Papacy from Habsburg influence meant that he was unwilling to excommunicate those Irish Catholics who did not take up arms with the Ulster rebels. Fabrizio Santafede, 'Pope Clement VIII Blessing Carmelite Nuns'. © Private collection

The contributions of Darren McGettigan, Henry A. Jefferies and Tadhg Ó hAnnracháin focus on the consequences of the flight and the efforts of elements of Ulster society to come to terms with the new realities for those who remained. Ó hAnnracháin's essay presents a succinct summation of the current scholarship on the survival and re-emergence of the Catholic Church in Ireland in Ulster in the first half of the seventeenth century. McGettigan's study of the rapid disintegration of the traditional power structures of Gaelic Ulster in the flight's aftermath reveals the difficulty of the task facing the earl of Tyrconnell in the period before the flight and the importance of strong lordship in holding Gaelic political structures together. Jefferies' analysis of Sir Cathair O'Doherty's rebellion illustrates how the situation in Ulster had been irrevocably altered after the flight. The fear of the earls' return, and the need to secure the province before such an eventuality, meant that even those Gaelic lords who had been prepared to collaborate with the crown were now treated as suspect.

Vincent Morley, Adrian Scahill, John Gibney, Elizabeth FitzPatrick and Antaine Ó Donnaile examine representations of the earls in the Irish historical imagination. Morley's article looks at the earls' excision from popular memory from the late seventeenth century which he attributes to their unsuitability as motifs in a political culture that sought to foreground loyalty to the crown. Their status as 'embarrassing skeletons in the closet of Catholic Ireland' meant that it was only with emergence of Romantic nationalism in the mid-nineteenth century that figures like John Mitchel recovered the earls as fundamental figures in forging a 'historic' Irish nation. This context may also explain Scahill's account of how the earls were remembered in traditional Irish music, a cultural mode that plays a key role in the construction and maintenance of collective cultural memory and an accurate means of reading the gap between popular tradition and the historical record. However, as Scahill admirably demonstrates, this too is laden with meaning. The tragic resonances of the flight became a key resource in the emergence of nineteenth century nationalism and its perpetuation of a 'cult of violent struggle, sectarian demeanour and anglophobia'.

Historians have found it much easier to agree on the flight's consequences than its causes. One of the few points of consensus on the episode is its profound consequences for the history of Ireland. Constantia Maxwell claimed that it created 'an entirely new situation' and that 'all schemes for the pacification of the North under Irish rule collapsed', compelling the government to step into the 'vacuum and erect a new sovereignty', in effect ushering in the Plantation of Ulster.[21] Yet this interpretation is grounded in hindsight. Very few contemporaries regarded the flight as a permanent departure,[22] and the return of the earls and later their descendants remained a possibility until Owen Roe's landing at Doe Castle in 1642.[23]

The decade after the flight saw a decline in the fortunes of the professional learned classes such as poets, scribes, brehons, historians, genealogists and chroniclers. A wholesale destruction of manuscripts and the carelessness of future generations have deprived us of much evidence with which we might tabulate the extent and influence of the *aos dána* [learned classes]. Nevertheless, surviving material vastly outstrips contemporary Scotland or Wales and is invaluable in shedding light on contemporary Irish society. The contributions of Mícheál

Mac Craith, Breandán Ó Buachalla, Diarmaid Ó Doibhlin, Marcas Ó Murchú and Máire Nic Cathmhaoil show that Ireland witnessed a remarkable flowering of poetic, literary and scribal activity in the decades after the flight. The Franciscan Order, operating from the Counter-Reformation power-houses of Louvain, Rome and Salamanca and utilising scions of the traditional learned families such as the Uí Chléirigh, Uí Mhaoil Chonaire and Uí Dhuibhgheannáin, drove this two-pronged effort to stem the tide of the Protestantism and preserve the nation's literary heritage. Throughout the reign of the first two Stuart kings (James VI & I, and Charles I) a stream of confessional and theological works, religious primers and catechisms emanated from these continental colleges, largely directed towards the clergy as opposed to the largely illiterate laity. They reflected the continental training of their authors and drew heavily on contemporary post-Tridentine Counter-Reformation works in Spanish, French, Italian and Latin.

Pivotal to the effort to preserve the nation's literary heritage was the enormous undertaking of the compilation of *Annála Ríoghachta Éireann* [Annals of the Kingdom of Ireland], assembled by the 'Four Masters' with the support of the Franciscans and the patronage of Fearghal Ó Gadhra, a Sligo nobleman. Mícheál Ó Cléirigh, the leading luminary among the quartet, also produced the *Martyrology of Donegal* and a revised version of the *Lebor Gabála* [Book of Invasions], comprising the origin myths of the Gaeil. Seathrún Céitinn [Geoffrey Keating], author of *Foras Feasa ar Éirinn* [Foundation of Knowledge on Ireland], employed his formidable pen against those Anglo-Norman and English writers such as

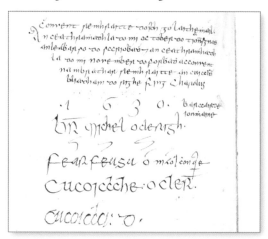

The autograph signatures of the 'Four Masters'.
© Mícheál Ó Cléirigh Institute

Giraldus Cambrensis, Edmund Spenser, Richard Stanihurst, Edmund Campion, Richard Hamner and Fynes Moryson, all of whom he dismissed as 'dall aineolach i dteangaibh na tíre' [blind and ignorant in the language of the country]. This monumental work proved immensely popular, the last 'best-seller' in the European manuscript tradition, the first book of the old testament of Irish Catholic nationalism, and the reference work for Irish poets until the nineteenth century.

The first decades of the seventeenth century also witnessed a proliferation of historical works, hagiographical biographies, diaries and social commentary, including Tadhg Ó Cianáin's *Imeacht na nIarlaí*, Lughaigh Ó Cléirigh's *Beatha Aodha Ruaidh Uí Dhomhnaill* [Life of Red Hugh O'Donnell], an heroic biography of the warriorprince of Tír Chonaill. Later in the century, *Cín Lae Uí Mhealláin* [O'Meallan's Diary] provided an eyewitness account of the Ulster army under General Owen Roe O'Neill, while the satirical *Pairlement Chloinne Tomáis* [Parliament of Clan Thomas], comprised a bitter invective from the learned classes at the effects of the social revolution which occurred in the aftermath the Cromwellian wars. It included a biting satirical eulogy for Cromwell, king of churls, who had established every boor and upstart and castigated the vile progeny of 'Clann Tomáis' who aped the manners, dress and language of the English settlers.

In the realm of poetry a general loosening of the traditional metres occurred during the course of the seventeenth century. Poets such as Seathrún Céitinn, Pádraigín Haicéad, Piaras Feiritéar, Muiris Mac Dáibhidh Dubh Mac Gearailt, Dáibhidh Ó Bruadair and the named and anonymous authors of five long narrative political poems (subsequently edited by Cecile O'Rahilly) continued the traditions of eulogy and satire. These writers invariably commented on the state of Ireland, the unprecedented suffering of the Irish, the wars, massacres, transportations and transplantations, as well as noting the effects on the Irish language, aristocracy and gentry and the Catholic Church.

Latin continued to be taught, studied and readily understood in sixteenth-century Ireland, but the great flowering of Hiberno-Latin learning was fuelled by the Irish Counter-Reformation. The language of politics and government in the middle ages, it remained important in the immediate post-Reformation period as the medium for communication with Catholic Europe. Various com-

'Close Quarters Kinsale', 'Massing for Attack' and 'Retreat from Kinsale'. © Brian Vallely

ments from the English Jesuit Edmund Campion, a survivor of the Spanish Armada and the papal nuncio Giovanni Battista Rinuccini would suggest that knowledge of vulgar Latin may have been widespread.

However accurate these individual testimonies may be, it is evident that there was an Irish tradition in Latin learning which could be traced from northwest Donegal to Vienna and from Naples to

Lisbon in the early modern period. The exiled Irish writer Philip O'Sullivan Beare lists in his *Zoilomastix* (c. 1626) some eighty-six Irish Catholic writers, and the full extent of this literary diaspora awaits the completion of the ongoing researches of Thomas O'Connor. The Jesuit schools and academies that flourished in most major towns in the fifty years after the Reformation fuelled this Latin learning. For example, a grammar school presided over by Peter White, a graduate of Oriel College, Oxford, boasted students of the calibre of Richard Stanihurst and Peter Lombard, the anti-hero of Brian Friel's *Making History* and a pivotal figure, as Ernan McMullin attests, in Galileo's trial.

Galway Academy, founded by Dominic Lynch, included scholars of such learning and renown as the historian, chronicler and genealogist Dubhaltach Mac Fir Bhisigh and John Lynch, archdeacon of Tuam and author of *Cambrensis Eversus* (1662) a firm rebuttal of Giraldus Cambrensis. Lynch also penned a hagiographical portrait of his uncle Bishop Francis Kirwan, as well as a Latin history of the Irish episcopate. Another eminent past pupil of this school was the historian Roderick O'Flaherty, associate of William Molyneux and the renowned Welsh Celticist Edward Lhuyd. O'Flaherty's famous work *Ogygia* (1685) comprised a learned exposition of Irish Catholic loyalty to the House of Stuart and asserted the antiquity of the kingdom of Ireland.

Throughout the course of the sixteenth and seventeenth centuries Archbishop Richard Creagh (Irish Catholic martyr and, as John McGurk shows, a long-time resident of the Tower of London), Richard Stanihurst, Conor O'Devany, Peter Lombard, David Rothe, Richard O'Ferrall, Robert O'Connell, Luke Wadding and the extraordinary literary talent

of the Franciscan friars of St Anthony's College in Louvain added to and enhanced a long and eminent tradition of history, hagiography, theology and genealogy. Similarly, John Colgan, the Inishowen-born friar credited with bringing Ó Cianáin's manuscript to Rome, also penned his *Trías Thaumaturgae* (1647), a tripartite hagiographical account of the lives of St Patrick, St Bridget and St Colum Cille. Canice Mooney did not exaggerate when he claimed that 'without Colgan, Irish history, and our knowledge of Irish history, would have been the poorer'.

Ó Buachalla, Ó Muraíle, Nic Cathmhaoil and Fitzgerald attest to the manner in which the flight has captured the imagination of Irish writers, including the Ó Cléirigh historians and the bardic families of Mac an Bhaird, Ó Dálaigh, Ó Gnímh and Ó hEodhasa. In more recent times, it inspired James Clarence Mangan, Thomas Davis, Sean O'Faolain, Thomas Kilroy and Brian Friel. Irish artists who have also rendered this iconic event in bronze and on canvas include Thomas Ryan, Brian Vallely, John Conway, Seoirse Ó Dochartaigh, Seán Ó Brógáin, John Behan and Maurice Harron whose wonderful paintings and sculptures adorn this volume.

The flight precipitated the emergence of an Irish Catholic military, religious and intellectual diaspora in continental Europe which made enormous contributions to the military, academic, political and diplomatic life of seventeenth-century Ireland, Britain and Europe. It is no exaggeration to say that Ireland's long-lived, far-flung, multifaceted European diaspora, inspired by the monastic and scholarly traditions of Colum Cille, Columbanus and John Scottus Eriugena, enabled a small, peripheral, under-populated island to box far above its weight in early modern European political, military, religious, diplomatic and literary circles.

Notes

1 *CSPI, 1606-08*, pp 270-4, 275-7. Against the lingering belief that the expression 'flight of the earls' was coined by historians, see M. Smith, 'Flight of the Earls? Changing views on O'Neill's departure from Ireland', *History Ireland*, iv: 1 (1996), pp 17-20.

2 N. P. Canny, 'Hugh O'Neill, earl of Tyrone, and the changing face of Gaelic Ulster', *Studia Hibernica*, x (1970), pp 7-35; H. Morgan, 'The end of Gaelic Ulster: a thematic interpretation of events between 1534 and 1610', *IHS*, xxvi (1988), pp 8-32.

3 TNA SPI 63/215/114.

4 C. Falls, *Elizabeth's Irish wars* (London, 1950), pp 79-95.

5 On the eve of the flight Tyrone was described as the Irish Catholic Mardochai; for the implications of this see David Finnegan's essay below.

6 Gerard Boate, *Ireland's naturall history* (London, 1652); Sir John Temple, *The Irish rebellion: or the history of the beginning and first progress of the general rebellion raised within the kingdom of Ireland, upon the three and twentieth day of October, 1641* (London, 1646).

7 J. MacErlean (ed.), *Duanaire Dháibhidh Uí Bhruadair: the poems of David Broderick* (3 vols, London, 1910-17), iii, pp 117-21, 127-41. B. Ó Buachalla, 'James our true king: the ideology of Irish royalism in the seventeenth century', in D. G. Boyce *et al* (eds), *Political thought in Ireland since the*

seventeenth century (London, 1993), pp 28-29.

8 Falls, *Elizabeth's Irish wars*, p. 338.

9 C. P. Meehan, *The fate and fortunes of Hugh O'Neill, earl of Tyrone, and Rory O'Donel, earl of Tyrconnel: their flight from Ireland, their vicissitudes abroad, and their death in exile* (2ⁿᵈ edition, Dublin, 1880); T. M. Healy, *Stolen waters: a page in the conquest of Ulster* (London, 1913), p. 42; Sean O'Faolain, *The Great O'Neill* (Dublin, 1942), pp 272-3.

10 This defeat was for some 'as inevitable as salutary' so Ireland could 'pass from barbarism to civilisation (Standish J. O'Grady, *Red Hugh's captivity* (London, 1889), p. 3); D. Matthews, *The Celtic peoples and Renaissance Europe* (London, 1933); A. L. Rowse, *The expansion of Elizabethan England* (London, 1955; repr., 1973).

11 A. Clarke, 'Alternative allegiances in early modern Ireland', *Journal of Historical Sociology*, v (1992), pp 253-66.

12 S. Meigs, *The Reformation in Ireland* (Basingstoke, 1997), pp 77-89.

13 P. J. Duffy, D. Edwards and L. FitzPatrick (eds), *Gaelic Ireland, c. 1250-c. 1650: land, lordship and settlement* (Dublin, 2001); K. Nicholls, *Gaelic and gaelicised Ireland in the later middle Ages* (Dublin, 1972); idem, 'Anglo-French Ireland and after', *Peritia*, i (1982), pp 370-403; K. Simms, 'The brehons of later medieval Ireland', in D. Hogan and W. N. Osborough (eds), *Brehons, serjeants and attorneys: studies in the history of the Irish legal profession* (Dublin, 1990), pp 51-76; idem, 'Bards and barons: the Anglo-Irish aristocracy and the native culture', in R. Bartlett and A. MacKay (eds), *Medieval frontier societies* (Oxford, 1989), pp 177-97; idem, 'The Norman invasion and the Gaelic recovery', in R. Foster (ed.) *The Oxford illustrated history of Ireland* (Oxford & New York, 1989), pp 53-102; H. Morgan, 'The end of Gaelic Ulster: a thematic interpretation of events between 1534 and 1610', *IHS*, xxvi (1988), pp 8-32.

14 Though this has sometimes been exaggerated: see for example T. Cahill, *How the Irish saved civilization: the untold story of Ireland's heroic role from the fall of Rome to the rise of medieval Europe* (London, 1995). A much more balanced view has been provided in D. Ó Cróinín, *Early medieval Ireland, 400-1200* (London & New York, 1995).

15 'The Irish welcomed them all gladly, gave them their daily food, and also provided them with books to read and with instruction, without asking for any payment', C. Plummer (ed.), *Venerabilis Baedae opera historica* (2 vols, Oxford, 1896; repr., 1969), i, p. 192). See also Dáibhí Ó Cróinín, *Early medieval Ireland*; K. Hughes, *The church in early Irish society* (London, 1966); idem, 'The golden age of early Christian Ireland (7th and 8th centuries)', in T. W. Moody and F. X. Martin (eds), *The course of Irish history* (Cork, 1967), pp 76-90; M. Richter, 'The European dimension of Irish history in the eleventh and twelfth cen-

turies', *Peritia*, iv (1985), pp 328-45; idem, *Medieval Ireland: the enduring tradition* (London & Dublin, 1988). John Ryan, *Irish monasticism: origins and early development* (Dublin, 1931); T. M. Charles-Edwards, *Early Christian Ireland* (Cambridge, 2000).

16 Many renowned Gaelic poets were of Anglo-Irish stock: see Simms, 'Bards and barons'.

17 R. E. Reynolds, 'The transmission of the Hibernensis in Italy: tenth to the twelfth century', *Peritia*, xiv (2000), pp 20-50; D. N. Dumville, 'Ireland, Brittany and England: transmission and use of the Collectio Canonum Hibernensis', in C. Laurent and H. Davis (eds), *Ireland et Bretagne: vingt siècles d'histoire* (Rennes, 1994), pp 84-85.

18 K. Simms, 'The contents of later commentaries on the brehon law tracts', *Ériu*, xlix (1998), pp 23-40; idem, 'The brehons of later medieval Ireland', in N. McLeod (ed. & trans.), *Early Irish contract law* (Sydney, 1994); F. Kelly, *A guide to early Irish law* (Dublin, 1988); D. Ó Corrain, L. Breatnach and A. Breen, 'The laws of the Irish', *Peritia*, iii (1984), pp 382-438; D. A. Binchy, 'The Linguistic and Historical Value of the Irish Law Tracts', *Proceedings of the British Academy*, xxxix (1943), pp 195-227.

19 A native style of architecture emerged (late Irish Gothic) which, while borrowing from England, went back to an earlier period and re-introduced some pure Irish features (stressing again the pervasive influence of native modes at the time), J. F. Lydon, *The lordship of Ireland in the middle ages* (Dublin, 1972), pp 180-1.

20 J. Lorimer (ed.), *English and Irish settlement on the River Amazon, 1550-1646* (London, 1989); A. Gwynn, 'Early Irish emigration to the West Indies (1612-43), *Studies*, xviii (1929), pp 377-93, 648-63; idem, 'An Irish settlement on the Amazon (1612-29)', *Proceedings of the Royal Irish Academy*, xli (1931-32), sect. C, pp 1-54; idem, 'The first Irish priests in the New World', *Studies*, xxi (1932), pp 213-28; idem, 'Documents relating to the Irish in the West Indies', *Analecta Hibernica*, iv (1932), pp 136-286; D. H. Akenson, *If the Irish ran the world: Montserrat, 1630-1730* (Liverpool, 1997).

21 C. E. Maxwell (ed.), *Irish history from contemporary sources (1509-1610)* (London, 1923), pp 44, 51.

22 See, for example, Sir John Davies to Salisbury, 12 Sept. 1607 (TNA SPI 63/222/138).

23 J. Casway, *Owen Roe O'Neill and the struggle for Catholic Ireland* (Philadelphia, PA, 1984); idem, 'Gaelic Maccabeanism: the politics of reconciliation', in J. H. Ohlmeyer (ed.), *Political thought in seventeenth century Ireland: kingdom or colony* (Cambridge, 2000), pp 176-88.

The Flight of the Earls

CAUSES

Opposite: Hugh O'Neill, second
earl of Tyrone (c. 1540-1616).
Lithograph after the Dunsany
portrait. © NLI

Why did the earl of Tyrone join the flight?

David Finnegan

On 4 September 1607, the earls of Tyrone and Tyrconnell – respectively heads of Gaelic Ulster's two greatest dynasties, the O'Neills and the O'Donnells – along with Cúchonnacht Maguire, the lord of Fermanagh, and accompanied by an unknown number of their relatives and closest followers, sailed from Lough Swilly for continental Europe, never to return. The 'flight of the earls' – as this bitter exodus has become known – remains one of the most poignant, as well as intriguing, episodes in Irish history. The mystery dates from the time as the fugitives' Gaelic contemporaries could not offer any explanation for such drastic action. Writing a generation after the event, the compilers of the *Annals of the Four Masters* could only lament:

> Woe to the heart that meditated, woe to the mind that conceived, woe to the council that decided on the project of their setting out on this voyage, without knowing whether they should ever return to their native principalities or patrimonies to the end of the World.[1]

Nor does contemporary Gaelic poetry offer any clues; it merely reflected the shock of those abandoned, and linked the flight, through the Ulster plantation, with the destruction of the Gaelic system.[2] Even Tadhg Ó Cianáin – who accompanied the earls on their fateful journey – failed to offer any analysis of their motives.[3]

Despite the government's proclaimed reaction to the flight, which asserted 'that the only ground and motive of this high contempt in these men's departure, hath been the private and inward knowledge of their own guiltiness',[4] English contemporaries, in the days immediately after the event, seemed equally confounded by the earls' exit. Most echoed Sir John Davies's description of it as an 'accident extraordinary'.[5] Perhaps the clearest contemporary evidences were the earls' statements of grievance addressed to King James after they had reached the continent. They listed a litany of injustices and injuries committed against them by the king's Irish servitors, ranging from religious persecution and attempts to deprive them of their property to practices against their lives and those of their followers. While these documents provide considerable insight into the earls' view of the events that forced them to abandon their homeland, their utility is undermined somewhat by their retrospective compilation.

Until recently historical opinion on the episode shaped by these sources divided into two camps. Historians of a nationalist persuasion and mainly influenced by the earls' claims, advanced the view that the fugitives had fled for their lives from a tyrannical English government.[6] Opposed to this view and echoing closely the conspiracy theory of the early seventeenth-century Irish government was the contention that the earls fled because they feared that their treasonable transactions with Spain had been discovered.[7] Nicholas Canny's article from 1971 offered a new synthesis of the existing evidence from the English state papers and, without wishing to disparage those who had previously considered the matter, brought a professional historian's critical acumen to bear upon those sources for the first time. Canny argued that while Hugh O'Neill may have lost the war, he won the peace between 1603 and 1607. Although Tyrconnell and Maguire had little to keep them in Ireland in 1607 (and indeed well before this), Tyrone had successfully thwarted the efforts of the Dublin administration to erode his influence in Ulster. It was the arrival of shipping to take his two malcontent relatives into European exile that caused Tyrone, then on the verge of going to court, to successively take fright and flight.[8]

Working on the continental sources associated with the earls after 1603, Micheline Kerney Walsh offered new evidence to suggest that 'the so-called "flight of the earls"' was neither a panicked 'flight' nor an acceptance of defeat in an impossible situation. Instead she presented it as a planned, tactical retreat, an attempt by Tyrone to secure military aid by presenting his case in person before Philip III, having decided that his position in Ireland under an English administration had become untenable.[9] Despite her provision of extensive translations of the documents on which she based her case, Kerney Walsh's argument failed to win universal acceptance, though the present author agrees with Aidan Clarke's suggestion that her work 'certainly

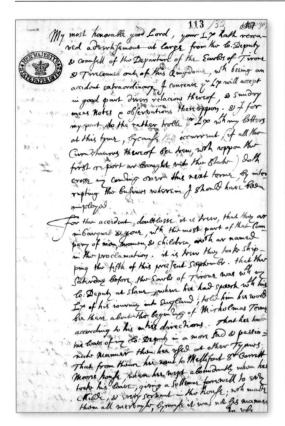

The Irish and English Governments' initial reactions to the flight are echoed in Sir John Davies's description of the event as an 'accident extraordinary'. © TNA

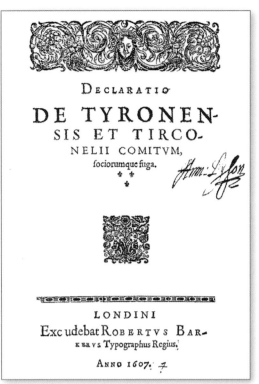

The London Government tried to ensure that the fugitive earls received little sympathy on the continent. In December 1607, Sir Thomas Edmonds, James's ambassador at Brussels, published a Latin translation of the king's proclamation against the earls. © Cambridge University Library

suggests that there may have been more to the allegations of conspiracy than the presently received version of the episode allows'.[10]

Building on Kerney Walsh's work, John McCavitt suggested that 'before leaving Ireland the earls had been engaged in conspiratorial machinations on two levels, international and domestic'.[11] As well as supporting Kerney Walsh's discovery that the earls had concluded a treasonable contract with the Spanish shortly after the conclusion of the Nine Years War in 1603, he demonstrated that they had also engaged in 'secret dealings' with members of the Old English community to foment rebellion against the Irish government in the two years before their departure. He shows that elements of the Old English population were amenable to such 'dealings' because the confrontational 'Mandates' campaign policy which aimed at the conversion of the Catholics of the towns to Protestantism had alienated them from the government. McCavitt argued that the flight hinged upon a change in James's attitude to Tyrone from friendly support to burgeoning hostility over the summer of 1607 as the extent of Tyrone's involve-

ment in a pan-insular Catholic conspiracy appeared to be confirmed. It was this information, relayed to Tyrone from sympathisers on the Privy Council via the Archduke Albert in the Spanish Netherlands, that persuaded him that if he did not flee, he would be deprived of liberty, if not life, when he travelled to London to settle his land dispute with Donal Ballagh O'Cahan.[12]

This essay contends that Tyrone's reason for joining the flight has still not been fully explained. It presents a new synthesis of the existing information to advance a more plausible explanation for Tyrone's abrupt departure and posits a fresh appraisal of the creeping encroachment of the agents of the state and the state church in Ulster and his reactions to these. The essay agrees broadly with Kerney Walsh's and McCavitt's view that Tyrone had engaged in conspiratorial dealings with Spain and with elements of the Old English community, findings borne out by the author's own work on the 1590s.[13] This brief contribution can devote minimal attention to the processes of confessionalisation that reshaped political and communal

Charles Blount (1563-1606), eighth Baron Mountjoy, finally brought the Ulster confederates to heel. This delicate, bookish figure displayed remarkable endurance as well as ruthlessness in ending the war. His leniency in negotiating terms was determined by his eagerness to return to England to claim his reward as much as his conviction that Ulster could not be pacified without enormous expense. © NPG

alignments in Ireland in the period, but will contend that the Old English community were by no means as hostile to Tyrone as received historical wisdom has suggested.[14]

Canny disproved Fynes Moryson's claim that Tyrone accepted terms 'as humble as the poorest rebel in Ireland', and demonstrated that the flight was not an inevitable consequence of Tyrone's defeat in the Nine Years War.[15] In accordance with the general principles laid down by the Treaty of Mellifont, the land settlement formalised by the English Privy Council in August 1603 restored Tyrone to almost the same estate allowed him by Elizabeth in 1587. This confirmed him in possession of all lands, tenements and hereditaments held by his grandfather, Conn Bacach O'Neill, at the time of his 'surrender and regrant' arrangement in 1542 with the exception of those portions allocated to Henry Óg O'Neill and Turlough MacHenry O'Neill and 600 acres surrounding the forts of Charlemont and

Mountjoy.[16] Yet it is also important to temper this with a recognition of the fact that despite this apparent return to favour, Tyrone's position was far from secure. There is evidence that James and his council did not regard the terms of the Hampton Court settlement as immutable. Tyrone also had good cause to remain on guard, for most of the king's Irish servitors who felt bitterly cheated at his return to favour remained openly hostile to him.[17] Indeed, many English Protestants could not believe that the enemy who had so long and successfully waged war against them was now decisively beaten.[18] This opinion was shared by the earls themselves, who, even as they conspicuously co-operated with the state, maintained contacts with Spain throughout the period 1603-07.[19] Tyrconnell 'went in person to speak of this matter secretly with the [Spanish] ambassador' in 1604, a mere year after James had restored the Ulster earls to most of their lands. The import of the message, as reported by the Spanish ambassador, was that, if King Philip III felt that the peace with England was unlikely to last, the earls 'and their friends, kinsmen and confederates will wait up to two years, even in their present difficult circumstances, to see what Your Majesty may wish to order for his service in that kingdom where they will continue with the same steadfast courage as always'.[20] If the king was certain that the peace with the English was to last, they requested that a ship be sent to take them wherever Philip III might wish 'while awaiting to see how the affairs of the world develop'. Their insecurity was palpable. They felt that their service to Spain meant that 'they cannot live in safety and they fear the power of the King who has inherited, along with the kingdom of Queen Elizabeth, the hatred which she bore them'.[21]

Their unease may also have been occasioned by a change in royal Irish policy. Reports began to filter through to London in early 1604 that the earls were deliberately exploiting the liberal tenets of the 1603 agreement in order to establish full possession over vast areas of Ulster.[22] This prompted a major transformation of the government's attitude towards Tyrone and the other Ulster lords, especially as Sir Robert Cecil came to exert increasing influence over Irish affairs with the collapse of Lord Devonshire's [Mountjoy's] career following his marriage to the sister of the disgraced second earl of Essex.[23] Over 1604-05, Cecil grew to fully support the efforts of Sir John Davies, the Irish solicitor general (November 1603 – May 1606),

James Stuart, who ruled Scotland as James VI from 1567 (directly after 1583 until his death in 1625), inherited the kingdoms of England and Ireland in 1603. He proved happy to uphold the Treaty of Mellifont and was anxious that the Ulster lords be incorporated into his new 'British Empire'. © NPG

to reduce the influence of the Ulster lords. It was Cecil, as Davies acknowledged, 'who moved the king to write special letters to the earl [Tyrone] and other northern lords requiring them to make a competent number of freeholders in their several countries'.[24]

Sir Arthur Chichester's appointment as lord deputy in February 1605 further intensified the earl's discomfort, as the new governor, who had played a key role in the earl's final reduction after Kinsale, had been outraged by the earl's re-establishment and the failure of the government to reward the captains.[25] From the outset, he seems to have encouraged both legal and illegal means to discomfit Tyrone. The month after Chichester's appointment Tyrone wrote to Cecil (after 4 May 1605 earl of Salisbury) complaining of the many wrongs done to him for which he could get no redress from the king's ministers in Ireland.[26] Three months later he complained that attempts were being made to take away his hereditary rights over the fishing of the River Bann and Lough Foyle.[27] That James did not respond promptly to these queries can hardly have reinforced the earl's confidence.[28] Indeed, it may have persuaded Tyrone of the wisdom of continuing his overtures to the king of Spain. In February 1606 Matthew Tully, the earls' agent in Spain, presented a petition requesting financial aid with which to bribe the heretical ministers of the crown to alleviate the earls 'present state of miserable servitude'.[29] Not everything in the earls' later list of grievances need be accepted for an impression of constant harassment and humiliation to be formed.

The government's assault on the Ulster lords began in earnest with a proclamation of denization of 1605, which prohibited all dependency on lords by declaring all Ulster's inhabitants 'the free natural and immediate subjects of his majesty'.[30] It also sounded an ominous warning to the earls by stating that, 'notwithstanding the said general words therein conveyed', the letters patent issued to Tyrone and Tyrconnell and other chieftains did not transfer to the lords the lawful freeholds that had formerly belonged to freeholders in accordance with the customs and traditions of Gaelic land law.[31] This promised all those who had been

The appointment of Sir Arthur Chichester (1563-1625) as lord deputy of Ireland in October 1604 proved a disaster for the Ulster earls.

bullied or cajoled into accepting the earls' interpretations of their patents after 1603 a sympathetic hearing from the government.[32]

Soon afterwards James appointed a commission which he empowered to grant common-law tenures in exchange for voluntary surrenders of Gaelic freeholds.[33] Equipped with this, the commissioners moved into the two Ulster earldoms in the autumn of 1605 determined to reduce the earls' influence. They had some success in Tyrconnell, compelling the earl to restore the rights of the MacSweeneys and the O'Boyles. They also undercut O'Donnell lordship by allocating to Sir Niall Garbh O'Donnell 12,900 acres in the vicinity of Lifford, considered the only 'jewel' in his lordship. The commissioners met with considerably less success in Tyrone. Although various cadet branches of the O'Neill family and some of the lesser septs subordinate to Tyrone's rule did present petitions claiming rights to freehold, the earl outmanoeuvred them by presenting his immediate kinsmen as freeholders instead. This disconcerted the commissioners and forced them to accept this as a temporary arrangement.[34] While he had forced the commissioners to exempt his country temporarily from Davies's scheme, Tyrone's machinations merely redoubled the Irish government's efforts to reduce him by fair means or foul. Attempts were now made to cast suspicion on the contacts he maintained with his son Henry, colonel of the Irish regiment in Spanish service in the Low Countries, and Tyrone later complained of attempts to suborn condemned criminals to implicate him in treasonous activities.[35] Yet it was the initially more trivial matter of a proprietal dispute between Tyrone and his tenant and erstwhile son-in-law, Donal Ballagh O'Cahan, which furnished the most insidious means to undermine the earl.

O'Cahan challenged Tyrone's claim, which Mountjoy had granted, that his country was an integral part of the Tyrone earldom. The solicitor general (Sir John Davies) took up O'Cahan's cause because he hoped to establish a precedent which would result in the dismemberment of the Tyrone lordship among several claimants, all of whom, including Tyrone himself, would then be ruled by a provincial president. Davies insisted that by his grant from the crown Hugh O'Neill had received 'all the lands, tenements and hereditaments' which Conn Bacach O'Neill held at the time of his surrender in 1542. Davies argued that the express words of Conn's patent merely conveyed the property and interest that Conn had enjoyed as The O'Neill.[36] Furthermore, he insisted that 'by [Gaelic] law' then 'the country of Colrane [O'Cahan's country] had not passed to the earl, Conn, the first earl, never having had any other possession of the country but the aforesaid rent and Irish exactions', and thus Davies extrapolated that Tyrone's 1587 grant had not accurately reflected the geo-politics of Gaelic Ulster.[37] To compound the injustice, Davies insisted that Tyrone lorded it over those he had cheated 'like the Turk or Tartar', seeking 'to have all in possession, and consequently all the tenants of that county to be his slaves and vassals'. Having 'drawn the case more exactly out of the records themselves', Davies also concluded that neither Montgomery, O'Cahan nor Tyrone had any title to the land in dispute; rather, since the attainder of Shane O'Neill those lands within the earldom which were not demesne lands of the ruling O'Neill were vested in the crown.[38] Tyrone, on the other hand, held rigidly to the view that both his grandfather in 1542 and he himself in 1587 and again in 1603 had been granted outright ownership of the entire lordship of Tyrone and that the only others who had property rights within his earldom were those appointed by him as tenants-in-chief after 1590 and again in 1605.[39]

Yet it seems clear that, notwithstanding his protestations, Tyrone both doubted his legal position and appreciated the looming threat. As late as 26 May 1607 he complained of the attempts of 'so many that seek to despoil' him 'of the greatest part of the residue' of his lands; such comment suggest that he had never been made privy to the king's resolution that Chichester take:

> More than ordinary care to free him [Tyrone] and protect him from any unnecessary molestation upon any ordinary process or information of any troublesome persons because it is a matter subject to charge and disgrace from both which, as long as he shall remain obedient to the state, his Majesty would have him freed.[40]

He bitterly lamented that the 'bishop of Derry [Montgomery] not only claims for himself lands whereunto none of his predecessors ever made claim, but also sets on others to call into question that which was never heretofore doubted to be his [Tyrone's] or his ancestors', and which Davies 'likewise also calls in question, namely Killetragh, Glanconkeine, Slewshees, Sliocht Art and Iraght-I-Cahan, as not being specially named in his letters patent', before despairingly concluding that 'in truth, there is not one parcel particularly named in them'.[41]

This runs counter to Canny's assertion that the grant to Tyrone of all but palatinate status in 1603 gave him the room to frustrate the designs of the Dublin government and meet the advance of anglicisation on his own terms.[42] Although Tyrone continued to struggle against the Dublin government's efforts to deprive him of his lands, there seems little doubt that he felt himself to be fighting a losing battle. In his last scheme, mooted towards the end 1606, he offered to accept Bishop Montgomery's right to the actual church lands, and not merely their rents, within his earldom in exchange for new letters patent for the remainder of his lands.[43] In such straitened circumstances, it was no surprise that Tyrone explored possibilities to reverse the situation.

Given the prevailing international political climate, the possibility of Spanish aid for a renewed rebellion seemed remote and Tyrone realised this fact. Yet the government's 'Mandates' campaign – a misconceived attempt to convert the Old English of the Pale and the towns to Protestantism by compulsion – presented an opportunity. The religious persecution associated with this policy persuaded one Catholic commentator that 'since peace has been concluded between our King and the King of Spain, the Neronian times have been inaugurated here'.[44] The two years preceding the flight ushered in a deeply traumatic time for thousands of Old English recusants and the experience of incarceration, fines and forced attendance at Protestant services provided considerable incentives for taking action.[45] McCavitt has established that by the late spring of 1607 the government believed that the planning of a rebellion by Old English recusants and the Gaelic Irish of the 'north' and 'west' had reached an advanced stage.[46]

This is not to suggest that Tyrone was not deeply opposed to the government's religious policies, and the present author would concur with

T. W. Moody's observation that the reading of the anti-Catholic proclamation in Tyrone's manor at Dungannon in July 1605 must have impressed upon the earl 'the reality of his eclipse', as well as warning that the mandates might soon be applied to Ulster's elite.[47] Yet it seems that the conspiracy sprang from elements within the Old English community, motivated by 'the general dislike of unchristian proceedings against them' and aimed at 'tolerance in religion'.[48] Recognising, as Sir John Davies surmised, that they had not 'a man of spirit and greatness among them to … make a war', they naturally turned to Tyrone – the self-proclaimed champion of Catholicism in Ireland.[49] Historians do not generally accept that the Old English recognised Tyrone's Catholic credentials, but it is significant that they chose him to present the petition of thirty leading nobles and gentlemen of Ireland to James in August 1603. The petition 'to have the public use of their religion, & to be governed with their own nation, and have their coin better' echoed the key points of Tyrone's famous proclamation of 1599 and suggests a shared vision of Ireland's future.[50] The affection for the earl in some Old English circles jars with the existing historical consensus, with some members of the old colonial community lamenting that 'even the most illustrious earl of Tyrone, the Catholic Mardochai, has been oppressed in various ways, and at the call of the Lord Deputy he has now come to Dublin … the inveterate hatred and malice of heretics towards him make us anxious about his fate'.[51]

Sir Christopher St Lawrence emphasised the role played by religious grievance in the alleged plot when he noted Tyrone's alleged claim that 'the assistance of the country' would be forthcoming because 'the punishment for religion had drawn the hearts of all the people from the King'.[52] This accorded with O'Neill's recollection that the mandates were the primary motivating factor in the nascent conspiracy. Tyrone's report also threw further light upon the religious and political attitudes of the Old English during the Nine Years War. He remained convinced that they had failed to join him and his confederates in rebellion and had 'temporised with her [Elizabeth] so as not to lose their estates and they hoped that, when she would die, there would come a change of religion'. This had not transpired, and the prospect 'of a continuous succession of heretics on the throne of England', coupled with the intensification of persecution marked by the mandates, provoked

'great resentment and anger' and rendered the Old English amenable to participation in a 'Catholic League'.[53]

Despite Kerney Walsh's and McCavitt's arguments to the contrary, no evidence exists of a fundamental change in James's attitude towards Tyrone at any point over the period 1603 to 1607. His advice to Chichester in July 1607 remained perfectly consistent with his earlier instructions. While James would have Tyrone freed from 'any ordinary process of troublesome persons … as long as he remained obedient to the state', Chichester was told in September 1606 that if Tyrone refused to accept the settlement negotiated in London he could 'proceed without regard of persons'.[54] James had imposed strict limits on what the earl could expect and it was certainly not permissible that he would intrude on the rights of other subjects.[55] There is absolutely no reason to suggest, as McCavitt has, that James's statement of July 1607 that 'if Tyrone means to encroach upon other subjects of little less condition than himself, and to draw them to such a dependency upon him as is inconsistent with the security of the state, I cannot forget what the authority is which God has committed unto me' meant that the earl faced a far more menacing situation.[56] This statement should hardly be taken to mean that the king had decided to rule against Tyrone; neither would James's decision to hear the case in London at the beginning of Michaelmas term, with both Tyrone and O'Cahan present, have unduly alarmed the earl.[57] While the dissident mood among the Gaelic leadership and the Old English population of the Pale and the towns disposed the London government to examine the information of an impending rebellion seriously, the source of most of it, Sir Christopher St Lawrence, had little credit with Chichester or Salisbury and it was deemed not 'worthy to draw on the king any sudden action'.[58] Moreover, if Tyrone had been forewarned, as Kerney Walsh suggests, up to a month before the flight that he was to be arrested and executed, he would have been most unlikely to have placed himself within the state's power as he did when he convened with Chichester at Slane.[59] Presumably he would have taken greater pains to retrieve his youngest son, Conn, from his foster-family. Finally, as Chichester explained, the earl seemed fully prepared to come to London to plead his case against O'Cahan. So Kerney Walsh's argument based on the supposed warning from an informant on the English Privy

The Treaty of London, 1604. © TNA

Council seems flawed. It has the appearance of a post-flight justification advanced to add weight to the earl's claims of persecution. This seems clear given the contemporary official correspondence, which hardly suggested that Tyrone was being lured to London to face a trial.[60]

Tyrone's flight therefore seems to have been based on a more immediate point of panic, and the sequence of events at Slane thus assumes crucial significance. There can be no doubt that Chichester wanted desperately to prevent his visit to London. This was because if even some of the allegations contained in the earl's later memorial of complaints from exile were sustained, then Chichester could have faced revocation and disgrace, as he would have been demonstrated to have deliberately disobeyed the king's advice regarding Tyrone: '[that] all occasion to be taken from him of just complaint, considering what a dependency the Irish have on him and how ticklish their disposition is towards the state, and he an instrument apt to make innovation'.[61] At Slane the deputy had the perfect opportunity to leak information to Tyrone that might preclude this embarrassing eventuality.

Tyrone claimed from exile that he had fled for a variety of reasons, not least that the deputy had been granted the lord presidency of Ulster.[62] This news seems to have convinced him that the king would have little time for his other petitions and that life in exile would be preferable to 'the misery he saw sustained by others through the oppression of the like government'.[63] Yet even this information was unlikely to have made Tyrone abandon his last chance to persuade the king to preserve him from his opponents.

Thus one must look for an alternative reason for the earl's flight. It is perhaps significant that government officials observed that St Lawrence, also suspiciously present at Slane, put 'buzzes' in Tyrone's ear by convincing him that 'if he went into England he should either be perpetual prisoner in the Tower of London or else lose his head and members'.[64] This supported Tyrone's claim from exile that he feared that Chichester had intended 'to come upon' him 'with some forged treason and thereby to bereave him both of his life and living'.[65] St Lawrence subsequently confessed that he had told Tyrone that the king had responded to Sir Patrick Murray's suggestion that the earl was an honest man by saying: 'Patrick, I pray God he prove so'. He also admitted warning the earl to be well provided with money to make friends on his visit to court 'for he had now but few there'.[66] This information, which was mentioned by Tyrone to Sir Garret Moore directly before his flight, would merely have confirmed the earl's impressions based on the short shrift that his suits seemed to have received at court.[67] That Tyrone faced reprimand, let alone execution, seems improbable, but the earl could not have known that, and when such 'buzzes'

were put in his ear he understandably panicked. While he had undoubtedly used middlemen to engage in treasonable transactions with the Spanish as well as within Ireland, events proved that it was not that sufficient evidence had been amassed to proceed against the earls on a charge of treason that caused them to become uneasy and take flight; rather, it was the apprehension that such a case had been compiled that proved decisive. This, converging with the news of Maguire's arrival with shipping at Lough Swilly, persuaded Tyrone successively to take fright and take flight.

Notes

1 *AFM*, vi, 2359.

2 For examples see: Fearghal Óg Mac an Bhaird, 'The Downfall of the O'Donnells' and Fear Flatha Ó Gnímh, 'The Death of Ireland', in O. Bergin, *Irish Bardic Poetry*, (eds) D. Greene & F. Kelly (Dublin, 1970), pp 230-1, 264-5. For a poem that hints at the harassment that the earls were subjected to see also Fearghal Óg Mac an Bhaird, 'The Flight of the Earls', (ed.) L. McKenna, *Irish Monthly* (1929), pp 471-5.

3 Tadhg Ó Cianáin, *The Flight of the Earls*, (ed. & trans.) P. Walsh (Dublin, 1916). John Bath, captain of the vessel that brought the earls from Ireland, claimed that it was the fear that their Spanish pensions had been discovered that persuaded the earls to flee; see C. P. Meehan, *The fate and fortunes of Hugh O'Neill, earl of Tyrone, and Rory O'Donel, earl of Tyrconnel* (Dublin, 1868), pp 247-9.

4 *Stuart royal proclamations: Royal proclamations of King James I, 1603-1625*, (eds) J. F. Larkin and P. L. Hughes (Oxford, 1973), pp 176-9.

5 Davies to Salisbury (Cecil), 12 Sept. 1607 (TNA SPI 63/222/133). Chichester to Privy Council, 7 Sept. 1607 (TNA SPI 63/222/126).

6 Meehan, *Fate and fortunes*, passim. T. M. Healy, *Stolen Waters: a page in the conquest of Ulster* (London, 1913), p. 42; Sean O'Faolain, *The Great O'Neill* (Dublin, 1942), pp 272-3. O'Faolain had no doubt of the earls' innocence: 'Felon-settlers, agents provocateurs, spies, petty officials of every kind dogged them like shadows. Failing to get any evidence to support the story of a plot, Chichester egged on his men to badger his victims into some indiscretion that would justify him in proclaiming them traitors'.

7 W. D. Killen, *The ecclesiastical history of Ireland: from the earliest period to the present times* (2 vols, London, 1875), i, 480; S. R. Gardiner, *History of England: from the accession of James I to the outbreak of the civil war, 1603-1642* (10 vols, London, 1883-84), i, pp 413-6; C. Falls, *The birth of Ulster* (London, 1936), pp 131-2; J. J. Silke, *Ireland and Europe, 1559-1605* (Dundalk, 1966), p. 28.

8 N. P. Canny, 'The Flight of the Earls, 1607', *IHS*, xvi (1971), pp 380-99.

9 M. Kerney Walsh, *'Destruction by peace': Hugh O'Neill*

after Kinsale (Armagh, 1986), p. 143. Tyrone subsequently explained his predicament to King Philip: 'In order to save our lives, there was no other remedy but to take up arms, or to escape from the Kingdom. We chose to escape rather than stir the whole Kingdom to rebellion without first being assured of the help and assistance of Your Majesty'.

10 A. Clarke, 'Bibliographical supplement: introduction', in *NHI*, iii, p. 707.

11 J. McCavitt, 'Lord Deputy Chichester and the English government's "Mandates policy" in Ireland, 1605-07', *Recusant History*, xx (1991), pp 320-35.

12 J. McCavitt, 'The Flight of the Earls', *IHS*, xxix (1994), pp 159-73, citing Kerney Walsh, *'Destruction by peace'*, docs. 11, 30, 35, 36, 43A, 56B, 72A.

13 M. D. Finnegan, 'Tyrone's rebellion: Hugh O'Neill and the outbreak of the Nine Years War in Ulster' (M.Litt. thesis, NUI Galway, 2001).

14 M. D. Finnegan, 'The impact of the Counter-Reformation on the political thinking of Irish Catholics, c. 1540-c. 1640' (PhD thesis, Cambridge, 2006).

15 N. P. Canny, 'The Treaty of Mellifont', *Irish Sword*, 9 (1970), pp 249-62.

16 N. P. Canny, 'Hugh O'Neill, earl of Tyrone, and the changing face of Gaelic Ulster', *Studia Hibernica*, x (1970), pp 13-15; *Calendar of the Patent and Close Rolls of Chancery in Ireland from the 18th to the 45th of Queen Elizabeth (1576-1602)*, (ed.) J. Morrin (3 vols, Dublin, 1861-63), ii, p. 130.

17 'I have lived,' wrote Sir James Harington, 'to see that damnable rebel Tyrone brought to England, courteously favoured, honoured, and well liked. Oh my lord: What is there that does not prove the inconstancy of worldly matters! How I did labour after that knave's destruction! I was called from my home by her Majesty's command, adventured perils by sea and land, was near starving, ate horseflesh in Munster; and all to quell that man, who now smileth in peace at those who did hazard their lives to destroy him; and now doth Tyrone dare us old commanders with his presence and protection': J. Harington, *Nugae Antiquae*, (ed.) H. Harington (2nd ed., 3 vols London, 1792), ii, pp 149-51.

18 A Spanish agent reported from London in April 1603

that 'A great number of people believe that Tyrone's submission is a feint in order to gain time and to improve his position' (anonymous, 6 Apr. 1603, cited in Walsh, *'Destruction by Peace'*, p. 28).

19 The Venetian ambassador reported in August that 'the earl of Tyrone, finding himself out of favour at Court, has asked leave to return to Ireland … but he has taken fright at the imprisonment of the Irish deputation, and is afraid that if he sets out now the King will have him killed on the road, and he wishes he had never left Ireland', (Scaramelli to the Doge and Senate of Venice, 27 Aug. 1603: *Calendar of state papers, Venice*, (ed.) R. Brown (8 vols, London, 1864-97), 1603-07, no. 118). Chichester and Council to Privy Council, 30 Dec. 1604 (TNA SPI 63/216/56). They later reminded Philip III that they had sent 'MacWilliam Burke with a message to Your Majesty in the year 1603 … begging you to send us help and declaring that we would continue in your royal service with the same good will and loyalty as always' and they offered their support if the peace that the English and Spanish were then negotiating (and which lasted until shortly after the accession of Charles I) broke down, Memorial of O'Neill and O'Donnell, undated but forwarded to King Philip III by the conde de Fuentes with his letter of 13 April 1608 (Kerney Walsh, *'Destruction by Peace'*, doc. 56B). This letter was sent in the same month that Tyrone sent Philip III a letter constructed by Mountjoy's secretariat renouncing his aid (see F. Moryson, *An Itinerary* (4 vols, Glasgow, 1907), iii, pp 304-5).

20 Tyrone and Tyrconnell to Philip III, 3 Dec. 1607 (Kerney Walsh, *'Destruction by Peace'*, doc. 56B).

21 Conde de Villamediana to Philip III, 23 Dec. 1604, in (ibid., doc. 11). They also implied that they had far more friends than during their rebellion.

22 R. Bagwell, *Ireland under the Stuarts* (3 vols, London, 1963), i, p. 13; *NHI*, i, p. 372.

23 M. Jones, *Mountjoy, the last Elizabethan deputy* (Dublin, 1958), p. 180.

24 Davies to Salisbury, 12 Nov. 1606 (TNA SPI 63/219/132). This assessment is supported by Sir Roger Wilbraham, who preceded Sir John Davies as Irish solicitor general. Writing on the eve of Cecil's death in 1612, Wilbraham noted that Cecil alone exercised responsibility for Irish affairs ('The Diary of Sir Roger Wilbraham', *Camden Miscellany*, x (1902), p. 106).

25 His animus against Tyrone had a personal edge to it as it was rumoured that Tyrone's troops had played a gruesome game of football with the severed head of his brother, Sir John Chichester (H. Pawlisch, *Sir John Davies and the Conquest of Ireland* (Cambridge, 1985), p. 86). Moreover, Chichester's hopes of gaining substantially from the expected confiscation of Tyrone's lands after the war had been bitterly disappointed.

26 Tyrone to Cecil, 3 Mar 1605 (TNA SPI 63/217/40).

27 Tyrone to Viscount Cranbourne (Cecil), 2 June 1605 (TNA SPI 63/217/36).

28 He can hardly have been reassured by the delay in granting his new letters patent for although he had received the privy signet bill for his grant in September 1603, his letters patent were not finally granted to him until September 1605.

29 Earls' Memorial to Philip III, 16 Feb. 1606 (Kerney Walsh, *'Destruction by Peace'*, doc. 22).

30 Proclamation by Chichester and Irish Council. 11 Mar. 1605 (TNA SPI 63/217/16). This was prompted by Sir John Davies' insistence that Tyrone's interests in the 'bodies of the King's subjects … neither standeth … with reason of state or … the law of England' (Davies to Cecil, 19 Apr. 1604 (TNA SPI 63/216/15)).

31 R. Steele (ed.), *A bibliography of royal proclamations of the Tudor and Stuart sovereigns* (2 vols Oxford, 1910), ii, nos 167a, 180, pp 15-17.

32 There is evidence that Tyrone had been particularly brutal in quashing dissidence in 1603 (Canny, 'Hugh O'Neill and the changing face of Gaelic Ulster', pp 12-15).

33 James I to Chichester, 27 June 1605, in *Desiderata curiosa Hibernica, or a select collection of state papers*, (ed.) John Lodge (2 vols, Dublin, 1772), i, pp 453-7; 'Commission for making shires, etc.', 19 July 1605, in J. C. Erck (ed.), *A Repertory of the Inrolments on the Patent Rolls of Chancery in Ireland Commencing with the Reign of James I* (Dublin, 1846), pp 182-4. There were in fact two separate commissions, one for the surrender of uncertain titles and one for the surrender of 'tanist' lands only. See also Steele, *Proclamations*, ii, nos 186 & 196, pp 18-19.

34 Lord Deputy and Council to Privy Council, 30 Sept. 1605 (TNA SPI 63/217/63).

35 Chichester to Salisbury, 12 Sept. 1606 (TNA SPI 63/217/105).

36 A fact Davies claimed was substantiated by the two jury inquisitions conducted prior to Hugh O'Neill's formal creation as earl of Tyrone in 1587: 'The metes, bounds and limits of Tyrone. The findings of the land commission', Apr. 1587 (TNA SPI 63/129/58). For the eventual ruling, one which supported the earl's interpretation of his patent see 'Record of the Inquisition of the earl of Tyrone's lands', 10 Jun. 1588 (TNA SPI 63/135/34). Davies to Salisbury, 12 Nov. 1606 (TNA SPI 63/219/132). Chichester and Council to Privy Council, 26 June 1607 (TNA SPI 63/221/88).

37 St John to Salisbury, 1 June 1607 (TNA SPI 63/221/59).

38 Davies to Salisbury, 1 July 1607 (TNA SPI 63/222/95). This was a return to Tyrone's pre-war policy of using his patent to claim all the lands of the earldom as his absolute freehold: see Finnegan, 'Tyrone's rebellion', pp 52-55.

39 His interpretation was in line with that of the patent granted him in 1587 which provided for the establishment of only one freeholder. Other observers were aware that Tyrone's patent was a regrant of the one granted him by Elizabeth in 1587; see Richard Hudson's 'A discourse presented to the King's Majesty touching Ireland', 1604 (TNA SPI 63/216/64).

40 Quoted in Canny, 'Hugh O'Neill and the changing face of Gaelic Ulster', p. 11.

41 Tyrone to James I, 26 May 1607 (TNA SPI 63/221/56).

42 Canny, 'Hugh O'Neill and the changing face of Gaelic Ulster', passim; idem, 'Flight of the Earls, 1607', p. 385; R. D. Edwards, 'Ireland, Elizabeth I and the Counter-Ref-

ormation', in S. T. Bindoff *et al* (eds), *Elizabethan government and society* (London, 1961), p. 335. Tyrone was further hampered by his undertaking that in terms of the future administration of law and justice, as well as in matters of the future landholding arrangements in his country, that he would be 'content to be informed and advised by her [the queen's] magistrates here, and will be conforming and assisting unto them': Moryson, *Itinerary*, iii, p. 301.

43 'Tyrone's petition to James I', n. d. c. 1606 (TNA SPI 63/219/153, 154).

44 Various Irish clergy and laity to Fitzsimons, 1 May 1607 in H. Fitzsimon, *Words of comfort to Persecuted Catholics. Written in exile, anno 1607. Letters from a cell in Dublin Castle and diary of the Bohemian war of 1620,* (ed.) E. Hogan (Dublin, 1881), pp 64-66.

45 The baron of Delvin admitted involvement in a plot naming Tyrconnell as his accomplice (Delvin's Confession, 6 Nov. 1607 (TNA SPI 63/222/174)). Chichester to Salisbury, 12 Sept. 1606 (TNA SPI 63/219/105).

46 J. McCavitt, *Sir Arthur Chichester, lord deputy of Ireland, 1605-1616* (Belfast, 1998), p. 136.

47 T. W. Moody, *The Londonderry plantation, 1609-41: the city of London and the plantation in Ulster* (Belfast, 1939), pp 27-28.

48 Tyrone and Tyrconnell to Philip III, 3 Dec. 1607, 24 Jan. 1610 (Kerney Walsh, *'Destruction by peace'*, doc. 43a). This affection of the 'Old English' clergy towards him on the eve of the flight of the earls challenges the historical consensus that the 'Old English' hated Tyrone (Various Irish clergy and laity to Fitzsimon, 1 May 1607, Fitzsimon, *Words of comfort*, pp 64-66).

49 Davies to Salisbury, 1605/6 (TNA SPI 63/217/94). McCavitt, 'Chichester and the "Mandates"', pp 320-35.

50 H. S. Scott, 'The journal of Sir Roger Wilbraham: solicitor-general in Ireland and master of requests, for the years 1593-1616', *Camden Miscellany*, 3rd ser., 4 (London, 1902), p. 62.

51 Various Irish clergy and laity to Fitzsimon, 1 May 1607 (Fitzsimon, *Words of comfort*, pp 64-6). For the story of Mardochai see the deuterocanonical Book of Esther.

52 Howth's charge against Sir Garret Moore, May 1608, HMC, *Hastings*, i, p. 156.

53 Chichester to Privy Council, 22 Jan. 1607 (TNA SPI 63/221/12); Carew's 'Brief relation of the passages in parliament summoned in Ireland in 1613', *Carew MSS*, vi, pp 278-85; Meehan, *Fate and fortunes*, pp 65-6.

54 Privy Council to Chichester, 2 Sept. 1606 (*CSPI, 1603-06*, pp 548-9).

55 Canny's argument that it was through him that oth-

ers were pardoned might well have been one of the chief means by which Tyrone reestablished his authority over his dependants but it was never understood this way by the government; Canny, 'Hugh O'Neill and the changing face of Gaelic Ulster', pp 8-18.

56 James I to Chichester, 16 July 1607 (*CSPI, 1606-08*, pp 220-2).

57 Ibid.

58 Chichester to Privy Council, 22 Jan. 1607 (TNA SPI 63/221/12); Chichester to Salisbury, 27 May 1607 (TNA SPI 63/221/57).

59 Chichester to Privy Council, 7 Sept. 1607 (TNA SPI 63/222/126).

60 'For although it is true that we do know this remnant of the northern Irish traitors, to have been as full of malice as flesh and blood could be, and no way reformed by the grace they had received, but rather sucking poison out of the honey thereof; yet because His Majesty had given them pardon and could not demonstrably prove new treasons against them so clearly *in foro judicii*, as they might have not suspected to savour of rigour, yet, *in foro conscientiae*, His Majesty hath known they have absolutely given commission to their priests and others to undertake for them a resolution to abandon their sovereign if they might be entertained, not sticking to avow their alienation of heart from the English government' (Salisbury to Sir Charles Cornwallis, 27 Sept. 1607 (Kerney Walsh, *'Destruction by Peace'*, p. 59)). The Archduke's embarrassed reaction when the refugees eventually arrived in Flanders suggests that they were quite unaware of their plans for flight; (ibid., pp 55, 70).

61 Lake to Salisbury, 27 Aug. 1606 (HMC, *Salisbury*, xviii, pp 254-6).

62 Articles exhibited by the Earl of Tyrone (TNA SPI 63/222/201).

63 Meehan, *Fate and fortunes*, p. 126.

64 Moore to Salisbury, 23 May 1608 (TNA SPI 63/224/110). Articles exhibited by the Earl of Tyrone (TNA SPI 63/222/201, item 20).

65 Cúchonnacht Maguire had been arrested and questioned closely by the lord deputy who was 'very desirous and earnest to aggravate and search out matters against him … and specially and very distinctly examined Maguire and used many persuasions to him to signify if he might lay any matters to [the earl's] charge' (articles exhibited by the Earl of Tyrone (TNA SPI 63/222/201), item 20).

66 Chichester to Salisbury, 8 Sept. 1607 (TNA SPI 63/222/128).

67 'Answer of Sir Garret Moore to Lord Howth's accusations', 16 Mar. 1609 (TNA SPI 63/226/53 i).

Christopher St Lawrence, ninth baron of Howth: conspirator and informer

Valerie McGowan-Doyle

Christopher St Lawrence, ninth baron of Howth, had a key role in the events surrounding the flight. However, whether Howth played the loyal informant or treacherous conspirator is a question that has vexed historians as much as it did his contemporaries.[1] Howth began his career as a member of the Old English colonial aristocracy fighting under Elizabeth I against Hugh O'Neill in the Nine Years War and ended as an intimate in the company of King James VI & I. Between these periods he fought alongside O'Neill's son Henry in Flanders, and he earned the confidence of some of O'Neill's closest associates, including Rory O'Donnell. He also spent time in prison in both Dublin and London as a suspected traitor. In the immediate aftermath of the flight, the precise nature of his relationship with O'Neill both concerned and confused the authorities. When Sir Arthur Chichester, lord deputy of Ireland, first wrote to London to inform the earl of Salisbury of the northern earls' sudden departure, he reported that O'Neill's very decision likely had something to do with the 'buzzes' that Howth had put in O'Neill's head.[2] Chichester suspected furthermore that Howth had been planning a second exodus. Writing to Salisbury again just two days later, he reported that several prominent members of the Old English community had gathered at Howth Castle, including the countess of Kildare, the Dowager Lady Delvin, her children

and several priests, and that Howth had secretly procured a boat which waited with its crew in Howth harbour.[3] In spite of his suspicions, Chichester was uncertain about how to proceed with Howth, the reason being that, during precisely the same period of time when Howth was apparently colluding with O'Neill, he was in fact operating as a spy and conveying information on the earl's activities to the government in Dublin. Between May and August 1607, up to the very week before the flight, he had made a series of detailed statements outlining an extensive and co-ordinated Spanish-backed plot to overthrow English rule in Ireland.[4]

It is these allegations – rather than Howth himself – that have traditionally captured historians' attention in their attempts to reconstruct the immediate context of O'Neill's departure. Micheline Kerney Walsh used them to assess the degree and detail of O'Neill's plans and the precise nature of his treasonous relationship with Spain.[5] John McCavitt considered Howth's allegations from another perspective, demonstrating that they contributed significantly to the flight by influencing the government's increasing pressure on O'Neill in the months preceding his departure.[6] Howth's allegations play a key role in understanding the flight, but he himself has even more to offer. By moving beyond the content of his allegations to consider them within the entire spectrum of his mindset and activities, a broader

'Howth Castle'. © Neptune Gallery

13

appreciation of the competing pressures that confronted both Howth and O'Neill can be attained. When considering the factors that bore on O'Neill, account must be taken of his relationship to the authorities in Dublin and in London, his traffic to the Spanish crown and his position within Gaelic Ireland. The Old English grouping (Conrad Russell's 'pigs in the middle' of Irish politics), to which Howth

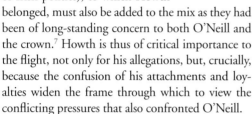

Coat of Arms of the St Lawrence family. © Neptune Gallery

belonged, must also be added to the mix as they had been of long-standing concern to both O'Neill and the crown.[7] Howth is thus of critical importance to the flight, not only for his allegations, but, crucially, because the confusion of his attachments and loyalties widen the frame through which to view the conflicting pressures that also confronted O'Neill.

Christopher St Lawrence availed of the opportunity to establish his loyalty to the Dublin administration during the Nine Years War. His lifelong proclivity for erratic, and often violent, behaviour caught the attention of officials who channeled it into military activity. This quickly earned him semi-legendary status and close association with influential figures such as the earl of Ormond and Sir George Carew, president of Munster, as well as several viceroys, in particular Robert Devereux, second earl of Essex, and Charles Blount, Lord Mountjoy.[8] In the war's aftermath, St Lawrence's loyalty and abilities also brought him land and military command in Ulster. As time wore on, his influence waned and he complained that he had been insufficiently compensated for his services to the crown. Citing economic need, he sought licence to offer his military services in Flanders, where many Irishmen, Gaelic Irish and Old English alike, had already gone.[9]

Taking recruits with him from Cavan, Fermanagh and Monaghan, where he had served as governor following the Nine Years War, St Lawrence arrived in Flanders in the summer of 1606 and took up a post as one of the six captains of the Irish regiment.[10] Just as he had quickly established himself with influential figures during the Nine Years War, he rapidly developed a close relationship with Henry O'Neill, colonel of the Irish regiment.[11] The Dublin administration's concerns about his activities with the Irish regiment heightened in the following winter when reports reached Chichester that St Lawrence and Henry O'Neill were together preparing their soldiers for an invasion of Ireland.[12] These reports led

Chichester, who had earlier attempted to prevent St Lawrence's departure from Ireland, to repeatedly seek his recall. Those efforts became unnecessary when St Lawrence's father, the eighth baron of Howth, died in May 1607 and his son immediately returned to Ireland to take up his inheritance.[13]

The new baron of Howth did not return directly to Ireland, however. He traveled to London, where he made the first of what would become a series of allegations against O'Neill.[14] Over the summer of 1607, Howth met with Chichester on several occasions and expanded on the details of the initial allegation. He claimed that O'Neill's plan was to begin by taking Dublin Castle and 'kill[ing] or otherwise dispos[ing] of the lord deputy and council'.[15] Lord Mountgarret would simultaneously capture the earl of Ormond and Viscount Butler, while Thomas Burke would seize the earl of Clanricard and storm Athlone Castle. Together with Randall MacDonnell, Cúchonnacht Maguire and other unnamed 'members of the nobility', they would lead a prearranged revolt of the cities and towns. Howth further claimed that ships were being built at Dunkirk and that Spain had agreed to send 10,000 soldiers and 200 cavalry under Spinola's command.[16]

However, Howth provided other information which suggested that he had not merely 'discovered' this conspiracy as he later claimed, but that he had been actively involved in it. Although consistently denying direct contact with O'Neill, Howth repeatedly sought to validate the authenticity of his claims with reference to his meetings with Rory O'Donnell, Father Florence Conry [Flaithrí Ó Maoil Chonaire] and Richard Nugent, baron of Delvin. Aware of the implied complicity, Howth offered even greater detail about these meetings in an attempt at self-defence. Thus he claimed, for instance, that the attack on Dublin Castle had originally been planned for Easter 1606, but that he had convinced O'Donnell to postpone it until Spanish forces arrived, arguing that without their assistance the enterprise would be unsuccessful. Furthermore, he used this statement to win praise from the authorities for personally thwarting that attack. Similarly, he sought credit for his unsuccessful attempts to persuade Conry to have Spanish forces land at Dublin rather than Waterford or Galway, a change of plan which Howth insisted he had encouraged in an attempt to draw the Spanish to a location where English forces might better defeat them.

He also attempted to defend himself – though only serving to draw attention now to the length of his complicity – by asserting that he had intended to reveal the plot on several occasions. Hence he claimed that having departed Ireland in the summer of 1606 with licence to go to Flanders, he actually intended traveling to London to seek either pension or employment from the king. Frustrated in his endeavours, and dismissing the plans for revolt as idle talk, he proceeded to Flanders, where he quickly became an intimate of Hugh O'Neill's son Henry. Howth also came into contact with Richard Stanihurst and Father Christopher Cusacke, who both assured him of imminent Spanish assistance.[17] Believing that the revolt was imminent, he left for England, intending once again to reveal the plot. Howth crossed the Channel in February 1607 and may well have intended to inform at that point, but was arrested upon arriving in Gravesend on charges stemming from an outstanding debt. He protested his arrest, claiming to be on Privy Council business.[18] Whatever his intent, he returned to Flanders on his release. Although given to understand from Father Conry that arrangements with Spain had been finalised, he made no move. It was only on his return to Ireland following his father's death that Howth, having stopped in London *en route*, made his first allegations. The rest emerged over the summer in Dublin. Howth claimed that duty compelled his revelations, but James's Privy Council attributed it to fear.[19] Panic may well have motivated the decision to turn against O'Neill as he moved into his in-

Robert Cecil, first earl of Salisbury (1563-1612), became Elizabeth's leading minister on his father's death in 1598, a position he retained after James's accession. He supported Chichester and Davies in their schemes against the Ulster earls. © NPG

heritance as Lord Howth – and, not surprisingly, he feared equally for his life from several different quarters. Whether out of fear or duty, or both, the more critical questions to be considered are the competing pressures that led Howth into the position in which he now found himself.

The intensification of English conquest in Ireland over the later Tudor and early Stuart periods put severe pressure on Howth's Old English community as well as on the Gaelic Irish. Old English responses to these pressures, which varied considerably, proved crucial to O'Neill. From the 1560s onwards in particular, the Old English had continued to adhere to Roman Catholicism. Because of their religious conservatism, they increasingly stood accused of adopting Gaelic culture and increasingly lost influential administrative, conciliar and military positions and offices to an *arriviste* Protestant colonial class who became known as the New English.[20] They struggled to maintain the position they had held in the medieval period as representatives of English control in the new climate that pitted them against both Irish and New English. Some preserved their security by acquiescing in the changing socio-political climate, while others engaged in open rebellion. Most, however, particularly in the Pale, resisted their deteriorating status by struggling to convince the authorities of their pliability and loyalty. This proved increasingly difficult over the later years of the Elizabethan period as their Marian compromises turned into Counter-Reformation recusancy. This only aggravated English suspicions about their loyalties.[21] In spite of the progress of the Reformation in England, the English authorities in Ireland baulked at pressing religious conversion on the Old English for fear of pushing them into an alliance with the Gaelic Irish on the basis of a shared Catholicism.

Hugh O'Neill appreciated their conflicted position and aggressively sought their alliance during the Nine Years War. He applied considerable pressure on the community at large as well as on influential individuals, the baron of Delvin in particular, reminding them that as Catholics their continued loyalty to England constituted heresy.[22] The Old English insisted they could be both Catholic and loyal, and few joined O'Neill at that point. With O'Neill's defeat, though, England not only sought to advance its control of Ulster, but believed that the enforced religious conversion of the Old English could be finally advanced through the mandates campaign.[23] This miscalculation, coupled with numerous fines and arrests, raised Old English hackles. Whereas the barons of Howth and Delvin had rejected O'Neill's overtures and threats during the Nine Years War, their sons now sought his support to challenge the government's religious reforms by force, and so too, as Howth's allegations asserted, did many more.

Howth's requests to pursue his military career in Flanders had intensified over the autumn and early winter of 1605 precisely as Chichester cranked up the pressure on the Old English.[24] Howth carefully avoided reference to religion, although both he and his father might have felt constrained in resisting the mandates campaign as forcefully as others because the Irish council had transferred its meetings to Howth Castle because of an outbreak of plague in Dublin.[25] Though the pressure to abandon Catholicism may have motivated many of the Old English to oppose the Dublin administration and drift towards O'Neill, Howth had additional cause, complaining of the insufficient compensation for his 'spent blood,' during the Nine Years War.

His failure to achieve adequate recompense for his loyal service left him, as many in Ireland and more than a few in England knew, a 'discontented' man. Although characterised variously throughout his lifetime as 'dangerous', 'unstaid', 'seditious', 'disordered', 'swaggering', and 'half-wild', he was most frequently described as 'discontented'.[26] Even O'Donnell attempted to utilise this spleen as a motivating factor to entice Delvin into an alliance.[27] In fact 'discontented' was frequently, consistently and strikingly used to describe him by a wide range of Gaelic Irish, Old English, New English and English figures. Not unlike Shakespeare's Richard III, who had only recently proclaimed the 'winter of [his] discontent' on stage, Howth's discontent and its remedy similarly both stemmed from political displacement and fuelled his attempt to regain status by any means necessary. In using this term, his contemporaries identified in him more than a passing phase of unhappiness, bad humour, or even restlessness that might have led to his Flanders adventure: this individual and his magnified position threatened the established order. From the 1570s on, Howth's grandfather the seventh baron, his father the eighth baron, and he as ninth baron too, had all been identified as influential members of the Old English whose loyalty was believed so tenuous. Chichester specifically reported that the ninth baron – unlike his father and grandfather – had now used his position to gain influence with the Irish.[28] Within the characterisation of Howth as 'discontented' lay the transformation

of the Old English that English authorities both feared and fostered: whereas the authorities had ultimately been able to control his forebears, who rejected any alliance with the Irish, Howth's new alliance threatened to eclipse the authorities' ability to control him. And, if an individual from an influential family as historically loyal to the Dublin administration as the St Lawrences should thus transfer his loyalty, it would not bode well for the Old English population at large and suggested that O'Neill now had the Old English support he had long sought.

Chichester and Salisbury communicated frequently over the summer of 1607 about Howth's allegations, referring to him in code, most often as 'A. B.' and occasionally as '600'. They did not wish to respond too hastily to his information, for fear of inciting a revolt if Howth was correct. However, they doubted his reliability.[29] Howth was ultimately imprisoned, first in Dublin and later in London, where he frantically sought to convince the authorities of his loyalty by implicating others and offering to assist in their arrest.[30] Once released, his continuing panic complicated an already tense situation in the Pale, and he lodged charges of treason against leading political figures, including Lord Deputy Chichester and Archbishop Jones of Dublin.[31]

O'Neill was on his way to Rome when he learned that Howth had been imprisoned.[32] According to Delvin, his decision to leave Ireland had been occasioned by his realization that the English council knew of his plot, though whether or not he was specifically aware of Howth's allegations is unknown. Howth's accusations cannot solely explain the flight, but are essential to an understanding of the complexities that confronted O'Neill. Howth's activities indicates that O'Neill had by 1607 gained the support of several key Old English figures if not the wider Old English community, which he had failed to achieve during the Nine Years War. Just as critically, Howth demonstrated the fragile nature of alliances made under the pressures of post-war consolidation in the early Stuart period. Those pressures created a situation in which many formerly loyal Old English were now ready to resist strenuously any perceived threat to their status, and it once more raised the possibility of an alliance with the Gaelic Irish. O'Neill's sudden departure undermined the possibilities for such an alliance, though they reemerged to vastly greater effect with the 1641 Rising.

1757

AND COVNCELL

ARTHVRE CHICHESTER.

Oɜ as much as it is knowne to the woɜld how infinitly the fugitiue Earles of Tyrone and Tirconnell, haue been obliged vnto the Kinges most excellent Maiestie foɜ his singular grace and mercy, not only in giuing free pardon to them both foɜ many heynous and execrable treasons, aboue all hope that they could in reason conceaue: but also in restoɜing the one to his lands and honoɜ, which he had most iustly foɜfaited by his notoɜious Rebellion, and in raysing the other from a very meane estate, to the degree and title of an Earle, giuing him withall, large possessions foɜ the suppoɜt of that honour, befoɜe either of them had giuen any new pɜoofe of loyaltie, oɜ merited the least fauour by perfoɜmance of any good seruice. And whereas since they were receiued to grace, neither of them can iustly pretend any pɜouocation oɜ cause of greeuance, no not in that poynt which serueth foɜ a Cloake foɜ al their Treasons, namely in point of Religion, touching which they haue not been called in question, ♣ haue been also boɜne withall in many other insolencies and outrages committed in their seuerall Countries.

And whereas Tyrone himselfe being lately sent foɜ into England, accoɜding to his owne desire (as hee pretended) to receiue oɜder in a controuersie betweene him and a pɜincipall Neighbour of his, did vnder colour of that Journey pɜepare himselfe foɜ that contrarie course which now he hath taken, and most vngratefully and contemptuously fledde from his Maiesties most gracious pɜesence, and together with Tirconnell, Cowconaght oge mac Guyre, ♣ the rest of the Fugitiues in their company and retinue, withdɜew himselfe out of this Realme into foɜraine parts, where they doe now lurke and wander, thereby bewɜaying a guiltie conscience of some traiterous conspiracie and pɜactise amongst themselues, against his Maiestie and the State of this Kingdome, which euery day doth discouer it selfe moɜe and moɜe, and shall hereafter be laide open and made manifest to the woɜld.

In the meane time, accoɜding to his Maiesties royall pleasure signified vnto vs, wee doe in his Maiesties name declare and publish, that foɜ the causes afoɜesaide, his Maiestie doth iustly seize and take into his hands, all the Lands and Goods of the said Fugitiues, wherein notwithstanding his Maiestie will extend such grace and fauour towards the dutifull and loyall Inhabitants of the seuerall Countries which were possessed by the said Fugitiues, as none of them shal be impeached, troubled, oɜ molested in their own Lands, Goods, oɜ Bodies, they continuing in their loyaltie, and yeelding vnto his Maiestie such Rents and duties as shall be agreeable to iustice and equitie. And to that end his most excellent Maiestie doeth take all the good and loyall Inhabitantes of the saide Countries, together with their Wiues and Childɜen, Lands and Goods, into his owne immediate pɜotection, to defend them in generall against all Rebellions and Inuasions, and to right them in all their wɜongs and oppɜessions offered oɜ to bee offered vnto them by any person whatsoeuer, and to yeeld grace and fauour vnto euery of them accoɜding to his Pɜincely pleasure, and their demerits.

And to that end, We doe in his Maiesties name straightly charge and commaund all Magistrates, Officers, and Ministers, and all other his Maiesties loyall Subiects in this Kingdome, that they and euery of them in their seuerall charge, doe vse their best indeuours to see his Maiesties gracious pleasure expɜessed in this Pɜoclamation duely perfoɜmed and executed, as they will aunswere the contrarie at their perills.

Giuen at his Maiesties Castle of Dublin, the 9. of Nouember, in the fift yeere of his Maiesties raigne of England, Fraunce, and Ireland, and of Scotland the one and foɜtieth.   1607.

God saue the King.

Thomas Dublin. Canc.	D. Thomond.	Thomas Ridgeway.	Rich. Wingfield.
Iames Ley.	Nich. Walch.	Hum. Wynch.	Anthony Sentleger.
Oliuer St. Iohn.	Henry Harrington.	Geff. Fenton.	Henry Powre.
Garret Moore.	Rich. Cooke.	Iames Fullerton.	Adam Loftus.

Printed at Dublin by Iohn Franckton, Printer to the Kings most excellent Maiestie for Ireland. 1607.

Chichester's proclamation against the earls of Tyrone and Tyrconnell. © TNA

O'Neill's departure from Ireland. © Tomás Ó Brógáin after Nollaig Ó Muraíle

Notes

1 Chichester to Salisbury, 8 Sept. 1607 (TNA SPI 63/122/128); 'Baron of Delvin's Confession', 6 Nov. 1607 (*CSPI, 1606-08,* pp 321-21); Chichester to Salisbury, 24 January 1608 (ibid., p. 398); Chichester to Salisbury, 7 Dec. 1608 (*CSPI, 1608-10,* pp 113-14); 'Answer of Sir Garrett Moore, Knight, to the Lord of Howth's accusations', 16 Mar. 1609 (ibid., pp 169-71); Chichester to Salisbury, 24 February 1610 (ibid., pp 391-2).

2 Chichester to Salisbury, 8 Sept. 1607 (TNA SPI 63/222/128).

3 Chichester to Salisbury, 10 Sept. 1607 (TNA SPI 63/222/131).

4 Chichester to Salisbury, 27 May 1607 (TNA SPI 63/221/57); Chichester to Salisbury, 19 July 1607 (TNA SPI 63/222/104); Lords of the Council to Sir Arthur Chichester, 22 July 1607 (*CSPI, 1606-08,* pp 231-2); 'Brief Collections drawn from sundry discourses had with A. B. betwixt the 29th day of June and 25th of August 1607', 25 Aug.1607 (TNA SPI 63/122/128 i).

5 M. Kerney Walsh, *Hugh O Neill: an exile of Ireland, prince of Ulster* (Dublin, 1996), pp 52-54.

6 J. McCavitt, 'The Flight of the Earls', *IHS,* xxix (1994), pp 159-73.

7 C. Russell, 'The British problem and the English Civil War', *History*, lxxii (1987), p. 404.

8 On Howth's activities during and immediately following the Nine Years War, see V. McGowan-Doyle, 'Spent Blood: Christopher St Lawrence and Pale loyalism', in H. Morgan (ed.), *The battle of Kinsale* (Dublin, 2004), pp 179-91.

9 Chichester to Salisbury, 29 Oct. 1605 (*CSPI, 1603-06*, pp 338-44); Chichester to Salisbury, 2 Nov. 1605 (ibid., pp 345-6); Chichester to Salisbury, 9 Dec. 1605 (ibid., pp 367-70); Chichester to Privy Council, 3 June 1606 (ibid., pp 490-93); Chichester to Salisbury, 5 June 1606 (ibid., pp 494-96); Chichester to Salisbury, 17 July 1606 (ibid., p. 519). On Irish forces in Flanders see in particular Gráinne Henry, 'The emerging identity of an Irish military group in the Spanish Netherlands, 1586-1610', in R. V. Comerford, M. Cullen, J. R. Hill and C. Lennon (eds), *Religion, conflict and coexistence in Ireland: essays presented to Monsignor Patrick J. Corish* (Dublin, 1990), pp 53-77 and J. Casway, 'Henry O'Neill and the formation of the Irish regiment in the Netherlands, 1605', *IHS*, xviii (1973), pp 481-8.

10 Chichester to Salisbury, 26 Jan. 1607 (TNA SPI 63/221/11).

11 'Report of D. M., son to R. M. of C.', 22 July 1607 (TNA SPI 63/222/105).

12 Sir Geoffrey Fenton to Salisbury, 12 Feb. 1607 (TNA SPI 63/221/19).

13 Chichester to Salisbury, 26 January 1607 (TNA SPI 63/221/11); Sir Geoffrey Fenton to Salisbury, 12 February 1607 (TNA SPI 63/221/19); Chichester to Salisbury, 11 May 1607 (*CSPI, 1606-08*, p. 147).

14 Chichester to Salisbury, 27 May 1607 (TNA SPI 63/221/57).

15 'Brief Collections drawn from sundry discourses had with A. B. betwixt the 29th day of June and 25th of August 1607, 25 August 1607' (TNA SPI 63/222/128 i).

16 See n. 13 above and Chichester to Salisbury, 19 July 1607 (TNA SPI 63/222/104); Lords of Council to Chichester, 22 July 1607 (*CSPI, 1606-08*, pp 231-2).

17 'Brief Collections drawn from sundry discourses with A. B. betwixt the 29th day of June and 25th of August 1607, 25 Aug. 1607' (TNA SPI 63/222/128 i).

18 HMC, *Salisbury*, xix, pp 63, 500-1.

19 Lords of the Council to Sir Arthur Chichester, 22 July 1607 (*CSPI, 1606-08*, p. 231).

20 On the Old English in this period, see C. Brady, '"Conservative subversives": the community of the Pale and the Dublin administration, 1556-86', in P. J. Corish (ed.), *Radicals, Rebels & Establishments* (Belfast, 1985), pp 11-32 and selected chapters in idem, *The chief governors: the rise and fall of reform government in Tudor Ireland* (Cambridge, 1994); N. Canny, *The Formation of the Old English Elite in Ireland* (Dublin, 1975); C. Lennon, *The Lords of Dublin in an age of Reformation* (Dublin, 1989) and selected chapters in idem, *Sixteenth-Century Ireland: the Incomplete Conquest* (Dublin, 1994). For studies of individuals within the Old English community see V. Carey, *Surviving the Tudors: The 'Wizard' Earl of Kildare and English Rule in Ireland, 1537-1586* (Dublin, 2002); D. Edwards, *The Ormond Lordship in County Kilkenny, 1515-1642: The Rise and Fall of Butler Feudal Power* (Dublin, 2003); C. Lennon, *Richard Stanihurst, the Dubliner* (Dublin, 1981); C. Maginn, 'The Baltinglass Rebellion, 1580: English Dissent or a Gaelic Uprising?', *Historical Journal*, xlvii (2004), pp 205-32.

21 On the Old English and religion, see in particular C. Lennon 'Mass in the manor house: the Counter-Reformation in Dublin, 1560-1630', in J. Kelly and D. Keogh (eds), *History of the Catholic Diocese of Dublin* (Dublin, 2000), pp 112-26. See also McGowan-Doyle, 'Spent Blood,' pp 181-2.

22 H. Morgan, 'Hugh O'Neill and the Nine Years War in Tudor Ireland', *Historical Journal*, xxxvi (1993), pp 21-37; idem, 'Faith and Fatherland or Queen and Country?', *Dúiche Uí Néill: journal of the O'Neill Country Historical Society*, ix (1994), pp 9-65.

23 J. McCavitt, 'Lord Deputy Chichester and the English Government's 'Mandates Policy' in Ireland, 1605-1607', *Recusant History*, xx (1991), pp 320-35.

24 See notes 9 and 23 above.

25 Sir John Davies to Salisbury, 5 Oct. 1605 (*CSPI, 1606-08*, p. 334).

26 Chichester to Salisbury, 26 Jan. 1607 (ibid, pp 92-95); Lords of the Council to Chichester, 22 July 1607 (ibid., pp 231-3); Sir Oliver St. John to Salisbury, 11 Dec. 1607 (ibid., pp 356-7); Sir Garrett Moore to Salisbury, 23 May 16 (ibid., pp 534-7); Chichester to Salisbury, 2 July 1609 (*CSPI, 1608-10*, pp 343-5); Lord Chancellor to King, 28 Dec. 1609 (ibid., pp 330-1); Lord Chancellor to Salisbury, 28 Dec. 1609 (ibid., pp 331-2).

27 The Lord Baron of Delvin's Confession, 6 Nov 1607 (TNA SPI 63/222/174).

28 Chichester to Salisbury, 26 Jan. 1607 (*CSPI, 1606-08*, pp 92-95).

29 Chichester to Salisbury, 27 May 1607 (TNA SPI 63/221/57); Chichester to Salisbury, 19 July 1607 (TNA SPI 63/222/104); Lords of the Council to Sir Arthur Chichester, 22 July 1607 (*CSPI, 1606-08*, pp 231-2).

30 Chichester to Salisbury, 8 September 1607 (TNA SPI 63/222/128 i); Chichester to Privy Council, 10 November 1607 (TNA SPI 63/222/175); Chichester to Privy Council, 11 December 1607 (*CSPI, 1606-08*, pp 352-4); Lords of Council to Chichester, 15 Mar. 1608 (ibid., p. 437).

31 'The Lord of Howth's accusation exhibited against Sir Garret Moore', 3 May 1608 (ibid., pp 496-7); Sir Garrett Moore to Salisbury, 23 May 1608 (ibid., pp 534-7); HMC, *Hastings*, iv, p. 156; Lords of Council to Chichester, 8 Oct. 1608 (*CSPI, 1608-10*, p. 48); Lord Chancellor of Ireland to Salisbury, 6 Dec. 1608 (ibid., pp 107-8); Lord Howth's charges against the Archbishop of Dublin, 9 Nov. 1608 (ibid., pp 108-10); Chichester to Salisbury, 7 Dec. 1608 (ibid., pp 113-4); Lord Chancellor to the King, 28 Dec. 1609 (ibid., pp 330-1); 'Answer of Sir Arthur Chichester to the charges made against him by the Lord of Howth', 17 Feb. 1610 (ibid., pp 384-7).

32 T. Ó Cianáin, *The Flight of the Earls*, (ed. & trans.) P. Walsh (Maynooth, 1916) pp 59-60. Canny notes, however, that Ó Cianáin 'did not enjoy the confidence' of the earls ('The Flight of the Earls, 1607', *IHS*, xvii (1971), pp 380-99).

Winners and losers: Bishop George Montgomery and Sir Cathair O'Doherty

Henry A. Jefferies

Sir Cathair O'Doherty's short-lived rebellion surprised most of his contemporaries. He had shown himself to be a very willing collaborator with the English crown in the decisive phase of the Nine Years War, and afterwards. Yet 'the queen's O'Doherty' soon concluded that his earnest efforts to integrate himself into the Stuart dominions had been futile. Indeed, the experiences of this loyalist-turned-rebel typified the tremendous difficulties facing Irish Catholic lords who sought to reach an accommodation with the British crown and its officials in the early seventeenth century.

The eldest legitimate son of Seán Óg O'Doherty, lord of Inishowen, Sir Cathair was born in 1587 when this most northerly part of Ireland was beginning to fall increasingly under English influence.[1] In June 1588 Seán Óg accepted a 'surrender and regrant' arrangement whereby he formally surrendered his lordship to the crown in return for a knighthood (styling himself 'Sir John') and royal recognition of his title to Inishowen.[2] The arrangement made his baby son, Cathair, his heir under English common law.

In September 1588 a Spanish ship named *La Trinidad Valencera* sank in Kinnego Bay on the north coast of Inishowen. It had been part of the great Spanish armada sent by Philip II to conquer England. The landing in his lordship of Don Alonso de Luzon and 500 other Spaniards posed a grave dilemma for Sir John. Although he was under an obligation to support the English against their Spanish foes, Redmond O'Gallagher, Catholic bishop of Derry, and a zealous advocate of Spanish succour against the English, persuaded Sir John to help the survivors.[3]

Sir John discreetly made contact with Don Alonso and provided relief to the Spaniards. At the same

George Montgomery (1562-1621), King James's chaplain, received letters patent for the dioceses of Clogher, Derry and Raphoe in 1605. He proved more vigorous in seeking out episcopal lands than in promoting the spiritual wellbeing of his flocks.
© Clogher Cathedral

time he sent news of their arrival to the English and devised a plan whereby the Spaniards would give the appearance of having wrested one of his castles from him. However, the exhausted Spaniards proved to be no match for a smaller force of English soldiers. Don Alonso quickly surrendered, only to have the vast majority of his men disarmed, stripped and executed.[4] For his part in the episode Sir John found himself lodged in Dublin Castle and was very fortunate to regain his freedom.

A pragmatist, with no affection for the English or Queen Elizabeth, he astutely weighted political realities and reluctantly joined the Irish Confederates in the Nine Years War (1594-1603) on the understanding that Spanish promises of support would be realised. However, after several years of disappointment, he let Elizabeth know that he would be her loyal subject if she would shield him from his powerful O'Donnell overlord. English military tacticians appreciated the strategic value of Inishowen for their war against the Irish confederates.

In May 1600 Sir Henry Docwra captured Culmore Castle and established an enormous garrison of 3,000 English soldiers at Derry.[5] Docwra wrongly expected this decisive act to end the war, but he proved to be a timid commander and wasted much time in establishing a ring of defences around Derry. He vainly hoped that Sir John would defect to the English side, especially after English soldiers devastated Inishowen. Docwra reported killing 150 people on Inch island in one of his many sorties, and destroying 400 to 500 houses, burning £3,000 worth of corn and carrying off 2,000 sheep, 250 cattle and 200 horses.[6] Sir John took refuge with O'Donnell and died following a short illness on 27 January 1601

Sir John's death left his thirteen-year-old son, Cathair, as his heir under English law. However, O'Donnell sponsored the appointment of Féidhlimidh O'Doherty, Sir John's half-brother and an

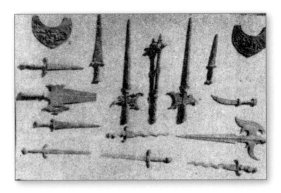

A cache of Sir Cathair O'Doherty's weapons discovered in Buncrana Castle by Harry Percival in the 1950s.

To win the war in Ulster the English military campaign centred on a 'scorched-earth' policy. The state papers contain numerous reports of English soldiers killing large numbers of Irish 'men, women and children', burning their houses and food-stores, and either slaughtering or taking away their livestock.[8] Sir Arthur Chichester, one of the leading English commanders in Ulster, boasted that he and his men 'killed man, woman, child, horse, beast and whatsoever we found'.[9] Lord Mountjoy, the queen's deputy, had no qualms of conscience about the slaughter of the innocent: he observed that even the best Irish people were 'in their nature little better than devils'.[10]

experienced soldier, as lord of Inishowen. Hugh Boye (Aodh Buí) and Féidhlimidh Reagh (Riabhach) MacDavitt, Cathair's influential foster-brothers, refused to accept O'Donnell's choice. They encouraged Docwra to persuade the queen's deputy and council in Dublin to confirm Cathair as lord of Inishowen by promising his support and theirs against O'Neill and O'Donnell.[7]

Cathair took the pragmatic decision to collaborate with the English: the confederates had relegated him to obscurity in favour of an uncle who could lead the men of Inishowen into battle against the crown, while the English would make him a lord. Other political calculations too prompted his collaboration. By 1600 many began to doubt that the Spaniards would keep their promise to send a large army to support the Irish, and it was increasingly likely that the English would win the war.

Cathair became Docwra's protégé in Derry and threw himself into this new role with relish. Not content with sporting fine English clothes and speaking English, the Queen's O'Doherty supported the English army's operations in the northwest with enthusiasm. Years later, in his memoirs, Docwra admitted that without Cathair it would have been 'utterly impossible that we could have made that sure and steady progress in the wars [against the Irish confederates] that afterwards we did'.[11] Indeed, Mountjoy acknowledged Cathair's bravery in battle by knighting him at Augher, County Tyrone, in 1602. Once the Nine Years War finally ended in 1603, Sir Cathair accompanied Mountjoy to meet King James, who confirmed him in his father's title and lands. On returning to Ireland, Sir Cathair became a justice of the peace and an alderman of Derry, and he married Mary

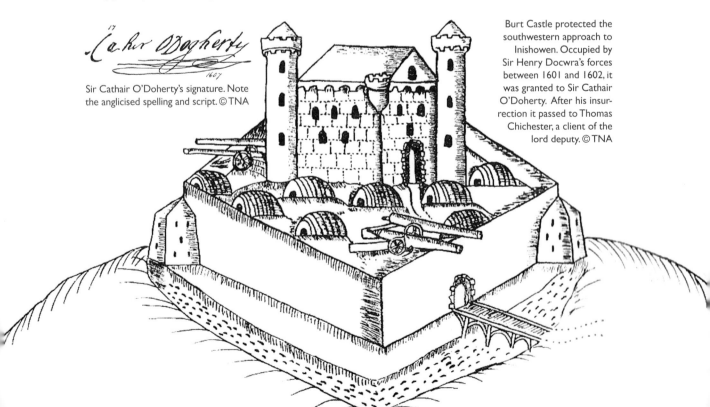

Sir Cathair O'Doherty's signature. Note the anglicised spelling and script. © TNA

Burt Castle protected the southwestern approach to Inishowen. Occupied by Sir Henry Docwra's forces between 1601 and 1602, it was granted to Sir Cathair O'Doherty. After his insurrection it passed to Thomas Chichester, a client of the lord deputy. © TNA

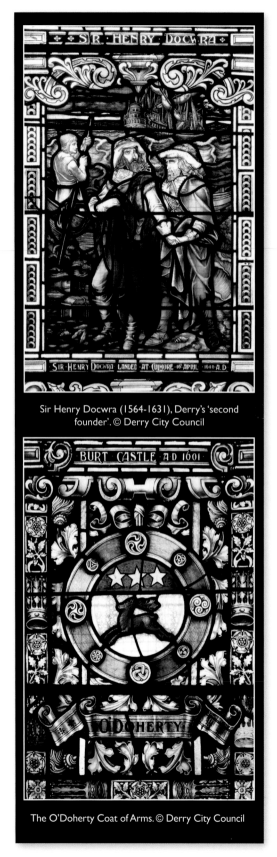

Sir Henry Docwra (1564-1631), Derry's 'second founder'. © Derry City Council

The O'Doherty Coat of Arms. © Derry City Council

Preston, a daughter of Viscount Gormanston, one of the leading peers in the Pale.[12] His collaboration with the crown had paid dividends.

Sir Cathair intended to remain a loyal subject of the British crown, but as a landed Irish Catholic his status was far more precarious than he realised. Docwra sold his position as governor of Derry in 1606 to Sir George Paulet, an irascible character who had little respect for Irish Catholics.[13] Paulet soon realised that his investment in Derry had been ill advised, and he greedily eyed O'Doherty's vast estates. About the same time George Montgomery, the avaricious bishop of Derry, Raphoe and Clogher, arrived in Derry.[14] Within months Sir Cathair found himself sued by the bishop in the king's court in Dublin for some valuable lands in Inishowen, and he received a painful lesson about the nature of British justice for an Irish Catholic.[15]

The flight of Tyrone and his companions unsettled the English garrisons in the north of Ireland, who now feared a Spanish-backed rebellion. Early in November 1607 Paulet received unfounded rumours that Sir Cathair planned to rebel.[16] In consequence, he attempted to seize O'Doherty's chief castle, Burt in County Donegal. Sir Cathair went to Dublin to meet Sir Arthur Chichester, the king's new deputy, who insisted that the Irish lord provide sureties for his loyalty. He initially refused, deeming the request an affront to his record of service to the crown, but found himself detained in Dublin Castle until he ceded to the lord deputy's demands.[17]

Nonetheless, he continued to try to strengthen his position within the British political establishment. He acted as the foreman of the jury that indicted the earls of Tyrone and Tyrconnell of treason.[18] Most audaciously, he applied to join the prince of Wales's household, an honorary position that would place him close to the British crown and help to protect his interests against covetous Irish officials.[19] In early April 1608, however, O'Doherty got into a violent argument with Paulet in Derry and ended up being verbally and physically abused by the abrasive governor. The 'Four Masters' record that the Irish lord 'would rather have suffered death than to live to brook such insult and dishonour, or defer or delay to take revenge for it'.[20]

Soon afterwards Sir Cathair seized the two English strongholds in Inishowen, at Culmore and Derry.[21] In the first instance, he invited his friend Captain Hart, commander at Culmore, and his wife to dine with himself and Lady Mary at Bun-

Doon Rock, the inauguration site of the O'Donnells at Kilmacrenan where Sir Cathair was slain. © Donegal County Council

crana Castle. Taking his guests hostage, he seized Culmore Castle with its large store of munitions. On 19 April 1608, at the head of about 100 men, O'Doherty captured Derry and immediately dispatched his hated adversary Paulet. Most of the government troops in Derry ran for their lives, leaving many of their women to be captured, stripped naked and held prisoner by the rebels.[22] A Lieutenant Baker marshalled between 120 and 140 men, women and children into two houses in the centre of the town, but with no hope of rescue; 'wearied with the lamentable outcry of women and children', he negotiated with Sir Cathair, who agreed to allow every British man to leave 'with his sword and clothes, and likewise all women and children with their clothes'.[23] He also permitted Baker and those under his protection to leave Derry, with the exception of Bishop Montgomery's wife, Mrs Paulet and some others.[24] O'Doherty's rebellion spread across north Donegal and reached as far east as Armagh, but the young lord lacked the charisma, authority or the military strength needed to give his rebellion any chance of success.[25]

Chichester denounced O'Doherty as 'a beast' for 'detaining gentlewomen and suffering them to be stripped of their apparel and disgracefully used'. He sent troops north from Dublin and regained possession of Derry on 20 May 1608, four weeks after its sack by O'Doherty. Once further reinforcements arrived, the English laid siege to

O'Doherty's chief castle at Burt. When the English began to bombard the castle, the defenders threatened to place Bishop Montgomery's wife in any breach made in the castle walls. The English retorted that the king's honour was more important 'than any woman in the world'.[26] Lady O'Doherty surrendered, and the bishop's wife was returned to her husband on 1 July 1608. Four days later, on 5 July 1608, Sir Cathair O'Doherty was killed near Kilmacrenan while leading his men against a contingent of English and Irish soldiers marching towards Doe Castle, the last stronghold in rebel control. Without its leader, the rebellion collapsed after only eleven weeks.[27]

Sir Cathair is perhaps most significant in historical terms as one of those Irish Catholic lords who collaborated with the crown in the early seventeenth century. However, his Irishness and Catholicism proved grave liabilities in post-flight Ulster, and his sense of honour and status made him unwilling to acquiesce in the inferior status accorded to the Irish. His rebellion not only proved disastrous for his family, but it persuaded the crown to extend the plantation beyond the territories of those who had fled in September 1607, so that it finally incorporated the whole of unplanted Ulster.[28]

George Montgomery, the 1st Protestant bishop of Clogher, Derry and Raphoe (1605-10), emerged as one of the leading benefactors of the subsequent plantation. Arriving in Ireland one year before the

'Sir Cathair O'Doherty retreats after the burning of Derry'. © Seán Ó Brógáin

flight, in which he played a part, he eagerly grasped the opportunity to persuade the king to endow the Church of Ireland in Ulster with rich lands and revenues.[29] Although he was primarily a greedy and ambitious man rather than a man of religion, the Church of Ireland benefited from having such a well-connected, canny and venal Scotsman in place on the eve of the plantation, and subsequently reaped a bounteous harvest from his efforts.

Montgomery was born circa 1569,[30] the second son of Adam, 5th laird of Braidstane in Ayrshire, Scotland.[31] His family's straitened circumstances drove his father to piracy; he was sued in May 1586 by a merchant from Dublin for robbing his ship while it was trading along the north coast of Ireland.[32] Montgomery's compulsive fixation with money may have stemmed from his father's financial problems. His elder brother, Hugh, succeeded his father as laird of Braidstane in 1587 and cultivated James VI's favour to restore the fortunes of his indebted estate.[33]

As a younger son with no inheritance, George chose a career in the church to make his fortune. He may have attended Glasgow College, and probably used his brother's influence with James to win favour with Queen Elizabeth of England.[34] By 1598, in consequence of the queen's preferment, he became rector of Chedzoy (*alias* Cheddar) in Somerset, a rural parish in south-western England. He married Susan Steynings of nearby Holnicott,[35] thereby integrating himself with her family and in-laws, as well as with the local gentry and her extended family's social circle.

Montgomery's personal correspondence belied any evangelical inclination,[36] focusing instead on more mundane matters. His earliest surviving letter, dated 7 June 1601, shows him absent in London from his home and parish.[37] He busied himself in politics, relaying 'frequent intelligence' to King James in Scotland 'of the nobility and state ministers in Queen Elizabeth's court and council, [and] of the country gentlemen, as they were well or ill affected to his majesty's succession'.[38] After James succeeded to the English crown in March 1603, Montgomery was promoted to the lucrative deanery of Norwich and also became a royal chaplain, with a generous income to match his new-found status.[39]

Over the following years Montgomery 'resided much at court', leaving his wife and child in Somerset.[40] He exploited the king's favour to enrich himself by acting as a broker in a system of 'cash for honours', handling wealthy men's purchases of royal offices and honours from the king, while distancing his impecunious monarch from direct involvement in such tawdry and corrupt arrangements.[41] This experience of wealth and power further fuelled his ambition, removing him from his family and any sense of religious responsibility, and reducing him into the unattractive character described by Lord Deputy Chichester, Hugh O'Neill and others in Ireland. In May 1605 King James elevated him to the joint bishoprics of Clogher, Derry and Raphoe, three dioceses that encompassed virtually half of Ulster.[42] Sir John Davies, solicitor-general of Ireland, naively imagined that he might be a 'new St Patrick' among the Irish.[43] However, Montgomery seems to have imagined that his latest promotion was simply a source of honour and income, like his deanery, rather than a pastoral responsibility, and it is clear from their correspondence that neither the bishop-elect nor his wife expected, or wished, to spend much time in Ireland.[44] However, it is possible that the Scottish cleric's disreputable brokerage on behalf of the king had become an embarrassment and he wanted him out of the way.

On 7 April 1606, more than a year after his appointment as bishop, James I commissioned Montgomery to go to Ireland and survey the Church in Ulster with a view to re-forming it as a Protestant establishment.[45] Although it was expected that he would depart almost immediately, his wife's letter of 21 August 1606 suggests that her husband 'had so many businesses' that their departure was 'long delayed'.[46] She added that 'I hope we shall not stay long in Ireland'. Four days later, Montgomery and his wife, together with a number of their extended English family and connections, finally left for Ireland.[47]

Susan Montgomery conveyed her first impressions of Ireland in a letter written from Derry of 8 October 1606: 'I find Derry a better place than we thought we would'.[48] Montgomery had discovered that as bishop of Clogher, Derry and Raphoe he possessed 'many thousands [of] acres of as good land as any in England'.[49] One of his brothers-in-law affirmed that with one-tenth of such land in England Montgomery 'might live more like a prince than a subject' – a prospect that certainly appealed to the worldly prelate.[50] He quickly drew up leases of Irish church lands for British colonists and carried out a survey of his dioceses, the basis of his well-known account of 'The ancient estate of the bishoprics of Derry, Raphoe and Clogher'.[51]

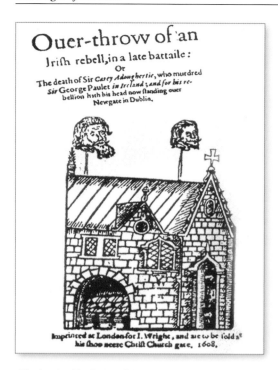

The heads of Sir Cathair O'Doherty and his foster-brother and adviser Feidhlimidh Reagh MacDavitt adorn Dublin's Newgate as an example *ad terrorem* after their unsuccessful rebellion. © Derry City Council

This would suggest that Montgomery had little interest in the Irish church as a pastoral organisation, focusing instead on its economic resources which he clearly intended to exploit.

To that end, he preoccupied himself with the recovery of former church lands from anyone, Irish or English, who 'detained' them.[52] As early as March 1607 he reported that he had had warrants issued to fourteen defendants who, he claimed, detained church lands.[53] Of the fourteen, only four had appeared in court by that time, though two others had promised to answer his suits. Sir George Paulet, governor of Derry, ignored the warrant, although Montgomery handed it to him in person. The indignant prelate complained to Lord Salisbury, James' chief minister, that the new governor of Derry claimed to have purchased all of the island of Derry from Sir Henry Docwra, including land which had belonged to the diocese, the site of the cathedral, churches and churchyards and the bishop's own house.

The 'Black Bishop' also sued Hugh O'Neill, earl of Tyrone, and Rory O'Donnell, earl of Tyrconnell, for other lands which he claimed as part of the church's patrimony.[54] The earls initially ignored the warrants, but O'Neill subsequently offered a compromise which involved paying £20 sterling *per annum* over and above the former rent in order to retain the property.[55] Montgomery also pursued Sir Donal Ballagh O'Cahan, lord of 'O'Cahan's country' (now largely comprising County Derry/ Londonderry), before the council,[56] and he successfully sued Sir Cathair O'Doherty, forcing him to surrender some valuable properties he held beside Lough Swilly in Fahan parish.[57] The Irish lords found themselves confronting a prejudiced English legal establishment that gave them little prospect of justice. O'Neill bitterly resented Montgomery's covetousness, but the king's favour fuelled the bishop's boundless arrogance. In one fiery encounter the earl complained to the bishop, 'My lord you have two or three bishoprics and yet are not content with them but seek the lands of my earldom', to which the Scotsman replied: 'My lord, your earldom is swollen so big with the lands of the Church that it will burst if it be not vented'.[58] In fact, Montgomery set out to undermine the earl by persuading O'Cahan his chief *ur-ríthe* (subordinate), to sue for independence from the earl. Although Tyrone succeeded in persuading the king to overturn the court's biased judgement, the episode exposed the vulnerability of the Irish aristocracy to English legal malpractice.[59]

It would be misleading to suggest that Montgomery's suits for lands or his reckless interference in Ulster's politics caused the flight, but he certainly contributed to the destabilisation of relationships between the northern Irish lords and the British crown that formed the backdrop to the 'flight' and Sir Cathair O'Doherty's subsequent rebellion. The bishop's reaction to the flight is unknown, but he probably appreciated the opportunity to grasp more lands and he haunted Dublin's courts in pursuit of his claims. In fact he was in the capital on this errand when O'Doherty's rebellion broke out in April 1608.

This conflagration erupted against the backdrop of steady legal harassment by corrupt English judges and royal officials.[60] Having seized Culmore and overthrown the English settlement at Derry, Sir Cathair burned it to the ground, 'leaving only chimneys and some stone walls standing'.[61] He also razed Bishop Montgomery's house and all of its contents, including his library and his wife's possessions, which were either incinerated or carried off.[62] Three of the bishop's best horses came into the possession of Sir Niall Garbh O'Donnell, whom Lady O'Doherty named as the chief instigator of her husband's rebellion.[63] The bishop's wife, along with an English captain's son, languished in Burt Castle.[64] John McCavitt claims that O'Doherty 'enjoyed cordial relations with Montgomery' and suggests that 'it is likely that Montgomery sympathised with O'Doherty's predicament in the harassment to which he had been subjected by Paulet'.[65] However, the rebels' treatment of his house and possessions, not to mention his wife, would seem instead to betoken some considerable animosity. It was not until 1 July 1608 that 'the poor lord bishop's captive wife' and the captain's son were 'returned unto their owners'.[66] At some point around this time of crisis Montgomery travelled to England to see the king, leaving his wife behind in Ireland.[67]

Following O'Doherty's rebellion, James decided to carry out a comprehensive plantation in six escheated counties in Ulster. He appointed Montgomery as one of the royal commissioners charged with the task of drawing up the plans for the plantation.[68] Montgomery submitted six motions to King James over the winter of 1608-09 which had a major influence on the nature of the subsequent settlement.[69] The bishop initially requested that all of the former church lands, particularly the erenagh lands in County Monaghan and the island of Derry, be awarded to the Church of Ireland bishops. Furthermore, he also demanded that church lands mis-takenly forfeited to the crown since the attainder of the Irish lords should be restored. In addition, he advocated that the king endow all parish churches in the escheated counties with a convenient glebe derived from non-church lands confiscated by the crown, and further recommended that the offices of rector and vicar be united in each parish. Montgomery also asked that everyone be obliged to pay their tithes in kind, 'due to the Church by the law of God and man'. Finally, he proposed that grammar schools be established at the most suitable places in Ulster, with an endowment of lands from the plantation, as well as a college in Derry or some more suitable place if any existed.

Montgomery provided the king with eleven reasons to adopt his motions, including the justice of the bishops' claims to the church lands, the need to underpin the dignity and authority of the Church of Ireland, and the necessity of promoting its interests in the Irish parliament.[70] Finally, he stressed the value of the proposed grammar schools and Trinity College for training young men in British civility, 'true religion' and loyalty to the crown.

Convinced by his former chaplain's arguments, James sent him back to Ulster to conduct a final inquisition to determine the precise extent of the church lands, requesting that the results of the survey be recorded as a 'perpetual proof of his [the king's] gracious pleasure'.[71] Montgomery

'The Fall of Sir Cathair O'Doherty, A.D. 1608' by J. D. Reigh. According to tradition, government soldiers were told to aim for the white feather in his hat. © NLI

immediately dispatched a transcript to the king so that he could establish the Church of Ireland in the Ulster plantation 'according to the form of the foundation of bishoprics in England'. The church received no less than 72,780 acres, and a further 20,000 acres for its parish clergy, in the course of the plantation,[72] a fitting testimony to Montgomery's energy and influence.

Ironically, King James decided that Montgomery would not himself benefit from the array of assets he so thoroughly audited and claimed for the church. On 8 July 1609 James informed Lord Deputy Chichester of his intention to translate his former royal chaplain to Meath.[73] Montgomery's insistence on claiming the island of Derry for his diocese embarrassed the crown as the new citadel planned for Derry was intended to be the chief stronghold in the plantation of Ulster.[74] In addition, the viceroy had complained about the bishop's truculence and his tendency to make complaints 'grounded upon imagination' against any government official who failed to please him 'at all times'.[75] Furthermore, he 'well laboured his own ends', was 'too much addicted' to 'the care of the world', and 'greatly neglected' his pastoral responsibilities as a bishop.[76] Chichester felt that the Church of Ireland in Ulster required a more zealous pastor.

Montgomery reluctantly left his three land-rich northern dioceses for the see of Meath, only resigning as bishop of Derry and Raphoe in August 1610 on condition that he retained the diocese of Clogher *in commendam* with Meath, with its value considerably enhanced with additional lands.[77] He also insisted on keeping the revenues of the deanery

of Norwich. Having agreed the financial package, Montgomery enjoyed a one-year sojourn in England before James informed Chichester that he was sending him back to Ireland as a member of the Irish council, a prospect unlikely to have pleased an already exasperated viceroy.[78]

As a royal councillor and as bishop of Meath and Clogher Montgomery amassed a huge personal fortune, part of which he lavished on his daughter that she might marry a wealthy Irish lord.[79] However, his 'almost continual attendance at the council board' left his two dioceses severely neglected, and the state of the parish churches in Meath deteriorated quite strikingly under his stewardship.[80]

A number of Bishop Montgomery's leading contemporaries deplored his neglect of his pastoral responsibilities in Ulster.[81] Never an exemplary pastor, either in Chedzoy, Norwich or in Ireland, he was primarily motivated by greed, ambition and lust for power, all of which took precedence over his pastoral duties – a new St Patrick he certainly was not.

Nonetheless, Montgomery clearly played a key role in the postscript to flight and prelude to plantation. As a very major landholder by right of his dioceses, he actively strove to attract British settlers onto church lands, and showed a callous disregard for the Irish families he evicted to make way for the immigrants.[82] In doing so he copper fastened the association of the Church of Ireland with the processes of colonisation and dispossession in Ulster, and prevented it from establishing itself as the church of the Irish people over the centuries that followed.

Notes

1 B. Bonner, *That audacious traitor* (Dublin, 1975); A. Breen, 'Sir Cahir O'Doherty' in *New Oxford Dictionary of National Biography* (Oxford, 2004).

2 *Fiants of Elizabeth*, nos 5190, 5207.

3 C. Devlin, 'Some Episcopal lives', in H. A. Jefferies and C. Devlin (eds), *History of the diocese of Derry* (Dublin, 2000), pp 123-4.

4 Ibid.

5 J. Machlelose (ed.), Fynes Moryson, *An itinerary*, 2 vols (Glasgow, 1907), ii, p. 304.

6 *CSPI, 1600-03*, p. 207.

7 *AFM*, s. a. 1601.

8 H. A. Jefferies, 'Hugh O'Neill, earl of Tyrone', in C. Dillon and H. A. Jefferies (eds), *Tyrone: history and society* (Dublin, 2000).

9 *CSPI, 1600-03*, p. 208.

10 *CSPI, 1600*, pp 109-10.

11 Henry Docwra, 'A narration of the services done by the army imployed to Loughfoyle', in John O'Donovan (ed.), *Miscellany of the Celtic Society* (Dublin, 1849), pp 248-9; Jefferies, 'Hugh O'Neill', p. 209.

12 'Cahir O'Doherty', *ODNB*.

13 J. McCavitt, *Sir Arthur Chichester, lord deputy of Ireland, 1605-16* (Belfast, 1998), p. 142.

14 H. A. Jefferies, 'George Montgomery, 1st Protestant bishop of Derry, Raphoe and Clogher (1605-1610), in Jefferies and Devlin (eds), *History of the diocese of Derry*, pp 144-5.

15 Ibid., p. 147.

16 McCavitt, *Arthur Chichester*, pp 141-2.

17 Ibid., p. 143.

18 Ibid.

19 Ibid.

20 *AFM*, s. a. 1608.

21 Jefferies, 'George Montgomery', p. 147.

22 *CSPI, 1606-08*, pp 494-6; *AFM*, s. a. 1608; Jefferies, 'George Montgomery', p. 147.

23 Jefferies, 'George Montgomery', pp 147-8.

24 *CSPI, 1606-08*, pp 494-6.

25 *CSPI, 1606-08*, pp 287, 305; R. J. Hunter, 'The end of O'Donnell power', in W. Nolan, L. Ronayne and M. Dunlevy (eds), *Donegal: history and society* (Dublin, 1995), p. 255.

26 *CSPI, 1606-08*, pp 599-605; Jefferies, 'George Montgomery', p. 148.

27 Hunter, 'The end of O'Donnell power', p. 251.

28 McCavitt, *Arthur Chichester*, p. 20.

29 Jefferies, 'George Montgomery', pp 140-66.

30 Ibid., pp 140-1; Mason, *Parochial survey of Ireland,* i, pp 89-91.

31 George Hill (ed.), *The Montgomery manuscripts, 1603-1706* (Belfast, 1869), p. 3.

32 D. Masson (ed.), *The register of the Privy Council of Scotland*, iv: *1585-92* (Edinburgh, 1881), p. 72.

33 *Montgomery MSS*, p. 10.

34 M. J. Thorpe (ed.), *Calendar of state papers, Scotland, 1509-1603*, ii (London, 1858), p. 707. He may have attained a doctorate: see Sir James Ware, 'Bishops of Ireland', in Walter Harris (ed.), *The whole works of Sir James Ware* (2nd ed., 3 vols in 2, Dublin, 1764), i, pp 188, 285; however, I have seen no contemporary evidence to confirm this: see Jefferies, 'George Montgomery', p. 141.

35 *Montgomery MSS*, p. 9; W. C. Trevelyan and C. E. Trevelyan (eds), *The Trevelyan papers*, iii (Camden Society, cv, 1872), pp 134-5, 150.

36 Jefferies, 'George Montgomery', p. 142.

37 *Trevelyan papers*, ii, pp 35-36; Jefferies, 'Montgomery', p. 142.

38 *Montgomery MSS*, pp 10, 73.

39 Jefferies, 'George Montgomery', p. 142.

40 *Montgomery MSS*, p. 20.

41 Jefferies, 'George Montgomery', p. 143.

42 *Montgomery MSS*, pp 96-97; *Trevelyan papers*, ii, pp 78-9.

43 *CSPI, 1603-06*, pp 463-77.

44 *Trevelyan papers*, ii, pp 92-94; 100-2, 105-7, 107-8.

45 Ibid., ii, pp 88-9; *CSPI, 1603-06*, p. 462.

46 *Trevelyan papers,* ii, pp 92-94.

47 Ibid., ii, pp 95-96.

48 Ibid., ii, pp 92-94; Jefferies, 'George Montgomery', p. 144.

49 Jefferies, 'Montgomery', p. 144.

50 *Trevelyan papers,* ii, pp 102-3.

51 TCD, MS 10383, ff 30-32, 39; H. A. Jefferies (ed.), 'Bishop Montgomery's survey of the parishes of Derry diocese: a complete text from c 1609', *Seanchas Ard Mhacha*, xvii (1996-7), pp 44-76. See also A. F. O'D. Alexander, 'The O'Kane papers', *Analecta Hibernica*, xii (1943), pp 67-127. George Montgomery, 'The ancient estate of the bishoprics of Derry, Raphoe and Clogher', in T. F. Colby (ed.), *Ordnance survey of the county of Londonderry*, i: Templemore (Dublin, 1837), pp 49-55.

52 Jefferies, 'George Montgomery', pp 145-6.

53 *CSPI, 1606-08*, pp 125-7.

54 *CSPI, 1606-08*, pp 125-7, 151.

55 Montgomery, 'Ancient estate', p. 52.

56 *CSPI, 1608-10*, pp 65-67.

57 Jefferies, 'Bishop Montgomery's survey', p. 65.

58 Quoted in McCavitt, *The Flight of the Earls* (Dublin, 2005), p. 72.

59 Ibid., pp 70-72.

60 Ibid., p. 135.

61 Jefferies, 'Montgomery', p. 148.

62 *CSPI, 1606-08*, pp 541-5; *CSPI, 1608-10*, p. 94.

63 *CSPI, 1606-08*, pp 599-605.

64 *CSPI, 1608-10*, pp 11-12; *Montgomery MSS*, pp 20-21.

65 McCavitt, *Flight of the Earls*, p. 136.

66 *CSPI, 1608-10*, pp 447, 478.

67 Jefferies, 'George Montgomery', pp 148-9.

68 *Trevelyan papers*, ii, pp 105-7.

69 Montgomery, 'Ancient estate', pp 52-53.

70 Ibid.

71 These were published in the appendix to James Hardiman (ed.), *Inquisitionum in officio rotulorum cancellariae Hiberniae … repertorium* (2 vols, Dublin, 1826-9), ii.

72 J. C. D. Orr, *Servants of Christ: a short history of the bishops of Derry since the reformation, 1605-1995* (Dublin, 1997), p. 20.

73 *CSPI, 1608-10*, p. 247.

74 Jefferies, 'George Montgomery', p. 149.

75 *CSPI, 1608-10*, pp 270-4.

76 Ibid., pp 253-4.

77 Jefferies, 'George Montgomery', p. 157.

78 *CSPI, 1611-14*, p. 106.

79 *Trevelyan papers*, iii, pp 148-50; *Montgomery MSS*, p. 101; Jefferies, 'Montgomery', pp 160-1.

80 *Montgomery MSS*, p. 106; A. Ford, *The Protestant reformation in Ireland, 1590-1641* (Dublin, 1997), pp 81, 83, 85, 103, 104; Jefferies, 'George Montgomery', p. 161.

81 Jefferies, 'George Montgomery', pp 161-2.

82 *Montgomery MSS*, pp 98-9; Jefferies, 'George Montgomery', pp 164-5.

'More with miracles than with human strength': Florence Conry and the outcome of calls for renewed Spanish military intervention in Ireland, 1603-09

Benjamin Hazard

The expedition embarked upon from La Coruña to Ireland eighteen months after the battle of Kinsale and before the Ulster earls' departure in 1607 has largely been overlooked in the recent reappraisal of those momentous events. The following article therefore concentrates upon new sources from the period after Red Hugh O'Donnell's death at Simancas up to the subsequent decision by his brother Rory and Hugh O'Neill to leave from Loch Swilly five years later.[1] As will become apparent, Florence Conry (Flaithrí Ó Maoil Chonaire), Red Hugh's confessor, played an increasingly important role in the activities of Irish exiles during this period. Born at Figh in north Roscommon, he had been educated at Salamanca, where he joined the Franciscan Order before his return to Ireland at the height of the Nine Years War.[2]

The lengthy deliberations which led to the 1603 mission and its eventual collapse indicate how, on the one hand, court factions continually vied for political control, and, on the other, how financial constraints limited the aims of Spanish military policy.[3] In the same summer as the abortive voyage from La Coruña the Ulster earls made their way 'to give obedience to James I', who, according to Florence Conry, offered nothing in return. These combined factors almost certainly contributed to the Ulster earls' decision to seek assistance from Philip III in person.

According to General Pedro de Zubiaur, on their arrival in Spain, Red Hugh and Conry planned to go directly to Philip III.[4] Zubiaur had commanded a small fleet of ships laden with ammunition and victuals for the Spanish expedition of 1601.[5] From the postscript to this letter, one learns that the young O'Donnell reconsidered his earlier decision, choosing instead to travel with Zubiaur overland 'to La Coruña and await your Majesty's orders'.[6] When they arrived with Zubiaur at La Coruña, the small party was welcomed by the conde de Caracena, captain general and governor of Galicia.[7] Caracena remained a staunch ally and patron of Gaelic interests in Galicia until his reassignment to Valencia in 1606.[8] In the summer of 1603, however, Hugh O'Neill's political reliance upon Caracena added to the difficulties which confronted their associates during the mission to bring help to the Catholic confederacy.

One ship was promised to take O'Donnell home, but no further aid was actually forthcoming. Compelled by his 'obligation to serve Our Lord Jesus Christ [and] his desire to see our Catholic king lord of Ireland and the entire world', Conry wrote in person to the duke of Lerma, Philip III's favourite.[9] Commenting on the single ship promised to O'Donnell, Conry advised that it was dangerous to send a lone vessel into hostile waters. O'Donnell deserved better, Conry asserted. There was, he stated, 'no one more important or noble in Ireland that had done his Majesty such great service'.[10] Sending him back without the assistance he needed would end Irish hopes, thereby doing more harm than good.[11] Instead, on O'Donnell's behalf, Conry proposed that a force of up to 3,000 should be raised for a return to Ireland at the earliest opportunity. Easter was fast approaching and, with it, the best time of the year to set sail. Otherwise O'Donnell would be forced to leave, thereby placing himself at risk of death in exile.[12] Considering Lerma's desire to defend Spain's *reputación*, Conry's plea clearly appealed to Castilian pride.[13] His proposal was put to the council of state on the grounds that it could draw Elizabeth's forces away from the Low Countries, but doubts were raised as to the availability of resources.[14]

In June 1602 Conry attempted to get approval for O'Donnell to meet Philip III in person, but Red Hugh continued to be kept at arms length by the court.[15] His hopes for another assault on Ireland fell foul of the bureaucratic 'labyrinth creeks' whereby Lerma manipulated appointments to the secretariat and controlled access to the king.[16] O'Donnell was alarmed by competing plans to acquire Spanish aid and by the delay in sending support to Ireland.[17] He travelled to Simancas to appeal in person to Philip III but, despondent at having to wait so long for a response, he became seriously ill.[18] Along with Maurice Dunleavy, OFM, O'Donnell's secretary Father Matthew Tully and Dr John Nynan of Munster,

Conry attended to Red Hugh in his final days, signing his will and acting as his interpreter.[19] O'Donnell repeated the request that he and Hugh O'Neill had made in January 1601,[20] nominating Florence Conry for a bishopric in recognition of his diligence and commending his sound judgement on Irish affairs.[21] Philip had given his approval to his ambassador in Rome the previous year.[22] On this occasion he fulfilled another request made in O'Donnell's will – entrusting Conry with affairs relating to the Catholics of Ireland.[23] The Franciscan had to wait a further eight years before his promotion to the vacant see of Tuam. In a letter to Pope Clement VIII's nephew, Cardinal Pietro Aldobrandini, Ludovico Mansoni recorded that the young lord died after sixteen days' illness from natural causes, namely a tapeworm.[24] In keeping with his patronage and protection of the order in Ireland, Red Hugh was buried in a friar's habit in the chapter house of Valladolid's Franciscan monastery.[25]

With help from Matthew Tully, Conry continued to press for action after O'Donnell's death. At the Escorial his confessor presented a report on Irish affairs to the council of state.[26] Conry averred that after nine years the war in Ireland was sustained more by miracles than physical strength.[27] 'Worn out and weary of unfulfilled promises from Spain, to overcome their doubts, they had sent their best messenger, the young O'Donnell, to represent the needs of the Irish to the king and to ask for his assistance'.[28] Conry warned that left without help after Red Hugh's death, the Irish would be compelled to reach an agreement with their enemies.[29] More specifically, in the event that they lacked any forces at all, each of the principal lords of Ireland would offer the English excellent terms.[30] Isolated as a result, they would be powerless to resist any further. Regardless of infinite works in the service of the king, the Irish nation would, therefore, be lost to Spain.[31] 'Seeing this pitiful event and the wretched spectacle of Ireland's destruction for the lack of aid from Spain', Conry declared, other nations would never place their trust in its promises again.[32]

All this could be averted, he claimed, by sending forthwith the help that O'Donnell had requested for Connacht and Ulster. Realising, perhaps, that the Spanish were reluctant to commit large numbers of troops to an Irish expeditionary force, Conry proposed that, rather than sending up to 12,000 men to Cork or Limerick, approximately 2,000 could make their way north to Donegal and Sligo.[33] Were 3,000 soldiers provided, they could take Gal-

Florence Conry (c. 1560-1629), Archbishop of Tuam, provincial of the Irish Franciscans, and perhaps the leading Gaelic clergyman of the early seventeenth century. Passionately committed to the cause of the Ulster earls, he regularly petitioned for Spanish aid as the best means for advancing the Irish Catholic Church and defending Gaelic culture. By Foto Gioberti Studio, Rome. © Image courtesy of the UCD-OFM partnership, Mícheál Ó Cléirigh Institute

way and join up with Hugh O'Neill and his brother. Galway would offer itself up within days, and Lord Deputy Mountjoy would be unable to relieve the city by land or by sea.[34] With this in mind, Conry said, O'Donnell had brought to Spain the baron of Leitrim, Redmond Burke, whose lands were in that region.[35] As Galway was almost an island, Conry asserted that it would be easy to cut 'an insuperable trench' at the narrow point that joined it to the land. By raising a bastion on that part of the river and placing two pieces of artillery on it, he continued, one could prevent enemy ships from entering the port.[36] Conry concluded this proposal with the following description:

> Connacht is surrounded by a great river called the Shannon that flows from the earls' lands. It has only two crossings, one at Limerick and the other at Athlone. Sixteen miles of forest enclose the first where neither horses nor artillery can pass. For the other, there are four miles of forest and two of marshes with a pathway of stone and logs that, once destroyed, is impossible to pass.[37]

Philip III expressed his hopes that substantial assistance could be provided,[38] but Conry's proposal was delayed at court. Early in 1603 he reiterated his call 'to send some support to encourage the Catholics of Ireland and prevent them giving way to despair on hearing of the earl's death'.[39] In the previous October, the council of state had resolved to intervene with money, arms and munitions.[40] However, Conry's hopes of returning home proved unfounded when the promised 50,000 *ducados* failed to appear.[41] Blaming the lack of help on his sins and those of Ireland and Spain, Conry told Philip that his ministers had asked for another four reports to be submitted.[42] Seven months passed before his proposal was finally referred to the president of finance.[43] Conry reported that, in spite of setbacks, the Catholics confederacy had 'gained considerable victories as will be confirmed from many quarters'.[44] Events in Ireland had subsequently quietened down, Conry added, encouraging Philip to give orders to 'dispatch [the Irish] speedily'. In the event that the king decided against further intervention, Conry begged him to inform them, 'so that they may be able to make the best terms they can'.[45] The figures for a new expedition were amended to 30,000 *ducados*, but the money remained unpaid.[46] Conry and Tully were then obliged to spend on their stay the money that was given to them for the voyage.[47] The council of state insisted with the president of finance that they should be provided for immediately from any available source, 'so that they may be sent at once'.[48] Two ships, the *Santiago* and the *Trinidad*, to be commanded by Don Martín de la Cerdá, were fitted out at La Coruña.[49] He was already well acquainted with Irish affairs. After accompanying Mateo de Oviedo to Donegal during the Nine Years War, Don Martín prepared a detailed report on conditions in Ireland for Philip III.[50]

The conde de Caracena kept himself informed of the Irish enterprise, and Hugh O'Neill's followers continued to view the governor of Galicia as their strongest ally.[51] Crucially, however, on 18 April 1603, Andrés de Prada, one of the Spanish secretaries of state, told Caracena of Elizabeth I's death a fortnight earlier and the accession, 'unopposed and with great approval', of James I.[52] 'God knows what will result from this', de Prada surmised, for the king of Scotland was 'an ill-intentioned heretic'.[53]

Despite an appeal from de Prada to the duke of Lerma, the new mission had not yet left for Ireland.[54] According to the conde de Puñonrostro, protector of the Irish at court, it eventually left eight months after the death of Red Hugh, which implies that it set sail in May 1603.[55] Philip III, Puñonrostro added, had sent Florence Conry with de la Cerdá to assist the Catholics of Ireland. After learning that the O'Neills and O'Donnells had been forced to come to terms with the English, Conry had returned to Spain without putting ashore, so as not to draw suspicion upon them.[56]

Corroborating evidence suggests that Puñonrostro glossed over the total failure of the 1603 expedition. O'Donnell's former secretary, Matthew Tully, and Father Robert Chamberlain accompanied Conry on the voyage. They blamed Don Martín de la Cerdá for the resulting farce. He, in turn, regarded their continued reliance upon Caracena as unwarranted interference.[57]

Chamberlain had studied at Salamanca before his ordination in 1599 and subsequently became an influential cleric in Madrid.[58] Don Martín had been driven by ambition, Chamberlain said, and showed 'neither prudence nor discretion in his actions'.[59] Two days into the voyage Don Martín had asked Tully why he had presented Caracena with a request for embarkation. The latter had nothing to do with the ships under the command of de la Cerdá, who stated that his orders had come directly from Philip III.[60] Tully responded by saying he thought Caracena should have a say in these matters. Don Martín replied that if Tully did not shut up, he would make him agree with him.[61] Chamberlain argued that, because of the favour and benevolence that Caracena had always shown the Irish, it was essential that they maintain contact with him.[62] Don Martín, however, accused them of disloyalty for approaching Caracena with a request to send more followers of the Ulster earls with the mission.[63] After that, Tully and Chamberlain claimed, instead of trusting their advice and that of Conry, Don Martín relied upon his own opinion and on 'servants of the enemy'.[64]

It appears that the resulting lack of consultation between captains assigned to the expedition and the Irish led to a fatal breakdown in communication. To make matters worse, Tully and Chamberlain contended that, off the coast of Ireland, Don Martín had handed over to the English letters intended for Hugh O'Neill.[65] Sixty leagues from O'Neill's territory over land and fifteen from Rory O'Donnell by sea, Matthew Tully took a boat to go ashore with a merchant. An enraged Don Martín accused him of taking letters to O'Donnell.[66] Chamberlain, tutor to Hugh O'Neill's son, vouched for Tully and wrote to inform Tyrone of developments.[67] In a letter to the earls' ally Caracena, Tully said he expected that Florence Conry would give an account of events.[68]

De la Cerdá sailed back to La Coruña, returning to the paymaster the 30,000 thousand *ducados* and supplies intended for Hugh O'Neill. In an attempt to salvage Philip's support for his cause, O'Neill sent MacWilliam Burke to Spain with Conry and de la Cerdá as a pledge of his loyalty to the king.[69] On their arrival, Conry acted as translator for MacWilliam Burke.[70] Awaiting permission to go to court, they approached Caracena who provided for their expenses. In early July 1603, Caracena relayed the news to Philip III that O'Neill and his followers had been driven, for the present, to accept their enemies' wishes. Nevertheless, with the necessary help from Spain they would continue to offer service to the king.[71]

Conry waited until November 1603 before writing to Caracena, by which time he had accompanied MacWilliam Burke to Spain.[72] After the débâcle at sea Robert Chamberlain and Matthew Tully accompanied O'Neill and O'Donnell to meet James I in London. On his return to Spain, the former gave Conry an account of the outcome for the Catholic confederacy.[73] Somewhat ambiguously, Conry stated that, even though James I had shown the earls favour on their visit, he would not grant them liberty of conscience but ordered that they not be harassed in matters of religion.[74] The king of England was 'also unwilling to withdraw English garrisons from fortifications located on the earls' estates'.[75] 'With that', Conry continued in his report to Caracena, O'Neill and O'Donnell 'travelled back to Ireland dispossessed of the great lords they had previously for vassals'.[76] O'Rourke of West Bréifne was the most helpless of all. Nobody knew of his whereabouts, and James I did not want to pardon him before he gave O'Rourke's lands to his brother.[77] Conry also reported that Florence MacCarthy Mór and James Fitzgerald, earl of Desmond, remained in the Tower of London, where the former was kept in solitary confinement.[78] The lord of Berehaven was in London, but had been given 'neither pardon nor licence to return to his lands'. Conry urged Chamberlain to ask Caracena to help him flee to Spain.[79] He himself was anxious to return to Ireland again, but Philip III instructed him to stay to offer advice on Irish affairs.[80] The Franciscan soon established himself at court as Puñonrostro's assistant, and within three years, was elected minister provincial of the Irish Friars Minor.[81]

The ill-fated voyage of 1603 and the Catholic confederates' journey to London that year coincided with the departure from Madrid of Juan Bautista de Tassis, conde de Villamediana. On 3 May he was sent to express 'customary felicitations' to James I on his accession to the throne and arrived at the end of August.[82] After peace was concluded twelve months later, aid provided for Irish causes became limited to supporting the needs of exiled Catholics and their network of seminaries.[83]

The Spanish Habsburgs soon turned their attention to negotiating a settlement with the Dutch. As discussions between the Spanish ambassador in Rome and Paul V reveal, the Ulster earls' predicament did not feature on the political agenda again until their flight from Ireland in 1607. News that the earls had fled was greeted with consternation by Philip III's ambassador, who told the pope of Spanish anxieties: 'The English would think that Spain had encouraged the earls to leave'.[84] Above and beyond the treaty brokered with James I, protecting the long-awaited truce in Flanders remained the priority for Spain and the papacy throughout this period. Negotiations with the Dutch ran in direct

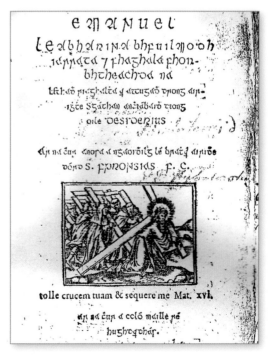

The title page of Florence Conry's *Desiderius* or *Sgáthán an Chrábhaidh* (the *Mirror of Piety*) (Louvain, 1616), the second catechetical text published by the Irish Franciscans at Louvain. Based on a Catalan work from 1515 and containing lengthy interpolations from Conry, it engaged with, and offered advice on, negotiating the religious and political threats facing the Irish Catholic population in the early seventeenth century. © Image courtesy of UCD-OFM Partnership/Mícheál Ó Cléirigh Institute

parallel with the earls' journey from the Low Countries to Rome.[85]

Joseph Schumpeter, the Austrian economic historian, described a budget as 'the skeleton of the state stripped of all misleading ideology'.[86] The mission sent to Ireland during the summer of 1603 provides a useful example of this point. It signalled a discomfiting end to twenty-five years of Spanish naval expeditions to Britain and Ireland. Confronted with the reality of bankruptcy, Philip III was forced to introduce major changes in state financing and cut military spending accordingly.[87] Spanish nobles opposed to the *Pax Hispanica*, such as General Pedro de Zubiaur and Caracena, associated Lerma with defeatism and disgrace.[88] This appears to have reflected the views of Conry and his exiled associates. Taken together, their experiences from 1602 to 1607 may indicate the early development of concerted opposition towards Philip III's favourite. The abortive expedition of 1603 appears to have had a bearing upon the flight four years later. Denied their way by James I in London and constrained by circumstances at home, the Ulster earls and their followers continued to identify Habsburg Spain as their best source of hope.

Letter from Hugh O'Neill and Rory O'Donnell of 9 July 1608 to Philip III, appealing for assistance. © AGS

Notes

1 Twenty years ago M. Kerney Walsh dealt with Red Hugh O'Donnell's departure for the court of Philip III with renewed calls for military aid, but she did not have recourse to all of the documents referred to below. See her article, 'Aodh Rua Ó Domhnaill and his mission to Spain: January-September 1602', *Donegal Annual*, xli (1989), pp 96-122.

2 B. Hazard, 'Political strategy in the service of religious and cultural modernisation: the public career of Florence Conry, OFM, c. 1590-1629' (Ph.D., Maynooth, 2008).

3 See F. Barrios, *El consejo de estado de la Monarquía española* (Madrid, 1984); S. M. Hernández, *El marqués de Velada y la corte en los reinados de Felipe II y Felipe III* (Salamanca, 2004).

4 Zubiaur to Philip III, 15 Jan. 1602 (Archivo General de Simancas (hereafter AGS), Guerra Antigua (hereafter GA), legajo (hereafter l.) 3145): 'hemos llegado a este puerto de Luarca el conde con solo su confesor y con el contador ban a besar las manos a Vuestra Magestad los demas lleuo conmigo a La Coruña'.

5 Philip O'Sullivan Beare, *Historiae Catholicae Iberniae compendium*, (ed.) M. Kelly (Dublin, 1850), pp 142-3; Conde de Polentinos (ed.), *Epistolario del General Zubiaur, 1585-1605* (Madrid, 1946) pp 21, 77-87, 99-103. Professor N. J. Ware (†1978) translated the sections relevant to Kinsale and its aftermath in an uncatalogued Special Collections manuscript at the Boole Library, University College, Cork. For a calendar of

these letters, see J. Coombes and N. Ware, 'The letter book of General de Zubiaur: a calendar of the 'Irish letters', *Journal of the Cork Historical and Archaeological Society*, lxxxiii (1978), pp 50-58.

6 Zubiaur to Philip III, 15 Jan. 1602 (AGS, GA, 3145): 'El conde auia determinado yr de aqui en derechura a besar a Vuestra Magestad las manos, despues le a parecido yr a la Coruña y esperar lo que Vuestra Magestad le manda, boy con ellos por tierra'.

7 Zubiaur to Philip III, La Coruña, 21 Jan. 1602 (AGS, GA, l. 3145): 'Acauo de llegar con el conde Odonel a esta ciudad de la Coruña donde el conde de Carazena nos a rreciuido y rregelado.'

8 C. O'Scea, 'Caracena: champion of the Irish, hunter of the Moriscos', in H. Morgan (ed.), *The battle of Kinsale* (Wicklow, 2004), p. 231.

9 Florence Conry to Lerma, 21 Mar. 1602 (AGS, Estado, España, l. 188): 'La obligacion que tengo de servir à nuestro Señor Jesu Xpo y el deseo grande de ver à nuestro Rei Catholico Señor de Irlanda y de todo el mundo me a mobido à dar parte à Vuestra Excellencia que no pareçe cosa conveniente que el Señor O'Donel se vaia agora con un solo navio a su tierra'.

10 Ibid: 'lo que es peor que todo por no aver en Irlanda una persona mas principal y mas noble y que a hecho maoires servicios a su Magd que el Señor'.

11 Ibid.: '… si le vean apportando sin gente perderan en todo esperanzas antes el mesmo Señor O'Donel no tendra esperanzas de socorro … Yo seguro a Vuestra Excellencia que la ida del Señor alla de aquella manera a de haçer mas daño que provecho.'

12 Ibid.: 'que si quisiesen embiarle accompañado de 2 o 3 mil soldados el servicio que pudiese haçer seria mui famoso y mas que de piensa y esto pareçe mas açertado por que sin duda si vee que el socorro se dilate mas de Pasqua de Flores (que es un poco mas tiempo asseñalado) tomara su viage por su tierra aunque no halla mejor comodidad para este camino sino ir a pie disfraçado por el camino de Escoçia hasta morir lastimosamente en el camino'.

13 Ibid.: 'Supplico a Vuestra Excellencia que me perdone este attrebimiento que no me metiera en esso, sino pensara ser servicio de Dios y nuestro Rei'. On the subject of *reputación* see Antonio Domínguez Ortiz, 'La defensa de la reputación', in *Arte y saber: la cultura en tiempos de Felipe III y Felipe IV* (Valladolid, 1999), pp 25-54.

14 J. J. Silke, *Kinsale: the Spanish intervention in Ireland at the end of the Elizabethan wars* (New York, 1970), p. 166.

15 Florence Conry to Philip III, 1603 (AGS, E., Inglaterra, l. 840, ff 200-1): 'fray Florencio yrlandes … desde el junio passado esta siguiendo esta corte en el Escurial y aqui primero tratando con Vuestra Magestad que diesse licencia al conde Odonel venir a la corte a tratar los negocios del reyno de Yrlanda'.

16 See C. O'Scea, 'The role of Castilian royal bureaucracy in the formation of early-modern Irish literacy', in T. O'Connor and M. A. Lyons (eds), *Irish communities in early-modern Europe* (Dublin, 2006), pp 200-39.

17 P. Walsh, 'James Blake of Galway', *Irish Ecclesiastical Record*, 50 (1937), pp 382-97; F. M. Jones, 'James Blake and a projected Spanish invasion of Galway in 1602', *Journal Galway Archaeological and Historical Society*, 24 (1950-1951) pp 1-18; D. McGettigan, *Red Hugh O'Donnell and the Nine Years War* (Dublin, 2005), pp 114-5.

18 Lughaidh Ó Cléirigh, *Beatha Aodha Ruaidh Uí Dhomhnaill*, ed. P. Walsh (2 vols, Dublin, 1948), vol. 1, pp 344-5.

19 C. Mooney, 'The death of Red Hugh O'Donnell', *Irish Ecclesiastical Record*, lxxxi (1954), pp 332-7.

20 O'Donnell and O'Neill to Philip III, 14 Jan. 1601 (AGS, E., España, l. 236).

21 'Testamento de Hugh O'Donnell hecho en Simancas ante el escribano del rey, a siete dias del mes de septiembre de 1602' (AGS, Guerra Antigua l. 596); see J. J. Silke, 'The last will of Red Hugh O'Donnell', *Studia Hibernica*, xxiv (1988), pp 51-60.

22 Philip III to the Duque de Sessa, Valladolid, 16 June 1601 (AGS, E., Roma, l. 1856).

23 Conde de Puñonrostro to Philip III, Madrid, Madrid, 28 Nov. 1606 (AGS, E., NP, l. 1797): 'despues que murio el dicho conde en Simancas dexo supplicado a Vuestra Magestad en su testamento, que en todos los negocios del Reyno de Irlanda oyesse al dicho padre y se fiasse del por saber bien la experencia que tenia en las cosas de aquel reyno y el Zelo a la causa catholica, lo qual Vuestra Magestad cumplio mandandole luego que solicitasse el negocio de los catholicos de Irlanda'.

24 Mansoni to Aldobrandini, 11 Sept. 1602 (Archivio Segreto Vaticano, Particolari I, pp 485-9; for details of which see F. M. Jones, 'Correspondence of Father Ludovico Mansoni, S. J., papal nuncio to Ireland', *Archivium Hibernicum*, xvii (1953), pp 1-51).

25 Ó Cléirigh, *Beatha Aodha Ruaidh*, i, p. 345.

26 Friar Florence Conry on Irish matters, 1602 (Archivo Histórico de Loyola, FH/Lerma t. I/c. 27, 26/9).

27 Ibid.: '… al cabo de nueve años que sustentan los Catholicos guerra contra el enemigo ingles mas con milagros que con poder humano'.

28 Ibid.: '… tan gastados y cansados con las promesas no cumplidas de España, que para salir de estas dudas, enviaron á España al mejor mensajero (que era el Conde de Odonel) para que representarse á su Magestad la necesidad de los yrlandeses y pidiesse socorro'.

29 Ibid.: 'Cuando agora separan la muerte del Conde y que sus ruegos no han aprovechado, y que no va allá socorro de gente sino algun dinero y otras cartas; haran por precision conciertos de algun modo con sus enemigos'.

30 Ibid.: 'Si tienen aún fuerzas haran convenios generales: si carecen de ellas y estan en mucho aprieto, á cada señor en particular ofrecera el enemigo de buena voluntad excelentes partidos'.

31 Ibid.: 'De esta suerte dejará aislados á los principales y sin poder resistir – Es gran lastima – que deste modo se pierda para España la nacion Irlandesa despues de los infinitos trabajos que se ha impuesto para servir a su Rey!'

32 Ibid.: 'Se ha de seguir de aqui que viendo las demas naciones este lastimoso suceso y miserable espectáculo de la destrucion de Irlanda por falta de este auxilio de España, nadie querrá ponerse jamas en peligro fiado en las promesas de esta nacion'.

33 Ibid.: 'Todo pudiera deshuirse enviando sin dilacion socorros á Irlanda de la manera que lo pidió el Conde de O'Donell. Si el socorro, decia este, fuese de diez ó doce mil hombres ir á Corque ó á Lumbrique; y si fuera de dos mil ó mil quinientos ir á su tierra y ponerlos … Dunigall y Sligo'.

34 Ibid.: 'Si tres ó cuatro mil ir á Galvay y tomar la dicha villa, donde el Conde O'Neill y su hermano pudieran unirseles sin que el enemigo pudiera estorbarles el paso. Puesto sitio á Galvay se rendirá á los pocos dias por no poder ser socorrido por el Virrey ni por mar ni por tierra … está rodeada por un gran rio llamado Sinon que viene de la tierra de los Condes'.

35 Ibid.: 'Por esto trajo el Conde de O'Donell en su compañia al Baron de Letrym de quien es todo aquel pais'.

36 Ibid.: 'Y siendo casi una isla con gran facilidad se puede hacer inespugnable haciendo una trinchera en la lengua que le une con la tierra, y levantando un baluarte por la parte del rio y colocando en él dos piezas de artilleria, se impide que puedan entrar en el puerto barcos enemigos'.

37 Ibid.: 'Conacia … está rodeada por un gran rio llamado Sinon que viene de la tierra de los Condes. No hay sino dos entradas, uno por Lumbrique y otra por Alóen. Por las diez y seis millas de bosque que cierra la primera no pueden pasar caballos ni artilleria. Por la otra hay cuatro millas de bosque y dos de pantanos con un camino de piedra y maderos que en destruyendole no es posible pasar'.

38 Ó. Recio Morales, *El socorro de Irlanda en 1601 y la contribución del ejército a la integración social de los irlandeses en España* (Madrid, 2002), p. 86.

39 Conry to Philip III, 1603 (AGS, E., Inglaterra, l. 840, ff 200-1): 'fray Florencio yrlandes confesor que era del Conde Odonel que aya de Gloria … desde la muerte de aquel noble conde en Symancas, procurando que Vuestra Magestad embiasse algun socorro a los catholicos de Yrlanda para animarlos para que no se demayassen oyendo la muerte del conde'.

40 Ibid.: 'como el mesmo [O'Donnell] suppca a Vuestra Magestad en su testamento fue la santa muerte del conde la gran christiandad y clemencia de Vuestra Magestad y Dios sobre todo servido que un mes despues fuesse resuelto en consejo de estado que se embiase socorro a Yrlanda'.

41 Council of state to Philip III, 13 Feb. 1603 (AGS, E., Inglaterra, l. 840, f. 37); *CSP Spain, 1587-1603*, pp 719, 732.

42 Conry to Philip III, 1603 (AGS, E, Inglaterra, l. 840, ff 200-01): 'pero por mis pecados y por los de Yrlanda y de España, el socorro y todos estamos aqui aun, porque quando fue esso resuelto nos respondian los ministros que era menester hacer otro acuerdo a Vuestra Magestad y una semana despues otro acuerdo, y un mes despues otro, y un mes despues otro'.

43 Ibid.: 'y assi passamos 7 meses hasta que al cabo llego el negocio dispachado al presidente de hacienda'.

44 Ibid.: 'Los Catholicos estan en pie aun, y an llevado buenas victorias como consta por muchos caminos gracias a Dios'.

45 Ibid.: '… parece que se mansillo algo en Yrlanda el año passado, mandando que nos despachen presto o si por nuestros pecados no ay lugar para esso que mande Vuestra Magestad avisar aquellos afligidos Catholicos que se concierten lo major que pudieren'.

46 Council of state to Philip III, 13 Feb. 1603 (AGS, E, Inglaterra, l. 840, f. 37): 'El consejo dize que por consulta de 3 de março del año passado resolvio Vuestra Magestad que se embiassen al conde Oneil 50V ducados y las armas y municiones que se pudiesse y despues por otra consulta de 2 de noviembre del mismo año fue servido de mandar que fuese 30V desde principio deste año'.

47 Conry to Philip III: 'Los que solicitamos este negocio como yo y el secretario del dicho conde tenemos gastado lo que nos dio Vuestra Magestad'.

48 Council of state to Philip III, 13 Feb. 1603 (AGS, E., Inglaterra, l. 840, f. 37); *CSP Spain, 1587-1603*, pp 719, 732.

49 L. F. Vega, *La Real Audiencia de Galicia* (2 vols, La Coruña, 1982), ii, p. 66 (AGS, E, l. 2797); Morales, *El socorro de Irlanda*, p. 92. The type of vessel used, the *pataje,* was a tender or advice-boat.

50 T. O'Connor, 'Diplomatic preparations for Kinsale: Lombard's *Commentarius*', in E. García Hernán, Ó. Recio Morales *et al* (eds), *Irlanda y la monarquía hispánica: Kinsale 1601-2001* (Madrid, 2002), p. 138.

51 See, for example, Esteban de Ibarra to Caracena, 22 Mar. 1603 (Archivo Histórico Nacional (AHN), Sección Nobleza, Frias, caja 66, f. 26), notifying him of the *entretenimiento* awarded to Matthew Tully by Philip III which was to be paid in La Coruña.

52 Andres de Prada to Caracena, Valladolid, 18 Apr. 1603 (AHN, Nobleza, Frias, caja 66, ff 39-40): 'Anoche se tuvo

aviso que la Reyna de Ynglaterra murio a los tres deste y que otro dia proclamaron por Rey sin contradiçion y con grande aplauso al de Escoçia'.

53 Ibid.: '[…] lo que desto resultara Dios lo sabe pero el es ereje y mal intencionado'.

54 Ibid.

55 Conde de Puñonrostro to Philip III, 28 Nov. 1606 (AGS, E, NP, l. 1797): 'y acabo de ocho meses despues … fue embiado por Vuestra Magestad con un socorro a los catholicos de Irlanda en la Jornada que hizo Don Martin de la Cerda'.

56 Ibid.: 'y hallando los Condes y los demas catholicos (por no poder mas) concertados con el enemigo, no quiso de desembarcarse por no traer los dichos Condes a sospecha, y bolvio a España'.

57 Matthew Tully to the conde de Caracena, 8 Jun. 1603 (AHN, Nobleza, Frias, caja 66, d2, ff 110-111v): 'Toda esta desastre á succedio por la suberuia de Don Martín que quijo hacer todas estas cosas de su cabesa'.

58 Enrique García Hernán, 'Irish clerics in Madrid, 1598-1665', in O'Connor and Lyons (eds), *Irish communities in early-modern Europe*, pp 275-6.

59 Robert Chamberlain to Caracena, 8 Jun. 1603 (AHN, Nobleza, Frias, caja 66, d2, ff 108-9v): 'su ambiçion no le da lugar de acertar en cosa alguna ni usar prudençia ni discreçion en sus actiones'.

60 Tully to Caracena, 8 Jun. 1603 (ibid., ff 110-11v): 'Don Martin de la Cerda dos dias despues que partimos de la Coruña me á llamado y pregunto porque á dado un memorial en La Coruna a Vuestra Excellencia pidiendo embarcaçion … y que Vuestra Excellencia no tenia que hacer con los navios teniendo el orden de su Majestad para venir con el despacho'.

61 Ibid.: 'y quando yo le respondi que pense que Vuestra Excellencia podia dar orden en lo que tocava a esto, Don Martin me dixo si no callasse que hiziesse accorder me del.'

62 Chamberlain to Caracena, 8 Jun. 1603: 'en el accustombrado favor y benevolencia que Vuestra Excellencia siempre ha muestrado y continuamente muestra a los criados del Señor O Neill del qual soy yo indignamente criado y capillan'.

63 Ibid.: '[Don Martín] dixo que eramos traydores a su Magestad por suplicar paraque diesse orden que algunos criados que traymos se embiassen para avisar a los Condes O Neill y Odonel'.

64 Tully to Caracena, 8 Jun. 1603: 'En llegando a estas costas Don Martin no á querido oyr una palabra mia ni de los padres Fr Florencio y Roberto Chamberlino, y fiacca se de los criados del enimigo'.

65 Chamberlain to Caracena, 8 Jun. 1603: 'entregaron al enemigo las cartas que escrivio al Señor O Neill'.

66 Tully to Caracena, 8 Jun. 1603: 'stuvo sesenta leguas por tierra del Conde O Neill donde aporto, y quinze leguas del Conde Donell por mar, jamas le a escrito … tomo un barco y un mercader al qual Don Martin dio tormentos para haçer le confessar si yo le mano llevar alguna carta al Conde O Donell'.

67 Ibid.: 'El Licenciado Roberto que es ayo del hijo del Conde O Neill escriviesse al Cond O Neill'; Chamberlain to Caracena, 8 Jun. 1603: '… por sospechar que Mattheo

escrivole algunas cartas al Conde O Donel, las quales no ha escrito como Dios es testigo.'

68 Tully to Caracena, 8 Jun. 1603: 'el padre fray Florencio va alla a dar cuenta de esto'.

69 MacWilliam Burke to Caracena, Valladolid, 18 Sept. 1604 (AHN, Nobleza, Frias, caja 67, d. 1).

70 Puñonrostro to Philip III, 28 Nov. 1606 (AGS, E, NP, l. 1797): 'bolvio a España, y despues de interpretar otra embaxada a Vuestra Magestad que los Catolicos embiaron con el Marques Macvilliam Burk'.

71 Caracena to Philip III, La Coruña, 5 July 1603 (AGS, E, l. 194); Kerney Walsh, *'Destruction by peace'*, pp 28, 150.

72 Conry to Caracena, Valladolid, 15 Nov. 1603 (AHN, Nobleza, Frias, caja 66, d2, f. 251): 'No escripto a Vuestra Excellencia hasta agora por poder deçir algo de los negocios del Marques Macguillerm Burk'.

73 Ibid.

74 Ibid.: 'Aqui a llegado de Londres el Padre Roberto capellan del Conde Onel, que viene con orden del Rey Ingles ... a me dicho que los condes Onel y hOdonel estuvieron en Londres y que aun alli mostraron su valor y christianidad, hizo les el Rey merced, aunque no quito dar libertad de consçiençia. Pero mando que no los molestassen en materia de religion'.

75 Ibid.: 'Tampoco el Rey quito sacar la guarniçion del Ingleses de las fortaleças de los estados de los Condes'.

76 Ibid.: 'Y con esto se an buelto a Irlanda desposados de los mayores señores que tenian por vassallos'.

77 Ibid.: 'El pobre ... Señor O Rorq es el mas desamparado porque no se sabe a donde esta, el Rey no le quiere perdonar antes dio su estado a su hermano'.

78 Ibid.: 'Don Florencio Macarte y el Conde de Desmon estan prestos en la torre de Londres y no dexan hablar a Don Florencio con nadie'.

79 Ibid.: 'El Señor de Viraven esta en Londres, no le dan ni perdon ni licençia para yr a su tierra, rogo mucho al Padre Roberto que tratase con Vuestra Excelencia si le convendria huyrse y venir a España destar se quedo'.

80 Puñonrostro to Philip III, 28 Nov. 1606 (AGS, E, NP. L. 1797): 'y queriendo bolver a Irlanda por otra camino Vuestra Magestad le mando que se quedasse para informar y ayudar en los negocios de aquel Reyno'.

81 Ibid.: 'sirviendo con mucho cuydado de lo qual soy buen testigo […] en el Capitulo general passado de Toledo fue electo por ministro provincial de los frayles menores del Reyno de Irlanda'.

82 J. P. Alzina, *Embajadores de España en Londres: una guía de retratos de la embajada de España* (Madrid, 2001), p. 89.

83 See, for instance the letter and memorial of Cardinal Pompeo Arrigone, protector of the Irish, to the duke of Lerma, Rome, 27 Oct. 1605 (Fundación Ducal de Medinaceli, Archivo Histórico, legajo 51, ramo 5).

84 Marqués de Aytona to Pope Paul V, Rome, 10 Nov. 1607 (Fundación Ducal de Medinaceli, Archivo Histórico, legajo 55, ramo 8): 'El conde de Tiron con su muger y tres higos, y el conde de Odoñel con otros señores y cavalleros se han ydo a España. Atribuiran esto los ingleses a fomentos de España'.

85 'Actas de las Audiencias', Rome, Jan. 1607-May 1609 (Fundación Ducal de Medinaceli, Archivo Histórico, legajo 55, ramo 8).

86 J. Schumpeter, *Die Krise des Steuerstaates* (Graz & Leipzig, 1918), cited in I. A. A. Thompson, 'Gasto público y unidad política: la Monarquía española', in A. M. Bernal (ed.), *Dinero, moneda y crédito en la monarquía Hispánica* (Madrid, 2000), pp 839-61.

87 E. M. García Guerra, *Las acuñaciones de moneda de vellón durante el reinado de Felipe III* (Madrid, 1999), pp 44-46.

88 See J. H. Elliott, 'Foreign policy and domestic crisis: Spain, 1598-1659', in idem (ed.), *Spain and its world, 1500-1700* (New Haven, 1989), pp 114-36.

The Flight of the Earls

COURSE

'Imeacht na nIarlaí'. © Seán Ó Brógáin

Cuntas Thaidhg Uí Chianáin ar Imeacht na dTaoiseach as Éirinn, 1607-08

Nollaig Ó Muraíle

Is féidir na príomhfhoinsí eolais atá againn faoin eachtra chinniúnach úd, *Imeacht na nIarlaí*, a roinnt ina dtrí aicme. Is iad seo a leanas na haicmí sin: páipéir stáit Shasana, a bhíonn naimhdeach de shíor – agus go minic clúmhillteach agus bréagach – i leith na nÉireannach a bhí páirteach san imeacht; cartlanna na Spáinne a bhfuil ábhar astu a bhaineann leis an imeacht curtha ar fáil i bhfoirm aistriúcháin ag Micheline Kerney Walsh ina sárshaothar *'Destruction by Peace'* (1986); an aicme is mó díobh sin – agus ceann a ndéanann lucht staire faillí inti go minic – mar atá, na foinsí éagsúla Gaeilge, idir phrós agus fhilíocht. Is ar cheann de na foinsí Gaeilge sin ba mhaith liom díriú sa pháipéar seo – ceann den dá chuntas próis atá againn mar gheall ar an imeacht. Is é an ceann is giorra den phéire an gearrchuntas corraitheach maorga atá le fáil in *Annála Ríoghachta Éireann*, nó Annála na gCeithre Máistrí mar is fearr aithne orthu, faoin mbliain 1607, ach ní hé an téacs sin is spéis liom anseo.

Nuair a sheol taoisigh Ghaelacha Chúige Uladh agus a lucht leanúna amach as Loch Súilí i lár mhí Mheán Fómhair na bliana 1607 ar an turas stairiúil úd a chríochnaigh sa Róimh beagnach naoi mí ina dhiaidh sin, bhí sa chomhluadar duine amháin ar a laghad den lucht léinn dúchais. Ba fhear é sin a bhain le teaghlach a raibh cáil an léinn air ar feadh na gcéadta bliain i gCúige Uladh – Tadhg Óg Ó Cianáin ab ainm agus ba shloinne dó.

Tá seans ann go raibh an dara duine den aos léinn in éineacht leo: b'shin file cáiliúil de chuid Thír Chonaill, Eoghan Ruadh Mac an Bhaird, ach níltear lánchinnte cé acu an raibh seisean ar an long a d'fhág Loch Súilí nó an amhlaidh a thaistil sé trasna na farraige as a stuaim féin. (Ghlac Tomás

Pedro Henriquez de Acevedo, conde de Fuentes (1560-1610), príomhghobharnóir Milan, 'a great respected earl, one of the most excellent soldiers in the world'. Chuir sé fáilte Uí Cheallaigh roimh na hiarlaí.

Ó Fiaich leis go raibh sé ar an long.) Chomh maith leis sin, b'fhéidir go raibh an tríú duine le cúlra den sórt céanna ina measc, mar atá, Doighre Ó Duibhgeannáin, a bhain le teaghlach léannta iomráiteach i dtuaisceart Chonnacht, ach ní heol dúinn gur fhág sé aon saothar liteartha ina dhiaidh. Is fíor a rá go bhfuil fiúntas thar na bearta, mar fhoinse eolais chomhaimseartha, leis an gcuntas a bhreac Tadhg Ó Cianáin le linn an turais.

Is ar ámharaí an tsaoil a mhaireann saothar sin Thaidhg, óir níl sé le fáil ach in aon lámhscríbhinn amháin. Leabhar beag páipéir atá i gceist, agus díreach faoi bhun 140 leathanach inti, agus is suimiúil an stair atá taobh thiar di. Tá beagán leathanach ag tús na lámhscríbhinne, agus cúpla ceann ag an deireadh, ar a bhfuil liostaí de na pápaí agus d'impirí na Róimhe breactha, ach tá 135 leathanach idir eatarthu tugtha do théacs próis a thosaíonn mar seo a leanas:

In ainm Dé. Ag so páirt do scéalaibh agus d'imtheachtaibh Uí Néill ón uair forfhágaibh sé Éire.

Aon duine amháin a bhreac an téacs ar fad, agus tá sé le tuiscint ó nótaí thall is abhus sa lámhscríbhinn gurb é údar an téacs, Tadhg Ó Cianáin, an scríobhaí. Níl aon teideal ar an téacs, ach níl sé sin ar aon tslí neamhghnách i gcás téacsanna próis i lámhscríbhinní Gaeilge. Tuairim is 37,000 focal atá sa saothar – thart ar an méid a bheadh in úrscéal gearr nó i ngearrscéal fada.

Tosaíonn cuntas Uí Chianáin ar 6 Meán Fómhair 1607 agus críochnaíonn sé ar 27 Samhain na bliana dar gcionn, 1608, ach tá nóta amháin sáite isteach ag bun lch 96 [*Turas* 7.7, p. 304] ar a bhfuil an dáta 24 Meán Fómhair 1609. Spreagann sé seo an cheist: an saothar neamhchríochnaithe é seo (faoi mar atá maíte ag údair éagsúla roimhe seo), nó an raibh sé i gceist ag an údar an scéal a thabhairt ar aghaidh tamall níos faide? Is cinnte nach raibh aon ábhar eile riamh sa bhreis *sa lámhscríbhinn seo* óir críochnaíonn an téacs ag bun lch. 135 agus tá an taobh eile den bhilleog fágtha bán ag an scríobhaí.

Ar an leathanach tosaigh tá spás fágtha folamh sa choirnéal clé os comhair na línte tosaigh, san áit a mbeifí ag súil le ceannlitir ornáideach (sa chás seo, A) i lámhscríbhinn traidisiúnta – rud a thabharfadh le tuiscint go raibh sé i gceist ag an scríobhaí a leithéid d'ornáidíocht a chur isteach ach nach bhfuair sé an deis chuige. Léamh amháin a d'fhéadfaí a dhéanamh ar an scéal ar fad gur chuir Tadhg an téacs le chéile ó nótaí comhaimseartha a bhí breactha aige i rith an turais agus nach bhfuair sé riamh an seans dul níos faide ná deireadh mhí na Samhna sa bhliain 1608 – toisc, b'fhéidir, gur stop sé de bheith ag breacadh na nótaí comhaimseartha, nó na dialainne, an t-am sin (seacht mí tar éis dó an Róimh a bhaint amach).

Braithim gur thart ar Mheán Fómhair na bliana dar gcionn, 1609, a bhí an téacs mar atá sé againn anois á chur le chéile, óir tá aontacht agus leanúnachas iontach sa stíl pheannaireachta ó thús deireadh. Is léir gur breacadh as éadan é, agus an nóta úd dar dáta 24 Meán Fómhair 1609 tá sé sa stíl pheannaireachta chéanna leis an gcuid eile den téacs; in ionad a bheith brúite isteach mar a bhíonn nóta imill de ghnáth, is amhlaidh atá sé scríofa go néata ag bun an leathanaigh ag an am céanna a raibh an saothar fré chéile á scríobh. Ar an lámh eile, tá roinnt den ábhar ar na leathanaigh dheiridh as ord ó thaobh na cróineolaíochta de agus an chuma air gurb amhlaidh a caitheadh le chéile faoi dheifir é. Mar sin féin, níl rian ar bith deifre le braith ar an bpeannaireacht sa chuid seo den leabhar.

Cuid de na sonraí sin – mar shampla an spás úd don cheannlitir nár breacadh ar an leathanach tosaigh agus an cuntas a bheith beagán in aimhréidhe sa chuid deiridh – spreagann siad an smaoineamh go mb'fhéidir gur drochshláinte (nó, fiú, bás) an údair faoi ndeara iad. Na sleachta sin atá beagán as ord, b'fhéidir gur cóip sách cruinn iad de bhunnótaí Uí Chianáin, dréacht nach bhfuair an t-údar an deis riamh a athscríobh ná a chur in eagar. Agus tharlódh go ndeachaigh na bun-nótaí céanna sin (*ur-text* an tsaothair atá againn go fóill) ar aghaidh thar Shamhain 1608 – ach ní cosúil go bhfuil

Ar Lá Fhéile Pádraig 1608, i gceann de na geimhridh ba mheasa i stair na hEorpa, thrasnaigh na hiarlaí Droichead an Diabhail. Chaill siad capall dá gcuid a raibh a maoin órga ar a dhroim. De réir an tseanchais aitiúil, tá an t-airgead seo (Stór Caillte Naomh Gottard) ann go fóill. Nochtadh leacht cuimhneacháin i gcuimhne ar an Niallach agus an Dálach in Andermatt ar Lá Fhéile Pádraig 2008.

tásc ná tuairisc orthu níos mó. Níl ansin ach aon cheann amháin den iliomad ábhar díospóireachta a spreagann saothar Uí Chianáin.

Pointe beag amháin eile faoin lámhscríbhinn féin is ea an nós atá ag an scríobhaí 'IHS' nó 'Emanuel' a scríobh ag barr gach leathanaigh, nach mór. Is é atá in IHS na trí litreacha tosaigh, i gceannlitreacha Gréigise, den ainm Iésous, agus bhí an siombal seo in úsáid mar a bheadh lógó ag na Proinsiasaigh Oibsearvántacha, go háirithe sa seachtú haois déag.

Maidir le stair na lámhscríbhinne, is féidir a bheith réasúnta cinnte de gur sa Róimh a scríobhadh í, ach am éigin i ndiaidh a scríofa – agus tar éis bhás an scríobhaí, ní foláir – tugadh go Lobháin í, go dtí Coláiste San Antaine, lárionad na nÉireannach san Ísiltír Spáinneach (.i. an Bheilg inniu), a bunaíodh, le tacaíocht ó rí na Spáinne, Pilib III, in 1606-07. Is cosúil go raibh an lámhscríbhinn tagtha go Lobháin faoi lár an seachtú haois déag, ar a dheireanaí, óir luaitear téacs Thaidhg i dtrí liosta atá ceangailte isteach sa lámhscríbhinn Phroinsiasach A 34 (atá anois i gColáiste Ollscoile Bhaile Átha Cliath) agus i liostaí eile (atá níos

sine, b'fhéidir) in dhá lámhscríbhinn a bhí go dtí
le deireanas i gColáiste San Iosadóir sa Róimh; is í
an t-ainm a thugtar uirthi sna liostaí sin *Turas na
nIarladh as Éirinn*. Tá an nóta Laidine seo a leanas
ag gabháil le ceann de na liostaí sin in A 34:

> Catalogus manuscriptorum tam Latinè quam
> Hibernicè olim in camera R. P. Colgani rep-
> ertorum; quibus postea R. P. Sirinus usus fuit
> (Clár na lámhscríbhinní Laidine agus Gaeilge
> a bhí tráth i seomra an Athar Mhic Colgáin,
> [agus] ar bhain an tAthair Ó Sírín úsáid astu
> ina dhiaidh sin.)

Tá sé le tuiscint uaidh sin go raibh lámhscríbh-
hinn Uí Chianáin i seilbh Sheáin Mhic Colgáin
i Lobháin sular cailleadh an mórscoláire Proinsiasach úd as Inis Eoghain sa bhliain 1658, agus go
raibh sí ina dhiaidh sin ag an Athair Tomás Ó Sírín
a fuair bás sa bhliain 1673. Ceisteanna nach féidir
a fhreagairt ag an bpointe seo, áfach, is ea cé thug
an lámhscríbhinn ón Róimh go dtí Lobháin agus
cén uair go baileach a tharla sé sin.

Maidir lena stair ina dhiaidh sin, is eol dúinn
gur fhan an lámhscríbhinn i Lobháin go dtí aimsir Réabhlóid na Fraince nuair a ghlac rialtas na
Fraince seilbh ar Choláiste San Antaine. Am éigin
i samhradh na bliana 1793, de réir dealraimh, is
ea a bogadh sciar de na lámhscríbhinní a bhí sa
choláiste go dtí Coláiste San Iosadóir sa Róimh.
Bhí na lámhscríbhinní, agus Coláiste San Iosadóir
féin, i mbaol mór arís nuair a ghabh na Francaigh
an Róimh in 1798-99, óir bhí sé ar intinn acu an
coláiste a leagan go talamh, ach d'éirigh leis an bhfoirgneamh agus na lámhscríbhinní teacht slán.

Rinneadh iarrachtaí éagsúla i rith an naoú haois
déag na lámhscríbhinní Gaeilge a thabhairt ar ais
go hÉirinn ach is beag dul chun cinn a rinneadh
go dtí tús na bliana 1872 nuair a measadh baol a
bheith ann go gcuirfeadh rialtas nua na hIodáile
aontaithe Coláiste San Iosadóir faoi chois agus go
ngabhfaí na saothair luachmhara léinn sa leabharlann. Tháinig ambasáid na Breataine sa Róimh i
gcabhair ar na lámhscríbhinní Gaeilge de bharr
impí ón Tiarna Seán Ó hÁgáin (1822-90), tiarna
seansailéir na hÉireann agus fear a bhí páirteach
tráth dá shaol le gluaiseacht Éire Óg. Le cúnamh
ó údaráis na Breataine, mar sin, cuireadh na seoda
cultúrtha seo ar ais go hÉirinn agus coimeádadh
go cúramach iad i gCé na gCeannaithe, Baile
Átha Cliath, go dtí gur bunaíodh Teach Staidéir
na bProinsiasach, Dún Mhuire, Cill Iníon Léinín

Ar Aoine an Chéasta, 4 Aibréan 1608, thug na hiarlaí cuairt ar Ardeaglais Santa Maria del Duomo agus chonaic siad na ceadta oilithreach á lascadh iad féin. Chuir sé Tadhg Ó Cianáin ag smaoineadh ar a shaol féin.

sa bhliain 1946. Sa bhliain 2000 bogadh na lámhscríbhinní Gaeilge go Coláiste na hOllscoile, Baile
Átha Cliath, agus tá siad le feiceáil anois ar an
suíomh idirlín an-úsáideach úd, ISOS (Irish Script
on Screen), a bhunaigh Scoil an Léinn Cheiltigh,
Institiúid Ardléinn Bhaile Átha Cliath.

Glactar leis gurbh é Tadhg (nó Tadhg Óg) Ó
Cianáin a scríobh an cuntas atá faoi chaibidil anseo. Fear é a bhain le ceann de na teaghlaigh léannta
ba iomráití i gCúige Uladh sa tréimhse idir teacht
na Normannach agus tús an seachtú haois déag.
D'áirigh an túdar cúigear is fiche den sloinne a
d'fhág a bheag nó a mhór de rian ar stair chultúrtha

nó pholaitiúil na hÉireann – idir fear díobh darbh ainm (1) Giolla na Naomh, a bhí ina ab ar Lios Gabhail, Contae Fhear Manach, agus a fuair bás sa bhliain 1348, agus (25) Brian Óg áirithe a bhreac lámhscríbhinn mhór do Bhrian Ruadh Mag Uidhir, barún Inis Ceithleann, i dTulaigh Mhaoil, Contae Fhear Manach, sa bhliain 1638.

Ní heol dúinn cén gaol a bhí ag Tadhg leis na daoine eile de Mhuintir Chianáin. Sna blianta deiridh dó in Éirinn (.i. sular imigh sé in éineacht leis na hiarlaí) bhí cónaí air féin agus ar sheisear eile den sloinne i gContae Ard Mhacha, i mbaile fearainn Phort Niallagáin, i bparóiste Thuíneáin, in iardheisceart an chontae – tamall gearr ó bhaile Ard Mhacha. Chuir Tomás Ó Fiaich an tuairim chun tosaigh gurb amhlaidh a bhronn Aodh Mór Ó Néill talamh orthu sa chontae sin – tharla nárbh é contae dúchais Mhuintir Chianáin é. Os a choinne sin, is fiú a chur san áireamh go bhfuil baile fearainn darb ainm Dromad Uí Chianáin – Drumadd i mBéarla – tamall ó thuaidh ó Phort Niallagáin, ar imeall Ard Mhacha, agus, ina theannta sin, go raibh Ó Cianáin ar phríomhshloinnte Chontae Ard Mhacha timpeall na bliana 1659 – de réir an tsaothair a dtugtar 'Census of Ireland' air.

Liostaítear an seachtar úd de Mhuintir Chianáin a bhí lonnaithe i bPort Niallagáin i measc lucht leanúna Éinrí Óig (mhic Éinrí mhic Sheáin) Uí Néill a fuair pardún ón gcoróin faoi Nollaig na bliana 1602, agus tá duine a bhfuil Tadhg air ina measc.[1]

Tar éis do Thadhg imeacht leis na hiarlaí rinneadh a shealús a choigistiú – de réir na bpáipéirí stáit ní raibh aige ach cúig bhó dhéag, ocht ngamhain, gearrán, beithíoch capaill agus cúig mhuc fhichead, arbh é £22 6s 2d a luach.[2] Tamall ina dhiaidh sin tugadh an t-iomlán ar ais do bhean Thaidhg ar iarratas ó Iarla Thuamhan, a raibh gaol éigin aige léi; thuairiscigh seisean 'that the said Teig sent him intelligence of importance from beyond the seas'.[3] Ceapann Tomás Ó Fiaich nach gciallaíonn seo ach go scríobhadh Tadhg abhaile ó am go chéile agus go seoladh sé corrphíosa nuachta gan tábhacht ar ais, ach go raibh an t-iarla Muimhneach (Donnchadh Ó Briain) in ann an méid sin a úsáid ar mhaithe lena bhean gaoil. Is cosúil gur timpeall na bliana 1610 a rinneadh an méid seo.

Is beag eile atá ar eolas againn faoi Thadhg – mar shampla, cén uair go baileach a fuair sé bás. Tá tagairt shuimiúil amháin dó sa bhfianaise a baineadh as fear darbh ainm Lodder McDonnell a gabhadh sa bhliain 1615. Luaitear freisin

dearthair le Tadhg darbh ainm Cúchonnachta a crocadh in eineacht le cúigear eile i gcathair Dhoire i mí Iúil na bliana sin. Ní féidir a rá le cinnteacht arbh ionann an Cúchonnacht seo agus an sagart den ainm céanna a luadh in éineacht le Tadhg sa bhliain 1602 (nuair a tugadh pardún ón gcoróin dóibh), óir is mar fhile nó mar sheanchaí a chuirtear síos air sa chuntas ó 1615:

Couconnagh O'Kernan [*sic*], a rhymer or chronicler to Conn Rory [Conor Roe?] Maguire … [*L*.] thinks he was brother of Teig Oge O'Kennan that went with Tyrone and died at Roome.[4]

Sula gcríochnaím an gearrchuntas seo ar Thadhg, is fiú a lua gur cosúil gur bhreac sé lámhscríbhinn eile, cé go ndealraíonn sé nach maireann an saothar sin inniu. Sa scríbhinn is luaithe dá bhfuil againn ó pheann Mhíchíl Uí Chléirigh, an mórscoláire Proinsiasach, ar a bhfuil an dáta 28 Márta 1627, mar atá, cóip de théacs dar teideal *Ionnarba Mochuda a Rathain*, tá colafon a deir: 'As an leabhar do scríobh Tadhg Ó Cianáin do scríobhadh an beagán sin ag Drobhaois.' Cé nach féidir a bheith lándeimhin de, meastar go coitianta gurb é an Tadhg s'againne atá i gceist anseo.

Tosaíonn cuntas Uí Chianáin ar an Déardaoin, 6 Meán Fómhair 1607. Bhí Aodh Mór Ó Néill i mBaile Shláine, Contae na Mí, in éineacht le Sir Arthur Chichester, tiarna iúistís na hÉireann, nuair a fuair sé scéala go raibh Cúchonnacht Mhag Uidhir agus roinnt daoine eile tar éis teacht go Ráth Maoláin i dtuaisceart Thír Chonaill i long Fhrancach. Rinne sé cinneadh gan mhoill, d'fhág slán ag a chara Sir Gearóid Múr agus ag a mhuintir ag an Mainistir Mhór [Mellifont], agus ghluais ó thuaidh trí Ard Mhacha go dtí an Chraobh [Stewartstown], in oirthear Thír Eoghain, agus uaidh sin go Ráth Maoláin. Bhain sé féin, a mhuintir agus a lucht leanúna ceann scríbe amach faoin Aoine, 14 Meán Fómhair; bhuail siad ansin le Ruaidhrí Ó Domhnaill, iarla Thír Chonaill, agus a chlann agus a lucht leanúna siúd, agus chuadar go léir ar bord loinge láithreach. Thart ar mheán oíche chuir siad chun farraige agus ghluais ó dheas, feadh cósta thiar na hÉireann. Choinnigh siad amach ón gcósta de bharr eagla roimh na longa Sasanacha a shíl siad a bheith ag fanacht leo i gCuan na Gaillimhe; faoi mar a tharla, ní raibh ansin ach an t-aon long amháin!

Is chun na Spáinne a bhí Ó Néill ag iarraidh dul, ach chuir stoirm mhór farraige dá dtreoir iad.

Níor thuigeadar gur tháinig siad i ngiorracht scór mile nó mar sin de chósta thuaidh na Spáinne, ach d'éisteadar leis na mairnéalaigh ar bord a mhol dóibh déanamh ar an bhFrainc. Rinneadar sin agus thángadar i dtír ar 4 Deireadh Fómhair (féile San Proinsias, mar a chuireann Ó Cianáin i gcuimhne dúinn). In áit bheag darbh ainm Quilleboeuf ('Cilbuf' ag Tadhg) i ngar do Le Havre i dtuaisceart na Normainne a tháinig siad den mbád, tar éis dóibh trí seachtaine fada a chaitheamh ar an bhfarraige. Faoin am ar shroicheadar cósta na Fraince is beag deoch ná bia a bhí fágtha acu. Cheap Ó Néill go bhféadfadh sé dul ó dheas trí lár na Fraince go dtí an Spáinn, ach ní cheadódh Anraí IV, rí na Fraince, é sin. Dá bhrí sin, b'éigean do na hÉireannaigh dul trasna na teorann isteach san Ísiltír Spáinneach.

Gach áit a ndeachaigh siad cuireadh na múrtha fáilte rompu, léiríodh ómós agus tugadh gach saghas onóra dóibh, ach cur i gcéill a bhí ansin, cuid mhaith; is amhlaidh a bhí na cinnirí polaitiúla éagsúla san Eoraip ag iarraidh iad a bhogadh ar aghaidh, isteach sa chéad ríocht nó ceantar eile. Mar a deir Tomás Ó Fiaich, 'Bhí na hiarlaí tagtha ar an mhór-roinn fiche bliain ró-mhall.' Faoin am seo bhí an Fhrainc agus an Spáinn araon tuirseach traochta spíonta ó bhlianta fada na cogaíochta, agus bhí siad ag féachaint le síocháin a dhéanamh leis an mBreatain; sa chomhthéacs sin, ní fhéadfadh taoisigh Uladh a bheith tagtha chucu ag lorg cabhrach ag am níos mífheiliúnaí. In ainneoin na reitrice ar fad faoi chearta na gCaitliceach a chosaint ar na heiricigh, b'fhearr go mór le ríthe na Fraince agus na Spáinne, agus go deimhin leis an bpápa féin, go mbogfadh na hÉireannaigh achrannacha seo ar aghaidh gan mhoill.

Coicís tar éis dóibh teacht i dtír ag Quilleboeuf chuaigh na hiarlaí, a gclanna agus a lucht leanúna, trasna teorainn na Fraince ag Arras ar 18 Deireadh Fómhair. Chuadar ó bhaile go baile agus d'itheadar agus d'óladar a ndóthain ag na fleánna agus na féastaí a tugadh ina n-onóir. Faoi dheireadh, ar 25 Samhain 1607 (Domhnach ab ea é), bhuail na fir an bóthar ó Lobháin ó dheas go dtí an Spáinn, mar a mheasadar – fágadh na mná ina ndiaidh, óir bheadh an turas ró-dhian orthu ag an tráth sin den bhliain. Ní raibh siad imithe ach daichead ciliméadar nuair a tháinig teachtaire suas leo, á ordú dóibh thar ceann an Ard-diúic Ailbeirt, gobharnóir na hÍsiltíre Spáinní, filleadh ar ais láithreach go Lobháin. Rinneadar amhlaidh, agus bhí orthu fanacht sa chomharsanacht sin go dtí deireadh mhí Feabhra (ó 28 Samhain go 28 Feabhra). Déanann Ó Cianáin cur síos ar an gcaoi ar mheill siad a gcuid ama ach ní thugann sé aon leide de mhífhoighid na dtaoiseach leis an mbac seo a bhí curtha ar a gcuid pleananna – is léir nár thuig sé cén polasaí polaitiúil a bhí taobh thiar den bhac sin, óir is beag tuiscint a bhí aige ar an *realpolitik* agus an bheartaíocht agus an ionramháil a bhain le gach cor dar chuir na h-iarlaí díobh.

Faoi dheireadh thiar thall, ar 28 Feabhra, bhuail scata de na hÉireannaigh an bóthar ó dheas arís – dhá fhear déag ar fhichid ar mhuin chapaill agus scata de na mná uaisle i gcóiste. Bhí sé ar intinn acu dul chun na hIodáile, le súil go bhféadfaidís a mbealach a dhéanamh as sin go dtí an Spáinn. Isteach leo go Lorráine, áit ar chuir an diúc fáilte chroíúil rompu i Nancy agus thug fleá agus féasta breá ina n-onóir – rud é seo a chuir an-olc ar ambasadóir Shasana sa dúthaigh, agus go deimhin ar an rí Séamas féin i Londain. Lean siad orthu ó dheas isteach in Alsace, áit a n-iompaíonn na logainmneacha ó Fhrancis go Gearmáinis. Nuair a shroich siad Bâle nó Basel san Eilbhéis luann Ó Cianáin:

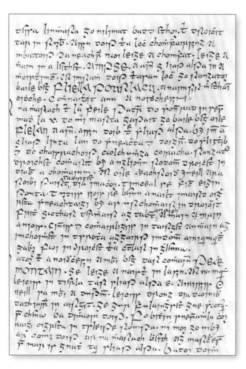

Cuntas Thaidhg Uí Chianáin ar thrasnú na nAlp.
© Institiúid Mhíchíl Uí Chléirigh

teampall ró-mhór i gceartmheán na cathrach ina bhfuilid dealbha agus pictiúirí Lúiteir agus Calvuin agus mhóráin de dhrochúdaraibh diabhlaí eile.[5]

Bhí na taistealaithe neirbhíseach in áit ina raibh na 'heiricigh' (mar a thugtar orthu in aimsir sin na gCogaí Creidimh) chomh láidir sin, agus is léir go mba faoiseamh dóibh fáil chomh fada le Liestal, agus ansin, ar Fhéile Phádraig, shroich siad 'droichead comhard … i nglionn ró-dhomhain, Droichead an Diabhail' (Die Teufelsbrücke sa Ghearmáinis), áit ar bhain tubaiste dóibh nuair a thit capall de chuid na nIarlaí le haill; agus ní haon ghnáthchapall a bhí ann ach an capall a raibh sciar maith d'airgead na nÉireannach – £120 san iomlán – á iompar aige. D'éirigh leo an capall a tharraingt aníos (cé nach ndeir ár n-údar linn cé acu an raibh sé beo nó marbh!), ach theip orthu teacht ar an airgead. Is léiriú ar a thromchúisí agus a bhí an timpiste seo go dtángadar ar ais an lá dar gcionn le súil go bhféadfaí an t-airgead a tharrtháil, ach ní raibh aon mhaith san iarracht – 'ba díomhaoin dóibh'.

Sula bhfágann siad an Eilbhéis tá roinnt rudaí suimiúla le rá ag Tadhg mar gheall ar an tír sin: luann sé go bhfuil siad 'gan ceannas umhla nó uachtaránacht ag rí ná ag prionsa ar talúin orthu' – i bhfocail eile, tá siad go hiomlán neamhspleách. Tuairiscíonn sé:

> Stát éagsúil iontach áirithe iad féin. Toghann siad a rogha de ghoibhearnóireacht na tíre gach bliain. Tá leath a bpríomhchathracha Caitliceach agus an leath eile eiriciúil, nó Protastúnach, agus iad comhcheangailte le chéile le coinníollacha agus le mionna móra chun iad a chosaint ar gach comharsa a dhéanfadh iarracht cur ina gcoinne, agus ar an tslí sin féachann siad leis an tairbhe phoiblí a choinneáil suas go measartha iomchuí.[6]

'Na hIarlaí ag trasnú na nAlp'. © Brian Vallely

Agus leanann sé air:

> Atá de thuarascáil ar lucht na tíre seo gurb iad is fírinní dírí neamhfhealltaí agus is lú a bhriseann a bhfocal ar domhan. Ní ligeann siad slad nó dúnmharú a dhéanamh ina dtír gan díoltas a bhaint as láithreach. As foirfeacht a bhfírinne is iad amháin is garda do ríthe agus prionsaí Catoilce na Críostaíochta [sin tagairt, gan amhras, do 'Gharda Suisear' an Phápa, mar a thugann Ó Cianáin air].[7]

Ardaíonn sé seo ar fad an cheist: an raibh Ó Cianáin ag féachaint ar an leagan amach seo san Eilbhéis mar eiseamláir a d'fhéadfaí a chur i bhfeidhm ina thír féin, a raibh a pobalsa roinnte freisin idir Caitlicigh agus Protastúnaigh?

Tar éis dóibh an turas fíorachrannach a dhéanamh trí Shliabh Alp agus an sneachta agus an leac oighir fós ar fud na háite, agus gan de mhórthrioblóid acu ach an eachtra úd leis an gcapall ag Droichead an Diabhail, rinne siad turas báid trasna Locha Lucerne agus Lugano agus isteach san Iodáil, ag sroichint chathair Milan – mórionad Spáinneach ag an am sin – ar 23 Márta. Chuir an gobharnóir, an saighdiúir clúiteach an cúnta de Fuentes, an-fháilte rompu agus tugadh gach onóir dóibh ar feadh na dtrí seachtaine a chaitheadar i Milan.

Rinne na hÉireannaigh a mbealach gan aon ró-mhoill síos feadh cósta thoir na hIodáile trí áiteacha mar Piacenza, Parma agus Bologna agus go leor bailte beaga. D'iompaigh siad ar leataobh chuig an scrín cháiliúil i Loreto, áit a bhfaca siad an Santa Casa, nó an Teach Naofa – de réir an tseanchais, ba é seo an teach ina raibh cónaí ar an Teaghlach Naofa i Nasaireat, ach rug na haingil leo é trasna na farraige go dtí Slavonia, i gCróit an lae inniu, agus ina dhiaidh sin thógadar arís é trasna Mhuir Aidriait go dtí an Iodáil.

In ainneoin an chuntais rífhada atá ag Tadhg ar an Teach Naofa, níor chaith na hÉireannaigh ach aon lá amháin i Loreto. Bhuaileadar an bóthar arís i dtreo na Róimhe ar 23 Aibreán, ach dhá lá ina dhiaidh sin (Dé hAoine, 25 Aibreán) d'iompaigh scata de na taistealaithe ar leataobh arís, an babhta seo le cuairt a thabhairt ar scrín cháiliúil na bProinsiasach, Assisi. Orthu siúd a chuaigh ansin bhí Rúraí agus Cathbharr Ó Dónaill, agus Aodh Óg Ó Néill (barún Dhún Geanainn agus mac le hAodh Mór), agus is dócha Tadhg Ó Cianáin, ó tharla go dtugann seisean cuntas ar an gcuairt. (Ar chúiseanna nach mínítear, ní dheachaigh Aodh Mór Ó Néill agus an chuid eile den dream go hAssisi.) Tá cuntas fíoraisteach ag Tadhg ar thuama Naomh Proinsias – tugtar le tuiscint go raibh corpán an naoimh ar foluain san aer sa sailéar faoi thalamh, agus deirtear nach bhfuil cead ag duine ar bith é a fheiceáil gan chead speisialta ón bpápa. De réir mar a thuigim, áfach, tá fadhb ar leith ag baint leis an gcuntas seo, óir is cosúil nárbh eol cá raibh corp an naoimh curtha ón am ar cailleadh é in 1226 go dtí go dtángthas air in Assisi sa bhliain 1818!

Ar deireadh thiar, Dé Máirt, 29 Aibreán 1608, shroich na hiarlaí agus a gcompánaigh cathair na Róimhe, agus fearadh fáilte rompu mar laochra an Chaitliceachais. Bhí Peadar Lombard, ardeaspag Ard Mhacha, ansin le fáiltiú rompu, mar aon le cóistí a bhí curtha amach go himeall na cathrach ag na cairdinéil. Chuir an pápa lóistín ar fáil dóibh i bpáláis mhaorga sa Róimh, ach dealraíonn sé go raibh an Pápa Pól V beagán sprionlaithe, óir fágadh iad 'gan bata troscáin' nó go dtáinig Pilib III, rí na Spáinne, i gcabhair orthu agus gur bhronn liúntas beag ar Ó Néill agus ar Ó Domhnaill – bhí liúntas Uí Néill beagán níos mó ná liúntas a chomrádaí.

Baineann an chuid eile den téacs, den chuid is mó, le mionchuntais ar na cuairteanna a thug na hiarlaí agus a lucht leanúna ar mhóreaglaisí na Róimhe – sraith oilithreachtaí a leagadh amach go cúramach, i dtreo is gur féachadh le gach cuairt díobh a cheangal le lá féile phátrún na heaglaise a bhí i gceist. Ceapann údair áirithe go ndearnadh na cuairteanna seo faoi dheifir mar go raibh súil ag Ó Néill bogadh ar aghaidh gan mhoill chun na Spáinne. Ach ní raibh sé i ndán dóibh an turas sin a dhéanamh. Ina ionad sin, tá againn liosta gruama básanna, go háirithe i measc na bhfear, ar chriog aeráid fhiabhrúil samhraidh na Róimhe ina nduine agus ina nduine iad.

Sa chomhthéacs seo, ní féidir gan cuimhneamh ar na caointe binne truamhéileacha a chum Eoghan Ruadh Mac an Bhaird, file, thall i gcathair sin na Róimhe i dtaca an ama seo: *Anocht is uaigneach Éire* agus *A bhean fuair faill ar an bhfeart*.

Is é an léamh a rinne Ó Fiaich ar Thadhg Ó Cianáin nach raibh ann ach 'a simple unsophisticated scribe, somewhat naïve and medieval in outlook'. Duine ar bith a léifeadh an téacs ní fhéadfadh sé gan suntas a thabhairt don chlaonadh a bhí ag Tadhg iompó ar leataobh go rialta le cur síos a dhéanamh ar na míorúiltí a bhain le taisí naomh agus le heaglaisí a chonaiceadar ar a mbealach tríd an Eoraip. Ar an lámh eile, d'fhéadfaí a áiteamh

nach bhfuil sé ach ag cloí le gnéithe de dhiagacht an Fhrithreifirméisin.

Tá stíl bheoga Uí Chianáin le moladh, mar aon leis an gcineál Gaeilge a scríobh sé – atá soiléir, sothuigthe, ach gan a bheith neamhshofaisticiúil. Ar an iomlán, is féidir a rá faoin téacs gur cuntas é ó ghnáthdhuine atá beag beann ar an ardpholaitíocht agus ar na pleananna agus ar an uisce faoi thalamh a bhíonn de shíor san áit a mbíonn státairí agus ceannairí polaitiúla bailithe le chéile. Dhealródh sé nach bhfuil ó Thadhg ach cur síos a thabhairt dúinn ar ar tharla ó lá go lá, céard a rinne na taistealaithe, céard a d'ith siad, cé mar a mhothaigh siad ag pointí áirithe, cé na cineálacha bailte a ndeachaigh siad tríothu, ag críochnú lenar tharla nuair a bhaineadar an Róimh amach sa deireadh. Deir Ó Fiaich faoi Ó Cianáin:

[He] was obviously not *au fait* with the political chicanery which revolved around his master's destination and wrote like an Irish country lad seeing the Taj Mahal for the first time.[8]

Is deacair, dar liom, an léamh géarchúiseach a dhéanann Breandán Ó Doibhlin ar an scéal a shárú:

Bhí Ó Néill sáite in iarrachtaí dioplomáideacha chun filleadh ar a thír dhúchais, agus feidhmeannaigh agus spíodóirí Sasanacha á chiapadh. Ní raibh Ó Cianáin ranpháirteach sa bheartaíocht seo, ní de dheasca aon mhímhuinín as, ach … nach raibh an taithí ná an chaolchúis pholaitiúil agus dioplomáideach ann a sholáthródh ionad dó i gciorcal cúng an dlúthchaidrimh. Cín lae taistil … atá scríofa aige a sceitheann go minic iontas béal-leata an tuathánaigh in áiteanna aduaine, chomh maith le saontacht agus róchreidmheacht. Ina dhiaidh sin, insint shimplí, sholéite atá aige ar cheann d'eachtraí móra stair na hÉireann … Finné súl atá ann a thugann spléachadh luachmhar dúinn ó phointe dearctha Éireannach ar Eoraip an Athleasaithe Chaitlicigh.[9]

Is léir ó ghrinnléamh ar théacs Uí Chianáin go bhfuil cuid mhór mionsonraí ann a léiríonn gur thug an t-údar aird chruinn chúramach ar a raibh ar siúl ina thimpeall, rud a thabharfadh le fios go mb'fhéidir go raibh Tadhg níos sofaisticiúla ná mar a mheastar go minic. Féach, mar shampla, an chaoi a bpléann sé leis na cultúir éagsúla a chonaic sé i dteagmháil lena

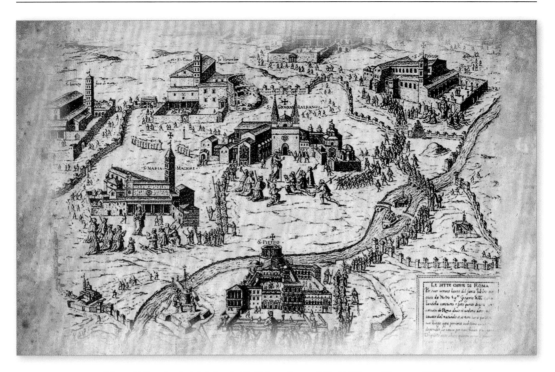

'Léarscáil Antoine Lafréri d'eaglaisí oilithreachta sa Róimh', Etienne Duperac (1575).

chéile. Gné ríspéisiúil den saothar is ea an chaoi a dtéann an t-údar i ngleic leis na teangacha éagsúla a chastar air ar feadh an turais. Tá sé soiléir nach leasc leis focail a thógáil ar iasacht ó na teangacha sin – idir an Fhraincis, an Spáinnis, an Dúitsis, an Iodáilis agus an Laidin, agus, gan amhras, an Béarla.[10]

Gan dul isteach go rómhion sa scéal anseo, tharraingeoinn aird ar roinnt pointí. Mar shampla, is anseo atá an sampla is túisce dá bhfuil againn den bhfocal *náisiún* sa Ghaeilge, ach gur cosúil gur mar *naisión* (ón Spáinnis *nacion*?) a bhí sé le scríobh – tá suas le dosaen samplaí de sa téacs. Féach freisin focail mar *bioláiste* agus *dorp* le haghaidh sráidbhaile, *seicreatáir* le haghaidh rúnaí, nó an chaoi a bhfuil an dá fhocal *ceol* agus *múisic* ann, nó *abhainn* agus *ruibhéar*, chomh maith le hiasachtaí mar *geastús* agus *stádús/státús*, gan trácht ar an gcomhfhocal aisteach úd *extraordinary-ambasadóir* agus an tagairt is luaithe sa Ghaeilge do chúirt leadóige (faoin bhfoirm *teinis-chúirt*)! Pointe suimiúil eile is ea an chaoi a scríobhann Ó Cianáin an focal *leorghníomh*, faoi dhó, mar *leabhairghníomh* – foirm a thiocfadh le fuaimniú an fhocail i gCúige Uladh! (An t-aon sampla amháin de chanúnachas sa téacs?) Is fiú a thabhairt faoi ndeara freisin nach n-úsáideann Ó Cianáin choíche an téarma *Gael*, ach tá deich samplaí den bhfocal *Éireannach* nó *Éireannaigh* aige ag tagairt do mhuintir an oileáin seo, bídís ó chúlra Gael nó Sean-Ghall.

Agus tá an téarma *naisión Éireannach* le tuiscint in abairt amháin ina luaitear an dá fhocal i bhfoisceacht dá chéile – 'd'Éireannchaibh agus do gach naisión archeana'.[11]

Chomh maith leis sin go léir, is fiú suntas a thabhairt don chaoi a láimhseálann Ó Cianáin na logainmneacha a dtagann sé trasna orthu ar an turas – tuairim is 240 ainm difriúil lasmuigh d'Éirinn atá i gceist ar fad (cé gur ainmneacha eaglaisí sa Róimh, agus in áiteacha eile, atá sa deichiú cuid díobh). Is léir, b'fhéidir i bhformhór na gcásanna, go bhfuil an t-údar ag brath ar an leagan a chuala sé sa chaint – bíodh sé sin ó strainséirí nó ó chuid de na compánaigh ba eolaisí ar an turas. Amanta tugann sé an leagan sin leis sách cruinn agus sách gar don fhoirm atá fós le fáil sa chaint, ach amanta eile is léir go bhfuil a bheag nó a mhór de phraiseach déanta aige de.[12]

Níl aon amhras ach go bhfuil tionchar láidir Proinsiasach le tabhairt faoi ndeara i dtéacs Uí Chianáin. Thagair mé níos luaithe don chaoi a bhfuil an lógó Proinsiasach úd IHS breactha ag Tadhg ar fhormhór na leathanach sa lámhscríbhinn, ach tá go leor samplaí eile lena chois sin. Luann Ó Cianáin féile San Proinsias (4 Deireadh Fómhair) sa bhliain 1608 go sonrach, agus insíonn sé mar a chuaigh Ó Néill an lá sin ar cuairt chuig San Francesco a Ripa in Trastevere, mainistir a raibh dlúthbhaint aige le scéal San Proinsias agus le bunú na bProinsiasach.

Tá trácht ag Tadhg freisin ar an gcuairt a tugadh ar an mórionad Proinsiasach ba thábhachtaí ar fad, Assisi, agus níos faide ar aghaidh tagraíonn sé d'eaglais cháiliúil Phroinsiasach eile, San Pietro in Montorio, a thuillfeadh cáil bhreise ar ball mar láthair adhlactha na n-iarlaí.

Tagraíonn Tadhg don Phroinsiasach aithnidiúil Flaithrí Ó Maoil Chonaire, proivinsial na bProinsiasach in Éirinn (agus a cheapfaí cúpla bliain ina dhiaidh sin ina ardeaspag ar Thuaim), agus insíonn sé mar a bhuail sé leis na hÉireannaigh i Douai. I gcomhluadar Fhlaithrí bhí an tAthair Roibeard Mac Artúir, nó Robert Chamberlain, a bhí ina ghnáthshagart deoisiúil go fóill ach a bhí ar tí dul isteach in Ord San Proinsias.

Is fiú a thabhairt dár n-aire an bhéim a leagann Ó Cianáin ar bhallaí na gcathracha agus na mbailte a dtéann sé tríothu, agus an chaoi a raibh cead speisialta ag Spáinnigh agus Éireannaigh amháin na ballaí sin a scrúdú. Leagtar béim ar leith ar na caisleáin agus na ballaí in Antwerp[13] i Milan[14] agus i bParma.[15]

Tá, gan amhras, mionchur síos ar na taisí naomh míorúilteacha go léir a leagann na hÉireannaigh súil orthu i rith an turais. Tá cuid de na cuntais ar sheaneaglaisí agus ar fhoirgnimh eile an-spéisiúil. I gcásanna áirithe maireann na foirgnimh sin agus is féidir a léiriú cé chomh cruinn is a bhíonn cuntas Uí Chianáin. I gcásanna eile tacaíonn an cur síos aige lena bhfuil ar eolas againn as seanfhoinsí eile faoi fhoirgnimh nach bhfuil tásc ná tuairisc orthu inniu.

Is ríshuimiúil an dá thagairt a dhéantar sa téacs do Shéarlas Borromeo, a bhí ina ardeaspag ar Mhilan agus ina chairdinéal go dtí go bhfuair sé bás sa bhliain 1584 – ní 'naoi mbliana roimhe seo [.i. 1599]', mar a deir Ó Cianáin. Duine fíorthábhachtach i stair an Fhrithreifirméisin ab ea Borromeo, agus bhí baint ar leith aige le Comhairle Thrionta.

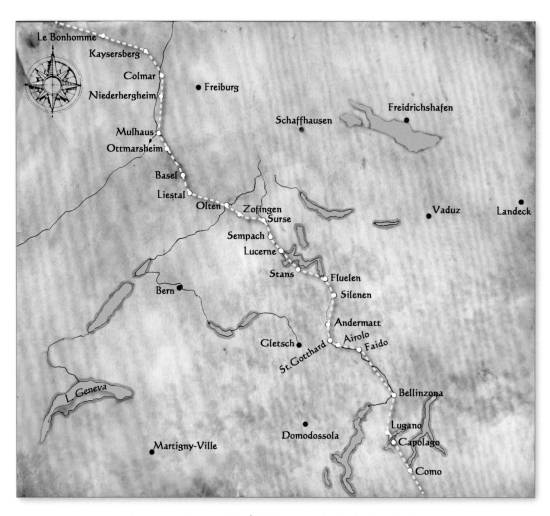

Ag trasnú na nAlp. © Tómás Ó Brógáin ag leanúint Nollaig Uí Mhuraíle

Is suimiúil go luann Ó Cianáin go bhfuiltear le naomh a dhéanamh de Borromeo go luath – rud a tharla go deimhin tamall gearr ina dhiaidh sin, sa bhliain 1610. Caithfidh, más ea, go raibh caint ar an gcanónú ag an am a raibh Tadhg ag breacadh a lámhscríbhinne.

Tá cur síos an-bheoga ag Ó Cianáin ar chanónú eile, sin an ócáid a ndearnadh naomh de bhean Rómhánach de chuid an cúigiú haois déag, Santa Francesca Romana. Caithfear cuimhneamh nach minic a dhéantaí naoimh a chanónú ag an am sin, agus rud níos neamhghnáiche fós ab ea bean Rómhánach a fhógairt ina naomh.

Cé gur féidir cur leis an gcuntas anseo is ansiúd ó fhoinsí eile, is cinnte go bhfuil go leor rudaí sa téacs seo nach bhfuil aon ní ag freagairt dóibh i bhfoinsí Gallda ar nós na bpáipéar stáit. Bíodh is nach cosúil go mbíodh Tadhg ar an eolas faoi phleananna Aodha Mhóir agus a chomhghleacaithe, bhí radharc aige ar a raibh ar siúl nach mbeadh ag mórán eile. Pé eolas atá le baint as na foinsí éagsúla eile, níl aon cheann acu in ann na mionsonraí a léiriú chomh gléineach céanna agus a dhéanann Tadhg. An cur síos aige ar na radharcanna, na hiontais a chonaiceadar, na h-ábhair imní a bhí ag na taistealaithe, an míchompord a bhain leis na drochbhóithre nó na hóstáin ina bhfuaireadar lóistín don oíche, an cruatan a bhain le dul trí Bhealach St Gotthard i lár na nAlp, an turas taitneamhach báid trasna Loch Lucerno agus Loch Lugano, an timpiste thragóideach ag an Teufelsbrücke (Droichead an Diabhail), na dinnéir leis an Ard-diúc Ailbeirt, le diúc na Lorráine, nó le daoine mór le rá eile, na ceoltóirí agus na damhsóirí a bhí i láthair, an teinis-chúirt nó an láthair ghiústála i Nancy, an zú i bParma – ní fhéadfaidís sin teacht ach ó dhuine a bhí ar an turas, a chonaic na rudaí céanna agus a d'airigh na rudaí ceannann céanna. Thar aon ní eile, is cuntas sa chéad phearsa atá againn ó Thadhg.

Fágann a bhfuil ráite agam faoi thábhacht an téacs go bhfuil sé dochreidte a laghad leasa atá bainte as ag staraithe. An beagán uaireanta a dtagraítear dó is go tarcaisneach a dhéantar sin go minic. Déantar beag is fiú den údar le hais foinsí naimhdeacha mar na páipéir stáit ghallda, nó ní dhéantar ach gearrthagairt achomair dó ag fíordheireadh fonóta. Ach bhí buntáiste ag Ó Cianáin a bhí ceilte ar na foinsí eile sin ar fad. Bhí sé in éineacht leis an taoisigh agus a lucht leanúna gach uile chéim den bhealach ó Ráth Maoláin go dtí an Róimh.

Nuair a léitear saothar na staraithe úd a dhéanann neamhshuim de leithéidí Uí Chianáin spreagtar an

smaoineamh: cé bheadh sotalach go leor le leabhar a scríobh, abair, ar stair na Fraince gan a bheith in ann foinsí Fraincise a léamh, nó ar stair na Rúise gan Rúisis? Ach ní bhíonn aon leisce ar staraithe áirithe scríobh faoi Éirinn roimh bhlianta tosaigh an naoú haois déag gan eolas maith acu ar theanga fhormhór na ndaoine ag an am sin, teanga a gcuid amhrán agus scéalta, a gcuid annála, dlíthe, ginealach, agus eile. Cuireadh an méid sin i gcuimhne dom tamall ó shin nuair a tháinig mé ar an ráiteas seo a leanas le scoláire Gaeilge as Albain, John Lorne Campbell; tá sé le fáil ina mhórshaothar *Highland songs of the Forty-five*:

> It is astonishing … that any historian should feel himself properly equipped to write the history of his country while remaining in ignorance of the language spoken over half its area.[16]

Nach fíre fós an ráiteas sin i dtaca le hÉirinn sa tréimhse atá i gceist anseo (1607-08), nuair a bhí an Ghaeilge á labhairt – gan aon chur isteach ó aon teanga eile – in gach coirnéal den tír?

Mar a dúras cheana, níor bhain Tadhg leis an 'gciorcal inmheánach'; ní thugann sé aon leide choíche gur labhair Ó Néill leis ná gur thug sé aon sonraí dó i dtaobh a dturais. Is tuairisceoir ón taobh amuigh é ó thús deireadh. Ach tá an méid sin intuigthe, ar ndóigh, tharla spiairí Sasanacha, nó spiairí ag gníomhú ar son na Sasanach, a bheith ar fud na háite; níor mhór a bheith san airdeall i gcónaí agus ríchúramach faoi chúrsaí slándála. Ba ré í, tar éis an tsaoil, ina raibh gníomhairí Shasana ina máistrí ar an bhfeallmharú – duine de na spiairí Sasanacha a bhí ag faire ar chomplacht na nIarlaí, d'iompaigh sé ar thaobh na nÉireannach agus chuir Ó Néill ar an eolas faoi chomhcheilg a bhí ar bun le nimh a chur ina chuid bia.

Mhíneodh sé sin, más ea, cur chuige Uí Chianáin. Is d'aon turas, dá réir sin – agus ar mhaithe le slándáil – a léiríonn sé na taoisigh agus a lucht leanúna ón taobh amuigh; tharlódh go raibh níos mó ar eolas aige ná mar a ligeann sé air. Léamh eile fós a bheadh níos inchreidte, dar liom, is ea go bhfuil sé ag cleachtadh nósmhaireacht an annálaí nó an chroiniceora Ghaelaigh gona stíl fhuarchúiseach, neamhphearsanta. Ós a choinne sin, áfach, féach an spéis agus an t-iontas a léiríonn sé go follasach agus é ag cur síos ar chuid de na radharcanna a chonaic sé.

Tá roinnt ceisteanna fós gan freagairt mar gheall ar shaothar Uí Chianáin. Mar shampla: cé dó a scríobhadh é? Cén aidhm a bhí leis? Cén fáth a stopann sé san áit a stopann? Freagra amháin a d'fhéadfaí a thabhairt ar an gcéad cheist acu sin gur do na Gaeil san Eoraip a breacadh é – ós iadsan amháin a thuigfeadh na focail nua ón iasacht a d'úsáid Tadhg. Caithfear a admháil nach saothar don ghnáthléitheoir é cuntas Uí Chianáin – go háirithe gnáthléitheoir ar ais sa mbaile in Éirinn i mblianta tosaigh an tseachtú haois déag. Ní gá ach cuimhneamh ar an dúil atá ag an údar i bhfocail a tógadh ar iasacht ó theangacha eile. Ní bheadh aon tuiscint ag na daoine sa bhaile ar fhocail mar sin, tharla gan aon taithí acu ar aon cheann de na teangacha sin.

Maidir leis an dara ceist, tá an smaoineamh curtha chun tosaigh ag scoláire amháin gurb amhlaidh a scríobhadh é le go léifí é sa bhialann i gcoinvint Phroinsiasach éigin. Is dóichí gur aidhm bholscaireachta a bhí leis go bunúsach – gur beartaíodh é mar shaothar a d'fhéadfaí a úsáid mar thacaíocht le feachtas Uí Néill, go háirithe i measc na nÉireannach a bhí ar deoraíocht ar an mór-roinn. Ach nuair

a thit na pleananna sin as a chéile – tar éis bhás na dtaoiseach, agus bhás Uí Chianáin féin – tharlódh gur úsáideadh an téacs mar ábhar léitheoireachta i bproinnteach na mbráithre i Lobháin, áit a dtabharfadh sé inspioráid do na deoraithe sin as Éirinn.

Chomh fada is a bhaineann leis an tríú ceist, tá an smaoineamh curtha chun tosaigh thuas go mb'fhéidir gurb é easláinte, nó fiú bás, an údair faoi ndeara críoch sách obann a bheith leis an saothar, agus go deimhin an t-iomrall ama nó aimhréidhe cróineolaíochta atá le sonrú gar don deireadh. Ach tá tuilleadh staidéir le déanamh ar an gceist seo agus ar go leor gnéithe eile den téacs.

Ceist amháin eile nár mhiste breis taighde a dhéanamh uirthi is ea: cé go díreach a bhí sa 'pearsa d'uireasa ar chéad [nócha is a naoí]' a bhí sa long a d'fhág Ráth Maoláin? Tá obair fhiúntach déanta ar an gceist seo ag scoláirí éagsúla – go háirithe Cainneach Ó Maonaigh, Tomás Ó Fiaich agus Micheline Kerney Walsh – ach is ar éigean atá an focal deiridh ráite go fóill.

Nótaí

1 *Fiants Eliz.*, 6735, pp 598-9 (6 Nollaig 1602).

2 *CSPI, 1608-10*, p. 537.

3 *CSPI 1608-10*, p. 543.

4 *CSPI, 1615-25*, p. 63.

5 *Turas*, p. 147.

6 Ibid.

7 Ibid., p. 148.

8 Kerney Walsh, '*Destruction by Peace*', p. xiv.

9 B. Ó Doibhlin (ed.), *Manuail de Litríocht na Gaeilge*, ii (Dublin, 2006), p. 200.

10 *audiens*: audience; *baingcéad*: banquet; *beinidicsión*: benediction; *bioláiste*: village; *coinseacráitión*: consecration; *cubhacal*: cubicle; *deavóisión*: devotion; *dorp*: village; *eacsaimean*: examination; *fondáisión*: foundation; *fortún*: fortune; *maiste*: match; *meilimheint, meiliveint, miliveint*: velvet; *múinisíon*: munition; *múisic*: music; *naipicín*: napkin; *naisión*: nation; *orphán*: orphan; *páitsidhe*: page[boy]s; *paspart*: passport; *peirseacúitión*: persection; *píleót, píolóit*: pilot; *piostail*: pistol; *preasántaidhe*: presents; *proiséisión*: procession; *réigión*: region; *reivireans*: reverence; *ruibhéar*: river; *runntábla*: round table; *searmóinias*: ceremonies; *seicreatáir*: secretary; *séicréide*: secret; *sliús*: sluice; *soiléar*: cellar; *stádús, státús*: stadhuis; *stáisión, stáitión*: station; *stannarda*: standards; *stioróipe*: stirrup; *suide, teaghdhas stuidéir*: study; *súibmisíon*: submission; *teinis-chúirt*: tennis-court;

traibhléaraidhe: travellers; *trongca*: trunk; *tubháille*: towel; *tucsaoid*: hogshead; *viseatáitión*: visitation

11 *Turas*, p. 93.

12 Aarschot: *Ascot*; Alpnachersee: *Ampse*; Amiens: *Amens, Amiaunce*; Antwerp: *Anverp, Anvuorp, Anvoeirp*; Assisi: *Asidhis*; Bale/Basle/Basel: *Basalea*; Bellinzona: *Bellusona*; Binche: *Bench*; Bruxelles: *Bruicséil*; Capolago: *Caput de Lacu, Codelacu*; Casenove: *Nuevocasa*; Castel Bolognese: *Castel Burneis*; Contay: *Pountau*; Die Teufelsbrücke: *Droichead an Diabhail*; Enghien: *Inginn*; Fillières: *Feilirs*; Foligno: *Fulino*; Ghent: *Gant*; Guernsey: *Goirge*; Jersey: *Gairsí*; Jodoigne: *Sidona*; Kaysersberg: *Ceizerspell*; La Bouille: *Laboil, Laboill*; Lisieux: *Liegeeuvaie*; Mars-la-Tour: *Malatur*; Niederhergheim: *Niderharga*; Notre Dam de Hal: *Noutre Dam de Hauer*; Ottmarsheim: *Hotmers*; Pesaro: *Pensaro*; Piedimonte: *Pede Montain*; Pont-à-Mousson: *Pontemountson*; Quilleboeuf: *Cilbuf*; Rouen: *Rodhán*; Saint-Die-des-Vosges: *Saungdi*; Savignano sul Rubicone: *Salignano Silenan*: *Flelan*; Slavonia: *Eschioua* [.i. *Eszék, Osijek*]; Vilvorde: *Filfort*; Willebroeck: *Milbruc*; Zofingen: *Ophingaraibh*

13 *Turas*, pp 67-69.

14 Ibid., p. 160.

15 Ibid., p. 170.

16 J. Lorne-Campbell (ed.), *Highland Songs of the Forty-five* (Edinburgh, 1933), p. xviii.

Imirce na nUaisle Ultacha, 1607[1]

Marcas Ó Murchú

Cosúil le clann Iosráél
Thoir san Eigipt ar éidréan
Mic Mhíle um Bhóinn abhus
Ag síneadh dóibh ón dúchas.[2]
(Fear Flatha Ó Gnímh, 1612)

Léacht a thug an Cairdinéal Tomás Ó Fiaich i Ráth Maoláin, áit ónar imigh na huaisle Gaelacha deiridh i Meán Fómhair 1607 is ábhar don leabhar a scríobh údar an ailt seo d'am comórtha na n-uaisle Ultacha. Rith smaoineamh le húdar an ailt seo gur beag ábhar éasca léitheoireachta ar an tonnbhriseadh seo i stair na tíre atá ar fáil ag Gaeil an lae inniu. Is é ab áil leis ná go n-amharcfadh idir óg is aosta ar an tréimhse chorraiteach seo inár stair, is go ndéanfadh siad athshealbhú ar stair an chultúir dhúchais Ghaeilge.

Bhí meas as cuimse ar scoláirí na hÉireann ar fud na hEorpa, lá dá raibh.[3] Is fada mainistreacha agus coláistí bunaithe ar mhór-roinn na hEorpa agus manaigh ag saothrú iontu, trí Ghaeilge is trí Laidin den chuid ba mhó. I ndiaidh scrios an chórais ghaelaigh in Éirinn a bunaíodh cuid mhaith acu, go háirithe ón tseachtú haois déag ar aghaidh. Ba chóir seans a bheith ag aos óg na tíre foghlaim cérbh iad na pearsana tábhachtacha a bhí iontu, Na Ceithre Máistrí, Aodh Mac Aingil (Mac Cathmhaoil), Flaithrí Ó Maoil Chonaire, Lúcás Wadding agus scríbhneoirí eile nach iad.

Mheall an tOrd Proinsiasach in Éirinn agus i gColáiste San Antaine sagairt agus bráithre d'ardchaighdeán intleachtúil chucu. Ba dhream iad sin a d'fhág lámhscríbhinní luachmhara againn mar oidhreacht,[4] *Annála Ríoghachta Éireann* agus *Imeacht na nIarlaí* ina measc. Nuair a ghlac rialtas na Fraince ceannas ar an choláiste i 1793 aistríodh cuid den bhailiúchán go dtí Coláiste San Iosodóir sa Róimh. Tugadh an bailiúchán go Teach na bProinsiasach, ar Ché na gCeannaithe, Baile Átha Cliath, sa bhliain 1872 agus as sin go Teach

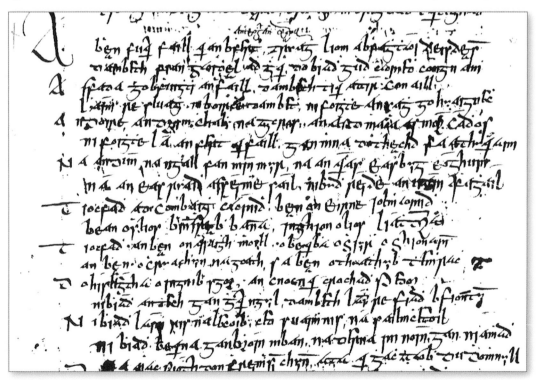

A bhean fuair faill ar an bhfeart (Eoghan Rua Mac an Bhaird). Leabhar Inghine Uí Dhomhnaill. In eagar, E. Knott, *Celtica*, 5 (1960), p. 161. © Royal Library, Brussels

Comóradh i n-onóir Mhichíl Uí Chléirigh. © Ionad an Léinn Éireannaigh, Teach Inse

Staidéir na bProinsiasach i nDún Mhuire, Cill Iníon Léinín, Contae Bhaile Átha Cliath, i 1946. Bogadh go Coláiste na hOllscoile, Baile Átha Cliath iad nuair a bunaíodh Fondúireacht Mhíchíl Uí Chléirigh um Thaighde ar Stair agus Sibhialtacht na nGael i 2000.

Ón tseachtú haois déag ar aghaidh, tháinig borradh mór faoi choláistí Éireannacha ar mhór-roinn na hEorpa agus na sagairt ag seachaint na géarleanúna sa bhaile. Agus tuaisceart na hEorpa ag tiontú ar an Phrotastúnachas, bunaíodh coláiste Éireannach i Lisboa na Portaingéile sa bhliain 1593 ('Collegio de Estudiantes Irlandeses sub invocaçaon de San Patricio'), Salamanca na Spáinne, 'El Real Colegio de Nobles Irlandeses', (1593), agus tosaíodh cuid mhór scoileanna léinn ar fud na mór-roinne i rith na haoise; Santiago de Compostela (1605); Lobháin (1607); Antwerp (c. 1629); Tournai (1689); Douai na Fraince (1577); Lille (1604); Bordeaux (1603); Toulouse (1659); Nantes (c. 1680); Poitiers (c. 1674), Páras (1578); Sevilla (1612); Maidrid (1629) agus Alcalá de Henares (1590).[5]

Is fiú fosta filíocht chomhaimseartha na Gaeilge a thabhairt san áireamh. Ba dhream iad na filí a raibh ardstádas orthu sa tsochaí, céim bheag i ndiaidh na n-uaisle. Ar an dóigh sin is féidir domhandearcadh lucht léinn Éire na linne sin a thuigbheáil trí fhocail agus trí smaointeoireacht na bhfilí:

Go bhfille tú ar shliocht Ghael Glas,
A mhic Aodha, a ua Mhánais,
Go mba dhímrí gach tonn dá dtuil,
Gach imní ann go mba soraidh.[6]

Níl le déanamh ach dán de chuid Eoghain Rua Mac an Bhaird a léamh, dán a cumadh mar bhuíochas croí as ucht na litreach a fuair sé ó ghasúr beag a bhí mar oidhre ar phrionsa Thír Chonaill. Ba mhac óg é an gasúr seo le Ruaidhrí Ó Domhnaill, duine a bhí ar bord na loinge a d'iompair na tiarnaí Ultacha chun na mór-roinne agus gan é ach bliain d'aois. Tugadh chun na Róimhe é ach ar bhás a athar ansin, d'fhill deirfiúr a athar, Nuala Ní Dhomhnaill go Lobháin leis sula raibh sé trí bliana d'aois le go gcuirfeadh Proinsiasaigh Éireannacha, Coláiste San Antaine, Ollscoil Lobháin, oideachas air:

Ionúin scríbhinn scaoiltear ann;
Mór an bíogadh a bhain asam.
Saor, a Dhé ó athleonadh sinn-
Athbheochan é do m'intinn …

… Aodh Ó Dónaill …
Gan d'aois ann ach seacht mbliana
Damhna mo rí róbhá liom
scoláire a scríobh thú, a scríbhinn.[7]

Bhí Eoghan Ruadh Mac an Bhaird i gcuideachta na n-iarlaí i 1607 nuair a ardaíodh ancaire na loinge i Loch Suillí, is tá mothúcháin phearsanta an fhile le brath ó na chéadlínte:

A bhean fuair faill ar an bhfeart,
trua liom a bhfaightheá d'éisteacht.
Dá mbeadh fian Gael i do ghar
bheadh ag do chaoineadh cúnamh.[8]

Luaitear sraith logainmneacha, cuid acu atá ann go fóill agus cuid a dhíbir an Phlandáil as éadan ar fad:

I nDún na nGall fán mhínmhuir,
nó in áras Easpaig Eoghain,
nó in Eas Rua is séimhe sáil'
ní ba réidhe an uain a fháil …[9]

Cuirtear in iúl don léitheoir is don lucht éisteachta gur thábhachtach ionad na n-uaisle i saol polaitiúil an lae agus gurb iad síol na ríthe atá ar bord agus gur boichte sinn ina n-éagmais:

Dhá mhac rí den fhréamh sin Choinn
atá ar gach taobh d'Ó Domhnaill

… dís den triúr sin tharla istigh
clann Aodh ardfhlaith Ailigh;
ua don Aodh sin duine dhíobh.[10]

Déantar tagairt do chathanna a troideadh in éadan fhórsaí na Banríona Eilíse i ndeisceart Uladh ina raibh bua cuimsitheach ag an Niallach:

Lá oirirc an Átha Bhuí
inar laoidheadh leacht sochaí,
dá dtiteadh uainn Aodh Ó Néill,
don taobh thuaidh ba thuirling …[11]

Agus arís agus é i gCúige Chonnacht, le cuidiú ó Chlann Diarmada agus ó Mhac Diarmada Ruadh throid Ó Domhnaill in éadan an tSasanaigh, Conyers Clifford, in aice le Mainstir na Búille i gContae Ros Comáin:

Lá an Chorrshléibhe ar chlaí na nGall,
dá bhfeicfí fuil le Cafarr
Ba leor d'urú a fheiceáil,
slua Mhuirbhigh a mhochachtáil.[12]

Déanann Eoghan Rua tagairt do dhúchas na nDálach fada siar go Clann Mhíleadh na Spáinne, a tháinig go hÉirinn ó iarthuaisceart na Spáinne, de réir an tseanchais. Bhí na hiarlaí ag iarraidh dul chun na Spáinne ach is tríd an Fhrainc ab éigean dóibh taisteal cheal cuidithe ón Fhrainc ná ón Spáinn. Fiú agus iad sa Róimh bhí siad ag iarraidh dul chun na Spáinne ar bád. Ba thráthúil mar sin go raibh lasta na loinge seo ag pilleadh ar a bhfód dúchais:

Aodh Mac Cathmhaoil (1571-1626), portráid i gColáiste San Antaine, Lobháin. © Coláiste San Antaine

Cén Gael nach gcaoinfeadh libh
bláth fréimhe mhacra Mhíle
Bhur n-ualach cé nach n-iompródh
Cé an croí sin nach gcreathnódh.[13]

Buille marfach do leanúnachas an chultúir dhúchais a bhí ann a chuir as ríocht ar fad é. Fágadh cuid mhór de na filí gan pátrúin agus na Gaeil gan cheannasaíocht is go leor díobh gan talamh. Bhí cosc ar cheol is glas ar Ghaeilge.[14] Cailleadh críocha atharta is cuireadh creideamh is cleachtais choimhthíocha eile i bhfeidhm. Tá cuid den fhilíocht is brónaí sa stór liteartha againn ón tréimhse sin: atá soiléir in 'Feartlaoi do náisiún

marbh' le Fear Flatha Ó Gnímh, file chlann Aoidh Bhuidhe Uí Néill (deisceart Chontae Aontroma):

Beannacht ar anam na hÉireann,
Inis na gcéimeann corrach;
Atá Treabh Bhriain na mbog-ghlór,
De mo dhóigh, ar dhobrón torrach.[15]

Tá pian an bhróin ag cur as go mór dó 'Ionann a's éag na Fódla Ceilt córa 's a creidimh'. Dar leis go bhfuil sé amhail is go bhfuair anam na tíre féin bás: 'Deacair nach bás don Bhanbha, d'éis an tread calma curadh, a thriall ar toisc don Easpáin -mo thrua iad'. Tháinig an tuar faoin tairngreacht i dtaca leis an chéad líne eile seo, mar a léirigh na céada bliain de neamart is neamhaird do na filí is do nósanna na hÉireann a lean an imirce: 'D'éag a huaisle a's a hoidhreacht, gan teacht aicí ón ollbhéim …' Thuig sé i gceart go raibh riocht na tíre athraithe go huile is go hiomlán is gur dheacair don mhuintir a fágadh gan bláthfhleasc féin i gcuimhne na hoidhreachta a cailleadh a leagan cois uaigh an traidsiúin dhúchais. '… gan bhláth i dtalamh – bíodh ar a hanam beannacht'.

Bhí 'coróin iontach Éireann' á baint den tír agus an tséú haois déag ag druidim chun deiridh. Chuir Eilís I Robert Devereux, iarla Essex agus 17,000 saighdiúir go hÉirinn, ach chonacthas di go raibh seisean, an fear ionaid s'aici, ag iarraidh déiléail leis an hÉireannaigh 'ar dhóigh róshíochánta'. Cuireadh chun báis é, i ndiaidh a bheith páirteach i gcomhcheilg thréasúil. Sa tsibhialtacht a bhí ann, bhí meas ar airm níb oilte is níor mhaith leis na Gaeil cogaíocht oscailte leanúnach a dhéanamh leis na Sasanaigh. Bhí a fhios acu dá dtiocfadh arm ollmhór go mbeadh deireadh leo is nach mbeadh seans feasta ag na Gaeil Chaitliceacha in Éirinn. Iarradh cuidiú ón Spáinn ach tháinig sé i dtír san áit chontráilte ag an am chontráilte. Le bás Eilíse, tháinig Séamas VI na hAlban i réim mar rí na dtrí ríocht is thiontaigh sé ar a ghéillsinigh Chaitliceacha i ndiaidh Chomhcheilg Guy Fawkes i 1605.

Tugann an dán seo a chum Fearghal Mac an Bhaird bás an Cairdinéil Uí Fhiaich féin i gcuimhne

'Imeacht na nIarlaí'. © Seán Ó Brógáin

dom i dtaca le cailliúint phearsanta is mothúcháin de 'Mairg atá an uairsi gan Aodh'. Thairis sin, tá Aodh Mag Uidhir, taoiseach Fhear Manach roimh aimsir Chúchonnacht (Mhig Uidhir), faoi thrácht sa dán eile seo a bhfuil an-chosúlacht aige leis an dán thuas ó thaobh téama de. Ba é file Mhig Uidhir, Eochaidh Ó hEodhasa a chum:

Fuar liom an oíche seo d'Aodh
Cúis tuirse, troime a ciot braon
Mo thrua é sin dár seise
Nimh fhuaire na hoíche seo.[16]

Cé gur ó pheann file anaithnid é an dán thuas luaite is léir é a bheith ar maos i mothúcháin, stair, gineolas, logainmneacha ach thar aon ní eile tá mothúcháin na hócáide le brath ann tríd síos. File gan ainm in *Leabhar Uí Chonchobhair Dhoinn* (413b) a chum agus a thug liosta díobh sin a bhí ar bord na loinge:

Seisear uainn fa Aodh Macha
Do-chuadar fa leith san luing,
cúigear do Chinéal Chonaill,
mór sníomh do chuir im chroidhe,
dhá fhuil ríogh le Rughraidhe
A-táid sa luingse thar lear
dá Iarla Inse Gaoidheal,
siar ar eachtra ó Iath Fhuinidh,
Is triath sleachta saor Uidhir.[17]

Is eol don fhile go díreach cé a bhí ar bord agus bhí sé in ann pobal na tíre a chur ar an eolas faoin imirce thragóideach a thug siad orthu féin. Is tábhacht leis an gineolas a thabhairt leis, bunaithe ar na blianta staidéir i scoileanna filíochta: 'Ar dtriall Aodha Í Néill a-nois … ar n-imtheacht mic mhic Mhagnois … Triath ó Néill, ceann ó gConuill … Art, Aodh Ruadh, Cathbharr, Cúchonnacht, Ceithre beithre Thoighe Táil'.[18]

Shín dúiche Uí Dhomhnaill isteach go Doire Choluim Cille féin sa tseachtú haois déag mar is léir 'dá Aodh Ó Domhnaill Doire', agus déantar tagairt do Thír Eoghain, ceantar an Niallaigh: 'ceithre leinb na laochroidhe … Brian Ó saoirNéill is Seáin'. Ní dhéantar faillí sna mná is sna máithreacha ach oiread: 'Triúr ban d'uaislibh Fhóid Bhanba, uainn san árthach ollmhardha, na réadhmhná ó Ráth na bhFionn, le téarna cáich go coiteann … Guidhim an Triúr as treise laoich is leinbh na loingeise … 's an triúr ríoghbhan …'[19]

Tugadh 'Aodh Doire' ar Aodh Ó Domhnaill i gcuid eile de dhánta comhaimseartha lena léiriú go raibh smacht an Dálaigh go forleathan ag barr tíre, fiú i gceantar Uí Dhochartaigh, Inis Eoghain is Doire Chalgaigh. Arís is eol don fhile ginealaigh bhantracht na loinge siúd chomh maith leis na fir, eolas a bhí an-luachmhar ag na clanna uaisle agus ag na filí araon 'Inghean ríoghfhréimhe Rosa, inghean airdríogh Bhearnasa, m'imneadh gan fhatha ní fhuil, is inghean flatha ó bhFiamhui'. Is tagairt eile é sin do shinsir Uí Dhochartaigh nó Clann Fiamhain agus Uí Dhomhnaill. Léirítear mar dhís mhóruasal iad a shíolraigh ó 'roighne Ó Néill is Clann gConuill'. Is saothar eisceachtúil é ina ndeir an file faoi na daoine gur 'd'fhuil ardfhlatha' iad.

Níorbh iad aimsir na hArmáide Dochlóite agus Cath Chionn tSáile amháin a chuir an Spáinn cuidiú míleata go hÉirinn.[20] Mar léiriú air sin, tháinig fianaise chun cinn ó chartlann na Spáinne le blianta beaga anuas.[21] D'fhág an Captaen Diego de Ortiz de Urizar baile Castro i 1574 agus é ar misean le heolas a bhailiú fá Éirinn. Bhí Fray Mateo de Oviedo, bráthair d'Ord San Proinsias as Santiago i láthair ag Dún an Óir i gCiarraí.[22] Bhí an-chumarsáid leis na húdaráis Spáinneacha aige. D'fhág Alonso Cobos agus Domingo Ochos cathair Santander agus tháinig go Dún na nGall i 1596 agus rinne pleanáil le lucht éirí amach sa chontae sin ag an am. Sheol Antonio de Cisneros agus Medinilla as Lisboa na Portaingéile agus iad ag triall ar Dhún na nGall i 1596. D'fhág Cristóbal Montero, Domingo Jiménez agus an piolóta Pantaleón González ó La Coruña i 1596 ar misean le cósta tuaisceartach na hÉireann a scrúdú le go bhfaigheadh siad áit chuí le teacht i dtír d'arm na Spáinne. Rinne Alonso Cobos ullmhúchán agus pleanáil le saighdiúirí a thabhairt i dtír in Éirinn sa bhliain 1596. Thug an Captaen Antonio de Cisneros eolas míleata go hÉirinn i 1597 fá phlean le hionsaí a dhéanamh, agus chuir sé eolas míleata le chéile ina thaobh. B'as San Sebastián a sheol Fernando de Barrionuevo i 1599 agus thug sé gunnaí go Dún na nGall agus bhailigh sé eolas míleata. Bhí cruinniú aige le fórsaí míleata a bhain le Ó Néill agus le lucht leanúna Uí Dhomhnaill i nDún na nGall.[23]

Ní hiad na hUltaigh amháin a bhí á gcoinneáil agus á gcothú ag an Spáinn. Bhí 'Cornelio [Conn] O'Driscoll, señor de Baltimore y Castelhaven', Dún na Séad, ón bhliain 1602 ar aghaidh, ar pinsean 80 escudo sa mhí. Cuireadh an mac s'aige, Cornelio Óg Ó Drisceoil, chun na Gailéise (iarthuaisceart

Aodh Mór Ó Néill. © NLI

Geata an Phobail (Porta del Popolo), An Róimh, ar thaistil na hiarlaí tríd ar a mbealach isteach sa chathair: ó Giuseppe Vasi (1710-82), *Delle Magnificenze di Roma Antica e Moderna*, 1747-61. © BL

na Spáinne) mar chruthú cairdis is comhartha muiníne sa Spáinn. Ina theannta luaitear 'Thadeo [Tadhg] O Driscoll', mac leis. Mhair 'Dionisio [Donncha] Ó Drisceoil, señor de Castelhaven' i La Coruña ar 80 escudo sa mhí i 1602 agus 'Juana O Driscoll' [Sinéad Ní Dhrisceoil] iníon leis, ina chomhluadar.[24]

D'imigh an 'Vizconde' [Leas-Chúnta] Baltinglass go Maidrid i ndiaidh éirí amach a stiúradh in Éirinn sna blianta 1580-81.[25] Bhí 'John Geraldine' [Seán Mac Gearailt], á chothú ag an Spáinn i La Coruña i dtuaisceart na tíre ón bhliain 1602. Chuaigh 'Juana Geraldine' [Sinéad Nic Gearailt], iníon Chúnta Dheasmhumhan, isteach sa bheatha chrábhaidh mar bhean rialta i gclochar Real Monasterio de las Huelgas (i gceantar Burgos).[26] Timpeall an ama sin, bhí uaisle na hÉireann scartha ar fud na ríochta; Donncha Ó Briain i La Coruña (ó 1602), Theobald Burke, mac 'el Marqués Mac Uilliaim de Búrca' i gcathair Valladolid i 1604, Walter Burke, a mhac agus a oidhre 'el marqués McWilliam Burke' ina 'paje real' (cúntóir ríoga) i gcúirt rí na Spáinne, agus ligeadh isteach é mar bhall de Orden de Santiago i mí an Mheithimh 1607 agus é aon bhliain déag d'aois. Lena chois, bhí 'Florence Carthy' is a chuid mac ('Dermicio

Florencio Carthy', 'Eugenio Florencio Carthy', 'Cornelio Florencio Carthy', 'Carolas Florencio Carthy', 'Fynyn Carthy') i La Coruña ar chostas rí na Spáinne, a bhí ag díol tríocha escudo sa mhí leis ó 1602.[27]

Bhí Gearaltaigh nó 'La Familia Fitzgerald, condes de Desmond y Kildare' (Cúntaí Dheasmhumhan is Chill Dara) ann fosta. Le himeacht aimsire, thosaigh Clann Mhic Mhathúna (Muineachán) is Clann tSuibhne (Tír Chonaill) ag triall ar an Leithinis Ibéireach.[28] Níos faide anonn sa tseachtú haois déag, d'imigh muintir Dhochartaigh agus Dálaigh agus Niallaigh Ard Mhacha chun na Spáinne fosta.[29] Ba iad seo an dream ba mhó Gael a raibh tionchar acu ar phobal is ar shochaí na Spáinne. Bhí na céadta saighdiúir de phór Gael i mbun gníomhaíochta ón Ostair go Flóndras agus ba dhream iad a tháinig a chogaíocht ansin ón tséú haois déag amach.[30] Tá teacht ar thaifid de mhóréachtaí na saighdiúirí seo i gcartlanna ar fud na hEorpa agus obair scolártha idir lámha acu ag saineolaithe Spáinneacha is Éireannacha lena dtréithe a thabhairt chun solais. Is ábhar spreagtha do thaighdeoirí ár linne go bhfuil an bhearna seo sa leanúnachas i dtraidisiún an léinn á líonadh le solas lonrach an eolais faoi dheireadh thiar.

'Imeacht na nIarlaí'.
© John Conway

Nótaí

1 *Imirce* agus *uaisle* in ionad *teitheadh/imeacht* agus *iarlaí* na téarmaí tagartha ar chloígh B. Ó Doibhlin (ed.), *Manuail de litríocht na Gaeilge* (Dublin, 2006).

2 Fear Flatha Ó Gnímh, 'Mo thruaighe mar táid Gaoidhil' (1612), ag T. F. O'Rahilly (ed.), *Measgra dánta*, ii (Dublin, 1927), p. 206 agus O. Bergin (ed.), *Irish bardic poetry* (Dublin, 1970). Aistrithe ar W. Cox's *Irish Magazine and Monthly Asylum*, iii (Dublin, 1810); agus J. Hardiman (eag.), *Irish Minstrelsy*, *ii* (Dublin, 1831).

3 T. Ó Fiaich, *Irish Cultural Influences in Europe* (Dublin, 1967); idem, *Gaelscrínte san Eoraip* (Dublin, 1986).

4 Scríobhtar na litreacha ISOS tríd an idirlín le tuilleadh den taisce luachmhar seo a bhrath.

5 P. Ó Mianáin, 'Na cólaistí Éireannacha ar an mhór-roinn: culra agus fóras', *Taighde is Teagasc,* iii (2003), pp 133-209.

6 Ó Doibhlin, *Manuail de litríocht na Gaeilge,* ii, ina bhfuil go leor ábhair léinn ón tréimhse seo.

7 C. Ní Dhomhnaill, *Duanaireacht* (Dublin, 1975), p. 188a, agus tagairt do Leabhar Uí Chonchobhair Dhuinn' agus fosta Ó Doibhlin, *Manuail* (2006), p. 250.

8 E. Knott, (ed), 'Mac an Bhaird's elegy on the Ulster lords', *Celtica* v (1960), pp 161-71. *A bhean fuair faill ar an bhfeart,* le hEoghan Rua Mac an Bhaird.

9 Knott (op cit. 1960), pp 161-71.

10 Ibid.

11 Ibid.

12 Ibid.

13 Ibid.

14 Léitear i bhfilíocht Fhear Flatha Uí Ghnímh gurb ionann is éag na Fódla ceilt a córa 's a creidimh … ní léigeann eagla an Ghallsmachta damh a hanstaid do nochtadh; atá an chríoch réidhse ríNéill de chrú fíréan dá folcadh" (.i. go raibh tailte Uí Néill á bhfolcadh i bhfuil neamhurchóideach – aistriuchán an údair). Feictear filíocht Mhuiris Mhic Gearailt le tuilleadh íomhánna den chineál seo a fháil

'Fearg Dé … is é a fháth dá n-ionnarbhadh díoltas Dé as adhbhar ann' (B. Ó Buachalla, 'Anocht is Uaigneach Éire', *History Ireland*, xv, no. 4 (2007), pp 33-4).

15 Ibid., passim.

16 Ó Doibhlin, *Manuail*, ii, p. 221.

17 Is do Mhag Uidhir taoiseach Fhear Manach a thagraíonn sé sa chuid dheireanach seo: Ní Dhomhnaill, *Duanaireacht*, p. 413b.

18 Ibid., p. 413b.

19 Ibid., p. 413b.

20 Is eiseamláir é an t-údar Spáinneach, E. García Hernán, agus a bhfuil ina leabhar *Irlanda y el rey prudente laberinto* (Madrid, 2000).

21 Ó. Recio Morales, *El socorro de Irlanda en 1601 y la contribución del ejército a la integración de los Irlandeses en España* (Madrid, 2002), p. 198.

22 Smerwick an t-aistriú a rinneadh ar Dhún an Óir.

23 Morales, *El socorro de Irlanda*, passim, agus taighde an údair.

24 Buíochas le Mairéad Ní Dhrisceoil as Baile Átha Cliath a chuir tuilleadh eolais chugam faoin teaghlach seo. Tá na hainmneacha pearsanta céanna le fáil ina sinsir féin.

25 Recio Morales, *El socorro de Irlanda,* p. 198 et seq.

26 Ibid.

27 Ibid.

28 M. Ó Murchú, Léacht Comórtha na nIarlaí, Ráth Maoláin, Meán Fómhair, (2007); Gabhtar buíochas fosta le Áine Ní Dhuibhne.

29 Taighde an údair agus M. Kerney Walsh, '*Destruction by Peace*': *Hugh O'Neill after Kinsale* (Armagh, 1986).

30 F. D'Arcy, *Wild Geese and travelling scholars* (Cork, 2001); R. A. Stradling, *The Spanish monarch and Irish mercenaries: the Wild Geese in Spain, 1618-68* (Dublin, 1994); G. Henry, *The Irish military community in Spanish Flanders, 1586-1621* (Cork, 1992).

'A garden in the very centre of Christendom': the earls' sojourn in the duchy of Lorraine

Mary Ann Lyons

The three most wonderful ceremonies in Europe – the coronation of the emperor in Frankfurt, the anointing of the king of France in Rheims and the funeral of the duke of Lorraine in Nancy.
(Proverb, early 1600s)

Immediately after Charles III, duke of Lorraine, died on 18 May 1608 his body was embalmed, clothed in golden raiment and placed on display for a month while the clergy sang daily psalms and litanies around it. Having fashioned an image of the corpse, clad in court robes, the court celebrated the 'dead man's supper' for another month. Courtiers feasted each day, placing the dead duke's portion in front of his empty throne. After several days of offices and masses of the dead, on 17 July the duke's funeral procession, comprising three hundred poor people, three hundred of the middle strata, and all of the gentry and clergy, processed through the streets of the ducal capital, Nancy, and on the following day his remains were interred in the Franciscan church beside his old palace where he routinely attended mass.[1]

Charles III, duke of Lorraine (1543-1608). This devout Catholic nobleman defied King James by extending generous hospitality to the Ulster fugitives as they moved through his duchy. © NPG

Conspicuously absent from this distinguished gathering was a representative of King James I of England and Ireland and VI of Scotland. James boycotted the ceremony to register his annoyance at the manner in which the duke had defied his wishes by warmly receiving the earls of Tyrone and Tyrconnell as they passed through his duchy *en route* to Rome in the previous March.[2] Among those who commented on this very public slight to the House of Lorraine was Antoine Le Fèvre de la Boderie, the French ambassador to London. He explained to the French minister for foreign affairs that King James took this course of action because he 'bears ill will towards the princes who have received and allowed freedom of travel in their coun-try to the earl of Tyrone'. James reportedly told a gentleman of his household that 'he would have more regret for the loss of that old man [Charles III] and would send messages of condolence to his children, had he not, before dying, caused him such grave displeasure by receiving the Earl [of Tyrone] and by the manner in which he did so'.[3] This article examines the Ulster earls' brief sojourn in the duchy of Lorraine within the context of the prevailing finely balanced international political and diplomatic relations. It aims to explain James I's reaction to the stance assumed by Charles III, thereby illuminating the wider political and diplomatic sensitivities and significance of the earls' presence on the continental stage.

After England and Spain signed the Treaty of London in 1604, James I committed himself to maintaining amicable relations with both Philip III of Spain and Henry IV of France while he sought a Spanish or French bride for his heir.[4] Henry IV's conspiratorial role in facilitating the Ulster earls' safe passage through France into Spanish Flanders in October 1607 exerted a short-term strain on relations with James. However, his refusal to permit the earls to journey southwards through France to their intended destination, Spain, his eagerness to see them pass out of his realm as quickly as possible, and their avoidance of French territory as they travelled from Louvain towards Italy in the early months of 1608 all demonstrated Henry IV's earnest commitment to maintaining good relations with 'the wisest fool in Christendom'.[5] Determined not to allow the earls to jeopardise his relationship with James, Philip III prevaricated and obfuscated for several months while the Irish party sojourned in Spanish Flanders, awaiting his decision on their ultimate destination. During that time spies and agents of the English ambassador, Sir Thomas Edmonds, actively sought their arrest and deliverance to James.

They grew acutely conscious that their presence caused embarrassment to their host, Archduke Albert, whom James accused of harbouring traitors to his crown. Likewise, they received little consolation from the papal nuncio, Guido Bentivoglio.[6] When the earls were finally notified by the marqués de Spínola, commander-in-chief of the Spanish army in Flanders, that the archduke wished them to leave, they remonstrated with King Philip that 'having arrived in these states, in safe haven as we thought … another misfortune has befallen us'. Their despair and resentment at having to leave Flanders 'so that he [Archduke Albert] may keep a promise he made to the king of England' was palpable. Intensely conscious of how the treatment afforded them as Catholic refugees would be viewed in England, Scotland and Ireland, as well as on the continent, the earls emphasised to Philip 'the sorrow and scandal this will cause to other Catholics, and the pleasure and satisfaction it will give the heretics to see us thus treated'.[7] However, Philip had decided that 'the best solution' was for the earls to go to Rome since 'the king of Great Britain may find cause for complaint should they come to Spain or be given a grant in the states of Flanders'.[8] With no option but to leave Flanders, the party of thirty-two men on horseback and a coach with the ladies left Louvain for Italy on 28 February. On the following Tuesday, 4 March, they entered the independent territory of Charles III, duke of Lorraine (now part of north-eastern France).[9]

The duchy of Lorraine stretched between Franche-Comté and Luxemburg, and from the River Meuse to the Rhine. It straddled the strategically vital 'Spanish Road', linking the Spanish Habsburg lands in Italy with those in Flanders, and it served as a gateway between the Bourbon and Habsburg domains.[10] Uniformly Catholic, partly French-speaking and open to French influence, during the period under review Lorraine remained an independent entity, although since 1559 the three bishoprics of Metz, Toul and Verdun, which lay within the ducal lands, were under the protection of the French crown.[11] Given that the Ulster earls had been effectively prohibited from re-entering the French king's jurisdiction (including these bishoprics), the duke of Lorraine's readiness to receive them after their expulsion from Flanders, and his permitting them pass unmolested through his territory, enabled them to take the shortest, safest route eastwards into the Empire. The significance of the duke's assistance in enabling the Irish to es-

cape the clutches of King James I's agents as they fled Flanders, is borne out by the hostility it elicited from both James and his Flemish ambassador, Sir Thomas Edmonds.

As the earls passed through his duchy, the sixty-five year old Charles ('the Great'), was approaching the end of his life. Born in Nancy in 1543, he ruled Lorraine for more than sixty years, during which time his duchy experienced unprecedented stability, peace, prosperity and progress.[12] Raised at the French court, where in 1559 he married Claude, daughter of Henry II of France, he maintained close personal and political connections with the militantly Catholic Guise faction, themselves members of a cadet branch of the House of Lorraine.[13] An ardent champion of Counter-Reformation Catholic orthodoxy, in the mid-1580s, at the height of the Wars of Religion in France, Charles adhered openly to the Catholic League sponsored by his Guise cousins, thereby gaining recognition as a prominent defender of Catholicism alongside the Spanish king on the international stage. Indeed, his level of involvement with the Guise campaign was such that in 1584 they placed Charles among those candidates considered for accession to the French throne. During that year he demonstrated his support for his French cousins by hosting a round in the negotiations attended by the dukes of Guise (d. 1588), Mayenne (d. 1611) and the cardinal of Guise (d. 1588), which led to the creation of their militant Catholic League. In December he joined Philip II of Spain, Henry of Guise and other members of that faction in signing the Treaty of Joinville. All pledged support for Cardinal Charles of Bourbon, the League's candidate for the French throne. In addition, the Spanish undertook to subsidise the League's military campaign for the defence of Catholicism in France, and Lorraine guaranteed his support for that venture.[14] Later, in exchange for the duke's renunciation of his own hereditary claim to the French crown, King Henry IV of France guaranteed the duchy's integrity as an independent entity under the Treaty of Folembray. In 1598 both France and Spain confirmed its neutrality under the Treaty of Vervins. A year later Charles consolidated relations with the French monarchy by the marriage of his son Henry (d. 1624) and Catherine of Bourbon (d. 1604), a sister of Henry IV.[15] By the early 1600s, therefore, Charles had secured his international reputation as a steadfast defender of Catholicism and effectively neutralised the French threat to his independent duchy. Then in his sixties, he retreated from involvement in international political affairs and spent his remaining years channeling his energies into developing the economy, administration and infrastructure of his flourishing dominion.

In January 1608, just weeks after James I issued his proclamation against the Ulster earls (15 November 1607), Sir Thomas Edmonds learned that Hugh O'Neill had sought and obtained a permit of free passage through Lorraine *en route* to Italy. Having failed to convince the archduke that the Irish should be arrested and sent to James I,[16] and animated by O'Neill's claim that the duke had promised him favourable treatment, Edmonds determined to stop the fugitives' progress as they departed Flanders. Immediately he set about dissuading Charles III from extending a welcome to Tyrone. Given the duke's standing as a champion of Catholicism, one can understand Edmonds's anxiety about how this hospitable reception would be interpreted and publicised in Catholic and Protestant circles on the continent and closer to home. He feared that 'the favourable entertainment which the duke may be apt to afford him [Tyrone]' owing to the latter's 'false suggestions of being persecuted for his conscience, may serve as an example to purchase him the like respect among other princes as he passes through their countries'. Determined to prevent this from happening, and anxious to ensure that Charles would have no excuse for receiving the earls against the expressed wishes of King James, Edmonds wrote to the duke in mid-January 1608 'to acquaint him how matters have passed concerning Tyrone, whereof he supposes the duke is not informed'.[17] He exerted strong moral pressure on Charles, emphasising that James had declared the earls 'fugitives and rebels' and that Philip III, with whose father Charles had been closely allied in the past, had refused them entry to his realm out of respect from his friendship with James. Edmonds counseled Lorraine to follow Philip's example in denying the earls admission to his territory. If he did so, Charles could not be accused of unintentionally allowing anything prejudicial to James's interests (or favourable to the rebels' 'malicious cause') to occur within his jurisdiction. The English ambassador took the precaution of providing the duke with a French translation of King James's proclamation against the fugitive earls.[18]

As news of Tyrone's forced departure from Flanders reached London there was a heightened sense of expectation within government circles. Reports

The Craffe Gate in Nancy, built at the end of the fourteenth century as part of the walls that completely encircled the town. The Cross of Lorraine on the facade is a reminder that the emblem was adopted after the victory of the Battle of Nancy. © Private collection

that his departure was 'not to his pleasure and satisfaction' gave rise to 'great rejoicing'. According to Don Pedro de Zúñiga, the Spanish ambassador to London, the English were so fearful of what Tyrone might do after he left the Spanish Netherlands ('their fear of him gnaws at their entrails and it will be all the greater if he may go to Rome') that they wished to kill him 'by poison or by any possible means'. Consequently, de Zúñiga urged the Spanish king to have Tyrone guarded.[19] At this important juncture in the Ulster earls' continental progress, Lorraine's readiness to grant them safe passage through his duchy proved vital in frustrating English efforts to arrest Tyrone and enabled the party to steal a march on those English agents who pursued them.

In contrast with Henry IV, Philip III and the Archduke Albert, Charles III was neither embarrassed nor apologetic about receiving the earls. He withstood considerable pressure and diplomatically veiled threats from Edmonds, and demonstrated his political independence and readiness to lend his protection to Catholics, regardless of their origin or circumstances, by extending a warm welcome to the earls during their sojourn in his patrimony (4-12 March 1608). It is clear

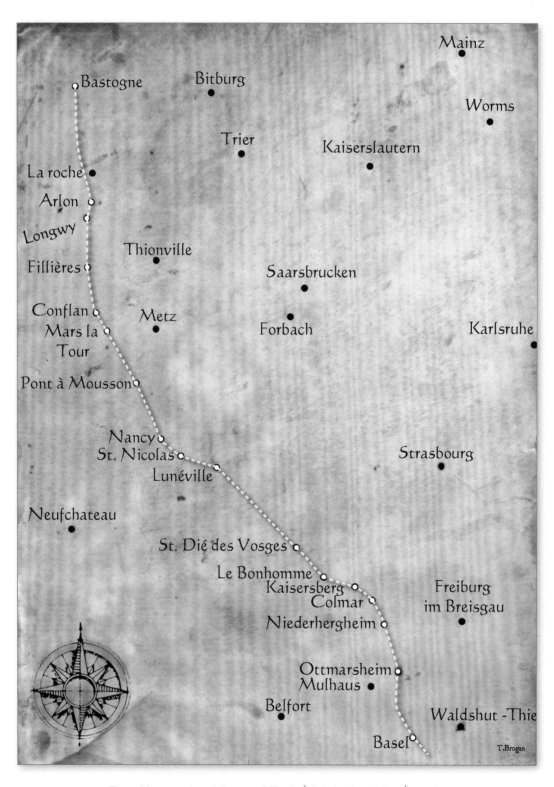

The earls' journey through Lorraine. © Tomás Ó Brógáin after Nollaig Ó Muraíle

from Tadhg Ó Cianáin's account that the earls' stay in Lorraine provided an unexpectedly comforting interlude, coming as it did in the immediate aftermath of their forced departure from Flanders. Having crossed into Lorraine via the town of Longwy on Tuesday 4 March, the party spent that night in Fillières before travelling via Malatur and Conflans to Pont-à-Mousson, a large university town which strove to rival the ducal capital of Nancy.[20] They stayed there for two nights and dispatched messengers to announce to the duke their imminent arrival at Nancy. As they approached the ducal capital they left behind 'bad, rough and water-filled roads' and passed through 'very beautiful and varied ... country ... with plenty of vines and wheat, fruitful forests, and many dwellings'. The awestruck Ó Cianáin described how they had entered a virtual Eden, 'a garden in the very centre of Christendom, giving neither obedience nor submission to any king or prince in the whole world, [but] ever steadfast, strong [and] unbending in the faith of God's Church'. For the duration of their stay there the Irish party enjoyed a sense of solace and security which is palpable in Ó Cianáin's narrative. This is especially evident in his wistful account of how, on Wednesday 12 March, 'they left behind them the duke's territory, with its abundance of vines and wheat and every good fruit, its beautiful rivers, its extensive, many-rivered, watery plains, and its tall, fruit-laden woods in the river of Nancy'.[21]

Intent on extending a warm welcome to the earls as they approached his capital on Saturday 8 March, Charles dispatched coaches and noblemen to meet them. His steward invited the earls directly to the duke's palace, but they declined his hospitality, pleading weariness from their travels. On the following day the steward again arrived with coaches at their lodgings to take Tyrone, Tyrconnell and the young baron of Dungannon to the palace. When they arrived, the duke was attending mass at the nearby Franciscan church and so they walked and passed the time in what Ó Cianáin described as 'the most extensive, excellent, beautiful gallery in the world'. Coming from Gaelic Ulster, the scribe was almost overwhelmed by the sheer opulence, modernity, comfort and magisterial grandeur of this continental ruler's palace. This is most striking in his evocative references to its 'many splendid well-populated apartments', its 'good tennis-court, which the duke's children and nobles frequent', its 'very long stable, with many beautiful, well-shaped

horses' and the place 'where horsemen and noblemen joust and ride, breaking lances on one another's breasts and chests'. When Charles emerged from mass, he summoned Tyrone, Tyrconnell and Dungannon to his hall, where 'he received them with honour and welcome, and his children did likewise'. Having conversed for some time, the duke and his two adult sons, Henry, duke of Bar (d. 1624), and Francis, count of Vaudemont (d. 1632), sat down to dinner with Tyrone, Dungannon and Tyrconnell, and they had many honourable noblemen waiting on them. After their meal, the party withdrew to the duke's private apartment for some time before retiring to their lodging in the company of the duke's head steward. In a further demonstration of the duke's generous support for the earls, his steward proclaimed, under severe penalty, that no one should accept gold or silver from the earls while they were in Nancy and that all their expenses would be borne by the duke.[22]

In Nancy, as in many other Catholic towns and cities which they visited on their journey to Rome, the earls highlighted their plight as Catholic exiles, deserving of the protection and support of their continental co-religionists, by making very conscious and public shows of their steadfast devotion to the Catholic faith. On the Sunday morning after they arrived in the capital they attended mass before going to the palace to meet with Charles. Ó Cianáin rejoiced at the vitality of the Catholic Church in the ducal capital, alluding to its 'very beautiful churches', its 'wealthy college, [and] a good monastery, with a community of Capuchins, built by the duke in proximity to the new city'. Furthermore, the exiles satisfied their fascination for Christian relics by discovering that a fourth part of the body of St George was 'splendidly and reverently enclosed in a shrine of silver with many bright [precious] stones ... in one of the churches'.[23] The earls also availed of the opportunity to visit the church of St Nicholas, situated two leagues outside the city, where they viewed a relic of one of the saint's hands.[24]

Having luxuriated in the warm hospitality afforded them as recognised aristocrats in a realm which vigorously celebrated and promoted Catholicism, the earls soon reverted to being anonymous travellers, experiencing anxiety and hardship as they made their arduous journey to Italy via German and Swiss cities and towns. In contrast with Lorraine, they were repeatedly obliged to pay tolls and customs for their horses, and their unease while

Henry IV of France (1553-1610, above left) famously described the earl of Tyrone as the 'third soldier of his age' but was unwilling to allow him and his fellow fugitives to tarry long in France or to proceed directly to Spain after they made landfall at Quilleboeuf. He told the English ambassador that he could not hand over the fugitives because Henry, duke of Montpensier (1573-1608, above right), had already given his word that they would be granted free passage. © NPG

staying in cities such as Basel, where they encountered 'statues and pictures of Luther and Calvin and many other bad, devilish authors', is palpable from Ó Cianáin's narrative. He was acutely aware that after they left Lorraine, the earls were treated no differently from other 'strangers' and 'travellers'. Even the reception they received at the home of an earl at Faido in northern Italy was unexceptional since he extended 'kindness and honour to every foreigner and every class of strangers who pass[ed] the way'.[25] Not until Sunday 23 March, eleven days after they left Lorraine, did the earls once again attended mass in public and receive an honourable reception from the local dignitary, the conde de Fuentes, Spanish governor of Milan and Lombardy.[26]

After the earls had passed safely beyond the border of his duchy, and before the end of March, Charles III replied to Ambassador Edmonds's correspondence advising him not to receive Tyrone in his duchy. Displeased with the duke's response, Edmonds forwarded the letter to the earl of Salisbury to whom he remarked: 'Your Lordship may perceive how much Tyrone's insinuations have wrought upon him [Lorraine]'.[27] Independent of Charles, Edmonds subsequently discovered that the duke did not 'fully declare [to him in that

communication] the entertainment which he gave to Tyrone' during his sojourn in his duchy. On 2 July 1608, during the 'dead man's supper' element of Charles's funeral rites in Nancy, Edmonds divulged to Salisbury (King James's chief minister) that the deceased duke had invited and entertained the earls at his own table, and that the duchess of Brunswick, the duke's sister, had visited Catherine, countess of Tyrone, at her inn. Although annoyed at the duke's secretive conduct, a rather self-congratulating Edmonds declared that the earls would have been afforded even greater 'respect and favour' by the duke at Nancy 'had it not been for the advertisement which came from him [Edmonds]' in advance of their arrival.[28] With Charles dead, no one could contradict his assertion.

Clearly the discovery of the extent of Charles's hospitable treatment of the earls at the precise time his elaborate funeral ceremony slowly proceeded in Nancy served to stoke the embers of James I's fury to the point that he boycotted the service. It is also likely that James had a personal reason for his acute sense of pique at Lorraine's actions. In addition to being annoyed at Charles's refusal to honour and preserve the interests of a fellow sovereign ruler, James's sense of disappointment at the duke's lack of support undoubtedly stemmed from their close blood-ties.[29] James's mother, Mary Queen of Scots, was a cousin of the duke (Mary's grandfather, Claude (d. 1550), founder of the Guise ducal line and Charles III's grandfather, Antoine (d. 1544), were brothers). Mary's and Charles's blood-ties were reinforced by their having been raised together at the French court and by Charles's marriage to the sister of Mary's first husband, Francis II. Moreover, they apparently enjoyed a relatively close relationship throughout most of her lifetime. Following the untimely death of Francis II in December 1560, Mary, then eighteen years old, took up residence for several months in Custines Castle, just north of Nancy. After she returned to Scotland she remained in contact with Charles, and in 1581, he supported her foundation of a Scottish seminary in his city of Pont-à-Mousson.[30] From an early age James claimed to have a real affinity with his powerful Lorraine and Guise relatives. Indeed, in the mid-1580s, when engaged in negotiations with the duke of Guise to secure his mother's release, the ingratiating prince sought to capitalise on this dynastic solidarity, telling the duke that he believed his (James's) own virtues and rare qualities, with which God had been pleased to endow him, could be attributed to his descent from the House of Lorraine.[31] While it subsequently became expedient for James to distance himself from intrigue with his Guise relatives, the close familial connection might have elicited more from Charles when James called for his support in capturing the fugitive Ulster earls.

The warm welcome afforded Tyrone by the duke of Lorraine and his sons in March 1608 clearly left a lasting impression on him. In February 1611, the conde de Castro reported how the earl complained bitterly to him that although he had written repeatedly to Philip III asking for a clear answer about what he intended to do on his [Tyrone's] behalf with the king of England, he had received no clear response. It was said that Tyrone 'greatly fears he must die if he spends this summer in Rome where many kinsfolk and children of his have died'. Consequently, he wanted to make it known to Philip III that he wished to move 'to the states of the duke of Lorraine [Charles III's son, Henry II (1608-24)] if the latter will grant him admission'. To that end, Tyrone asked that Philip grant him and members of the earl of Tyrconnell's family permission to return to Lorraine.[32] Whether he genuinely entertained the prospect of returning there, or whether he hoped to return to Spanish Flanders, or perhaps just sought to exert pressure on the Spanish king to respond to his petitions, is unclear and ultimately irrelevant since the earl ended his days in Rome. Over forty years after the earls were received by Charles III, Charles IV, his exiled grandson, who had a strong association with the House of Stuart and a reputation for militant Catholicism, emerged as a key figure in Irish affairs and the only foreign ally of Catholics in their campaign against Oliver Cromwell and the New Model Army. This opened a new, if brief, chapter in the history of Ireland's strengthening relations with the House of Lorraine.[33]

Notes

1 *Turas*, p. 525.

2 Kerney Walsh, '*Destruction by peace*', p. 75.

3 Antoine Le Fèvre de la Boderie to Pierre Brulart, viscount of Puisieux, 20 June 1608 (Bibliothèque Nationale, Paris, MS, Fr. 7109, f. 146).

4 M. Greengrass, *France in the age of Henri IV: the struggle for stability* (2nd ed., London & New York, 1995), ch. 9; D. Buisseret, *Henri IV* (London, 1984).

5 M. A. Lyons, *Franco-Irish relations, 1500-1610: politics, migration and trade* (Woodbridge, 2003), ch. 7; idem, 'French reactions to the Nine Years War and the Flight of the Earls, 1589-1608', in H. Morgan (ed.), *The battle of Kinsale* (Dublin, 2004), pp 421-54.

6 Kerney Walsh, '*Destruction by peace*', ch. 3; idem, *An exile of Ireland: Hugh O Neill, prince of Ulster* (Dublin, 1996), chap. 3; *Turas*, p. 489.

7 See Kerney Walsh, '*Destruction by peace*', pp 196-7.

8 Ibid., p. 200.

9 *Turas*, pp 133-5.

10 Greengrass, *France in the age of Henri IV*, p. 188; M. Ó Siochrú, 'The duke of Lorraine and the international struggle for Ireland, 1649-1653', *Historical Journal*, xlviii, 4 (2005), p. 907.

11 Y.-M. Bercé, *The birth of absolutism: a history of France, 1598-1661* (Basingstoke, 1996), p. 131. After 1559 the three bishoprics of Metz, Toul and Verdun were under the protection of France.

12 *Turas*, p. 525; M. Parisse (ed.), *Histoire de Lorraine* (Toulouse, 1977); L. Bély, *Dictionnaire de l'ancien régime. Royaume de France XVIe-XVIIIe siècle* (Paris, 2006), p. 759.

13 See J. Garrisson, *A history of sixteenth-century France, 1483-1598: Renaissance, Reformation and rebellion*

(Basingstoke, 1995), pp 274-6; Bercé, *Birth of absolutism*, p. 46; F. J. Baumgartner, *Henry II, king of France, 1547-1559* (Dubuque, Iowa, 1996), pp 48-9, 150, 153; R. J. Knecht, *The rise and fall of Renaissance France, 1483-1610* (London, 1996), p. 253; idem, *The French Wars of Religion, 1559-1598* (2nd ed., London & New York, 1996); S. Carroll, *Noble power during the French Wars of Religion: the Guise affinity and the Catholic cause in Normandy* (Cambridge, 1998).

14 F. J. Baumgartner, *Radical reactionaries: the political thought of the French Catholic League* (Geneva, 1975), pp 59-61, 171, 188; Bercé, *Birth of absolutism*, p. 131; Knecht, *French Wars of Religion*, p. 16; M. P. Holt, *The French Wars of Religion, 1562-1629* (Cambridge, 1995), ch. 4.

15 Bély, *Dictionnaire de l'ancien régime*, p. 759.

16 Kerney Walsh, *'Destruction by peace'*, pp 67, 186.

17 Sir Thomas Edmonds to the earl of Salisbury, 13 Jan. 1608 (*CSPI, 1606-08*, p. 644).

18 Edmonds to Charles III, duke of Lorraine, 12 Jan. 1608 (*CSPI, 1606-08*, pp 644-5 (enclosure)).

19 See Kerney Walsh, *'Destruction by peace'*, p. 201.

20 During the 1580s there had been a small but significant Irish and Scottish presence in this town. Irish clerical students attended both the newly founded university (which had an Irish Jesuit, Richard Fleming, as its chancellor for the period 1584-90) and also the Scottish seminary, which Mary Queen of Scots established in 1581. However, in 1591 the seminary transferred to Douai. See *Turas*, p. 524.

21 *Turas*, pp 135, 137, 143, 145.

22 Ibid., pp 139, 143, 526.

23 Ibid., pp 139, 141.

24 Ibid., p. 143; C. P. Meehan, *The fate and fortunes of Hugh O'Neill, earl of Tyrone, and Rory O'Donel, earl of Tyrconnel; their flights from Ireland, and death in exile* (3rd ed., Dublin, 1886), p. 164.

25 *Turas*, pp 143-53.

26 Ibid., p. 159.

27 Thomas Edmonds to the earl of Salisbury, 30 Mar. 1608 (*CSPI, 1606-08*, p. 650).

28 Thomas Edmonds to the earl of Salisbury, 22 June 1608 (*CSPI, 1606-08*, p. 663).

29 On the Guise faction's connections with Scotland during the sixteenth century see Lyons, *Franco-Irish relations*; D. Potter, 'French intrigue in Ireland during the reign of Henri II, 1547-59', *International History Review*, v (May 1983), pp 159-80; Carroll, *Noble power*, pp 46-48.

30 *Turas*, p. 524.

31 D. H. Willson, *King James VI & I* (London, 1962), p. 51.

32 See Kerney Walsh, *'Destruction by peace'*, pp 274-5.

33 Ó Siochrú, 'The duke of Lorraine and the international struggle for Ireland', pp 905-32.

French policy and Irish emigration, 1607

Éamon Ó Ciosáin

This essay will examine how events in France and French policy towards the Ulster earls cast light on the international context of their journey across Europe. It also suggests that evidence from European archives provides pointers as to a reevaluation of the process of colonisation which was under way in contemporary Ireland. Considering the Ulster leaders' position in relation to France also provides a useful vantage-point from which to view their history, as opposed to the usual framework in which the high politics of the Gaelic Irish leaders are set (Spain, Rome, England). Moreover, it is particularly relevant to do so given that the ship which carried the party came from Nantes in Brittany in western France, that a sailor attempted to guide the ship into the salt trading port of Le Croisic (near Nantes) after the storm, and above all because of the earls' French landfall.

The voyage of the O'Neill-O'Donnell party through Europe took place in a context of large-scale migration from Ireland to the continent which had been ongoing for some years previously. By 1607 literally thousands of Irishmen and women of all social stations were on the move in Europe. This movement had been no more than a trickle in the 1590s, when Irish soldiers had joined Spanish armies in Flanders and Brittany and clerics left to study in Spain and France, but it swelled considerably in the years following Kinsale, running into thousands. Ciaran O'Scea has estimated that up to 10,000 Irish went to Spain in the first decade of the seventeenth century, and has described the large numbers arriving in Spain and Flanders, and their subsequent further movements as the Spanish government sought to deal with the challenge the situation posed.[1] The present writer has elsewhere proposed an estimate that up to 3,000 Irish men and women migrated to or through France between 1600 and 1633.[2] Some of these passed through France *en route* from Flanders to Spain or vice versa; others were clerics, following a peripatetic course of study. A large majority of the Irish who found themselves on the continent at this time were humble, indeed poor. Mary Ann Lyons and the present author have written on the situation of these people in France and French administrative reactions to

'Irish kern, woman and young piper', watercolour by Lucas de Heere after a lost drawing by the artist.
© University Library, Ghent

the problem over the first third of the seventeenth century.[3]

The earls' departure in 1607 should not be viewed in isolation, either apart from the broader migration just mentioned or from other cases of elite migration. As regards noble migration, 1607 followed other 'flights' (a term put into circulation by the English authorities, as Ó Buachalla has pointed out)[4] such as that of Red Hugh O'Donnell to Spain in 1602. Other departures not authorised by the crown, no more than that of 1607, were those of the O'Driscolls, several prominent O'Sullivans Beare and the MacWilliam Burke of Lower Connacht. These nobles left various parts of Ireland between the defeat at Kinsale and 1607. The so-called flight of the earls was thus one of a sequence, albeit the most important. The motives which led those other noblemen to go into exile and the practice of imprisoning other Gaelic noblemen for the duration of their lives, which continued for some time under James I, should be taken into consideration when the flight is being discussed.

Tadhg Ó Cianáin's account of the voyage has previously been analysed for political and ideological ideas and terms by Mícheál Mac Craith, Brendan Kane, Diarmaid Ó Doibhlin, Nollaig Ó Muraíle, Clare Carroll and others. To take the section of most interest in this essay, it is clear that the style and atmosphere in the section of the text relating to France neatly conform to a political analysis. The initial section is infused with fear: fear of the uncontrollable sea, of course, but, of greater interest politically, fear of being cast ashore or wrecked in English-controlled Jersey or Guernsey, where imprisonment would be the voyagers' fate. The French section of the text is fretful, repeatedly expressing fear: fear about the attitude of local governors, worry about the members of the party becoming separated, that those who have gone a different way have come to harm, about Matthew Flood's [Matha Ó Maoltuile's] time away at court. There was the politically well-founded fear that the English ambassador to France would seek to have them arrested, and other sources confirm that he was active in this regard during their sojourn in France.[5] Members of the O'Neill-O'Donnell party had indeed been put under *gné riastála* – a form of arrest – by the governor of Normandy while he awaited instructions as to what to do with his unexpected guests. Up until the last hour before their crossing into Flanders, fear predominated. The last hours before crossing the border were the most nervous of all, according to Ó Cianáin. People stayed up on night watch in the inn for fear of harm. All of the preceding narrative contrasts sharply with the descriptions which follow: civic receptions in Flanders, fellow Irish coming to meet them, feasting, viewing splendid sights, detailing the privileges of the Irish in Spanish territories, rejoicing, relief in safety and political protection, all far from the fugitive status Ó Cianáin's text implies was theirs in France.

The earls would, of course, have been aware of the international politics of the time. Henry IV of France had come to power with the support of 11,000 English soldiers sent by Elizabeth I to aid in his wars with the French Catholic League and the Spanish. His relations with England remained very cordial, although they became less dependent in time, as Mary Ann Lyons has shown. Even setting Anglo-French relations aside, O'Neill might not have been welcome in France. As one who had had contact with elements of the Catholic League and who had appealed to his fellow Irish Catholics in the language of a Catholic league, O'Neill had little chance of winning the trust of a king who had

fought long and hard against such a Spanish-supported Catholic League. France had little inclination then or afterwards to a militant Catholic position in international relations, for several reasons. Relations with Rome were distant at times; the French regime had to deal with the reality of the Huguenots in France, with whom they had negotiated the Edit of Nantes in 1598. The French church clung tenaciously to its own liberties, and neither king nor church inclined to yield certain prerogatives to Rome. This contrasted sharply with Spain, where the Habsburgs strenuously promoted religious and racial purity. France was an enemy of Spain and was surrounded by Habsburg territories. The Ulster lords' alignment with Spain would have been well known in France, notwithstanding Henry IV's high opinion of Hugh O'Neill as a military commander. Allowing the earls passage through France was all that would be contemplated in such a context. This in itself was not exceptional, as the legal principle of innocent transit – *transitus innoxius* – allowed Spanish persons and even troops to cross French territory since the Franco-Spanish Treaty of Vervins in 1598. This agreement is what lies behind Ó Cianáin's statement that the French king had said that all Catholics could travel through France without fear of hindrance.

In fact, during the years preceding 1607, Henry IV of France had facilitated the passage of Irish troops going to Flanders who had landed in France, while instructing local officials to ensure the Irish groups moved on as rapidly as possible. Indeed, evidence survives of small groups or individual Irish persons passing through France in the early decades of the seventeenth century which leads one to take a less than categorical view about passage through France being avoided by Habsburg elements, as proposed by Geoffrey Parker and Robert Stradling.[6] As regards the use of the land route, O'Scea has detailed the transfer of companies of Irish troops through France by the Spanish authorities as a means of reducing the numbers of Irish arrivals in Galicia and at the court.[7] It is quite conceivable that strays and stragglers from these companies formed part of the large numbers of Irish reported to be begging in Paris and Rouen, for example, in the years after 1604. Be that as it may, engaging in a holy war for Catholicism, in Ireland or elsewhere, was out of the question in France. This was still the case when Richelieu was approached by militant Catholic elements such as Vincent de Paul on the issue at the outbreak of the 1640s wars. Equally, France did not baulk at alliances with Protestant kingdoms and states, notably England. This pragmatic stand, noticeable during the reign of Henry IV, was confirmed and articulated at various junctures later in the century.[8]

Other events confirm that French policy on Irish matters was, if not aligned, at least generally similar to that of England. The Franciscan Order, which found favour with the Gaelic Ulster leaders, encountered various forms of opposition to their attempts to set up a bridgehead in France, as attested by the research of Canice Mooney and Benignus Millett.[9] Efforts by the Franciscans and other regular orders such as the Dominicans and Cistercians to open houses in France failed in the 1620s and 1630s.[10] Hugh MacCaughwell (Aodh Mac Aingil) of Louvain, actively tried to open a Parisian residence. Sources indicate that government indifference or even hostility contributed to their failure. Even the strong support of Cardinal de Sourdis in Bordeaux was not sufficient for the Irish Franciscan project there.[11] At this very time, however, a secular or diocesan college for Irish clergy had been founded in Bordeaux and secular communities existed in Paris and Toulouse, the former enjoying royal recognition by Louis XIII from 1623 onwards. The Bordeaux college, founded in 1603 by Dermot Mac-Carthy, had been strongly supported by Cardinal de Sourdis. It may be no coincidence that his family, the MacCarthys of Muskerry, were aligned with the English administration in Dublin. The distinction between favour for secular clergy and the difficulties encountered by the regular orders appears from the historical facts in France in this instance. It is tempting to compare it to the distinction made by the English administrators between the 'seditious' friars on the one hand and the parish clergy, whom one viceroy deemed more 'amenable'. It may also be ascribed to the situation within France itself, where some religious orders were seen as being too 'Roman' and therefore distrusted by the authorities. However, this interpretation is not confirmed in the case of the most Roman of orders, the Jesuits, towards whom Louis XIII was favourable.

It is possible to ascertain French attitude towards the earls. Apart from king Henry IV's studied neutrality, other contemporary Paris-based sources, reflecting French elite opinion, mention the earls' passage. Two such documents give an indication of the effectiveness of James I's relaying abroad of his declarations and other statements in print and in translation. The diary of Pierre de L'Estoile, a Parisian magistrate, contains valuable material on the Irish in France in the first decade of the century.[12] In an entry written in August 1608 he summarised a French translation in pamphlet form of James I's declaration concerning the earls.[13] De L'Estoile noted that according to the king the earls left for fear that Ireland would be cleared of Catholic nobles. They had, however, left 'less on pretext of religion than for fear of the judgement which could be made on their past misbehaviour, having rebelled against their king and delivered their land to enemies. They were thus 'disloyal rebels and bad rascals (*mauvais garnemens*) who did not deserve to be given asylum'. Of course, leaving the jurisdiction of their king without his permission was reprehensible in itself in France as it was in the eyes of the English administration. They stayed very few days in France, de L'Estoile says in this 1608 entry. He does not note that the ship which carried them came from France. In October 1607, at the time of the earls' journey to France and Flanders, de L'Estoile had described a coin which carried the bust of James I, declaring that the kingdoms of Scotland and England were joined, and bore the motto *Faciam eos in gentos unam*.[14] De L'Estoile did not add one of his frequent sardonic comments to this account, which suggests that he noted and accepted the idea.

Some years later the French royal historiographer André Duchesne published his *Histoire générale d'Angleterre, d'Escosse et d'Irlande* (Paris, 1614). Duchesne laid great stress on the amicable relations between France and England, which continued after Henry IV's assassination in 1610. Most of the final page of Duchesne's bulky volume (p. 1444) is devoted to a sustained paean of praise for James I and his many qualities. His history makes no allusion to Kinsale, which is blotted out by the Essex affair in the narrative, but the earls' voyage does get mention, shortly before the book ends. To summarise Duchesne: these 'rebels' saw that King James had fortified the ports of Ireland and would purge the country of all sedition and revolt. This, according to Duchesne, so frightened the earls that they suddenly crossed to France and thence to the Archducal court in Flanders, where they were honourably received. They claimed publicly that they were fugitives for religion, to which the king replied in print that they were ungrateful to him and to the queen (Elizabeth) who had raised them to the dignities they held. They had fled, wrote the king, for reasons which were particular and related to the state. When some of their party later seized castles, the English pursued them and forced them into obedience.[15] The

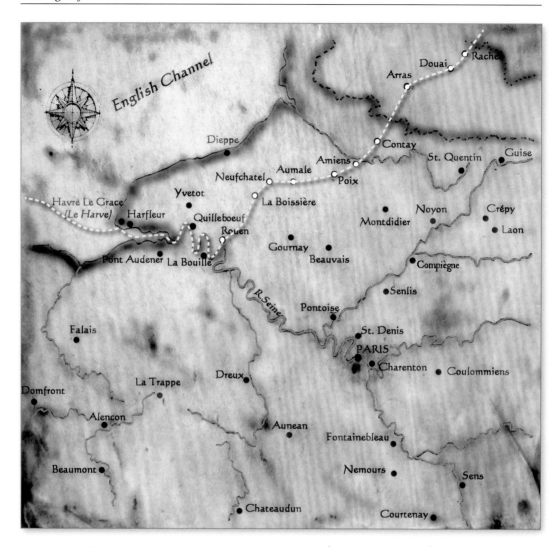

The earls' journey from Quilleboeuf to Douai. © Tomás Ó Brógáin after Nollaig Ó Muraíle

legitimist thrust of Duchesne's account is clear from the context and was coloured by events in France since 1607. As G. Ascoli noted, French elite opinion in the early seventeenth century was remarkably receptive to the ideas of James I, his religion notwithstanding. French pamphlets drew parallels between the plot against the English parliament by Guy Fawkes and others and attempts on the life of Henry IV.[16] Pierre de L'Estoile represented the legitimist, pragmatic standpoint, receptive to such opinion. As a young man he had had a Huguenot tutor, and he frequently shows his dislike of over-enthusiastic Catholic activity in his diaries. His fellow legal officer, Jacques-Auguste de Thou, also a noted historian who corresponded with Camden, gives a strongly pro-English account of the sixteenth-century wars in Ireland in his *Histoire de son temps* (translated

from the Latin original *Historia sui temporis*), laying stress on native Irish barbarity. Judging on the writing of these men, there existed a Paris-centred French intelligentsia which was unsympathetic to the plight or the political discourse of such as the Ulster earls.

The flight did not mark a turning-point as regards Ireland and France. Migration had reached noticeable proportions some years earlier. Some of this migration was direct, some was a spill over from England or cases of migrants who headed for Spain making landfall in France, as noted in some Spanish documents. Kinsale and Mellifont (1601 and 1603) marked the real turning-point in Irish migration to France. Groups of visibly poor Irish appeared in French cities – Paris, Nantes, Angers. Proclamations were issued against them in Nantes in 1605, they were cleared in a chartered ship from Paris in 1606, and excluded from Saint Malo in 1606 by a royal order banning them from all ports. Rouen barred Irish vagabonds in 1607 and took additional measures against them in 1609. Expulsion orders against Irish vagrants and stray soldiers recur from the 1620s to the 1640s, notably in Brittany, where many Irish landed and a number stayed. Edicts range from local decrees in times of pestilence against allowing hogs, dogs and Irish vagabonds in the streets, to orders of the Breton *parlement* (legal assembly) against stray Irish soldiers who encumbered the urban centres of Brittany. A variety of phenomena are involved in these crisis situations. To mention only those applicable to the years around 1607: a wave of migration of mainly Munster allies of O'Neill and the Spanish, followed by their dependants; some migrants driven abroad by food shortages in Ireland; and probable seasonal migration. Pilgrimages to places such as Santiago de Compostella may also explain a small number of appearances of wandering Irish. These migrants moved between various kingdoms, and there are cases of persons migrating to several countries and later returning to Ireland. Irish migration to the continent is marked at this time by considerable mobility, and there was some circular migration through Spain, France and England, not necessarily in that order.

However, this migration continued well after 1607. Archival sources in various locations in France and Spain indicate that a steady movement occurred in times which are not usually associated with Irish emigration in any tradition of historiography, be it Irish or other. Brittany and Anjou witnessed a trickle of migrants arriving from Ireland in the second decade of the century, and a quickening of the rate of appearances in the late 1620s and early 1630s. In studying the long-term phenomenon in France, and comparing it with Ciaran O'Scea's work on Spain for the same period, some conclusions emerge. Firstly, civilian migration to France, especially Brittany, is continuous right down to 1690, and is not solely the result of military recruitment for the French army, important as that was after 1635. Secondly, the vast

majority of Irish migrants in France before 1690 originated from Munster and Leinster. Ulster names are extremely rare in France before the 1650s, and constitute a minority between the 1650s and 1680s. The Spanish situation as regards the origins of Irish migrants during the period 1600-40 is broadly similar. A survey of the migrant Irish population in Spain, Flanders and France shows that the majority of these migrants had Gaelic family names. This is scarcely a surprise, given the composition of the population of Ireland at the time. Sources such as parish records in France and Flanders, lists of petitioners in Spain, and the names of soldiers in Flanders as calendared in Brendan Jennings's *Wild Geese in Spanish Flanders*, further illustrate the fact that the majority of Irish, be they of Gaelic or Old English origin, came from Munster and southern Leinster. In the first half of the seventeenth century there are striking similarities between the family names encountered in Spanish records, those found in parish records in Brittany and Anjou, the names of Irish priests and seminarians training in Bordeaux and Toulouse, and the family names of early migrants to Montserrat and Barbados.[17] West Munster surnames are strongly represented in all of these records, those of west Cork and south Kerry reaching a proportion of two-thirds of some samples in western France during this period. This suggests a considerable degree of migration to the various destinations listed above.

The relatively low status of those of Gaelic origin who went to France makes it difficult to construct individual profiles, as they flit in and out of parish records and do not leave papers or letters of naturalisation. However, they would appear to be members of lesser branches of Gaelic families, together with their possibly landless vassals. No major Gaelic figures appear in France, as opposed to Flanders and Spain, and indeed no major Old English figures are found there before the 1640s. Given the aforementioned difficulty of profiling the migrants to France, mapping of migrants in Brittany by traditional location of family name in Ireland has provided pointers and suggests causes for their departure.[18] While

Jacques-Auguste de Thou (1553-1617) stressed the barbarity of the Irish in his *Historia sui temporis* (Paris, 1604-08).

one must be aware of the risks of movement of population when charting family names by distribution, many Irish surnames were localised, some very much so, before the Cromwellian period. Further clues can be found in French records, which sometimes provide mentions of geographical origins in Ireland. Maps based on data from parish records indicate that there is a clear correspondence between the core locations of Gaelic surnames found abroad and the zones of plantation during the early seventeenth century: south Munster, Wexford, Offaly, Longford. It is noticeable that there is an increase of appearances of Munster Irish in Brittany during the 1620s and 1630s, before large-scale military migration began. Munster names predominated in eastern France (leaving aside Saint Malo) until the 1680s. The 1620s increase could be related to the 'second plantation of Munster'.[19] Munster areas where mapping indicates clusters of families also correspond to the area of activity and influence of Richard Boyle, earl of Cork and notorious Jacobean land-grabber.

Unfortunately a standard work such as Michael MacCarthy-Morrogh's *The Munster plantation* pays scant attention to the situation of the displaced 'Irishry', and such compositions are of little assistance in tracing the Irish who ended up on foreign shores, be they O'Keeffes, Donovans, Barretts or Barrys. In this area, the dated works of W. F. Butler provide material which corresponds very well to the French data.[20] As regards plantations which followed Ulster and developed the English administration's model, articles by Henry Goff on the plantation in north Wexford and Brian Mac Cuarta on the midlands plantation also give an insight into what was occurring between 1607 and the Ulster rising of 1641, and provide further background facts related to migration towards France.[21] Again, mapping of surnames points to clusters in these areas. The forces at play include a mixture of dispossession by 'undertakers' and 'adventurers' using titles to lands and the English legal system which was taking effect across Ireland at the time, displacement of vassals in the reorganisation of Gaelic lands under English law (as in the case of the MacCarthy Muskerry), and the reduction of the Gaelic Irish in economic terms in the new money economy, in which they were at a disadvantage both in relation to the colonists and to the Old English of the towns. There were departures of groups led by clan or kin leaders, some of whom turn up in France and Flanders offering themselves for military service. French data indicates a ten to fifteen-year delay between the plantation of areas

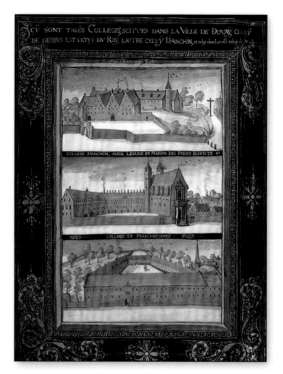

The earls received a wonderful reception at Douai. An oration characterised O'Neill as a religious warrior and anticipated his triumphant return to Ireland.

and the appearance of native Irish from those areas in western France. This timespan corresponds to the view of Nicholas Canny, according to which displaced and dispossessed Irish (Gaelic in particular) remained near their former lands for some time afterwards, before eventually leaving. Their departure took place either as economic migration (in Brittany, for example) or by enlisting in the various regiments raised for Spain and France, in plantation areas among others.[22]

The study of the Irish emigrants on continent provides evidence on the outcome of these processes and may, with further analysis, cast light on the workings of the forces which were de-gaelicising Ireland, as David Edwards has put it. The continuous movement to continental Europe in the decades following the earls' departure and the plantation of Ulster hints at the pressures on Gaelic and indeed lesser Old English groups (for example, the Cork Old English are represented among the Irish in Brittany). Edwards has written of the pressure applied during those decades, most notably by the imposition of martial law, which created the impression of peace and calm at a time when the Gaelic social system was being undermined.[23] However, this strategy was not altogether success-

'Quilleboeuf, mouth of the Seine' by J. M. W. Turner (1775-1851). This stormy scene was similar to the one that greeted the earls when they made landfall in France.

ful, as could be seen in the mid-century wars. The present writer has argued elsewhere, that in military terms at least, Gaelic Ireland's last stand was not Kinsale or O'Neill's vain efforts to rally support from Spain and the papacy, but in 1651-52, when the remnants of the Catholic Confederate armies held out for some time.[24] The events of those two years bring into focus the fact that the Old English military and political commanders (and their circle, such as MacCarthy Muskerry) had left (fled) Ireland on Cromwell's arrival, and those who remained in the field, poorly equipped as they were, were under the command of Gaelic military men. The poet Pádraigín Haicéad's final poems reflect this fact, with the older term *Gael* replacing his previous use of the catch-all *Éirionnach*. A letter in the Tanner papers from the Ulster and Leinster commanders in 1652 is worthy of analysis in this regard.[25] They

were making a last and rather hopeless stand, before the Cromwellian settlement radically changed land-ownership in Ireland and the politics of the island.

During the commemoration year of 2007 Diarmaid Ó Doibhlin stated that Imeacht na nIarlaí is elite history,[26] and this is largely the case. Of course it had repercussions for the other social orders of Gaelic Ireland, but it in no way sums up the broader situation. The story of the Irish migrants in France, Spain and Flanders in the first half of the seventeenth century is in some respects at odds with the traditional emphasis on the Ulster migration as being the most prominent phenomenon, but it provides much material for study of the situation affecting the broader spectrum of Gaels and Catholics in Ireland in the decades following 1607, and also supports a longer-term analysis of migration out of Ireland before and after the earls' voyage.

Notes

1 C. O'Scea, 'The significance and legacy of Spanish intervention in west Munster during the battle of Kinsale', in T. O'Connor, and M. Lyons (ed.), *Irish migrants in Europe after Kinsale, 1602-1820* (Dublin, 2003), pp 32-63; idem, 'Irish emigration to Castile in the opening years of the seventeenth century', in P. Duffy (ed.), *To and from Ireland: planned migration schemes c. 1600-2000* (Dublin, 2004), pp 17-37. See also idem, 'In search of honour and a Catholic monarch: the acculturation and integration of the Old-Irish aristocracy in early seventeenth-century Castile' (PhD thesis, Florence, 2006).

2 É. Ó Ciosáin, 'Les Irlandais en France 1590-1685, les réalités et leur image' (thesis, Université de Rennes 2, 2007).

3 É. Ó Ciosáin, 'Les Irlandais en Bretagne 1603-1780: invasion, accueil, intégration', in C. Laurent and H. Davis (eds), *Irlande et Bretagne: Vingt Siècles d'histoire* (Rennes, 1993), pp 152-66; idem, 'A hundred years of Irish migration to France, 1590-1688', in T. O'Connor (ed.), *The Irish in Europe 1580-1815* (Dublin, 2001), pp 93-106; M. Lyons, '"Vagabonds", "mendiants", "gueux": French reaction to Irish immigration in the early seventeenth century', *French History*, xiv (2000),

pp 363-82; idem, *Franco-Irish relations, 1500-1610* (Wood-bridge, 2003), pp 173-186.

4 For analysis of the terms used by the various parties, see B. Ó Buachalla, 'Ó Néill agus an t-aos léinn', in T. Ní Mha-onaigh and T. Ó Dúshláine (ed.), *Léachtaí Cholm Cille*, xxx-viii: *Éire agus an Eoraip sa 17ú haois* (Maynooth, 2008), pp 18-21.

5 Lyons, *Franco-Irish relations, 1500-1610* presents documentation in this regard.

6 G. Parker, *The Army of Flanders and the Spanish Road, 1567-1659: The logistics of Spanish victory and defeat in the Low Countries' wars* (Cambridge, 1972); R. Stradling, 'Military Recruitment and Movement as a Form of Migration: Spain and its Irish Mercenaries, 1598-1665', in S. Cavaciocchi (ed.) *Le Migrazioni in Europa Secc. XIII-XVIII*, (Florence/Firenza, 1994), pp 477-90, see p. 478 for comparison with 'a traffic-island'. For an example of the passage of Spanish troops through French territory in June 1605, see Berger de Givrey (ed.), *Recueil des Lettres Missives de Henri IV* (Paris, 1876), pp 458-9.

7 The O'Driscoll and Stanihurst companies left Spain to travel to Flanders via France in June 1606: see O'Scea, 'The significance and legacy of Spanish intervention', p. 63; further information in idem, 'Irish emigration to Castile', p. 33.

8 For example see Cardinal-Minister Mazarin's letter to the Confederate Council, 16 Oct. 1643, in J. Gilbert (ed.), *History of the Irish Confederation and the War in Ireland* (7 vols, Dublin, 1882-91), iii, pp 33-34.

9 M. Mooney, *Irish Franciscans in Rome* (Dublin/London, 1964), p. 26-27 and B. Millet, *The Irish Franciscans, 1651-65* (Rome, 1964), p. 184.

10 See T. Flynn, *The Irish Dominicans, 1534-1641* (Dublin, 1993), pp 210-13 regarding proposals for Dominican houses in the West of France in the 1630s. For similar proposals regarding the Cistercians see T. J. Walsh, *The Irish continental college movement* (Cork & Dublin, 1973), p. 71.

11 B. Millett summarises letters in Roman sources by Hugh Burke OFM concerning the Bordeaux scheme in *Collectanea Hibernica*, xi (1968), p. 9.

12 P. de L'Estoile, *Mémoires*, (eds) C. Brunet *et al* (12 vols,

Paris, 1875-96); Irish material in vols viii, ix and xii.

13 See H. Morgan (ed.), *The battle of Kinsale* (Dublin, 2004), p. 252, for an illustration based on the cover of the tract.

14 De L'Estoile, *Mémoires*, viii, p. 354.

15 A. Duchesne, *Histoire générale d'Angleterre, d'Escosse et d'Irlande* (Paris, 1614), p. 1444.

16 G. Ascoli, *La Grande-Bretagne devant l'opinion française au XVIIe siècle* (2 vols, Paris, 1930), i, pp 1, 2, 7, 11.

17 A. Gwynn, 'Documents relative to the Irish in the West Indies', *Analecta Hibernica*, iv, 1932, pp 139-286; D. H. Akenson, *If the Irish ran the world: Montserrat 1630-1730* (Liverpool, 1997), p. 34.

18 See maps in A. Le Noac'h and É. Ó Ciosáin, *Immigrés irlandais au XVIIe siècle en Bretagne/Iwerzhoniz o tivroañ e Breizh (XVIIvet kantved)* (Vannes, 2006) and *Immigrés irlandais en Bretagne au XVIIe et XVIIIe siècles*, ii (Vannes, 2009).

19 D. B. Quinn, 'The Munster plantation', *Journal of the Cork Historical and Archaeological Society*, lxxi (1966), pp 19-40.

20 W. F. T. Butler, *Confiscation in Irish History* (London, 1917; repr., Washington/London, 1970); idem, *Gleanings from Irish History* (London, 1925).

21 H. Goff, 'English conquest of an Irish barony: the changing patters of land ownership in the barony of Scarawalsh 1540-1640', in K. Whelan (ed.), *Wexford: history and society* (Dublin, 1987), pp 122-149; B. Mac Cuarta, 'The Plantation of Leitrim 1620-41', *IHS*, xxxii (2001) pp 301-17.

22 N. Canny, *Making Ireland British, 1580-1650* (Oxford, 2001), pp 326-8.

23 D. Edwards, 'Legacy of defeat: the reduction of Gaelic Ireland after Kinsale', in H. Morgan (ed.), *The battle of Kinsale*, pp 279-99.

24 É. Ó Ciosáin, 'Imeacht na nIarlaí agus imirce na nGael don Fhrainc', *Léachtaí Cholm Cille*, xxxviii (Maynooth, 2008), pp 231-2.

25 Sir Phelim O'Neill and others to the parliamentary commissioners, 4 Aug. 1652, in C. MacNeill (ed.), *The Tanner letters* (Dublin, 1943), p. 379.

26 In a lecture broadcast on Raidió na Gaeltachta at the time.

Flight of fancy: journeying into the miraculous

Patricia Palmer

Hugh O'Neill died in Rome on 20 July 1616. Some three months before, on 23 April, Miguel de Cervantes expired in Madrid, in a country off limits to O'Neill throughout his exile.[1] The links between O'Neill and the greatest writer of the Spanish Golden Age, however, extend beyond the mere coincidence of a shared date on a tombstone. There is a strong likelihood that the first English-language translation of *Don Quixote* was done by a Palesman who had once found refuge with O'Neill. Edwin B. Knowles's identification of Thomas Shelton, the translator of Part I of *The History of Don-Qvichote* (London, 1612) with a Dubliner of that name exiled in Brussels is now generally accepted. Shelton's brother, John, was hanged in 1598 for plotting to seize Dublin Castle on behalf of O'Neill. By March 1600 Shelton had fled to O'Neill in Dungannon. In February 1612 Shelton, by then long exiled in Brussels, put out feelers on behalf of both O'Neill and the rector of the Irish College about the possibility of a rapprochement with the English authorities in exchange for religious toleration in Ireland. There are fleeting glimpses of him in the following decades: teaching Spanish in exchange for lodgings, working as a messenger, begging to support 'a prettie newe wife'.[2] Our last sighting of him is in Rome in 1629, in the habit of a Franciscan.[3]

'Don Quixote'. © John Behan

One wonders whether O'Neill, in the tedium of his last years in the Palazzo Salviati, ever turned over the pages of Shelton's remarkable translation. The question is not entirely fanciful. To wonder about the literary tastes and practices of a figure like O'Neill is to think about the relationship between literature and politics, between violence and aesthetics, and to recognise the links between them. For the New English, the interplay between Gaelic poetics and political praxis was manifest –

and manifestly pernicious.[4] Thomas Gainsford, in his *History of the earle of Tyrone*, repeatedly ascribes O'Neill's 'hurliburlies' to his willingness to give 'all credit to his bards and rhymers', whom Gainsford saw as 'enscorcering wretches' and 'the very bane and confusion of Ireland'.[5] Hugh O'Neill's exposure to literature was not confined to Irish. A precious sighting of O'Neill as a reader – or, at least, one who tolerated being read to – is given by Sir John Harington. Harington, Elizabeth's godson and the translator of Ariosto's *Orlando Furioso*, visited Tyrone in October 1599 with Sir William Warren.[6] Left to amuse O'Neill's 'freckle-faced' sons, Hugh and Henry, both dressed 'in English cloths like a nobleman's sons; with velvet gerkins and gold lace, both of them learning the English tongue', Harington 'pos[ed] them in their learning' and gave them a copy of his translation which he had bought in Dublin. When the boys showed O'Neill their present, he 'call'd to see it openly, and would needs hear some part of it read. As it had been by chance',[7] Harington turned to the start of Canto XLV and began to read:

> Looke how much higher Fortune doth erect
> The clyming wight on her unstable wheele,
> So much the nigher may a man expect
> To see his head, where late he saw his heele.[8]

Having listened to that 'and some other passages of the book, which he seemed to like so well', O'Neill 'solemnly swore his boys should read all the book over to him'.[9] Despite the politeness all round, there is an element of war by another means about this encounter.[10] O'Neill, who carried a price on his head since June 1595,[11] would not have needed to be a gifted close-reader to have picked up the menace in the lines 'So much the nigher may a man expect / To see his head, where late he saw his

The queen's godson, Sir John Harington (1561-1612), famously met with Hugh O'Neill in 1599 and the earl's sons read Harington his own translation of Ariosto's *Orlando Furioso* under the direction of 'Friar Nangle' (Aodh Mac Aingil), their English-language tutor. © NPG

heele'. The illustration on the facing page – the Saracen Ruggiero being led away as a prisoner by a band of helmeted soldiers[12] – underlined the barbed message of Harington's far from 'chance' selection. Four years later Harington would react with considerable bitterness 'to see that damnable rebel Tir-Owen broughte to Englande, curteouslie favourede, honourede, and well likede. Oh! my Lorde … How did I labour after that knave's destruction!'[13]

Harington's letters from Ireland evince a fascination with witchcraft,[14] and, in his commentary 'historicising' the Saracen Ferraù's possession of a magic girdle, he explains that:

> It is a great practise in Ireland to charme girdles and the like, perswading men that while they weare them they cannot be hurt with any weapon, and who can tell whether the divell may not sometime protect some of his servants?

Moreover, he insisted, Rory Óg O'More was only able to take his cousin, Sir Henry Harington, prisoner during 'a vile and treacherous Parlee' because he used 'meere witchcraft'.[15] But there is a quality

of magical thinking too, of recitation-as-malediction, about Harington's own performance.[16] Harington's wishful invocation of a head brought to heel is in service to power in a way that mirrors the 'ensorcering' conjurations which Gainsford ascribed to O'Neill's poets and rhymers. Sir Philip Sidney asserted that 'Poetry is the companion of camps. I dare undertake, *Orlando Furioso* … will never displease a soldier'[17] – and certainly, its translator wielded it that day as a threatening weapon. To imagine O'Neill reading Cervantes, however, is to explore the possibility of a different relationship between literature and conflict, a relationship where literature is not indentured to power – unless it be the power of the imagination to assuage conflict and magic it away.

Whether O'Neill ever got any further with his reading of *Orlando Furioso* – and it would seem that he left his presentation copy behind him in Ulster[18] – it is known for certain that he never read Cervantes's *Persiles y Sigismunda*, published posthumously a year after the death of both men.[19] Yet its plotline would have seemed surprisingly familiar to him in at least one respect. It is the story of a party of northern nobles 'exiled from their homeland' (*desterrados de su patria*) (232), making a slow and perilous journey to Rome and its 'holy relics' (*reliquias santas*) (233); a journey that slowly becomes a pilgrimage. The title, *Los trabajos de Persiles y Sigismunda*, might be translated as *The trials of Persiles and Sigismunda*, but the journey of these northern lords exposes them to the wondrous as well as the perilous. It is a work of storm tossed voyages, of migrancy and displacement.[20] Though its polyglot, pan-European characters are themselves safely ensconced within the charmed bubble of a romance, they skirt a world of darker possibilities as they cross a continent beset by wars of religion, dynastic disputes, the Turkish threat, injustice, torture and sudden eruptions of violence. Furthermore, Cervantes's imports into this highly stylised, fantastical Europe tropes of the New World and its conquest: flint blades hover over the hearts of sacrificial victims; natives run down to greet strangers who seem to arrive on every tide.[21] Everywhere, we meet barbarians. However, in Cervantes's refracted meditation on colonial encounter and conquest,

An illustrated Irish translation of Ariosto's *Orlando Furioso* by the south Ulster scribe Uilliam Ó Loinsigh c. 1690.
It is possible that Ó Loinsigh may have had access to the actual copy which O'Neill left behind
after the flight. © Trinity College Dublin

these barbarians are not naked Indians. The 'island of wild barbarians' (*tierra de bárbaros salvajes*) of the opening action is an island in the region of Iceland, and we quickly meet 'el bárbaro Español' and a barbarous-seeming Italian (159, 185). For *Persiles y Sigismunda* entertains, among other things, a fantasy of reverse colonisation. The savage indigenes of this northern island believe, on the promptings of a demonic sorcerer, that a king will emerge from among them 'who will conquer and win a large part of the world' (*que conquiste y gane gran parte del mundo*) (138). The ritual for identifying the prophesised leader – drinking without blinking a potion made from powdered hearts harvested by ritually sacrificing all male visitors to the island – transposes the lurid ethnography of the New World to Europe with defamiliarising effect.[22] This arrestingly polyglot contact zone – where Castilian, Tuscan, Danish, English, Portugese and Norwegian criss-cross and even the occasional wolf speaks decent Spanish (169) – throws up another figure familiar from the literature of encounter: the female interpreter. For much of the early part of the book the *lingua franca* is, unaccountably, Polish, and the interpreter who moves between it and this septentrional Babel is 'la hermosa Transila', the lovely Transila. Living up to the transmutability

signalled by her name, Transila, celebrated for her 'manly brio' (*varonil brio*) (157) crosses, in Amazon fashion, boundaries of gender as well as language. Betrothed to one Ladislao, she finds herself on her wedding day, in accordance with the custom of 'my barbarous homeland' (*mi bárbara patria*) (218), subjected to the attention of Ladizlao's brothers, intent on 'gathering the flowers' (*coger las flores*) of a garden which she had been keeping intact for her prospective husband (215). But – and an allegorical reading of her assertion is there for the taking – she is not minded to let outsiders 'cultivate others' fields without the licence of their rightful owners' (*cultivar los ajenos campos sin licencia de sus legítimos dueños*) (217). Seizing her phallic lance, she sees off the brothers and casts herself into 'a little boat which, unquestionably, the heavens provided for me'. Though hotly pursued and oarless in this 'boat of romance',[23] she drifts with fair winds and favourable currents into the main story. Only at the end of Chapter XI, when an English warship approaches the island, blazing fire from two artillery pieces and twenty arquebuses at the rag-tag cluster of nationalities waving white flags on the shore, is her nationality – and this backstory – revealed. For out of the English warship steps, inexplicably, a 'Hibernian' gentleman, Mauricio, who turns out to be none other than Transila's father. Having found his daughter, his only remaining desire is to regain his ancestral home and die back in his homeland (326).[24] It must be a testimony to the hold which James Fitzmaurice had on the English and Spanish imagination that the name 'Maurice' came so readily to hand when an Irish character needed naming. But if Macmorris in Shakespeare's *Henry V* with his catch-cry 'there is throats to be cut' is a figure of unfocused violence, Cervantes's Mauricio is an astronomer-astrologist and astute literary critic. Interestingly, however, he is the only character in Cervantes's benignly counter-reformation romance who voices anti-Protestant sentiments (213).

The relevance of Cervantes's *Persiles y Sigismunda* for those primarily interested in the flight of the earls goes far beyond the superficial coincidence of another band of (fictional) northern exiles making their storm-tossed pilgrimage towards Rome in the enlivening company of two 'Hibernians'. Its most resonant correspondence is not with the 'factual' dimension of the flight but with its most esoteric-seeming interlude. In structuring the earls' journey around miracle-working relics, Tadhg Ó Cianáin's

Imeacht na nIarlaí crosses the historical with the miraculous to the point where chronicle shades into romance. Geraldine Heng defines romance as the genre that 'transact[s] a magical relationship with history';[25] *Persiles y Sigismunda* does precisely that and in a way that throws an unexpected sidelight on the peregrinations of Ó Cianáin's displaced Hibernians. *Persiles* reflects Cervantes's serious commitment to harnessing romance's effortless switching between the marvelous and the real (and the genre's tolerance of 'contradictory worldviews')[26] to reflect on the pressing debates of his day. The intellectual case for the importance of romance as a heuristic tool of this kind is articulated by none other than Mauricio. An exacting critic of the narrative styles of the storytelling pilgrims, Mauricio demands that 'the powers of the imagination' (*fuerzas de la imaginación*) (386), be tempered by reason and verisimilitude. An 'implacable neo-Aristotelian', he upholds Tasso's notion of the 'legitimate marvellous'.[27] When Persiles (disguised as Periandro) recounts leaping, on horseback, from a high cliff and landing unscathed on the frozen sea below, Mauricio opines that he should at least have

Engravings from Cantos 3 and 42 in Ludovico Ariosto's *Orlando Furioso* translated into heroical verse by Sir John Harington (London, 1591). There is strong circumstantial evidence that these images are from the actual edition which Sir John Harington presented to O'Neill. © Private collection

This image characterises Rory Óg O'More (who had imprisoned Sir John Harington's cousin by 'meer witchcraft') as a cowardly woodkerne, too frightened to engage Englishmen on the open field, a charge frequently levelled at the Ulster chiefs during the 1590s rebellion. From John Derricke's *The Image of Irlande* (London, 1581). © Trinity College Dublin

had the narratorial decency to have broken some bones for credibility's sake (415). The 'legitimate marvellous' brings us, as Childers points out, into a world cognate with magic-realism,[28] where the solidity of the quotidian comfortably rubs shoulders with the wondrous and the supernatural.

The imaginative space opened up by the 'legitimate marvellous' is matched by the fantastical space of 'Hibernia' itself. Recycling the old tale about barnacle geese breeding from logs, Cervantes locates that prodigy of reproduction in 'the provinces of Ireland *and* Ireland', (*las provincias de Hibernia y de Irlanda*) (212; my emphasis), as though 'Ireland' and 'Hibernia' were quite separate places. Later we meet corsairs who turn out to be not from Ireland, as was first thought, 'but from an island in rebellion against England' (*sino de una isla rebelada contra Inglaterra*) (262). This 'confusion' has been seized upon as evidence of Cervantes nodding.[29] But this is, rather, an imaginatively fertile reduplication: Hibernia and Ireland are split apart to make a third space of the imagination.[30] Cast adrift from the co-ordinates of the real, the space *between* Ireland and Hibernia becomes available for utopian play. The pivotal location in Book II is Policarpo's kingdom which is found on one of Hibernia's offshore islands (265);[31] the travellers' arrival among its harp-playing natives is described as a 'rebirth' (*parto*) (285, 295), and it provides them with a perfect play-space of romance.

The 'Hibernian' contribution to the discourse of the 'legitimate marvellous' and the utopian in *Persiles y Sigismunda* offers an unexpected perspective on the world of marvels – as well as perils – into which the fleeing earls embarked. Speaking of Shakespeare's late romances, Kiernan Ryan celebrates the way the ageing playwright 'expand[s] the scope of the possible and whet[s] our appetite for change by forging from the theatrical dialect of his day a discourse for the future'.[32] In a similar way, Cervantes's late romance (with Mauricio, the magus, and his motherless daughter reminding us of Prospero and Miranda in *The Tempest*) exploits romance's 'marvelous alteration of reality' to imagine a troubled world differently.[33] Violence threatens, like the artillery round and blunderbusses from the English warship, but the white flags waving on the shore prevail. No scenes of violence are directly witnessed, only, on rare occasions, their painful aftermath is encountered. Rutilio, a Portuguese sailor, is washed up on the island which, in the manner of romance, serves as a place of encounter and discovery for a diverse and contingent cast. He sees 'a hung man hanging from a tree' and therefore knows that he has come to 'a land of savage barbarians' (192). Later the pilgrims come alongside a boat drifting without a crew. They go abroad and find pirates hanging from the yard-arms like rotten fruit; the boarding party's feet squelch across a deck bloody with severed heads and amputated hands (373, 376). And once, on the highway to Rome, near Perpignan, they enter a castle and find a beautiful woman in mourning weeds, contemplating the severed head of her dead husband. She is Ruperta, a Scottish noblewoman. A year previously the elderly suitor whom she had rejected in favour of a young Scottish count had sheathed his sword in his young rival's chest. In her grief, she ordered that her husband's head be severed from his dead body, stripped of its flesh and placed in a silver casket. She then set out on the long journey to Rome to seek aid from its princes. She travels with her 'sad relics' (*dolorosas reliquias*) (589), namely the head in its silver reliquary and the fatal sword still uncannily wet with her husband's blood. 'The blood of your husband is calling to you', she tells herself; 'and through that head without a tongue it is saying to you "vengeance!"' (*y en aquella cabeza sin lengua te está diciendo ¡Venganza!*) (592). Romance proceeds by the logic of coincidence, and that very day the killer's son rides up to the castle. At nightfall the Scottish widow places her right hand on the severed relic-head and swears to obey its tongueless entreaty. Invoking Judith's beheading of Holofernes,

she sneaks into the young man's chamber, carrying a knife and a lantern. As she stands over his sleeping form, poised to strike, the light from the lantern falls on the young man's face, and the knife drops instantly from her hand. His handsome visage arrests her as surely as if it were the petrifying face of Medusa. Meanwhile the flame from the lantern starts to burn his chest and he wakes with a start to find the beautiful widow in her white mourning weeds standing before him. Morning finds them in bed, in the embrace of love: 'that night, gentle love won out over hard war; the field of battle became a marriage bed; peace was born from anger; from death, life' (*Triunfó aquella noche la blanda paz desta dura guerra; volvióse el campo de la batalla en tálamo de desposorio; nació la paz de la ira; de la muerte, la vida*) (596). Next morning Ruperto's elderly squire is seen slipping out of the bridal chamber with the skull in its silver case and the bloody sword, carrying them off to where 'they would never reawaken old misfortunes amid present glories' (*no renovasen otra vez en las glorias presentes pasadas desventuras*) (597).[34]

The emollience of Cervantes's romance in seeking to bury the sword and silence death-heads calling for vengeance is the other side of literature's complex relationship with violence. But in the real field of battle, in the harsh world outside romance, the violence which the severed head represented and incited could not be so sweetly set aside. In June

English soldiers take the heads of defeated Irish rebels. From John Derricke's *The Image of Irlande* (London, 1581).
© Trinity College Dublin

'These trunckles heddes do playnly showe, eache rebeles fatall end, / And what a haynous crime it is, the Queene for to offend'. From John Derricke's *The Image of Irlande* (London, 1581). © Trinity College Dublin.

1602 Sir Arthur Chichester was expressing his confidence of finding 'a speedy course for beating, and, as I hope, beheading, that wood-kearn Tyrone'.[35] Behind the flight lay O'Neill's fear that 'if he went in to England he should either be perpetual prisoner in the Tower, or else lose his head and his members'.[36] For those left behind, there was no respite. Cathair O'Doherty's head would end up on a spike on Newgate, while the victor of the unseemly scramble to cut a trophy-head from his lifeless body collected a £500 bounty.[37] Most terrible of all was the final death-spasm of the rebellion on Tory Island, where sixty rebels took refuge. When the constable of the island, Maolmhuire MacSweeney, offered to surrender the castle, he was told that he would be pardoned only if he presented the heads of the other defenders. Racing against time, MacSweeney set to the grisly task, until 'a desperate villain, with a skione' [*scian*, knife] stabbed him in the heart and the wretched MacSweeny was 'afterwards himself … cut in pieces'.[38]

The earls did not leave severed heads and body parts entirely behind them when they went into exile. However, they encountered them in a context that utterly transformed their meaning. With the flight, the earls enter a different storyline, leaving behind a narrative of war to enter one that combines elements of the quest, the Grand Tour and the pilgrimage. Tadhg Ó Cianáin's record of their journey

registers that shift. It starts with the solid materiality of chronicle-writing as he intones the route 'from Sráidbhaile by the high road of the Fiodh, to Béal Átha an Airgid, across Sliabh Fuaid, to Ard Mhacha, over the Abha Mór, to Dún Geanainn, to the Craobh'.[39] As the wind blocks their passage to Spain, however, the reader enters a world without coordinates. The ship's company is astray and confounded (*seachrain ⁊ aineoluis*) (10). They have no pilot for French waters, and the small craft they meet cannot guide them ashore. At the height of the storm they trail relics, including O'Neill's gold crucifix containing a piece of the True Cross, in the scudding wake – just as Astolfo's pilot had streamed fenders and guys astern in Book XIX of *Orlando Furioso* – and a pair of merlins perches wondrously on deck. We have entered something like the narrative logic of romance.

Landfall brings no return to the old solidities. Denizens now of the floating world of exile, Ó Cianáin narrates the northern lords' journey onwards as a pilgrimage, written under the sign of wonder. The continent has marvels unknown in Ulster: the duke of Lorraine's tennis-court; the leopard, lions and two camels they see in the duke of Parma's gardens (80, 103). This is a journey that hugs close to the supernatural. The exiles have hardly lost their sea-legs when they detour to Amiens to behold the head of John the Baptist in its glass case. In Arras the

Governor of Flanders sends coaches and a priestly guide who shows them a piece of the True Cross, a cup from which Christ drank, a tress of Mary Magdalene's hair – and another head (St James's). The terrible mutilations of the battlefield – the head of Henry Hovenden, O'Neill's foster brother, sometime interpreter and nemesis of Armada survivors, struck off and presented to Docwra;[40] the arm of a knight named Seagrave, sheared off by O'Cahan's son as it struck at O'Neill[41] – give way to hallowed relics of dismemberment: the hand of St Nicholas, 'the fourth part of the body of St George', the forefinger of St Anne's left hand (81, 169). Later, in their avid church-visiting in Rome, they see not only the heads of Saints Andrew, Luke, Sebastian and Thomas of Canterbury, but also the unlikely head of the Samaritan woman.[42] Just as conflict had turned marvellous in *Persiles,* it turns miraculous in Ó Cianáin. The earls hear how Notre Dame de Hal, besieged by Protestant heretics, was saved by an apparition of the Blessed Virgin who caught their impotent bullets in her napkin. They see the bullets – and the hands of a heretical captain who, having threatened to strike the statue of the wonder-working Virgin, had his hands severed in battle. As the texts grows cluttered with sites of miracles and turns from travelogue to miracle-tale, its keywords become 'wonder' (*ingantus*) and 'marvels and miracles' (*fert ┐ mirbal*) (30, 38, 66).

Years later O'Neill would become the 'old man [who] every night … sleeps with his sword naked by his bedside';[43] but there is no report of a book by his bed. Yet Gainsford imagined him as the hero of a very different kind of story: had times been otherwise, he 'would have shewed himselfe as brave and complete an Amorist, as the formallest Courtier in England'.[44] As it was, his 1607 adventure, at sea and on the road from Quilleboeuf to Rome, could be woven seamlessly into the interlaced plotline of *Persiles y Sigismunda.*

Notes

1 J. McCavitt, *The Flight of the Earls* (Dublin, 2002), pp 102-5.

2 E. B. Knowles, 'Thomas Shelton, translator of *Don Quixote*', *Studies in the Renaissance*, v (1958), pp 164-75.

3 J. George, 'Thomas Shelton, translator, in 1612-14', *Bulletin of Hispanic Studies*, xxxv (1958), p. 164.

4 P. Palmer, *Language and conquest in early modern Ireland* (Cambridge, 2001), p. 138.

5 Thomas Gainsford, *The history of the earle of Tyrone* (London, 1619), p. 26; see also p. 48.

6 On his visit, see C. Carroll, *Circe's cup: cultural transformation in early modern Ireland* (Cork, 2001), pp 69-90; D. Gardiner, '"These are not the thinges men live by now a days": Sir John Harington's visit to The O'Neill, 1599', *Cahiers Elizabethains*, lv (1999), pp 1-16.

7 *The letters and epigrams of Sir John Harington,* (ed.) N. E. McClure (Philadelphia, 1930), p. 77.

8 Sir John Harington, *Orlando Furioso*, (ed.) R. McNulty (Oxford, 1972).

9 Harington, *Letters and epigrams*, p. 77.

10 Just as there was later at lunch, served on a 'fern table … spread under the stately canopy of heaven', when the ebullient Harington recorded that 'it was mine hap to thwart one of his priests in an argument', Harington, *Letters and epigrams*, p. 78.

11 Proclamation of the lord deputy and council, 22 Nov. 1600 (*CSPI, 1600-01,* p. 41).

12 On the conflation of the Irish and the Moors see B. Fuchs, 'Spanish lessions: Spenser and the Irish Moriscos', *Studies in English Literature, 1500-1900,* xlii.1 (2002), pp 43-62.

13 Harington, *Letters and epigrams*, p. 107.

14 Ibid., pp 12, 70.

15 Harington, *Orlando Furioso*, p. 140.

16 Something of the same dynamic operates in Sir Henry Wotton's recommendation, as English ambassador in Venice, that Salisbury 'proscribe him [O'Neill], that he may walk in the more fear' (Wotton to Salisbury, 20 June 1608 (*CSPI, 1606-08,* p. 662)) and his friend John Donne's recommendation that O'Neill, whom he saw as Ireland's 'head-vein', be 'let blood' (John Donne, 'Elegy 20: Love's War', in *The complete English poems,* (ed.) A. J. Smith (Harmondsworth, 1986), p. 126). Harington and Wotton were together at Essex's infamous parley with O'Neill at the ford of Aclint (Sir John Harington, *Nugae antiquae*, (ed.) T. Park (2 vols, London, 1804), i, p. 300).

17 K. Duncan-Jones (ed.), *Sir Philip Sidney: a critical edition* (Oxford, 1989), p. 237.

18 Personal communication from Clare Carroll.

19 Miguel de Cervantes, *Los trabajos de Persiles y Sigismunda,* (ed.) C. Romero Muños (Madrid, 2003). Translations in the text are mine but see *The trials of Persiles and Sigismunda,* trans. C. F. Weller and C. A. Colohan (Berkeley, 1989).

20 By far the most troubling *destierro* is the expulsion of the Moors after 1609 (Chapter 11). For a fascinating reading of *Persiles* as a work that crosses boundaries of genre, gender, religion and politics, see W. Childers, *Transnational Cervantes* (Toronto, 2006).

21 *Persiles*, p. 130 n. 11. The definitive study of *Persiles's* American context is D. de Armas Wilson, *Cervantes, the novel and the New World* (Oxford, 2003).

22 The old reflexes die hard. When Antonio, a Spanish castaway, courts a native of the barbarous island, he instructs her in the true faith; in exchange, she brings him gold and pearls (p. 177).

23 D. Quint, *Epic and romance* (Princeton, 1993), p. 248.

24 In the event, he is last seen heading off on a boat for France, though there is a later report of him at the court of Queen Mary in England (pp 424, 679).

25 G. Heng, *Empire of magic: medieval romance and the politics of cultural fantasy* (New York, 2003), p. 9.

26 Childers, *Transnational Cervantes*, p. 46.

27 A. K. Forcione, *Cervantes, Aristotle and the 'Persiles'* (Princeton, 1970), pp 32, 194.

28 Childers, *Transnational Cervantes*, p. 45.

29 Cervantes, *Persiles*, p. 213 n. 7. For a flavour of the once-widespread view of *Persiles* as a work of either Cervantes's inexperience or his dotage see M. Singleton, 'The *Persiles* mystery', in A. Flores and M. J. Beruardete, (eds), *Cervantes across the centuries* (New York, 1969), pp 237-48. W. J. Entwhistle's exasperated view is that Transila's *jus primae noctis* story 'is set in Ireland because its inverisimilitude would not permit a nearer approach to Spain'; see 'Ocean of story', L. Nelson (ed.), *Cervantes: a collection of critical essays* (Englewood Cliffs, 1969), p. 166.

30 See H. K. Bhabha, *The location of culture* (London, 1994), p. 53.

31 See J. Baena '*Los trabajos de Persile y Sigismunda*: la utopía del novelista', *Cervantes*, viii (1998), pp 127-40

32 *Shakespeare: the last plays*, (ed.) K. Ryan (London, 1999), pp 15-16.

33 Childers, *Transnational Cervantes*, p. 46. In a related way B. Fuchs sees *Persiles* as 'a plea for tolerance' towards *conversos, moriscos* and *mestizos*, in *Passing for Spain: Cervantes and the fictions of identity* (Urbana, 2003), p. 98.

34 Cervantes later 'forecasts' Don Juan's beheading of Ali Pasha at Lepanto (p. 602). But the fact that the pilgrims are given this analeptic prophecy by Padre Soldino, who has himself abjured the battlefield where he served Charles V to find peace as a hermit (p. 601), somewhat mutes the triumphalism.

35 Sir Arthur Chichester to Cecil, 22 June 1602 (*CSPI, 1601-03*, p. 415).

36 Sir John Davies to Salisbury, 12 Sept. 1607 (*CSPI, 1606-08*, p. 272).

37 McCavitt, *Flight*, p. 146.

38 Sir Henry Folliott to Sir Arthur Chichester, 8 September 1608 (*CSPI, 1608-10*, p. 36).

39 Tadhg Ó Cianáin, *The Flight of the Earls*, (ed. & trans.) P. Walsh (Dublin, 1916), pp 5-7.

40 D. McGettigan, *Red Hugh O'Donnell and the nine years war* (Dublin, 2005), p. 95; H. Morgan, 'Slán Dé fút go hoíche': Hugh O'Neill's murders', in D. Edwards *et al* (eds) *Age of atrocity* (Dublin, 2007), p. 98.

41 McCavitt, *The Flight of the Earls*, p. 14.

42 L. Swords, *The Flight of the Earls* (Dublin, 2007), p. 76.

43 C. P. Meehan, *The fate and fortunes of Hugh O'Neill, earl of Tyrone and Rory O'Donel, earl of Tyrconnel* (Dublin, 1868), p. 406.

44 Gainsford, *Earle of Tyrone*, p. 16.

Tadhg Ó Cianáin's *Imeacht na nIarlaí* as European pilgrimage

Clare Carroll

The story of the pilgrimage to Loreto takes up about one-fifth of Tadhg Ó Cianáin's account of the earls' journey from Rathmullan to Rome. So much space is devoted to Loreto because it was one of the most important sites of pilgrimage in Europe in the sixteenth and seventeenth centuries. In the absence of access to the Holy Land, a journey to Loreto provided contact with the greatest representative of that world in Western Europe: the house of the Blessed Virgin from Nazareth that had been borne over the sea to rest on the eastern coast of Italy. In response to the criticism of the Loretan tradition by Pier Paolo Vergerio, a Catholic bishop who converted to Protestantism, there arose a vast literature of defence in the sixteenth century. Chief among these was the work of St Peter Canisius, S. J., but there were also those by those by Cirillo, Riera, Martorelli, Torsellino, Torres and Benzoni.[1]

As Nollaig Ó Muraíle has pointed out in his splendid new edition and translation of *Turas na dTaoiseach nUltach as Éirinn*, 'One would love to discover the source of Tadhg's narrative' of the 'detour to the famous shrine of Loreto'.[2] He rightly calls for new research on this section of the 'Turas', it having been slighted by earlier editors. The imitation of and variations upon

The Holy House of the Virgin Mary, where Jesus was conceived, born and raised was said to have been carried by angels from Nazareth to Italy via Dalmatia in 1294.

a variety of texts that can be observed in this first Irish account of the Loreto story show that it was hardly a detour, at least in the author's imagination. Ó Cianáin gives us a hint that he is basing his account on written sources when he begins with the following words: 'Do réir mar fuaramar scríobhtha i seanstarthachaibh, i n-ainm Dé laibheóram uaite do ilibh .i. beagán do mhórán, ar shubháilcibh Loreta'.[3] The author draws the reader's attention to the source of these miracles 'written in ancient histories' (*scríobhtha i seanstarthachaibh*). One of these ancient histories appears to be either indebted to or identical with a Latin account written by Pietro Giorgio Tolomei, called Il Teramano. From 1455

until 1473, Teramano served as administrator of the shrine, and penned his account between 1465 and 1473. Until the recovery of Giacomo Ricci's *Historia* of 1469, and the *Rosarium* of 1449 by St Catherine of Bologna, scholars considered Il Teramano's *Traslazione miraculosa* to be the oldest document containing the story of how the Blessed Virgin's House had been miraculously conveyed from Nazareth to Loreto.[4] Ó Cianáin mentions Teramano twice in the text, describing him as the bishop of the city of Recanati. He describes how Bishop Teramano (*an espaig Terremano*) heard the witnesses Paulus Rinalducii and Francisco testify that each had heard his grandfather swear that 'go bhfcadar a shúile féin an séipéal ag ascnamh agus ag céimniughadh tar an bhfairrge gur thoirinn agus gur thoirling go míorbhaileach isin diamharchoill adubhramar'.[5]

The text of Teramano's Latin manuscript of the late fifteenth century has been edited by Floriano Grimaldi, the major expert on the textual tradition of Loreto.[6] An abbreviated version of Teramano's *Origin and Translation of the Church of Our Lady of Loreto* was translated into Welsh, Lowland Scots and English in widely disseminated broadsides published in Loreto in 1635 by Francesco Serafini.[7] There may have been still earlier Latin or vernacular versions of the text of these broadsides that Ó Cianáin might have read. It appears that Serafini always intended a written version of Teramano's full Latin text to be available for pilgrims visiting the Holy House. The three broadsides were written by Robert Corbington, whose 1634 Gaelic translation of Teramano's text 'out of the original Latin hung up on this church' (*as an original langhie a ta ar croughe sna themapoill so*) can still be read on the walls of the shrine today.[8] Born in Dublin in 1596 to a Protestant English convert father, Corbington entered the Jesuits in 1626 and became English penitentiary at Rome and Loreto.[9] That he translated the text into Gaelic for both publication

The Basilica (above) and papal altar (below) at the burial place of St Francis was a considerable draw for the O'Donnells whose family had long venerated the Franciscans. After their deaths later that year, Rory and Cathbharr O'Donnell were buried in the Franciscan cowl as was the tradition in their family.

and to be inscribed on the walls of the shrine suggests that Loreto was clearly on the map of Gaelic-speaking pilgrims in the seventeenth century.

While Corbington's text is later than Ó Cianáin's, a comparison of their respective word choices highlights differences in their style and themes. For example, Ó Cianáin uses *séipéal Loreta* where Corbington opts for *Teampoll Loreto* (*séipéal* is a Middle Irish loan word from the Middle English and Old French *chapel*, and has a more colloquial and familiar feel than *Teampoll* from the Latin *templum*, reflecting the Biblical and Judaic *temple*). Ó Cianáin also utilises *ró-onóir* rather than *devosión mór* which may be in line with the general emphasis on the concept of honor, both secular and religious, throughout the text.[10] Even Ó Cianáin's rendering of names is different. For example, he uses *Paulus dela Silva* rather than *Pol na Sylva*, and *Francisco* rather than *Proinsias*. On the whole, his text contains more loan words than Corbington's, which could be construed as a reflection on the linguistic level of the attempt in the *Turas* to demonstrate the international European rather than the local Gaelic character of the earls' journey. As we shall see, there is a greater degree of artful variation on Teramano's text in Ó Cianáin's account than there is in Corbington's workmanlike translation.

Nevertheless, Ó Cianáin's opening five paragraphs of the description of the Holy House closely resembles the beginning of Teramano's text. Just as the latter tells us that the house was made in the 'city of Galilee which was named Nazareth' (*que domus fuit … in civitate Gallilee cui nomen Nazareth*) so too Ó Cianáin, amplifying the description of the city with adjectives, tells us that it was 'i bpríomhchathraigh oirdhirc adhamhra oirdnidhe Nasaret Galale, conrótacht an teagh sin ó thús'.[11] Teramano describes how 'in this room the Virgin Mary was born, educated and saluted by the archangel Gabriel' (*in qua camera virgo Maria fuit nata et ibi educate et poste ab archangel Gabriele salutata*). Similarly, Ó Cianáin tells us that 'An fós ro compreadh, ro geineadh, ro hileamhnaigheadh an naomhógh' and that 'isin teagh chéadna sin dosrad an t-archaingeal uasal Gabriel an teachtaireacht ón Athair neamhdha go naomh-Muire trias dtáinig saoradh'.[12] As Teramano relates 'in this said room she nourished her son Jesus Christ' (*in dicta camera nutrivit filium suum Jhesum Christum*), so Ó Cianáin conveys, again with some elegant descriptive variation: 'ar Slánaightheóir Íosa Críost. Ro hoileamhnaigheadh as a haithle ar gheilchíochaibh naomhlachtmhara na hóige'.[13] Both Teramano and Ó Cianáin tell about how the house contained the image of Mary crafted by the evangelist Luke with his own hands, while our Irish author adds: 'Is í amháin is míorbhaileach gan imreasain fón uile dhomhan.[14] Both Teramano and Ó Cianáin comment that the 'house was honored with great devotion and reverence' (*dicta ecclesia fuit … honorata cum magna devocione et reverantia*), while Ó Cianáin intensifies the adjectives to make this 'ro-onóir go priviléid ndearmháir ndíochre dó'.[15]

The way that Ó Cianáin's at once follows Teramano's narrative while adding new details is underscored by the story's next turn. The Loretan author makes an abrupt transition from the way in which so many revered the Holy House to the story of how 'the people dismissed the faith of Christ and received the faith of Machomet' (*ille populius dimisit fidem Christi et recepti fidem Machometi*).[16] Similarly, the Irish diarist suddenly mentions the people's conversion to Islam. Adding information not found in Teramano, Ó Cianáin inserts the names of the instigators of this apostasy and the persecution of Christians: the emperor of Rome (Heraclius) and the king of Persia (Chosroes). These references make it clear that Ó Cianáin used sources other than Teramano in his text. Beyond this, he gives a fuller explanation of why the house had to be moved: 'Ní ro léig iomorra an t-iomfhaitcheas do lucht áitreabhtha na cathrach nó an régióin umhla nó adhradh do chreideamh Dé 'sa naiomh shéipéal sin'.[17] His version of the story also gives a more precise historical context as well. Whereas Teramano's narrates how the house is 'carried by angels to Sclavonia to a town called Flumen',[18] following the peoples' conversion to the faith of Mahomet,[19] Ó Cianáin locates the event in relation to the crusades: 'An Pápa an chethramhadh Nioclás bhuí isin Róimh triallais cogadh agus coinbhlíocht igceartaghaidh na n-eiritcheadh sin'.[20] He also notes that this pope, who reigned from 1288 to 1292, was a Franciscan and the gen-

eral of the order who took over from Bonaventure. That he should mention this makes sense given the many Franciscan references in the text, including the visits to Assisi and to San Francesco a Ripa in Trastevere.[21] Interestingly enough, neither Teramano's earlier account nor the later, also widely disseminated, *Historia Lauretana* by the Jesuit Orazio Torsellino (Rome, 1597) mention this Franciscan pope or his crusade. In this instance, Ó Cianáin may be trying to draw a highly topical analogy between Christians persecuted by heretics in the Holy Land and the Irish who now sought papal aid in their own conflict with heretics. Whatever his rhetorical aim, Ó Cianáin certainly amplifies Teramano's account with a wealth of specifics.

As Teramano continues the story of the Holy House, the reader learns that no sooner was the house moved to Sclavonia than it was lifted up again and brought to Recanati. Here, Teramano mentions, 'innumerable crimes were committed' (*innumerabilia mala commitebantur*), so that the angels had to rescue the house again bearing it to the 'hill of two brothers' (*in montem duorum fratrum*).[22] When these brothers fought over the money that they were making from the pilgrims to the shrine, the angels moved the relic to the common crossroads, where it stands to this day.[23] Teramano narrates how 'all the people of Recanati came to the house which was over the ground without any foundation … Considering what a great miracle this was, they built a church with a great big wall around it with the best foundation which is seen manifestly today. No one knew where this shrine originally came from nor where it originally departed from'.[24]

Although Ó Cianáin does eventually tell about the translation of the house from Tersato in Sclavonia to Recanati in Le Marche, and from the 'garden-hill' (ghairdin-chnoc) of the 'two brothers of one another' (dís dearbhráthar diaroile) to 'the very center of a royal high road between the great city of Recanati and the old sea' (gceartlár an ríoghróid ríoghdha thairmnigheas eidir príomhchathraigh Recanati agus an seanfhairrge), he does not relate this information at the same point as Teramano's narrative, but delays it until later.[25] Instead of immediately telling of the second and third flights of the house, Ó Cianáin relays the story of the first person to whom Mary revealed the origins of the house. This story of the 'very noble prior who was superior in the monastery of St George … Alexandro' (prióir ro-onórach ros-buí i n-a uachtarán i

The Pilgrim Churches of Rome, from a seventeenth-century guide book.

mainistir Sanct Seóirse … Aileacsandro) appears to be based on yet another famous Loretan text – the *Historia Lauretana* by the Jesuit Orazio Torsellino.[26] Published in Rome in 1597, and translated into Italian, French, German and Catalan, it finally appeared in an English translation in 1608, early enough for Ó Cianáin to have read it.[27] The Roman edition of this Jesuit text carries the symbol that order appropriated from the Franciscans: the IESU or Holy Name of Jesus, first described by San Bernardino da Siena. It is also a symbol that appears on many leaves of Ó Cianáin's manuscript. The story of Alexandro follows the outlines of Toresellino's account. Alexandro is struck with an illness, and prays to Mary, who appears to him and reveals how she was raised in the house and gave birth to Jesus there, and that after her death the Apostles lived in the house, where they 'made a tabernacle

and venerable, honoured, holy place of prayer'.[28] His story then comes to the attention of the ruler of the country, who decides to send Alexandro and other witnesses to the city of Nazareth to investigate and confirm the story.[29] Some of the significant details of Torsellino's account that appear to be picked up by Ó Cianáin include: the 'heavenly odour' that Mary emits as she ascends to heaven after appearing to Alexandro, which Ó Cianáin renders 'pleasantness of the divine glorious odor' (subháilcighe an bholtanaighe dhiadha ghlórmhair bhuí); Alexandro's awakening to immediate health after the vision of Mary; the story coming to the attention of Nicolas Frangipane, or, as Ó Cianáin renders it 'Fransifane'; Frangipane's order to send four worthy men with Alexandro to the holy land to verify the vision; their measuring of the foundations of the spot where the house once stood in

Nazareth, which are found to be exactly the same as the dimensions of the house in Sclavonia.[30] Its story of Alexandro is not in the 1635 broadsides, suggesting that it had to have come from either Torsellino's text or one of his sources.

Following the story of Alexandro, Ó Cianáin continues with the account of how the house moved from Sclavonia to Recanati. After this point his text again appears to follow Teramano's closely, but he also manages, while following Teramano's more abbreviated plotline, to weave in some of the details which Torsellino adds in his much longer and more detailed version in five books. As Teramano does, Ó Cianáin relates the story of yet

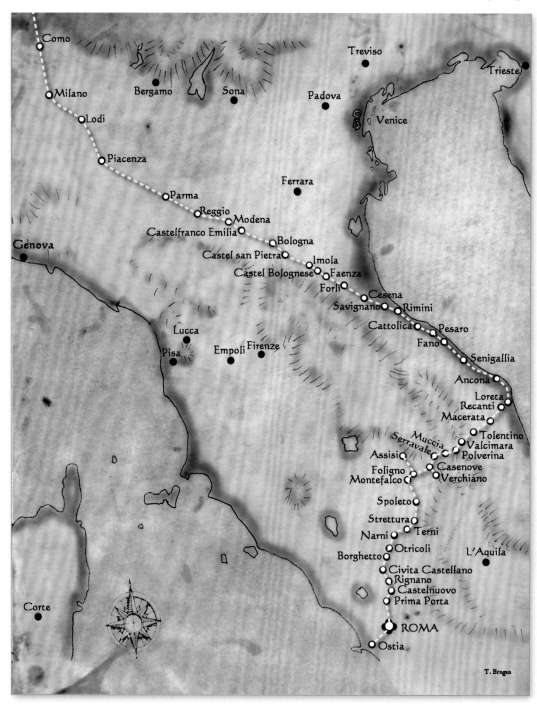

The earls' journey down the Italian peninsula. © Tomás Ó Brógáin after Nollaig Ó Muraíle

another witness to a Marian apparition in the house's new Italian location. Teramano, Torsellino and Ó Cianáin all portray this new witness as a 'holy man of great sanctitie'.[31] In all three accounts 'sixteen notable men' are sent to Nazareth to investigate the story. Ó Cianáin imitates Torsellino more closely that Teramano in this part of the story, as he recounts how they went first to Tersato in Slavonia, which he calls Sinonia, rather than directly to the Holy Land. In all three versions the dimensions of the house in Loreto are again verified by measurement of its foundation left behind in Nazareth. Neither the trip to Slavonia nor the measuring of the foundations of the house appears in the abbreviated account of the 1635 broadsides.

The Irish diarist then proceeds to the story of Paulus de Silva or, as he calls him, Paulus dela Silva. Both Ó Cianáin and Torsellino appear to follow Teramano's account of the hermit's spectacular vision of a 'great shining torch, descending on the chapel'. Only Ó Cianáin picks up Teramano's detail that the light was 'twelve feet in length and six in breadth'.[32] All three accounts agree on the timing of this event: once a year for ten years on 8 September, the feast of the nativity of the Blessed Virgin Mary. This vision was important enough to be included even in the short 1635 broadsides.

In his next story Ó Cianáin again follows Teramano in telling how Paulus (whom he calls Rinaltinus) spoke to Teramano, bishop of the city of Recanati, who had come on pilgrimage to Loreto. Paulus testified under oath concerning the sworn witness of his grandfather, who had himself witnessed the translation of the house first over the sea (*per mare*) into this aforesaid wood (*in dicta silva*) and to the hill of the two brothers, and where it had been set down and placed (*ibi sita et collocata*).[33] Torsellino mentions that his source is Franciscus Angelita, whose *Laurentanae historia* was published at Macerata in 1579. Torsellino also refers to Teramano, whom he praises for having:

> set up in the House of Loreto, the summe of that historie (gathered out of that little booke which in time past, as we shewed before, was published at Recanati) that all might have meanes to know it; which he caused to be set down in simple and plaine stile, conformable to the understanding of the Communalitie, that it might be an acceptable and Gratefull repast to the Pil-

grimes not altogether unlearned, and no small ornament to the House of Loreto itself.[34]

It seems therefore certain, that Ó Cianáin must have had access to Teramano's widely disseminated account, which he would have found posted in the shrine for pilgrims to read.

Torsellino's account also provides stories for Ó Cianáin to imitate and embellish. If one removes the material about papal relations with Loreto, added by Torsellino, Ó Cianáin's narrative follows a sequence common to Teramano and Torsellino, but it also picks up new material only found in the latter's text. For example, Ó Cianáin takes the first of the two miracle stories that he relates from Book Two, Chapter VII of Torsellino's *History*. Here Petrus Orgetorix (Petro Orgentoris) brings his wife Antonia to Loreto because she has been unable to find a cure for her demonic possession anywhere else, not even at the sacred pillar at St Peter's in Rome. Ó Cianáin adds a psychological motivation and human agency to the possession, absent from Torsellino's account: she has been bewitched by a woman who is jealous of her:

> Gabhais tra bean oile isin gcathrigh gcéadna dóigh éada, iomthnúith, agus acaise di im an bhfearscál réamhráidhte. Dealbhais breachta diabhlaidheachta agus draoidheachta, íodhalachta agus ainchreidmhe, in-a haghaidh.[35]

Going to Loreto as a last resort, Antonia is exorcised by Stephanus Francigena. In both Torsellino's and Ó Cianáin's descriptions the expelled devils confess that they have been constrained by the power of Mary to proclaim publicly that Loretan house is her home. Ó Cianáin appears to add more fascinating details to Torsellino's account, which is in turn based on that of Franciscus Angelita, cited as his source for the story of Antonia's exorcism. In the Irish text the devils are far more haunting and macabre. Menacingly, they reveal the names of those whom they had previously possessed. Ó Cianáin's description of the devil Herot is hair-raising:

> Iar sin ro ghreamaigh do lóchrann oile dia mbuí isin séipéal. Dos-rad a cheartaghaidh ghránna ghráineamhail forsan athair réamhráidhte. Nochtais agus glomhais a dhraintfhiacla iomdhorcha aidhéidche.[36]

The next miracle he describes is also taken from Torsellino's text, where he attributes his source to Raphael Riera.[37] In Book IV, Chapter III, he describes the bishop of Coimbra being struck with a near fatal illness after taking a stone away from the Holy House at Loreto. Even though this has been done with the pope's permission, the bishop comes to realise the arrogance of his action. Two cloistered nuns counsel him to return the stone. Ó Cianáin again shows his flare for the uncanny:

> I gcéadóir iomorra greamaighis agus coimhleannais an chloch go míorbhaileach éagsamhail iogantach dia coigéilibh comhadhasa clochchomharsnach oile mar nach biadh eadarscaraidh eatorra riamh ón chéad ló gusan tan sin.[38]

There are still many unanswered questions about Ó Cianáin's relation to his sources and what his crafting of those sources means for the text as a whole. For example, it is unclear whether he read Torsellino in its original Latin or in the English translation of the recusant T. P. To what extent, if at all, is his text indebted to Torsellino's sources Angelita and Riera, or some lost popular broadside that preceded these 1635 imprints. It might also be useful to explore this part of the text as an interpolated narrative. But then, why, besides the importance of Loreto as a European pilgrimage site, would he place this pilgrimage within the larger pilgrimage? If any credence is given to the Irish title of this text in the late seventeenth-century inventory at Louvain, then it is necessary to think of the narrative as a *turas*, or pilgrimage, and the images of exile, banishment, physical suffering and miraculous cure may have a bearing on those motifs as they are woven throughout the entire story of the earls' journey to Rome. Indeed, the length and careful craft in Ó Cianáin's rendering of the Loreto story suggests that it was hardly a detour. In some sense, as a *turas*, or pilgrimage, it may be considered as a kind of microcosm of the text as a whole.

Given the inventive and elegant variations in Tadhg's retelling of these miracles of Loreto, it is regrettable that nowhere among the 673 texts listed in the Abbé Joseph Faurax's *Bibliographie Loretaine* (Bruges, Tournai, Rome, 1913) and nowhere in Floriano Grimaldi's *La Historia della Chiesa di Santa Maria di Loreto* is there a mention of Ó Cianáin's account of the pilgrimage. A preliminary examination of Ó Cianáin's text against those of Teramano and Torsellino goes at least some way towards giving the Irish author a place in the tradition of one of the most widely written about pilgrimages in Renaissance Europe.

The earls are received by the pope in Rome. © Inch House Irish Studies Centre

Notes

1 G. Santarelli, *La Santa Casa di Loreto* (Loreto, 2006), pp 13-17.

2 *Turas*, p. 25.

3 'According as we have found them written in ancient histories, we shall, in the name of God, narrate a few of the many, that is, a small number of the multitude, of the miracles of Loreto', *Turas*, pp 180-1.

4 Santarelli, *La Santa Casa di Loreto*, p. 41; G. Ricci, *Virginis Mariae Loretae historia*, (ed.) G. Santarelli (Loreto, 1987); F. Grimaldi, *La historia della Chiesa di Santa Maria di Loreto* (Loreto, 1993).

5 'His own eyes saw the chapel advancing and coming over the sea until it alighted and descended miraculously into the dark wood we have mentioned', *Turas*, pp 210-11.

6 Grimaldi, *Historia*, pp 15-17.

7 *Dechrevad a rhyfedhus esmudiad Eglwys Yr Arglwydhes Fair o Loreto* (Loreto, 1635); *The wondrous flittinge of the Kirk of Our B. Lady of Loreto* (Loreto, 1635); *The miraculous origin and translation of the Church of Our B. Lady of Loreto* (Loreto, 1635).

8 For an excellent article on Corbington and his translations into Gaelic, Lowland Scots and English, which traces the reprinting of Corbington's translation in the edition of Bonabhentura Ó hEodhasa's *An Teagasg Críosaidhe* printed in Rome in 1707, see P. Ó Mianáin, 'An tAthair Robert Corbington, C. Í., agus Inscríbhinn Ghaeilge Loreto, 1635', *Taighde agus Teagasc*, iv (2004), pp 94-110. See also A. Ó Fachtna, 'An tráchtas ar Teampoll Mhuire Loreto i *Teagasg Críosdaidhe* Uí Eodhasa', *Éigse: A Journal of Irish Studies*, xix (1983), pp 373-5.

9 H. Foley, *Records of the English Province of the Society of Jesus* (7 vols, London, 1875-83), iii, p. 65; vii, p. 169.

10 See B. Kane, 'Making the Irish European: Gaelic honor politics and its continental contexts', *Renaissance Quarterly*, lxi (2008), pp 1139-66; idem, *The politics and culture of honour in Britain and Ireland, 1541-1641* (Cambridge, 2009).

11 'In that great, famous, remarkable, worthy city of Nazareth in Galilee that house was first built'; Grimaldi, *Historia*, p. 15; *Turas*, pp 180-1.

12 'It was there too that that the Holy Virgin was conceived, born, and reared; in that same house the noble archangel Gabriel delivered the message from the heavenly Father to Mary', *Turas*, pp 181-3.

13 'Our Saviour Jesus Christ. He was nourished afterwards on the white, milky, holy breasts of the Virgin', (ibid., p. 183).

14 'It is alone the most miraculous one, without contention, in the whole world'; Grimaldi, *Historia*, p. 15; *Turas*, pp 182-3.

15 'Great honour and exceeding great devotion to it'; Grimaldi, *Historia*, p. 15; *Turas*, pp 184-5.

16 Grimaldi, *Historia*, p. 15.

17 'The inhabitants of the city and the region were prevented by fear from submitting to or adoring God's religion in that holy chapel', *Turas*, pp 184-5.

18 Grimaldi, *Historia*, p. 15.

19 Ibid.

20 'Pope Nicholas IV, who was in Rome, commenced a war and conflict against those heretics', *Turas*, p. 185.

21 C. Carroll, 'Turas na nIarladh as Éire: international travel and national identity in Ó Cianáin's travel narrative', *History Ireland*, xv, no. 4 (July/August 2007), pp 56-61.

22 Grimaldi, *Historia*, p. 16.

23 Ibid.

24 Ibid.

25 *Turas*, pp 195, 201.

26 Ibid., pp 186-7.

27 Grimaldi, *Historia*, p. 21.

28 *Turas*, p. 189.

29 Ibid., p. 191.

30 Orazio Torsellino, *The History of our B. Lady of Loreto* (1608) (facsimile reprint London, 1976), pp 17-27; Ó Muraíle, pp 186-92.

31 Toresellino, *History of our B. Lady of Loreto*, p. 61; *Turas*, pp 202, 203; Grimaldi, *Historia*, p. 16.

32 *Turas*, p. 209; Grimaldi, *Historia*, p. 16; Torsellino, *History of our B. Lady of Loreto*, p. 81.

33 Grimaldi, *Historia*, p. 16.

34 Torsellino, *History of our B. Lady of Loreto*, p. 121.

35 'Another woman in the city being smitten with jealous, envy, and hatred of her in relation to the man aforementioned. She performed charms of devilry and witchery, idolatry and heathenism against her', *Turas*, pp 212-3.

36 'After that it struck to another torch that was in the church. It turned its ugly face on the father aforementioned, [and] grinned and bared its dark, ugly teeth', *Turas*, pp 218-9.

37 R. Riera, *Historia Domus Lauretanae liber singularis* (1565) in P. V. Martorelli, *Teatro istorico della S. Casa* (Roma, 1732-35).

38 'At once the stone miraculously, strangely and wonderfully took hold and adhered to the corresponding proper adjoining stones as if there had never been a separation of them from the first day until that time', *Turas*, pp 236-7.

The links between St Colum Cille and Scotland anticipated connections between Ulster and Scotland in the early modern period, as did his exile anticipate the eventual fate of the earls themselves. © Seán Ó Brógáin

The Flight of the Earls

CONTEXTS

Facts and fabrications: the earls and their Ulster ancestry

Brian Lacey

Commenting on the departure of the earls of Tyrone and Tyrconnell from Rathmullan on 4 September 1607, the Annals of the Four Masters reads:

> Bá maith an lucht aon luinge battar ainnsidhe ar as dearbh deaimhin ná ro thaoscc muir, ⁊ na ro fogluais gaoth a héirinn is na deaidheancoibh lucht aon luinge báttar fearr, ⁊ báttar aireagdha ⁊ ba huaisle ar aoí ngeainelaigh …[1]

On their arrival in Rome in April 1608, Hugh O'Neill and Rory O'Donnell were ceremoniously received as befitted significant aristocratic figures, despite the diplomatic complications that existed then between England, Spain and the papacy. Sir Henry Wotton, the English ambassador at Venice, reported on their reception:

> Tyrone arrived on the 29th of April. About two miles out of the town he was met by eight coaches, and six horses to every coach, sent by the Cardinals Montalto, Farnese, Colonna and Barberini. The English papists by commandment of the pope went to meet him, and he was thus conducted to St Peter's Church in the Vatican where he first set foot on the ground.[2]

That account matches Tadhg Ó Cianáin's narrative, which described the earls' arrival at the Ponte Molle, the famous Milvian Bridge across the Tiber north of the city:

> Dos-riacht Petrus Lombardus, ardeaspag Aird Mhacha agus príomháidh na hÉireann, go ndeisceabal onórach i n-a choimhideacht go líonmhaireacht cóistidhe ó chairdeanálaibh i n-a gcomhdháil agus i n-a gcomhairicis gusan dú sin. Téid stíobhard gach aoin fo leith do dhroing áirighthe do na cairdeanálaibh i n-a gcoinne d'fhorbháiltiughadh friú agus dia nglacadh go honórach in ainm na gcairdeanál. Éirghid i gcóistidhibh as a haithle …

> Chéimnighid go ro riachtsad an Róimh. Porta Popule comhainm an gheabhta do shonnradh ar a ndeachsad isteach isin gcathraigh. Gluaisid iar sin go ro-onórach tré phríomhshráidibh oireagdha na Rómha. Níor hoiriseadh leó go ro riachtsad prímhtheampall Peadair in Vaticano. Scuirid a n-eachraidh ann. Éirghid isteach isin eaglais. Do-ghníd sléachtaine. Timchillidh i modh thurais, na seacht bpríomhaltóra príviléideacha mórlóíghidheachta fuilead isin eaglais.[3]

Mural of St Colum Cille, formerly in the Bogside, Derry. © Liam Campbell

It is significant that this description compares fairly closely with a fictional account of St Colum Cille's alleged arrival in Rome over a thousand years earlier, given in Manus Ó Domhnaill's magnificent *Betha Colaim Chille*, composed eighty years before Ó Cianáin's account:

> Gluaisis C[olum] C[ille] andsin, & ar techt fa cuig mile decc don Roimh dó, do beanatar cluicc na Romha uile uatha fen; & nir fedadh cosc doib & do bidhgatar lucht na Romha uile uime sin. Et do gab ingnadh mór íad. 'Na bidh ingnadh oruib fan ní úd,' bar an Papa, 'Colum Cille an naem erlumh ata ag techt am cend-sa, & as dó doberid an cluic an onóir úd; ⁊ ni fedfaider cosc doib no co ti se fén don baile.' Is andsin do erich an Papa amach ⁊ morán do mhaithibh na Romha farís, maille re honóir ⁊ re reverians mór a coinde C[olum] C[ille]; ⁊ ar rochtain a celi doibh, do pogsad a celi ⁊ doronsad luthgaired ⁊ gairdechus imarcuch re roile; ⁊ do filleatar don baili ar sin; ⁊ ar ndenamh sléctana do C[olum] C[ille] a tempull mor na Romha, do coiscetar na cluic uatha fen.[4]

Colum Cille came away from the Città Eterna with the gift of a valuable indulgence that lead to the establishment of a pilgrimage in Derry:

> ⁊ tuc an Papa tidluicthe mora do C[olum] C[ille] andsin .i. gebé baile da bailtibh fen a n-oiredeochadh C[olum] C[ille] do cach oilithri do denamh, luaigidhecht sdasioín na Romha do beith ag an duine dodenadh an oilithre sin. Acus as é baile dá tucc C[olum] C[ille] an onóir sin .i. do Doire ⁊ ssé fen a nAlbain.[5]

This fictional story provided the basis of a real, late medieval pilgrimage in Derry developed by the O'Donnells. From other details in the text, it is evident that main pilgrimage *turas* proceeded along what is now Magazine Street, effectively the only irregularly aligned street inside the otherwise very geometrically laid-out walled plantation city of Londonderry.[6] Manus Ó Domhnaill had not been to Rome himself, but he undoubtedly heard accounts about it from his father, Aodh Dubh, who had made a celebrated pilgrimage in 1510-11. In fact, Manus first came into historical focus at that time, having been left in charge of Tír Chonaill in his father's absence. That experience must have left a deep, albeit surrogate, impression of the eternal city on him.

Rory O'Donnell, first earl of Tyrconnell, was Manus's grandson (Table 1). Like all the Gaelic aristocracy, Donegal's 'Renaissance prince' had a very conscious, indeed inordinately proud, sense of his noble ancestry. In the introductory material to the *Betha Colaim Chille*, he outlined his recent pedigree, five generations back:

> Bidh a fhis ag lucht legtha na bethad-sa gorab é Maghnas, mac Aeda, mic Aeda Ruaid, mic Neill Gairb, mic Toirrdelbaigh an fhina hi Domhnaill, do furail an cuid do bi a Laidin don bethaid-si do cur a n-Gaidhilc, ⁊ do furail an chuid do bi go cruaid a n-Gaidilc di do cor a m-buga, innus go m-beith si solus sothuicsena do cach uile.[7]

A few lines later he proceeds even further back in his supposed ancestry, claiming a relationship with what he calls his 'ard-naem', the 'high saint' Colum Cille, his 'comhbrathair genelaig':

> Et ar n-gabhail báidhe ⁊ brathairsi dó rena ard-naem ⁊ réna combrathair genelaig & réna pátrún gradhach fen, da raibe se ró-duthrachtach. A caislen Puirt na tri namat, umorro, do dechtagh in betha-so an tan ba shlan, da bliadain dec ar .xx. ar cuic .c. ar .m. bliadan don Tigerna.[8]

The O'Donnell family thus claimed kinship with Colum Cille's own people, the Cenél Conaill, thereby copper fastening their impeccable aristocratic credentials in the sixteenth and seventeenth centuries.

On 15 November 1607, two months after the earls had left Ireland, James I issued a proclamation denouncing them as traitors and conspirators. The text of the proclamation subsequently appeared as a pamphlet and circulated among the king's ambassadors and associates throughout Europe. It attempted to discredit the earls among their potential hosts and allies and, in the words of Micheline Kerney Walsh, criticised them 'as men of low extraction who claimed titles of ancient nobility to which they were not entitled'.[9] Paradoxically, the earls probably had as ancient and as noble an ancestry, if not a better one, as King James himself.

Fascination with genealogy and the length of ancestry, whether factual or fictional, characterised medieval Gaelic society and has preoccupied those who have written about it in more recent times. There is a telling illustration of this phenomenon in the history of County Derry/Londonderry. In 1076 there occurred what the annals described as the battle of Belat in which the king of Aileach, Áed ua Máel Sechlainn, defeated the Ciannacht, a local petty kingdom that nestled in the Roe Valley, between Dungiven and Limavady.[10] The location of the battle, Belat, has been identified as the townland of Gorticross, east of the River Foyle and a few miles outside Derry. Whatever the circumstances of this relatively minor battle, it can hardly be described as one of the great turning-points of European history. However, in the 1950s Dr Séamas Ó Ceallaigh, the eminent historian of the medieval period in the county, used the opportunity provided by his account of the battle for a wonderful piece of high-flown County Derry patriotism, as well as a celebration of the longevity of the Gaelic aristocracy. The Ciannacht, Dr Ó Ceallaigh said:

claimed to have arrived there about the year 400 A.D., and had been established in the valley of the Roa for a period which might excite the envy of some enduring dynasty of Continental history. The year of this battle, for instance, was the very time when Henry IV [the Holy Roman Emperor] was preparing to cross the snows to Canossa. If that monarch had his finger on the pulse of European politics, as any reputable Emperor should have had, he must have got first word of the current calamity at Belat. And as he reflected on the evils that were threatening his dynasty, was his mind awed by the fate of Ciannachta, in comparison with which his own house, back through Henry the Fowler, even to the baptism of Wittekind, was really nothing but a thing of mushroom growth, making the whole galaxy of the Salic Emperors a procession of the merest parvenus? Indeed, if, as well as thinking back, he could have seen forward to Conradin and the end of the Hohenstaufens, even then the Irish family would have maintained its footing for a longer time than his.[11]

On 13 April 1608, six months after King James issued his denunciatory proclamation, the earls themselves penned a memorial to King Philip III of Spain, part of the purpose of which attempted to counteract this negative propaganda which included allegations about the falsity of their ancient ancestry. The text contained the following scenario (Table 2):

The Earls are direct descendants of King Gathelo [Goidel Glas] who was married to Scota, daughter of the Pharao King of Egypt. This Gathelo fled from the plagues with which god punished Egypt through the agency of Moses; he embarked with his people and his wife Scota and did not land until he reached Galicia and, having conquered Biscaya, Asturias and Galicia, he proclaimed himself king of that territory. One of his descendants, a king called Milesius, sent his sons with a fleet of sixty ships, which sailed from the port of La Coruña, to conquer and populate Ireland. This was one thousand years before the birth of Our Lord, according to all the ancient chronicles of Ireland …

Since the time of King Eremon who was the first conqueror of Ireland and son of the said King Milesius until the reign of King Nel [Niall of the Nine Hostages], one hundred and fifty kings of that house reigned successively. This King Nel had three sons; the eldest son and heir became king and was called Lagerio [Lóegaire]; he died without sons and in his reign the catholic faith was received in Ireland, which was about three hundred years after the birth of Christ. The other two sons of King Nel were of the one birth [i.e. twins] and from them are descended the Earls Onel and Odonel. Because of the rivalry as to which of the two houses would succeed to the kingdom of King Nel, they agreed that each would reign in turn, that is to say that when the heir of Onel was king, on his death the heir of Odonel would succeed to him, and when the latter died, the heir of Onel would reign. After that agreement there were twenty-six kings of those houses and they were kings of all Ireland.[12]

The earls derived this propagandistic account of their ancestry from the traditional Irish origin legends as outlined in texts such as the *Lebor Gabála Érenn* and in the standard interpretation of the Uí Néill pedigrees which had been in existence from

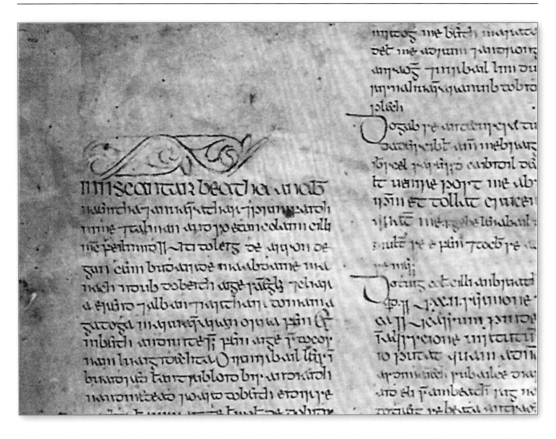

St Colum Cille remained a figure of considerable significance in the cultural life of the inhabitants of Tyrconnell as evidenced by Manus O'Donnell's compilation of *Betha Cholaim Chille* in 1532. © Bodl., Oxford

about the middle of the eighth century. Almost certainly untrue, it nonetheless reflected the earls' understanding of their background which had been current in Ireland for about eight or nine hundred years preceding the seventeenth century.

Although the Irish of the medieval period were fascinated by their own history, much of what was written about it was influenced by the propaganda requirements of the great families and the great monasteries where most of the writing was done. A substantial amount of genealogical composition exists, but it is clear that these pedigrees had been subjected to considerable manipulation and falsification, as and when circumstances required. This prompted ridicule and hostility from English servitors, as expressed in F. J. Byrne's famous observation that 'Elizabethan officials complained that most Irishmen were bastards [but] claimed to be gentlemen'.[13] More surprising, perhaps, is that those fictions continued to be believed for over a thousand years; it is only in recent times that historians have begun to see what really lies behind them.

The O'Neills of Tír Eógain ultimately derived from the Donegal kingdom of Cenél nEógain, originally based in Inishowen (Inis Eógain). Their surname comes from the king of Tara, Niall Glúndub ('Black Knee'), who died in 919, fighting the Vikings at a battle at Islandbridge in Dublin. Niall himself descended from a celebrated line of kings (Table 3). His immediate ancestors for five generations – i.e. his father, grandfather, great-grandfather, great-great-grandfather and great-great-great-grandfather – had been not only kings of their own vast territories in the north, but had also managed to secure the most important office in the country – the kingship of Tara – which they shared alternately with the Southern Uí Néill kings of the east midlands.

At that time the north of Ireland – roughly corresponding to the nine-county province of Ulster – was effectively divided into three. To the west lay the Donegal kingdoms that Niall and his family controlled directly. The collection of relatively unimportant kingdoms, the Airgialla, nestled in the middle of the province but increasingly came

Archbishop Lombard met the earls' party at the Milvian Bridge, site of the 312 battle that marked the beginning of the Emperor Constantine's conversion to Christianity. If the earls missed such symbolism, it would not have been lost on Lombard, still anxious to advance Tyrone's cause. Pieter Lastman's 'Schlacht bei der Milvischen Brücke' (1613).

under Cenél nEógain control, ultimately giving us Tír Eógain. East Ulster came under the suzerainty of the Ulaid, from whom the province of Ulster's name was derived. Tradition claimed that the Ulaid had originally ruled over everything north of the Rivers Boyne and Drowse but, certainly by the tenth century, the people who retained that name had been confined to the lands east of the Bann. At the time of Niall Glúndub the Ulaid remained nominally independent, although they had given allegiance to the kings of Tara. Niall Glúndub, however, tried but failed to make them subject to him in right of his kingship of the north.

Although Niall Glúndub provided the eponym for the O'Neills, his grandson Domnall Ua Néill was the first king to actually bear that surname.

Domnall's father for instance was not an O'Neill. Known as Muirchertach na gCochall gCroicenn, Muirchertach 'of the Leather Cloaks', he had, in his bid to become king of Tara, departed from the Grianán of Aileach just west of Derry on a famous tour of Ireland in the winter of 941. To protect his troops from the wintry weather, he allegedly dressed them in leather; hence his soubriquet. Unfortunately Donnchadh Ó Corráin has shown that the detailed account of that journey – the long poem, *A Mhuircheartaigh mhic Néill náir*, also known as the 'Mórthimpeall Érenn' – dates to more than two hundred years after the events which it purports to describe and is, in reality, a *roman-à-clef* about the affairs of a later high-king, Muirchertach Mac Lochlainn, who died in 1166.

The latter Muirchertach almost certainly lived in Derry. Muirchertach 'of the Leather Cloaks' died in 943, before he could attain his objective of the kingship of Tara. His son Domnall Ua Néill, also known as Domnall Ardmacha, became king of Tara in 956 and died in 980. He was, strictly speaking, the first of the O'Neills to have attained that kingship and also the last as no O'Neill ever again became king of Tara.

The name Niall, however, figures prominently in what might be called the 'prehistory' of the O'Neills, i.e. before they adopted the O'Neill surname. Niall Glúndub's grandfather, Niall Caille, acquired his nickname because he drowned in the river Caille or Callan in County Armagh in 846. His grandfather, Niall Frossach, 'Niall of the Showers', acquired his nickname from the miraculous shower of honey which fell at his birth allegedly on Inishowen and an ominous shower of blood that covered Leinster – the traditional enemy of his people. Other miraculous showers of silver, wheat and honey are said to have fallen on the occasion of his inauguration as king of Tara. These stories may have also reflected Niall Frossach's piety; he abdicated from the kingship of Tara about 770 and died as a pilgrim or penitent on Iona in 778.

Of course, the O'Neills had an association with an older and more famous Niall, the legendary Niall Noígiallach, Niall of the Nine Hostages, the reputed founder of the group of early ruling dynasties from various parts of Ireland collectively known as the Uí Néill, from whom both the O'Neills and the O'Donnells are traditionally said to have descended. It should be pointed out, however, that in Irish the plural of the surname O'Neill is Uí Néill, but there is a huge difference between that and the homonymous dynastic name Uí Néill.

The traditional understanding of the history of the Donegal kingdoms, which ultimately gave rise to those two families, maintained that, some time in the late fifth century, four of the sons of Niall Noígiallach – Cairpre, Conall, Énna and Eógain – had launched an invasion into that territory from Tara. The fullest account of this is found in a wonderful thirteenth-century O'Donnell propaganda text; *Gabhaltas Conaill Gulban mic Néill ar Gairbhtrian Uladh*, better known as *Echtra Conaill Gulban*.[14] The *Echtra* tells us that, having defeated and conquered the indigenous people – the Ulaid – the brothers divided the territory comprising modern County Donegal between them, each establishing a kingdom that consequently bore his name. Col-

lectively those kingdoms and their ruling dynasties became known as the Northern Uí Néill and they subsequently conquered the rest of western and central Ulster. Two of the kingdoms – Cenél nEógain in Inishowen and Cenél Conaill elsewhere in present-day Donegal – allegedly shared the overkingship of the whole territory between them. In addition, each kingdom provided alternate incumbents of the prestigious kingship of Tara.

However, that story is a later propagandistic fiction rather than a summary of what actually happened.[15] It almost certainly acquired its classical form by and on behalf of the Cenél nEógain during the reign of Áed Allán, a powerful mid-eighth-century king who died in 743. Áed's dramatic rise to power arose from violent offensives and *realpolitik*. However, a set of deliberately created fictional historical and genealogical texts framed and underlined his victories, giving his ancestors a more glorious past than they had actually enjoyed in reality.[16] Whatever the initial reaction to them, these political fictions endured and became accepted as 'history' by most commentators over the past thirteen hundred years. Áed's 'spin doctors', probably led by Congus, bishop of Armagh, (d. 750), did an astonishingly effective job, and the latter exploited the opportunity provided by his alliance with the king to advance the case for the primacy of his own church.

The historical reality, however, proved to be much more complex. Recent genealogical work almost certainly shows that neither the Cenél nEógain nor the Cenél Conaill came into Donegal from outside at all, but were actually native to it. Furthermore, the eponymous founders of those dynasties, or whatever groupings their names represented, almost certainly had no blood connection whatsoever with the allegedly Tara-based Niall Noígiallach. Instead they probably descended from the range of peoples whose origins lay in Ulster itself. The Cenél nEógain seem to have had connections with the people from County Down known as the Dál Fiatach, while the Cenél Conaill similarly seem to have been connected with the people from Antrim, Down and Louth, known as the Dál nAraidi, the Uí Echach Coba, and their namesakes the Conailli Muirtheimne. In other words, instead of the Donegal kingdoms being Uí Néill conquerors of the Ulaid as the legends suggest, it now seems clear that these people were actually Ulaid themselves.

There is a further twist to this story. The O'Donnell family represented themselves in the later middle ages as the very epitome of the Cenél Conaill but, as Dónal Mac Giolla Easpaig originally suggested,[17] it now seems clear that the O'Donnell family descended from an entirely different people, the Síl Lugdach, who originated around Gortahork (Gort a' Choirce) and Falcarragh (An Fál Carrach). Their eponym, or primary 'ancestor' figure, was the god Lug or Lugh Lamhfhada, whose cult is memorialised in that area in a number of monuments and placenames, most especially at Dunlewey (Dún Lúiche, i.e. the 'fort of Lug') and at Tullaghobegley.[18] The Cenél Conaill proper, on the other hand, had originated in the lower Finn Valley in east Donegal, the area anciently known as Mag nItha and had expanded from there up to Derry by about 578, and south through the Barnesmore Gap into the fertile lands of south Donegal by the middle of the seventh century. The Cenél nEógain from Inishowen, who themselves simultaneously moved into what are now Counties Derry and Tyrone, provided the main opposition to this expansion. At the battle of Clóitech or Clady on the Donegal/Tyrone border in 789 these two opposing kingdoms clashed. The Cenél nEógain drove their Cenél Conaill enemies out of east Donegal, and the Síl Lugdach partly filled the ensuing vacuum, appropriating the very title of the defeated Cenél Conaill in a massive display of cheek. Almost nothing is heard about the Síl Lugdach until the ninth century; they do not really figure in the records until the eleventh century, and their rise to power really begins two centuries later.

About that time the O'Donnell family emerged among the Síl Lugdach, deriving their surname from Domnall mac Échnecháin who had lived about the middle of the tenth century (Table 4) and whose brother Adhlann (d. 952) had allegedly been *comarb* (coarb, abbot) of Derry, although some confusion exists in the ancient sources between the latter ('Doire Calgach') and Doire Eithne – actually Kilmacrenan, County Donegal. Their grandfather, Dálach, became a very significant ancestral figure for the people of Donegal, most especially for the O'Donnells (alternatively known as 'Na Dálaigh').

Manus Ó Domhnaill has Colum Cille make an important, retrospective prediction about that Dálach to a sixth-century ancestor:

'Genfider mac ar do shlicht-sa ⁊ bud Daluch a ainm ⁊ is ar a shlicht beid riga & tigernadha sleachta Conaill Gulpan go brath. Acus an

uair bus mesa a shlicht coichce biaidh siad mar chach, ⁊ an uair nach bia dimgha Día orra ina mo dimgha-sa, budh ferr iad iná cach. Acus bud é an Daluch sin an sectmadh glun uaid-si fen.' Acus do fírad an faidhedóracht-sin C[olum] c[ille]. Gonad ar slicht an Daluig-sin ataid Clann Dáluig ó sin ille. Acus asse an Daluch-sin mac dob óige don cuiger mac do bi gá athair fen ⁊ nír slan dó acht a .uíí. mbliadhna ag ég dá athair uadh, ⁊ tucatar na braitri ba sine ina sé fein tigernas dó orra fen tré mirbhuilib de ⁊ C[olum] c[ille]; oir nír fédadh faidhedóracht C[olum] c[ille] do brécnugad.[19]

Despite this retrospective greatness, the *Annals of Ulster* tells us that Dálach was killed (*iugulatus est*) by his own people (*a gennte sua*) in 870.

Following the death of Domnall Ua Néill in 980, that family went into a decline among the Cenél nEógain to be replaced by the Derry-based Mac Lochlainns. It was not until the mid-thirteenth century, following war between these two families, that the O'Neills re-emerged. However, because of the belief that the O'Neills and all the Cenél nEógain were really Uí Néill, it was not until 1364 that the conservative Annals of Ulster referred to an O'Neill as 'rí Ulaidh'.[20] Later, in 1387, Niall Ua Néill legitimised his claim as king of Ulster in the eyes of the learned classes by holding a great feast for the poets of Ireland at Emain Macha.[21] F. J. Byrne highlighted an apparent paradox: 'The restoration of the name Ulster to cover once again the whole of the North was made possible only by the extinction of the kingdom of Ulaid'.[22] But the real paradox is that the O'Neills and the O'Donnells, instead of being descended from Uí Néill outsiders who had conquered Donegal in the fifth or sixth centuries, were descended from the Ulaid themselves, even if they did not know it.

Hugh O'Neill allegedly argued that he did not want to become king of Ireland, but in the event of a victory, he would offer that position to the king of Spain. However, in spite of, and maybe because of, his complicated factual and fabricated genealogy, no one was better entitled to that honour than he. The concept of the Northern Uí Néill as a group of dynasties descended from Niall Noígiallach was a propagandistic invention, most probably of the eighth century, but the earls of Tyrone and Tyrconnell, and most especially the O'Neills, could boast an ancient and noble lineage.

Notes

1 In John O'Donovan's famous translation: 'This was a distinguished crew for one ship; for it is indeed certain that the sea had not supported, and the winds had not wafted from Ireland, in modern times, a party of one ship who would have been more illustrious or noble, in point, of genealogy', (*AFM*, iv, pp 2358-9).

2 M. Kerney Walsh, *An exile of Ireland: Hugh O'Neill, prince of Ulster* (Dublin, 1996), p. 80.

3 'Peter Lombard, the archbishop of Armagh and primate of Ireland, came to them with a noble young man in his company, having a large number of coaches sent by cardinals, to meet them in that place. The steward of each in turn of a certain number of the cardinals came to them to welcome them and receive them with honour, in the cardinals' name. Then they proceeded in coaches ... They went on until they came to Rome. The Porta del Populo was the name of the gate by which they entered the city. They went on after that through the principal noble streets of Rome in great splendour. They did not rest until they reached the great church of St Peter's in the Vatican. They put up their horses there [and] entered the church. They worshipped [*do-ghníd sléachtaine*], [and] went around, as on a pilgrimage, the seven chief altars of great merit that are in the church', *Turas,* pp 266-7.

4 Manus Ó Domhnaill, *Betha Colaim Chille*, A. O'Kelleher and G. Schoepperle, (repr., Dublin, 1994), p. 210. 'Colum Cille set out then and, when he had come to within fifteen miles of Rome, all the bells of the city rang by themselves and they could not be stopped. All the people of Rome were startled and filled with wonder. "Don't be amazed at this," said the pope. "The holy patron, Colum Cille, is coming to see me and the bells rang in his honour, and they will not be silenced until he comes to the city." Then the pope went out with great honour and reverence to meet Colum Cille, together with many of the nobility of Rome. They embraced when they met each other and were truly joyful and glad towards each other. Then they returned to the city and, when Colum Cille had bowed down [*ár ndenamh sléctana*] in the great church of Rome, the bells stopped by themselves', *The Life of Colum Cille by Manus O'Donnell*, (ed. & trans.) B. Lacey (Dublin, 1998), p. 114.

5 *Betha Colaim Chille*, (eds) O'Kelleher and Schoepperle, p. 212. 'And then the pope gave important gifts to Colum Cille, that is, that, whichever of his own foundations Colum Cille would appoint as a pilgrimage destination for everyone, there should be the same indulgence there as for a pilgrimage to Rome. And, although he himself was in Scotland [at the time], the place that Colum Cille gave that honour to was Derry', *The Life of Colum Cille*, p. 114.

6 B. Lacey, 'A lost Columban turas in Derry', *Donegal Annual,* xxxix (1997), pp 39-41; idem, 'Revival or re-invention: Columban Traditions in Nineteenth-century Derry', *Ulster Folklife*, l (2004), pp 27-50, 33-34.

7 *Betha Colaim Chille*, (eds) O'Kelleher and Schoepperle, p.

6. 'And be it known to the readers of this Life that it was Manus (son of Aodh, son of Aodh Ruadh, son of Niall Garbh, son of Toirdelbach of the Wine) O'Donnell who had the part of this Life that was in Latin put into Gaelic, and the parts that were in difficult Gaelic made easy, so that it might be clearly comprehensible for all', *The Life of Colum Cille*, p. 17.

8 *Betha Colaim Chille*, (eds) O'Kelleher and Schoepperle, p. 6. 'And having developed an affection and brotherly love for his high saint and kinsman in blood, and for his own dear patron to whom he was fervently devoted, in the castle of Port na Trí Namat ... in truth, this Life was composed in the year of our Lord 1532', *The Life of Colum Cille*, p. 18.

9 Kerney Walsh, *An exile of Ireland*, p. 71.

10 B. Lacey, 'County Derry in the early historic period', in G. O'Brien, (ed.), *Derry and Londonderry: history and society* (Dublin, 1999), p. 12.

11 S. Ó Ceallaigh, *Gleanings from Ulster history* (repr., Draperstown, 1994), p. 24.

12 Kerney Walsh, *An exile of Ireland*, pp 137-8.

13 F. J. Byrne, *Irish kings and high kings* (London, 1973; repr., Dublin, 2001), p. 1.

14 M. Dobbs and S. Mac Airt, 'Conall of Tír Conaill', *Donegal Annual*, iii (1957), pp 25-65.

15 B. Lacey, *Cenél Conaill and the Donegal kingdoms: AD 500-800* (Dublin, 2006).

16 Ibid.

17 D. Mac Giolla Easpaig, 'Placenames and Early Settlement in County Donegal', in W. Nolan, L. Ronayne and M. Dunlevy, M. (eds) *Donegal: history and society* (Dublin, 1999), pp 149-82, 154-5.

18 Lacey, *Cenél Conaill and the Donegal kingdoms*, pp 84-96.

19 *Betha Colaim Chille,* (eds) O'Kelleher and Schoepperle, p. 110. 'There will be born a son of your descendants, Dálach will be his name, and there will be kings and lords of the people of Conall Gulban from his descendants forever. And at their worst times they will be like everyone else, and when God's displeasure or mine is not directed towards them they will be better than anyone. And that Dálach will be the seventh generation after yourself. That prophecy was fulfilled so that the descendants of that Dálach are the Clann Dálaigh since then. Dálach was the youngest of his father's five sons and was only seven years old when his father died. And his older brothers gave him the lordship over them through the miracles of God and Colum Cille, for it was not possible to belie his prophecy', *The Life of Colum Cille*, p. 65.

20 F. J. Byrne, *Irish kings and high-kings*, p. 129.

21 Ibid.

22 Ibid.

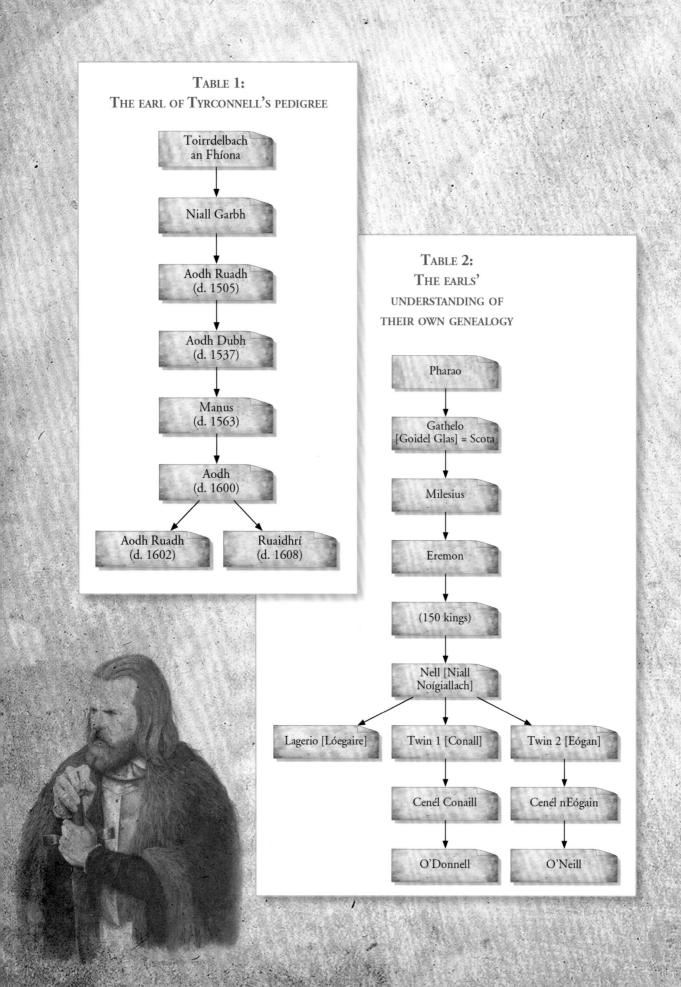

TABLE 1:
THE EARL OF TYRCONNELL'S PEDIGREE

Toirrdelbach an Fhíona
↓
Niall Garbh
↓
Aodh Ruadh (d. 1505)
↓
Aodh Dubh (d. 1537)
↓
Manus (d. 1563)
↓
Aodh (d. 1600)
↓
Aodh Ruadh (d. 1602)   Ruaidhrí (d. 1608)

TABLE 2:
THE EARLS'
UNDERSTANDING OF
THEIR OWN GENEALOGY

Pharao
↓
Gathelo [Goidel Glas] = Scota
↓
Milesius
↓
Eremon
↓
(150 kings)
↓
Nell [Niall Noígiallach]
↓
Lagerio [Lóegaire]   Twin 1 [Conall]   Twin 2 [Eógan]
↓
Cenél Conaill   Cenél nEógain
↓
O'Donnell   O'Neill

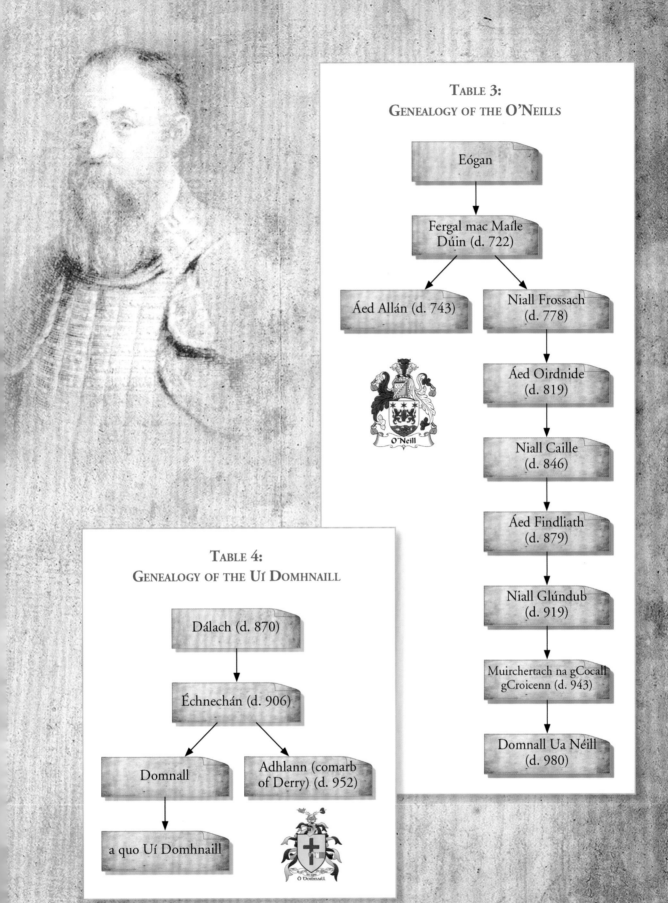

TABLE 3:
GENEALOGY OF THE O'NEILLS

Eógan

Fergal mac Maíle Dúin (d. 722)

Áed Allán (d. 743)

Niall Frossach (d. 778)

Áed Oirdnide (d. 819)

Niall Caille (d. 846)

Áed Findliath (d. 879)

Niall Glúndub (d. 919)

Muirchertach na gCocall gCroicenn (d. 943)

Domnall Ua Néill (d. 980)

O'Neill

TABLE 4:
GENEALOGY OF THE Uí Domhnaill

Dálach (d. 870)

Échnechán (d. 906)

Domnall

Adhlann (comarb of Derry) (d. 952)

a quo Uí Domhnaill

Ó Domhnaill

An Leabhar Eoghanach: clabhsúr leabhar a mhuintire

Malachy Ó Néill

Is ionann An Leabhar Eoghanach [LE] agus scéal gineolaíochta Uí Néill agus Chineáil Eoghain ó chianaimsir go dtí an seachtú haois déag. De réir mar a thagann deireadh le réimeas glórmhar Uí Néill mar dhream de mhórúdarás na hÉireann, cuirtear clabhsúr nádúrtha le ginealach maisithe Chineáil Eoghain. Is ann a aithristear scéal Uí Néill idir aimsir Néill Naoighiallaigh agus bás an Niallaigh Mhóir sa Róimh sa bhliain 1616 agus is í an iontráil atá dírithe ar Aodh Mór Ó Néill atá mar dhlaíóg mhullaigh ar an téacs. Tá LE mar chuid lárnach den chnuasach chlúiteach liteartha sin de chuid mhuintir Uí Néill, Leabhar Cloinne Aodha Buidhe [LCAB][1] Maireann dhá chóip den téacs sa ls. seo agus tá mionathruithe i bhfoirm na bhfocal agus in ord na bparagraf idir an dá chóip. Is beag difear atá i sonraí an scéil, áfach.

Léirítear san intreoir a théann le LE sa ls. gur saothraíodh an buntéacs idir 1577 agus 1580,[2] tamall de bhlianta sular rug Aodh Mór Ó Néill ar an chumhacht iomlán ó thuaidh. Is do Thoirrdhealbhach Luineach, a bhí lonnaithe ar an Srath Bán, Contae Thír Eoghain, a thiomnaítear an saothar seo ach is fiú cúpla gné a shoiléiriú maidir leis an tiomnú seo. Baineann an chéad chuid seo leis an tréimhse idir 1577 agus 1580 nuair a bhí Toirrdhealbhach Luineach i réim agus tamall sula bhfuair Aodh Mór an lámh in uachtar ó thuaidh. Cuireadh an téacs iomlán seo (.i. LCAB agus LE mar chuid de) le chéile céad bliain ina dhiaidh sin (1680) do Chormac Ó Néill ó Éadan Dúcharraige, Contae Aontroma. Ní foláir gur cuireadh iontráil Aodha Mhóir leis an téacs idir an dá linn, seal éigin idir bás Uí Néill (1616) agus toirbhirt an leabhair (1680). Deirtear ann gur chaith Aodh Mór Ó Néill 'bliaghain is fiche [i]na Thighearna', tagairt don seal idir bás Thoirealaigh Luinigh (1595) agus bás Aodha Mhóir féin (1616) nuair a bhí seilbh iomlán aige ar thiarnas Uí Néill. Is féidir gur baineadh d'iontráil Thoirrdhealbhaigh Luinigh san am céanna agus gur scríobhaí eile a chum an chuid dheireannach seo den téacs, Ruaidhrí Ó hUiginn féin, go fiú, tamall maith i ndiaidh na bliana 1580. Séard atá sa dá chóip de LE a mhaireann ná peannaireacht Ruaidhrí Uí Uiginn, scríobhaí as Contae Mhaigh Eo, a scríobh an bheirt acu. Maítear ann gur chríochnaigh sé a chuid oibre ar

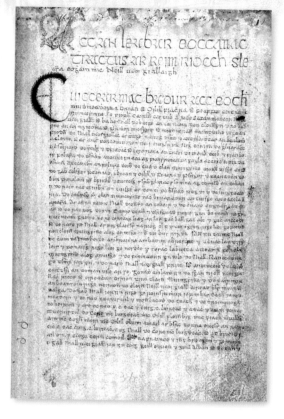

'An Leabhar Eoghanach', scéal ginealais Uí Néill agus Chineáil Eoghain ó chianaimsir go dtí an seachtú haois déag. © RIA

17 Meitheamh 1680. Tháinig an-athrú ar an dreach polaitiúil ó thuaidh sa chéad sin idir tionscnamh an téacs (c. 1580) agus scríobh LCAB sa bhliain 1680: briseadh Chionn tSáile (1601), Imeacht na nIarlaí (1607), Plándáil Uladh (1609), Éirí Amach 1641, cogadh Chromail, an Chomcheilg Phápaireachta, agus go leor eile.

Déantar fréamhacha Uí Néill Thír Eoghain a chuardach siar a fhad leis an chúigiú haois agus Niall Naoighiallach (d. 405), Rí Éireann, agus ach ab é gurbh éigean d'Aodh Mór imeacht i gcuideachta na dtaoiseach eile ó Ráth Maoláin, is féidir gur deireadh eile ar fad a bheadh ar an saothar seo.

Is iomaí craobh de bhunadh Uí Néill a fheictear sa scéal teaghlaigh seo agus is iomaí casadh a fheictear sa ghinealach féin de réir mar a bhogtar ríghe agus tiarnas ó dhream amháin go dream eile, a thugann an-léiriú agus an-léargas ar chomharbas Gaelach. Tá tábhacht nach beag leis an dearbhfhine, an córas ceapacháin a bhí ag na Gaeil chun comharba ríoga a roghnú. Níor chloígh teaghlaigh ríoga na hÉireann le *primogeniture*, an dóigh a dtoghtar monarc na Breatáine agus ríthe eile de chuid na hEorpa agus ar fud na cruinne go fóill sa lá atá inniu ann. Ba chóras ar leith é de chuid na nGael an dearbhfhine. Níor tugadh tús áite don mhac is sine ag an rí mar

Lámh dhearg Uladh, an Niallach ag teacht go hÉirinn.

a tharlaíonn nuair a chloítear le *primogeniture*. Ba leithne i bhfad an rogha a bhí ar fáil ag na hoifigigh a d'oirnigh an rí úr i gcóras na nGael. Bhí ceithre ghlúin i gceist leis an dearbhfhine: athair mór an rí reatha agus seacht n-aicme eile:[3] athair mór an rí; clann an rí; athair an rí; dearthaíreacha an rí; clanna dhearthaíreacha an rí; dearthaíreacha athair an rí; clanna dhearthaíreacha an rí agus clann clainne dhearthaíreacha an rí.

Is féidir an córas *patrilinear* a fheiceáil agus é i bhfeidhm i laethanta tosaigh Chineáil Eoghain. Bogtar an ríghe idir athair agus mac ó Eochaidh Muighmheadhóin (b. 365) go dtí Aodh Uairiodhnach (b. 607), agus is annamh a fheictear rídhamhna nár shuigh a athair ar 'leac na rí' ag dul chun tosaigh mar rí an chineáil.[4] Pléitear seacht rí is daichead sa ghinealach ar fad[5] idir Eochaidh Muighmheadhóin (b. 365) agus Aodh Mór Ó Néill (b. 1616) agus tá cúig athrú is daichead le feiceáil sa ríghe: aistrítear an ríghe ó athair go mac in aon chás is tríocha acu. Mar sin de, cé nár chloígh Gaeil Éireann le *primogeniture*, níor imigh córas na dearbhfhine i bhfad ar strae ó fhuil ríoga Chineáil Eoghain ach oiread.

Is fiú go mór nóta a dhéanamh anseo ar chúrsaí sloinnte, ar a dtionscnamh agus ar na nósanna a théann leo. Ní cuntas ar chlann Uí Néill amháin

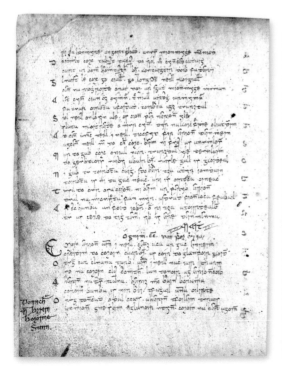

'Imdha sichar ag siol Neill'; 'Coróin Eirionn ainm Í Neill'; 'Maith do suidhigheadh siol Neill', dánta a bhronn Tadhg Dáll Ó hUiginn, Fearflatha Ó Gnímh agus Fearghal Óg Mac an Bhaird ar Thoirrdhealbhach Ó Néill, pátrún *An Leabhar Eoghanach*.
© Meamram Páipéar Ríomhaire le Caoinchean Clonalis House/Teach Cluain Mhalais

é LE ná orthu siúd amháin a tugadh 'Ó Néill' mar shloinne orthu; tá go leor sloinnte le fáil go flúirseach sa lá atá inniu ann i gCúige Uladh (Ó Néill, Ó Coinn, Ó Donnaile, Ó Catháin, Ó Dochartaigh, Ó Domhnaill, Ó Baoill, Ó Gallchóir, agus go leor eile) a bhfuil baint acu le sliocht Néill Naoighiallaigh.[6]

Bíonn go leor den bharúil gur Niallaigh iad uilig an dream a shíolraigh ó Niall Naoighiallach agus *faux pas* nádúrtha atá ann. Ní hamhlaidh an scéal, áfach, ar ndóigh agus níor baineadh feidhm as an teideal sin 'Ó Néill' go dtí an dara mílaois agus Niall eile ar fad a bhí i gceist .i. Niall Glúndubh, Rí Éireann (b. 919). Ar shliocht Néill Ghlúnduibh a cuireadh an sloinne 'Ó Néill' i dtosach báire.

Ba é an tábhacht le fréamhacha an duine, le cúlra, le dúchas agus le sinsir a chuir béim faoi leith ar luach an ghinealaigh in Éirinn san aimsir seo. Tá ginealaigh na hÉireann ar cheann de na seánraí is tábhachtaí i litríocht na nGael agus is ón bhéaloideas a breacadh an chéad chuid acu i dtrátha na séú haoise. Is mó bolg soláthair na nGael sa ghort seo ná na caipéisí scríofa atá ar fáil i dtír ar bith eile de chuid na hEorpa.[7]

Bhí tréimhsí ann, ar ndóigh, nuair a theip ar mhuintir Uí Néill taoisigh eile Chineáil Eoghain a cheansú. Is dual d'fhoinsí ginealaigh a bheith claonta ó tharla go bhfuil clú agus oidhreacht ghrúpa amháin á cheiliúradh iontu. Ní eisceacht é LE claonta ar fad: admhaítear ann gur le Mac Lochlainn a thit tiarnaí Uí Néill idir 1033 agus 1160, ach ní ghlactar leo mar rí an chineáil sa téacs in aon chor. Cruthaíonn an claontas seo deacrachtaí do lucht na staire ó tharla nach 'impartial history' é,[8] ach aithnítear gur nasc iad na tiarnaí seo idir dream 1033 agus Aodh 'an Macaomh Tóinleasc' (b. 1177) ónar shíolraigh an ríora. Ba í a stair féin í mar a thuig siad féin í.

Cruthaítear ann 'ríthe' de mhuintir Uí Néill don tréimhse sin nuair a bhí an lámh in uachtar ag Mac Lochlainn, rud a fhágann líne ghlan dhaingean de bhunadh Uí Néill i gceannas ar an tuaisceart agus a thugann seasmhacht do chomharbaí na gceannairí seo a tháinig i réim ina ndiaidh: an ghlúin a thionscain LE, mar shampla. Cibé scoilt a bhí idir Uí Néill an Tuaiscirt san am (1680), bhí na bunfhréamhacha ginealaigh céanna ag Cormac Ó Néill, pátrún LCAB, is a bhí ag Seán an Díomais, ag Toirrdhealbhach Luineach agus ag Aodh Mór féin.

Is ar charachtar i bhfad siar sa stair a fhilleann an mhórchuid de na ginealaigh, figiúr neamhshaolta a

bhíonn i gceist minic go leor. Baineann na Sasanaigh agus na Lochlannaigh feidhm as an té céanna mar atá Woden,[9] agus is doiligh muinín iomlán a chur sna taifid luatha seo, go háirithe sa phearsanra a bhaineann leis an tréimhse réamh-Chríostaí.[10] I gcomhthéacs na hÉireann, cruthaíodh nasc le Míl na Spáinne, figiúr miotaseolaíoch a ndearnadh comhshinsear na nGael ar fad de[11] Is mó an *corpus* atá ar fáil i nginealaigh na hÉireann roimh A.D. 1200 ná an méid atá ar fáil do thír ar bith eile de chuid na hEorpa agus is ó thobar an eolais seo a fhaightear ginealaigh cheannairí na tíre, mar atá againn in LE.

Tá áit ag an ghinealach i gcroílár chorp na staire ó tharla go gcruthaítear ann comhthéacs réadúil stairiúil do bheathaisnéisí agus scéalta a mhaireann i stair an phobail. Is leis an ardaicme a bhaineann an chuid is mó acu agus cuirtear ar chumas an léitheora tuiscint ar leith a aimsiú ar an dóigh ar mhair ríthe agus flatha na cianaimsire, ar an tsochaí féin agus ar na nósanna a cleachtaíodh san am. Ba i bhfoirm filíochta a caomhnaíodh an t-eolas seo roimh theacht na Críostaíochta go hÉirinn agus maireann iarsmaí den fhilíocht sna ginealaigh féin.

Méadaítear léargas an léitheora le scéilíní agus le ranna filíochta; pléitear cúrsaí polaitíochta agus eachtraí cogaíochta; soiléirítear teorainneacha ársa cúigeacha nach bhfuil ann dóibh sa lá atá inniu ann; agus tráchtar ar chúrsaí dlí agus socheolaíochta. Is iomaí scéal atá le haimsiú in LE: an scéilín faoi Niall Naoighiallach a thug póg don arracht ag an tobar chun uisce a fháil dó féin agus dá dheartháireacha; nó an bhreith a thug Niall Frassach ag Aonach Taillten don bhean a mhaígh nárbh eol di athair a mic. Tugtar creatlach don stair tríd an ghinealach ina bhfuil leanúnachas agus comharbas le sonrú agus is féidir aithne áirithe a chur ar na carachtair éagsúla a thagann chun cinn mar ríthe cineáil. Is é an creatlach leanúnach seo atá mar bhunchloch sa LE.

D'éirigh le Cineál Eoghain spréadh amach ó Inis Eoghain de réir a chéile tríd an tuaisceart agus an ruaig a chur ar Uí Tuirtre ó lár Chúige Uladh.[12] Ba dhream iad Uí Tuirtre a bhain le hOirghialla ach cuireadh faoi chois iad agus glacadh seilbh ar a gcuid tailte de réir mar a chuaigh Uí Néill an Tuaiscirt chun cinn. Thit an scoilt idir dhá shliocht Néill – Uí Néill an Deiscirt agus Uí Néill an Tuaiscirt – ar leataobh ón aonú haois déag i leith agus bhí ionad cumhachta Uí Néill socraithe ó thuaidh faoin am seo.[13] Rinneadh dún daingean den tuaisceart go léir agus socraíodh ceannáras nua do Chineál Eoghain ag Tulach Óg, Contae Thír Eoghain, faoin am a raibh na Normannaigh ag triall ar an deisceart. Úsáidtear an téarma 'Rí Éireann' nó 'Ardrí Éireann' uair déag in LE chun cur síos ar cheannairí áirithe Chineáil Eoghain.[14] Tugtar an teideal céanna ar an triúr is túisce a luaitear sa téacs chomh maith, mar atá Eochaidh Muighmheadhóin (§1), Niall Naoighiallach (§2) agus Lughaidh mac Laoghaire (nach mbaineann leis an ghinealach). Ní thugtar 'Rí Éireann' ar Eoghan féin, ná ar a mhac, Muireadhach ('Rí Ailigh' an bheirt acu), ach ba é Muircheartach Mac Earca (§5) an chéad rí de Chineál Eoghain a shuigh mar Ard-Ríghe, de réir LE.

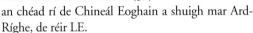

Tullach Óg, an cnoc ar a n-oirnítí Ó Néill.

Tá clú leitheadach ar an teideal a bhaineann le hArdríghe Éireann agus Cnoc na Teamhrach, ach is fiú a thabhairt faoi deara gur mhó i gcónaí an teideal ná an chumhacht a bhain leis. Bhí *tuath* ar leith faoi cheannas ag gach rí sa tír agus b'amhlaidh an cás don té a raibh Ard-Ríghe Éireann ina sheilbh aige. Níor rí uilechumhachtach é ó cheann ceann na tíre, stádas a chuirtear chun cinn mar gheall ar an teideal féin a cruthaíodh sna meánaoiseanna.[15] Ba é 'Rí Ailigh' nó 'Rí Uladh' an teideal a bhronntaí ar ríthe eile Chineáil Eoghain atá le fáil sa ghinealach agus bhí suí rí na nEoghanach ag Aileach in Inis Eoghain, Contae Dhún na nGall sular bogadh go Tulach Óg, Contae Thír Eoghain é ag tús na dara mílaoise.[16]

Thugtaí 'Rí Ailigh' ar rí Chineáil Eoghain go fóill, ach oirníodh an rí ag Tulach Óg, Contae Thír Eoghain, agus cuireadh sa 'mausoleum regum' iad in Ard Mhacha i ndeireadh na mbeart.[17] Ba le muintir Uí Ágáin an t-ionad ríoga sin ag Tulach Óg nuair a aistríodh ceannáras Chineáil Eoghain ó Aileach in Inis Eoghain ag tús na dara mílaoise. Bogadh 'Leac na Rí' chuig an ionad úr seo agus tugadh ról faoi leith do mhuintir Uí Ágáin sa searmanas a bhain le hoirniú Uí Néill ag Tulach Óg ina dhiaidh sin.

Is é dul chun cinn Uí Néill an Tuaiscirt atá i gceist in LE ó tharla gur cumadh an téacs le freastal ar riachtannais Uí Néill Thír Eoghain ag deireadh an séú haois déag. 'Ulaidh' a thugtaí ar thuaisceart na tíre sular cuireadh deireadh le ríocht Uladh le dul chun cinn Uí Néill ó thuaidh ón chúigiú haois i leith. Brúdh fir Uladh chuig imeall an chúige, ar

chósta an oirthuaiscirt, agus ghlac Cineál Eoghain seilbh iomlán ar lár Uladh de réir a chéile. Faoi dheireadh ghlac siad le teideal 'Rí Uladh' sa tríú haois déag agus nuair a chuir Domhnall Caol Ó Néill (.i. Domhnall Mac Bhriain Chatha Dúin, b. 1325) scéal chuig an Phápa sa bhliain 1317, shínigh sé an litir 'Donaldus Oneill Rex Ultoniae'.[18]

Le blianta beaga anuas tá géineolaithe in Institiúid Smurfit atá mar chuid de Choláiste na Tríonóide, Baile Átha Cliath, i ndiaidh taighde a fhoilsiú a mhaíonn gur shíolraigh duine as gach dáréag d'Éireannaigh ár linne ó Niall Naoighiallach.[19] Feictear gur in iarthuaisceart na tíre a mhaireann an chuid is mó dá shliocht agus creidtear go bhfuil baint fola ag fear as gach cúigear le Niall Naoighiallach sa chearn sin den tír.

Maireann trí mhilliún de shliocht Néill ar fud an domhain de réir an staidéir seo a rinneadh. Bunaítear an taighde ar Y-chromasóm atá le haimsiú go fóill i sliocht Néill sa lá atá inniu ann. Rinneadh mionscrúdú ar an chromasóm i gColáiste na Tríonóide agus chonacthas gur iompraíodh an cromasóm gan athrú idir athair agus mac. Bailíodh samplaí seileagair ó shaorálaithe ar fud na hÉireann agus rinneadh taifead den áit inar rugadh a n-athair mór. Fuarthas an cromasóm ceannann céanna in ocht faoin chéad de mhéarloirg na samplaí agus treisíodh an ceangal leis an iarthuaisceart, áit a raibh an cromasóm le feiceáil in 21 faoin chéad dc na samplaí.

Is é an tomhas a bhí ag na taighdeoirí gur mhair sinsear na ndaoine seo (an chéad duine a raibh an cromasóm ar leith seo ann) timpeall 1,700 bliain ó shin. Dar le *Annála Ríoghachta Éireann*, rinneadh Rí Éireann de Niall Naoighiallach ag Teamhair sa bhliain 379, dáta atá ag teacht leis an tomhas gurbh eisean sinsear na líne fola seo. Cuireann an tiúchan fola agus loirg Y-chromasóim san iarthuaisceart leis an chás chomh maith agus is é an ceantar sin, iarthuaisceart na tíre, an áit is flúirsí do shleachta Néill Naoighiallaigh sa lá atá inniu ann.[20]

Is ar scáth a chéile a mhaireann an dá eolaíocht seo sa lá atá inniu ann, ginealas agus géineolaíocht. Teastaíonn ó dhaoine go fóill tuiscint a bheith acu ar an chianaimsir ach tá cíocras úr orthu anois léiriú gur mhair na daoine seo ar an fhód chéanna mar

Armas Uí Néill. © Halla na Cathrach, Doire

Bás Aoidh Mhóir Uí Néill as *Annála Ríoghachta Éireann*
(1616). © RIA

a seasann siad féin ag tús na dara mílaoise. Freasta-
laíonn an ghéineolaíocht ar an riachtanas seo anois
ar dhóigh anois atá inchurtha leis an dóigh a bhfuil
lucht an ghinealais á sásamh leis na cianta agus ba
chuid an-tábhachtach go deo de sheanchóras na
nGael é an ginealas; ealaíon a bhí ann, ceird a bhí
teoranta don lucht léinn agus don aos dána.

Ba é an file a chaomhnaigh an seanchas seo de
ghnáth agus oileadh ábhar filí chuige sin. Ba dhual-
gas ar leith é ag an fhile eolas a chur ar stair agus ar
ghinealach mhuintir a phátrúin agus ba mhinic an
t-eolas sin mar bhunchloch ag a chuid filíochta.[21]
B'ionann stair agus stádas, cuimhne agus cumhacht. An file a raibh stair an chineáil ar a thoil
aige, b'fhurasta dó stádas an phátrúin a ardú agus a
chanadh ina chuid saothar. Bhí cumhacht faoi leith
ina láimh aige, cumhacht draíochta go fiú, a chuir
ar a chumas an stair a lúbadh agus a athmhúnlú de
réir a mhéine féin agus is mar chuid den traidisiún
seo a cuireadh LE i dtoll a chéile.

Luaitear seacht bpríomhphearsa is daichead sa
téacs ar fad: ríthe agus taoisigh, iarlaí agus flatha.
Tuilleann daichead is a cúig acu sliocht dóibh
féin in LE agus roinntear sliocht amháin idir beirt
mhac de chuid Mhuircheartaigh Mhic Earca, mar
atá Domhnall Ilchealgach agus a bhráthair, Fearghus, a raibh comhréimeas acu i ndiaidh a n-athar.
Tugtar an buneolas céanna ar an tromlach acu:
na páistí a rugadh dóibh; máithreacha na bpáistí;
scéilíní faoina saol; na cathanna inar throid siad;
agus an dóigh a ndeachaigh siad in éag i ndeireadh
na mbeart. Leantar den scéal le tuarascálacha ina
bpléitear na gnéithe céanna de bheatha a gcom-
harba. Tugtar níos mó eolais sa téacs, ar ndóigh,
ar na príomh-cheannródaithe i stair mhuintir
Néill. Osclaítear an cuntas le cur síos ar Eochaidh
Muighmheadhóin ach is í breith Néill Naoighiallaigh an ghné is tábhachtaí de shaol a athar. Tugtar
beathaisnéis Néill agus leantar ar aghaidh lena mhac
shíolraitheach, Eoghan, ónar shíolraigh Cineál
Eoghain uile. Cuirtear síos ar ríthe na gCineálacha,
ríthe Ailigh agus ar ríthe na hÉireann ach léann sé
mar ghinealach ar dhream amháin a raibh sé ar a
gcumas acu dul siar a fhad le Niall Naoighiallach
agus a athair, Eochaidh Muighmheadhóin, chun
a mbuanseasmhacht féin a léiriú. Tar éis Eoghain,
tagann a mhac, Muireadhach, agus cuirtear síos ar
phríomhphearsana Chineáil Eoghain sa dóigh sin
go mbainimid Aodh Mór amach ag deireadh na
séú haoise déag.

Is iad na ceannairí eile a raibh go leor tábhachta
ag baint leo chun cur síos níb iomláine a fháil sa

téacs ná Muircheartach Mac Earca, Domhnall Ilchealgach agus Fearghus Mac Mhuircheartaigh Mhic Earca, Aodh Uairiodhnach, Fearghal Mac Maoldúin, Niall Frassach, Aodh Oirdnidhe, Niall Caille, Aodh Finnliath, Niall Glúndubh, Muircheartach na gCochall gCraiceann, Domhnall Ard Macha, Aodh Craoibhe Tulcha, Flaithbheartach an Trostáin, Aodh 'an Macaomh Tóinleasc', Brian Chatha Dúin, Domhnall Caol, Aodh an Fhraochmhoighe agus Niall Óg. Na taoisigh eile a bhfuil trácht déanta orthu sa téacs, ní thuilleann siad ach cúpla líne: a dteacht chun cinn mar cheannaire, a gcuid éachtaí sa ríghe agus a mbás. Toirrdhealbhach Luineach, go fiú, an fear a luaitear agus a mholtar go hard na spéire sa chéad pharagraf den réamhrá, ní thugtar ach cúpla líne dó sa téacs féin, cé go dtráchtar air nuair a bhíothas á threascairt nó á thuargaint ag Aodh Mór i mbáire na fola.

Is é Aodh Mór an té is mó clú as na ceannairí seo uile go léir sa lá atá inniu ann agus is féidir a rá gurb é an t-aistear áirithe sin ó Ráth Maoláin is cúis le cuid mhór den chlú sin. Scéal iontach é scéal a bheathasan agus maidir lena shinsir, tá an scéal iontach sin faoi chaibidil in An Leabhar Eoghanach.

'Toirrdhealbhach Ó Néill', pictiúr a tharraing Barnaby Googe i 1575. ©TNA

Nótaí

1 *ARÉ*, 24 p. 33. www.isos.dias.ie.

2 Bhí Ruaidhrí m. Maghnusa m. Donnchadha Í Chatháin 'ina thríath for Chiannachta' agus Seaán m. Oilbhérus Búrc 'ina Mhac Uilliam Íachtair' san am. Bádh Aibhne Ó Catháin sa Bhanna sa bhliain 1577 gur oirníodh Ruaidhrí m. Mhánuis m. Dhonnchaidh ina ionad (*ARÉ* 1577) agus cailleadh 'Mac Uilliam Búrc Seáin m. Oilibhéaruis m. Sheáin' sa bhliain 1580 gur oirníodh Risteard in Iarainn ina ionad (*ARÉ* 1580). Ní foláir gur idir an dá bhliain sin a tionscnaíodh *LE*.

3 F. J. Byrne, *The rise of the Uí Néill high-kingship* (Dublin, 1969), pp 122-3.

4 Idem, *Irish kings and high-kings* (London, 1973), p. xxxix.

5 Féach Aguisín I: 'Príomhphearsana' in LE.

6 M. Ó Néill, 'Niall Naoighiallach agus a shliocht', *An tUltach*, Eanáir 2006.

7 N. Ó Muraíle, (ed.), *Leabhar Mór na nGenealach: The Great Book of Irish Genealogies, compiled (1645-66) by Dubhaltach Mac Fhirbhisigh*, i, *Pre-Gaels; early Gaels; Northern and Southern Uí Néill; Connachta* (Dublin, 2003), p. ix.

8 S. Ó Ceallaigh, *Gleanings from Ulster history* (Cork, 1951), p. 85.

9 J. Ingram, *The Anglo-Irish Chronicle* (London, 1893).

10 T. F. O'Rahilly, *Early Irish history and mythology* (Dublin, 1946), p. 267.

11 Ó Muraíle (ed.), *Leabhar Mór na nGenealach: The Great Book of Irish Genealogies*, p. 10; J. Carey, 'Did the Irish come from Spain?: the legend of Milesius', *History Ireland*, ix, no. 3 (2001), pp 8-11.

12 Byrne, *Irish kings and high-kings*, p. 112.

13 Ibid., p. xxxi.

14 Muircheartach mac Earca (b. 534); Domhnall Ilchealgach (b. 561) agus Fearghus (b. 566), Aodh Uairiodhnach (b. 612); Fearghal mac Maoldúin (b. 722); Niall Frasach (b. 778); Aodh Oirdnidhe (b. 819); Niall Caille (b. 846); Aodh Finnliath (b. 879); Niall Glúndubh (b. 919); agus Domhnall Ard Macha (b. 980).

15 Byrne, *Irish kings and high-kings*, p. 42.

16 Ibid., p. 94; D. Ó Doibhlin (ed.), *O'Neill's own country and its families* (Monaghan, 1996), pp 12-16.

17 Byrne, *Irish kings and high-kings*, p. 125.

18 D. Flanagan and L. Flanagan, *Irish place names* (Baile Átha Cliath, 1994), pp 4-5.

19 L. Moore *et al*, 'A Y-chromosome signature of hegemony in Gaelic Ireland', *American Journal of Human Genetics* (Smurfit Institute of Genetics and School of Histories and Humanities, Coláiste na Tríonóide, Baile Átha Cliath, 2006), pp 334-8.

20 Ó Néill, 'Niall Naoighiallach agus a Shliocht', pp 8-9.

21 J. Carney (ed.), *The Irish bardic poet* (Baile Átha Cliath, 1967), p. 10.

'Saint Patrick blesh vs': *Captain Thomas Stukeley*, textual quirks and the Nine Years War

Kevin De Ornellas

In the anonymous 1605 play, *Captain Thomas Stukeley*, a gang of Irish rebels approach an English garrison at Dundalk. The action is set some time in the 1560s. It is rare enough to see such an Irish-based event in a late-Elizabethan / early Jacobean play. However, what makes this particular scene remarkable is that just after the scene is described through the anonymous dramatist's dialogue and stage directions the same scene is replayed again. Even for the standards of the ephemeral play quarto of the period, *Captain Thomas Stukeley* is a muddled, disorganised text. Inchoate, discombobulated 'bad' quartos of the early 1600s are common; but the repetition of a scene is extremely unusual. The inherent unusualness of this repetition immediately confers an antiquarian curiosity to this particular scene and to the play as a whole. The present author would argue that the disparate way in which the Irish characters are constructed in the two versions of the scenes carries much cultural significance.

In the first version of the scene the Irish speak almost as English characters would – with sober, controlled, conventional early modern blank verse. In the second version, though, the characters have become 'stage Irishmen', racially 'othered' rogues who speak in lowly prose with sibilant slurring – and, crucially, with the addition of some authentic Irish-language words. This essay contends that the change in the construction of the Irish characters carries with it a substantial amount of freight for cultural historians to intercept. Similarly, it is argued here that the second version of the scene is written some time during the Nine Years War, and that its simultaneous construction of racially stereotyped yet more authentically Irish warriors suggests a clear anxiety about how Irish characters should be portrayed on stage. As the play was published just two years before the flight of the earls, one could suggest that the

Sir Thomas Stukeley (c. 1525-78), the notorious English courtier, pirate, adventurer and soldier. He died at the Battle of Alcazar (Morocco) in 1578, while serving in the army of King Sebastian 'The Desired' of Portugal.

often-overlooked text of *Captain Thomas Stukeley* reflects a growing English anxiety about the Nine Years War. The scene is rewritten in a manner that tells us that the audience is being invited to laugh ever more heartily at the hapless Irish characters – but the authentic Irish words and the slack-jawed satire both work to betray an anxiety. Only a serious threat is worth laughing at. So what seems like a quirk of late Elizabethan drama and / or early Jacobean printing becomes crucial for those seeking to gauge English attitudes towards Ulster prior to the flight. The dramatist tries hard to rewrite a scene that will encourage the audience to laugh at this 1560s-set drama of the abortive approach on the English at Dundalk. A similar attack in 1605 might not be so hapless. Rather than demonising the Irish, the rewritten scene reveals deep-seated English anxieties about the seeming intractability of their ever-repetitive efforts to pacify Ireland.

Having argued for the general marginality of Ireland in English Renaissance drama, the next section of the essay will introduce *Captain Thomas Stukeley* and its messy text, while highlighting its importance as a source text for English attitudes towards Ireland. The final section offers a straightforward 'compare and contrast' reading of the two versions of the Dundalk scene, concluding by insisting that the scene affords us an insight into early seventeenth-century English anxieties about the durability of the Irish resistance to England's ongoing imperial adventure in Ireland. The conditions of early modern drama before the publication of *Captain Thomas Stukeley* (1605) were not conducive to sustained dramatic engagements with the Irish problem. To read through the accounts of the businessman and theatre producer Philip Henslowe is to confront a lot of realities about theatre of the late Elizabethan period.[1] English Renaissance drama was commercial, organised on sophisticated financial models whereby the playing companies performed in their permanent playhouses and toured the country and beyond working on strict budgets. As well as depending on public support, the companies relied on patronage – official patrons ranged from rich noblemen to, after 1603, the monarch himself. Early modern dramatic writing was, at this point, also primarily collaborative – with very few plays being composed by a single playwright. Henslowe's accounts are packed with references to multi-author payments and payments for additions or rewrites. The cult of the dramatic author was non-existent. Most play quartos were published anonymously in the years before the cult of the playwright became cemented with the publication of the Ben Jonson and William Shakespeare Folios of 1616 and 1623. In addition, censorship presented a major hazard for early modern dramatists. Naturally dramatists sought to avoid annoying the Master of the Revels with overt jibes about monarchical and Privy Council policies in Ireland or anywhere else.[2] In other words, early modern drama comprised a fast-moving, written-to-order medium; an art form not conducive to sustained lucumbrations about the complexities of the Irish situation.

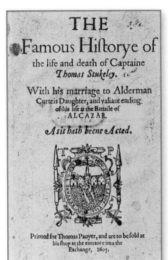

Title page of *Captain Thomas Stukeley*. © Cambridge University Library

Prose and poetry writers – John Derricke and Edmund Spenser immediately come to mind – had the opportunity to produce long, involved works about the efficacy of Elizabethan subjugation of the Irish. Playwrights had no such luxury. Writing popular drama for a mass audience, they could refer to Ireland only in passing or very allusively. It is perhaps unsurprising, then, that references to the conflict with the remaining rumps of Irish resistance are conspicuous through their absence. Ireland is alluded to rather than addressed in detail. Take, for example, the corpus of Shakespeare. In the *Henry IV* plays, written in the late 1590s, a determined Welsh rebel resists a troubled English king. Glendower is articulate and civilised – but in his detestation of the English he is brutal and ruthless too. It is easy to surmise that a late-1590s audience may have seen in the construction of Glendower a sort of unspoken analogy to the

complicated, troublingly half-English and half-Irish figure of Hugh O'Neill. This is also a back projection from contemporary critical preoccupations. While the two *Henry IV* plays may *allude* to Ireland, they cannot be said to be *about* Ireland. Similarly, *Macbeth* (1606) overtly refracts anxieties about the Union of Crowns (1603) and Gunpowder Plot (1605) and inspires fear of professional treason, but its investment in discourses about 'regime change' and 'cross-border' interference may suggest that Shakespeare had half an eye on the ongoing changes in Ulster. But it is not reasonable to assert that *Macbeth* is *about* Ireland. Similarly, *The Tempest*, one of Shakespeare's final plays, may allude to Ireland because its depiction of an island exploited by colonial powers works as an abstraction of all colonial adventures.[3] The play alludes to Ireland rather than actually engaging with the specifics of the Irish question.

When Ireland is mentioned directly in Shakespearean drama, there is often a vaguely racist joke – if, that is, it is not anachronistic to think of racism as a clearly defined phenomenon in those pre-Enlightenment times. For example, in *The Comedy of Errors* Dromio of Syracuse delivers a hideous burlesque of the blazon, as he compares the grotesque body of a kitchen-maid to the earth:

DROMIO OF SYRACUSE:
She is spherical, like a globe. I could find out countries in her.

ANTIPHOLUS OF SYRACUSE:
In what part of her body stands Ireland?

DROMIO OF SYRACUSE:
Marry, sir, in her buttocks. I found it out by the bogs.[4]

The connection made here between Ireland and a sort of sodden anality is obvious – but no more obvious than the masculine fear of the fully-grown woman in full feminine corporality. In other words, Dromio delivers an ephemeral conceit, an elaborate but fundamentally insubstantial comparison of the basest part of a base female with the supposed base-ness of wild, kern-infested Ireland.[5] In a play written perhaps just a year or two before Shakespeare's early comedy, Christopher Marlowe dramatises an historical English nobility worrying about the rebellious O'Neills. In the 1594-published *Edward II*, set in the early fourteenth century, Lancaster complains that Edward's dalliances are distracting the English from the dangerous resistance to their foreign interests:

LANCASTER:
Look for rebellion, look to be depos'd.
Thy garrisons are beaten out of France,
And lame and poor lie groaning at the gates.
The wild O'Neill with swarms of Irish kerns,
Lives uncontroll'd within the English pale.[6]

Annoying, massed and noisome, the Irish warriors are like an invasion of insects that will infest the English realm, Marlowe's character may refer to an Irish rebel of the 1300s, but, of course, the 1590s audience will think about Hugh O'Neill, the contemporary thorn in the English side. Again, though, Ireland is a mere detail in a play that delivers a more generalised depiction of a crisis-immersed English monarch. The play is *about* the clash between private satisfaction and political duty, not *about* Ireland.

For a play to be said to be about Ireland, it must have Irish characters and an Irish location. Thirty-three plays dating from 1588 to 1645 have Irish characters – though the vast majority of these characters are very minor.[7] Few of these plays have any sort of Irish location. One of the more substantial English dramatic investments in Irish issues is Shakespeare's 1599 history play, *Henry V*. There, in a much-analysed passage, an Irish mercenary, Captain Macmorris, seems to undermine the king's patriotic integrity by lambasting any concept of national service, concluding that his nation – any nation – is 'a villain and a bastard and a knave and a rascal'.[8] Critics have also seized on the play's very contemporary reference to the real-life mission of the earl of Essex.[9] The chorus, briefly disregarding historical events in France to mention real-life events of the present-day, anticipates that Essex will return to London having 'rebellion broachèd on his sword'.[10] I would argue that plays of the period worked more to make audiences forget about national embarrassments such as the Essex débâcle rather than to engage thoughtfully with them. A

letter dating from late 1599 suggests that the earl of Southampton consciously watched plays to forget about politics – and about the Essex failure in particular; he passed 'away the Tyme in London merely in going to Plaies euery day'.[11] In other words, Southampton attended plays not to think about Ireland but to consciously *not* think about Ireland. Early modern playwrights could not or would not engage directly with the Irish problem. This lacuna can be filled to an extent by *Captain Thomas Stukeley*, a play written some time around the beginning of the Nine Years War and published near its end, with Irish characters who change from one version of a scene to another.

Only one early text of *Captain Thomas Stukeley* is extant: the highly corrupt 1605 quarto. The title-page furnishes readers with the basic plot: the Famous Historye of the life and death of Captaine *Thomas Stukeley*. With his marriage to Alderman Curteis Daughter, and valiant ending of his life at the Battle of Alcazar.[12] The play centres on an ambitious but hopelessly impetuous young unthrift, Stukeley, and its action seems to take place from the early 1550s and ends in 1578. He marries Nell Curtis, to the chagrin of his rival, Vernon. Stukeley abandons Nell to fight against Shane O'Neill and other Irish rebels. Travelling from one country to the next, constantly seeking 'honour', Stukeley arrives in Spain (enjoying an encounter with the Spanish queen) and later fights in King Sebastian of Portugal's hare-brained attack on the Moors in northern Africa. Like Stukeley, Sebastian dies young: the play ends with the rather anti-climatic death of Stukeley at the hands of African-based Italians. This death is anti-climatic simply because the story of Stukeley's death has already been told, a fact which alone encapsulates the inherent disorder of the text.

There are other problems. It is impossible to work out from the dialogue whether two Moorish characters, Muly Hamet and Muly Mahamet, are one and the same person. The play starts with reasonable order – the opening scenes in London and the Irish scenes (barring the anomalous repeated scene) progress smoothly enough, before degenerating into chronological chaos in the later continental European and African scenes. This textual disorder reflects the disorder of Stukeley's mind: as he gets more messily involved in the internal affairs of other nations, so the text gets more muddled up in narrative confusion. The play, then, may work as a morality play about reckless, parent-ignoring youth; or it may function as a tragic warning about England's propensity to get involved in scarcely understood military adventures far afield. The play is identified as a history play on the title-page. The character of Stukeley is based on the real-life adventurer, Thomas Stukeley (c. 1520-78).[13] The play offers an abbreviated and only slightly sensationalised account of the historical individual's activities. It is also a hotchpotch of various genres as well as that of the history play; a prodigal son play gone wrong, in which a careless youngster is not tamed of his wild ways and winds up dead rather than reformed (as in, for example, the anonymous, 1605-published *The London Prodigal*). Its early scenes depict a reasonably realistic London in a way that mirrors citizen comedy of the period (Thomas Dekker's *The Shoemaker's Holiday*, published in 1600, being an obvious analogue). It is also a tragedy because of the sheer inevitability of the headstrong Stukeley's fall. Finally, the play's vast geographical sweep and increasingly bizarre adventures anticipate the *Winter's Tale*-like romances made popular by John Fletcher and Shakespeare in subsequent years.

The dating of the play is vexed. It was probably written in the early to mid-1590s. *Henslowe's Diary* suggests that some version of the play had been performed in 1596 and 1597, with a long gap before its 1605 publication. It possibly appeared in print that year because of its unusual, even unique, investment in Irish characters and Irish locations. It has other appealing characteristics: the single-mindedness of its hero, the doomed Stukeley, is magnetic if alarmingly uncompromising. He casts aside his father, his friends, his wife and ultimately his life to the pursuit of 'honour'. One heavily iambic line of verse conveys his single-mindedness:

STUK[ELEY]:
I must haue honour, honour is the thing.[14]

Alliterative and full of aggressive consonance, this line underlines Stukeley's self-centred egotism as well as his profound self-abnegation and devotion to

Sebastian 'The Desired', King of Portugal (d. 1578), disappeared after the Battle of Alcazar where Captain Thomas Stukeley was killed.

'honour' – a concept that is almost anthropomorphised as an entity that Stukeley seeks both to conjoin with and to become defined by. One of his initial problems, though, is that English military leaders and politicians have rarely found 'honour' in Ireland. They find expense, headaches and embarrassment. Rather than being some sort of celebration of English 'honour' in Ireland, the Irish scenes in *Captain Thomas Stukeley* work to reveal a sense that Ireland is a monstrous problem, not a place where 'honour' is to be found.

Even before the English characters head off to Ireland, Stukeley's rival, the decent but sensible and dull Vernon, has a conversation with a friend that revels deep-seated English anxieties about Ireland. Upset that Stukeley has stolen Nell's hand, Vernon says that he will fight in Ireland:

VER[NON]:
yet whilst I breath this natiue ayre of mine …
And whilst I tread vpon this English earth …
vnderneath is hid
a bed of crawling Serpents.[15]

This speech is intriguing because of its possible allusion to the snake-thwarting myth of St Patrick, but, more crucially, it explains why one character in particular will go to Ireland – to get away from England. It is a negative, not a positive reason to seek victory over the Irish. His friend, Ridley, clearly sees this:

RID[LEY]:
Yet since you needs will leave vs and the Realme,
go not to Ireland: The Countries rude
and full of tumult and rebellious strife,
Rather make choice of Italy or France.[16]

Ridley neatly articulates a dystopian vision of an uncontrollable Ireland, one unfit for sensitive Englishmen to visit, let alone fight in. Even Catholic, continental places are safer than Ireland. It is very significant that Ireland is seen as outside 'the Realme'. Despite English gains (at the vague time of the play's setting and at the time of the play's writing and later publication), the western island is still something 'other', something 'outside', ruled in theory but not in actuality. Later, though, Vernon leaves Ireland, infuriated to find that Stukeley has crossed the Irish Sea as well. He suggests that it is not Ireland that is monstrous and 'rude' but Stukeley. The betrayed rival complains about Stukeley with withering contempt:

VER[NON]:
I gaue my loue to such a Prodigall,
For which I hate the clymate where he liues,
as if his breath infected all the aire,
And therefore Ireland now farewell to thee,
For though thy soile no venime will sustaine,
There treads a monster on thy fruitfull brest.[17]

At a time when the likes of John Derricke and Edmund Spenser (and Dromio of Syracuse) demonised Ireland and the Irish, it is remarkable that Vernon suggests that England is the problem in Ireland, not the wild Irish themselves. If Stukeley metonymically represents English masculine, martial recklessness, then Vernon cannot support any engagement with Ireland. In other words, Vernon struggles to see Ireland as unproblematically 'other'. The play's most remarkable scene has a monstrous anomaly: a repeated Ireland-based scene suggests that there is an even greater struggle to define how exactly Irish guerrillas are so different from English soldiers.

Captain Thomas Stukeley has received little attention from scholars over the years, a probable consequence of the muddled state of the anonymous text. Unlike many other Renaissance plays, it has rarely been edited. It is necessary here to account briefly for editors' treatments of the repeated scene. In the original 1605 quarto, there is no self-consciousness about the repetition. The seventh scene comes naturally after the sixth. Then, with no explanation, the dramatically charged scene is repeated again, with a stage-Irish tone to the dialogue. Presumably, the compositor(s), like all his peers as a printer rather than an editor, worked from a playhouse manuscript into which had been inserted the second version of the scene. Messy and ignored, the play was not published again until 1878. This Victorian edition came in a bizarre, posthumous, two-volume collection assembled by Richard Simpson, the Catholic antiquarian scholar. Simpson managed to make a confused play even more confusing, conflating characters, introducing many silent emendations, and generally failing to clarify the text's vexed provenance. He claimed,

without foundation, that the play's writing had been somehow 'supervised' by Shakespeare. He kept the two versions of Scene VII within the text, confusingly describing the rewrite as 'an alternative scene, instead of the preceding one',[18] meaning that a playing company would select one version of the scene rather than another – not that any known production of the play has occurred since the 1590s. His crude modernisation of the language, though, undermines the differences between the two versions of the scene.

The very nature of the two twentieth-century editions of the play ensured that no editorial innovations were possible. A useful 1911 facsimile reproduced the layout of the original quarto, as does the type facsimile prepared for the Malone Society by Vivian Ridler in 1975.[19] Ridler's edition is particularly useful for its short but dense introduction that outlines the play's myriad textual problems, its vexed dating, confusing chronology and sometimes discombobulated depiction of character. The new century has seen the most sophisticated edition of the play to date. Charles Edelman presents a modernised yet meticulous rendering of the text together with *The Battle of Alcazar* – a play that features another construction of Thomas Stukeley as a major character. Edelman, however, does a disservice to the repeated scene, using the first version as a straightforward scene between Scenes VI and VIII. He relegates the second, 'Irish' version to an appendix, effectively suggesting that the first version is 'better' than the other.[20] This glides over the idiosyncratic nature of the text and somehow suggests that one version of the scene is less worthy of critical study than the other. In his introduction Edelman makes no effort to explain the repetition of the action in the original quarto, referring briefly and blandly to the scene being 'inexplicably followed by a shorter, alternative version in "stage-Irish" prose'.[21] With little editorial help, then, it is up to the reader to make sense of the consequences of the dually rendered scene. The Irish characters are not only made more Irish in the rewritten version through their use of the Irish language, but the gravity of their language changes too. Despite the lowly prose and sibilant slurring, the Irish seem much more threatening in this second version.

Scene VII, the first scene set in Ireland, takes place at night, just in front of a garrison at Dundalk, County Louth. A group of three Irish rebels approaches the gates, but withdraw in what could be considered to be cowardice or intelligent awareness of limitations. The three are Shane O'Neill, a character based on the historical 'Seán an Diomhais' (c. 1530-67), Neil Mackener, his secretary, and Rory O'Hanlon. In the first version of the scene, hereafter referred to as 7a, the Irish speak in calm, organised blank verse – in other words, they sound just like the English characters of the previous six scenes. After a cautious approach over water, the Irish hear a cough from within the walls. Mackener seems spooked, but O'Neill reacts with calm, murderous intent:

MACK[ENER]:
Be whist I heare one stir. *On[e] Coughs within.*

ONEALE:
Some English Soldior that hath got the cough,
Ile ease that griefe by cutting off his head.[22]

Here, O'Neill comes across as a sort of sardonic, blackly comic pantomime villain from a revenge tragedy. Although his motive is defined by a ferocious desire to launch a guerrilla-style attack on the English base, his language does not define him as Irish. Threatening and menacing, but controlled and calm, he reminds one of Aaron from *Titus Andronicus* or Bosola from *The Duchess of Malfi* rather than a shaggy-haired Irish kern from Derricke or Spenser. But see how the same passage of action is scripted in the second version of the play – scene 7b:

One coughs within.
[O']HAN[LON]:
Cresh blesh vs, so ish tat ishe coughes.

MACK[ENER]:
Saint Patrick blesh vs we be not betraid.

ONEALE:
Mackener, Mack Deawle, marafastot art thou a féete liuered kana.[23]

Immediately one can tell that the Irish in this version of the scene are to be orally clumsy and probably physically disorganised. Oaths are interpolated. Ireland's patron saint is invoked, his name peeking out with clarity through the fog of sibilance and haste. More significant than the association of the Irish with a Catholic veneration of a saint is the reference to the son of the devil – 'Mack Deawle' (Mac An Deabhail). Casual with their oaths, these Irishmen wilfully veer in their allusions between ex-

alted saints and loathed serpents. It is unclear who O'Neill is wishing death upon (marafastot/marbh feasta ort), and it is unclear whom he is calling the son of the devil; he may be simply swearing with impotent fecklessness. The point is that in 7b, these Irish rogues, now speaking a slurred English that is augmented awkwardly with Gaelic oaths, have lost control of their language as well as their military discipline. They are linguistically reckless, militarily inchoate and vocally irresponsible.

In Scene 7a, O'Neill imagines an Irish success in the near future. They will attack, kidnap and ransom some of the more valued English leaders:

[O']NEALE:
O Hanlon, captaine Harbart shall be thine,
and Gainsfords ransome shall be Maekeners.

[O']HAN[LON]:
Thanks greate Oneale.[24]

Although anti-English and brutal, the Irish seem organised and competent: O'Neill is dividing labour and promising rewards to his followers; O'Hanlon is as modest, as obsequious and as ingenuous as any English follower of an English nobleman would be. In the second version, however, both rank and organisation have disappeared:

ONEALE:
O Hanlon zée will giue you trée captaines to ransome.

[O']HANLON:
Zée wil take trée prishoners and giue thee too and take de turd my self.[25]

Here O'Hanlon is neither deferential nor modest. In this later version of the same scene, these lines have been rewritten to make the Irish seem somehow more disreputable, more chaotic – in other words, unEnglish. They are, superficially, less competent guerrillas because they struggle even to say a basic English word such as 'three'. English, however, is not their first language.

To an English audience, the vagueness of the Irish in 7b is more threatening because they come across as more unknowable as well as more unpredictable and spontaneous – in other words, more foreign. Compare, too, the contrasting manner in which the scene ends in the two versions. In 7a, after withdrawing because another English cough

Hugh O'Neill, above, and on right 'The Death of Shane O'Neill' (1567) from John Speed's map (1599). Shane appears as an anti-hero in *Captain Thomas Stukeley* but analogies with his more famous nephew are irresistible. ©TNA and Brian Vallely

Oneal kild by the wild Scots.

is heard, O'Neill remains confident and defiant, retaining his sardonic, controlled disposition:

ONEALE:
One coughes againe, lets slip aside unséene,
to morrow we will ease them of their spléen.
[*Exit*].[26]

The rhyme is significant because it would force an actor to articulate the two lines with patient, measured balance. A callous threat to kill is delivered with a comic, faux-medical concern to ease an ailment – a conceit already used by O'Neill when he promised to cure a cold through beheading. The regular, rhyming verse makes these two lines seem smooth and almost matter-of-fact and proverb-like. In 7b, however, the departure is less organised. This time, just before O Neill departs, he waffles somewhat, ordering one of his men to prepare his 'bagpiper' who must 'be ready to peep'

at the obscure location of 'Ballootherie'.[27] Before the men take their leave from each other – and with a noticeable lack of ceremony or formality – they simply speak casually in Irish:

[O']HAN[LON]:
Slaue haggat Bryan MacPhelemy.

MACK[ENER]:
Slaue lets Rorie beg. *Exit*.[28]

Although these speeches are foreign and therefore inexplicable to an audience that does not know Irish, there is clear affection between the men. United through language, these Irishmen seem here to be more loyal to each other.

If the Irish language confuses and English audience, then the inexplicable appearance of an unexplained name may confuse further bafflement. Why does O'Hanlon call Mackener 'MacPhelemy'? Is this

116

a simple case of a muddled manuscript, a rewrite of the scene done in excessive haste just prior to a performance? Or did the compositor make a mistake, or does O'Hanlon allude to Mackener's father, Phelemy, or is O'Hanlon too stupid to know which of his comrades is standing beside him; or is 'MacPhelemy' another Irishman on stage, a shadowy one who says nothing and who is not mentioned even in the stage directions? In other words, these characters have been mixed up by whoever wrote this new version of the scene and have been made to look clumsy, haphazard and ridiculous. They just appear less tangible and less distinctive and have become more Irish through their language. Furthermore, they are now more threatening because it is much harder for English men and women to distinguish their motives and plans. Remember the outdoor nature of a performance in an early modern auditorium such as Henslowe's Rose Theatre. In these testing theatrical conditions it would not be easy for even an educated English theatre-goer to understand what the Irish are saying to each other – even when calling each other by the right names. The present writer is convinced, then, that 7b appears more alarming for an English audience. The realities of the Nine Years War may bear little resemblance to the realities of the Shane O'Neill struggles of the 1560s, but analogies between Shane and Hugh O'Neill are irresistible. The Shane O'Neill of Scene 7b may be no more confused or confusing a figure than the contemporary bogeyman, Hugh O'Neill. In a scene rewritten at some point during this crucial period of conflict, some time just before 1605, we have a brief yet illuminating glimpse of English anxieties about the half-foreign and half-English Hugh O'Neill. In 7b, the anonymous dramatist has managed to both caricature and strengthen 7a's representation of the Irish threat. English men and women who saw this play performed or who read the 1605 quarto may well have been pleased to be able to say 'Slaue haggat' to this particular O'Neill as he departed from Lough Swilly in September 1607.

Notes

1 For help in completing this essay and on delivering the conference paper on which it is based, I thank Maria Campbell, Éamonn Ó Ciardha, Anoush Simon and Ramona Wray.

A seminal transcription of Henslowe's accounts has recently been made available in a new edition: R. A. Foakes (ed.), *Henslowe's Diary* (Cambridge, 2002).

2 For a classic account of dramatic censorship in the period see R. Dutton, *Mastering the Revels: The Regulation and Censorship of English Renaissance Drama* (Iowa, 1991).

3 On this, see D. J. Baker, 'Where is Ireland in *The Tempest*?', in M. T. Burnett and R. Wray (eds), *Shakespeare and Ireland: History, Politics, Culture* (Basingstoke, 1997), pp 68-88.

4 Shakespeare, *The Comedy of Errors*, III.ii.120-5, (ed.) S. Wells (Harmondsworth, 1984).

5 On the connection between the blazon and overseas territories see A. Hadfield, *The English Renaissance, 1500-1620* (Oxford, 2001), pp 31-32.

6 Marlowe, *Edward II*, II.ii.161-5, *The Complete Plays*, (ed.) J. B. Steane (Harmondsworth, 1986).

7 See under the entries for 'Ireland' and 'Irishman' in T. Berger at al. (comps.), *An index of Characters in Early Modern English Drama* (Cambridge, 1998).

8 Shakespeare, *Henry V*, III.iii.63-64, (ed.) G. Taylor (Oxford, 1994).

9 For a very thorough analysis of the play's reference to Essex see C. Highley, '*Henry V* and Essex's Irish Campaign' in idem, *Shakespeare, Spenser and the Crisis in Ireland* (Cambridge, 1997), pp 134-63.

10 *Henry V*, V.o.32.

11 For this marvellous insight into the escapist possibilities afforded to supporters of drama during Shakespeare's period see C. Whitney, *Early Responses to Renaissance Drama* (Cambridge, 2007), p. 75.

12 All quotations from the play are taken from the original 1605 quarto: *The famous historye of the life and death of Captaine Thomas Stukeley* (London, 1605; STC 23405).

13 P. Holmes, 'Thomas Stucley (c. 1520-78)', www.oxforddnb.com, 2004 (accessed 22 Nov. 2009); J. E. Tazón, *The life and times of Thomas Stukeley, c. 1525-78* (London, 2003).

14 *Captain Thomas Stukeley*, sig. D1r.

15 Ibid., sig. C1v.

16 Ibid.

17 Ibid., sigs E1v-E2r.

18 R. Simpson (ed.), *The School of Shakspere* (2 vols, London, 1878), i, 192.

19 *Captain Thomas Stukeley, 1605* (London, 1911); V. Ridler (ed.), *The famous history of Captain Thomas Stukeley* (Oxford, 1975).

20 C. Edelman (ed.), *The Stukeley Plays* (Manchester, 2005), pp 236-7.

21 Ibid., p. 34.

22 *Captaine Thomas Stukeley*, sig. D3r.

23 Ibid., sig. D3v.

24 Ibid., sig. D3r.

25 Ibid., sig. D3v.

26 Ibid., sig. D3r.

27 Ibid., sig. D3v.

28 Ibid., sigs. D3v-D4r.

Craobhsgaoileadh Chlainne Suibhne: the story of MacSweeney Fanad

Áine Ní Dhuibhne

'As buaine aon rann maith a deir Colum Cille ná sliabh óir' ('One good poem is more enduring than a mountain of gold,' says Colum Cille)

This proverb is found on a page accompanying a manuscript collection relating to the MacSweeney clan of Fanad in north Donegal. The collection contains a number of poems (*rannta*) addressed to MacSweeney Fanad chiefs, together with an account or narrative of the lordship of the Mac-Sweeneys. This narrative is a history of the clan and its doings and is entitled 'Craobhsgaoileadh Chlainne Suibhne' (The Broadcasting of Clan Sweeney).

This kind of narrative history can be seen as an extension of the praise poem (*rann* or *dán*) of the *file* (poet) and serving the same purpose. The poets and historians of a Gaelic lordship maintained close links to its chief or lord. Each would-be chieftain sought the lordship on certain merits – these ranged from an individual's physical strength to the military might and the support that he could muster. In the system of 'tanistry' which decided succession, it was incumbent on the chieftain to validate his position in a number of ways. These included justification of his claim to his patrimony – the territory inherited from his ancestors; the antiquity of his clan's claim to that territory, and his own ability to defend his people as a constable and a hero-warrior and by reason of his many virtues and desirable attributes. It also necessitated the chief to command the good services of the poets and historians who would place his pedigree and achievements within the formulaic framework required to validate him in his lordship and to record or broadcast this.

The compositions of the poets and historians recording the qualities and achievements of the chief were meant for recitation at gatherings of the Gaelic elite as well as at public gatherings. Recitation and reiteration reinforced the message concerning patrimony, extent of territory, achievements and attributes of the individual chieftains. With repetition these passed into the lore of the people and gained further permanence by being written down by the poets and chroniclers.

Bernadette Cunningham illustrates this in her recent book, *O'Donnell histories: Donegal and the Annals of the Four Masters*.[1] The great compilation known as the Annals of the Four Masters is particularly a record of the kingships and lordships of Gaelic Ireland. The annals record key aspects of the careers of illustrious clan members and chiefs, especially those exploits that enhance the clan's image. Cunningham makes the case that because of the connection of the Four Masters with the former O'Donnell lordship and with Donegal, there is a bias in favour of the O'Donnell clan. In the annals for instance, the Ó Cléirigh chroniclers faithfully recorded O'Donnell victories, while regularly ignoring their defeats.[2] Cunningham explains that the attributes and achievements of the O'Donnell chieftains through the centuries were regularly developed in the obituaries, which effectively became microhistories of individual chiefs, culminating in the heroic cult of Red Hugh O'Donnell.[3]

Just as the O'Donnell lordship and others had their poets and historians so too did the Mac-Sweeneys of Fanad, Doe and Banagh. They maintained close connections with their overlords, the O'Donnells, particularly in the late medieval period. These clans' histories show an interdependence and many parallels, not least because as the wealth and power of the O'Donnell lordship grew, so too did that of the MacSweeney clans of Fanad, Doe and Banagh (Doe is in the mid-west and Banagh in the south-west of Donegal). These galloglass clans, of which the MacSweeney clan of Fanad comprised the senior branch, provided the military might that contributed to the great power and wealth the O'Donnell lordship commanded by the beginning of the sixteenth century.

References to the MacSweeneys of Fanad can be found in records of Gaelic Ireland such as the various annals, genealogies and poems. The manuscript known as Leabhar Chlainne Suibhne constitutes a specific history of the clan. Now housed in the Royal Irish Academy, it comprises poems, religious and secular tracts and a narrative account of the clan of MacSweeney of Fanad.

The narrative, or *Craobhsgaoileadh*, translated by Paul Walsh, who edited and published it as

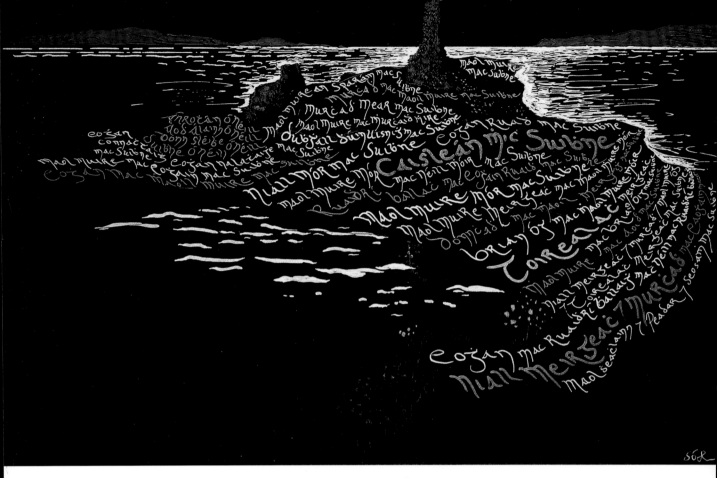

'Mac Suibhne Boghaine'. © Seoirse Ó Dochartaigh

Leabhar Chlainne Suibhne in 1920, sets out to introduce the clan and assess their significance in Gaelic Ireland. Máire Ní Mháille, wife of the MacSweeney chief, Ruaidhrí (d. 1518), commissioned this history of MacSweeney Fanad. It furnishes all the necessary criteria to validate the MacSweeney lordship, over hundreds of years; by establishing an Irish origin for the clan and most importantly in Tír Chonaill, giving it a connection with Colum Cille. Fate and fortune directed the clansmen to Scotland, where they prospered as professional soldiers. They resumed closer ties with Ireland through conquests and marriage alliances and were recorded in the annals as established in Ireland by the second half of the thirteenth century.[4]

Numbers of the clan settled permanently in the Fanad peninsula, around 1262, having ousted the O'Breslins. Following this settlement, 'there was a new influx of the clan into Tír Chonaill under the leadership of Murchadh Mear, Murchadh the Crazy, the common ancestor in all the Mac Suibhne pedigrees now extant'.[5] His descendants established the branch of MacSweeney of Doe. As the narrative unfolds the patrimony and its expansion is traced and the warring deeds and military successes of numerous chieftains over a period of three hundred years are recorded.

The first MacSweeney chief of Fanad noted in the Annals of the Four Masters was Toirdhealbhach (Tarlach) Caoch.[6] He received many concessions for his clansmen from his O'Donnell overlord, who:

bestowed on them six scores of axes of buannacht bona (that is, axe-men to be maintained) out of Tír Chonaill itself, a gift, in perpetuity from himself and his posterity after him: the making of a circuit of Tír Chonaill once in the year: the spending of three nights in each house in Tír Chonaill: the fishing of the Erne every Friday between Patrick's Day and the Feast of the Cross in Harvest; if they should happen to be encamped by the Erne to oppose the men of Connacht: two ballybetaghs of Tír Mic Caorthainn which are now called Bráighid Fánad [the Braid of Fanad], and to sit by the right side of Ó Domhnaill whenever Mac Suibhne would visit him.[7]

119

In return, the MacSweeneys supplied a stated number of galloglass to serve the O'Donnell chieftain as he needed them.

Toirdhealbach's son, Toirdhealbhach Ruadh, gained a most significant concession from O'Donnell by being allowed to be inaugurated as chieftain at Doon Rock near Kilmacrenan, the inauguration site of the O'Donnells:

> He was the first Mac Suibhne whom Ó Domhnaill ever inaugurated. It was the successor of Colum Cille who used to inaugurate Mac Suibhne in Iona as long as they remained in Scotland, but after their coming to Ireland, when they were not at enmity with one another, and they had power, they used to give the task of inauguration to Ó Frighil [O'Friel], instead of having it done in Iona by Colum Cille's successor. A proof of this is this: no Mac Suibhne was ever proclaimed except in Colum Cille's precinct (that is Kilmacrenan), and if any were inaugurated elsewhere, he could not be long in power.[8]

'Craobhsgaoileadh Chlainne Suibhne', commissioned by Máire Ní Mháille, wife of the MacSweeney chief Ruaidhrí (d. 1518), stresses the importance of the MacSweeneys of Fanad. © RIA

According to the *Craobhsgaoileadh*, this Toirdhealbhach accompanied the O'Donnell on a major military expedition through Ulster, Meath and Connacht. In 1461 when Aodh Ruadh Ó Domhnaill claimed the O'Donnell chieftainship, he sought and received the assistance of Maolmhuire MacSweeney at the battle of Kinnaweer between the Fanad and Ros Goill peninsulas. Following their victory, Aodh Ruadh championed Maolmhuire in securing the lordship of Fanad, and 'On that day Aodh Ruadh Ó Domhnaill granted the ballybetagh of Gort Cathlaighe (Gortcally) free of charge to Maolmhuire Mac Suibhne, without any contribution at all in return'.[9]

At Maolmhuire's death in 1472 he was succeeded by his son Ruaidhrí, who married the aforementioned Máire Ní Mháille of Mayo. Tadhg Mac Fhithil, author of the *Craobhsgaoileadh,* records many of Ruaidhrí's remarkable military exploits:

> It was he who, together with Aodh Ruadh O Domhnaill, won the battle of Gairbh-Eiscir, which is called Bealach na gCorrghad to-day; and the Battle of the Moy against Clanwilliam; and the battle of Béal an Droichid [Ballydrehid] against Clanwilliam … wherein were slain … son of Toirdhealbhach Carrach [the Scabby] O Conchubhair, lord of Connacht from the Mountain, i.e. Corrshliabh na Seaghsa, northwards, and Maolmhuire na Samhthach [of the Battleaxes], the son of Mac Domhnaill; and the battle of Móin Leasg, wherein was slain the son O hAinnli [O Hanley]; and the famous battle of Ard an Ghaire, [Ardingary] in conjunction with Conn O Domhnaill, against Aodh O Domhnaill and Clann Suibhne na dTuath; it was Ruaidhrí also who, along with Aodh Ruadh O Domhnaill, burned Srádbhaile [Dundalk].[10]

The author also catalogues Máire's establishment of the Carmelite Friary in Rathmullan and her commission of the *Craobhsgaoileadh* to record the history of MacSweeney Fanad. In light of that, it is to be expected that Ruaidhrí and Máire are accorded the greatest eulogies and finest obituaries in the whole narrative (these are quoted below). The narrative ends with a typical entry:

> This Toirdhealbhach built the castle of Carraig Fheile, by means of which he reduced and

annexed all the country to himself. The Age of the Lord when Mac Suibhne (Toirdhealbhach, son of Ruaidhrí, son of Maolmhuire) commenced this castle of Carraig Fheile in Magh Ross [Moross] was 1532 …[11]

Paul Walsh concluded his description of the MacSweeney families by noting that 'no other family in Tír Chonaill except only the O'Donnells can present such an unbroken record of lordship'. Such a record was an important part of the clan's ratification within the Gaelic system.

The other cornerstone in authenticating or validating a lordship was in the recalling, reiteration and broadcasting of the personal achievements, virtues and attributes of the individual chief. Very often obituaries for the chief served as an important part of the process of authentication and validation as one chieftainship ended and another began. An excerpt from the *Craobbhsgaoileadh* extols the generosity of Maolmhuire, son of Murchadh Óg, son of Murchadh Mear, and illustrates the dependency of the chief on his poets and his reluctance to offend them:

At one time this Maolmhuire was in Fanad, and he set out on a certain day to hunt. A number of poets were sent to him with their compositions, and he sat down to hear them on the brink of a certain lake in Fanad. They commenced to chant and recite for him, and then demanded their fee. Mac Suibhne asked what kind of fee they wished for, and they replied that they would accept no payment except of gold, and no drink except of wine, and no light except of wax. Mac Suibhne answered that, if they came with him to his house, they would receive whatever he would be able to procure them. But they said they would not go, and that, unless they there obtained what they had demanded, they would subject him to satire. And he replied that he had not in that place what he demanded. 'We see with you here' said they, 'a gold ring; give it to us, and we shall not lay blame on you for whatever else we have not'. Now this gold ring was an heirloom with successive generations of the MacSweeneys, and it had in it a precious stone, which whosoever possessed was never beaten in battle or in combat. And Maolmhuire stretched forth his hand to them that they might take off

The ruins of St Mary's Friary Rathmullan, founded by Máire Ní Mháille in the late fifteenth century.

the ring. They took his hand, but they were unable to remove the ring. Then they said that if he thought that they could, that he would not have offered it to them. And he himself said he would take off the ring from his hand, but he was unable to do that, and was much ashamed for that reason. Whereupon he produced a sharp, blue-bladed knife which he had, and, striking his finger, cut it off and threw it, together with the ring, into the bosom of the chief of the poets.[12]

Maolmhuire's son, Toirdhealbhach Caoch, shows another example of 'flaithiúlacht', demanding to share his food with one hundred more:

On a certain day that this Toirdhealbhach we are speaking of was in his own house his servant offered him dinner. And, having looked about him in all the house, he considered that all those who were in the house were too few, and he said: 'May this cheek be not mine own if it move in absence of an hundred more, on which a beard growth, moving contemporaneously therewith'.[13]

The obituaries of Ruaidhrí and Máire contain many of the important constituents in remembering and reinforcing the message of the lordship and in extolling aspects of the traditional ways of Gaelic lordship:

And it was this Mac Suibhne [Ruaidhrí] who first built the castle of Ráith Maoláin [Rathmullan]; and it was his wife, namely, Máire, daughter of Eoghan, son of Diarmaid Bacach [the Lame] Ó Máille [O Malley], who erected the monastery of Ráith Maoláin. It was

Mac Suibhne and this wife who brought to that monastery a community from the south, from Munster … The year of the Lord when the monastery was founded was 1516. At the end of two years after his founding of the monastery Mac Suibhne died – he who was the constable of the greatest name and fame, and who, of all that came in this latter age, bestowed most on poets and schools (he had been forty-six years in the chieftainship of his family, and was seventy-eight years of age when he died) – having gained victory over the devil and the world, in the habit of the friars of Mary, in the monastery which he himself had founded in her honour, on the seventh day of the month of April, on the Wednesday between the two Easters, in his own seat of Ráith Maoláin.

And at the end of four years after that, his noble, loveable wife, the daughter of Ó Máille, the most generous and the best mother, and the woman of most fame in regard to faith and piety of all who lived in her time, died. This is the manner in which she passed her days: she used to hear Mass once each day, and sometimes more than once; and three days in each week she used to spend on bread and water fare, with Lenten fast, and winter fast, and the Golden Fridays. She also caused to be erected a great hall for the Friars Minor in Dún na nGall [Donegal]. Not only that, but many other churches we shall not here enumerate that woman caused to be built in the provinces of Ulster and Connacht. It was she also who had this book of piety above copied in her own house, and all affirm that in her time there was no woman who passed her life better than she. And the manner of her death, after victory over the devil and the world, was, in the habit of the friars of Mary, in the monastery which she herself had founded.[14]

Having assisted Aodh Ruadh Ó Domhnaill (1427-1505), centre, to secure the O'Donnell chieftainship, Maolmhuire Mac Suibhne received the lordship of Fanad. © Ian Broome/Maurice Harron

In *Leabhar Chlainne Suibhne* Paul Walsh focuses on the narrative account, the *Craobhsgaoileadh*, and his introduction ends with the transcription of a tribute written in a vacant column of the manuscript by the scholar Tadhg Ó Rodaighe:

Truagh liomsa go fíor na tuir chatha et comhla(i)nn na Gúaireadha et na laoich Liathmhuine air fheile air dhaonnacht et air einioch .i. Clann tSuibhne fhearrdha fheidhmlaidir (do fhág na signeadha onaracha so na ndiaidh mar ghnáthchuimhne ar a maith et orra pfein) do díosc et do dhul arccul go leir mar an ccuid eile do shliocht Gaoidhil Ghlais. Monúar monúar bunadha na féile do dhul ar neimhní queis nulli aequales quondam re militari doctrina liberalitate hospitalitate sanctitate antiquitate nobilitate etc. Hibernia insula sanctorum genetrix sophiaeque magistra at nunc omnia e contra le dúrsmacht achtrannach do gach uile chinel do léirscrios ar nuaisle go dith fine gurab é an tanuasal as uasal ann anoiss ge go raibh gan tsean gan tseinnsior ó thainic clanna Milidh go hEirinn anno mundi 3500 ante Xristum natum 1699 (natusenim Christus secundum septuaginta duos Eusebium etc. anno mundi 5199). Acht ata seanchus na mbachlach anois na ccinnlitribh ┐ na cceapuibh ria seanchus sleachta EimhirIr ┐ Eireamhoin ┐ Iotha mhic Breogain fós. Acht biodh oramsa nach bfuil i nEirinn aon chairt ag cothugadh sheanc(h)uis na ndaor nuaibhrioch ndobheo(l)usach úd óir atáid na cartacha agumsa ┐ ag morán eile ar ndoigh ┐ gabhuim orum nach bfuil an bachlachsheanchus úd ionnta. As buaine áon rann maith mar adeir Colum Cille ina sliabh óir. Is iomdha dan romhaith annso ar shliocht Suibhne. Bennacht leo go flaithios oir as cinte go bfuilid san dún sin uile.[15]

This laudatory passage dates from 1697, ninety years after the flight of the earls. Ó Rodaighe's reflections on the Gaelic system of lordship, a cornerstone of Gaelic civili-

An Irish lord (Mac Suibhne) dines in the open-air. Taken from John Derricke's notorious text *The Image of Irlande* London, 1581). © Trinity College Dublin

sation as exemplified in the *Craobhsgaoileadh* can be paraphrased as follows:

> My true regret is for the leaders in hospitality, humanity – Clann tSuibhne – who left this honourable document after them as a remembrance of their great and good antecedents and of themselves, because they were being diminished, like many more of the Gaeil. Sad indeed it is that the essence of hospitality, freedom, holiness, antiquity and nobility is militated against. Now all is conquered by foreign oppression in the destruction of the nobility so that now the ignoble have become the noble and these have no pedigrees to be found in any charter which I or others have. One good poem is more lasting than a mountain of gold. In this compilation are many good poems on the clan of Sweeney. Farewell to them in heaven because it is certain that it is in that fort that they all dwell]

Tadhg Ó Rodaighe penned his tribute at a time when the lives of poets and chieftains had been fractured and when no inaugurated or traditionally validated MacSweeney Fanad chieftain existed, to reward him for his eulogy or obituary on 'Clann tSuibhne' Fanad. Nevertheless, his sentiments reflect the opinions of a scribe or scholar of the Gaelic tradition who was deeply influenced by the narrative to which he was adding his own epilogue. He set down a final valedictory accolade to 'Clann tSuibhne' Fanad, sustained by the premise of the ancient proverb attributed to Colum Cille: 'As buaine aon rann maith ná sliabh óir'.

Notes

1 B. Cunningham, *O'Donnell histories: Donegal and the Annals of the Four Masters* (Rathmullan, 2007).

2 Ibid, pp 19-20.

3 Ibid, pp 59-61.

4 P. Walsh (ed), *Leabhar Chlainne Suibhne* (Dublin, 1920), pp xvi-xvii.

5 Ibid., p. xxi.

6 Ibid., p. xxiv.

7 Ibid., p. 43.

8 Ibid., p. 51.

9 Ibid., p. 61.

10 Ibid., p. 65.

11 Ibid., p. 73.

12 Ibid., p. 33.

13 Ibid., p. 47.

14 Ibid., p. 67.

15 Ibid., lxiii.

A dynastic nation? Re-thinking national consciousness in early seventeenth-century Ireland[1]

Brendan Kane

Scholars of early modern Europe have recently focused attention on the role of monarchical and familial interests in the character of the developing state. The resultant category of the 'dynastic state' has been very useful for conceptualising emergent early modern political systems: increasingly complex and impersonally bureaucratic in structure, yet still closely connected to the interests of royal families and their attendant aristocratic elites.[2] Although there was no independent Irish 'state' in the early modern period outside of the Tudor and Stuart government, it can be argued that dynastic considerations are crucial for understanding the peculiarities of late sixteenth- and early seventeenth-century Irish politics and political imaginings. In short, this article suggests that one should think of the nation envisioned by Old English and Gaelic elites in the period of the flight of the earls as a 'dynastic nation'.

Numerous scholars have argued for the presence of a form of 'national consciousness' in the thought and actions of early modern Irish elites.[3] Interests in 'faith and fatherland' are posited to have lain at the heart of this newly imagined nation, but exactly what that entity, and its attendant state structure and apparatus, were supposed to look like remains unclear. Was it to be a monarchy or a republic?[4] What was the basis of its sovereignty, and who would wield it? How could the heads of aristocratic dynasties like the O'Neills and O'Donnells claim to bestow that sovereignty upon foreign potentates such as the kings of Spain? Whatever the answers to these questions – and there is certainly not the opportunity here to address them – a concept of the 'dynastic nation' became central to the political future pursued by a variety of Irish actors. By 'dynastic nation' I mean a concept that held Ireland to be a pan-insular political entity the legitimacy of which was inextricably linked to the claims of lineal elites to positions of hereditary authority.

The Nine Years War and its aftermath, including crucially the flight of the earls, offer an excellent opportunity to explore early modern Irish national imaginings and their dynastic elements. The writings and actions of Queen Elizabeth and her aristocratic statesmen during the years of the

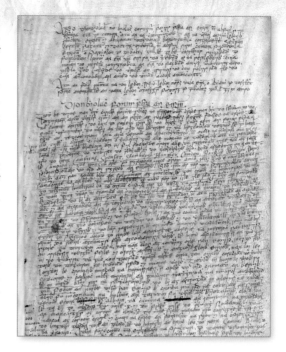

Geoffrey Keating's (Seathrún Céitinn's) 'best-selling' manuscript history of Ireland, *Foras Feasa ar Éirinn*, elided the ethnic difference between the Gaelic Irish and the Old English in favour of the shared designation 'Irishmen' (*Éireannaigh*). © RIA

conflict clearly display the language of the dynastic Tudor state. Crucially, the language of the Irish 'rebel' leaders and their apologists reveals similarly clear evidence of an understanding that corporate political power inextricably linked itself to the interests of hereditary elites and would be grounded in a hierarchical division of society. Unlike their English opponents, however, Irish elites could not in any practical terms speak the language of the state: no pan-insular government existed outside the central administration of Dublin.[5] Rather, they had to speak in the more hypothetical and abstract terms of the nation though not, however, an abstraction as famously employed by Benedict Anderson. Writing of the modern period, Anderson describes a sense of national attachment that is believed to bind people together regardless of the fact that those people will never know more than a minute fraction of their compatriots.[6] This is a necessary conceit for a modern democratic nation-state whose sovereignty is held to derive from the voting public. It was not, however, a necessary conceit for the imagined early modern Irish nation, the legitimacy of which would lie in the participation of recognised elite families rather than in a concept of manifest popular will. Not only could and did those elites know each other, but they argued for a very clear sense of the emergent Irish nation as dynastically bound.

This essay looks at the Nine Years War as a key period in the articulation of the Irish dynastic nation. Specifically, it explores the intersection of corporate political interests (statist or national) and particularistic familial/dynastic ones in the pronouncements of the war's leaders. The lens to do so is provided by the language of honour. Initially it will highlight the attention paid to honour by Queen Elizabeth I and Robert Devereux, second earl of Essex, in order to demonstrate that these English leaders held state and dynasty (be it monarchical or aristocratic) to be inextricably bound together. It will then proceed to explore an analogous obsession with honour and politics as revealed in the discourse of the Irish leaders Hugh O'Neill, second earl of Tyrone, and Red Hugh O'Donnell, chief of the O'Donnells. Surveying these English and Irish cases will demonstrate that all combatants, regardless of ethnic, social or cultural background, saw political legitimacy as tied to hereditary social legitimacy and articulated in part through reference to honour. There is, however, a crucial difference between the English and Irish positions: whereas the English government and its supporters spoke a language of the dynastic 'state' – positioned as they were at the centre of one of Europe's most precociously centralised polities – the Irish leaders and their supporters invoked a less tangible, more hypothetical 'nation'. But while that nation lay in an imagined future, it was legitimated by a past and present grounded in the authority of local dynasties.

Thinking of the emergent Irish nation as a dynastic one may help us to understand better a number of aspects of the conflict and its later representations. First, it may bring out more fully the complexity of Irish motivations. Historians have focused on various aspects of the Irish leaders' efforts to defend faith, fatherland and culture. But the obsessive deployment of a language of honour in negotiations with London and its representatives demonstrates the concerns these men had for family as well as faith and fatherland. Second, this focus on family honour and its relationship to political legitimacy reveals the Irish combatants to be less exotic and/or retrograde when compared with their English counterparts. Men like Hugh O'Neill and Red Hugh O'Donnell were not barbarous Gaelic 'others', nor were they hopeless medievals destined to cede the stage of power to English and anglicising moderns. They were members of the European nobility and were recognised as such by their English and continental peers.[7] Consequently, their conflict with the crown cannot be viewed as a winner-take-all struggle of cultural, confessional or ethnic difference – as it has sometimes been portrayed – but rather one that was very much (if not exclusively) about the relationship between the expanding Tudor/Stuart dynastic state and its peripheral elites.

A focus on the Irish dynastic nation may also offer insight into larger historical questions. First, it may allow us to think more critically about the analytical usefulness of a term frequently used to describe Irish lords throughout the entirety of the early modern period: 'conservative'.[8] Conservative they may have been, but they do not appear to have been necessarily any less so than their Eng-

William Cecil, Lord Burghley (1521-98), Elizabeth I's chief advisor for most of her reign. He familiarized himself with the genealogies of the noble families of Gaelic Ireland and compiled a number of family trees in his own hand. © NPG

lish counterparts. So what do, or should, historians mean when deploying the term? Second, it may also allow us to think more critically about how we use the term 'nation' when discussing the early modern period. Again, numerous scholars have identified the articulation of an Irish nation in the thought of contemporaries. But the contours and character of that imagined Irish polity remain underdefined and undertheorised. Thinking more critically about them may not only help us to understand early modern Ireland and Britain better, but perhaps even help to historicise the nation itself.

That Ireland's Tudor monarchs saw their expanding state as linked to dynastic interests is revealed in their concern for honour.[9] As much as the Nine Years War was driven by tensions over money, confession, socio-cultural 'reform' and territorial sovereignty, participants noted its effects on the honour of the state's leaders. Elizabeth believed her honour to be deeply engaged in the conflict, and that the defence of monarchical honour could not be separated from the defence of the state.[10] A particularly revealing example of this position appears in her command to Lord Deputy Sir William Russell in May 1596 to engineer a submission of the Irish leaders that would be 'completed for our honour [and] with such conditions as we may find to be derived only from public respect and not for particular end.'[11] Practical details of the arrangement mattered little to Elizabeth. What mattered was the restoration of her honour before the eyes of the world, an honour that had been bruised by ungrateful provincials.

English aristocrats also had dynastic interests to protect as the Tudor state expanded westward, as most clearly evidenced by the words and actions of the second earl of Essex. Although his family was of only recent elevation, Essex linked the proper function of the state to the honourable conduct and exploits of its great persons and families.[12] The Irish were to have no doubt about this. Thus Essex warned Feidhlimidh MacFeagh O'Byrne that he would execute the Wicklow leader's messengers if they 'dishonoured' him and the state by seeking to parley without first demonstrating contrition for their rebellious behaviour.[13] To Essex's mind, Ireland required the stabilising force of aristocratic greatness. Military adventures there could in turn confirm, or even increase, the honour of the state's great men – even if doing so impinged upon monarchical honour imperatives. His choice of the earl of Southampton to be general of the horse struck

Elizabeth as a frustrating case of status trumping experience, and his knighting men in the field enraged her. She would later complain to Lord Deputy Mountjoy that 'the excesse which other governors have used in that particular [i.e. the bestowal of knighthoods] hathe not only made that degree soe Common, as the Honorable Callinge it self is generally become more contemptible'.[14] The Tudor state's dynastic proposition now stretched into Ireland, and the new kingdom became as much a plaything of crown and nobility as was the domestic realm.

This intersection of political theory and dynastic politics, expressed through concerns for noble honour, was not a uniquely English concern. The Irish too thought in terms of honour and believed that the state legitimised itself in part by its concordance with aristocratic interests. This precise understanding lay at the heart of the policy of 'surrender and regrant'. Men like Conn Bacach O'Neill agreed to link themselves to London and its interests provided that the state in turn would make room in the new dispensation for their hereditary claims to political power. His successor to the earldom, Hugh O'Neill, whatever the controversy over his 'true' parentage, took as sacrosanct O'Neill preeminence in the Irish arena of the new state. He repeatedly castigated the crown for allowing low-born and 'mechanical men' to serve in his territories: in March 1594 he complained that places of 'credit or government' had been denied to those who bore him 'affection' and given instead to 'base men' allied with his nemesis Sir Henry Bagenal, marshal of the army.[15] In doing so he accused the crown and its representatives of flouting the divinely ordained right of the better born to lead the lesser. Even the more impetuous and seemingly impolitic Red Hugh O'Donnell deployed this language of dynastic legitimacy when negotiating with the crown. When, for instance, asked by crown commissioners why he had taken up arms given that his ancestors had been so loyal to the crown, he responded flatly with reference to his illegal imprisonment by that very same government.[16]

Tyrone's private parleying with Essex in 1599 represents perhaps the most audacious of Gaelic attempts to insert themselves into the expanding Tudor dynastic state. His claim that he would negotiate with Essex on account of their shared nobility, rather than with him as a representative of a socially levelling queen, represented an extraordinarily aggressive articulation of aristocratic rights.

The meeting between the earls of Essex and Tyrone at Aclint destroyed the former's career. © NLI

Unsurprisingly, Elizabeth flew into a rage when informed of it, decrying the 'dishonour that a traitor must be so far from submission as he must first have a cessation granted'.[17] What angered, and indeed frightened, her was not ethnic or confessional revolution but rather the possibility of cross-realm noble revolt. She would later inform the Irish secretary of state, Sir Geoffrey Fenton, that Tyrone must surrender to her and to her alone as he was, in her words, 'our subject born, and raised to honour by us only, and not born to depend upon any second power (as long as he shall carry himself as a good subject)'.[18] Essex, for his part, would later face accusations from his English contemporaries that he had conspired with Tyrone to combine against the queen. Tudor monarchs and Tudor peers, English and Irish alike, may not have always seen eye to eye, but they all saw the state as predicated on dynastic entitlement.

The events of 1594-1603 revealed, however, the limits of the London-centred state's accommodation of Gaelic dynastic interests.[19] With their loss at Kinsale and eventual submissions, Gaelic aristocrats faced a new reality regarding their claims to wield power in the new state: the claims may have been accepted, but the power was greatly curtailed. King James had confirmed Hugh O'Neill and Rory O'Donnell as earls following their surrender: the former to his erstwhile title of Tyrone, the latter to the newly created earldom of Tyrcon-

nell. Confirmed too, however, was the state's desire to have its own men-on-the-spot so that the earls' interests did not take precedence over the crown's. Base-born men would once again enjoy authority in Ireland that Gaelic elites held to be their historic prerogative. And this time the northern earls could do little to alter the situation. As Hans Pawlisch has brilliantly demonstrated, legal imperialism would take the place of physical force.[20] In this new imperial contest, there would be no feats of arms or aristocratic parleys and the descendants of ancient warrior elites would prove no match for commoners learned in the law.

Rather than abandon their dynastic interests, however, many Irish grandees chose to question their association with the state. This, in turn, required envisioning some new political arrangement that could accommodate those interests. Tyrone wrote revealingly to the Spanish king of the need for a new Irish 'state' to be founded upon true religion and allied with Spain.[21] Details on this new political entity are lacking, however. It could hardly have been otherwise: a tradition of high-kingship was not the same as a tradition of centralised institutions, and a kingdom did not a state make. Consequently, the language employed by Irish political theorists tended increasingly to the abstraction of nation rather than to the specifics of state. This was not a dominant discourse, and many contemporaries sought simply to in-

The obsession of Robert Devereux (1565-1601), second earl of Essex, with his own honour brought him to the block in 1601. © NPG

gratiate themselves with the Stuart state on the latter's terms. Nor was it a new one: Brendan Bradshaw and Marc Caball, for instance, have argued for the emergence of national consciousness from the late sixteenth century.[22] But it became an increasingly sophisticated and explicit one in the early seventeenth century.

A sign of its sophistication and subtlety was that the questioning of Irish relations with the London-centred state did not require rejection of the Stuart monarchy. Irish national imaginings did not necessarily equate to separatism. Fearghal Óg Mac an Bhaird's political genealogy of James's right to the three crowns is merely the most dramatic example of Gaelic efforts to strike a better arrangement with the Scottish Stuarts than had been enjoyed under the Tudors. Loyalty to the monarch, however, still left open the option to envision a new political definition of the kingdom of Ireland. Breandán Ó Buachalla has argued that while the Irish intelligentsia accepted the Stuarts as legitimate monarchs at the beginning of the seventeenth century, they claimed that Ireland had its own separate history as a political entity, totally unconnected to England.[23] The effort, indeed necessity, to construct the 'national' history of this separate kingdom of the Stuarts would occupy some of the greatest minds of the early seventeenth century. Most famously this would be the work of

Seathrún Céitinn (Geoffrey Keating), whose *Foras Feasa ar Éirinn* drew out the history of an Irish nation inclusive of Gaelic and Old English *Éireannaigh* alike.

The earlier imaginings of Tadhg Ó Cianáin are equally striking. His account of the Ulster lords' travels from Lough Swilly to Rome is our only contemporary account of the so-called flight. The near-hagiographic quality of his treatment of O'Neill and O'Donnell left centuries of readers to dismiss the work as mere fluff and flattery. Ó Cianáin is now taken seriously as a witness to contemporary events and as a figure of some political vision. Crucially, it has been pointed out by Mícheál Mac Craith that Ó Cianáin's is the first to link the terms *nasión* (nation) and *Éireannach* (Irish person) together.[24] What that nation would look like, however, seems to have been only crudely developed by contemporaries, if at all. Mac Craith sees Ó Cianáin's Irish nation as based on common faith (Catholicism), a sense of homeland, and a cultural affinity shared by Gaels and gaelicized Galls alike (i.e. *Éireannaigh*). These elements, he adds, would prove the foundations of Irish identity throughout the seventeenth century and beyond.[25]

To this description of Ó Cianáin's imagined Irish nation must be added the crucial element of dynastic interest. The focus by numerous scholars on the innovative collapsing of Gael and Gall into the geo-political neologism of *Éireannaigh* can leave a false impression that this polity's legitimacy rested within the sovereign power of the Irish people. This is not the case. Potential leaders in this new *nasión* of *Éireannaigh*, like all good seventeenth-century elites, believed that their churls had been born to serve, and roundly ridiculed and despised any of them who refused to know or accept their place in the divine hierarchy. The anonymous satire *Pairlement Chloinne Tomáis* is merely the most spectacular of the many assaults by Gaelic elites and intelligentsia on those Irish who sought to rise above their betters.[26] And thus, when one considers the political innovation suggested in Ó Cianáin's chronicle of the earls' flight across Europe, attention must be paid to the one factor that he held to be nearly as important as religion: namely the nobility of his subjects and their natural 'right' to govern. His obsession with hierarchy, one of the text's defining features, must therefore be added to our list of characteristics descriptive of the early modern Irish nation.

Acknowledging this essential 'class' element should caution us against assigning too 'modern' a quality to Ó Cianáin's *nasión*. Moreover, his fascination with the Swiss republican system was combined with an unequivocal praise of continental monarchies. This suggests the catholicity of his interests in political systems and, thus, demonstrates his lack of any particular state vision for Ireland. In spite of the inchoate nature of his political theorising, however, one element of it is indisputable: whatever state form an Irish nation would take, it was Ó Cianáin's firmly held position that some were born to lead, some to follow. Grandees like Hugh O'Neill and Rory O'Donnell were Ireland's natural leaders, whatever the system through which they were to rule. Ó Cianáin's nation, therefore, was a dynastic one.

In theorising the dynastic nation, Ó Cianáin simply made explicit the political assumptions of his contemporaries. Tyrone's discussion of an Irish state (noted above) presumed aristocratic participation. The earl, and Ó Cianáin's contemporary Philip O'Sullivan Beare, exiled aristocrat-turned-historian, had a clear vision of the necessity for noble power in any legitimate Irish political formulation. The latter's history of Catholic Ireland, written while in exile on the continent, has rightly been plumbed to demonstrate the importance of faith and fatherland in contemporary Gaelic political thinking and national imaginings. Largely overlooked, however, is his obsessional concern for the flower of Ireland's nobility. His trinity of crown sins consisted of efforts to suppress the faith, to take Irish land, *and* to kill off the nobility. Thus he appealed to Spain for aid 'against our enemies who are diabolically suppressing the Catholic faith, vindictively killing our nobles, and unlawfully coveting our patrimony'.[27] According to such an analysis, any new, legitimate, pan-insular political arrangement would have to satisfy requirements of faith, fatherland *and* family. It is little surprise, then, that Gaelic supplicants to Spain couched their appeals in terms of family honour imperatives: the Spanish must help the Irish lords on account of fictive kinship bonds.[28] Ó Cianáin's genius combined the political vision of a Tyrone with the dynastic concerns of an O'Sullivan Beare.

This brief trawl through materials dating from the Nine Years War and the flight of the earls may offer ways by which scholars may more subtly consider early modern Irish political thought and action. First and foremost, it highlights the extent to which Irish 'rebels' against the crown sought to

Ambrogio Spinola Doria, first Marquis of the Balbases (1569-1630), the scion of an ancient Italian noble family in Spanish service in the Netherlands. He treated the earls as fellow members of an extended European nobility.

defend family, faith and fatherland. This is not, however, to categorise this conflict as some species of tribal resistance to change. Debora Shuger's reference to Ireland's 'dangerous clan revolts of the 1590s' captures clearly the dynastic elements of the period's troubles.[29] However, to refer in this way to the series of events that most scholars term the Nine Years War is an arresting dismissal of the Irish lords' expectations to be treated as Tudor nobles.

This prompts the second concluding point: namely that the Irish fascination with personal and family interests placed them firmly in the mainstream of European aristocratic conduct. The Irish leaders O'Neill and O'Donnell spoke much the same language of aristocratic honour as their English counterparts. This is not to say that their honour claims were exactly coterminous with those of Elizabeth I and Essex, but that they existed along the same spectrum. English and Irish theorists alike thought of political legitimacy as something based in a proper relationship between governing power and social status. Seeing the points of contact in English and Irish honour politics, therefore, highlights the extent to which the war and its aftermath were episodes in an extended internal struggle between a centralising state and its peripheral elites rather than a winner-take-all struggle over faith, fatherland and/or culture.

Thirdly, therefore, one should be more careful when characterising Irish elites as conservative, a term frequently used in reference to Irish lords but never defined. The unfortunate result is that 'conservative' can come across as simply shorthand for the sort of pre-modern warlordism implied in Shuger's reference to 'dangerous clan revolts'. But if Essex and Elizabeth I were also conservative in that they too linked political legitimacy to dynastic interests, then perhaps scholars should be more open to exploring the creative and *avant-garde* possibilities of aristocratic conservatism. Ciaran Brady has famously explored the subversive aspects of Old English conservatism.[30] O'Neill and O'Donnell too, like many of their English (and even continental) contemporaries, appear to have been able to imagine quite radically new political arrangements while simultaneously holding conservatively on to their dynastic interests. These men were courtiers and Machiavels not tribal chieftains. An exploration of the intersection of Gaelic aristocratic conservatism with nascent national consciousness may increase the precision of the terms we use when describing early modern Irish politics and political thought. Doing so, finally, may also tell us something more definite about the character and contours of the emergent Irish nation in the seventeenth century. This was an innovative development, but more *early* modern than modern. The modernity of this imagined polity – as discussed above – has been linked to its ethno-cultural collapsing of Gael and Gall into *Éireannaigh*, its focus on the binding power of shared confession, and a sense of shared homeland. One should be wary, however, of seeing that nation as attached to the interests of the Irish people. It might be more accurate to see it as linked to the interests of Irish *persons*, namely elites. That does not mean we cannot see links to present-day definitions of nationalist thought: genealogical connection across ages is, of course, simply one more type of imagined community – one that sacrifices breadth (a nation of people separated across space) for depth (a nation of particular persons separated across time). Yet one thing that Irish political thinkers and actors seem significantly to have lacked was any sense of an acephalous polity.[31] To them, cut off the nobility and there would be no Irish nation. Thus, while the Irish may have been thinking of a nation, it was a 'dynastic' one. Enduring Irish fascination with the Stuarts throughout the eighteenth century and the consequent socio-political hold of Jacobitism speak to the tenacious power of the relationship between proper lineage and political legitimacy well past the collapse of the Gaelic order.[32] An Irish nation arising from the sovereign interests of its people would be a later phenomenon. Recognising these stages in national consciousness may assist us to understand more richly the development of Irish politics and identity. Doing so may also serve as one more reminder that the nation, as much as the state, had historical stages and peculiarities that require sensitivity.[33] A road from Tyrone to Pearse, or from Ó Cianáin to Anderson, can be traced, but it is an awfully convoluted, if fascinating, one.

Notes

1 This article draws on material and ideas discussed at greater length in B. Kane, *The politics and culture of honour in Britain and Ireland, 1541-1641* (Cambridge, 2010), cha. 3. I wish to thank the Syndics of Cambridge University Press for their kind permission to reprint that material here.

2 See, for example, M. Braddick, *State formation in early modern England c. 1550-1700* (Cambridge, 2000); W. Beik, *Absolutism and society in seventeenth-Century France: state power and provincial aristocracy in Languedoc* (Cambridge, 1989); G. Rowlands, *The dynastic state and the army under Louis XIV: royal service and private interest, 1661-1701* (Cambridge, 2002); R. Bonney, *The European dynastic states, 1494-1660* (Oxford, 1992); J. Dewald, *The European nobility, 1400-1800* (Cambridge, 1996); Ronald Asch, *Nobilities in transition, 1550-1700: courtiers and rebels in Britain and Europe* (London, 2003).

3 See, for example M. Caball, *Poets and politics: continuity and reaction in Irish poetry, 1558-1625* (Notre Dame,

1998); M. Mac Craith, 'Literature in Irish, c. 1550-1690: from the Elizabethan settlement to the battle of the Boyne', in M. Kelleher and P. O'Leary (eds), *The Cambridge history of Irish literature* (2 vols, Cambridge, 2006), i, pp 191-231; B. Ó Buachalla, *Aisling ghéar: na Stíobhartaigh agus an taos léinn, 1603-1788* (Dublin, 1996); J. Leerssen, *Mere Irish and fíor-Ghael: studies in the idea of Irish nationality, its development and literary expression prior to the nineteenth century* (Dublin, 1990); B. Bradshaw, 'Native reactions to the Westward Enterprise: a case-study in Gaelic ideology', in K. R. Andrews, N. P. Canny and P. E. H. Hair (eds), *The Westward Enterprise: English activities in Ireland, the Atlantic, and America, 1480-1650* (Detroit, 1979), pp 65-80.

4 N. Canny, *Making Ireland British* (Oxford, 2001), p. 419.

5 Historical sites of island-wide authority like Tara were ceremonial not administrative. The Confederate Catholics establishment of a new state centre at Kilkenny was a

phenomenon of true novelty in Ireland.

6 B. Anderson, *Imagined communities: reflection on the origin and spread of nationalism* (revised ed., New York, 1991), p. 6.

7 B. Kane, 'Making the Irish European: Gaelic honor politics and its continental contexts', *Renaissance Quarterly*, xli (2008), pp 1139-66.

8 On the 'conservatism' of Gaelic and Old English elites alike see for instance Canny, *Making Ireland British*, especially ch. 7; R. Gillespie, 'Negotiating order in early seventeenth-century Ireland', in M. Braddick and J. Walter (eds), *Negotiating power in early modern society: order, hierarchy and subordination in Britain and Ireland* (Cambridge, 2001), pp 188-205; C. Lennon, *The lords of the Dublin in the age of reformation* (Dublin, 1989); and, crucially, C. Brady, 'Conservative subversives: the community of the Pale and the Dublin administration, 1556-86', in P. J. Corish (ed.), *Radicals, rebels and establishments* (Belfast, 1985), pp 11-32.

9 Braddick employs the concept of 'dynastic state' precisely to describe this territorial expansion of the Tudor and Stuart state: see Braddick, *State formation*, pp 337-419.

10 H. Morgan, *Tyrone's rebellion: the outbreak of the Nine Years's War in Tudor Ireland* (Woodbridge, 1993), pp 177, 194, 201, 202, 206, 220.

11 Elizabeth I to Lord Deputy Russell and council, 25 May 1596 (*Cal. Carew MSS,* iii, p. 176).

12 For detailed discussion of Essex's views of honour and politics see P. Hammer, *The polarization of Elizabethan politics: the political career of Robert Devereux, 2nd earl of Essex, 1585-1597* (Cambridge, 1999).

13 Proceedings of Essex, 1 July 1599 (*Cal. Carew MSS*, iii, pp 311-2).

14 Lambeth Palace Library, Carew MSS, iii, p. 208 r.

15 *Cal. Carew MSS*, iii, p. 87.

16 Commissioners (Wallop and Gardiner) to the lord deputy and council, 23 January 1596 (ibid., p. 142).

17 Elizabeth I to Essex, 17 Sept 1599 (ibid., pp 235-7).

18 Elizabeth I to Secretary Geoffrey Fenton, 5 Nov 1599 (ibid., p. 343).

19 Essex's rebellion and execution similarly revealed limits to aristocratic honour politics in England: see M. James, '"At the crossroads of a political culture": the Essex Revolt, 1601', in M. James, *Society, politics and culture: studies in early modern England* (Cambridge, 1986), pp 416-65.

20 H. Pawlisch, *Sir John Davies and the conquest of Ireland: a study in legal imperialism* (Cambridge, 1985).

21 *Cal. Carew MSS*, iii, p. 349.

22 Bradshaw, 'Native reactions to the Westward Enterprise'; Caball, *Poets and politics*.

23 B. Ó Buachalla, '*Annala Ríoghachta Éireann* is *Foras Feasa ar Éirinn*: an comhthéacs comhaimseartha', *Studia Hibernica*, xxii-xxiii (1985), pp 59-105; idem, 'James our true king: the ideology of Irish royalism in the seventeenth century', in D. G. Boyce, R. Eccleshall and V. Geoghegan (eds), *Political thought in Ireland since the seventeenth century* (London, 1988), pp 7-35.

24 Mac Craith, 'Literature in Irish, c. 1550-1690', p. 208.

25 Ibid., p. 219.

26 N. J. A. Williams (ed.), *Pairlement Chloinne Tomáis* (Dublin, 1981).

27 Quoted in C. Ó Scea, 'The significance and legacy of Spanish intervention in west Munster during the battle of Kinsale', in T. O'Connor and M. A. Lyons (eds), *Irish migrants in Europe after Kinsale, 1602-1820* (Dublin, 2003), p. 39.

28 Lughaidh Ó Cléirigh, *Beatha Aodha Ruaidh Ui Dhomhnaill*, (ed. & trans.) P. Walsh (2 vols, Dublin, 1948-57), i, p. 121; D. Downey, 'Purity of blood and purity of faith in early modern Ireland', in A. Ford and J. McCafferty (eds), *The origins of sectarianism in early modern Ireland* (Cambridge, 2005), pp 216-28.

29 D. Shuger, 'Irishmen, aristocrats, and other white barbarians', *Renaissance Quarterly*, i (1997), p. 506.

30 The subversion described by Brady was, of course, innovative too in that it necessarily implied changed political arrangements in Ireland and with the crown. See Brady, 'Conservative subversives'.

31 On English notions of such a possibility based in common law thought see A. Cromartie, 'The constitutionalist revolution: the transformation of political culture in early Stuart England', *Past & Present,* clviii (1999), pp 76-120.

32 See Ó Buachalla, *Aisling ghéar*; É. Ó Ciardha, *Ireland and the Jacobite cause, 1685-1766: a fatal attachment* (Dublin, 2004).

33 Anderson, for example, opposes the dynastic realm and national community. Anderson, *Imagined communities*, pp 12, 19-22.

The view from Scotland: the Scottish context to the flight of the earls

Alison Cathcart

Despite the significance of the flight of the earls within Irish history, and regardless of its importance for James VI & I's subsequent policy of plantation in Ulster, Scottish historians have made little reference to the event. Indeed, quite apart from the growing body of literature, a product of the current trend for all things Irish-Scottish, and highlighting the close connections between Irish and Scottish Gaeldom, recent work on the Scottish Highlands and royal policy towards the region pays scant attention to the fact that after 1603, James was a king, no longer of Scotland, but of Great Britain and Ireland. If scholars are to appreciate fully the Scottish context to the flight, its repercussions for that kingdom must be examined within a British context. This essay aims, not simply to jump on the bandwagon of British history (even if its wheels are about to come off), but to highlight the importance of such a context in understanding events in one of the three kingdoms.

An integrated British or 'three kingdom' approach towards the history of the Atlantic Archipelago has produced much scholarly research. It has informed the work of medieval historians such as Robin Frame, Rees Davies and Alexander Grant, highlighting both the similarities and differences in the emergence of the four nations within the British Isles during the period from the eleventh to the fourteenth centuries.[1] Furthermore, a British perspective has also reinvigorated research into the civil wars of the seventeenth century and the acquisition of overseas territories as well as debates regarding issues such as nationalism, confessionalism and identity.[2] In short, this integrated, non-anglocentric approach to the understanding of the archipelago has produced a significant body of scholarly research. However, for the period from the mid-fifteenth through to the early seventeenth century this adoption of a British approach has its limitations. Apart from the work of some notable scholars, including Steven Ellis and Jane Dawson, a British perspective has yielded less.[3] This is not to assert that a British approach ought to be, or indeed should be, adopted; such a perspective carries its own limitations.[4] In late medieval and early modern Scotland, a continental perspective is of greater significance, especially if analysing political development at the so-called 'centre'. During this period, as recently argued by Jane Dawson, Scotland was a country of regions, and to focus solely on politics as defined and formulated at Edinburgh or London is to miss a great deal regarding Scotland's political development.[5]

This essay will also examine the extent to which the events of 1607 impacted on the formulation and execution of royal policy towards Scottish Gaeldom, and the reaction of Highland society to that policy. While Scottish historians have been reluctant to consider the wider context, it is unfair to point the finger solely at them. After all, contemporaries paid little attention to Irish affairs and, to a large extent, did so out of necessity. On 18 September 1607 the Privy Council in Edinburgh noted that:

> Some noblemen of the cuntrey of Ireland, with a nowmer of thair speciall freindis and dependairis, hes of lait, without the previtie, knawlege, and consent of his Majestie, or of the Lord Deputie of Ireland, tane schipping in Lochfuillie for some treasonable deseygne and practize aganis his Majesties estate and cuntrey.[6]

In response, the Privy Council ordered the sheriff of Wigtown, the steward of Kirkbudbright and the magistrates of the burgh of Kirkcudbright and all other towns along the west coast to give 'diligent attendance … upoun thair coistis and harboreyis, to espy gif ony Ireland men sall cum willinglie in thair boundis'.[7]

Irishmen who landed in Scotland would be arrested and handed over to the authorities. Apart from this, Scotland, or at least the Scottish administration, barely raised a collective eyebrow over the flight. An initial glance may suggest a negligible impact. However, this essay argues that Hugh O'Neill and Rory O'Donnell's dramatic departure had long-term repercussions for Scotland. These can be appreciated properly only by taking a long-term view and considering, not just events in Scotland and Ireland, but wider plantation projects of the early seventeenth century.[8]

From the moment James began his personal rule in Scotland, in 1584-85, he sought to bring the Highlands and Isles to order. Throughout his reign he initiated a number of policies that aimed to extend royal authority throughout the west. These efforts met with occasional success and during the course of the late 1580s and 1590s various Highland chiefs submitted and gave assurances for their good behaviour. Unfortunately for James, these submissions often proved tenuous; lawlessness and blatant flouting of royal authority remained the rule rather than the exception. He needed a more systematic, far-reaching policy, expressed in James's 'civilising' of the region, which aimed at 'reducing ... the rebellious inhabitants thairof to obedience ... establishing of peace, justice and quietnes', transforming the barbarous nature of the Highlanders, stimulating commercial development, increasing crown revenue, and fully integrating the region into Scottish society.[9] He packaged such policies in the rhetoric of religion, law and order, designed to appeal to the civic society of the Lowlands, many of whom, at times, were reluctant to support the king's expensive expansionist expeditions to the west.[10]

The employment of seasonal mercenaries from the islands and Highlands of Scotland – the Redshanks – greatly stimulated the militarisation of Ulster's lordships in the sixteenth century. © David Swift (Claoímh)

By the late 1590s, with the programme of civilising the Highland Gaels under way, James oscillated between various policies, including plantation. In his advice to his son Henry, he discussed the Highland problem and the best way to deal with the situation. Published in 1598, the *Basilicon Doron* offers some insight into James's contemporary mindset, as well as his plans for plantation, internal conquest and the imposition of crown authority. James asserted that his plan for the Highlanders was to plant:

> Colonies among them of answerable In-lands subiects that within short time may reforme and ciuilize the best inclined among them; rooting out or transporting the barbarous and stubborne sort, and planting ciuilitie in their rooms.[11]

Initial efforts to plant the west Highlands and Isles had begun in 1596 when Angus MacDonald of Clan Donald South submitted in writing to the king.[12] MacDonald agreed to hand over his eldest son James as a hostage, to 'remove himself, his family and dependers, and all others who are not actual tenants or possessors of the ground, out of the bounds of Kintyre and isle of Giga', and accept new crown tenants, notably in Islay, the traditional patrimony of his clan.[13] Although this particular scheme floundered, the policy of plantation soon extended to other parts of the region.[14] The foundations were laid by legislation passed in 1597 which required all landowners to appear before the council and show titles to land they inhabited. Plans for the plantation of Lewis followed suit.[15] Torquil Macleod, chief of the Macleods of Lewis, upon failure to produce his titles, lost the lands of Lewis, Ronalewis and Ilandschand, all of which reverted to the crown. Theoretically, this cleared the way for James to plant civic, God-fearing, rent-paying, obedient Lowland subjects into the Highland region.[16] In doing so, the king hoped to imbue the barbarous inhabitants with Lowland values and behaviour, resulting in the full assimilation of the Highlanders into the Scottish realm. However, he grossly underestimated the level of opposition to the planters from the inhabitants of the Isles, and the first attempt ended in 1601 with the planters either meeting their deaths at the hands of the islanders or fleeing back to the safety of Fife. These initial setbacks did little to dampen the king's enthusiasm, and he initiated a second attempt in August 1604.

By this time James VI of Scotland had become James I of England and Ireland and no longer resided in Edinburgh but managed the affairs of his three kingdoms from London. In 1603 he had also inherited an acute law and order problem in Ireland, most notably in the north. As king of Scotland he had been all too aware of how events in one realm could have repercussions elsewhere, and although he was now based in London, the situation in Scotland continued to warrant his attention. Knowledge that lawlessness in Scotland had the potential to spill over into Ireland, and vice versa, resulted in the proclamation 'that it cannot stand with his Hienes honour and princely dignitie that sic a unfamous byke of lawles lymmaris salbe sufferit in ony pairt of his Majesties dominions'.[17] Consequently, in February 1605 the king wrote from London to the three estates in Scotland encouraging the promotion of royal policy. Understandably, he turned his attention to the Isles, expressing his hope that 'the Yllis may be reduceit to oure obedyence, coloneis of civile and industrious people planted thair' whereby barbarity and poverty would be stamped out, while trade and profit would increase.

Despite ongoing opposition to plantation from the inhabitants of the Isles, on 18 July 1605 James asserted his intention that:

> The interpryse of the conques of Lewis … sal be yit prosequuted … in a mair substantious maner nor it wes befoir, as alswa that the haill remanent Ilis and lands nixt adjacent quha are now disobedient sal be reducit to his Hienes obedience.[18]

On 8 August 1605, James granted a commission of lieutenancy in the Western Isles and Kintyre to David Murray, Lord Scone, to undertake an expedition to the region for 'the furtherance and advancement of His Majesteis authoritie and service'.[19] In preparation, warrants were issued for Angus MacDonald of Clan Donald South and

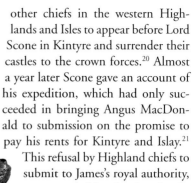

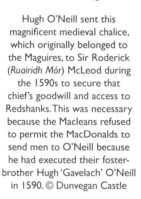

Hugh O'Neill sent this magnificent medieval chalice, which originally belonged to the Maguires, to Sir Roderick (*Ruairidh Mór*) McLeod during the 1590s to secure that chief's goodwill and access to Redshanks. This was necessary because the Macleans refused to permit the MacDonalds to send men to O'Neill because he had executed their foster-brother Hugh 'Gavelach' O'Neill in 1590. © Dunvegan Castle

other chiefs in the western Highlands and Isles to appear before Lord Scone in Kintyre and surrender their castles to the crown forces.[20] Almost a year later Scone gave an account of his expedition, which had only succeeded in bringing Angus MacDonald to submission on the promise to pay his rents for Kintyre and Islay.[21]

This refusal by Highland chiefs to submit to James's royal authority, compounded by the situation in Lewis, was 'a matter twitching His Hienes in honour'.[22] Indeed, James had declared to the three Scottish estates a year previously that bringing the Isles to order would benefit the whole nation economically and increase Scotland's reputation in Europe.[23]

James appreciated the problem of his 'north', the north and west Highlands and Islands where men followed clan chiefs and lived according to their own rules.[24] Highland lawlessness had been of concern to Scottish monarchs throughout the previous centuries, but James, as monarch of three kingdoms, could no longer choose to ignore it.[25] In July 1604 he confirmed an earlier grant of all the lands of the Route and the Glens of Antrim to Sir Randall MacDonnell. This grant contained a clause which authorised Sir Randal to divide the territory into parts of around 2,000 acres and build a castle or mansion house in each. Later, between December 1604 and February 1606, James issued instructions and grants which laid the foundations for the Hamilton-Montgomery plantation of Down and the Ards in the north-east of Ireland.[26] The future success of such endeavours depended on limiting the movement of his lawless subjects from the west of Scotland to the north of Ireland. In short, and as far as James was concerned, the situation in the Highlands was of 'grite hurt' to 'the commonweill', but it was also offensive to his position as sovereign.[27] Although James liked to theorise about kingship (as highlighted in *The Trew Law of Free Monarchies*), he chose to compromise in pursuit of a workable solution (as suggested in *Basilicon Doron*).[28] He would not, however, concede on the fundamental principle of royal authority.[29] The Highland chiefs' refusal to acknowledge his sovereignty heightened James's determination to deal with lawlessness in the west. In doing so he fell back on the tried and tested methods of his predecessors and relied on local and regional magnates to help execute royal policy in the west.

Throughout the sixteenth century successive Scottish monarchs had delegated responsibility for Highlands and Island affairs to the Gordons of Huntly in the North Isles and the Campbells of Argyll in the South Isles, and James again turned to the heads of these houses. On 3 December 1606 he declared his intention that George Gordon, sixth earl and first marquis of Huntly, should 'reduce the North Yllis … to civilitie and oure obedyence'.[30] Having thrashed out the finer details of the plan by 30 April 1607, Huntly agreed to settle the region, by extirpating its inhabitants, specifically the Clan Donald.[31] Fortunately for them, the Clan Donald and the rest of the inhabitants of the North Isles received an eleventh-hour reprieve, albeit indirectly, when James finally succumbed to pressure from an increasingly outspoken Protestant kirk that sought to push ecclesiastical proceedings against Huntly on account of his Catholicism. In June 1607 he ordered Huntly to confine himself within the burgh of Elgin, thereby ensuring that he played no further part in plantation in the Isles.

Huntly's fate contrasted sharply with the fortunes of Archibald Campbell, seventh earl of Argyll, in the Isles. The Campbell clan had been steadily acquiring further territory and influence in the south-west Highlands and Isles since the forfeiture of the MacDonald lordship of the Isles in 1493. Moreover, successive earls of Argyll had gained crown commissions to pursue unruly Highland clans, specifically the Clan Donald, and had benefited from such service. Nevertheless, the Campbells had faced internal weakness during the minority of the seventh earl, and James appeared reluctant to allow further extensions to Campbell jurisdiction in the west. However, in the early years of the seventeenth century Argyll had been instrumental in executing James's action against the Macgregors. In return, the king

An image of a galloglass.

'maid promise to give to the Erle of Ergyle ane worthie reward, to remayne heretablie with him and his aires heirafter'.[32] This reward, bestowed in 1607, comprised a 'gift of the landis of Kintyre' which had been previously held by the Clan Donald South. In putting forward Argyll's case, the Privy Council reminded James that the lands were small and that he had not received due rents or profits from them.[33] Moreover, it assured the king that a grant of Kintyre to the earl would assist him in his actions against the Clan Donald:

> the scoolemaisteris and fosteraris of all barbaritie, savaignes, and crueltye … addicit nocht only to rebellioun within this continent land and the iles, bot evir wer assisteris of the northern Irische people, dwelling in Ireland, in all thair rebellionis.[34]

Thus, it was asserted, Argyll's action against the Clan Donald would 'procuire thair ruitteing out and utter suppressing' and 'be ane feir to those in the northe of Ireland to rebel, having ane enemye lyand sa neir to thame'.[35]

The Scottish Privy Council fully appreciated the wider context of James's policy and highlighted that the gift of Kintyre to Argyll would assist in establishing law and order in Scotland – and Ireland. Indeed, in advocating 'the removeing of that mischevous Clan … thair utter extirpatioun and ruitteing out', the council argued that:

> sa lang as the said Clan Donald remaynes unremoveit furth of the saidis landis, his Majestie nor na utheris sal half any proffeit, and the uncivilitie and barbaritie sall continew nocht only thair bot in the Iles.[36]

James needed little more persuading, and Argyll promptly received infeftment of the lands of Kintyre on 30 May 1607.[37]

The acquisition by the Campbell chief of Clan Donald South's land precipitated a spontaneous outbreak of rebellion. On 16 July 1607, Sir Arthur Chichester, Lord Deputy of Ireland, informed the English Privy Council that Angus MacDonald and his men were planning an attack on Kintyre,[38] intelligence which he also imparted to the earl of Argyll. Two weeks later, on 31 July, the Scottish Privy Council likewise noted that Angus MacDonald and others of the Clan Donald had amassed a force of men and galleys with the intention 'to invaid and persew his Majesteis guid subjectis be sey and land'.[39] On 12 August, in consequence of this highlander unrest, Argyll received a commission of lieutenancy and justiciary that extended across much of the South Isles.[40]

In presenting Argyll's case to the king, the Scottish Privy Council noted the importance of his actions against the Clan Donald South in a Scottish and wider archipelagic context. In a calculated move, the council fully appreciated the king's belief that unrest in one of his kingdoms had repercussions in another. James had emphasised the importance of his policies towards the Highlands as being not just for the commonweal of Scotland, but for his 'haill impyre'. Thus the council's assertion that Argyll would bring stability to the Highlands and secure the coastal borders against the Irish rebels deliberately attempted to ensure that James would grant Kintyre to Argyll, rather than continue to work towards a solution involving the MacDonald chief himself and his son James.[41]

Earlier in the 1590s Argyll had been threatened by the king's preference for an accommodation with the Hebridean elite. The crown had made plantation agreements for the Western Isles with Angus MacDonald of Clan Donald South (1596) and Sir James, his son (1599), although these were never implemented.[42] In 1597 James MacDonnell of the Glens had won the king's favour and, although denied title to Kintyre and Islay, was knighted Sir James MacDonnell of Dunluce in December of that year. He also received lands in south Kintyre.[43] MacDonnell sought to reunite the Clan Donald lands, but Argyll, fearful of a reunited and reinvigorated MacDonald lordship that straddled the Irish Sea, thwarted his endeavours.[44] Failure to reach a workable solution with the Highland chiefs, combined with the reactions of the MacLeod chief to the Lewis plantation, prompted the king to look to regional magnates and Lowland lords to implement his policies. Argyll was well placed to benefit from this strategy. While the MacDonalds continued to feud amongst themselves, the Campbells worked to extend their influence at Clan Donald's expense. By 1607 Argyll appeared to be the clear winner.

The flight of Tyrone, Tyrconnell and their associates in September 1607 frustrated James's hopes of reaching a workable compromise with the former. Their departure, and fears of their imminent return, focused many minds. The Scottish Privy Council feared that the fall-out would exacerbate an already unstable situation in the west of Scotland and legislated to contain the situation.[45] The subsequent outbreak of Sir Cathair O'Doherty's rebellion in April 1608 resulted in a spate of communication between the Scottish Privy Council and Lord Deputy Chichester regarding the deployment of both land and naval forces in Ulster and the Isles, as well as the framing of additional legislation to prevent movement of rebels between Scotland and Ireland. By July the rebellion was over, which, according to the Scottish Privy Council's declaration of 2 August 1608, was nothing short of a sign from God 'manifesting his divyne providence and cair quhilk he hes … for the preservatioun and mantenance of all lauchfull authoriteis'.[46]

Indeed, the flight proved providential for James, offering him the opportunity to consider his plans for Ireland on a much grander scale.[47] With the removal of the elite from a large swathe of Ulster, James could readily plant loyal, obedient Protestants to advance commercial activities in the area. In some cases there was no need to remove the tenants, as they could be used to work the land, and, according to the English point of view, it had been the elites who bound the ordinary people to the Catholic religion.[48] James preferred loyal Protestant undertakers, but happily accepted Catholic undertakers such as Randal MacDonnell of Antrim, so long as they acknowledged his royal authority. With large tracts of the north and west of Ireland now vacant, and with the key MacDonnells onside and the Hamilton-Montgomery plantation under way in Down and the Ards, the king had the opportunity to introduce plantation on a much wider scale in Ulster. This would offer no refuge to his unruly Highlanders whose mercenary activities were being curtailed at home. Until then, the extirpation of Highlanders from their lands had the potential to create havoc in Ireland. Now the king could anticipate both regions becoming pacified and commercially orientated. James adapted his policy accordingly and sought instead to reach agreement with the Highland elite, an easier and more profitable solution.

'A Galloglass Wields His Great Axe'. The axe was rendered increasingly obsolete by Hugh O'Neill's military modernisation. Nevertheless, the MacDonnell galloglass provided the nucleus of his pike regiment in the 1590s. © Seán Ó Brógáin

The impact of 1607 is also evident on the attitude of the Highland chiefs themselves. They had recently witnessed the crown's repeated attempts at the Lewis plantation despite opposition from the Macleods; the Clan Donald South faced displacement as the earl of Argyll acquired legal rights to their lands; their allies across the Irish Sea had fled to the continent. As the crown made preparations for another expedition to the Isles, the wording of the commission issued to Andrew Knox, bishop of the Isles, alluded to the king's threat of 'all kynd of hostilitie yf thay continuew rebellious and dissobedyent'.[49] Ongoing opposition to the crown looked distinctly unappealing. At the same time, Angus MacDonald of Dunivaig could look to Randal MacDonnell in Antrim and recognise the benefits that came from co-operation with the crown. Rather than be forced from their land by Argyll or see their patrimonial lands planted like Lewis, when Lord Ochiltree's expedition reached the Isles with orders from James to negotiate with the clan chiefs, Bishop Knox found the Highland elite amenable. Historians have proffered differing interpretations on this change of heart. Macinnes's claim that the 'aversion of chiefs and leading clan gentry to collaborate with Ochiltree and Knox was ... remedied after brief gaoling in the Lowlands' is rather too simplistic.[50] In contrast, Martin MacGregor has suggested that a 'constant factor conditioning the behaviour of the Hebridean elite since spring 1608 must have been fear'.[51] Certainly these factors contributed, but the realisation on the part of Highland chiefs that ongoing resistance to crown policy would prompt further ruthless, coercive government action ultimately

encouraged their compliance and willingness to negotiate terms and acknowledge royal authority. In the resulting Statutes of Iona, James achieved what he had originally intended: not the removal of the clan elite, but instead their assimilation into Scottish landed society.[52]

James's plan for Scotland had originally envisaged integration. While the Highlands and Isles were a 'member of your awne body', in contrast Gaelic Ireland was 'no parte of this kingdome'.[53] As Macinnes has argued, 'concerted British action did not require a uniform policy for civilising the Gael'.[54] Certainly James did not have a blanket policy for Gaeldom, but instead was responsive to events as they happened. In Ireland, the flight of the earls allowed James to embark on a scheme for the plantation of Ulster. In Scotland, it heralded an end to plantation programmes and instead prompted the creation of a new set of circumstances within which a negotiated, conciliatory agreement could be reached. The events of 1607 had brought home to the Highland chiefs the seriousness of their situation and their realisation that continued opposition to interventionist crown policy was not going to reap the rewards they wanted. For both parties, the negotiations that resulted in the Statutes of Iona of 1609 were the best outcome and a direct result of events that occurred in Ireland. The flight, then, had a significant impact on the development and implementation of crown policy in Scotland, initiating a shift from coercion to conciliation and ultimately paving the way for the integration of the Highland elite into Scottish society and the new commercial world of the seventeenth century.

Notes

1 N. Davies, *The Isles: A History* (London, 1999); R. Frame, *The political development of the British Isles, 1100-1400* (Oxford, 1995); R. R. Davies, *Domination and Conquest: the experience of Ireland, Scotland and Wales 1100-1300* (Cambridge, 1990).

2 A. I. Macinnes, *The British Revolution, 1629-60* (Basingstoke, 2005); J. Kenyon and J. Ohlmeyer (eds), *The Civil Wars: a military history of England, Scotland and Ireland, 1638-1660* (Oxford, 1998).

3 A number of invaluable edited collections have stimuled further work in this field; S. G. Ellis & S. Barber (eds), *Conquest and union: fashioning a British state, 1485-1725* (London, 1995); B. Bradshaw and J. Morrill (eds), *The British Problem c. 1534-1707: state formation in the Atlantic Archipelago* (Basingstoke, 1996); S. G. Ellis & C. Maginn,

The Making of the British Isles: the state of Britain and Ireland 1450-1660 (Harlow, 2007); J. Dawson, *The politics of religion in the Age of Mary, Queen of Scots. The earl of Argyll and the struggle for Britain and Ireland* (Cambridge, 2002); C. Kellar, *Scotland, England and the Reformation 1534-61* (Oxford, 2003); M. Merriman, *The rough wooings: Mary Queen of Scots 1542-1551* (East Linton, 2000).

4 A. I. Macinnes, 'Making the plantations British, 1603-38', in S. G. Ellis & R. Esser (eds), *Frontiers and the writing of History, 1500-1850* (Wehrhahn Verlag, Laatzen, 2006), pp 95-125.

5 J. Dawson, *Scotland re-formed* (Edinburgh, 2007).

6 *Register of the Privy Council of Scotland*, vii, p. 439 [henceforth *RPCS*]

7 Ibid.

8 Macinnes, 'Making the plantations British, 1603-38', pp 95-125.

9 *RPCS*, iii, pp 87-88.

10 Ibid., viii, p. 502.

11 James VI, *Basilicon Doron* in J. P. Sommerville (ed.), *King James VI & I: Political Writings* (Cambridge, 1994), p. 24.

12 Otherwise known as the MacDonalds of Dunivaig. They had separated from the MacDonalds of the Glens, the Irish branch of the family, in 1589.

13 *RPCS*, vi, p. 321; D. Gregory, *History of the western highlands and islands of Scotland, 1492-1625* (Edinburgh, 1836), pp 268-74.

14 *RPCS*, vi, pp 24-25.

15 *Acts of the Parliament of Scotland*, iv, pp 138-9; *RPCS*, v, pp 455, 462-3; Gregory, *Highlands and islands*, pp 276-7.

16 *APS*, iv, pp 160-4; *RPCS*, v, pp 462-3; Gregory, *Highlands*, p. 279.

17 *RPCS*, vii, p. 89.

18 *RPCS*, vii, pp 84-90, especially p. 87; M. Perceval-Maxwell, *The Scottish Migration to Ulster in the Reign of James I* (London, 1973), p. 12.

19 *RPCS*, vii, pp 59-60, 69-70, 115-7.

20 Ibid., p. 59.

21 Ibid., p. 229.

22 Ibid., p. 229.

23 Ibid.. p. 466.

24 R. Bartlett, *Gerald of Wales* (Oxford, 1982), pp 158-77; D. B. Quinn, 'Ireland and sixteenth century European expansion', in T. D. Williams (ed.), *Historical Studies*, i (London, 1958), pp 20-32; D. Shuger, 'Irishmen, aristocrats, and other white barbarians', *Renaissance Quarterly*, l (1997), pp 494-525.

25 A. I. Macinnes, 'Crown, clan and fine: the 'civilizing' of Scottish Gaeldom, 1587-1638', *Northern Scotland*, xiii (1993), p. 31.

26 Perceval-Maxwell, *Scottish Migration to Ulster*, pp 47-56; Grant to James Hamilton, 26 July 1607, *CSPI*, xii, p. 233.

27 *RPCS*, vii, p. 89.

28 Sommerville (ed.), *James VI & I: Political Writings*, pp 1-61, 62-84.

29 R. Mason, 'Renaissance and Reformation: the Sixteenth Century', in J. Wormald (ed.), *Scotland. A History* (Oxford, 2005), pp 138-9.

30 *RPCS*, vii, pp 504, 516.

31 Ibid., pp 60-61.

32 Ibid., p. 749.

33 Ibid.

34 Ibid.

35 Ibid.

36 Ibid., p. 750.

37 *Registrum Magni Sigilli Regum Scotorum*, vi, no. 1911, p. 750, *RPCS*, vii, 750 n.1; *APS*, iv, pp 559-60.

38 Chichester to the Privy Council, 16 July 1607, *CSPI, 1606-08*, p. 223.

39 *RPCS*, p. 423.

40 Excluding the north isles: ibid., pp 426-7.

41 After Angus MacDonald's submission in the wake of Lord Scone's expedition, the chief had attempted to negotiate with council and had submitted proposals see *Criminal trials in Scotland, from A.D. M.CCC.LXXXVIII to A.D. M.DC.XXIV, embracing the entire reigns of James IV and V, Mary Queen of Scots and James VI. Compiled from the original record and MSS with historical notes and illustrations, by Robert Pitcairn*, iii (Edinburgh, 1833), pp 365-6.

42 Gregory, *History*, pp 288-90.

43 *Registrum Magni Sigilli Regum Scotorum*, vi, p. 554.

44 *Criminal trials in Scotland*, pp 365-6; Gregory, *Highlands and islands*, pp 310-1.

45 *RPCS*, vii, p. 439.

46 *RPCS*, viii, p. 140.

47 Perceval-Maxwell, *Scottish Migration to Ulster*, pp 49, 53, 71-77.

48 'A discovery of the decayed state of the Kingdom of Ireland, and of the means to repower the same', *CSPI, 1603-06*, pp 217-28

49 *RPCS*, viii, p. 756.

50 Macinnes, 'Making the plantations British, 1603-38', p. 104.

51 M. MacGregor, 'The Statutes of Iona: text and context', *The Innes Review*, lvii: 2 (2006), p. 115.

52 Macinnes, 'Making the plantations British, 1603-38', p. 105.

53 *RPCS*, pp 742-6 quoted in MacGregor, 'The Statutes of Iona', p. 132.

54 Macinnes, 'Making the plantations British, 1603-38', p. 104.

What if the earls had landed in Spain? The flight's Spanish context

Óscar Recio Morales

At the beginning of 1606, in a revealing report presented to the king of Spain by Mathew Tully, the Irish agent dispatched by the Ulster earls to Philip III, it emerged that Hugh O'Neill and Rory O'Donnell were 'forced and determined to flee for their lives to the succour of Your Majesty'. Tully also forewarned of the consequences of such a decision: 'If they come to Spain, their land will be lost and Your Majesty, in conscience and in honour, will be obliged to maintain them here, in accordance to their services and 'nobility' (*calidades*) as noble princes who had rendered great and heroic deeds in your royal service'.[1]

While the flight might have appeared as a surprise, a hasty, impulsive choice which facilitated the colonisation of Ulster, the document demonstrates that the Irish had already given serious notice to Philip III on the possibility of escaping Ireland at least one year in advance. The earls had considered the possibility of leaving Ireland for Spain long before September 1607, and the Spanish councillors had been made aware of this. Tully had also given careful consideration in his report to the serious consequences that would ensue in Ireland ('their land will be lost') if they came to Spain and became the Spanish king's responsibility. Tully's *if* was perhaps intended to sound menacing to the ears of the Spanish councillors. After all, following the defeat at Kinsale (1601), Philip III asked O'Neill to resist in Ulster for as long as possible, 'and I will take special care and succour of you, and having this in mind I am preparing and carrying the means'.[2]

Fortunately for the Spanish interests, Tully's threat did not materialise. On their arrival on the continent, Hugh O'Neill and Rory O'Donnell did not make landfall in Galicia, but in Normandy, and from there they sought the protection of the governor of the Spanish Netherlands. Irish and Spanish sources tell of their warm reception in Brussels. On 3 November 1607 Ambrogio Spinola, the famous Genoese general in the service of Spain, received the exiles and sent Madrid a list of the Irish 'who travel to Spain' (*que van a España*).[3] Two days later Archduke Albert and the Infanta Isabel received them at the royal palace.[4] Active Spanish diplomacy

Donal Cam O'Sullivan Beare (1561-1618) joined the Spanish stragglers from the Kinsale expedition who had landed at Castlehaven to fight the English. In the process, he swore fealty to Philip III and this placed him in a favourable position at the Spanish court when he fled there after 1603. Lithograph of a portrait in St Patrick's College, Maynooth. © Inch House Irish Studies Centre

in Europe actually prevented the earls journeying to Spain, instead plotting a logistically complicated operation to direct them to Rome, a non-Spanish territory where the Spaniards exercised considerable political influence.[5] So while the authorities in Madrid ignored all the extradition petitions from James I of England, they also neglected the exiles' requests for refuge in Spain.

The end of the story is well known. Until his death in 1616 Hugh O'Neill received the spiritual backing of the Holy See and the financial support, via secret funds, from the Spanish embassy in Rome.[6] The Spanish ambassador paid his funeral expenses. Although buried far from Spain, he was

Philip II's El Escorial functioned as monastery, royal palace and Habsburg mausoleum. From here, the king governed his affairs with solomonic deliberation.

interred in Spanish soil – in the Franciscan church of San Pietro in Montorio, Rome.[7] Madrid attained its goal of keeping the earls under control in Italy, a bitter experience for the Irish exiles. Abandonment and powerlessness became their lot from 1608: too far from any centre close to Ireland (Galicia, Lisbon or Flanders) and removed from the Spanish court at Madrid, the main font of the Spanish king's enormous patronage and the real centre of the empire. Yet, what could have happened if the earls *had* come to Spain in 1607, as Matthew Tully intimated in his report?

Tully had warned Philip III in his 1606 report that *if* the earls reached Spain, 'Your Majesty will be obliged to maintain them'. Providing for the earls and their immediate retinue would not have been a problem for Madrid, but the pull factor created by their presence might well have given rise to difficulties. The first generation of Irish arriving in Spain in the wake of Kinsale coincided with the beginnings of a reign which was rather open-handed in the concession of privilege, in contrast to Philip II's practice. Consequently, these newly arrived families reaped maximum benefits in compensation for the help they had previously rendered the Spanish in Kinsale. They thus did no more than follow the trend of the hundreds of *memoriales* pouring into the Chamber of Castile, requesting compensation from the Spanish monarch for their services in Ireland or for their defence of the Catholic religion there.[8]

The Irish College at Salamanca confirmed that 'news of the form of generosity and alms from Your Majesty is spreading throughout Ireland'.[9] The arrival of Irish refugees to the northern ports of Spain and Portugal became a major problem for the local authorities. To prevent them from heading for the Spanish court – exceptionally located in Valladolid between 1601 and 1606 – the Spanish administration issued a precise order to impede their landing and to repatriate them immediately.[10] The order failed to produce the desired effects, since it was later repeated, insisting that all royal officials ensure 'that no Irish land in your district and [that you] should punish the royal officer through whose carelessness or fault they get in'.[11] By mid-1605 the viceroy of Galicia admitted being overwhelmed by the situation and reported that 'I await every single day an answer on what to do with these Irish who arrive in great numbers day after day'.[12] The *corregidor* of Asturias found himself in a similar situation, informing the king of the arrival at the port of Candás of a ship with sixty Irish aboard, 'and because there is word of five more ships loaded with the same people on the way, I beseech Your Majesty to give me orders as to what is to be done with them'.[13]

If the earls had landed in northern Spain, they would have been received according to their 'nobility' (*calidad*). After all, in a memorandum submitted to the Holy See, Tyrone and Tyrconnell considered themselves as 'descendants from the kingdoms

141

of Galicia, Asturias and Cantabria'.[14] Following Kinsale, Red Hugh O'Donnell had already been received at La Coruña in February 1602 by the viceroy of Galicia, Luis Carrillo de Toledo, count of Caracena.[15]

The increasing importance of Galicia in the Atlantic military strategy of the Spanish monarchy made this territory a favoured destination for Irish emigrants at the time. From 1602 Galicia served as a 'shock-absorber' for the Irish, mitigating the hardships of exile, especially thanks to the personal involvement of Caracena. The incorporation of Portugal into the Spanish empire in 1580 and the preparations for the Armada of 1588 dramatically upgraded Galicia's strategic importance. During the 1590s the territory served as the base of operations for the successive fleets entrusted with the protection of the convoys from the New World and for Brittany. Its participation in the rescue of the survivors of Kinsale and its prominence in the sea route to Flanders from the 1580s confirm the strategic role of Galicia in the Atlantic military system of the Spanish monarchy.[16]

In the aftermath of Kinsale, the Irish were fortunate in having a viceroy so favourable to their cause as was Caracena. He followed closely the Kinsale affair, and he took into his own house four Irish nobles – Berehaven, Castlehaven and Baltimore, accompanied by Castlehaven's brother and some of his servants.[17] He did not hesitate in supporting the Irish allies when, in the wake of the disaster of Kinsale, criticism of them had reached fever-pitch within Spanish military circles seeking to play down their own military shortcomings.[18] Hugh O'Neill signed the Treaty of Mellifont (1603), and Caracena tried to mitigate Spanish disappointment – even if their Irish allies had already begun definitive peace talks with England. The Galician governor declared that O'Neill had done 'everything humanly possible to the limits of his supplies and strength'.[19] Caracena also acted as intermediary with the Spanish court for numerous Irish petitions and gained a reputation as genuine protector among the exiles in Galicia.[20] He continually warned that a considerable number of Irish would abandon Galicia for the court, if adequate resources were not provided for him to satisfy them in Galicia. This is precisely what happened after 1607.

Even if Hugh O'Neill and Rory O'Donnell had been received according to their nobility, they would probably not have found the favourable disposition Irish exiles encountered in Caracena. The circumstances of the Irish in Galicia had changed radically with the arrival of Diego Parragués de las Mariñas as acting governor in 1606. Only a month after his arrival he lamented that 'maintaining these people [Irish exiles] so far has caused me great ef-

The ruins of Dunboy Castle, seat of the O'Sullivans of Beare.

fort and labour'.[21] His correspondence bristled with references to the Irish as 'foreigners' (*extranjeros*) and 'tiresome ones' (*inoportunos*); they had even become a security problem: 'no matter how Catholic they are and how faithfully they serve … so many of them are coming and spies could easily be concealed in their midst'.[22] The difficult situation got completely out of hand in 1607 with the breakdown in payments of pensions to the Irish refugees.

If the earls had landed in Galicia, most probably the Spanish authorities would have tried to delay their arrival at the Spanish court, as had been done with Red Hugh O'Donnell in 1602. Had they been granted licences to come to court, they would have been faced with a difficult economic situation which stemmed from the only bankruptcy of Philip III's reign.[23] Total state debt in 1607 amounted to more than 23 million ducats, resulting in bankruptcy, the suspension of payments and the conversion of the current short-term debts of about 12 million ducats to a long-term debt with lower interest rates (5 per cent in nineteen years). The immediate interruption of the pensions to the Irish in Galicia triggered a wave of petitions for licences to attend the court. While Caracena had struggled to avoid such an exodus, Mariñas put no obstacles in their way. Luis de Luján Enríquez, who replaced Mariñas as governor in 1607, followed his predecessor's policy.[24] Thus John Geraldine obtained permission to reside at court for a four-month period; Dermicio O'Sullivan moved from La Coruña to Madrid to demand his monthly assignment of fifty escudos. Eugenio Carthy, the rector of the Irish College in Santiago, turned up at court to claim his twenty escudo grant. In June 1607 Dermicio and Thadeo O'Driscoll, together with their wives and children, totalling twenty people, had already reached Madrid, not having received their pensions in Galicia over the previous eighteen months.[25]

The pursuit of noble title provided a surer means of receiving more regular pension payments. In 1607 Daniel O'Sullivan Beare, son of Donal Cam O'Sullivan, entered the military Order of Santiago. Towards 1607, Walter Burke, a page to the king and son of Theobald Burke, lord of MacWilliam Burke, joined the same order. The recognition bestowed upon the O'Sullivan family continued with the entry into the same Order of Santiago of another son, also a page to the king, Dermicio O'Sullivan, in 1613.[26] Donal Cam O'Sullivan entered the order

Philip III (1578-1621) was less hard-working and gifted than his father. But Spain's disengagement from war against England and the Dutch rebels owed more to Spanish exhaustion and the need for financial retrenchment than his limited abilities. © Prado Museum, Madrid

in 1617, and also obtained in the same year the Castilian title *Conde de Birhaven* for himself and his descendants.[27] The court turned out to be the ideal milieu for the social ascent of this family. Dermicio O'Sullivan held the posts of treasury councillor, *gentilhombre de la boca* and royal butler.[28] Thus, in the years immediately following Kinsale, other Irish families of lesser influence in Ireland than the O'Neills and the O'Donnells were to fill the roles these latter could have filled in Spain. Instead the Ulster families came to occupy prominent places in the Spanish Army of Flanders – particularly the O'Neill family, who monopolized the position of Colonel of the Irish *tercio* since 1604, when Madrid conceded the first colonelship to Henry O'Neill.[29]

Had the earls, like other Irish lords, managed to establish themselves at the Spanish court, they would have been integrated into the Irish lobby group.[30] This group upheld a firmly pro-interventionist attitude, and the Spaniards believed that the presence of the earls in Madrid would only radicalise the group's position, as the Ulster lords would vigorously pursue new military aid. In July 1608 just three months after their arrival in Rome the earls sent news to Madrid on a new uprising in Ireland – Sir Cathair O'Doherty's revolt in Ulster – and pleaded for Spanish support. However, the

The Anglo-Spanish peace of 1604 made it less likely that Spain would intervene militarily in Ireland. It also explains why the earls were not permitted to stay in Spanish lands after their flight. © NPG

new international context hampered any Spanish military support for the Irish.[31] The 1604 peace with England – and with Spain at peace also with France from 1598 – heralded a new period of appeasement in the Spanish global strategy, the so-called *Pax Hispanica*. A welcome relief for an exhausted Spain, it in no way favoured the interests of Irish Catholics. Moreover, in 1609 Spain and the United Provinces signed a truce in the Eighty Years War (1568-1648). This confirmed 1609 as an *annus horribilis* for the Irish as James I of England announced his plans for the Ulster plantation. It also marked the maximum degree of tension between the aspirations of the Irish group and the Spanish policy of appeasement. This turned the Irish into a troublesome and problematic group: they openly blamed Madrid for doing nothing to stop the land confiscations. Father Florence Conry underlined the despair among the Irish 'to see their affairs going so badly and Your Majesty not favouring them so much as was initially expected'.[32]

Within the groups of Irish close to the Spanish court, the most prominent were members of the religious orders. However, they did not succeed in presenting a united front. The Franciscan Conry and the Jesuit James Archer (c. 1551-1620) exemplify this division. Conry became one of the most influential figures among the Irish exile from 1602 until his death in Madrid in 1629. His career at court began following the death of his protector, Red Hugh O'Donnell, at Simancas in 1602.[33] From 1604 to 1610 Conroy worked as assistant to the Spanish 'Protector of the Irish', drawing up lists of fellow countrymen and certifying the condition and nobility of each one of them. On the other hand, Archer played a key role in the foundation of the Irish College at Salamanca in 1592.

The aspirations of the Jesuits with respect to the Irish colleges immediately clashed with those of the Irish community of Gaelic origin, predominantly of Ulster and Connacht origin and traditionally close to the Franciscans. The Franciscans had a very well-placed figure in Conry, who headed a radical opposition to Jesuit claims in the early years of the seventeenth century. The confrontation served to clarify the ultimate aims of these institutions, fundamentally their nature as seminaries. This clash proved detrimental to an Irish nobility interested in an education that would prepare their offspring for posts in the civil administration, because the dispute caused a notable loss of prestige for the Irish clergy among the Spanish councillors and among the different foreign groups present at the court.[34]

As we have seen, a series of pragmatic reasons can explain the Spanish insistence from 1607 that the Irish earls should not be permitted to reside in Spain. Conry's departure from the Spanish court after receiving Philip III's permission to establish a Franciscan college at Louvain in 1606 not only facilitated the manoeuvres of the Jesuits in Spain, but also relieved the pressure on the court of a influential lobbyist. His position almost always advocated military action to recover the confiscated states in Ulster. He also regularly disavowed any accommodation with England and criticised Madrid's diplomatic and military inaction. During the period of the *Pax Hispanica* the Spanish authorities had been successful in their policy of keeping significant Irish lords and their agents away from the Spanish court. Significantly, the Irish had colleges in such important cities on the Iberian peninsula as Lisbon (1590), Salamanca (1592), Santiago (1605) and Seville (1612), but they did not count on a similar institution in the very centre of the Spanish empire until 1629 – St Patrick's College in Madrid.[35]

Despite the intense diplomatic activity between the Spanish monarchy and their Ulster allies during the Nine Years War, the lack of stories in Spain about the flight of the earls is somewhat paradoxical. This contrasts with the rich references in the Spanish Golden Age literature about the Irish community.[36] Apart from the official reports there appear to be no Spanish stories about the flight.[37] This suggests two possibilities. The first is that the story was not deemed worthy to be narrated or collected in the popular Spanish literature of the age. I do not think this is the case, given the popular interest in 'Irish matters' (*asuntos de Irlanda*) in seventeenth-century Spain, the Spanish links with the Ulster earls before and after Kinsale, and the heroic nature of their flight throughout Europe. It is more likely to be related to the second possibility: that the Spanish authorities tried to contain this episode within the strictest official diplomatic circle.

Notes

1 Matthew Tully to Philip III, 16 Feb. 1606 (Archivo General de Simancas (AGS), Estado (E), legajo (leg.) 1797). Hugh O'Neill (c. 1550-1616) and Hugh O'Donnell (c. 1571-1602) had formally transferred their sovereignty to king Philip II of Spain (1556-98) 4 Apr. 1597 (AGS, E, leg. 492). In 1599 they renewed their allegiance to the Spanish crown when they received from Spain a set of gold chains and a portrait of the new king, Philip III. Assembled at the Franciscan monastery in Donegal, O'Neill and O'Donnell, with other 60 Irish lords, 'received the gold chains and Your Majesty portrait with particular ceremonies, saying they will not receive another yoke or other chain, but those of Your Majesty' Fr Mateo de Oviedo, archbishop of Dublin, to Philip III, 24 Apr. 1600 (AGS, E, leg. 840, f. 74), Oviedo accompanied the Spanish agent Martín de la Cerda to Donegal in 1600 and thereafter remained in Ireland as Philip III's permanent envoy to the Irish confederates.

2 Philip III to Tyrone, 24 Jan. 1603 (AGS, E, leg. 2571, f. 3). To this end, in March 1602 the council of state ordered to send 50,000 ducats to Tyrone, together with arms and ammunition; in November the amount was reduced to 30,000 ducats, but with the promise to send 10,000 ducats a month until 6 Jan. 1603 (AGS, Consejo y Juntas de Hacienda (CJH), leg. 431-6). It was not until April 1603 when the two ships loaded with weapons, ammunition and money departed from La Coruña. One year had passed since the first order and a month after O'Neill had been forced to capitulate in Mellifont. Consequently, the Spanish ships returned to Spain: Philip III to Caracena, Segovia, 22 Aug. 1609 (AGS, Guerra Antigua (GA), leg. 717).

3 Spinola's report, 3 Nov. 1607 (AGS, E, leg. 625, f. 113-4).

4 Ibid., f. 115.

5 See T. J. Dandelet, 'Spanish conquest and colonization at the centre of the Old World: The Spanish nation in Rome, 1555-1625', *Journal of Modern History*, lxix: 3 (1997), pp 479-511; idem, *Spanish Rome, 1500-1700* (New Haven, 2001).

6 The Spanish council of state conceded 700 ducats monthly each to O'Neill and O'Donnell: Aytona to Philip III, Rome, 22 July 1608 (AGS, E, leg. 988).

7 Council of State to Philip III, 27 Aug. 1616 (AGS, E, leg. 1002, f. 46).

8 On the concession of favours by Philip II and the contrast with the new policy followed by his son, see A. Feros, *El Duque de Lerma. Realeza y privanza en la España de Felipe III* (Madrid, 2002), pp 122-6.

9 Irish College, Salamanca to Philip III, 29 July 1603 (AGS, CJH, leg. 429-12).

10 Orders to the Viceroy of Portugal after the arrival of another vessel with 60 Irish aboard: 'they must return in the same ship in which they arrived, providing them with supplies for the journey and 50 *reales* each. And the same is to be done with future arrivals': 29 Mar. 1604 (AGS, E, leg. 198). Similar orders were given to the viceroys of Galicia and Navarre, and to the *corregidores* (representative of the royal jurisdiction) of Biscay and Cantabrian ports: 24 Nov. 1604 (AGS, E, leg. 202).

11 Philip III to all Spanish viceroys, governors and port authorities, 15 Sept. 1605 (AGS, E, leg. 202).

12 Caracena to King Philip III, 12 June 1605 (AGS, E, leg. 843, f. 18).

13 Diego Bazán to Philip III, 19 Nov. 1605 (AGS, E, leg. 200). The previous month, the *corregidor* had informed of the arrival of another 160 Irish soldiers: Bazán to Philip III, 3 Oct. 1605 (AGS, E, leg. 200).

14 Archivio Segreto Vaticano, Fondo Borghese, Serie II, xv, pp 161-5.

15 Caracena to Philip III, La Coruna, 28 Feb. 1602 (AGS, GA, leg. 603). Caracena was appointed governor and captain general of the kingdom of Galicia in 1596 and he remained in this post until his appointment as viceroy of Valencia between 1606 and 1615. In 1615 he moved to Madrid to serve in the presidency of the Council of Orders and died there in 1626.

16 C. Saavedra, *Galicia en el camino de Flandes: actividad militar, economía y sociedad en la España noratlántica, 1556-1648* (La Coruña, 1996), pp 157-95, 203; idem, 'La participación de Galicia en el socorro de Irlanda y la comunidad irlandesa de La Coruña', in E. García Hernán *et al* (eds), *Irlanda y la Monarquía hispánica: Kinsale, 1601-2001* (Madrid, 2002), pp 113-36.

17 Caracena to Philip III, 25 Feb. 1602 (AGS, GA, leg. 603).

18 Ó. Recio Morales, 'Spanish army attitudes to the Irish at Kinsale', in H. Morgan (ed.), *The battle of Kinsale* (Dublin, 2004), pp 91-100.

19 Caracena to Philip III, 4 July 1603 (AGS, E, leg. 194).

20 Recommendation from the Irishman, Eugenio Egamus, in favour of Tadeo Carthy, Irish lord, 29 May 1602 (AGS, GA, leg. 596). Egamus points out that Carthy had also been received by Caracena, 'who treated him in accordance with his deeds and with the goodness and kindness with which he is wont to deal with Catholic lords of our land'. Caracena was clearly aware of the misgivings which the continuous stream of memoranda from the Irish was causing at the court: 'Being a work of mercy to attend those Irish who have forfeited their homes for the upkeep of our Holy Religion, let Your Honour pardon the burden caused by recommending them': Caracena to Ibarra, 27 July 1602 (ibid.) This comment was occasioned by a request for aid for another Irishman, Juan Ris.

21 Mariñas to Alonso Núñez de Valdivia, 30 June 1606 (AGS, CJH, 468).

22 Diego de las Mariñas to Philip III, 12 June 1607 (AGS, GA, leg. 681).

23 There were three bankruptcies under Philip II (1560, 1575, 1596) and four under Philip IV (1627, 1647, 1652, 1662).

24 'My policy will be not to give a single *real* to any *entretenido* (pensioner). And if they request licence to go to the court, I shall gladly concede it': Enríquez to Philip III, 13 Sept. 1608 (AGS, GA, leg. 706).

25 Council of State to Philip III, 3 Apr. 1604 (AGS, E, leg. 198). The basic coin for the gold was the ducat (*ducado*), being substituted in 1537 by the *escudo*. The *real* was the silver coin and the abstract unit of account was the *maravedí*. A *real* was

34 maravedís worth and a *ducat* was equivalent to 375 maravedís (1 *escudo* to 350 maravedís, 400 in 1566, 440 in 1609 and 450 c. 1700). The salary of a Spanish foot-soldier remained in three *escudos* monthly since 1534 until 1634, when it went up to four.

26 Archivo Histórico Nacional (AHN), Órdenes Militares, Santiago, exp. 5809, Daniel O'Sullivan; ibid., exp. 7957, Dermicio O'Sullivan. In virtue of the services of the earl of Berehaven to the Spanish crown, Philip III granted him and his descendants a perpetual rent from the Royal Treasury of 1,000 ducats, Cedule signed by the king and ratified by the Duke of Lerma, 28 Aug. 1607 (AGS, CJH, leg. 566-27-10-1).

27 Royal Cedule granted in Madrid, 5 July 1617 (AHN, Consejos, leg. 4482, exp. 68).

28 Archivo Histórico de Protocolos, Madrid, MSS 7393, f. 81, 27 July 1638. Originally the post of *gentilhombre de la boca* was in charge of serving the king's table – hence its name. Later it became more of an honorific title, following the monarch in the religious functions in public or in the royal exits on horseback.

29 Council of State to Philip III, 13 Nov. 1604 (AGS, E, leg. 1851). The *tercio* was the Spanish standard unit of troops and they could vary in size from less than 100 to over 1,000 (normally between 1,200-1,500 men).

30 On this group see I. Pérez Tostado, *Irish influence at the court of Spain in the seventeenth century* (Dublin, 2008) and Ó. Recio Morales, *Ireland and the Spanish Empire, 1600-1825* (Dublin, 2010).

31 'Several times it has been reported this to the Council [of State] and to His Majesty, and in substance we believe this is not the time to think on these things, because of the lack of money and resources': Council of State on the letter sent by Aytona to Philip III, Rome, 22 July 1608 (AGS, E, leg. 988).

32 Conry to Philip III, Rome, 1 May 1609 (AGS, E, leg. 992).

33 In his will, O'Donnell 'recommended' Conry as advisor to the king in everything concerning Irish affairs: Sept. 1602 (AGS, GA, leg. 596).

34 The confrontation can be followed in Ó. Recio Morales, *Irlanda en Alcalá: la comunidad irlandesa en la Universidad de Alcalá y su proyección europea, 1579-1785* (Alcalá de Henares, 2004), pp 79-99.

35 No monograph study of this institution is yet available. For an initial approximation see E. García Hernán, 'El colegio de San Patricio de los irlandeses de Madrid (1621-1937)', *Madrid: revista de arte, geografía e historia*, viii (2006), pp 219-46.

36 Ó. Recio Morales, "*De nación irlandés*: Percepciones socio-culturales y respuestas políticas sobre Irlanda y la comunidad irlandesa en la España del XVII", en García Hernán *et al* (eds), *Irlanda y la monarquía hispánica: Kinsale, 1601-2001*, pp 315-40.

37 An online copy, edited by Paul Walsh, can be found at the CELT Corpus of Electronic Texts: a project of University College, Cork http://www.ucc.ie/celt (2005) (last access Dec. 2008).

Galileo Galilei, Robert Bellarmine and Peter Lombard

Ernan McMullin

In 1979, in one of the first public addresses of his pontificate, Pope John Paul II called for a new study of the long-contested 'Galileo affair' which would permit 'a frank recognition of wrongs from whatever side they come'.[1] Needless to say, the initiative was widely welcomed, and when the pope established a formal commission in 1981 to carry through the plan, expectations ran high. Over the course of the next ten years a small number of studies appeared, until finally, in 1992, the acting chair of the commission, Cardinal Paul Poupard, in a public session submitted a final report to the pope, who himself went on to read a further statement prepared for him which would wind up the inquiry. The two discourses, taken together, were generally interpreted as a belated (if still somewhat half-hearted) acknowledgement of fault on the church's part in its dealings with Galileo.[2]

One feature of the assessment delivered in 1992 should be of special interest to an Irish audience. Blame is laid on 'some theologians', unnamed, who (it is said) should have examined their own criteria of Scriptural interpretation in the light of the new science but 'most of them did not know how to do so'. Exactly whom did the author of the papal address have in mind? Who were those erring theologians? Presumably, by implication, the committee of theologian-consultors appointed by the Holy Office, the Roman Inquisition, to advise on the Copernican issue. And who presided over that committee? None other than Peter Lombard, archbishop of Armagh, living in exile in Rome. Lombard, as committee president, might then seem to be first among those who are being

Pope John Paul II issued a qualified apology for the church's prosecution of Galileo.
© *Connaught Tribune*

held responsible, on the church's side, for the Copernican ban and its disastrous after-effects. The matter is clearly worth a further look.

In 1609 Galileo improved on what had been until then no more than a toy and turned it to observe the heavens. Over the next few years he made a series of significant discoveries: what appeared to be mountains on the moon, four satellites circling Jupiter, slow-moving sunspots, and, most significantly, phases of Venus, like the quarter and half phases of the Moon. Taken together, they undermined the long-standing Aristotelian world-system: the heavenly bodies could no longer be regarded as unchanging; there was more than one cosmic centre of circular motion; and Venus circled the Sun, not the Earth. The work in which he announced the earliest of these discoveries, *Sidereus nuncius* (1610), became an instant sensation, owing to the evidence it presented in support of Copernicus's *De revolutionibus orbium coelestium* (1543) and the claim that the Sun and not the Earth was the centre of the planetary rotations, which was still not widely accepted.[3]

Galileo met with vigorous opposition from two quarters: first from the Aristotelian philosophers who dominated the philosophy faculties in most universities, and secondly from the theologians who saw in the new ideas a challenge to the inerrancy of Scripture. There are several passages in the Old Testament that mention the movement of the Sun across the sky and others that describe the Earth as immobile. Galileo brushed aside the philosophers, but the theologians were a different matter.

In a letter to a friend, Benedetto Castelli (1612), he set out 'to examine some general questions about the use of Holy Scripture in disputes involving physical conclusions'.[4] He adopted a commonsense approach. Of necessity, Scripture would have had to be accommodated to the capacities of its hearers, and must thus use their language to convey its message. It frequently departs, therefore, from the literal, as in such expressions as the 'right hand' of God. Secondly, Scripture is directed to truths that bear on human salvation, not to issues about nature that are already accessible to human reasoning. Thirdly, it is open to multiple interpretations; knowledge of nature, if demonstrated, is not. Finally, prudence should dictate that the church not commit itself prematurely on an issue that could later be decided otherwise by physical investigation: 'Who would want to assert that everything knowable about the world is already known?'

This did not persuade his critics among the theologians and he was ultimately denounced to the Holy Office in Rome, with a copy of the letter to Castelli submitted as evidence.[5] The first consultor called upon found some of the wording of the letter poorly chosen, but concluded that on balance it contained nothing that would threaten orthodoxy. In a later well-crafted defence of his position addressed to the Grand Duchess Christina, Galileo cited the early theologians of the Christian Church, notably St Augustine, in support of his position. This now-famous document did not come to the notice of Rome at this time, so far as we can tell; Galileo had probably been advised by his friends not to circulate it. Months passed, and the word from Rome was that the theological orthodoxy of the Copernican position was being actively debated there. Galileo decided on a direct confrontation with his critics in the 'Città Eterna'. It proved to be a bad decision. One of those who saw him in action as he argued with guests 'in one house after another' wrote that he 'showed up as worthless' most of his opponents' arguments, making them 'look ridiculous'.[6] He evidently had theological Rome in turmoil.

'Galileo Galilei' (1567-1642) in crayon by Ottavio Leoni.

At this point, after consulting his close theological adviser, Cardinal Bellarmine, an irritated Pope Paul V decided that the increasingly troublesome issue should be settled by the Holy Office. Galileo's aggressive campaigning probably accelerated the decision, though it was probably in the making for some time. Several months earlier an essay by a respected theologian, Paulo Foscarini, arguing for the compatibility of the Copernican position with Scripture, had already been rumoured to risk official condemnation and its author's suspension by the Holy Office.[7] Following custom, as a first step, a group of the regular consultors to the Holy Office was assigned to advise on the matter. Peter Lombard, by that time one of Rome's most trusted theologians, was appointed to preside over the eleven-member committee.

Fifty years earlier two young men had arrived at around the same time at the University of Louvain in Flanders. One came from Italy: Robert Bellarmine, twenty-eight years old, in 1570 was the first Jesuit to be appointed to the faculty of the prestigious university. The other came from Ireland: Peter Lombard, aged eighteen, in 1572 enrolled in philosophy at Le Fauçon, one of the four colleges of the university. There is no direct evidence of their having interacted in the six years that Bellarmine would spend in Louvain but Lombard would quite certainly have heard much about the teaching of this immensely popular and widely influential young theologian. What can be learned about his teaching will help explain the momentous condemnation of the Copernican doctrine many years later.

Bellarmine taught theology to those students preparing for the priesthood. These proved difficult years for Catholic theologians in the immediate wake of the Protestant Reformation. The reformers had called for a return to Scripture as the sole rule of faith and had set aside much of Catholic practice and the entire mode of Catholic church governance which drew on the history of the early church. Their emphasis on Scripture led them to put a great deal of effort into translating

'Galileo facing the Roman Inquisition' by Cristiano Banti (1824-1904). One of the judges represented in this romantic picture could have been Peter Lombard.

the Bible into the various vernaculars from the Latin (in which it had hitherto been taught), devoting much attention to the exegetical issues involved in establishing the authentic original text.

The Holy See responded with the Council of Trent (1545-63). In the circumstances, the issue of biblical interpretation, not surprisingly, became one of the council's main concerns. A decree of the fourth session laid down that only the church could determine the authentic sense of Scripture passages in 'matters of faith and *mores* (morals and practices generally)'; the authentic sense is also conveyed by the unanimous consensus of the Fathers of the Church.[8] It permitted no departure, then, from the traditional interpretation of Scripture texts of the sort advocated by the reformers. Although this did not intend to enforce the literal sense overall (the traditional interpretation allowed for metaphor and allegory, and the decree was in any event restricted to matters of faith and mores), it led some Catholic theologians to lean heavily in that direction.

This, then, was the context in which the young Bellarmine began his teaching. He decided to meet the biblical challenge head-on by teaching theology through biblical commentary, working systematically through the *Summa Theologica* of Thomas Aquinas and laboriously acquiring the language skills needed for careful exegesis.[9] Because his carefully kept lecture notes are preserved, we can follow him as he began with the work of the creation in *Genesis*.[10] Instead of interpreting the six-day account of cosmic creation metaphorically as St Augustine had done and as countenanced by Aquinas,[11] he treated it quite literally. Furthermore, his strong devotion to the literal meant that he gave it preference when treating *Genesis* passages dealing with cosmological issues, in contrast to the majority of Catholic theologians of the day who favoured Aristotelian alternatives. Thus he argued on biblical grounds against the Aristotelian doctrine of the nature of the heavens: they are made of fire, not of some mysterious fifth element; there are no carrier spheres for the planets (they move 'like the birds of the air'); they are not incorruptible (they will perish on the last day).

One particularly striking instance of this preference for the strictly literal is his interpretation of the description in *Genesis* of the Sun and Moon as the 'two great lights'. He acknowledged that the astronomers of the day regard the Moon as the smallest of the heavenly bodies except for Mercury. But he disagrees: it appeared 'most probable' to the Church Fathers that the Moon is the greatest except for the Sun, 'both because the Scriptures called these two bodies *luminaria magna* and because the Moon appears to our senses incomparably larger than any other of the heavenly bodies'.[12]

This contrasted sharply with John Calvin's writings about the same text a few years earlier in his *Commentary on Genesis* (1554). Despite the description of the Moon in *Genesis*, he writes:

> astronomers prove by conclusive reasons that Saturn … is greater than the Moon. Here lies the difference: Moses wrote in a popular style things which without instruction all ordinary persons endowed with common sense are able to understand; but astronomers investigate with great labour whatever the sagacity of the human mind can comprehend.[13]

Calvin departed from the literal in this case, allowing for accommodation to common perception; Bellarmine did not. The Council of Trent had evidently made even such departures suspect.

Bellarmine's growing fame as a lecturer and preacher had reached Rome. Subsequently recalled in 1576 to teach on the reform 'controversies' at the Jesuit Collegio Romano; his comprehensive work on that topic became and long remained a theological classic. Appointed rector of the college in 1592, he became personal theologian to Pope Clement VIII in 1597, who once remarked that the church 'had not his equal in learning'. He fulfilled the same office for Paul V on the latter's accession as pope in 1605; that pontiff would mainly depend on him for advice on the eruption of the Copernican controversy in 1615-16.

Peter Lombard was born in Waterford to a well-off family in 1554.[14] Young Irishmen who wished to study for the priesthood in those difficult days had to go abroad, and the University of Louvain became one of their favourite destinations. Enrolling there in 1572, he met with conspicuous success in his studies and was honored as the outstanding student of the year on completion of his philosophy degree in 1575. He may well have studied theology with Bellarmine in the latter's last year in Louvain (1575-76). Given what we know of Bellarmine's

St Robert Bellarmine (1542-1621), the leading champion of the Tridentine Reformation, wrote his *Disputationes de Controversiis Christianae Fidei* (1581-92), the most celebrated early modern Catholic controversial work.

impact on the student body, a very bright student like Lombard would undoubtedly have come to know his views on biblical interpretation, perhaps even on the primacy of the Bible in matters cosmological. In any event, his theological formation would have been shaped by the same Counter-Reformation forces that had already led to a much more conservative approach to the biblical text.

Lombard gained his doctorate both in philosophy and theology at the university. Intriguingly, in 1580 he was the only student in the *Collège du Pape* not to have his bursary cancelled by the embattled head of that college, Michel Baius, himself under perpetual investigation by Rome for his unorthodox theological views.[15] Appointed to the faculty of theology of the university, Lombard received acclaim for his teaching of Aristotelian philosophy to beginning students. In 1598 he repaired to Rome as an emissary of the university and rapidly became a major figure there in matters political as well as theological. Hugh O'Neill, still in Ireland, took advantage of his presence in Rome and appointed him as his agent in his multifarious political and diplomatic initiatives. This was probably a major factor in Lombard's elevation to the archbishopric of Armagh in 1601.

In the 1580s an exceedingly acrimonious debate had broken out between Dominican and Jesuit theologians about the relationship between the influence of grace on human action and free will, the Dominicans emphasising the efficacy of grace (thereby, according to the Jesuits, undermining human freedom, Calvin's error) and the Jesuits emphasizing the reality of human freedom (thereby, according to the Dominicans, compromising the action of grace as Pelagius did).[16] Eventually, Clement VIII instituted the Congregation *de Auxiliis* in 1598 to resolve the issue. The matter dragged on, with Bellarmine taking a formal part from 1599. In 1602 the pope decided that he would personally oversee the sessions of the Commission and appointed Lombard as session president. Sixty-eight lengthy sessions followed, Lombard strongly favouring the Dominican view, which Bellarmine regarded as Calvinist. In 1605 Clement died. His successor, Paul V, continued Lombard as congregation president and made him a member of his official household. The congregation's work continued for seventeen more sessions. Eager for a resolution, Lombard submitted a detailed draft decree condemning the Jesuit position. On its being amended, he refused to sign. Paul V, weary of the interminable strife, terminated the deliberations of the congregation (1607) and ordered both sides to desist from further discussion of the matter.

Although reputedly parsimonious, Pope Paul V (1552-1621) was relatively generous to the earls, despite the fact that he was financing much public building in Rome. © NPG

Lombard also came to serve Paul V as an adviser on Irish political matters. The new king in England, James I, began bearing down on Catholics in his dominions and was in the process of replacing most of the native Irish elite in Ulster with settlers from Scotland and England. In the circumstances, fundamental political and theological questions arose. Did Catholics owe the king their loyalty? Could the pope depose him? Lombard tended on the whole to be conciliatory and worked for some years on a lengthy response to these delicate issues, resulting in a thousand-page manuscript, *Ad quaestiones XII*, completed around 1616. It is likely that he was in the final stages of this task in February of that year when the pope took the fateful decision to convoke the committee of consultors to assess the orthodoxy of the Copernican world-view. One can well imagine that Lombard's attention and his energies would have been focused elsewhere at that particular moment.

The committee convened on 19 February 1616 and was expected to report by 23 February. The issue had been under active discussion in Rome for months, so that many of the committee members would have had their minds made up already. Dominicans comprised the majority of its members (six), and their hostility to Galileo was already suspected; Lombard would very likely have aligned himself with them as he had done during the sessions of the Congregation *de Auxiliis*. The committee arrived at a decision on time and reported back to the Holy Office a day later. Their verdict was that the assertion that the Sun is at rest is 'foolish and absurd in philosophy [we might say 'natural science'] and formally heretical, since it explicitly contradicts the sense of Holy Scripture in many places'. It passed a similar philosophical judgement on the assertion that the Earth is in motion, but gave the less condemnatory verdict: 'at least erroneous in the faith'.[17]

At that point the Holy Office took over. On the following day the pope attended the meeting which discussed the censures agreed on by the consultors. He ordered Cardinal Bellarmine, his principal theological adviser, to instruct Galileo privately that he must abandon the Copernican views he had been defending, and to specify the penalties of not complying. They turned the matter over to the Congregation of the Index, which formulated the terms of the condemnation. Members of the congregation met on 1 March at Bellarmine's house and, after a discussion, they apparently decided, at the urging of Cardinals Caetani and Barberini (the future Pope Urban VIII),[18] not to accept the consultors' finding of formal heresy.

Peter Lombard (1555-1625), above right, composed a manuscript account of Ireland's history, below, subsequently published as *De Regno Hiberniae Sanctorum Insula Commentarius* (Louvain, 1632), in an effort to persuade Pope Clement VIII to support the Ulster confederates by excommunicating Irish Catholics who sought to remain neutral. In the scene from Brian Friel's *Making History* directly above, Lombard (Niall Tóibín) drinks *poitín* sent from his native Waterford while O'Neill (Stephen Rea, seated) looks on.

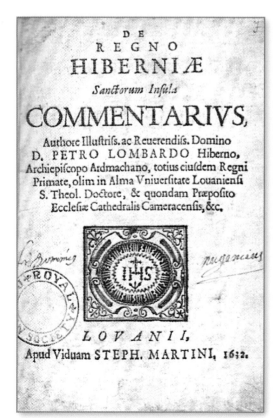

Instead the Copernican theses would be simply described as 'false and altogether opposed to Holy Scripture' in the decree banning the work of Copernicus 'until corrected'.[19] This was the decision that the condemnation of Galileo seventeen years later would cite as warrant.[20]

It would never have occurred to those involved that at this point they were setting theology and science at odds with one another, as would later be charged. It is doubtful that they would have considered the epistemic ('scientific') merits of the Copernican world-view worth serious discussion. For one thing, hardly any natural philosophers (the 'scientists' of the day)[21] had accepted Copernicus's claims as early as 1616. The Aristotelians among the consultors, including almost certainly Lombard, would have seen no reason to abandon the Aristotelian physics that had provided the foundation of their philosophical formation.[22] And that physics was undoubtedly incompatible with the Copernican view. Cosmology was admittedly another matter: Bellarmine, for one, as far back as 1611 had been assured of the reliability of Galileo's telescopic discoveries.[23] But the better informed among them would undoubtedly have settled for Tycho Brahe's Earth-centred alternative. So the consultors would have felt justified in declaring the Copernican view 'absurd'. As far as they were concerned, the issue on which they had to decide was strictly theological.

Should Lombard and the other consultors be held responsible for a decision that proved to be a very costly theological error?[24] They were certainly accountable for their recommendation, one that did much to shape what came after. Indeed, had their recommendation been followed, describing the Copernican view as formally heretical, the error would have been even more serious.[25] It was within their power to recommend dismissal of the theological charge; after all, a previous consultor had found nothing seriously wrong with the argument of Galileo's *Letter to Castelli*. But the legacy of Trent, fortified by a long standing commitment to Aristotelian philosophy, made that earlier verdict from this particular jury unlikely.

Yet all they could do was to recommend: the final decision was not theirs. At this stage, the theologians mainly responsible were Cardinal Bellarmine and, to a lesser extent, Pope Paul V, who made his own (negative) view of the Copernican innovation abundantly clear.[26] Indeed, it seems likely that Bellarmine's opposition to the Copernican claims on Scriptural grounds which he had already signalled more than once would have carried a great deal of weight with the consultors in their own discussions, just completed.[27] He was after all the pre-eminent biblical scholar in Rome; and had he been known to countenance taking the disputed Scripture passages to be accommodated to common usage, the others just *might* have gone along.

Galileo's telescope.

In an earlier letter, jointly intended for Foscarini and Galileo, Bellarmine had made his position quite clear: taking the Copernican claim to be anything other than a convenient mathematical device was impermissible. After a career devoted to countering the reform challenge, his opposition to proposed departures from the traditional understanding of the biblical text ran deep. It would be as heretical (he declares) to say that Abraham did not have two children as to say that Christ was not born of a virgin. The motion of the Sun must likewise be regarded as 'a matter of faith as regards the speaker' since the speaker is God. Apologists[28] have tried to present Bellarmine as open-minded towards the Copernican issue by quoting this same letter to the effect that if a demonstration *were* to be given, it would be necessary to reconsider how to read the biblical passages in question. But this apparent concession, obviously included for po-

liteness' sake, was not what it seems, since he then goes on to say that, for several reasons which he specifies, a demonstration is out of reach.[29] Of all those involved in the Copernican decision, Bellarmine in retrospect would seem the theologian most responsible.[30]

How *serious* a failure *was* this, in fact? One can argue both sides of the case. The biblical passages mentioning the motion of the Sun or the stability of the Earth could plausibly be regarded as being accommodated to the capacities of the original audience, as Galileo had argued. This was how the Sun and Moon would have *appeared* (as they still do) and hence were so described. But that does not commit the Bible to the reality of their motion or stillness. An ample precedent for this principle of interpretation existed in both Augustine and Aquinas,[31] two authors familiar to Roman theologians and whose authority was unquestioned. Bellarmine attached too much weight to the immediate evidence of the senses in this case, as he had done earlier in regard to the size of the Moon.[32]

The exegetic principle on which Bellarmine and the consultors relied was that where the literal interpretation of a text conflicts with a contrary claim about nature, the former should be maintained unless the latter can be demonstrated.[33] This leads to error (as it did in this case) when a conflicting claim whose evidence leaves it short of demonstration is later validated on the basis of new evidence or revised theory. The whole idea of natural science as a progressive enterprise was as foreign to the theologians as to the philosophers of that day. Nevertheless, in his *Letter to Castelli* Galileo had already alerted them to this possibility and had appealed to ordinary prudence in an effort to prevent them from relying on this defective principle of interpretation.[34] The discoveries he had already announced and of which they had at least heard should have warned them that this was a time when old certainties were being challenged on new grounds and thus not the moment to commit the church in a definitive manner.

There is also a case to be made that if this was an error it was one of a much less serious stripe. At the heart of the theological controversies that had so bitterly divided Christendom over the previous century was the issue of biblical interpretation, on which the Council of Trent had taken so uncompromising a stand. Bellarmine's entire career had been shaped by those controversies and by the church's response to them. Part of that response emphasised a renewed dependence on the Aristotelian philosophy that the reformers had found wanting. Galileo's discoveries had already put that philosophy on the defensive. Now he and others were presuming to interpret the Scripture to their own ends. It was all too reminiscent of what the reformers had been doing to such effect.

Church theologians such as Bellarmine and Lombard had for decades past been led to distrust proposed changes, particularly changes involving Scripture. Their vocation, as they saw it, was to protect the precious past, to hand on what had been given them, not to revise it. Innovation, particularly innovation that cut as deep as did the Copernican proposal, was automatically suspect. In short, the theologians who voted to declare his

innovation 'contrary to Scripture' simply acted as one might have expected Catholic theologians of that day to act. They should indeed have 'examined their own criteria of Scriptural interpretation', as the address in 1992 declared, but whether their failure to do so was because they 'did not know how to do so' or because doing so would have run contrary to their entire theological formation is not hard to guess.

One wonders what Lombard made of the whole matter. It seems doubtful that he would have spent more time on it than the couple of days allotted. The later significance for the church of that discussion none of those involved could ever have imagined. If Galileo's criteria for how the disputed passages of Scripture should be read gave Lombard pause (and one hopes that they did!), there was the weight of authority and tradition on the other side of the debate to quiet his doubts. And there was, after all, his encyclopedic response to James I's treatment of his Catholic subjects that still needed finishing touches.

Notes

1 John Paul II, 'Faith, science, and the search for truth', *Origins,* ix (1979), pp 389-92.

2 The two addresses, 'Lessons of the Galileo case' and 'Report on the Papal Commission findings', appear in *Origins,* xxii (1992), pp 370-5. G. V. Coyne, comments in 'The church's most recent attempt to dispel the Galileo myth', in E. McMullin (ed.), *The Church and Galileo* (Notre Dame, 2005), pp 340-59.

3 See, for example, S. Drake, *Galileo at work* (Chicago, 1978), pp 157-76; E. McMullin (ed.), *Galileo: Man of Science* (New York, 1967), pp 31-42.

4 A. Favaro (ed.), *Opere di Galileo Galilei* (1890-1909, repr., Florence, Giunti Barbera, 1968), v, pp 281-8; M. Finocchiaro, *The Galileo Affair* (Berkeley, 1989), pp 49-54.

5 For a full account see A. Fantoli, *Galileo: For Copernicanism and for the Church* (3rd ed., Rome, 2003).

6 Antonio Querengo to Cardinal d'Este, in *Opere,* xii, pp 226-7.

7 Giovanni Ciampoli to Galileo, in *Opere,* xii, p. 160.

8 R. Blackwell, *Galileo, Bellarmine, and the Bible* (Notre Dame, 1991), ch. 1; O. Pedersen, *Galileo and the Council of Trent* (Vatican City, 1983), pp 15-16.

9 J. Brodrick, *Robert Bellarmine: Saint and Scholar* (London, 1961).

10 U. Baldini and G. Coyne, *The Louvain lectures of Bellarmine* (Vatican City, 1984).

11 See, for example, E. McMullin (ed.), *Evolution and creation* (Notre Dame, 1985), pp 9-21; N. Kretzmann, *The metaphysics of Creation: natural theology in the 'Summa contra gentiles'* (Oxford, 1997), pp 190-3.

12 Baldini and Coyne, *Louvain Lectures,* p. 22.

13 J. Calvin, *Commentary on Genesis,* trans. John King (2 vols., Grand Rapids, 1948) i, p. 6.

14 J. J. Silke, 'The Irish Peter Lombard', *Studies,* lxiv (1975), pp 144-55; T. Ó hAnnracháin, 'Peter Lombard', in *RIA Dictionary of Irish Biography* (Cambridge, 2009).

15 He was, for example, accused of being Calvinist in his deeply pessimistic view of the effects of original sin on human nature, and is sometimes described as a forerunner of Jansenism.

16 T. Ryan, 'Congregation *de Auxiliis*', *New Catholic Encyclopedia* (Detroit, 2003), iv, pp 110-3.

17 Finocchiaro, *The Galileo Affair,* pp 146-7. The reason for the difference between the two verdicts was that the biblical texts regarding the stability of the earth were less explicit.

18 According, at least, to a diary entry long afterwards (1633) by G. Buonamici, *Opere,* xv, p. 11.

19 The work was never actually withdrawn and a short list of 'corrections' was issued a couple of years later.

20 Whether it was of itself sufficient to play that role without a further action on the part of the later Pope involved (Urban VIII) is discussed at length in E. McMullin, 'The Galileo affair: two decisions', *Journal of the History of Astronomy,* xl (2009), pp 191-212.

21 The 'science' of the day was still Aristotelian.

22 Galileo's effective critique of that physics would not ap-

pear until 1632, in his great *Dialogue on two chief world systems.*

23 By his Jesuit astronomer-colleagues at the Collegio Romano whom he asked to verify them: see *Opere,* xi, 87-88, pp 92-93.

24 This is J. J. Langford's conclusion; *Galileo, science, and the church* (New York, 1966), p. 90. The consultors were not 'rubber stamps', he argues. Most of them were eminent theologians in their own right, and some, like Lombard, he points out, had been quite vocal in the heated exchanges of the Congregation *de Auxiliis.*

25 Had that happened, however, Galileo almost certainly would not have been allowed to go forward with the writing of the *Dialogue* ... the makings of an intriguing 'what if?'.

26 In a report back to Florence a week later, the Florentine ambassador, Piero Guicciardini, wrote that the Pope and Galileo, discussing the consultors' verdict, 'decided that the opinion was erroneous and heretical' even before the Holy Office had officially met to discuss their own verdict (*Opere,* xii, p. 242). The reliability of this report has been questioned.

27 It was said that when Bellarmine served on the thirteen-member Congregation of Rites, the other members sometimes altered their decision when his was the sole dissenting voice. R. S. Westfall, *Essays on the trial of Galileo* (Vatican City, 1989), p. 4.

28 Including the author of the pope's address in 1992.

29 E. McMullin, 'The church's ban on Copernicanism', in idem (ed.), *The Church and Galileo,* pp 177-82.

30 This is also Westfall's conclusion, *Essays on the trial of Galileo,* pp 21-24.

31 See, for example, Aquinas, *Summa Theologica,* i, q. a.3. The *Summa* would have been the consultors' primary theological text.

32 A wise man, he wrote to Foscarini and Galileo, 'clearly experiences that the Earth stands still and that the eye is not in error when it judges that the Sun moves' (*Opere,* xii, p. 172). He obviously thought that the Copernicans would call those perceptions themselves into question.

33 As early as 1612, Galileo wrote to Cardinal Conti to ask about the authority of the Bible on cosmological issues. The Cardinal, answering, mentioned the Copernican case and said that it could be reconciled with Scripture only if the Bible was supposed to speak in 'the language of the common people' but that this 'should not be admitted unless it is really necessary' (*Opere,* xi, 355; Fantoli, *Galileo,* 116). This same restriction would overrule an appeal to accommodation in the consultors' deliberations in 1616.

34 In his *Letter to the Grand Duchess Christina* Galileo presented Augustine's version of this prudential principle in a particularly telling way. One wonders whether it would have made a difference had Bellarmine and the Roman theologians generally had the opportunity to work through that document.

Early-modern Catholic self-fashioning "Spanish style": aspects of Tadhg Ó Cianáin's Rome

Mícheál Mac Craith

On 29 May 1608, the third anniversary of his coronation, Pope Paul V canonised Santa Francesca Romana in the basilica of St Peter's in Rome. The pope obviously regarded this event as one of the highlights of his pontificate in that it was chosen, alongside the canonisation of St Charles Borromeo in 1610, as one of the achievements to be depicted in bas relief on his funerary monument in the Cappella Paolina in the basilica of Santa Maria Maggiore. Hugh O'Neill and Rory O'Donnell both attended the canonisation as honoured guests of his holiness, and their chronicler, Tadhg Ó Cianáin, wrote a vivid account of the occasion and the subsequent celebrations. In order to gain a proper appreciation of Ó Cianáin's description, it will be helpful to investigate the nature and frequency of canonisations in early modern Europe, as well as the contemporary impact of the newly canonised saint. Our understanding of Ó Cianáin's narrative is further enhanced by comparing it with other descriptions of the same event in English and Italian.

The public veneration of saints in the Christian Church goes back at least as far as the second century. The local community had particular veneration for those who gave the ultimate witness to their religious belief in shedding their blood for the faith. The word 'martyr' itself means 'witness' and the faithful generally believed that a person who died for the faith was certainly in heaven and could intercede for those who invoked his/her intercession. When the era of persecution and martyrdom ceased, however, a different kind of saint, *confessor fidei*, came to the fore, the term denoting one who lived for the faith, professing it, defending it, even suffering for it, but not compelled to give the ultimate witness of dying for his/her beliefs. This group gradually expanded to include missionaries, teachers, and those worthy of veneration in consequence of their exemplary charity or asceticism. In the early years of Christianity the local community, *vox populi*, ultimately decided a person's worthiness for veneration. While the faithful in general could decide to visit a saint's tomb, implore his intercession or proclaim his miracles, this informal procedure was deemed insufficient. Something more authoritative was needed, and this was initially provided by the approbation of the local bishop.

By the eleventh century many felt that the status of a local saint could be further enhanced if his or her cult received formal papal sanction. In 993, Pope John XV raised St Udalricus/Ulric in the first known papal canonisation. Liutolf, Ulric's successor as bishop of Augsburg, presented a book of his life and miracles to a council at the Lateran. The council examined this work, and the pope subsequently canonised the saint. The following centuries saw the elaboration of formal procedures and the provision of authenticated documents that would help to overcome the danger of abuses present in the informal spontaneous approach to the veneration of saints. In 1234 Pope Gregory IX finally sanctioned the norms regarding the methods of investigating the life and miracles of candidates for sainthood.

By the sixteenth century, however, the cult of the saints came under attack from both humanists and reformers alike. The reformers claimed that the intercessory power of the saints had no basis in Scripture and that it undermined the role of Jesus Christ as unique mediator between humanity and God. Although Luther had sharply criticised the 5,005 relics in the chapel of Frederick the Wise at Wittenberg, he later tried to control his followers who smashed images: 'Of course there are abuses, but are they eliminated by destroying the objects abused? Men can go wrong with wine and women. Shall we then prohibit wine and abolish women? Such haste and violence betray lack of confidence in God'.[1] While he advocated the removal of images of saints who had not received biblical sanction, he did not in any way condone their destruction: 'Crucifixes, manger scenes, and apostles could stay; Saints Ursula, George and Christopher, along with myriad others, must ultimately go'.[2]

'Ultimately' is the operative word in the above quotation. Luther hoped his followers could be gradually weaned away from reliance on the saints, in parallel with his own religious development.[3] He envisaged a similar process regarding the use of images. Writing to Nikolaus Hausmann in 1522, he suggested that images would fall on their own

The Spanish Steps, emblematic of the extensive Spanish influence in seventeenth-century Rome.

when people would learn that they were nothing in the presence of God.[4] Luther's attitude to images appeared much more nuanced than that of his contemporary Zwingli, who held all use of images both idolatrous and contrary to Scripture. Both Erasmus and St Thomas More criticised the cult of spurious and unauthorised relics, and Erasmus claimed that the veneration of saints constituted little more than the superstition of the ancients.[5]

In the light of the criticisms from both humanists and reformers, the Council of Trent reaffirmed the validity of venerating saints, while at the same time attempting to eradicate abuses. Henceforth a critical scientific approach would be applied to the writing of hagiography. Spurious and legendary material would be eradicated in favour of verifiable details. However, despite this reaffirmation of the cult of the saints and their relics, together with the affirmation of the propriety of undertaking pilgrimages to their shrines and Trent's upholding of canonisation as a prerogative of the papacy, the Roman Catholic Church had been quite shaken by the vehemence of the attacks on the cult of the saints. In one way it had been caught in a bind. The creation of new saints would have left the church open to further derision, while refusing to create new saints conceded the field to her enemies who created their own martyrs as victims of Catholic persecution.[6] The upshot was what Peter Burke has termed 'a crisis of canonisation' in the Catholic Church. Pope Adrian VI elevated St Benno and St Anthony of Firenze in 1523, the canonisation of the former incurring Luther's wrath.

These proved to be the last canonisations until 1588, a gap of sixty-five years when Pope Sixtus V canonised Diego di Alcalá, the Spanish Franciscan. Only one other saint, the Polish Dominican Hyacinth Odrovaz, in 1594, was canonised between then and the end of the sixteenth century. The church elevated fourteen more between 1588 and 1665: seven Spaniards, four Italians, one Pole, one Portuguese, and one Frenchman (Francis de Sales in 1665).[7] Twenty-four saints were canonised during the seventeenth century, and thirty in the eighteenth. Among the seventeenth-century saints, only Francis de Sales was neither Italian nor Spanish (including Spain and its dominions). No canonisations occurred between 1629 and 1658, with a further gap between 1767 and 1807.[8] The contrast between this and the pontificate of John Paul II, who canonised 483 saints between 1982 and 2004, not to mention beatifying more than 1,300 others, is most striking.

Ronnie Po-Chia Hsia's survey of Counter-Reformation saints provides further fascinating statistics. Of those that lived between 1540 and 1770, he notes twenty-seven male and five female canonisations, not to mention a further six beatifications. If these are arranged according to nationality, there are eighteen Italians and fourteen Spaniards. Of the grand total of thirty-eight, canonised and beatified taken together, nineteen came from the new religious orders, including six Jesuits, five Capuchins, and three Theatines. The new saints included founders of new orders and reformers of the old, as well as missionaries and implementers of the de-

157

O'Neill sits behind Pope Paul V during the canonisation of Santa Francesca Romana. Mural in the Paul V Gallery.
© Mícheál Mac Craith and the Vatican Museum

crees of the Council of Trent. Strangely enough, despite the frequency of religious wars during this period, only one martyr is included among the thirty-eight.[9]

The process of Diego di Alcalá (1400-63), the Spanish Franciscan, marked the first canonisation in sixty-five years and the first canonisation of the post-Tridentine era.[10] Furthermore, it signalled the beginning of a concerted campaign by the Spanish monarchy to create Iberian saints as a means of promoting Spanish prestige, it being a source of great disappointment to the crown that only one Spaniard, St Dominic (1234), had been canonised between 1198 and 1431. Philip II actively involved himself in the campaign to have Diego canonised from the 1560s onwards, writing letters to Rome in support of his candidate, along with other Spanish nobles and ecclesiastical dignitaries. Don Carlos, Philip's son and heir, fell seriously ill in 1562 as a result of a fall down the stairs of the royal palace in Alcalá. When medical intervention proved fruitless, the king ordered that Diego's body be brought into the patient's room. Diego had been venerated as a local saint since his death in the friary in Alcalà in 1463. As soon as the prince's hand touched the holy man's body, it was claimed, the sickness left and he recovered soon afterwards.[11] This prompted a series of letters from Philip II to the pope citing this impressive

miracle in support of Diego's canonisation. Pius IV remained unimpressed. Both of his successors Pius V (1566-72) and Gregory XIII (1572-85) showed the same reluctance to proceed with the canonisation in the absence of more evidence. In 1566 the Spanish ambassador in Rome wrote to Don Carlos that the pope needed a biography (*vita*) of Diego as well as other important details. In the absence of an available *vita*, Ambrosio de Morales, the royal historian, received a commission to provide one, and he became official procurator of Diego's cause in the following year. Despite de Morales's best efforts, however, he only managed to produce a document of six pages. A dearth of biographical details to prove Diego's sanctity during his lifetime forced the Spanish crown to resort to the other criterion for canonisation; the miracles worked through Diego's intercession during his lifetime and after his death. The healing of the king's son was the most important of these. Although the Spanish bishops succeeded in assembling a list of 130 miracles wrought through Diego's intercession, the majority of the witnesses who could authenticate these miracles were long dead.[12] They interviewed eighty-three witnesses regarding Don Carlos's cure, including the two doctors who had treated him. All of these testified to the miraculous nature of the cure and Diego's intercession.[13]

Pope Sixtus V (1585-90) eventually decided to canonise his fellow Franciscan in 1588. Given the reluctance of the pope's three predecessors, it is difficult to ascertain what exactly prompted Sixtus V's change of heart. Quite a number of contemporary commentators linked that decision to the Spanish invasion of England in the same year. Sixtus has been pressing Philip II for some time to attack England and overthrow her heretical queen; and in recompense for Philip's preparation of the Armada, the pope offered the Spanish fleet a heavenly intercessor through the canonisation of Diego. As well as being the first canonisation in sixty-five years, it was also the first canonisation of an Iberian saint in more than a century, which explains the strong Spanish stamp on the ceremonies. The Spanish royal coat of arms was just as prevalent as the papal coat of arms; Philip II's agents in Rome oversaw the decoration of St Peter's and the king himself promised to pay the necessary expenses. If Philip had gained a heavenly intercessor for himself and his kingdom, the ceremony itself and the subsequent celebrations showed the extent of Spanish influence and prestige in Rome.[14] It is no great surprise that the recently rediscovered painting of Diego di Alcalá at the Catholic University of Louvain originally belonged to the Irish Franciscan College of St Anthony. This college had been founded and sustained by Spanish patronage, which explains Irish veneration of the Spanish Franciscan.

In January 1588 Pope Sixtus V established the Congregation of Rites to oversee the whole process of canonisation and the authentication of relics, although he allowed the commission of cardinals appointed in 1587 to conduct the official examination into Diego's cause to complete their work.[15] This new congregation initiated a more stringent investigation of the life and miracles of subsequent candidates as well as the centralisation of more power in the Roman ecclesiastical bureaucracy. Though it is possible to see this decision as a reaction to the pressure waged by the Spanish crown in the process of Diego di Alcalá, it must be stressed that it amounted to little more than a refinement and improvement of the procedures that had been honed during this long-drawn out process, procedures which had not changed since the middle ages.[16]

Clement VIII's canonisation of the noble Polish Dominican, Hyacinth Odrovaz (d. 1257) in 1594 was the last canonisation in the sixteenth century. A strong political dimension also marked this el-

evation. Clement saw a strong Catholic Poland as having an important strategic role to play in creating a united European front against the Turk, and the creation of a Polish saint fostered this aim.[17] The turn of the century, however, saw the Spanish campaign for their own national saints bear fruit. Raymundo di Peñaforte (1175-1275), another Dominican, was canonised in 1601. Though his cause had been advanced soon after his death, the attempts by both the king of Aragon and the Dominican Order had failed to impress the pope in 1318. Philip II recommended the campaign in 1595, and the king's personal letter became a central item in the dossier of evidence placed before the Congregation of Rites. The process only lasted six years, and the new king, Philip III, also played a leading role. Once again, a strong Spanish imprint characterised the celebrations accompanying canonisation. A large procession followed the ceremony in St Peter's to the Catalan church of Santa Maria de Montserrat and from there to the Dominican church of Santa Maria sopra Minerva. Most of the participants were Spaniards and Dominicans, and these celebrations provided yet another example of Spanish triumphalism on the Roman stage.[18]

Peter Delooz has noted that the seventeenth century was the century of Spanish canonisations.[19] The climax of Spanish saint-making occurred on 12 March 1622 when Pope Gregory XV canonised four Spaniards on the same day: Teresa of Avila (1515-82), Ignatius of Loyola (1491-1556), Francis Xavier (1506-52) and Isidore the Farmer (1077-1130). Although one Italian, Philip Neri (1515-95), joined the four Spaniards, the greatest canonisation ceremony of the whole seventeenth century was essentially a Spanish occasion, providing another opportunity to display Spanish grandeur and prestige in Rome. It is significant that four of the new saints were heroes of the Counter-Reformation, and that two of them belonged to the newly founded Society of Jesus. Given that these four belonged to the sixteenth century, it was reasonably easy to provide documentary evidence and personal witness. Isidore provides a striking exception to this, having died almost six hundred years earlier. Yet his association with Madrid, and the Spanish court's transfer to its new capital by the middle of the 1590s, prompted Philip III to promote a cause that would provide the Spanish court with its own heavenly patron, even if the biographical details were even scarcer than those of Diego di Alcalá. The royal court threw its considerable weight behind Teresa of Avila's campaign. Philip II, Philip III, his wife, Queen Margarita, and the secretary of the kingdom of Castile, Don Juan de Henestrosa, all wrote letters to the Congregation of Rites in support of her cause. The latter not only emphasised the importance of saints in general to Spain, but also placed special emphasis on Teresa's role in the empire, seeing that the convents she established had a powerful influence for good on human behaviour.[20]

All the above serves as a background to the role of canonisation in Ó Cianáin's narrative. Three aspects of the process are prominent in the early seventeenth century: the reluctance of the papacy to canonise indiscriminately; the development of stricter criteria in authenticating the sanctity and miracles of the candidate for canonisation; and the enthusiasm of the Spanish monarch in promoting the creation of Spanish saints as a method of enhancing Spanish prestige.[21] Pope Paul V (1605-21) raised only two saints to the altar during his pontificate: Francesca Romana (1384-1440) in 1608 and Carlo Borromeo (1538-84) in 1610. In the light of the above discussion, it is remarkable that neither of these were Spaniards. Nevertheless, it must be pointed out that Philip II granted a large sum of money in 1562 to the nephews of Pius IV, among whom was Carlo Borromeo.[22] His successor, Philip III, firmly supported Borromeo's candidature for canonisation because the archdiocese of Milan, where Borromeo had served as pastor, belonged to the Spanish dominions at the time. In addition to the Spanish support, the Roman curia held Borremo in high regard for his swiftness and efficiency in implementing the decrees of the Council of Trent, particularly those decrees that pertained to the reform of the clergy. He became a role-model for reforming bishops and the first exemplar of the Counter-Reformation to be canonised. The earls visited Borromeo's tomb in Santa Maria del Duomo during their visit to Milan, some time between 23 March and 12 April 1608. Ó Cianáin refers to this visit as follows: 'O fuair bás measaid cách a bheith naomtha agus atá cano(n)sásion chom a dhéanta go hobann 'sa Róimh air'.[23]

Ó Cianáin testifies to the existence of Borromeo's Milanese cult over two years before his canonisation and expresses confidence of his swift, impending elevation. The clergy and people of Milan had in fact petitioned Clement VIII for his canonisation on 4 May 1604, but the inves-

tigations at Milan had been conducted without a mandate from the Holy See. Paul V, who became pope in 1605, ordered a new and searching inquiry that examined more than three hundred witnesses. Petitions supporting the cause came from the whole college of cardinals as well as from Philip III of Spain. Because Borromeo had himself been a cardinal, Paul V demanded a most rigorous investigation to avoid the slightest accusation of partiality to one of their own. Three auditors discussed the case and presented a favourable vote to the pope on 9 December 1609, which he passed on to the Congregation of Rites five days later. Although they had already given their assent in the spring of 1610, the discussions finally concluded in three consistories that took place 30 August, 14 and 20 September 1610.[24] Ó Cianáin's informants had been somewhat ahead of themselves in what they saw as an inevitable decision, and the Irish account provides an interesting vignette of the tension between local enthusiasm and Paul V's well-known circumspection. The reference to Borromeo's impending canonisation is the first evidence of the influence of the Counter-Reformation on Ó Cianáin's narrative, an influence that becomes much more pronounced on the rest of his account, especially the section that deals with the earls' residence in Rome between 29 April 1608 and 27 November 1608. The Irish exiles had only spent a month in the Eternal City when they received a papal invitation to attend the canonisation of Santa Francesca Romana. Before dealing with Ó Cianáin's account of this event, it is necessary to give an outline of Francesca's life and the context of her times.

Francesca Bussi was born into a noble Roman family in the year 1384. At the tender age of twelve, and in accordance with her parents' wishes, she married Lorenzo de' Ponziani, a rich landowner in the Trastevere quarter of Rome who commanded the papal troops in the city. They had three children, two of whom died very young. Francesca gained renown for her love and concern for the poor of Rome during a turbulent era when the city frequently fell prey to the invading armies of the Great Schism between pope and anti-pope. In 1425 she founded the Oblates of Mary, a group of lay women who affiliated themselves to the Benedictine monastery of Santa Maria Nova. The Oblates received official confirmation from Pope Eugenius IV in 1433. On the death of her husband in 1436, Francesca left her home to become superior of the community in the monastery they had ac-

Four Spanish saints were canonised on 12 March 1622. L-R: Francis Xavier (1506-1552), Ignatius Loyola (1491-1556), Teresa of Avila (1515-82) and Isidore the Farmer (1077-1130). The last of these, Isidore the Farmer, gave his name to the Irish Franciscan College in Rome.

quired in Tor de' Specchi abandoning her surname for the simple adjective 'Romana'. She died of the plague in 1440.

Four formal inquiries had been established into the sanctity of Francesca's life, 'la più romana tra tutti i santi'.[25] The first took place in the year 1440, only some months after her death; the second and third followed in 1443 and 1451-53, with the final definitive hearing in 1604.[26] She was considered a saint by popular acclaim, *vox populi*, from the very beginning, and the faithful venerated her image in the church of Santa Maria in Trastevere from as early as 1448.[27] It became customary to abstain from work 'in Curia Capitolina' on 9 March, the anniversary of her death, at least from the papacy of Alexander VI (1492-1503).[28] The short reigns of a number of popes, allied to the unsettled nature of the times, resulted in a protracted delay in her canonisation. Clement VIII took up the process in 1604, a year before his death. His successor, Leo XI, reigned less than four weeks before being succeeded by Paul V, who showed interest in the process from the very beginning of his reign. Paul's concern was less than impartial, however, seeing that this Roman pope, Camillo Borghese, descended on his mother's side from both the Bussi and the Ponziani families. Furthermore, his sister-in-law, Ortensia Santacroce, was a descendant of Vannozza Santacroce, Francesca's close friend and sister-in-law, and one of the first oblates in the monastery

of Tor de' Specchi.[29] Despite his personal interests, Paul V, with his customary regard for ecclesiastical procedures and rules, observed the letter of the law in regard to the process. After its favourable completion on 21 May 1608 he sanctioned the decision in the bull *Coelestis aquae flumen* and fixed 29 May, the anniversary of his own coronation, as the date for the canonization. Between 1608 and his death in 1625, Paul V regularly celebrated mass in the church of Santa Maria Nova, the new saint's burial place.

The canonisation of Francesca became a religious and specifically Roman occasion, commemorating the city's first saint in more than a thousand years, and the civic authorities contributed 20,000 scudi to defray the expenses and supply 'richissimi e sontuosissimi ornamenti'.[30] They also laid aside 200 gold ducats to provide bread for the poor (*ai fornari per li pani dispensati ai poveri*).[31] Both St Peter's and Santa Maria Nova were adorned in a lavish fashion; the latter was festooned with drapes and new carpets, while the ground outside the church was strewn with rose petals and violets. From the columns and arches of St Peter's hung banners bearing the coats of arms of the Bussi and Ponziani families, the papal coat of arms and the arms of the city. Rome had never seen such a celebration (*Roma ne aveva viste de simili*).[32] Everybody wished to celebrate the saint of the city with all the magnificence possible and there was marvellous emulation between the citizens of Rome and the nobility. The patriciate wished to exalt one of its most noble members.[33] Firework displays lit up the night sky, and the festivities continued for a number of nights, particularly in the Campidoglio, where a very great quantity and variety of fireworks had been ordered.[34]

It is this specifically Roman dimension to the canonisation of Santa Francesca Romana that made it such a lavish occasion, unusually opulent even according to the magnificence normally associated with canonisations. If canonisations in themselves were rare, unusual and marvellous events, the canonisation of a Roman saint was much more so. It is essential to bear this in mind when reading Tadhg Ó Cianáin's account of this splendid occasion.[35]

There are many points of interest in his description. It is obvious that he appreciated both the importance of the occasion in itself and the honour accorded to the earls, not only in receiving an invitation to attend, but also in being seated so close to the pope. He refers specifically to the Spanish ambassador, the most powerful foreigner in Rome at the time, being in their midst. The exiled earls were conscious of and appreciated the extent of their dependence on Spanish protection and patronage. At the same time, Ó Cianáin is particularly exercised,

not only on this occasion but throughout his narrative, to present the earls as Catholic European princes of equal standing with the Spanish nobility.[36] As regards his choice of language, one of the most intriguing features is the frequency of the word *onórach*, honourable, which occurs ten times in this passage, and which is not always reflected in the translation. It is the frequency of this word more than anything else that demonstrates how much the chronicler appreciates the importance, rarity and splendour of the occasion, not only as an ecclesiastical ceremony, but as a specifically Roman ceremony as well.

Ó Cianáin is quite accurate in his details, as when he notes that Santa Francesca's canonisation is taking place on the anniversary of the pope's coronation. It is interesting that Cardinal Scipione Borghese, the pope's nephew, is the one chosen to carry the invitation to the earls, as he too, along with his uncle, could trace his lineage to the new saint. When the chronicler refers to Francesca Romana's holy life and the miracles that God performed through her, he shows himself to be well aware of the two criteria necessary for canonisation. His use of language, indeed, in this instance is meticulously precise and technical from a theological point of view: 'triasa ndearna

Church of Santa Francesca Romana.

Dia d'fheartaibh agus do mhíorbhailibh tríthe', ('all the wonders and miracles that God worked through her'). The text studiously and deliberately refrains from discussing *her* miracles. Ó Cianáin is well aware of the distinction between God's power to work a miracle and the intercessory prayer of the saint, which, despite its efficacy, is always subsidiary to the divine power. One is inclined to think that Ó Cianáin is well versed in the criticisms of the reformers against the cult of the saints, and deliberately articulates orthodox doctrine to show that these criticisms are without foundation. If the poor and uneducated are unaware of the distinction between divine power and intercessory prayer, the fault is not in church teaching, but is rather due to a lack of proper instruction. Ó Cianáin here shows himself to be a well-educated lay representative of the Catholic Counter-Reformation.

Whether the chronicler had received this education in Ireland before his departure for the continent is, indeed, a moot point. It is most likely something that he acquired during the course of his travels. We must also remember that the earls' party was accompanied from Louvain to Rome by the Franciscan Florence Conry, a graduate of the University of Salamanca, well versed in the Counter-Reformation, who would later come to prominence as a noted theologian. Conry met the earls in Douai in November 1607 and acted as mentor to the exiles during their travels. Even as early as December 1607, James Loach, cook to Colonel Henry O'Neill of the Irish regiment in Flanders, reported to the English authorities that 'the earl of Tyrone was instantly bound to Rome, accompanied by Father Flarie O'Molconery as his principall guide'.[37] One suspects that the specifically Franciscan, Spanish and Counter-Reformation dimensions of Ó Cianáin's narrative owe much to Conry's promptings and guidance.

Another aspect of Tadhg Ó Cianáin's account of the celebrations associated with the canonisation of Santa Francesca Romana is his vivid description of the fireworks displays. It is obvious that this was his and the earls' first encounter with fireworks, as his narrative exudes a mixture of wonder, delight and fear. He makes deft use of alliteration to convey his emotions, which does not come across in the translation. An interesting feature of the Irish text is how close it agrees with an earlier Italian account that conveys the impression that this was no ordinary fireworks

display but something exceptional, even though an ordinary display would have been more than exceptional for the Irish exiles.

In his work on the representation of fireworks in early modern Europe, Kevin Salatino makes a very pertinent observation on the use of fireworks in Rome:

> Throughout the seventeenth and eighteenth centuries Rome was perhaps the most cosmopolitan of European urban centres. It was also the most ritualised. Like the Church that gave it meaning, Rome existed in time and out of time by nature of its symbolic presence; it betook of the eternal. Any ceremony, any festival, thus participated in the numinous aura of Holy Rome, assuming a significance greater than was possible elsewhere. The symbolic and the celebratory merged there in unique ways. Fireworks also assumed a resonance consistent with Rome's larger meaning. The annual fireworks display from the Castel Sant'Angelo (the so-called Girandola), became, over a period of several centuries, the most famous and most enduring pyrotechnical spectacle in Europe, while the eighteenth-century 'Festival of the Chinea', also celebrated annually, achieved a similar authority, not the least because it was scrupulously documented.[38]

If Salatino's remarks are true regarding any ceremony in Rome, they must ring much truer for the canonisation of a Roman saint. The present writer has been unable so far to source any illustration or print showing the fireworks associated with the canonisation of Santa Francesca Romana, but has acquired a copy of a 1580s print showing the annual fireworks display from Castel Sant'Angelo, which conveys some impression of what Tadhg Ó Cianáin witnessed. It would seem, too, that dragons and eagles regularly featured in good fireworks displays.[39] A contemporary English account of the canonisation of Francesca Romana also mentions the fireworks: 'On the evening of the canonisation, the pope's niece took all the Irish ladies to see the illumination of St Peter's and the fireworks in St Angelo – the grandest that can be imagined'.[40]

Ó Cianáin's account refers specifically to the Sunday after the canonisation rather than the actual day, but as the celebrations lasted four full days, he probably deemed one account as sufficient. The

The Palazzo del Quirinale from an etching by Giovanni Battista Piranesi in the middle of the eighteenth century. This was where the earls had their first formal meeting with Paul V on Sunday, 4 May 1608.

main event that took place on the following Sunday was a procession from St Peter's to Santa Maria Nova, the saint's final resting-place, a church subsequently named Santa Francesca Romana. The Irish account does not specifically state that the earls actually walked in this procession, but merely relates the fact of its taking place. This church is built on the fringes of the Roman Forum, then in poor repair and disparagingly referred to as a cow field (*un campo vaccino*) by the city's inhabitants. It is little wonder, then, that Ó Cianáin makes no mention of it. What is surprising, however, is that he does not make the slightest reference to the Colosseum, an imposing edifice in close proximity to the church, and one that has captivated visitors to the Città Eterna throughout the ages. A possible explanation for this glaring omission is that Ó Cianáin's narrative is neither a travel book nor a tourist's diary. The emphasis is totally centred on the procession to the tomb of newly created saint as part of the celebrations associated with her canonisation. That the Irish exiles participated in the splendid ceremonies and solemn liturgies of the Counter-Reformation church as honoured guests of the pope alongside the Rome's ecclesiastical and lay nobility, and loyal allies of Spain, is what the narrator wants to relate. The Colosseum and the relics of antiquity do not feature in Ó Cianáin's scheme of things.

Ó Cianáin, in fact, refers to only one monument of Roman antiquity in his chronicle, the Pantheon. He marvels at the dimensions of the building, noting that it as long as it is broad as it is high. He mentions the single thirty-foot window, circular and wide, which admits light to all the altars in the church ('éanfhuinneóg amháin i n-a bhfuilid deich dtroighthe fichead i n-a fíormhullach 's í comhchruinn comhfhairsing dos-gní soillse d'uile altóiribh an reigléasa i n-a fíormhullach').[41] Nevertheless, despite this precise attention to detail, Ó Cianáin is much less preoccupied with the architectural wonders of the Pantheon than with the religious feast that coincides with O'Neill's visit. The date is 1 November, the feast of All Saints, the Christian celebration that displaced the pagan origins of the Pantheon, a temple dedicated to all the gods. The Emperor Phocas actually presented the temple to Pope Boniface IV in 608, who consecrated it to Santa Maria and Martyres (subsequently All Saints). The earl's visit coincided with the thousandth anniversary of the Pantheon's use as a Christian place of worship. While Ó Cianáin does not specifically allude to this particular aspect of the Pantheon's history, he is much more concerned to present O'Neill as a Catholic prince participating in a public Catholic event, one of the major feast-days in the liturgical year. Indeed, if one reads the chronicle carefully, the vast majority of the events described by the narrator in Rome are public liturgical events. Ó Cianáin is engaged in an exercise of deliberate Catholic self-fashioning, portraying the earls as exemplars of the self-confident early modern Catholicism that had emerged in Rome after the *débâcle* of the Reformation. The deliberate crafting of his text is an accurate reflection of O'Neill's own conduct, a public representation that did not deceive Sir Henry Wotton, the English ambassador to Venice from 1604 onwards: 'In his coach, it is written, he commonly sits in *portella a basso*, (peradventure to be seen, with the Primate *in capo* and Tyrconnell on his left hand'.[42]

Italian accounts of the canonisation of Santa Francesca Romana and the associated celebrations have already been cited, as has an English-language account of the fireworks. As soon as O'Neill and O'Donnell set foot on European soil, the English ambassadors at the various continental courts meticulously catalogued their activities and reported back to London. Though Sir Henry Wotton was far enough removed from Rome at his post in Venice, he employed informants in the Eternal City who kept him fully posted on the earls' movements. One of these ciphers provided him with an account of the ceremonies of Santa Francesca Romana's canonisation that closely mirrors Ó Cianáin's, including a number of details not found in the Gaelic text. One can sense the disappointment and annoyance of the English diplomat at the marks of honour shown to the Irish exiles on this occasion:

> Reports the canonisation on this holiday, the Thursday before Trinity Sunday, of St Francesca, in St Peter's, with great splendour, and at the cost to the Romans of 20,000 crowns. Never saw a more stately sight or more religious ceremonies. The Pope himself in his patriarchical habit sang mass; all the cardinals, bishops, prelates, canons, and religious were for the most part present. Overnight his Holiness gave order that the Earl of Tyrone and the rest with him, should have the best place in the church. Saw this order carried out; and to grace the matter more, his Holiness's niece went in coach to the Earl's house, and brought with her the Countess to St Peter's, giving her both in place and church the better hand, which she had also of the Pope's sisters, amongst all the duchesses and other nobility of Rome. And when all the ceremonies were

ended, the same niece that fetched the Countess, carried her home again to her own palace, from whence she took her … Italians speak much good and very honourably of these Earls; and the Earls themselves keep their state gallantly. It seemeth some good vein of gold as yet flows with full tide, which he prays God may not soon fall to a low ebb.[43]

Wotton's correspondent took the precaution of including a picture of St Francesca of Rome with his report, as well as forty Agnus Deis. An accompanying note adds that these advertisements from Rome 'were written with some clauses to disguise the affection of the intelligence'.[44] The cost of mounting the ceremonies must have occasioned much comment, as it is interesting to note that both Wotton's informant and Francesco Penia, auditor of the Roman Rota, both mention the same amount, 20,000 scudi. Much the same information is given in another memo from Rome, dated 14 June 1608:

> The Count Tyrone, it is supposed, will live at Rome this summer at least; he and his are much esteemed and much pitied there of all sorts, as having lost all for conscience and religion; and the Pope and cardinals make great account of them, for at the canonising of the late saint, the Countess had place above all the Pope's sisters-in-law, and at the procession on Corpus Christi day the Pope gave them the honour to carry the canopy over him, eight of them only throughout the procession.[45]

Though we now realise with the benefit of hindsight that the kindness and marks of respect shown by Paul V to the exiled Irish lords were little more than empty gestures, this would not have been so obvious in the beginning of the summer of 1608, with the earls barely a month in Rome. It is hardly an exaggeration to claim that the canonisation of only the fourth saint since the Reformation, and the first Roman saint in a thousand years, was the highlight of the Roman year. Depending on one's political outlook, one could either be highly encouraged or deeply dismayed at the signs of esteem Paul V showed to the earls during this event. Tadhg Ó Cianáin provides us with invaluable insights on the earls' encounter with early modern Catholicism in the Eternal City and its accompanying political realities.

Notes

1 D. Farmer, *The Oxford Dictionary of Saints* (5th ed., Oxford, 2004), p. xvii.

2 S. C. Karant-Nunn, 'Ritual in early modern Christianity' in R. Po-Chia Hsia (ed.), *The Cambridge History of Christianity*, vi, *Reform and expansion 1500-1660* (Cambridge, 2007), p. 373.

3 C. P. Heming, *Protestants and the cult of the saints in German-Speaking Europe, 1517-1531* (Missouri, 2003), p. 8.

4 Ibid., p. 61.

5 P. Burke, 'How to be a Counter-Reformation saint', in idem (ed.), *The historical anthropology of early modern Italy: Essays on perception and communication* (Cambridge, 1987), p. 49.

6 Ibid., p. 50.

7 S. Ditchfield, 'Tridentine worship and the cult of the saints', in *The Cambridge History of Christianity*, vi, pp 203-4.

8 Burke, 'How to be a Counter-Reformation saint', p. 50.

9 R. Po-Chia Hsia, *The world of Catholic renewal, 1540-1770* (Cambridge, 1998; revised ed., 2005), pp 127-31.

10 L. J. A. Villanon, 'San Diego de Alcalá and the politics of saint-making in Counter-Reformation Europe', *Catholic Historical Review*, lxxxiii (1997), pp 691-715.

11 T. J. Dandalet, *Spanish Rome, 1500-1700* (New Haven, 2001), p. 172; Villalon, 'San Diego de Alcalá, pp 695-704.

12 Dandalet, *Spanish Rome*, pp 173-4.

13 Villanon, 'San Diego de Alcalá', p. 707.

14 Dandalet, *Spanish Rome*, pp 176-8.

15 Villanon, 'San Diego de Alcalá', p. 713.

16 Ditchfield, 'Tridentine worship and the cult of the saints', p. 207.

17 Ibid., p. 216.

18 Dandalet, *Spanish Rome*, pp 178-80.

19 P. Delooz, 'Towards a sociological study of canonized sainthood in the Catholic church', in S. Wilson (ed.), *Saints and the cults* (Cambridge, 1983), p. 252.

20 Dandalet, *Spanish Rome*, pp 180-2.

21 Simon Ditchfield cautions against taking a too simplistic view of the dearth of canonisations (universal cults) between 1525 and 1588. This must be balanced against the fourteen non-universal cults that were recognized by the papacy during the same period (Ditchfield, 'Tridentine worship and the cult of the saints', pp 207-8). The big innovation regarding canonisations after Trent was the determination of the papacy to differentiate clearly between the investigation at local level and the universal authority of the apostolic trial. The former did not constitute official recognition of sanctity, neither could it prejudge the result of the apostolic trial. It was this determination that resulted in Clement VIII's establishment of a 'Congregazione dei Beati' in 1602. The pope was particularly concerned at minimising the influence of pressure groups such as royal houses and religious orders to canonise recently deceased candidates with a reputation for sanctity. These 'holy' men and women were effectively the recipients of public cult without papal sanction. Clement made a clear distinction between these *beati moderni* and candidates who had been the recipients of a long-established local cult (ibid., p. 209).

22 Dandalet, *Spanish Rome*, p. 62.

23 'Since he died everyone thinks he is a saint, and he is soon to be canonised in Rome' *Turas*, pp 162-3.

24 L. von Pastor, *The History of the Popes*, xxv (London, 1937), pp 258-60.

25 A. Esch, 'Santa Francesca Romana ed il suo ambiente sociale a Rome', in Giorgio Picasso, *Una santa tutta Romana saggi e ricerche nel VI centenario della nascita di Francesca Bussa dei Ponziani (1384-1984)*, (Siena, 1984), p. 33.

26 G. Barone, 'La canonizzazione di Francesca Romana (1608): la riproposta di un modelo agografico medievale' in Gabriella Zarri (ed.), *Finzione e santità tra medioevo e età moderna* (Rome, 1991), pp 268-75.

27 Esch, 'Santa Francesca Romana', p. 51.

28 Barone, 'La canonizzazione di Francesca Romana', p. 265.

29 Ibid., pp 266-7.

30 Ibid., p. 265.

31 M. L. Ronco Valenti, *Francesca Romana La Santa della Solidarietà e della Speranza* (Milano, 2005), p. 20.

32 Ibid.

33 Ibid.

34 F. Penia, *Relatione sommaria della vita, santità, miracoli e atti della canonissazione di Santa Francesca Romana o de Pontiani. Cavata fedelmente dalli processi autentici di questa ausa. Da Monsig. Francesco Penia Auditor di Rota* (Roma, 1608), p. 44.

35 *Turas*, pp 289-97.

36 M. Mac Craith, 'Creideamh agus athartha: idé-eolaíocht pholaitíochta agus aos léinn na Gaeilge i dtús an seachtú h-aois déag', in M. Ní Dhonnchadha (ed.), *Nua-léamha: gnéithe de chultúr, stair agus polaitíocht na hÉireann c. 1600-c.1900* (Dublin, 1996), pp 13-14; C. Carroll, 'Turas na nIarladh as Éire: International Travel and National Identity in Ó Cianáin's Narrative', *History Ireland*, xv, no. 4 (July-August 2007), pp 56-61.

37 *CSPI, 1606-08*, p. 359.

38 K. Salatino, *Incendiary art: the representation of fireworks in early modern Europe* (Los Angeles, 1997), pp 36-37.

39 Ibid., p. 41. It is worth noting that the coat of arms of Paul V shows a dragon surmounted by an eagle.

40 C. P. Meehan, *The fate and fortunes of Hugh O' Neill, earl of Tyrone, and Rory O'Donel, earl of Tyrconnel* (3rd ed., Dublin, 1886), p. 171.

41 *Turas*, pp 386-7.

42 *CSPI, 1606-08*, p. 225.

43 Ibid., pp 655-6.

44 Ibid., p. 656.

45 Ibid., p. 662.

Roman religious and ceremonial music in the time of the earls[1]

Noel O'Regan

The Rome which the Irish earls entered on 29 April 1608 was a city with a rich and varied soundscape. A continual background of church bells marked out the day, street criers and trumpeters announced public notices, litanies and other pieces sung in plainchant or improvised harmony accompanied constant processions. The sounds of priests or choirs singing the offices in chant and/or polyphony filtered intermittently through the doors of churches. Music in the broadest sense invested the fabric of the city just as much as the architecture, the paintings, the sounds and the smells. Unlike buildings and paintings however, music survives only in prints and manuscripts and needs to be continually reconstructed; much of it was ephemeral and never committed to paper. This, with the difficulties of reconstituting historical performance practices, has led to a comparative ignoring of music's role in both forming and articulating Roman society in the 'Seicento'.

Music had a variety of functions in the religious life of the city and was provided by a range of musical groups. Like other princes, the pope maintained his own choir, the *Cappella Pontificia*, also commonly called the *Cappella Sistina* after the chapel in which it most regularly performed. It did not just perform there, however, but accompanied the pope to St Peter's and other basilicas and churches when he visited. Its singers were, on the whole, among the best in Europc, though some owed their places more to their ability as composers or the influence which they had attained with previous popes and important cardinals.[2] It was unusual among Roman choirs, firstly in performing unaccompanied by organ or other instruments,[3] and secondly consisting entirely of adult male singers, with no boys, relying on *castrati* and *falsettos* to sing the soprano parts. The pope also maintained two instrumental groups, based at Castel Sant'Angelo: six trumpeters for fanfares and for accompanying official announcements and a wind-band of six or so virtuoso players on cornets, sackbuts and other wind instruments who played on ceremonial occasions such as banquets and processions. Analogous groups to these were maintained by the S P Q R on the Campidoglio, and players from both groups

were regularly hired by basilicas and other institutions to play during processions and patronal feast day celebrations.[4]

Rome had about fifteen other church choirs in 1608. These were small in size: usually two or three adult males on each of alto, tenor and bass, and three or four boys on soprano. The largest was the *Cappella Giulia*, the resident choir in St Peter's basilica (it had twelve adults and six boys when at full strength);[5] the basilicas of St John Lateran and S. Mary Major also had choirs,[6] as did S. Lorenzo in Damaso (attached to the Cancelleria palace of the cardinal vice-chancellor),[7] the French national church of S. Luigi dei Francesi,[8] hospitals such as S. Spirito in Sassia, and other important churches such as S. Maria in Trastevere, S. Giovanni dei Fiorentini and S. Maria in Vallicella (the Chiesa Nuova).[9] The Germano-Hungarian College and the Roman Seminary (whose choir also sang at the main Jesuit church of the Gesù) had choirs which might include some talented seminarians.[10] Individually or collectively members of these choirs also carried out freelance work for the much larger number of institutions which did not have a regular choir.

Each church, hospital or confraternity celebrated at least one major patronal feast-day per year – and many had two or more – on which mass and both sets of vespers were celebrated solemnly with some polyphonic music, as well as processions which were also accompanied with music. The focus of the procession might be a relic, a prisoner released by concession of the pope to mark the occasion,[11] young girls to whom the institution had granted dowries, or floats illustrating the life of the patron saint.[12] There were normally at least two groups of singers and/or instrumentalists from the wind-bands based at Castel Sant'Angelo and the Campidoglio. There were other occasions for general processions such as Rogation days (especially the feast of St Mark on 25 April), Holy Thursday, during the octave of Corpus Christi. From time to time the pope also asked for processions with indulgences attached to pray for particular causes such as relief from plague or victory in religious wars. There was a constant flow of pilgrims, both as individuals and in organised groups, who often brought musicians, or hired them in the city, to accompany them around the major churches. Devotional confraternities such as SS. Crocifisso in S. Marcello maintained oratories in which prayer services with music were celebrated, especially during Lent and Holy Week.[13] Finally, at least one of the city's 240 or so churches celebrated the Forty Hours devotion at any one time. All of this meant a never-ending carousel of ceremonies, liturgies and processions, which visitors commented on, pointing out that virtually every day of the year had a ceremony of some sort in at least one institution. The French viol player André Maugars, for example, wrote in 1639:

> There is not a day of the week on which there is not a feast in some church and on which there is not some good music … every day new compositions are being performed.[14]

For singers and instrumentalists, including organists, this provided a constant source of work making early 'Seicento' Rome a very attractive place. By the early 1600s the musicians were mainly Italian (although some still came from north of the Alps as they had been doing for nearly two hundred

years). Rome had its own music printing-presses, serving both the local and export market,[15] while constant manuscript copying filled the demand for ceremonial music written for multiple choirs. The type and scale of music performed reflected its function. Patronal masses and vespers favoured large-scale music for three, four and more choirs; with platforms on which groups of singers and instrumentalists, each accompanied by a portable organ, performed; this surround-sound was designed to impress and to attract people.[16] It alternated with more intimate music for one or a handful of voices accompanied by the new 'basso continuo', favoured for antiphons and motets at more intimate moments such as Communion or during the Forty Hours devotion.[17] The organ played in alternation with polyphony or with plainchant in smaller institutions. Processions used groups of singers and instrumentalists at strategic points to draw attention to crucifixes, relics, floats or important personages. Oratory devotions included Gospel dialogues, performed by virtuoso singers and instrumentalists as a complement to the sermon, and psalm singing. Marian antiphons such the *Salve Regina* were sung devotionally on Saturday evenings before images of the Virgin. Plainchant was ubiquitous in the churches of friars and nuns,

as well as filling the major part of even the most solemn services in all churches. It formed the constant background against which polyphony in four or more parts shone as something special.

All this formed the musical backdrop to the earls' heady first months in Rome when they were treated as visiting princes, given places of honour at papal ceremonial and led around the liturgical carousel of patronal feast-day celebrations. The English writer Thomas Gainsford spoke at the time of the Irish as having been 'blessed with the Holy Father's entertainment'.[18] The table below lists the ceremonies which, Ó Cianáin informs us, they attended during the first seven months before his journal breaks off; between them they included a representative sample of the city's ecclesiastical institutions and of ceremonial events. There were four major papal occasions: the Ascension Thursday blessing, First Vespers of Pentecost, the canonisation of Santa Francesca Romana, and the Corpus Christi procession. Of the rest the largest number were patronal celebrations: Pentecost at S. Spirito in Sassia, St Michael at S. Angelo in Borgo, All Saints at the Pantheon, the Assumption at S. Maria in Trastevere; St Bartolomew, St Francis of Assissi, St Gregory, St Onofrio and St Peter's Chains at the eponymous churches. Processions took place on Whit Monday and Trinity Sunday as well as two processions specially called for by the pope to pray for the resolution of conflicts in the Habsburg dominions. The earls also undertook two visits to the seven major basilicas, an informal one on 17 May and a more formal one on 12 June.

Liturgical Events Attended by the Earls in Rome, 1608
(as chronicled by Ó Cianáin)

15 May Ascension Thursday: papal benediction from the loggia in front of St Peter's
24 May Vigil of Pentecost: First Vespers in the Cappella Sistina
25 May Pentecost Sunday: Mass and Second Vespers in S. Spirito in Sassia: patronal feast-day
26 May Whit Monday: procession of orphaned girls (*zitelle*) at S. Spirito in Sassia
29 May: Canonisation of Santa Francesca Romana at St Peter's
1 Jun Trinity Sunday: Irish ladies received by the pope. Procession by religious and young clergy to S. Francesca Romana (also known as S. Maria Nuova)
5 Jun Corpus Christi: the Earls carried the

canopy over the Pope and monstrance during the Papal procession around St Peter's Square
12 Jun: Visit to the seven major basilicas. S. Onofrio: patronal feast-day
1 Aug St Peter's Chains: S. Pietro in Vincula: patronal feast-day
15 Aug Assumption: S. Maria in Trastevere: patronal feast-day
24 Aug S. Bartolomeo (Tiber island): patronal feast-day
3 Sept: Special procession from S. Maria degli Angeli to S. Maria Maggiore
5 Sept: Special procession from S. Maria sopra Minerva to S. Maria della Pace
29 Sept St Michael the Archangel: S. Angelo in Borgo: patronal feast-day
4 Oct St Francis of Assissi: S. Francesco a Ripa: patronal feast-day
1 Nov All Saints: S. Maria ad Martyre (the Pantheon): patronal feast-day and millennial celebration
13 Nov St Gregory the Great: S. Gregorio Magno: patronal feast-day

The first major ceremonial occasion Ó Cianáin describes was on Ascension Thursday, when the earls watched the papal benediction given from the loggia in front of St Peter's basilica after solemn mass, watching from the palace of Cardinal d'Ascoli immediately opposite. In fact the earls would have been facing a building site, since the facade of the new basilica had been started in the previous November, with the first stone laid on 10 February 1608.[19] The old benediction loggia, however, remained in place until demolished in July, with the facade completed in 1615. Ó Cianáin mentions the blare of the papal trumpets and the beating of drums which accompanied the occasion, followed by the firing of canons from both the Vatican palace and Castel Sant'Angelo.

On the vigil of Pentecost the earls attended First Vespers in the Sistine Chapel. Ó Cianáin calls it the Cappella Paolina, but the 'Diario del Puntatore' (a diary kept each year by one of the papal singers recording all events and fines for lateness) for 1608 tells us that it was held in the Cappella di Sisto – the Sistine Chapel, the usual venue for such important public papal ceremonies at this period.[20] That diary entry simply says that the pope celebrated in the presence of the sacred college and lists a couple of absent singers.[21] Later in the reign of Paul V, a replica of the Cappella

Sistina was built in the Quirinale Palace, called the Cappella Paolina, which increasingly hosted papal services. The Vatican also had a smaller Cappella Paolina, but this was not used for large-scale *cappelle papale* such as that at Pentecost. For whatever reason, it seems that Ó Cianáin mistook the name of the chapel. The celebration of First Vespers on major feasts such as this was carried out on a grand scale, having as much of the political about it as the liturgical. It showed the pope officiating at the head of his court attended by ambassadors, heads of great Roman families, cardinals and a host of Vatican officials. Strict ceremonial laid down the precise position allotted to those attending, and precedence was a matter of national or family pride.[22] The decision to give Hugh O'Neill a place of honour opposite the pope, as described by Ó Cianáin, had a political significance, placing him among princes and ambassadors of the major European powers. Ó Cianáin makes no mention of music on this occasion, and it is quite possible that the general hubbub in the Sistine Chapel made the music difficult to hear.[23] While it is not known precisely which musical settings would have been performed, some fairly detailed information survives about the papal singers' repertory at this time. For one year only, 1616, the *puntatore* of the Cappella Pontificia, Carlo Vanni, recorded the precise repertory sung on each major occasion.[24] On the vigil of Pentecost the first psalm, *Dixit Dominus*, was for four voices by Felice Anerio, official composer to the chapel; the third psalm, *Beatus vir*, was for eight voices by Ruggiero Giovanelli, the hymn, *Veni creator*, by Vincenzo de Grandis, was for four voices, and the *Magnificat*, by Giovanni Maria Nanino, for eight. Giovanelli and Grandis were members of the chapel in 1608, and Nanino had died the previous year.[25] This repertory was pretty typical of the time, and the music in 1608 would have been similar. Only the first and third psalms, the hymn and the Magnificat were sung in polyphony; the other psalms would have been in plainchant or in *falsobordone* (improvised harmony) while some of the antiphons might well have been in improvised counterpoint over the plainchant, the *contrappunto alla mente* for which the papal singers were famous.

On Pentecost Sunday the Irish attended the patronal feast-day mass and vespers at the church of S. Sprito in Sassia, just beside St Peter's in the Borgo. Ó Cianáin described it thus:

On Pentecost Sunday there was a splendid station and an indulgence for all sins in the great church of Santo Spirito. The princes came to Mass and vespers there. There was a divine service, the most beautiful in all Christendom, in the church, with many worthy priests and exalted prelates, and a choir the most excellent in the world; also two or three pairs of sweet musical organs, and many instruments of music and harmony besides.[26]

He called it a 'stáisiún onórach', using the term normally used for the series of Lenten masses which moved from church to church throughout the city; an appropriate term for the continuous celebration of patronal feasts in various churches. He also mentions the plenary indulgence, routinely granted for Roman confraternities and other institutions on the occasion of their patronal feast-day, which acted as a draw for crowds of people. S. Spirito had its own choir, albeit a relatively small one: in May 1608 there were seven adult singers and a few boys led by Giovanni Francesco Anerio, one of the best composers of the post-Palestrina generation, as *maestro di cappella*.[27] Ó Cianáin later called it 'the finest choir, and the most worthy and best fathers for divine service, in the greater part of all Christendom'. This would certainly not have applied to the small regular choir, but, boosted as it would have been by extra singers and instrumentalists hired in for the patronal feast-day, it could well have seemed so to the Irish. We know from the archives of S. Spirito that Anerio was given 12 *scudi* to pay for extra musicians for the festal mass and vespers on this occasion,[28] enough to hire between eight and twelve extra singers and players.

S. Spirito in Sassia, one of Rome's most important institutions (part hospitaller order, part lay confraternity), ran one of the city's premier hospitals (still in use today) and an orphanage for both boys and girls.[29] Ó Cianáin gives a detailed account which described the instruction of the male orphans (or 'children of the pope') in doctrine, singing, music and 'every learning and proper instruction'. The best of these boys sang in the choir. He also describes the Whit Monday procession of female orphans, or *zitelle* who received dowries, a common practice among Rome's lay confraternities since poor girls needed dowries in order to get married and escape prostitution. Ó Cianáin was clearly impressed with all he saw and heard at S. Spirito, and this might explain his singling out of

Antonio Tempesta's engraving of the procession to the canonisation of Santa Francesca Romana (1608).
© Biblioteca Angelica Rome

the choir there for praise while he ignored the Cappella Pontificia the previous day. In fact this is also explicable if one imagines the different impressions that would have been made by the unaccompanied papal choir, singing in an already conservative style in a single balcony, and the brash modern-style singing at S. Spirito of multiple choirs accompanied perhaps by cornets, sackbuts, violins, lutes and theorbos as well as organs. It was common by this period to have at least some music for three and even four choirs, using platforms built specially for the occasion, with small organs on each platform; some of these platforms were placed in the nave, leading to a surround-sound effect for the congregation. Thus Ó Cianáin's mention of two to three pairs of organs and musical instruments is exactly in line with contemporary Roman practice.

The earls also took part in the ceremonies marking the canonisation of Santa Francesca Romana on Thursday 29 May. Unlike today, canonisations were very rare in the sixteenth and seventeenth centuries, the Lutheran attack on saints having led

A detail from the engraving above of the procession to the canonisation of Santa Francesca Romana.
© Biblioteca Angelica Rome

to something of a loss of nerve on the part of the Vatican.[30] The Roman Santa Francesca, who had founded an important convent in the city in the fourteenth century, proved a popular choice for the Roman Pope Paul V's first canonisation, which he held on the third anniversary of his own coronation, in the tribune of the new St Peter's – the first major ceremony to be performed there. He sent an invitation to the earls and their households, and his own sister came herself to fetch the countess of Tyrone in her carriage. Ó Cianáin gives his most detailed description of any ceremony:

> On Thursday, the twenty-ninth day of May, 1608, the anniversary of the day on which the Holy Father, Paul V, was crowned, Cardinal Borghese sent one of his noblemen as a grand messenger to invite the lords to solemn Mass which, in honour of the holy Father, was celebrated in the great church of Saint Peter. A position of honour and a fitting place was selected for them close to and near the Pope. They, and the ambassador of the King of Spain, and a great number of other great princes, were in the same place. Beautiful, splendid, reverent, remarkable, and wonderful was the precious Mass which was celebrated there. His Holiness the Pope himself said it and offered the Body of Christ. On either side of him was the melodious, sweet choir, the most harmonious in all Christendom. To increase the glory and the solemnity of that particular day, a noble, wonderful, holy woman named Saint Francesca Romana, who was in the city two hundred years before, was canonized … it would be tedious to narrate all the state, and splendour, and ceremony connected with her canonisation. Whoever had been present at the wonderful sight that was there, might say that his eyes never saw anything like or similar to it for piety, splendour, reverence, music, earthly state, and all the other virtues besides. When the Mass and the ceremony was finished, the holy Father gave a holy blessing to all Catholics who were present. He went to his palace after that. Then the trumpets of the guard, horse and foot, were sounded, and the drums beaten.[31]

A fresco in the Vatican depicts this canonisation and shows what appear to be between five and eight singers on a purpose-built balcony or platform on the right-hand side of the tribune.[32] Ó Cianáin speaks

of the choir being divided on both sides of the pope. It is possible that the papal choir, which would have been the principal choir on this occasion, was divided, but it is more likely that he is referring also to the choir of St Peter's, the Cappella Guilia, which probably performed on another platform on the other side. They normally sang a single motet as the papal procession entered St Peter's – *Tu es Petrus* or *Ecce sacerdos magnus* for example. According to the instructions given in Andrea Adami in 1711, on the way down from the Vatican Palace in procession the papal choir sang the hymn *Ave maris stella* alternating plainchant and polyphony, probably in Palestrina's setting. During the ceremony the Litany of the Saints was sung in plainchant, with the *Veni Creator* and *Te Deum* in polyphony.[33] The mass ordinary would have been sung in polyphony, as well as motets during the offertory and communion. On the following Trinity Sunday the earls observed one of three processions which carried an image of the new saint, this one to her burial place of S. Maria Nuova overlooking the Forum, afterwards renamed S. Francesca Romana.[34]

The papal Corpus Christi procession on 5 June marked the high point of the earls' ceremonial participation, since eight of the party had been given the honour, normally reserved to the ambassadors of foreign princes, of holding the canopy over the pope as he carried the Blessed Sacrament from the Vatican Palace, out into the Borgo and back into St Peter's. Ó Cianáin describes the pomp and ceremony which attended the procession, but makes no mention of music. We know from other chroniclers and contemporary engravings that the route was lined with poles supporting a canvas covering and decorated on the sides with tapestries and coats of arms of the pope and cardinals. Gregory Martin in his *Roma Sancta* of 1581 described the occasion:

> At the very appearing of him in the Palace gate to come forth the trompeters play their part with melodious blastes, and the gonnes are heard thicke and thundering from Castel Sant Angelo. The peale being finished, the pope's quyer continue all the way with the most excellent musicke. In the middle way by the Cardinal of Trent's palace there is a stage and new music of the best, for the time that the procession resteth there. Then they go forward to St Peter's church and so to his chapel and altar, where the solemn mass is sung by the pope himself or one of the cardinals.[35]

'O'Neill in Rome'. © Brian Vallely

The only piece of music mentioned anywhere in connection with this feast is Cristóbal de Morales's *O sacrum convivium* sung in 1616 during the mass which preceded the procession.[36]

During the rest of the summer the earls continued a round of visits to patronal feast-day celebrations at various churches. In each case Ó Cianáin does not say anything about the ceremonies or the music, concentrating instead on particular features of each church and its relics. Archival information does not survive for many of those institutions attended by the earls. In the case of the millenial celebrations at the Pantheon on All Saints' Day 1608, a payment of nine *scudi* is recorded to the singers of the Cappella Giulia from St Peter's, which was directed at the time by Francesco Soriano.[37] S. Maria in Trastevere had eight singers and a *maestro di cappella*, Giovanni de Gentili, in 1608;[38] there is no record of extra musicians being hired in.

It is not possible to know whether or not Ó Cianáin's descriptions include all of the patronal feast-days visited by the earls. He may have been selective in his inclusions: it has been suggested, for example, that he wrote particularly for Irish exiles in a continental Irish Franciscan milieu.[39] Two of the churches listed were Franciscan: S. Bartolomeo in Isola and S. Francesco a Ripa. Another Franciscan church, S. Pietro in Montorio, received the earl of Tyrconnell's mortal remains (clad in the robes of St Francis) on 29 July 1608. Ó Cianáin tells us that:

> a large and splendid funeral in grand procession was ordered by his Holiness the Pope, and on either side of the body there were large numbers of lighted waxen torches and sweet, sad, sorrowful singing.

The pope may have sent some of the singers from the papal choir for the occasion. They would most likely have sung the responsory *Libera me domine*, always sung at the funerals of papal singers and other members of the papal household.

The Irish participated in two of Rome's periodic special jubilee processions on 3 and 5 September which took in four of the principal Marian churches. In this case the pope sought divine assistance to solve a crisis in the Habsburg dominions, where the Emperor Rudolf II and his brother Matthias were at loggerheads, with the emperor reluctant to name his brother as his successor, while also making concessions to Protestants in Bohemia, Moravia and Hungary of which the pope disapproved.[40] The presence of the Irish party at such a politico-religious event is significant and would, of course, have reminded them of their own situation as a result of religious and political strife.

The final occasion described by Ó Cianáin was the state entry of the French ambassador, the duke de Nevers, and his party on 20 November. After describing in great detail the entry procession with all its pomp, including two groups of trumpeters, he concludes:

> As they entered by the gate of Sant' Angelo the Romans commenced a great burst of music. They had numbers of trumpets and of every musical instrument. At the great palace were the trumpeters of the Pope.

This must have reminded the Irish of their own entry into the city seven months previously. By this time the novelty had probably been wearing off and little practical help was forthcoming. The English ambassador to Brussels reported to Lord Salisbury on 3 August 1608:

It is written from Rome that Tyrone and his company are very much discouraged to find that the spiritual and temporal treasure of the church produces nothing more in their favour than a good welcome and the entertainment which they receive.[41]

Music formed an integral part of that 'entertainment' – and not just church music, though little is known of any secular music at banquets etc, which the Irish might have heard. As Mícheál Mac Craith has pointed out, Ó Cianáin wished to portray the earls as leaders of a Catholic nation on a par with others in Europe and used their participation in the Roman liturgical cycle to emphasise their commitment to Tridentine doctrines and practices.[42] Church music is believed to have played an important part in that cycle, and it is gratifying to the music historian to have this confirmed by a chronicler coming from a distant land.

Notes

1 Aspects of this topic have already been covered in N. O'Regan, '"Blessed with the Holy Father's Entertainment": Roman ceremonial music as experienced by the Irish Earls in Rome, 1608', in G. Gillen & Harry White (eds), *Irish Musical Studies II: Music and the church* (Dublin, 1993), pp 41-61; idem, 'Descriptions of music in Tadhg Ó Cianáin's *Imeacht na nIarlaí*', *Irish Archives*, xiv (2007), pp 40-44. The present article develops some aspects in more detail and provides a broader overview of Roman sacred musical practice in the early 'Seicento'.

2 R. Sherr, 'Competence and incompetence in the papal choir in the age of Palestrina', *Early Music*, xxii (1994), pp 606-30.

3 Except on four occasions in the year (Christmas, Easter, Pentecost, SS. Peter and Paul) when the choir sang Second Vespers privately for the pope and his household, not in the Cappella Sistina. At these services more up-to-date music than usual was sung and organ accompaniment was used. See J. Lionnet, 'Vespri papali nel seicento: primi considerazioni', in A. Roth (ed.), *Studien zur Geschichte der päpstlichen Kapelle: Tagungsbericht Heidelberg 1989, Capellae Apostolicae Sixtinaeque Collectanea Acta Monumenta 4* (Vatican City, 1994), pp 431-45.

4 A. Cametti, *I Musici del Campidoglio* (Rome, 1925).

5 A. Ducrot, 'Histoire de la Cappella Giulia au XVIᵉ Siècle', *Mélanges D'Archéologie et D'Histoire*, lxxv (1963), pp 179-240, 467-559; G. Rostirolla, 'La Cappella Giulia in San Pietro negli anni palestriniani', in G. Rostirolla & L. Bianchi (eds), *Atti del Convegno di Studi Palestriniani, 28 settembre – 2 ottobre 1975* (Palestrina, 1977), pp 99-283.

6 R. Casimiri and L. Callegari, *Cantori, maestri, organisti della Cappella lateranense negli atti capitolari (sec. XV-XVII)* (Bologna, 1994). For S. Maria Maggiore see J. Burke, 'Musicians of S. Maria Maggiore, Rome, 1600-1700: a social and economic study', *Note d'Archivio per la Storia Musicale*, nuova serie, ii (1984), supplement.

7 L. Della Libera, 'l'Attività musicale nella Basilica di S. Lorenzo in Damaso nel cinquecento', *Rivista Italiana di Musicologia*, xxxii (1997), pp 25-59.

8 H. W. Frey, 'Die Kapellmeister an der französischen Nationalkirche San Luigi dei Francesi in Rom im 16 Jahrhundert', *Archiv für Musikwissenschaft*, xxii (1965), pp 272-93; xxiii (1966), pp 32-60; J. Lionnet, 'La Musique a Saint-Louis des Français de Rome au xvii siecle', *Note d'Archivio*, nuova serie, iii (1985), supplement (pt. 1); iv (1986), supplement (pt. 2).

9 G. Dixon, 'The Capella of S. Maria in Trastevere (1605-45), *Music and Letters*, lxii (1981), pp 30-39; H. Wessely-Kropik, 'Mitteilungen aus dem Archiv der Arciconfraternità di San Giovanni dei Fiorentini', *Studien zur Musikwissenschaft*, xxiv (1960), pp 43-60; A. Morelli, Il tempio armonico: musica nell'Oratorio dei Filippini in Roma (1575-1705): *Analecta Musicologica* 27 (Laaber, 1991).

10 T. Culley, *Jesuits and Music. I: A Study of the Musicians connected with the German College in Rome during the 17ᵗʰ Century and of their Activities in Northern Europe* (Rome and St. Louis, 1970). R. Casimiri, '"Disciplina Musicae" e "mastri di Capella" dopo il Concilio di Trento nei maggiori istituti Ecclesiastici di Roma: Seminario Romano – Collegio Germanico – Collegio Inglese (sec. XVI-XVII)', *Note d'Archivio per la Storia Musicale*, xii (1935), pp 1-26, 73-81.

11 Many Roman confraternities had obtained this privilege

over the years. A prisoner condemned to death or to the galleys would be released on the vigil of the patronal feast, forming the focus of a procession from the prison and being present at mass and vespers, dressed in the habit of the confraternity as a living representation of its charitable endeavours.

12 N. O'Regan, 'Processions and their music in post-Tridentine Rome', *Recercare*, iv (1992), pp 45-80.

13 D. Alaleona, *Storia dell'Oratorio Musicale in Italia* (Turin, 1908; repr., Milan, 1945); N. O'Regan, 'Roman confraternities and their oratories 1550-1600', in A. Pompilio *et al* (eds), *Atti del XIV Congresso della Società Internazionale di Musicologia, 1987* (Bologna, 1989), pp 891-8.

14 A. Maugars, *Response faite à un curieux sur le sentiment de la musique d'Italie, escrite à Rome, la premier Octobre, 1639*, given in the original French and in Italian translation in J. Lionnet, 'André Maugars: risposta data a un curioso sul sentimento della musica d'Italia', *Nuova Rivista Musicale Italiana*, xix (1985), pp 681-707.

15 S. Franchi, *Annali della Stampa musicale romana dei secoli xvi-xviii*, I/I (Rome, 2006).

16 N. O'Regan, 'The performance of Roman sacred polychoral music in the late 16th and early 17th centuries': evidence from archival sources', *Performance Practice Review*, viii (1995), pp 107-46.

17 N. O'Regan, 'Asprilio Pacelli, Ludovico da Viadana and the origins of the Roman Concerto Ecclesiastico', *Journal of Seventeenth-Century Music*, vi (2000) http://www.sscm-jscm.org/jscm/v6/no1/Oregan.html

18 T. Gainsford, *The history of the earle of Tirone* (London, 1619; repr., Amsterdam & New York, 1968), p. 49.

19 L. von Pastor, *The History of the Popes*, xxvi (London, 1930), pp 388-9.

20 Biblioteca Vaticana, Fondo Cappella Sistina, *Diario Sistina*, XXVIII (1608).

21 Francesco Soto, dean of the papal singers, who was retired, and Luca Orfeo, who was ill.

22 N. K. Rasmussen, 'Maiestas Pontificia: liturgical reading of Etienne Dupérac's engraving of the *Cappella Sistina* from 1578', *Analecta Romana Instituti Danici*, xii (1983), pp 109-48. See also C. Reynolds, 'Rome: a city of rich contrast', in I. Fenlon (ed.), *Man and music: The Renaissance* (London, 1989), pp 63-101.

23 The papal singers were consulted on the position of their cantoria in the new Cappella Paolina at the Quirinale and asked for it to be closer to the altar and sticking out more from the wall so that they could both hear and see the ceremonies better.

24 H. W. Frey, 'Die Gesänge der sixtinischen Kapelle an den Sonntagen und hohen Kirchenfesten des Jahres 1616', *Studi e Testi della Biblioteca Apostolica Vaticana, Mélanges Eugène Tisserant* vi (1964), pp 395-437.

25 For details of these composers see the relevant articles in *The New Grove Dictionary of Music and Musicians* (London, 2001).

26 Tadhg Ó Cianáin, *The Flight of the Earls*, (ed.) P. Walsh (Dublin, 1916), pp 175-7. The particular Gaelic words used by Ó Cianáin to describe musical performance have been discussed in O'Regan, 'Descriptions of music'.

27 Archivio di Stato, Fondo Ospedale S. Spirito in Sassia, 1912 (unfoliated). See the article 'Anerio, Giovanni Francesco', in *The New Grove Dictionary of Music and Musicians* (London, 2001).

28 Archivio di Stato, Fondo Ospedale di S. Spirito in Sassia, 1912 (Copie di mandati, 1608), unfoliated.

29 The most comprehensive recent collection of writing on S. Spirito in Sassia, which includes substantial bibliographies, is V. Cappelletti and F. Tagliarini (eds), *L'Antico Ospedale di Santo Spirito dell'istituzione papale alla sanità del terzo millenio: convegno internazionale di studi, Roma, 15-17 Maggio 2001* (2 vols, Rome, 2001-02). For the choir at S. Spirito see Pietro de Angelis, *Musica e musicisti nell'arcispedale di S. Spirito in Sassia del Quattrocento all'Ottocento* (Rome, 1950).

30 S. Ditchfield, *Liturgy, sanctity and history in Tridentine Italy* (Cambridge, 1995). Other canonisations had included: Diego of Alcalá (1588), Hyacinth of Poland (1594) and Raymond of Penafort (1601).

31 Ó Cianáin, *Flight*, (ed.) P. Walsh, pp 183-7.

32 Reproduced in R. Sherr, 'Performance practice in the papal chapel during the sixteenth century', *Early Music*, xv (1987), pp 453-61. Sherr speaks of seeing five singers but in fact there seem to be more than five. Sherr also shows paintings of other canonisations around this time, all of which show a single platform with some singers.

33 These are the items mentioned for canonisation ceremonies in Andrea Adami, *Osservazioni per ben regolare il coro dei cantori della Cappella Pontificia* (Rome, 1711), pp 139-43.

34 The other two processions went to the convent of Tor di Specchi, which S. Francesca had founded, and to the church of Ara Coeli on the Campidoglio, the official church of the S. P. Q. R.

35 Gregory Martin, *Roma Sancta*, (ed.) George B. Parks (Rome, 1969), p. 88.

36 See footnote 24.

37 G. Dixon, 'The Pantheon and music in minor churches in seventeenth-century Rome', *Studi Musicali*, x (1981), pp 265-77.

38 Dixon, 'The Capella of S. Maria in Trastevere'.

39 C. Carroll, '*Turas na nIarladh as Éire*: international travel and national identity in Ó Cianáin's narrative', *History Ireland*, xv: 4 (2007), pp 56-61. See also M. Mac Craith, 'Early modern Catholic self-fashioning Spanish style: aspects of Tadhg Ó Cianáin's Rome', in this volume.

40 Pastor, *The History of the Popes*, xxvi, p. 283.

41 Sir Thomas Edmonds to Lord Salisbury, 3 Aug. 1608 (*CSPI, 1606-08*, p. 666) quoted in the introduction to Tadhg Ó Cianáin, *The Flight of the Earls,* (ed. & trans.) P. de Barra and Tomás Ó Fiaich (Dublin, 1972).

42 M. Mac Craith, 'An Irishman's Diary: Aspects of Tadhg Ó Cianáin's Rome', a paper read to the conference: 'Irish Europe: Language, Text and culture 1600-1640', NUI Maynooth, 14-15 September 2007. I am grateful to An tOllamh Mac Craith for letting me see a copy of this paper.

'Imeacht na nIarlaí'.
© Seoirse Ó Dochartaigh

The Flight of the Earls

CONSEQUENCES

Exempt from the authority of the earl: the failure of the second-rank nobles of Tír Chonaill in post-flight County Donegal

Darren McGettigan

Rory O'Donnell, the first earl of Tyrconnell, enjoyed his earldom for only four and a half years, from his creation in early 1603 to his flight in September 1607. As earl, he experienced much opposition from various members of his extended family who either sought the traditional lordship of Tír Chonaill for themselves or opposed his efforts to rebuild the lordship through tenurial and fiscal reform in the aftermath of the Nine Years War. These rivals included the O'Donnells of Castlefinn, led by Niall Garbh, as well as two first cousins of the earl, Shane MacManus Óg of Tory Island and Cathbharr Óg of Glen Swilly. The other major second rank Gaelic noble in County Donegal was Sir Cathair O'Doherty, the young lord of Inishowen. Rory had no authority over O'Doherty during this period and frequently complained of his loss of revenues from the peninsula. Indeed, some of these lords were regularly in a state of what might best be termed 'rebellion' against the earl's authority between 1603 and 1607. Although possibly overjoyed at his flight, none of these nobles survived as local power brokers in County Donegal for more than a year after his abrupt departure. This essay attempts to explain why.[1]

A short description of the power and landholdings of the second-rank nobles of Tír Chonaill is essential to understanding the process. Niall Garbh O'Donnell, a second cousin of the earl, headed a warlike band of brothers – only two of whom survived the Nine Years War – based at Glenfinn on the eastern frontier of Tír Chonaill. Niall had a castle at Castlefinn and extensive estates along the River Finn totalling forty-three quarters, or 12,900 acres.[2] Despite his support for the government in the later stages of the Nine Years War, he lost most of his military resources for having himself proclaimed O'Donnell in 1603. Nevertheless, he continued to maintain a band of sixteen woodkerne in upper Glenfinn. The earl's patent of 1603 listed Niall's holdings:

> the castle or manor of Finn or Castlefinn, with its rights and appurtenances, and all other castles, lordships and estates whatever, late in the tenure of Sir Niall O'Donnell, knight, called Niall Garbh O'Donnell, which he possessed when he lived under and in amity with Red Hugh O'Donnell', were exempted from the earl's authority and were ordered to be at the disposal 'at pleasure of the said Niall'.[3]

Shane MacManus Óg, the earl's first cousin, held land on Tory Island, centred upon an impressive castle. He also had land at Drumboy on the eastern side of Lough Swilly and was very powerful in western Tír Chonaill, in the Rosses and among the many small islands off the coast. His small fleet of boats and a retinue of well-armed men enabled him to defy the authority of the earl between 1603 and 1607.

Burt Castle – the main residence of Sir Cathair O'Doherty.
© Liam Campbell

Cathbharr Óg, another cousin of the earl's, owned Scarriffhollis Castle on the River Swilly and possessed scattered estates in Glen Swilly. He also maintained a bodyguard of armed men who seem to have retained their weapons after 1603.

Another important noble in the O'Donnell family was the earl's grand-uncle Hugh Dubh O'Donnell, a very old man by 1607, having been born c. 1537. He had once been tánaiste of Tír Chonaill and had challenged the earl's brother Red Hugh O'Donnell for chieftaincy in 1592-93. Following his submission to the latter, he became one of O'Donnell's most loyal adherents and only submitted to the English in 1602, when it was obvious that the cause of the Ulster confederacy was lost. He still retained a castle at Rathmelton on the shore of Lough Swilly, and thirteen quarters of land between the Rivers Swilly and Leannan.[4] By 1608 Hugh Dubh had entered his retirement and his eldest son, Cathbharr, led this branch of the O'Donnell family.

The O'Doherty had traditionally been accepted as O'Donnell's most important sub-chieftain. He raised substantial bodies of horsemen and kerne for his army and provided food and shelter for the billeting of his overlord's soldiers ('bonnaghta').[5] Cathair O'Doherty's father, Seán Óg (Sir John), had been lord of Inishowen from 1582 until his death in January 1601. The Annals of the Four Masters said of him that 'there was not among all the Irish of his time a lord of a *tríocha-chéd* (thirty cantreds) of better hand or hospitality, or of firmer counsel, than he'.[6] His teenage son, Cathair, managed to establish himself as lord of Inishowen, despite the opposition of Red Hugh O'Donnell, who backed Cathair's uncle, Feidhlimidh Óg O'Doherty. He achieved this through the support of his foster-family, the MacDavitts, led by Hugh Boy and Feidhlimidh Reagh, and other influential Inishowen families such as the MacCallions.

The young Cathair initially managed to make a success of life in post-war County Donegal. Knighted by Lord Deputy Mountjoy, his lands were exempted from the authority of the earl.[7] O'Doherty subsequently received 'the manors, lordships, [and] castles ... in the country called Inishowen' by order of King James in 1604,[8] became a justice of the peace and an alderman of Derry, and served as the foreman of the jury which later indicted the earls of Tyrone and Tyrconnell in the wake of their flight in September 1607. Indeed, by this time Cathair was also petitioning to be appointed to Prince of Wales's household, which would have secured the young

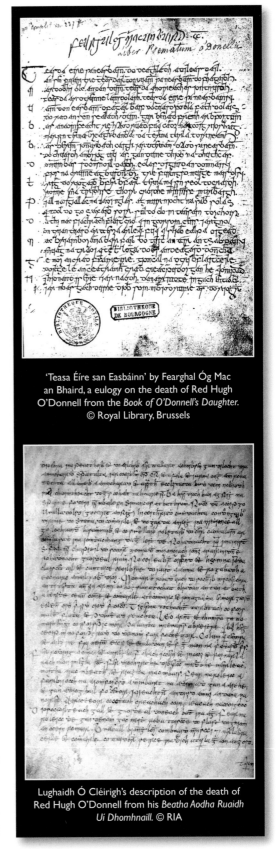

'Teasa Éire san Easbáinn' by Fearghal Óg Mac an Bhaird, a eulogy on the death of Red Hugh O'Donnell from the *Book of O'Donnell's Daughter*. © Royal Library, Brussels

Lughaidh Ó Cléirigh's description of the death of Red Hugh O'Donnell from his *Beatha Aodha Ruaidh Uí Dhomhnaill*. © RIA

O'Doherty's position into the future.[9]

The other sub-chieftains of Tír Chonaill, Turlough O'Boyle, the lord of Boylagh, Donal MacSweeney Fanad, Maolmhuire MacSweeney Doe, Donough MacSweeney Banagh and the O'Gallagher chieftain, held well-defined smaller territories stretching along the Donegal coastline. Traditionally they had closer ties to O'Donnells than the O'Dohertys, providing hereditary galloglass chieftains in the case of the three MacSweeneys and commanders of the household families of Tír Chonaill, in the case of O'Gallagher. The O'Gallagher chieftain at this time (possibly Brian MacTurlough O'Gallagher of Tirhugh),[10] as his foster-father, had close ties to the earl. However, these ties between the earl and the other chieftains listed here had been breaking down in the years leading up to the flight as a consequence of his tenurial reforms. These sub-chieftains had been tricked into surrendering ownership of their lands to the earl, but this later led to violent op-

Coat of Arms of the O'Donnells.
© Derry City Council

position among the MacSweeneys of both Fanad and Doe.[11]

Cathair O'Doherty and the major O'Donnell nobles had also experienced difficulties with the English administration in the county before the outbreak of his rebellion in 1608. Although Cathair, in particular, seemed to be doing very well in post-war Donegal, he did have a number of disputes with English officials in both Donegal and Derry. Inch Island in Lough Swilly, traditionally an important part of the lordship of Inishowen, had been granted in May 1604 to Captain Ralph Bingley, an English veteran of the war, now on the make in the county.[12] The loss of Inch rankled with the young O'Doherty, and he regularly petitioned for its return. In addition, George Montgomery, the new Protestant bishop of Derry, Raphoe and Clogher seized O'Doherty's tribute of 'four methers of butter and eight methers of meal per annum, every mether containing two gallons English measure', which the O'Doherty chieftains 'had anciently' received from every quarter of coarb, erenagh

and termon land in Inishowen, but none of which had been paid 'in the time of the now lord bishop of Derry'.[13] Cathair also had a difficult relationship with Sir George Paulet, the new English governor of Derry, who had replaced his patron, Sir Henry Docwra. Paulet was a man of arrogant and abrasive personality, and he did not respect the local nobles as had his predecessor.

Niall Garbh experienced similar difficulties.

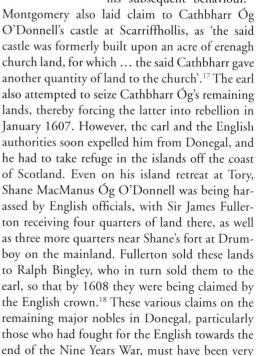

Although he had won a land dispute with Hugh O'Neill in 1605 over ownership of the territory of Moentacht, he too fell foul of the rapacious Bishop Montgomery,[14] who seized revenues of 'four methers of butter and eight methers of meal coshering' which, the 1609 inquisition states, the erenaghs of Donaghmore 'did … pay yearly unto the temporal lords of Glenfinn'.[15] Niall may also have been in a desperate financial situation at this time, as he owed £1,314 to the Dublin merchants Patrick and John Conley, and this may have contributed to his subsequent behaviour.[16]

Montgomery also laid claim to Cathbharr Óg O'Donnell's castle at Scarriffhollis, as 'the said castle was formerly built upon an acre of erenagh church land, for which … the said Cathbharr gave another quantity of land to the church'.[17] The earl also attempted to seize Cathbharr Óg's remaining lands, thereby forcing the latter into rebellion in January 1607. However, the earl and the English authorities soon expelled him from Donegal, and he had to take refuge in the islands off the coast of Scotland. Even on his island retreat at Tory, Shane MacManus Óg O'Donnell was being harassed by English officials, with Sir James Fullerton receiving four quarters of land there, as well as three more quarters near Shane's fort at Drumboy on the mainland. Fullerton sold these lands to Ralph Bingley, who in turn sold them to the earl, so that by 1608 they were being claimed by the English crown.[18] These various claims on the remaining major nobles in Donegal, particularly those who had fought for the English towards the end of the Nine Years War, must have been very

'Red Hugh O'Donnell'. © Seán Ó Brógáin

vexatious to a proud group of Gaelic chieftains. The lowly origins of some of the said English officials added insult to injury. Only the aged Hugh Dubh O'Donnell lived quietly in retirement in Rathmelton, realising that the traditional ways would have to be altered. His accommodation to the new English authority in Donegal may have been made easier by his taking refuge in writing bardic poetry.

The English administration in Ireland in 1607 certainly did not expect trouble in post-flight Ulster. In September 1607 Lord Deputy Chichester issued a proclamation 'to assure the inhabitants of Tyrone and Tyrconnell that they will not be disturbed in the peaceable possession of their lands so long as they demean themselves as dutiful subjects'.[19] The carrying of arms such as firearms and 'long skeanes' by 'idle kernes, [and] loose and master-less men' had also been prohibited by the lord deputy since 1605.[20] Cathair O'Doherty's problems in particular seemed insufficient cause to drive him to rebellion, and indeed he was about to be regranted Inch Island. Yet the power and position of almost all of the influential Donegal nobles was destroyed in 1608. The spark which seems to have ignited the rebellion is recorded in the opening Annals of the Four Masters entry for 1608: 'Great dissensions and strife arose between the Governor of Derry, Sir George Paulet, and O'Doherty (Cathair, the son of Seán Óg). The Governor not only offered him insult and abuse by word, but also inflicted chastisement on his body'. This was such an insult that Cathair:

> would rather have suffered death than live to brook such insult and dishonour, or defer or delay to take revenge for it; and he was filled with anger and fury, so that he nearly ran to distraction and madness. What he did was, to consult with his friends how he should take revenge for the insult which was inflicted upon him.[21]

Façade of the Church of St Francis, Valladolid, final resting place of Red Hugh O'Donnell. The church was destroyed during the Napoleonic War.

Thus the O'Doherty revolt sprung from a young man's desire for revenge after being insulted and injured. Yet O'Doherty's decision to attack Derry and kill Paulet proved very costly, both for himself and his Gaelic neighbours in Donegal. He was only twenty or twenty-one years of age at the time and his principal adviser was Feidhlimidh Reagh MacDavitt, a great warrior but no politician. His brother Hugh Boy MacDavitt, an intelligent and capable man, had been killed in 1602, and his loss would be keenly felt in 1608. In the end, Cathair assembled around one hundred half-armed men and stormed Derry on the morning of 19 April 1608, killing Governor Paulet and some of his men. Although O'Doherty and his followers devised a number of clever stratagems, they did not have a wider plan or the support of many of the surviving leaders in Gaelic Ulster. Besides Shane MacManus Óg O'Donnell, the only other noble to support O'Doherty was his brother-in-law Oghy Óg O'Hanlon in County Armagh. Cathair based himself at Glenveagh, in the heart of the Derryveagh Mountains, from where he launched raids on south Donegal and into Fermanagh and Tyrone. He was killed on 5 July 1608 in the course of an ambush he had laid for an English force marching past Kilmacrenan. His men soon scattered and many were hunted down and executed.

Even with the shock of 1603, and indeed after the flight of the earls, the O'Donnell nobles, especially Niall Garbh and Shane MacManus Óg, continued to aspire to succeed as O'Donnell. Niall never took out a patent for the lands he had been granted, since, as Lord Deputy Chichester later put it, he was 'expecting greater quantities and pretending title to the whole country, which I think will hardly satisfy his ambition'.[22] In 1604 Niall attempted to drive the earl out of the county, and three years later he must have felt that his hour had finally arrived if he could engineer some situation whereby the English would have to turn to

'The Gaelic Chieftain' by Maurice Harron, representing Red Hugh O'Donnell, stands in the Curlew Mountains, scene of O'Donnell's greatest military triumph. © Roscommon County Council

him and make him lord of Tír Chonaill.[23] Shane MacManus Óg O'Donnell 'who would needs pretend greatness in Tyrconnell',[24] also appeared to be preparing to make a bid for the chieftainship. He saw O'Doherty's rebellion as an opportunity to have himself created lord of Tír Chonaill and assembled a force of 240 well-armed men in the mountainous west of Tír Chonaill and on the offshore islands. Chichester claimed that his strategy was 'there to lie safe far off and difficult to come at and thereby to increase in number and reputation after our departure'.[25]

Shane reckoned without the determination and ruthlessness of the lord deputy. Chichester arrived in County Donegal in the weeks after Cathair O'Doherty's death and set about crushing all signs of resistance in the county. He executed Feidhlimidh Reagh MacDavitt and twenty others at Lifford,[26] and seized Niall Garbh and his brothers, as well as Cathbharr Óg, who had unwisely returned to Tír Chonaill. He also apprehended an infant nephew of the earl who had been left behind after the flight.[27] Chichester then marched to Lough Gartan crannog near Glenveagh, where he forced one of the O'Gallaghers, who commanded the fort, to put three or four of his men to death before he would accept his surrender.[28] The lord deputy then pursued Shane to Tory Island, where he left Sir Henry Folliott to finish the job. Shane's

force dwindled from 240 men on the Donegal mainland to sixty on the island, and when he finally fled for Aranmore Island he did so in the company of a mere four companions.[29]

It is likely that Niall Garbh had been heavily involved in the outbreak of Cathair's rebellion. Immediately before the attack on Derry Cathair had a secret conference at Castlefinn with Niall where the latter agreed to send a band of woodkerne under the command of Dualtach MacGilduff, described as 'kerne in Glenfinn and … a natural follower to Sir Niall O'Donnell',[30] as well as being foster-father to Niall's son.[31] It was stated that while O'Doherty only intended 'to have taken the munition and arms with the spoil of the town', Niall 'earnestly laboured and persuaded him that in anywise he should burn the town and to massacre the people'.[32] Feidhlimidh Reagh MacDavitt claimed that Niall advised O'Doherty, through Dualtach MacGilduff, to 'let him divide his men 3 parts, one in the market place, one in the upper fort, & the third in the lower fort, & in any case him not fail to take the star-fort'.[33] The government received other information that Niall promised Sir Cathair that he and his brothers would seize Lifford, Ballyshannon and Donegal town and capture Sir Richard Hansard, the commander of the English troops in Donegal, and kill all his men.[34] However, Niall never attacked these

183

places, contenting himself with the seizure of the fort of Mongavlin, home of Finola (Iníon Dubh) MacDonnell, the earl's mother.[35] Various reasons are given for Niall and his brothers' failure to join O'Doherty's revolt: Niall's inability to secure his son Neachtan's escape from Dublin; O'Doherty's refusal to share the arms captured at Derry, thereby breaking their agreement; or because the treasure taken at Derry was too small. However, Dualtach MacGilduff and his woodkerne did take part in the assault on Derry and remained with O'Doherty until his death. Indeed, their involvement in the rebellion only ended when sixteen of them were cornered and almost wiped out in a surprise attack on a house in Upper Glenfinn by Sir Richard Hansard.[36]

Dualtach MacGilduff and Sir Richard Hansard participated in one of the murkiest episodes of the entire rebellion. Dualtach later alleged that Sir Richard 'sent unto them one Rory Ballagh MacBoy Vally willing him to kill the party that should bring him notice of the charge the marshal left with him to cut off his head where-so-ever he got him'. He further claimed that 'soon after this, Sir Richard sent Donough Boy O'Shiel [one of Niall Garbh's most important and trusted followers] to the examinate to declare what charge the marshal had left with him'. Dualtach concluded that 'he knew him to be the man Sir Richard would have to be killed,

which he performed accordingly'.[37] This incident suggests that Donough Boy knew too much about the origins of the rebellion for his own good and as a result was eliminated by Sir Richard Hansard. Hansard's involvement in this killing points to the ambush of MacGilduff's woodkerne in Glenfinn also being intended to silence more potential witnesses to the plotting which preceded the outbreak of the rebellion. That Dualtach later received a grant of sixty-four acres in the plantation of Ulster suggests that he succeeded in making a deal which insured that he survived the rebellion and its aftermath.[38] Niall Garbh bitterly resented MacGilduff's evidence against him. He later singled him out of all his accusers, calling him, 'a base fellow and then out in rebellion', and adding that he 'had been a special actor in all ye mischief done at ye Derry [and] became his accuser not knowing how to get his pardon otherwise'.[39]

Perhaps Niall Garbh did not openly join the rebellion because he wanted to engineer a situation whereby the small English army in Ireland would fail to suppress O'Doherty's revolt and would turn to him as the only man powerful and ruthless enough to do the job for them. Unfortunately for Niall's plans, English officials immediately suspected this. Chichester believed that he wished to set himself up as a local king or 'roytelett', 'as all his predecessors have been'.[40] Niall stood accused of continuing

Red Hugh's welcome home silhouette from *The Fighting Prince of Donegal* by Robert T. Reilly.
© Inch House Irish Studies Centre

to give O'Doherty information on the movement of English troops, and of urging him to abandon Glenveagh without a fight. However, Niall had reckoned without the sudden death of Sir Cathair and Chichester's utter ruthlessness in killing rebels throughout Ulster, which struck fear into the hearts of any survivors. Indeed, Niall's behaviour after the beginning of the rebellion seemed quite strange and lethargic. In May 1608 he panicked and sought five pardons in fifteen days from the English.[41] His inactivity may have stemmed from the fact that he had not recovered from 'a blow ... got ... in the service' when assaulting Doe Castle on behalf of the government in March 1607.[42]

Although Lord Deputy Chichester could not conclusively incriminate Niall, the Irish attorney general, Sir John Davies, built up a powerful case against him, by collecting confessions and carefully collating information. When brought 'to his trial of life and death', Niall felt that the jury had been 'picked out of his most notorious enemies', the followers of Red Hugh O'Donnell. Although he failed to have the jury members replaced with twelve English, Welsh or Scots or even Palesmen:

(after nine hours spent in his arraignment) he was by their verdict acquitted, notwithstanding they were two days kept together after they had resolved upon ye verdict, which known to tend to his acquittal, they were three or four several times dealt with all to change'.[43]

This failure did not faze Lord Deputy Chichester. According to a later account from Niall himself, Chichester stated that O'Donnell's 'acquittal proceeded not of his innocencey, but from ye corruption of ye jury, saying ye Irish will find no man guilty'.[44] The lord deputy simply ignored the verdict of the jury and imprisoned Niall along with his son Neachtan, 'though he was never charged with anything', in the Tower of London.[45] In a petition to the English Privy Council written in 1610, Niall Garbh asked the lords:

to consider how little reason there was to think him to be partaken of O'Doherty's plots. He had experience in ye late Queen's time, how unable Tyrone was to prevail against ye state of England. What should make him think ye now king less able to keep Ireland under. They had ye assistance of Spain, then in enmity with England, now in amity.[46]

Niall Garbh died in the Tower in 1626, predeceased two years earlier by his son Neachtan. However, both were more fortunate than Cathbharr Óg O'Donnell, whom Chichester had executed in Dublin in 1609.[47]

During 'the war of O'Doherty', as one Gaelic annalist called the rebellion,[48] Hugh Dubh O'Donnell of Rathmelton remained quiet, although his son Seán participated in the storming of Derry.[49] The three MacSweeneys, the O'Boyles and the O'Gallaghers also remained aloof, while Maolmhuire MacSweeney Doe assisted the English in their assault on Tory Island.[50] In June 1608 Cathair O'Doherty wrote to the O'Gallagher chieftain stating: 'If you have any hope at the present or hereafter in your foster-son and your earthly lord, or the good of O'Doherty, then cause your sept and yourself to aid O'Doherty'.[51] However, far from joining O'Doherty, O'Gallagher surrendered both the letter and Lough Eske Castle to Sir Henry Folliott.

All the nobles discussed in this essay, with the exception of Hugh Dubh O'Donnell, O'Boyle and the MacSweeneys, lost their lands either as a direct result of their participation in the rebellion, or by the failure of the English authorities to grant their families estates in the plantation of Ulster in 1610. Chichester personally received the entire O'Doherty lordship of Inishowen, and because Niall Garbh had failed to take out a patent for his lands in Glenfinn, his lands too were given away in the plantation. Although his family continued to live in Glenfinn until the 1650s, they fell on hard times after the plantation and survived in poverty after their tenants turned against them in 1613.[52] Niall himself remained in great poverty in prison until his death. Cathbharr Óg and Shane MacManus Óg were also swept away. In contrast, Hugh Dubh received a 1,000-acre estate and his castle at Rathmelton in the plantation, though only for the term of his life. Upon his death in 1618 the estate came into the possession of Sir Richard Hansard.[53] O'Boyle and the three MacSweeneys did well out of the plantation of Ulster, all receiving estates of 2,000 acres. The O'Gallagher chieftain, who fostered Earl Rory, possibly received nothing, or at the most a very small estate. In the plantation no O'Donnell received a permanent grant of more than 128 acres. Niall Garbh could have become one of the largest native landowners in the province if he had taken out a patent for his lands in Glenfinn and settled down to a quiet life under the new regime. However, the lure of traditional

J. D. Reigh's idealised portrait of Red Hugh O'Donnell's inauguration in April 1592 hardly reflects historical reality. His collateral rivals attended 'wholly through fear'. © NLI

O'Donnell lordship proved too strong for him and these other Gaelic nobles in post-flight Donegal.

The second-rank nobles of Tír Chonaill left behind after the flight were too powerful to be left undisturbed by the English authorities, but not sufficiently powerful to resist the changes. They did not help themselves by either gambling all for personal revenge or in the hope of O'Doherty's revolt creating sufficient unrest in Gaelic Ulster to enable them to assume the lordship of Tír Chonaill. In this, Shane MacManus Óg O'Donnell probably came closest to achieving his aims. In his impregnable castle on Tory Island, he must have felt confident that he could sit out the initial English invasion of Donegal, increase in power and possibly have himself inaugurated as the

O'Donnell chieftain after the English campaign petered out. However, Chichester's attack on Tory Island scattered his army and ended his ambitions. Niall Garbh O'Donnell played a more subtle role in O'Doherty's revolt, participating in the initial plotting and then holding aloof from outright involvement. Again, Chichester's ruthlessness wrecked his plans, a situation already hampered by his slow recovery from a serious wound. Residual English gratitude to Niall for his support during the Nine Years War probably saved his life but did not secure his freedom. Cathair O'Doherty played a tragic role in the drama. Too young and inexperienced to prevent himself being used by older and more cunning men, his rash actions in April 1608 led to his own death and the ruin of his family.

Notes

1 J. McCavitt, 'The flight of the earls, 1607', *IHS*, xxix (1994), pp 159-73; idem, *The Flight of the Earls* (Dublin, 2002); idem, *Sir Arthur Chichester, Lord Deputy of Ireland* (Belfast, 1998). See also N. Canny, 'The Flight of the Earls, 1607', *IHS*, xvii (1971), pp 380-99; B. Bonner, *That audacious traitor* (Dublin, 1975).

2 Lord deputy and council to the privy council, 30 Sept. 1605 (TNA SPI 63/217/154).

3 *Irish Patent Rolls of James I* (Dublin, 1846) p. 13.

4 'Agso an mhed tuatha a Tir cuill' ('And that is the number of septs in Tyrconnel') 1607 (TNA SPI 63/222/265).

5 D. McGettigan, *Red Hugh O'Donnell and the Nine Years War* (Dublin, 2005), pp 130-1.

6 *AFM*, 1601.

7 'Grant from the king to Rory O'Donnel, earl of Tyrconnell, 1604' (*Irish Patent Rolls of James I*, p. 13).

8 Ibid., p. 59.

9 Sir Cathair O'Doherty to the Prince of Wales, 14 Feb. 1608 (TNA SPI 63/223/20).

10 'General pardon to Brian MacTurlough O'Gallagher of Tihugh, 1603' (*Irish Patent Rolls of James I*, p. 29).

11 *Inquisitionum in Officio Rotulorum Cancellariae Hiberniae asservatarum, repertorium* (2 vols, Dublin, 1826-9), ii, app. v: Donegal, p. 7. Tadhg Ó Cianáin, *The Flight of the Earls*, (ed.) P. Walsh (Dublin, 1916), pp 8-9. 'A note or brief collection of the several exactions, wrongs and grievances as well spiritual as temporal, wherewith the earl of Tír Chonaill particularly doth find himself grieved', 1607 (TNA SPI 63/222/308). Sir Arthur Chichester's instructions to Sir James Ley and Sir John Davies, 14 Oct. 1608 (TNA SPI 63/225/225).

12 Grant from James I to Captain Ralph Bingley, 18 May 1604 (*Irish Patent Rolls of James I*, p. 15).

13 *Inquis. in Officio Rotulorum*, ii, app. xv, p. 2.

14 *AFM*, 1606.

15 *Inquis. in Officio Rotulorum*, ii, app. xv, p. 3.

16 'The humble petition of Patrick Conley to the right honourable the Earl of Salisbury, Lord High Treasurer of England', c. 1610 (TNA SPI 63/232/45). R. Gillespie, *Conspiracy: Ulster plots and plotters in 1615* (Belfast, 1987), p. 28.

17 *Inquis. in Officio Rotulorum*, ii, app. xv, p. 7.

18 'An abstract of his majesty's title to the lands in the county of Donegal' [1608-09] (Carte Papers 61/130); A. Gwynn and R. N. Hadcock, *Medieval Religious Houses Ireland* (Dublin, 1988), p. 268.

19 R. Steele (ed.), *A bibliography of Royal Proclamations of the Tudor and Stuart Sovereigns, 1485-1714* (2 vols, Oxford, 1910), p. 18; *CSPI, 1606-08*, p. 263.

20 Proclamation by lord deputy and Council, 20 Feb. 1604/05 (TNA SPI 63/217/29).

21 *AFM*, 1608.

22 Chichester's instructions to Sir James Ley and Sir John Davies, 14 Oct. 1608 (TNA SPI 63/225/225).

23 S. Ó Domhnaill, 'Sir Niall Garbh O'Donnell and the rebellion of Sir Cahir O'Doherty', *IHS*, iii (1943), pp 34-38; D. Finnegan, 'Niall Garbh O'Donnell and the rebellion of Sir Cahir O'Doherty', *Donegal Annual* (2007), pp 60-82.

24 Dudley Norton to Sir Thomas Edmondes, 6 Oct. 1608 (BL, MSS 170, enclosure).

25 Sir Arthur Chichester to the privy council, 12 Sept. 1608 (TNA SPI 63/225/17).

26 Ibid.

27 Chichester's instructions to Sir James Ley and Sir John Davies, 14 Oct. 1608 (TNA SPI 63/225/225).

28 Chichester to the privy council, 12 Sept. 1608 (TNA SPI 63/225/184).

29 It was said that Shane MacManus Óg fled to the earl of Clanrickard in Connacht for protection; Dudley Norton to Lord Sir Thomas Edmondes (BL, MSS 170, enclosure).

30 The voluntary confession of Dualtagh MacGilduff, 8 Mar. 1609 (Bodl., Carte Papers 61/272).

31 The state of the cause touching Sir Niall Garbh O'Donnell, 3 Aug. 1608 (ibid., 61/107).

32 The examination of Feidhlimidh Reagh MacDavitt, 3 Aug. 1608 (ibid., 61/279).

33 The state of the cause touching Sir Niall Garbh O'Donnell, 1609 (ibid., 61/107).

34 Letter in Irish from Iníon Dubh (Finola MacDonnell) to George Montgomery, bishop of Derry, Raphoe and Clogher, 1608 (ibid., 61/251).

35 The examination of John Lynshall touching what he can say or what he heard by Sir Niall Garbh O'Donnell considering the late conspiracy in betraying of the Derry taken before Sir Thomas Ridgeway his majesty's treasurer, 15 June 1608 (ibid., 61/282). *Inquis. in Officio Rotulorum*, ii, app. v: Donegal, p. 5.

36 A branch of Sir Richard Hansard's letter written, 30 Aug. 1608 (TNA SPI 63/225/42).

37 The voluntary confession of Dualtagh MacGilduff taken 8 Mar. 1609 (ibid., 61/272).

38 G. Hill, *An historical account of the Plantation in Ulster at the commencement of the seventeenth century 1608-20* (Belfast, 1877), p. 330; T. W. Moody, 'Ulster Plantation Papers 1608-13', *Analecta Hibernica* (1938), p. 210.

39 The humble petition of Sir Niall O'Donnell [1610] (TNA SPI 63/228/167).

40 Chichester to privy council, 19 May 1608 (TNA SPI 63/224/58). At the same time Sir Thomas Ridgeway wrote to O'Donnell that 'We neither fear Sir Niall O'Donnell, nor need him if he be ill affected, or of he come slowly or too coldly on, but will love him as long as he loveth the King, our master …' (Ridgeway to Sir Niall O'Donnell, 20 May, 1608, *Hastings MSS*, IV (London, 1947), p. 4).

41 Ibid., pp 3-4.

42 Chichester to Salisbury, 28 Mar. 1607 (TNA SPI 63/221/34).

43 The humble petition of Sir Niall O'Donnell.

44 Ibid.

45 Humble petition of Niall O'Donnell knight prisoner in the Tower of London, Aug. 1609 (TNA SPI 63/228/166).

46 The humble petition of Sir Niall O'Donnell [1610] (TNA SPI 63/228/167).

47 *AFM*, 1609.

48 P. Walsh, 'Short Annals of Fir Manach', *Irish Chiefs and Leaders* (Dublin, 1960), pp 62-63.

49 *AFM*, 1608.

50 Sir Henry Folliott to Chichester, 8 Sept. 1608 (TNA SPI 63/225/42).

51 An Irish letter from Cathair O'Doherty to O'Gallagher, chief of his name, at Lough Eske Castle, 28 June 1608 (TNA SPI 63/224/181).

52 The names of the tenants of Sir Niall O'Donnell, and the number of forty in-calf cows imposed upon them (Niall Garbh O'Donnell to Lord Deputy Chichester, 9 Oct. 1613, *Philadelphia Papers*, 4, pp 329, 331); *CSPI 1611-14*, pp 391-2.

53 Hill, *Historical account of the plantation in Ulster*, p. 329.

'Anocht is uaigneach Éire'

Breandán Ó Buachalla

Is mó dán a ghin an tarlang a dtugtar 'Imeacht na nIarlaí' go coitianta air. Baineann dhá cheann de na dánta sin leis an imeacht féin agus leis an long a d'iompair na hiarlaí thar lear: ainmníonn ceann acu (7) cuid den lucht taistil a bhí sa long, insíonn an dán eile (8) gurbh é Cúchonnacht Mag Uidhir a sholáthair an long is a thug na hiarlaí is a lucht leanúna thar lear. Is leis an iarmhairt a lean an t-imeacht is mó a bhaineann na dánta eile; dánta éagaointeacha den chuid is mó iad a chaoineann imeacht na n-iarlaí agus anstaid na hÉireann de bharr na himeachta féin agus na plandála a lean é. Mar a scríobh Aindrias Mac Marcais:

> Anocht is uaigneach Éire,
> do bheir fógra a fírfhréimhe;
> gruaidhe a fear 's a fionnbhan fliuch,
> treabh is iongnadh go huaigneach.

> Uaigneach anocht clár Connla,
> gé lán d'fhoirinn allmhardha;
> sáith an chláir fhionnacraigh fhéil,
> don Spáin ionnarbthair iaidséin. (2: §§1-2).

Ní féidir gan díol suntais a dhéanamh dá bhfuil á chur in iúl go grinn sa líne dheireanach sin: gur 'ionnarbadh' a bhí i gceist. Faightear an briathar céanna i bhfoinsí eile ach níl ann ach briathar amháin i sraith líonmhar briathar is ainmfhocal ('imeacht', 'síneadh', 'toisc', 'triall', 'turas') a chuireann an t-aos léinn in ócáid ag tagairt dóibh d'eachtra léanmhar na bliana 1607.[1] Léiríonn sin go beacht tábhacht uathúil na ndánta seo: nochtann siad dúinn *mentalité* an aosa léinn, tugann léargas dúinn ar idé-eolaíocht an intleachta dhúchais, tugann peirspictíocht ar an stair dúinn atá difriúil go maith le stair oifigiúil na bpáipéar stáit. Is suimiúlaide an líne sin gur don 'Spáin' a ionnarbadh na hiarlaí, dar leis an bhfile; nochtar an tuairim chéanna in trí dhán eile:

> Deacair nach bás don Bhanbha
> d'éis an tréid chalma churadh
> do thriall ar toisc don Easpáin
> mo thruaighe beangáin Uladh. (3: §3)

> Do chuaidh oireachas bhfear bhFáil
> anonn uainne don Easpáin. (7: §7)

> A leithéid d'éin-chreich oile níor ghluais …
> le Mag Uidhir don Easpáin. (8: §9)

> rug dá choróin chláir na bhFionn
> don Spáin is onóir Éireann. (8: §10)

> Do chuir fháilte ar croidhthibh cáigh
> toisc na nIarladh don Easpáin. (8: §37)

'Trua liom Máire is Mairgréag' (Fearghal Óg Mac an Bhaird), *Leabhar Inghine Uí Dhomhnaill.* © Royal Library, Brussels

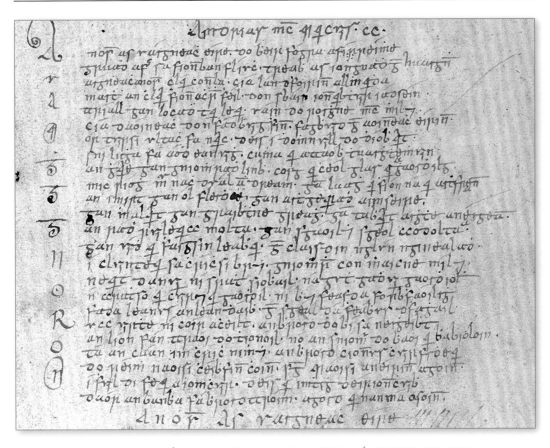

'Anocht is Uaigneach Éire' (Aindrias Mac Marcais). In eag., E. Knott, *Ériu* 8 (1915), p. 181. © RIA

Tá le tuiscint as na tagairtí sin don Spáinn gur scríobhadh na dánta áirithe sin ag am an imeachta féin nó go gearr ina dhiaidh: níl an scéal tagtha abhaile fós nár bhaineadar an Spáinn amach – an ceann scríbe a bhí beartaithe acu.[2]

Tá na dánta a bheidh á bplé agam san aiste seo liostálta agam thíos; tugann a gcéadlínte féin chun solais go gléineach dúinn ní hamháin meanma na ndánta, ach an bhuntuiscint atá laistiar díobh. Mar cé gur filí Ultacha a scríobh na dánta seo agus gurb é *toisc* na n-iarlaí Ultacha is mó a ghin na dánta, is í Éire trí chéile, agus ní cúige Uladh amháin, atá thíos leis; tragóid d'Éirinn uile agus do na Gaeil trí chéile é:

> Anocht is uaigneach Éire. (2)
> Beannacht ar anmain Éireann. (3)
> Cáit ar ghabhadar Gaoidhil. (4)
> Fríoth an uain se ar Inis Fáil. (6)
> Mór an lucht arthraigh Éire. (8)
> Mór do mhill aoibhneas Éireann. (9)
> Mo thruaighe mar táid Gaoidhil. (11)
> Tairnig éigse fhuinn Ghaoidheal. (12)

Faightear an tuiscint chéanna i ndánta eile de chuid na tréimhse, fiú i ndánta nach í polaitíocht na tréimhse is príomhfhócas dóibh. Sa tuireamh a chum Fearghal Óg Mac an Bhaird ar mhuintir Dhomhnaill, nach bhfuil fágtha díobh anois ach an bheirt deirféar, ní hé cás na beirte sin amháin is cás leis:

> Ní hí Mairgréag ná Máire
> chaoinim, is cúis diombáidhe,
> acht an corsa ar chró na bhFionn,
> mó sa mhó osna Éireann. (15: §14)

Sa dán a chum Eoghan Ruadh Mac an Bhaird ar Ruadhrí Ó Domhnaill, ní hé a ainriocht sin amháin atá ag cur isteach ar an bhfile 'acht cás oiléin na hÉireann' (14: §10). Sraith éifeachtach íomhánna a tharraingíonn Fear Flatha Ó Gnímh chuige féin agus an cás sin á léiriú aige:

> Baramhail do-bearar dóibh:
> fuidheall áir d'éis a ndíobhdhóidh,
> gá sníomh ó chróluighe a gcneadh,
> nó is líon tóraimhe ar dtilleadh.

189

Nó is lucht báirce fár bhrúcht muir,
nó is drong fuair fios a saoghail,
nó is géill i ngéibheannaibh Gall
Éireannaigh fá fhéin eachtrann. (11: §§2,3)

Bhí na filí ar aon fhocal i dtaobh an ancháis sin is
litríonn siad amach go neamhbhalbh an anstaid a
rug ar Éirinn:

Gan gháire fa ghníomhradh leinbh,
cosc ar cheol, glas ar Ghaoidheilg;
meic ríogh, mar nár dhual don dream,
gan luadh ar fhíon nó ar aifreann. (2: §5)

Ionann is éag na Fódla
ceilt a córa 's a creidimh … (3: §2)

Coimhthionól tuatha i dtigh naomh,
seirbhís Dé fá dhíon bhfionnchraobh … (4: §13)

Tarla ó Bhóinn go bruach Laighean
dligheadh is fhiú aindligheadh,
gur bhreath shaor le fianaibh Fáil
an riaghail chlaon do chongbháil. (11: § 6)

'Beannacht ar anmain Éireann' (Fear Flatha Ó Gnímh). In
eag., O. Bergin, *Irish Bardic Poetry* (Dublin, 1970). © RIA

Ní hé an saol polaitiúil amháin atá as riocht ach an
uile ghné de shaol na hÉireann idir chultúr (ceol,
Gaeilge), reiligiún (creideamh, aifreann, seirbhís
Dé), reacht (aindlí, riail chlaon), is comhdhéan-
amh an daonra fiú (fuil chranda, d'fhuil Ghall):

Atá againn 'na n-ionadh
dírim uaibhreach eisiodhan
d'fhuil Ghall, de ghasraidh Mhonaidh,
Saxain ann is Albanaigh. (4: §8)
Fuil chranda dá cora i gcion
's na fola arda ísiol. (12:10)

Tá an Gallsmacht i réim, an tír á folcadh le fuil, an
talamh féin á scrios:

Ní léigeann eagla an Ghallsmaicht
damh a hanstaid do nochtadh;
atá an chríoch réidhse ríNéill
de chrú fíréin dá folcadh. (3: §4)

Roinnid í eatorra féin,
an chríoch-sa chlainne saoirNéill,
gan phoinn de mhuigh lachtmhair Fhlainn,
nach bhfuil 'na acraibh again. (4: §9)

Aonuighe in áitibh sealga,
sealga ar slighthibh suaitheanda … (4: §14)

D'fhearaibh Fódla is fáth orchra –
do threabhsad daimh dhanartha,
in áit graifne a ngroigheadh seang,
gach faithche um oirear Éireann. (11: §8)

Dob fhéidir tráchtaireacht mhionchúiseach a
dhéanamh ar na sleachta sin agus ar na dánta dar
díobh iad; ní bhacfad ach le dhá ghné díobh anseo.
Meabhraíonn an líne sin Uí Ghnímh 'dligheadh is
fhiú aindligheadh' an taobh eile – an pheirspictíocht
inmheánach – den 'sibhialtacht' a bhí á cur siar ar
na Gaeil: dlí arbh ionann é agus aindlí, reacht nach
raibh ann ach 'riaghail chlaon' (11: §6). Léiríonn
na línte 'gan luadh ar fhíon nó ar aifreann' (2: §5)
agus 'ceilt a córa 's a creidimh' (3: §2) a tháite le
chéile a bhí reiligiún agus náisiúnachas anois; aon
chúis amháin a bhí i gceist. Léiriú eile ar an gcumasc
ríthábhachtach sin is ea a lárnaí, sa litríocht chomh-
haimseartha agus sa dioscúrsa poiblí trí chéile, atá
an Deonú: an tuiscint gurbh í toil Dé a stiúraigh an
saol go léir ó thus ama anuas go dtí imeachtaí uile
an tsaoil láithrigh idir olc agus mhaith; dá réir sin,
dob fhéidir mífhortúin an tsaoil a mhíniú go loigh-

'Imeacht na nIarlaí'. © John Behan

iciúil réasúnta mar réaladh ar fhearg Dé lena phobal peacúil. Mar a chuir Lochlainn Ó Dálaigh é:

> Díbirt Ghaoidheal ghoirt Bhanbha,
> gé atá a chlú ar chath n-allmhardha,
> fearg Dé ré gcách dá gcolgadh
> is é is fháth dá n-ionnarbadh.
>
> Díoghaltas Dé is adhbhar ann –
> fir Alban, óghbhadh Lunnann
> do anadar 'na n-áit sin –
> cáit ar ghabhadar Gaoidhil? (4: §§19, 26)

Ach ní mór a thuiscint nach téama liteartha amháin atái gceist, ach buntuiscint choiteann uilí:

> Providentialism was not a marginal feature of the religious culture of early modern England, but part of the mainstream, a cluster of presuppositions which enjoyed near universal acceptance. It was a set of ideological spectacles through which individuals of all social levels and from all positions on the confessional spectrum were apt to view their universe.[3]

Dob fhéidir an t-áiteamh céanna a dhéanamh i dtaobh na hÉireann, dar liom; léiriú uathúil ar an teagasc sin a craobhscaoileadh i measc an ghnáthphobail is ea an tuairisc atá againn ar an seanmóir cháiliúil a thug 'Tyrlogh M'Crodyn, a Franciscan Friar' i gContae Thír Eoghain sa bhliain 1613:

> He prayed long, exhorting them to reform their wicked lives, telling them of drunkenness, whoredom, and lack of devotion and zeal; he willed them to take heed that they were not tempted for fear, or desire of gain to go to the English service … and that they should not despair nor be dismayed; though for a time God punished them by suffering their lands to be given to strangers and heretics, it was a punishment for their sins; and he bad them fast and pray and be of good comfort, for it should not be long before they were restored to their former prosperities.[4]

Ní athnuachan reiligiúnda amháin a bhí i gceist ach athnuachan náisiúnta chomh maith; ach pobal na hÉireann aithrí a dhéanamh, thiocfaí slán:

Aithrighe a-nois dá nós sin,
truagh nach déanaid meic Mhílidh … (4: §24)

Do gheall fáidh, fada leam
a fhearg re huaislibh Éireann,
nach maithfidhe le Dia dháibh
go dtia a n-aithrighe dh'éanláimh …
Fada an tréimhse a-táithí i mbroid,
freagraidh so, a phobal Pádraig,
th'aire ribh, a chlann chridhe,
ag sin am na haithrighe. (6: §8, 23)

Straitéis uilí ag na filí é, gné bhunúsach dá n-oiliúint ghairmiúil é, analach cuí a aimsiú a d'fhreagródh d'éirim an bhunábhair in aon dán faoi leith. Stair is litríocht na hÉireann, an litríocht chlasaiceach, an Bíobla a chuir na hapalóga[5] ar fáil. Agus é ag cur síos ar an mbád a thug na hiarlaí thar lear, cuireann Fearghal Óg Mac an Bhaird (8) i gcomparáid é leis an áirc a bhí ag Naoi agus le long *Argho* i scéal na Traí; 'i dteidhm galair' ó 'bhéim súl Balair' a bhí ithir na hÉireann dar le Ó Gnímh (3: §17); 'meic Israhél' is sliocht Judas Maccabaeus a úsáideann Lochlainn Ó Dálaigh mar analach (4: §§21,22); scéal na Traí, anchás Bháibiolóin, 'an bhroid do bhí san Éigeipht' is ábhar comparáide ag Mac Marcais (2: §10); b'ionann 'mic Mhíleadh' agus 'clann Israhéal', dar le Fearghal Óg Mac an Bhaird (9: §39); chuir Ó Gnímh an-soiléir é:

Cosmhail re Cloinn Isra-héal
thoir san Éighipt ar éidréan,
mic Mhíleadh um Bhóinn a-bhus
ag síneadh dhóibh ó a ndúthchas. (11: §17)

B'shin, gan aon cheist, meafar lárnach litríocht na haoise, meafar a ghin idir dhobrón is dhóchas: bhí clann Iosrael ar deoraíocht i ndaoirse san Éigipt gur shaor Maoise iad agus gur threoraigh ar ais dá dtír dhúchais iad. Bhí a shamhail sin de dhobrón blaiste ag mic Mhíle freisin – an deoraíocht, an daoirse, an bhroid – ach b'í an cheist anois, an raibh an t-athaoibhneas i ndán chomh maith?; an raibh Maoise na nGael ar fáil?:

A Tríonóid gá dtá an chumhacht
an mbia an dream-sa ar deoradhacht
níos sia ó chathaoirlios Coinn
nó an mbia an t-athaoibhneas againn? (11: §21)

Ó tá an cuan um chrích bhFeimhin
an bhroid cionnus chuirfidhir
den fhréimh naoi-se chéibhfhinn Choinn
's gan Maoise in Éirinn againn? (2: §11)

Ní hé atá á áiteamh ag an bhfile 'ná fuil teacht anois ar leithéid Mhaoise chun na Gaeil a tharrtháil', mar a deir an tOllamh Pádraig Ó Macháin,[6] ach nach raibh Maoise 'in Éirinn againn'. Is mór eatarthu mar bhí Maoise ar fáil, dar leis na filí, cé gur thall sa Róimh a bhí: Aodh Ó Néill b'é é. Mar a chuir Fearghal Óg Mac an Bhaird é, is é Ó Néill a bheadh mar 'athMhaoise againn', d'fhillfeadh sé 'le buaidh' agus is é a bhainfeadh 'fine Coinn … a broid' (9: §§29,40, 44); ba mhithid dó 'druid le hÉirinn'(5: §19), a dúirt Muiris Óg Mac an Bhaird.

Meabhraíonn Ó Néill a bheith sa Róimh dúinn nach foláir an saothar fileata sin atá scrúdaithe go hachomair againn, nach foláir é a shuíomh sa chom-

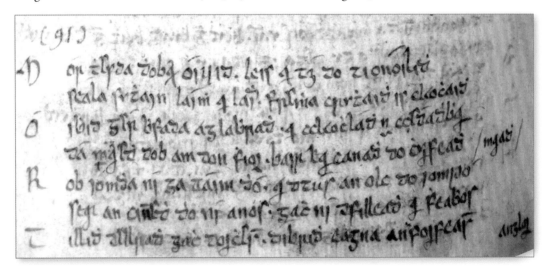

'Mór theasda dh'obair Oivid' (Eochaidh Ó hEodhasa). In eag., P.A. Breatnach, *Éigse* 17 (1977-79), p. 169. © RIA

'Mochean don loing-se tar lar' in eag., P. Walsh, *Beatha Aodha Ruaidh Uí Dhomhnaill*, ii (Dublin, 1948), p. 18.
© Meamram Páipéar Ríomhaire le caoinchead Clonalis House / Teach Cluain Mhalais

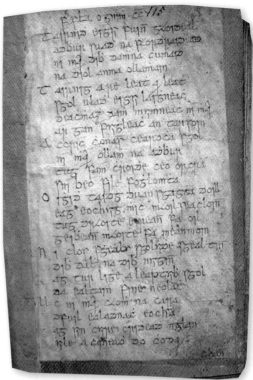

'Tairnig Éigse fhuinn Ghaoidheal' (Fear Flatha Ó Gnímh). In eag., P. de Brún *et al.* (ed.), *Nua-dhuanaire*, i (BÁC, 1971), p. 1.© RIA

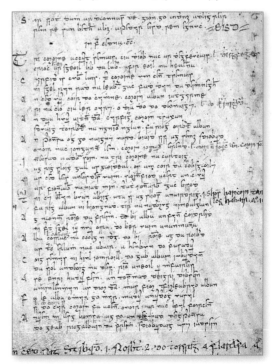

'Trí coróna i gcairt Shéamais' (Fearghal Óg Mac an Bhaird). In eag., L. McKenna, *Aithdhioghluim dána* (London, 1939).
© Meamram Páipéar Ríomhaire le caoinchead Clonalis House / Teach Cluain Mhalais

hthéacs iomlán, idir chomhthéacs inmheánach (*oeuvre* iomlán na bhfilí) agus chomhthéacs seachtrach – an comhthéacs Eorpach nach mór a chur i bhfáth agus stair nó litríocht na tréimhse á plé againn. Thall sa Róimh freisin, agus é ina chónaí sa teach céanna ina raibh Ó Néill, bhí Peter Lombard, ardeaspag Ard Mhacha, an té is mó a raibh cluas an phápa aige maidir le cúrsaí na hÉireann. Ba thaca mór ag Ó Néill é Lombard tráth, ach ó thus na haoise amach ba léir do Lombard go raibh gá ag an eaglais le hatharach polasaí in Éirinn chun déileáil leis na cúinsí difriúla a bhí anois i bhfeidhm.[7] Ní deacair an t-athrú a léiriú: sa bhliain 1570 chuir an pápa Pius V Eilís I faoi choinneallbhá agus scaoil Caitlicigh na hÉireann óna ngéillsine di; ar chorónú Shéamais I sa bhliain 1603, d'aithin an pápa Pól V mar rí *de jure* ar na trí ríochta (Alba, Éire, Sasana) é. Agus b'shin feasta, ar chomhairle Lombard, polasaí na hEaglaise in Éirinn: b'é Séamas I an rí ceart a raibh géillsine dlite do mar rí Éireann. Léirítear an polasaí nua agus a impleachtaí praiticiúla an-luath i litríocht na haoise: ar 'na trí coróna' a shealbhaigh Séamas I, dúirt Fearghal Óg Mac an Bhaird, bhí 'coróin iongantach Éireann', b'é Séamas 'céile' na hÉireann, dar leis (13: §§5, 23); bhí sé i ndán do Shéamas, dar le Eochaidh Ó hEodhasa, an bhuairt a bhaint de phobal 'imshníomhach Éireann', b'é 'scaoileadh gach ceo' acu é (10: §§13,14); 'ár rí uasal óirdheirc … ár rí uasal' a thugann Mac Aingil ar Shéamas, agus teagasc morálta á chur ar fáil aige 'don mhuintir atá fá mhórdhacht an ríogh'; ba chuid bhunúsach den teagasc sin é go raibh 'd'fhiachuibh ar an uile Chríosduidhe … gan aitheanta a uachtarán dtuaithe do bhriseadh'.[8]

Aon phobal a ndeintear concas nó coilíniú air, bíonn, de ghnáth, ceithre rogha ar fáil chun déileáil leis: troid, géilleadh, comhshamhlú, comhréiteach. Dob fhéidir a áiteamh gur triaileadh gach ceann acu in Éirinn, cé gur go páirteach agus nach go huilí é. Is cinnte gur triaileadh troid, ach le géilleadh Uí Néill sa bhliain 1603, agus le himeacht na n-iarlaí sa bhliain 1607, ba léir go raibh an troid thart (go fóill pé scéal é); b'é an comhréiteach, is é sin le rá teacht chun réitigh éigin le Séamas, a bhí le triail feasta. Faoin am ar scríobhadh *Iomarbhágh na bhFileadh* (1618)[9] ba pholasaí coiteann uilí é an comhréiteach. Luaim an téacs sin go háirithe mar sa monagraf atá scríofa ag an Ollamh Leerssen ar an téacs,[10] áitíonn sé gur choimhlint idé-eolaíochtúil go bunúsach a bhí laistiar den iomarbhá liteartha agus gur réaladh í an choimhlint liteartha idir Leath Coinn is Leath Mogha, gur réaladh í ar dhifríocht bhunúsach pholaitiúil idir an t-aos léinn sa dá chuid den tír – filí Uladh ceannairceach trodach traidisiúnta, filí na Mumhan[11] géilliúil réasúnta nua-aoiseach:

> The Contention narrows down to a *querelle des anciens et des modernes*. Tadhg heralds what he feels is the new ascendancy of Eberian Gaels surviving in the New Order. His opponents invoke the full moral weight of time-hallowed tradition, martyrdom and glory and loathe Tadhg with the approbrium of forsaking the old traditional values.[12]

Ach ní thagann an fhianaise leis an téis sin. Is iad na filí Ultacha Fearghal Óg Mac an Bhaird (13) is Eochaidh Ó hEodhasa (10) is túisce a d'fháiltigh roimh Shéamas I agus roimh 'the New Order'. Dar leis na Ceithre Máistrí (*ARÉ* vi, 2362) go raibh éirí amach Uí Dhochartaigh sa bhliain 1608 ar na tarlaingí ba chúis le h-imeacht na n-iarlaí agus plandáil Uladh. Is cinnte gur chaoin Fear Flatha Ó Gnímh ainstaid na tíre is díothú na huaisle i sraith dánta éagaointeacha (3, 11, 12), ach is é an radharc deireanach a fhaighimíd air dánta molta á scríobh aige do Sir Éinrí Ó Néill (Clainne Aodha Buí), dá bheansan Martha, iníon Sir Francis Stafford, do Raghnall Mac Domhnaill, iarla Aontroma, agus do Sir Art Mag Aonghusa – uaisle a raibh glactha acu le Séamas I agus a raibh conách orthu faoin reacht nua.[13] Ní hamháin gur tugadh pardún d'Eochaidh Ó hEodhasa sa bhliain 1586, ach bronnadh 200

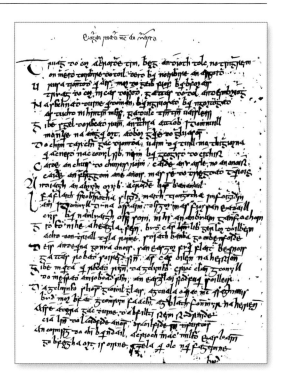

'Trua do chor a chroidhe tim' (Eoghan Rua Mac an Bhaird), Leabhar Inghine Uí Dhomhnaill, in eag., O. Bergin, *Irish Bardic Poetry*, p. 35. © Royal Library, Brussels

acra talún air faoi fhorálacha na plandála sa bhliain 1610.[14] File Ultach, Aodh Ó Domhnaill, a fhógraíonn san *Iomarbhágh* gur 'le Séamas aniú ma le / Sacsa, Alba agus Éire'.[15] Lughaidh Ó Cléirigh féin, a thóg páirt thionscantach san *Iomarbhágh*, bhí talamh ar cíos aige ón rí.[16] Níl difríocht pholaitiúil dá laghad idir a dhearcadhsan agus dearcadh Uí Bhruaideadha nó dearcadh na bhfilí Muimhneacha trí chéile: táid araon anois ag glacadh leis an *status quo* is níl d'ábhar aighnis eatarthu maidir le Séamas ach ceist ghinealaigh – cé acu ó ríthe na Mumhan nó ó ríthe Uladh a shíolraigh sé? Cé go bhfuil an-chuid fianaise curtha ar fáil ag an Ollamh Leerssen maidir le cúlra stairiúil an *Iomarbhágh*, níor sholáthair sé aon fhianaise théacsúil, is é sin le rá, fianaise as an téacs féin a léireodh an téis go raibh, um an dtaca seo, difríocht bhunúsach pholaitiúil idir filí Leath Mogha is Leath Coinn; ní hionadh sin, dar liom, mar nach raibh aon difríocht pholaitiúil i gceist. Léiríonn *Iomarbhágh na bhFileadh*, mar a léiríonn téacsanna eile na linne (*Scáthán Shacramuinte na hAithridhe, Foras Feasa ar Éirinn, Annála Ríoghachta Éireann*), an polasaí nua i leith an stáit – ar dearcadh ceannasach anois é – a bhí leagtha amach agus á chleachtadh ag éilíteanna soch-chultúrtha na hÉireann: gur trí theacht chun réitigh le Séamas is fearr a d'fhéadfaí teacht slán. Níor séanadh go hiomlán riamh bagairt na n-arm, ach nuair a chuathas i mbun na n-arm arís, mar a rinneadh sa bhliain 1641, ní mór cuimhneamh i gcónaí gur 'in ainm an rí' a éiríodh amach. Mar a chuir Eoghan Ruadh Ó Néill é: 'We are in no rebellion ourselves, but do really fight for our Prince in defence of his Crown and Royal prerogatives'.[17]

Imeacht na nIarlaí. © An Post

Nótaí

1 Féach B. Ó Buachalla, 'Ó Néill agus an tAos Léinn', *Léachtaí Cholm Cille,* xxxviII (2006), pp 18-21.

2 Nochtann P. Walsh (Lughaidh Ó Cléirigh, *Beatha Aodha Ruaidh Uí Dhomhnaill* (2 vols, Dublin, 1948-57), ii, p. 125) an tuairim: 'It may be that Flanders, being at that period in the Spanish dominions, is loosely spoken of as Spain.' Ach fiú más fíor sin, rud nach dóigh liom, d'fhágfadh sé fós gur scríobhadh na dánta sular bhain na h-iarlaí an Róimh amach (fómhar, 1608).

3 A. Walsham, *Providence in early modern England* (Oxford, 1999), pp 2-3.

4 B. Ó Buachalla, *Aisling ghéar* (Baile Átha Cliath, 1996), p. 45.

5 Féach L. P. Ó Caithnia, *Apalóga na bhfilí, 1200-1600* (Baile Átha Cliath, 1984).

6 P. Ó Macháin, *Téacs agus údar i bhfilíocht na scol* (Baile Átha Cliath, 1998), p. 3.

7 J. J. Silke, 'Later relations between Primate Peter Lombard and Hugh O'Neill', *Irish Theological Quarterly,* xxii (1955), pp 15-30.

8 Aodh Mac Aingil, *Scáthán Shacramuinte na hAithridhe* (Lobháin, 1618; eag. C. Ó Maonaigh, Baile Átha Cliath, 1952), línte 5457, 5494, 5632, 3140.

9 L. McKenna, *Iomarbhágh na bhFileadh* (London, 1918).

10 J. Leerssen, *The Contention of the Bards* (Dublin, 1994).

11 Tá géarghá le staidéar cuimsitheach ar fhilíocht na Mumhan sa chéad cheathrú den seachtú haois déag.

12 Leerssen, *Contention of the Bards*, p. 61.

13 Tadhg Ó Donnchadha, *Leabhar Cloinne Aodha Buí* (Baile Átha Cliath, 1931), pp xxii, xxiii, xxv, xxx, xxxi, xxxvi; Ó Buachalla, *Aisling ghéar*, p. 51.

14 'Pardon to Cowchonaght Maguire, chief of his nation ... Aghye O Hossye of Baelle Hossey ... granted on the submission of Cowchonaghte ... ' (*The Irish fiants of the Tudor sovereigns* (Dublin, 1994, no. 4810; *CSPI, 1608-10*: p. 210; C. Mhag Craith, 'Í Eodhusa', *Clogher Record,* ii (1957), pp 13-14.

15 McKenna, *Iomarbhágh na bhFileadh*, 138, §26.

16 Ó Cléirigh, *Beatha Aodha Ruaidh* (ed.) P. Walsh, ii, pp 3-4; *Analecta Hibernica*, viii (1938), p. 211.

17 Ó Buachalla, *Aisling ghéar*, p. 106.

Gan tuisle gan teibheadh: gnéithe de litríocht na Gaeilge sa seachtú haois déag[1]

Diarmaid Ó Doibhlin

De bhrí go n-áilíosaíonn nó go santaíonn gach tír a bheith freacnaithe go maith ina dteangacha máthartha agus dúchais, agus a bheith eolach foirfe go beacht agus caingne nó cúise a dtíre a thuiscint go maith iomlán ionas go dtuilchéimnidís nó go dtéidís ar a n-aghaidh gan tuisliú gan teibeadh chomh maith i neithe diadha agus daonna in éinfheacht; gonadh aire sin do shantaíos féin, de réir m'acfuinne cuidiú le mo choimhthíoracha le cruinniú agus le cur síos ár dteanga nádúrtha, an Ghaeilge, beagnach, nó go mórmhór ionnarbtha óna tír, tréigthe óna dúchasacha, agus dísbeagaithe óna haois leanúna, i bhfoirm fhoclóra ó choinne cháich, dochum go n-aithnidís a saine, nó a n-idirdhealú féin ó chiníocha eile rann an domhainse.

Mícheál Ó Cléirigh.[2]

Agus a shoiléire agus a oscailte is tá cuspóir Uí Chléirigh sa dréacht beag sin as an réamhrá a chuir se leis an *Sanasán* a scríobh sé, is doiligh liom aon chiall a bhaint as meon an fhile Patrick Kavanagh nuair a roghnaigh sé tarraingt ar 'Brother Michael' agus trácht a dhéanamh ar sheoltóireacht 'in puddles of the past / pursuing the ghost of Brendan's mast',[3] agus ba scigiúla ná sin arís an véarsaíocht bheag shuarach a chum William Allingham:

> MacMurlagh kill'd Flantagh, and Cormac kill'd Hugh,
> Having else no particular business to do.
> O'Toolle killed O'Gorman, O'More killed O'Leary
> Muldearg, son of Phadrig kill'd Con son of Cleary
> If you wish for more slaughter and crimes and disasters
> See passim, those Annalists called 'the Four Masters.[4]

B'fhurasta, ar ndóighe, a bheith ag béalastánaíocht ó chompord chroílár na himpireachta i Londain i seirbhís do mháistrí. Agus tá díobháil nach beag sa tuairim sin fosta a chludaíonn Mícheál Ó Cléirigh i gclóca ceoch an rómánsachais, agus nach bhfeic-

Coláiste San Antaine, Lobháin, liotagraf ón ochtú haois déag.

tear de ach bráithirín bocht gona aibíd dhonn, ag imeacht cosnocht ó áit go háit, an tóir i gcónaí air, agus sceimhle agus scéin mar chomhluadar aige de shíor. Nó i ndeireadh na dála ba réalaí é Mícheál Ó Cléirigh a raibh fócas, oiliúint agus tabhairt suas a aimsire féin air, agus an fuinneamh agus an diongbháilteacht ann a chuid beartanna liteartha a thabhairt chun críche.[5]

Bhí, ar ndóighe, Éire ina cíor tuathail ceart nuair a bhí an Bráthair Mícheál Ó Cléirigh i mbun saothair agus slabhra an choncais agus an choilíneachais a theannadh ar shaíocht agus ar shaibhreas na tíre. Bhí dlí sainiúil na hÉireann, cultúr sainiúil phobal na hÉireann, ealaín dúchasach na hÉireann, bhí siad sin á gcur as a ríocht agus á mbascadh. Bhí Chichester ag alpadh agus ag alfraitsíocht leis anseo ó thuaidh, plandáil agus transphlandáil ar bun, comhcheilgeanna á gcothú agus á bhfabhrú.

Próiseas leanúnach é an coilíniú agus cuirimis i gcónaí san áireamh go raibh pobal na hÉireann fágtha gan cinnirí ná taoisigh dá gcuid féin agus a gcóras maireachtála in aimhréidh. B'é an t-iontas é gur cruthaíodh litríocht ar bith sa tréimhe seo a raibh buanna ealaín inti, ach cruthaíodh agus is sna blianta áirithe seo – i ndeireadh an séú haois déag agus tús agus lár an seachtú haois déag á cumadh téacsanna móra canónda litríocht na Nua-Ghaeilge.

Is é fírinne an scéil go raibh tús úr ann sna blianta seo agus ré nua i stair an duine i mbéal an dorais agus tuiscintí agus struchtúir nua ag teacht chun cinn. Bhí dhá fhórsa mhóra ach go háirithe ag feidhmiú sa saol. Sa chéad áit bhí an tAthbheochan Léinn ann nó an Renaissance mar a thugtar air agus bhí a spiorad sin ag siúl na hEorpa, agus is minic an

196

mheánaois agus an nua-aois seo an tAthbheochan Léinn i ndeabhaidh a chéile agus ag iomrascáil le chéile sa litríocht féin.

Is as spiorad an tAthbheochan Léinn sin a d'fhás agus a bhláthaigh an bhéim ar an teanga náisiúnta, cé gurbh í an Laidin i gcónaí bunteanga an dioscúrsa léannta ar fud na hEorpa. Agus de thairbhe sin tá againn an Bráthair Mícheál ag soláthar Sanasán nó Foclóir Gaeilge,[6] Giolla Bhríde Ó hEodhasa ag soláthar leabhar gramadaigh don Ghaeilge,[7] agus Aodh Mac Cathmhaoil (Aodh Mac Aingil) agus Flaithrí Ó Maoil Chonaire agus iad ag soláthar téacsanna ina dteanga dhúchais féin.[8]

Chuir an tAthbheochan Léinn béim ar na foinsí, rud a d'fhág scoláire agus lucht léinn ag triall siar go dtí bunfhoinsí na staire agus na buntéacsanna. Agus b'é an ghairm sin *ad fontes* (chuig na foinsí) a sheol Ó Cléirigh agus Seathrún Céitinn ó theach go teach agus ó sheanleabhar go seanleabhar gur chuir siad le chéile stair agus scéal a muintire, agus ó tharla go raibh teanga ársa na hÉireann ar a dtoil acu is go raibh teacht acu ar na seanlámhscríbhinní, is acu a bhí an t-údarás le ceart an scéil a lorg agus a insint. Agus sa deireadh thiar léiríonn idir *Fhoras Feasa ar Éirinn* agus *Annála Ríoghachta Éireann* a shainiúla is a bhí cultúr phobal na hÉireann.

Agus ansin sa séú haois déag bhí fórsa mór eile ag feidhmiú agus ina ábhar imreasáin idir dhaoine, mar bhí, an réabhlóid i gcúrsaí creidimh. Bíonn sé doiligh againn in iarthar na hEorpa sa lá atá inniu ann tuiscint a bheith againn ar a phráinní is a dhiongbháilte is a bhí an taos léinn agus eagna agus prionsaí ríochtaí as ceisteanna creidimh sna meánaoiseanna agus ina dhiaidh.

B'é Jan Hus (c. 1372-1415) Déan Dáimh na Fealsúnachta in Ollscoil Phraha a chéad thugann tuaileas uaidh nach raibh rialú na hEaglaise sa Róimh mar ba chóir agus sna seanmóirí agus sna hóráidí a thugadh sé uaidh, bhémnigh sé an gá a bhí le leasú a chur i bhfeidhm ar ghnóthaí na hEaglaise. Fógraíodh Hus ina eiriceach agus dhíol sé as a chuid barúlacha lena bheo. Mar sin féin, bhí tacaíocht uaisle na Boihéime aige agus ba ghearr go raibh eaglais neamhspleách ar an Róimh agus ar phápa na Róimhe ag feidhmiú sa Bhoihéim agus leas á bhaint san eaglais neamhspleách sin as teanga an phobail sin i seirbhísí eaglasta in ionad na Laidine.

Ach b'é Liútar (1483-1546) agus an Liútarachas a bhris ón eaglais agus a scoilt an Eoraip. Mar is eol don saol, shéan Liútar údarás an phápa agus dhiúltaigh sé do prolaiféarú loghanna, ach dáiríre bhí ceisteanna níos bunúsaí agus níos achrannaí

taobh thiar den bhris. Scríobh Liutár trí cinn de dhuilleacháin inar bheachtaigh sé a chuid tuiscintí – san *Aitheasc d'Uaisle na Gearmáine* labhair sé ar eagrú na heaglaise agus ar an deighilt a bhí ann idir an chléir agus tuataí agus dar leis, ba fheall é an deighilt sin. B'é an pápa an tAinchríost, dhearbhaigh sé; ansin sa duilleachán *Braighdeanas Babailionach na hEaglaise* a scríobhadh le haghaidh na cléire, chuir sé an ruaig ar na sacraimintí go dtí nach raibh fanta aige ach mar bhí an Baisteadh agus an Eocairist. Agus sa mhullach air sin, rinne sé ionsaí fíochmhar ar an aifreann agus ar chleachtais an aifrinn; ansin bhí Liútar ag fógairt ré úr saoirse nó *libertas* mar a thug sé air agus sa duilleachán *Saoirse an Chríostaí* dhearbhaigh sé nach raibh feidhm le dea-oibreacha i saol an duine mar gurbh é Críost agus Críost amháin an Slánaitheoir.

Bhí an lasóg sa bharrach agus ba ghearr go raibh lucht leanúna Liútair, Zwingli (1484-1531), Melanchthon (1497-1560), Bullinger (1504-75) Cailvin (1509-64), Beza (1519-1605)[9] ag achrann eatarra féin fá phointí achranna diagachta, a bhí, dar leo, substaintiúil agus d'imigh siad a mbealach féin ach bhí an Protastúnachas lonnaithe anois san Eoraip agus roghanna le déanamh ag ag aos léinn agus ag uaisle agus ag tíortha.

D'imigh uaisle Uladh an cuan amach i Meán Fómhair 1607, agus a n-aghaidh ar an Spáinn. Bhí ar bord loinge leis na huaisle sin – Ó Néill agus Ó Domhnaill – bhí ar bord loinge leo, Tadhg Ó Cianáin, staraí profisiúnta a raibh tógáil na meánaoise air agus d'fhág sé ina dhiaidh cuntas ar thuras sin na n-uaisle thar sáile.[10] Is doiciméad tábhachtach staire agus doiciméad tábhachtach sóisialta é an cuntas sin ach bíonn díomá go minic ar mhuintir na staire agus iad ag plé leis an téacs. Nó, bíodh go raibh Ó Cianáin i gcuideachta Uí Néill agus Uí Dhomhnaill, agus, ní foláir, cóngarach go maith dóibh, níl aon lua aige ná léargas ar pholasaíthe ná ar mhana na dtaoiseach; agus, is é an bhrí is féidir a bhaint as sin nach raibh sé dáiríre ar an taobh istigh agus nach raibh sé páirteach sa bheartaíocht agus sa phlé pholaitíochta a bhíodh ar bun ag na huaisle. Bhí, ar ndóighe, ar Ó Néill agus ar Ó Domhnaill a bheith cúramach rúnda mar bhí an tír foirgthe le spiairí, agus fágann sin go bhfuil againn ó Ó Cianáin insint dhíreach shimplí ar thuras na n-uaisle seo ó bhaile go baile, ó áit go háit agus ó dháil go dáil. Dáiríre is geall le hoilithreacht é an turas agus iad ó eaglais go heaglais, agus ó thaisí naomh go taisí naomh. Agus bíodh gur insint shimplí í, gineann a réidhe agus an ghné nádúrtha atá le braistint inti, gineann sin go minic tnuthán uaignis i ndiaidh saoil a bear-naíodh orainn, agus a bhí leis an turas seo ar shéala a bhasctha. Is sonraíche an ghné seo, b'fhéidir, agus na huaisle go fóill in Éirinn:

Ghabh Ó Néill a chead ag an nGiúistís an Satharn ina dhiaidh sin, agus chuaigh sé an oíche sin gus an Mainistir Mhór, áit a raibh Sir Gearóid Moore. Arna mhárach dó go Sráidbhaile Dhún Dealgan. Ghluais sé Dé Luain as an tSráidbhaile trí Bhealach Mór an Fheadha go Béal Átha an Airgid, thar Shliabh Fuaid, go hArd Mhacha, agus thar an Abhainn Mhór go Dún Geanainn, gus an gCraobh, baile oileáin dá bhailte. Rinne sé cónaí agus oireasamh ar an gCraobh Dé Máirt. Ghluais sé in ainm Dé, Dé Chéadaoin ón gCraobh thar Shliabh Síos, agus bhí sé an oíche sin i Muintir Luinigh ar chóngar Loch Begfhine. Arna mhárach dó go Bun Dianaide agus bhí sé ina chónaí ó aimsir mheán lae go comhthitim na hoíche. Air sin chuaigh sé thar Fhearsaid Mhór ar Loch Feabhail gach ndíreach go Droichead Adhamhnáin. Bhí mac Uí Dhónaill – Cafarr mac Aodha mhic Mhánais – ar a gceann ansin.[11]

Ní hé amháin go bhfuil fócas an tsaothair seo a chur i láthair – is é sin gur turas é – ach meabhraíonn carnadh sin na logainmneacha, meabhraíonn sin gluaiseacht mhear Uí Néill ó thuaidh agus dúisíonn siad cuimhní a bhfuil a n-éifeacht féin leo ag léitheoirí a thuigeann go bhfuil Ó Néill ag fágáil slán anseo leis na 'ciníocha beaga' a bhí dílis dá mhuintir thar cheithre chéad blian agus gur gearr uilig go mbeadh an Chraobh ina Stewartstown agus Achadh an Dá Charad ina Charlemont.

Agus Ó Cianáin ar mhór-roinn na hEorpa, samhlaím go raibh teacht aige ach go háirithe ar leabhráin agus ar dhuilleacháin a raibh eolas, nó cur síos iontu ar na heaglaisí agus ar na páláis ar casadh iontu iad, mar a ndearna na huaisle seo na hÉireann teagmháil leis an ealaíon is gleoite, idir phéinteireacht agus dhealbhóireacht, a bhí ar caomhnú san Eoraip san am. Admhaíonn sé anonn i ndeireadh an chuntais gur thóg sé an t-ábhar atá aige ar theach míorúilteach úd Loreto gur thóg sé sin 'ó sheanleabhar', agus creidim féin go raibh ar an deasc aige sa Róimh leabhráin le haghaidh lucht oilithreachta a bhí san am sin ar fáil sa Róimh agus in áiteacha eile.[12]

Tá an cineál céanna fócais, ach é a bheith níos loime, le nótáil sa téacs a sholáthraigh Lughaidh Ó

Cléirigh ar Aodh Ruadh Ó Domhnaill, prionsa mór Thír Chonaill a fuair bás sa Spáinn.[13] Is beathaisnéis é go bunúsach agus níl de rún na de chuspóir ag an údar ach Aodh Ruadh a cheiliúradh mar laoch mór na haimsire, mar fhear cogaidh nach raibh a shárú ann, agus mar shaighdiúir a raibh misneach aige agus buanna móra beartaíochta agus straitéise aige. Sa dréacht seo thíos tá léiriú an-bhreá ar bheart dena beartanna sin cogaíochta ag Aodh Ruadh nár éirigh leis. Chuir sé díorma beag fear amach leis na Gaill a mhealladh go dtí áit a bhí roghnaithe ag Aodh Ruadh le slad a dheanamh a dhéanamh orthu. Thug sé ordú docht nach ndéanfaí teagmháil leis na Gaill ach go díreach iad féin a thaisbeáint, agus ansin tiontú ar a gcúl agus an namhaid a threorú isteach sa ghaiste a bhí réidh ag Aodh Ruadh agus a chuid saighdiúirí. Ach duine de mhuintir Uí Dhónaill- Feidhlimidh Riabhach Mac Daibhéad- tháinig an tóir chomh géar sin air go raibh air urchar a scaoileadh, agus captaen na nGall a mharú. Sheasaigh na Gaill ansin, agus thiontaigh siad ar ais, agus bhí beart Aodha Ruadh curtha ó mhaith. Bhí Aodh Ruadh ar mire:

Nuair a chonaic Ó Dónaill na Gaill ag filleadh ar ais, líonadh é le fearg lanábhal i leith na laochra, ó nach bhfuair sé mian a mheanman agus áilíos a intinne i gcoinne na n-allúrach mar a bheartaigh sé ar tús. Tháinig fianlach na fásruaige i láthair na flatha (cé go mba doiligh dóibh de bharr méid a fheirge) agus d'inis mar a tharla. Mhóidigh siad uile thar cheann an churaidh a ghoin Captaen Martin nach raibh aon ní, seachas cumhacht an Choimdhe, a thabharfadh as é mura scaoilfeadh sé an t-aon urchar sin. Shuaimhnigh sin fearg Uí Dhónaill agus tláthaíodh a aigne da bharr, agus insíodh dó arnamárach gur bhásaigh an Captaen, mar adúramar. Ba lúide a imní ansin, cé nár ba shlán leis a mheanma ar fad ar théarnamh do na Gaill mar a rinne siad agus a chealg agus a eadarnaí a dhul ar neamhní, seachas marú an aon fhir adúramar.[14]

Éiríonn le Lughaidh Ó Cléirigh scéal inspéise réalaíoch a chruthú as beatha Aodha Ruadh. Arís agus arís eile sna heachtraí éagsúla tá tnúthán mór na beatha ann, agus an gean agus an t-ómós a bhí ag Ó Cléirigh dá chomhChonallach. Seandacht na teanga agus maorgacht sa chur i láthair a dhíbríonn léitheoirí an lae inniu agus is trua sin nó bhí de bhua ag an scríbhneoir seo go raibh sé i dteagmháil le laoch mór de mhuintir na hÉireann, go gcuala sé seanchas agus anacdóid fá dtaobh de, agus go bhfuil blas na fírinne agus na daonnachta ar an chuntas a d'fhág sé faoi.[15]

Tá leabhar Lughaidh Uí Chléirigh luaite ag na Ceithre Máistrí ar na foinsí a bhí acu don tréimhse 1586-1602. Ma ba é ba chuspóir ag Lughaidh Ó Cléirigh ná *virtu* úd an Athbheochan Léinn, bhí cuspóir i bhfad níos leithne ag Mícheál Ó Cléirigh.[16] Chuir sé roimhe scéal agus stair a mhuintire, pobal na hÉireann a chur i dtoll a chéile agus chuaigh sé a thriall ar na bunfhoinsí agus roghnaigh sé modh na croineolaíochta – modh a raibh taithí aige air taobh istigh de thraidisiún liteartha na Gaeilge agus a raibh glacadh leis ag an Athbheochan Léinn.[17] D'aithin sé go raibh Éire Nua á dealbhú agus á cruthú sa tréimhse chorrach sin agus theastaigh uaidh go mbeadh an Éire nua sin préamhaithe i stair agus i seanchas na hÉireann mar a bhí sin ar fáil sna foinsí dúchais. Agus sin é ag cuartú na bhfoinsí agus beachtaíocht an Athbheochan Léinn ann agus é ag breacadh síos san iliomad gluaiseanna an t-am agus an áit a raibh sé ag saothrú ann, na patrúin a bhí aige agus na téacsanna a raibh se ag tarraingt orthu. Chan ag caointeoireacht a bhí sé ar dhomhan agus ar chultúr a bhíodh ann, ach ag leagadh síos ó na foinsí dúchais dúshraith na hÉireann Nua a bhí le tógáil, agus b'Éire í sin a mbeadh an teanga shinseartha i réim ann agus a mbeadh a stair shainiúil féin aici, agus siabhaltas a mbeadh spás agus bheith istigh ag an uile Éireannach ann.

Bhí beartas agus mana den chineál céanna idir lámha ag Seathrún Céitinn (c. 1570-c. 1650), sagart Muimhneach a raibh oiliúint scoileanna an dúchais air ag teaghlach de Chlann Mhag Craith – b'aos dána iad muintir Mhag Craith ag Buitléaraigh na Mumhan – agus in éineacht leis sin fuair sé ollscolaíocht i Rheims, agus bhí sé ina dhiaidh sin ina ollamh i gColáiste Ríoga na nÉireannach i mBordeaux. Bhí mar sin oiliúint ar leith aige – oiliúint traidisiúnta an dúchais in Éirinn agus oiliúint na nÍosánach ar an mhór-roinn.

Is é an saothar mór scríbhneoireachta a rinne an Ceitinneach ná *Foras Feasa ar Éirinn*, agus ba

'Dochum glóire Dé agus Onóra na hÉireann'. Stampa ag ceiliúradh na gCeithre Máistrí. © Ionad an Léinn Éireannaigh, Teach Inse

shaothar liteartha é sin a raibh gean ar leith ag pobal na Gaeilge air, agus é a léamh go forleitheadach ar fud na tíre. Is é an bunchuspóir a chuir a Céitinneach roimhe ná Éire agus pobal na hÉireann a chosaint ar an ionsaí gránna á bhí á dhéanamh uirthi ag scríbhneoirí Gallda an choilíneachais agus iad ag dearbhú nach raibh i muintir na hÉireann dáiríre ach barbaraigh agus gur tír bharbartha amach is amach í tír na hÉireann, agus gur fhág sin an coilíniú ceart ó thaobh na moráltachta de:

Bíodh a fhianaise sin ar an dteist a thugann Cambrensis, Spenser, Stanihurst, Hanmer, Camden, Barckly, Moryson, Davies, Campion, agus gach Nua-Ghall eile dá scríobhann uirthi ó shin amach, ionas gurb é nós, beagnach, an phriompalláin a dhéanann siad, ag scríobh ar Éireannaigh. Is é is nós don phriompallán, an tan a thógann a cheann sa samhradh, a bheith ar foluain ag imeacht agus gan cromadh ar mhionscoth dá mbíonn sa mhachaire nó ar bhláth dá mbíonn i luibhghort, cé go mba rós nó lile uile iad, ach a bheith ar fuaidreamh go dteagmhaíonn bualtrach bó nó otrach capaill leis go dtéann sé á únfairt fein iontu'. Agus arís eile 'Bíodh gurb iomaí ní a chuireann siad síos ina startha a d'fhéadfaí a bhréagnú, de bhrí, furmhór a scríobhann siad go maslach ar Éirinn, nach bhfuil d'údaras acu lena scríobh ach insint scéalta ainteastach a bhí fuafar d'Éirinn agus aineolach ina seanchas.'[18]

Is beag tathag a baineadh as saothar an Chéitinnigh taobh amuigh d'eolas a chnuasach ar na foirmeacha teanga, agus neamhaird a dhéanamh ar an chumas a bhí ann meafair a chruthú ar nós meafar an phriompalláin ansin thuas agus cuimhnímid ar struchtúrú agus ar chur i láthair scéal Deirdre, cuirim i gcás, mar atá sé ag an Chéitinneach, ar an truailliú a ghintear ag an ollchumhacht, ar an neamh-mheánacht a éiríonn leis a chruthú le sliochtanna comhrá, agus an traigéide a bhaineann le cúrsaí casta an duine sa saol. Ní dóiche go bhfuil scéal stairiúil á sholáthar aige, ach scéal atá bunaithe

Aodh Mac Cathmhaoil (1571-1626).
© Institiúid Mhíchíl Uí Chléirigh

cogaíocht mharfach de shíor ann, agus plánna rialta ag ruaigeadh sa phobal, agus gan aon leigheas ar éagruas ar fáil, agus bhí ina cheist mhór 'cad é bhí i ndán don duine i saol an alltair?' Is rabhadh dúinn uilig an bás agus láithreacht an bháis sa saol a bhfuil muid beo ann, agus de réir an Chéitinnigh, is chóir don duine beatha mhorálta a chaitheamh, peacaí a sheachaint agus dea-oibreacha a chleachtadh, is é sin le rá, tuiscint dheimhneach a bheith againn ar an bhás nó is é an bás a sheolann an duine fíréanta isteach in aoibhneas an alltair.

Tá go leor dréachtaí sa téacs toirtiúil seo a bhfuil áilleacht ar leith iontu agus ionramháil tomhaiste ar an ábhar. Sa sliocht seo thíos tugtar spléachadh dúinn ar ghnéithe de shaol na haimsire sin in Éirinn:

> Ni thuigtear cor na cinniúna go cuimhneach le hóga uallacha eigríonna haimsire seo an tan a bhíonn siad ag breith a ruaigeanna reabhraidh agus ag imirt a mbáire baoise, ag déanamh cluiche lúibe agus liathróide, ag lámhach bonsach agus biorghathanna, ag eatrasa agus ag iomáin, agus fós ag ól agus ag imirt, ag sibhreanadh agus ag breasnaíocht. Mo thrua nach dtuigeann siad mar a thagann an bás go tobann, á bhfuadach leis go minic, nuair is mó a bhíonn siad i mbun a n-ilchleas agus a n-antlás.[19]

An carnadh nó an liostáil sin 'eigríonnachta', tá blas láidir na seanmóireachta air agus bhí sé á léamh, ní foláir, go fonnmhar ag aos léinn agus uaisle na hÉireann gur dhaingnigh sé sa seanchreideamh iad.

Ach b'iad na 'perfidious Machiavellian friars at Louvain' a sheol isteach an ré nua dáiríre, agus a dhearbhaigh arís an teanga shinseartha mar theanga choitianta na hÉireann. Flaithrí Ó Maoil Chonaire (1560-1629), ar de mhuintir Uí Maoil Chonaire é a bhíodh ina n-ollaimh agus ina bhfilí ag muintir Uí Chonaire agus ag Mac Diarmada Chonnacht, bhí Flaithrí ar bhunaitheoirí Choláiste na mBráthar nÉireannach i Lobháin, agus bhí sé gníomhach i gcúrsaí eaglasta agus polaitíochta na haimsire – agus ina anamchara ag Aodh Ruadh Ó Domhnaill. Deir Wadding go raibh sé 'per Anglos proscriptus'. Bhí tógáil agus oiliúint na mbard in Éirinn aige sula ndeachaigh sé go dtí an Spáinn agus le sagartacht, agus bhí sé ar feadh a shaoil ina throdaí buansheasmhach ar son chúis na nGael agus ar son chúis an tseanchreideamh. D'fhoilsigh sé dhá leabhar Laidine agus scríobh sé Teagasc Críostaí i nGaeilge atá ar caomhnú i lámhscríbhinn.[20] Ach b'é an saothar ba

ar sheanchuimhne dhoiléir, b'fhéidir, ach scéal san am céanna a dheimhníonn buanna samhlaíochta mhuintir na hÉireann. Agus tar éis an tsaoil, nach gné bhunúsach den stair an cumas sin samhlaíochta agus ealaíon? Agus is doiligh liom a shamhlú gur chuir an s-préitiríteach as a bheag nó a mhór don Chéitinneach.

Sholáthraigh an Céitinneach dhá théacs mhóra eile a bhfuil a dtábhacht féin leo. In *Eocharsciath an Aifrinn* chosain sé Aifreann an tseanchreidimh in aghaidh na bProtastunach a dhearbhaigh gur sacrailéid agus diamhasla a bhí ann. Dealraíonn sé gur ag scríobh don chléir Chaitliceach a bhí sé, agus tá béim ann ar leanúnacht theagasc an tseancheidimh agus ar údarás an Scrioptúir. Scríobh sé fosta leabhar mór ar an bhás, mar a bhí *Trí Bhiorghaoithe an Bháis*. Leabhar toirtiúil é seo a bhfuil suas le céad agus fiche míle focal ann, agus aghaidh a thabhairt ann i nGaeilge chlasaiceach na linne ar cheist de na ceisteanna sin a bhí ina ábhar mór dioscúrsa san am agus téama á chaibidil aige a bhfuil infheistiú ag an uile dhuine ann. Agus bhíodh an duine daonna sna blianta sin ag bású go hóg go minic, mar bhíodh

thábhachtaí a rinne sé ó thaobh na Gaeilge de na *Desiderius* nó *Sgáthán an Chrábhaidh*. Tiontó ata ann ar bhunleabhar Spáinnise a foilsíodh i 1515. Is mó d'athchoiriú é ná tiontó, áfach, agus arís agus arís eile sánn sé dréachataí dá chuid féin isteach sa chuntas agus ó línte 3,411 go 5,050 nuair a ionsaíonn sé feal-súnacht agus dearcadh nua 'na n-eiriceach' nó 'na madraí gaoithe' mar a thugann sé ar lucht an leas-aithe, agus é ag cosaint seasaimh airteagail an tseanchreidimh. Is mac an diabhail aige 'Lútéur lobhtha mhac Lusifeir' mar go mbíodh 'deamhan do ghnáth ag imeacht ar mháthair Liútair agus gurb uaidh do ghlac sí Liútar mar thoircheas'[21] agus bhí Cailbhin 'chomh salach agus chomh madrúil sin agus gurb í pian phoiblí fuair sé trés an bpeaca sodamach do níodh do ghnáth .i. tré choimhriachtain ré buach-aillí, creachaireacht do dhéanamh ar a dhroim le hiarann dearg'.[22]

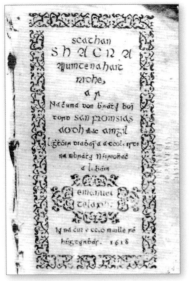

Aodh Mac Aingil, *Scáthán Shacramuinte na hAithridhe* (Lobháin, 1618).
© Institiúid Mhíchíl Uí Chléirigh.

Tá dhá rud le tabhairt faoi deara anseo. Tá, ar tús, an saothar seo a fhoilsiú mar leabhar, nó bhí bráithre seo Lobháin tar eis clólann dá gcuid féin a cheannacht agus bhí ar a gcumas téacsanna crábhaidh a sholáthar agus a sheoladh ar ais go hÉirinn.[23] Nó bhí, dar leo, ré na lamhscríbhinní thart agus ré fhoilsiú na leabhar i láthair.[24] Bhaineadh Liútar agus an tAthleasú creidimh feidhm éifeachtach as leabhair agus as duilleacháin lena dtuiscintí a chur abhaile ar an phobal i gcoitinne agus ba léir gur acra teicneolaíochta é an fhoilsitheoireacht a raibh fónamh ar leith ann. Thuig Proin-siasaigh Lobháin an méid sin agus ní raibh leisc orthu dul ina bhun. Agus chomh maith leis sin, tá simpliú á dhéanamh ag Ó Maoil Chonaire ar an teanga, gnéithe den stolpacht agus den chúirialtacht á bhaint di aige, agus an t-ábhar mar sin á fhágáil níos sochaideartha ag cách.

Imeasc na mbráithre féin, áfach, bhí tús áite ag Giolla Bhríde Ó hEodhasa (b. 1614) i ngnó seo na foilsitheoireachta, agus i simpliú na teanga. Bhí an cúlra céanna aige a bheag ná a mhór agus a bhí ag Flaithrí Ó Maoil Chonaire. Bhain sé le teaghlach a raibh cúram na filíochta agus an léinn orthu i gContae Fhear Manach agus bhí tabhairt suas na scol air. Is go Douai a chuaigh sé ar tús agus is ansin a

ghnóthaigh se céim MA i samhradh na bliana 1607. Chuaigh sé isteach in Ord San Proinsias i Lobháin, agus rinneadh sagart de i 1609, agus bhí sé ina ghairdian sa choláiste sin nuair a fuair sé bás i 1614.[25] D'fhoilsigh sé *An Teagasc Críostaidhe* in 1611 in Antwerp agus leabhar a bhí ann a raibh tionchar ollmhór aige ar fhorbairt phrós an chrábhaidh. Éiríonn le Ó hEodhasa téarmaíocht chuí a aimsiú, gluaiseacht réidh stíle a shrianadh agus íomhanna tíriúla a chruthú. Coincheapa agus tu-iscintí atá dorcha agus doiléir go maith agus a bhíonn ina h-ábhair diospóireachta agus imreasáin ag scolairí agus ag diagairí, éiríonn leis a leithéidí sin a chur i láthair sa tslí is go dtig leis an léitheoir nó an éisteoir seilbh a fháil orthu mar go bhfuil na híomhanna tógtha as an saol atá thart orainn. Seo Ó hEodhasa ag míniú na Trionóide:

Cuireann daoine foghlamtha an tAthair i gcosúlacht le tobar óna mbeadh sruth ag si-leadh chun locha, an Mac i gcosúlacht leis an sruth féin, agus an Spiorad Naomh i gcosúlacht leis an loch. Óir de réir mar is é an t-aon uisce amháin a bhíonn sa tobar a shileann chun an tsrutha agus ón sruth chun an locha, mar sin is aon diagacht amháin, aon nádúr agus aon substaint atá san Athair agus sa Mhac agus sa Spiorad Naomh. Ón Athair téann an diagacht seo ionsar an Mhac agus uathu araon ionsar an Spiorad Naomh. An tAthair mar sin tobar na diagachta, níor gineadh agus ní dhearnadh riamh é ná níor tháinig ó neach eile. An Mac fós ní dhearnadh ariamh é ach tá sé ann riamh gan tús gan deireadh, mar atá an tAthair. Gid-hea is ón Athair a gineadh é agus a ghintear é. An Spiorad Naomh leis, ní dhearnadh agus níor gineadh é, gidhea thainig agus tagann ón Athair agus ón Mhac in éineacht.[26]

Bhí bás Ghiolla Bhríde Uí hEodhasa ina thubaiste ollmhór, dar le hAodh Mac Cathmhaoil, agus chro-naigh se uaidh go mór é. Sa saothar mór a scríobh Mac Cathmhaoil *Scáthán Shacramuinte na hAithrid-he,* ina luann sé:

mo dhearthair chroí … is mór a bhí faoi a scríobh a rachadh i leas anma agus in onóir shaolta don náisiún dá mhaireadh, ach faraor, tré fheirg Dé leis an bpobal peacach goireadh air in am a thoraidh agus i dtosach a saothair a chur i gcló agus sul ráinig leis sinni a theagasc i dteanga ár máthar ionas go dtiocfadh linn ní éigin a rachadh i leas na n-anamacha a scríobh ó nach ligtear dúinn tré bhoirbe an pherseacuision foircheadal do dhéanamh ó bhéal.[27]

Agus má b'fhíor don tuairisc a thug Pádraig Modartha Mac Giolla Eoin do Sir Toby Caulfield bhí taithí áirithe ar an 'persecution' sin ag Aodh Mac Cathmhaoil féin nó de réir na tuairisce sin thug Torlough McCrodyn seanmóir 'in the woods of Loughensolyn' agus bhí ina chuideachta ansin 'two other friars who are his consorts. One is Hugh McKale (.i. Aodh Mac Cathmhaoil), born in Evagh or Lecale and Henry O'Mellan'.[28]

Giolla Brighde Ó hEodhasa, (d. 1614), *An teagasg Críosdaidhe* (Antwerp, 1611; Louvain, 1614).© Institiúid Mhíchíl Uí Chléirigh

An leabhar a scríobh Aodh Mac Cathmhaoil, *Scáthán Shacramuinte na hAithridhe*, léiríonn sé arís an simpliú sin teanga ag feidhmiú, agus ó thaobh stíle de cloisim arís agus arís eile coiscéimeanna an tseanmóirí. Agus sa deireadh thiar is é an beartas atá ar bun aige nósanna agus cleachtais córa shacraimint na hAithrí a sholáthar don ghnáthphobal, mar a bhí déanta chomh héachtach sin beagán beag blianta roimh a am ag Cairdinéal Carlo Borromeo (1538-84), ardeapag Milan.[29]

B'éachtach agus ba fhadcheannach an beart acu é – ag Ó hEodhasa, ag Ó Maoil Chonaire, agus ag Mac Cathmhaoil ach go háirithe – nó bíodh gur cúrsaí staire nó cúrsaí crábhaidh a bhí idir chamáin acu bhí siad ag leagan amach dúshraith an tsaoil úir agus dúshraith liteartha Ghaeilge seo ár linne. Bhí siad sásta réidh cuibhreacha na sean a scaoileadh, muinín a chur i dteicneolaíocht nua na haimsire, agus aghaidh a thabhairt ar cheisteanna agus ar fhadhbanna an ama i láthair agus toradh a éileamh ar ghnáthmhuintir na tíre.

Nótaí

1 Féach sa chomhthéacs seo ach go háirithe C. Ó Maonaigh, 'Scríbhneoirí Gaeilge an seachtú h-aois déag', *Studia Hibernica*, ii (1962) pp 182-208; B. Ó Buachalla '*Annála Ríoghachta Éireann* agus *Foras Feasa ar Éirinn*: An Comhthéacs Comhaimseartha', *Studia Hibernica*, xxii-xxiii (1982-3), pp 59-105; Féach fosta B. Ó Doibhlin *Manuail de litríocht na Gaeilge*, faisicil ii (Baile Átha Cliath, 2006); idem *Manuail de Litríocht na Gaeilge*, faisicil iii (Baile Átha Cliath, 2007).

2 D. Ó Floinn, *An éigse ilcheasach* (Maynooth, 1953). Tá simpliú deanta agam ar an litriú. Is as *Sanasán Uí Chléirigh* dó. Tá an léargas is iontaofa, dar liom, ar shaol agus ar imeachtaí Uí Chléirigh ag B. Jennings, *Michael O'Cléirigh and his associates* (Dublin, 1936).

3 Féach Ó Maonaigh, 'Scríbhneoirí Gaeilge an seachtú h-aois déag'. p. 207. Is cóir a rá go raibh de gheanúlacht i Patrick Kavanagh gur admhaigh sé ina dhiaidh sin nach raibh feabhas ar bith mórán filíochta ar an dán sin aige ná feabhas ar bith staire ach oiread.

4 Féach ibid., p. 185.

5 Féach Jennings, *Michael O'Cléirigh and his associates*, passim.

6 E. Knott, '"O'Clery's Glossary" and its forerunners A note on glossary-making in medieval Ireland', in *Measgra i gcuimhne Mhichíl Uí Chléirigh* (Dublin, 1944), pp 65-69.

7 Féach P. Mac Aogáin, *Graiméir Ghaeilge na mBráthar Mionúr* (Baile Átha Cliath, 1968); S. de Napier *Comhréir agus Gramadach Ghaeilge Uladh i 1600* (Baile Átha Cliath, 2001).

8 Aodh Mac Aingil, *Scathán Shacramuinte na hAithridhe* eag. C. Ó Maonaigh (Baile Átha Cliath, 1952).

9 D. MacCulloch, *Reformation Europe's house divided, 1490-1700* (London, 2003), go háirithe pp 115-57.

10 Tá siad seo uilig (ach amháin Bullinger) luaite ag Flaithrí Ó Maoil Chonaire: *Desiderius otherwise called Sgathán an Chrábhaidh* eag. T. F. O'Rahilly (Dublin, 1955), línte 4159-63.

11 Tadhg Ó Cianáin, *The Flight of the Earls,* (ed. & trans.) P. Walsh (Dublin, 1916).

12 Chuir P. de Barra agus T. Ó Fiaich leagan taitneamhach nua-aimseartha faoin teideal *Imeacht na nIarlaí* ar fáil (Dub-

lin, 1972), maraon le nótaí cuimsitheacha.

13 Féach D. Conway, 'Guide to documents of Irish and British interest in Fondo Borghese', series 1, *Archivium Hibernicum,* xxiii (1960), pp 1-148; féach ach go háirithe mír 803, p. 58.

14 Ó Doibhlin, *Manuail de litríocht na Gaeilge,* ii, pp 186-95; Conway, 'Guide to documents in the Fondo Borghese'; series 1; féach ach go háirithe mír 803, p. 58.

15 Lughaidh Ó Cléirigh, *Beatha Aodha Ruaidh Uí Dhónaill,* (eds) C. Ó Lochlainn and P. Walsh (Dublin, 1957).

16 Féach ach go háirithe Ó Buachalla, '*Annála Ríoghachta Éireann* agus *Foras Feasa ar Éirinn*: An Comhthéacs Comhaimseartha', passim.

17 Maidir leis an Athbheochan Léinn féach Ó Doibhlin *Manuail de Litríocht na Gaeilge,* ii, pp 1-4.

18 Ibid., iii, pp 43-44.

19 B. Ó Doibhlin, 'Athléamh ar '*Trí Bhiorgha an Bháis*' in *Bliainiris,* vi (2009).

20 B'é Roibeard Mac Artúir, OFM (1571-1636) a d'fhág a chuid airgid 're haghaidh an cló Gaoidhlige agus neithe do chur a gcló do rachas a n-onóir do Dhia, a gclú dár naisíon agus d'ord San Proinsias'.

21 *Desiderius,* línte 3805-6. Tá nóta inspéise ar an fhrása sin 'ag imeacht ar' ag Ú. Ní Bheirn, 'Tábhacht na gcanúintí don Fhoclóireacht', *Meascra Uladh,* iii (Monaghan, 2004) lgh 207-20.

22 *Desiderius,* línte 3814-19.

23 Insíonn an *Dublin Courant* dúinn gur gabhadh 'three chests of Popish books' ar chéanna Bhaile Átha Cliath i 1724: féach J. Brady *Catholics and Catholicism in the eighteenth century-press* (Maynooth, 1965), p. 42.

24 Mar sin féin lean soláthar na lámhscríbhinní ar aghaidh go bisiúil sa bhaile in Éirinn agus ní féidir a shéanadh, is dóigh liom, gur traidisiún lámhscríbhinne é traidisiún liteartha na Gaeilge. Agus gheobhaidh tú go minic – arís is arís eile dáiríre – leabhair clóite seo Lobháin á gcoípeáil isteach sna lámhscríbhinní in Éirinn.

25 Féach Bonabhentura Ó hEodhasa, *An Teagasg Críosduidhe* eag. F. Mac Raghnaill (Dublin, 1976).

26 B. Ó Doibhlin, *Manuail de litríocht na Gaeilge,* iii, p. 69.

27 Aodh Mac Aingil, *Scáthan Shacramuinte na hAithridhe* eag. C. Ó Maonaigh (Dublin, 1952), línte 3080-3088.

28 *CSPI James I,* vol iv, pp 429-30.

29 D. MacCulloch, *Reformation Europe's house divided 1490-1700,* pp 410-7.

Foinsí Gaeilge Leath Chuinn: fuinneog ar an phlandáil

Máire Nic Cathmhaoil

Bíodh go raibh brú mór tubaisteach ar achan ghné de chóras na nGael sa chéad leath den tseachtú haois déag, tháinig bláthú ar chúrsaí litríochta agus léinn. Bhí litríocht don scoth á cumadh sa tréimhse sin sna réimeanna éagsúla. Tá *Annála Ríoghachta Éireann*,[1] *Foras Feasa ar Éirinn*,[2] *Cín Lae Uí Mhealláin*[3] agus dréachtaí staire agus seanchais eile againn, litríocht chráifeach, graiméir, foclóirí, beathaí na naomh agus dinnseanchas le fáil. Ar ndóigh, bhí ardchaighdeán filíochta á scríobh agus tá crá agus díshealbhú na nGael go minic mar phríomhábhar san fhilíocht sin. Ba é chéad leath na seachtú haoise déag ré órga na bProinsiasach, ar ndóigh, agus d'fhág siad rian buan ar shaol agus ar litríocht na hÉireann. Chomh maith le tithe nóibhíseacha agus coláistí a rialú agus diagacht agus fealsúnacht a theagasc, bhunaigh siad cineál institiúid staire agus léinn Éireannaigh i Lobháin agus in áiteanna eile ar an mhór-roinn. Cheap siad scéimeanna le gach blúire a bhain le stair na hÉireann i leabharlanna na hEorpa agus in Éirinn a aimsiú, a mheas agus a chur i gcló. Chuir siad ar fáil cuid mhaith buntéacsaí a chum siad féin agus aistriúcháin ar chuid de théacsaí clasaiceacha na hEorpa. Bhí Proinsiasaigh Lobháin go háirithe ag foilsiú leabhar Gaeilge agus á scaipeadh i measc na nGael a bhí ar deoraíocht ar an mhór-roinn.[4] Tá flúirseacht foinsí Gaeilge ann mar sin ina léirítear dearcadh agus meon na nGael ar imeachtaí comhaimseartha. Tá cuid de na foinsí Gaeilge a scríobhadh i Leath Chuinn sa tréimhse sin idir plandáil Uladh agus léirscrios Chromaill faoi chaibidil san alt seo. D'ionannaíodh an lucht léinn le Leath Chuinn nó Leath Mogha in áit chúige ar bith – rud a bhí ríshoiléir le linn *Iomarbhágh na bhFileadh* (c. 1618).[5] Sníonn plandáil Uladh trí fhoinsí Gaeilge agus litríocht na Gaeilge ó aimsir na plandála ar aghaidh. Chaill muintir an tuaiscirt na taoisigh mhóra sin a ba bhun le córas na nGael le linn Imeacht na nIarlaí dhá bhliain roimhe sin agus chuir plandáil Uladh deireadh le cibé dóchas a bhí ann go bpillfeadh na taoisigh chéanna faoi lán cumhachta arís. Thuig Mícheál Ó Cléirigh agus scríbhneoirí eile *Annála Ríoghachta Éireann* go maith gurbh é imeacht na n-iarlaí sin agus éirí-amach Chathair Uí Dhochartaigh (1608) a thug

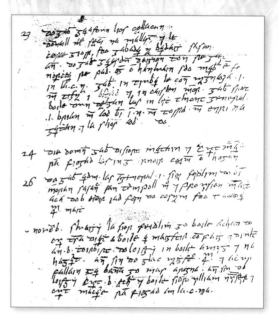

Leathanach ó *Chín Lae Uí Mhealláin*.
© Boole Library, NUI, Cork

faill do rialtas na Sasana plandáil Uladh a chur ar obair. Mar a scríobh Ó Cléirigh faoi éirí amach Uí Dhochartaigh sna 1630í le bua an iarchoinn:

Bá de eiccin, ⁊ do imtheacht na n-iarladh att-rubhramar, tainicc a n-domhnus ⁊ a n-dúthaigh, a f-forba, & a f-fearann, a n-dúine, ⁊ a n-diongnadha, a c-cuanta caomhthur-carthacha, ⁊ a n-inbeara iaiscc iomdha do bhein do Gaoidhelaibh Chóiccidh Uladh, ⁊ a t-tabhairt ina f-fiadhnaisi do eachtair chenélaibh ⁊ a c-cor-somh for athchur, ⁊ for ionnarbadh in aile criochaibh comhaigthibh go ro éccsat a n-ermhór.[6]

Is foinse an-tábhachtach staire í filíocht na seachtú haoise déag ina dtáispeántar dearcadh an aosa léinn ar chúrsaí na linne sin. Ní mór an gaol speisialta siombóiseach idir an lucht léinn agus an t-uasalaicme Gaelach a chur san áireamh agus filíocht na tréimhse á léamh againn. Bhí na filí i gcroílár an chórais traidisiúnta agus iad ag brath ar phatrúnacht an uasalaicme le slí bheatha rathúil a bhaint amach. Ar ndóigh, bhí na taoisigh go mór i

204

dtuilleamaí na bhfilí agus an ról a bhí acu i mbuanú agus i neartú na taoiseachta. Ní ábhar iontais é mar sin gur chaoin na filí imeacht na dtaoiseach thar lear agus an phlandáil a tháinig ina diaidh mar bhí siad go bunúsach ag caoineadh deireadh a réime féin. Is sa chomhthéacs seo a chaithfimid freagairt na bhfilí ar phlandáil Uladh a léamh. B'ionann na hathruithe a lean Imeacht na nIarlaí – coigistiú a ndúichí agus Plandáil Uladh – agus bás d'Éirinn, dar le Fear Flatha Ó Gnímh (a d'fhreastail mar fhile ar theaghlaigh mhóra oirthear Uladh):[7]

> Ionann is éag na Fódla
> Ceilt a córa 's a creidimh,
> Táire a saormhac 's a saoithe,
> Más fíor laoithe ná leitir.[8]

Ba mhinic an port céanna á bhualadh aige féin agus ag go leor de na filí eile le linn na mblianta éidearfa sin. Tá againn dánta mar *Tairnig Éigse fhuinn Ghaoidheal* leis an fhile chéanna ina chaoineann sé deireadh ré na bhfilí agus na filíochta in Éirinn:

> Tairnig éigse fuinn Ghaoidheal;
> adhbhar suadh ná saordhraoidheadh
> Ní mhair díobh – damhna cumhadh –
> Ná díol anma ollamhan.[9]

Is marbhna é ar fhilí móra agus ar theaghlaigh léannta na hÉireann agus is iad na fodhaoine atá i gceannas anois is ciontaí le himeacht na héigse, dar le Ó Gnímh:

> Thug fógra dhámh an domhain
> Is col d'fhagháil d'ealadhain
> Fuil chrannda dá cora i gcion
> 's na fola arda íseal.[10]

Ar ndóigh, chuaigh plandáil Uladh trom ar na filí. Ní hamháin gur chaill siad cuid de na patrúin a ba thábhachtaí agus an ról agus an stádas a bhí acu sa chóras traidisiúnta ach chaill go leor filí dá raibh acu féin. Cé gur éirigh le roinnt acu greim a choinneáil ar a gcuid dúichí faoin chóras úr is dócha gur chuir focail Fhearghail Óig Mhic an Bhaird síos ar chúinsí pearsanta na bhfilí agus na dtaoiseach i gcoitinne ag an am:

> Do choilleas onóir m'anma,
> 's mo bhuar 's mo lucht leanamhna,
> 's mo dhuthchas – gidh dál pudhair –
> i gClár chlúmhchas Chonchubhair.[11]

Sior Féilim Ó Néill. © BL

Chaill sé an sealúchas a bhí aige i dTír Chonaill am éigin i ndiaidh na bliana 1616 ach mar is léir óna línte thuas chaill sé níba mhó ná talamh de dheasca na plandála.[12] Chum Mac an Bhaird, a raibh Brían na Múrtha Ó Ruairc, Toirealach Luineach Ó Néill, Aodh Mhag Aonghusa, Cormac Ó hEadhra agus Cúchonnacht Mag Uidhir i measc na bpatrún a bhí aige, chum sé na línte thuas i ndiaidh dó teacht go dtí an Ísiltír agus é ag cuartú tacaíochta ó Fhlaithrí Ó Maoil Chonaire, ardeaspag Thuama.[13]

Ní amháin gur athraigh plandáil Uladh timpeallacht pholaitíoch, eacnamaíoch, shóisialta agus intleachtúil an aosa léinn ach rinneadh athruithe móra ar an timpeallacht fhisiciúil dá bharr. Tá marbhna spéisiúil ann a scríobh file gan ainm ar bhás Néill Ghairbh Uí Dhomhnaill[14] sa bhliain 1626 ina luaitear cuid de na hathruithe sin a tháinig isteach leis an Phlandáil:

> Foithre a sealg i n-a sráidibh,
> a hoirecht n-a n-acáidibh,
> a taoisigh gan treabha a bprémh,
> cneadha an laoigh-sin a leithsgél.[15]

Maíonn an file seo gur tharla plandáil Uladh mar gur cneádh Niall Garbh – b'fhéidir go raibh cuid den cheart aige sa dóigh is gurbh airsean a bhí cuid den locht. Fear páirte na Sasanach a bhí in Niall Garbh le linn Chogadh na Naoi mBliana, ar ndóigh, agus chuir a chuid cealgaireachta go mór le treascairt Ghaeil Uladh a d'ullmhaigh an bealach don phlandáil.[16]

205

'Imeacht na nIarlaí'.
© Ionad An Léinn
Éireannaigh, Teach Inse

Caoineann Lochlainn Ó Dálaigh na hathruithe céanna i gceann de na dánta is cáiliúla a scríobhadh ar thionchar na plandála *Cáit ar ghabhadar Gaoidhil?*[17] Cuireann sé síos ar mhilleadh na timpeallachta dúchasaí le tógáil na bhfoirgneamh agus na mbailte úra agus leis na hiarrachtaí a rinne na plandóirí an talamh a thabhairt chun míntíreachais. Tá anois 'dorchfhoithre sealg 'na sráidibh',[18] 'sliabh 'na gortoibh gabhála'[19] is an t-ord nádúrtha trína chéile mar go bhfuil:

Aonuighe a n-áitibh sealga,
Sealga ar slighthibh suaitheanda,
Creasa tar fhaithche d'fhál air,
Gan dál ghraifne fá a ngruadhaibh.[20]

Scriostar áiteanna cónaithe na n-uaisle, 'bruidhne flaithfhear'[21] agus tógtar 'líne lios bhfrosuaidneach bhfionn'[22] ina n-áit. Is spéisiúil léamh an fhile ar an tionchar trom síceolaíoch a d'fhág cúrsaí comhaimseartha ar na Gaeil. Deir sé gur ghoid anfhorlann agus éagóir na plandála na hanamacha uafa agus gur fágadh laochra na nGael leathbheo:

Daoire na mbreath bhíos orra,
Gadaidh asda a n-anmanna;
Laoich ghleogharbha ghuirt Lughaidh,
Cuirp bheómharbha a mbaramhuil.[23]

Léiríonn Ó Dálaigh an turraing, an mearbhall agus an dobrón a d'fhág athruithe tobanna na plandála

ar na Gaeil. Tá cúrsaí chomh holc sin go bhfuil an file cinnte gur pionós Dé atá ann agus go gcaithfidh na Gaeil pheacacha maithiúnas a iarraidh. Taobh istigh de dhá scór bliain, áfach, fágann údar an dáin 'An Síogaí Rómhánach'[24] an locht go daingean ar Rí Séamas I:

I ndiaidh na mná seo tháinig Séamas.
Níor thuar faoiseamh do chríocha Fhéilim,
An fear do thógaibh a bpór as a bhfréamhaibh
Is d'órdaigh a dtalamh do thamhas le téadaibh,
Do chuir Saxanaigh i leabaidh na nGaol nglan
Is *transplantátion* ar chách le chéile.[25]

Cuireann sé in iúl go bhfuil sé sínte ar thuama Aoidh Uí Néill agus Ruaidhrí Uí Dhomhnaill in Eaglais San Pietro in Montorio sa Róimh agus é ag cumadh an dáin seo.[26] Níl ainm an fhile ar eolas againn ach is cinnte gur scríobhadh an dán idir mí Mheithimh 1650 agus mí Mhárta 1653 nuair a básaíodh Sior Féilim Ó Néill.

Tá foinse thábhachtach Ghaeilge Uladh eile againn ón tréimse chéanna, a scríobh Ultach mar atá, é *Cín Lae Uí Mheallláin*. Cuntas reatha ar imeachtaí éirí amach na nGael 1641-47 i gCúige Uladh agus i gCúige Laighean atá ann. Glactar leis gurbh é Toirealach Ó Mealláin, sagart Proinsiasach as Tír Eoghain, á scríobh. Cuireann leathanaigh thosaigh *Chín Lae Uí Mheallláin* na hUltaigh sin a bhí fágtha i ndiaidh Imeacht na nIarlaí os ár gcomhair agus iad ag athghábháil a dtailte dúchasacha: ghlac Féilim Ó Néill Charlemont agus Dún Geanuinn ar an tríú lá is fiche de Dheireadh Fómhair; gabhadh Iúr Cinn Trá ag Sior Conn Mag Aonghusa; tháinig Ruaidhrí Mag Uidhir i réim arís i bhFear Manach; ghlac Clann Uí Anluain athsheilbh ar Thóin re Gaoith is ghabh Clann Uí Chuinn agus Cormac Ó hÁgáin Muinseo, Muine Mór, Machaire Fiogad agus Béal Átha:

Do gabhadh Serlimont, agus tigherna an bhoile My Lord Caulfilld, agus a roibh ann ó sin síos. Do gabhadh Dún Genuinn, a chaptin, .i. Parcens, agus an boile ó sin síos le Raghnall Mac Domhnaill, .i. mac an Fhir Dorchae, mhic Eoin, etc., agus le Pád[raic] Modarra Ó Donn[gh]aoile; 's do gabhadh garasdún mór Muinseoigh, agus a shaighdiúirigh lasan ccaptin Toirdhealbhach Gruamdha Ua Coinne; 's do [gabhadh] cúirt Mí Lord Caulfilld a mBoile Í Dhonnghoile le Pád[raic] Modarra Ó Donnghoile, Captin.[27]

I gceann dhá lá gairid rinneadh máistrí Thír Eoghain agus Ard Mhacha de na Gaeil agus bhí codanna de Mhuineachán, d'Fhear Mánach, den Dún agus de Dhoire faoina smacht fosta. Milleadh go leor d'obair na plandála lena léarscáileana agus suirbhéanna. Cuireann Ó Mealláin síos go héifeachtach ar an chumhacht a mhothaigh na Sean-Ghaeil agus an bua acu in aon abairt amháin. Insítear dúinn gur ordaigh Sior Féilim:

… mart ramhur, meadur ime, agus ceithre sgill[inge] d'airgiod san mboili bhó ón Ghlas Dromuinn go Tulaigh Óg.[28]

Mar a chuireann forógra Sior Féilim in iúl, shíl na Sean-Ghaeil agus Ó Mealláin go raibh córas na nGael agus a chuid dlíthe agus nósanna i réim arís. Ní raibh, áfach, agus thug teacht Chromail agus an léirscrios a tharla dá bharr bráchbhuille do mheanmarca polaitaíochta na nGael ar feadh fada go leor.

Nótaí

1 *AFM,* (ed.) John O'Donovan (7 vols, Dublin, 1848-56).

2 Geoffrey Keating (Seathrún Céitinn), *Foras Feasa ar Éirinn: The History of Ireland* (4 vols, Dublin, 1902-14).

3 M. Nic Cathmhaoil, 'The seventeenth century text "Cín Lae Uí Mhealláin", with introduction, translation and notes' (D. Phil. Thesis, University of Ulster, 2006).

4 C. Mooney, 'St Anthony's College, Louvain', in N. Ó Muraíle (ed.), *Mícheál Ó Cléirigh, his associates and St Anthony's College, Louvain* (Dublin, 2008), pp 200-25.

5 J. Leerssen, *The Contention of the Bards (Iomarbhágh na bhFileadh) and its place in Irish political and literary history* (London, 1994).

6 *AFM*, vi, p. 2358.

7 B. Ó Doibhlin, *Manuail de litríocht na Gaeilge*, faisicil ii (Dublin, 2006), p. 236.

8 O. Bergin, *Irish bardic poetry* (Dublin, 1984), p. 115: *Beannacht ar anmain Éireann*, lines 5-8.

9 P. de Brún, B. Ó Buachalla and T. Ó Concheanainn (eds), *Nua-dhuanaire i* (Baile Átha Cliath, 1971), p. 1: *Éigse fhuinn Ghaoidheal*, línte 1-4.

10 Ibid., p. 2; *Éigse fhuinn Ghaoidheal*, línte 37-40.

11 B. Ó Doibhlin, *Manuail de litríocht na Gaeilge*, faisicil ii, p. 251: *Éist le m'éagnach, a fhir ghradh*, línte 9-12.

12 M. Ní Mhurchú and D. Breathnach, *1560-1781: Beathaisnéis* (Baile Átha Cliath, 2001), p. 56.

13 B. Ó Doibhlin, *Manuail de Litríocht na Gaeilge*, faisicil ii, p. 251.

14 P. Walsh, *Gleanings from Irish Manuscripts, chiefly of the Seventeenth Century* (Dublin, 1918): *Bean do lámhaigeadh Leith Cuinn*, pp 27-52.

15 Ibid., pp 34, 121-4.

16 B. Fitzpatrick, *Seventeenth-century Ireland: the war of religions* (Dublin, 1988), pp 23-24.

17 B. Ó Doibhlin, *Manuail de litríocht na Gaeilge*, faisicil ii, pp 245-7.

18 Ibid., p. 246: *Cáit ar ghabhadar Gaoidhil?*, líne 48.

19 Ibid., líne 52.

20 Ibid., línte 53-6.

21 Ibid., líne 57.

22 Ibid., líne 59.

23 Ibid., línte 69-72.

24 C. O'Rahilly, *Five seventeenth-century political poems* (Dublin, 1977), pp 12-32.

25 Ibid., p. 21: *An Síogaí Rómhánach*, línte 89-94.

26 Ibid., línte, 7-12.

27 M. Nic Cathmhaoil, 'The seventeenth century text "Cín Lae Uí Mhealláin", p. 1, línte 14-20.

28 Ibid., p. 3, línte 62-63.

'… the false and crafty bludsukkers, the Observauntes':
'… na súmairí bréagacha beartacha: na hObsarvaintigh'

Mícheál Mac Craith

Nuair a d'fhógair Annraoi VIII in Aibreán na bliana 1527 go raibh fadhb choinsiasa aige, imní air nach raibh sé pósta go bailí le Caitríona Aragon ar chor ar bith, thacaigh na Proinsiasaigh Obsarvainteacha go huile is go hiomlán leis an mbanríon. D'íoc siad go daor as an dílseacht seo, áfach. Nuair a d'éag Caitríona in Eanáir na bliana 1536, ní fhéadfaí beart a dhéanamh de réir a tola agus í a adhlacadh i séipéal Obsarvainteach toisc nach raibh teach ar bith fágtha acu i Sasana faoin am sin. Ach sula ndeachaigh an crú ar an tairne, d'éirigh le Francis Faber, proibhinsial na bProinsiasach i Sasana, cead a fháil sa bhliain 1534 chun fiosrú a oifigiúil thabhairt ar thithe an oird in Éirinn. Roimh imeacht dó gheall sé d'Eustace Chapuys, ambasadóir an impire i gcúirt Annraoi:

> … that he would brew up there all he could for preservation of the authority of the Holy See … in which he may do wonderful service, especially among the wild Irish, by whom these Cordeliers (Obsarvaintigh) are feared, obeyed and almost revered not only by peasants but by the lords who hold them in such reverence as to endure from them blows from a stick.[1]

Ar an drochuair níor tháinig aon eolas anuas chugainn faoi chuairt Faber ar Éirinn, ach dealraíonn sé go raibh rath ar an turas, arae bhí Proinsiasaigh na tíre seo chomh diongbháilte in aghaidh pholasaí reiligiúnda an rí is a bhí a macasamhal i Sasana. Is léir frustrachas na n-údarás leis na bráithre bochta i ráiteas Thomás Aagarde, oifigeach de chuid na corónach i mBaile Átha Cliath sa bhliain 1538, ráiteas atá mar cheannteideal leis an aiste seo. Mhéadaigh ar fhreasúra na bProinsiasach in imeacht na mblianta agus is eiseamláir cruthanta é den fheachtas a chothaigh an t-órd in Éirinn ar son an leasúcháin chreidimh Chaitlicigh gníomhréim Eoghain Uí Dhubhthaigh (c. 1530-90), fear a raibh cáil na seanmóireachta air agus a rialaigh proibhinse na hÉireann ar feadh trí bliana idir 1580-83. Bhain sé le clochar an Chábháin agus scríobh Donnchadh Ó Maonaigh an cuntas seo ar a chuid seanmóireachta i Lobháin sa bhliain 1617:

Antoin Gearnon (1610-c. 1677), *Parrthas an Anama* (Lobháin, 1645). © Institiúid Mhíchíl Uí Chléirigh

I ndeireadh gach seanmóra dá fhaid í cheana féin, thugadh sé uaidh achoimre ar an méid a bhí ráite aige i bhfoirm véarsaí deas-snoite Gaeilge, mar ní hámháin go raibh sé oilte i gceird na filíochta ach is mó fós a bhí sé arna theagasc ón Spiorad Naomh. Bhí sé go dian ar na heiricigh, á bhfeannadh i ndán agus i bprós, ach mar sin féin bhíodh anmheas air ag cuid mhaith acusan ba mhó a cháin sé i ngeall ar a mailís agus a n-earráidí, agus ba leasc leo aon ní a dhéanamh ina choinne i ngeall ar a bheatha chrábhaidh agus a dhíograis chreidimh, arae, murar thaitin leo ar fad an cineál beatha a thug sé isteach, ar a laghad bhí meas acu air.[2]

Níor tháinig ach dhá dhán leis an Dubhthach anuas chugainn, *A Bhanbha, is truagh do chor* agus *Léig dod chomórtas dúinn*. Ar éigean is achoimre ceachtar acu ar cheann dá sheanmóintí, ach ní lúide is díol spéise iad ar an nasc a dhéanann siad idir an concas Eilíseach agus an Reifirméisean. Sa chéad dán acu seo, *A Bhanbha is truagh do chor*, dán gearr seacht rann, deir an Dubhthach gur díol trua í Éire agus sluaite Saxan agus Albanach sa tóir uirthi. Mura mbíonn Éire dílis di féin agus

208

dá dúchas creidimh, ní bheidh inti ach 'Saxa óg'. Léiríonn an Proinsiasach an t-achrann creidimh in Éirinn mar choimhlint idir 'Caiptín Lúitéir 's Caiptín Cailbhín' ar láimh amháin agus 'Pádruig do ghénerál féin' ar an láimh eile. Nascann an file an creideamh a thóg Pádraig go hÉirinn fadó le feachtas an leasúcháin chreidimh Chaitlicigh. Chomh fada agus a bhain leis an Dubhthach de, níorbh fhéidir idirdhealú a dhéanamh idir an concas Eilíseach agus agus an Reifirméisean in Éirinn, ba dhá thaobh den bhonn céanna iad.[3]

Chum Ó Dubthaigh an dara dán, *Léig dod chomórtas dúinn*, sa bhliain 1578, dréacht fada a bhfuil naoi rann is ochtó ann. Fitear dhá théama le chéile sa dán seo, moladh na Maighdine Muire agus fogha fíochmhar faoi thriúr Éireannach a thréig an creideamh Caitliceach ar mhaithe le bheith ina n-easpaig in eaglais nua an stáit. Tá an chuid is binbí den ionsaí seo dírithe ar Mhaolmhuire Mac Craith, iarPhroinsiasach agus ardeaspag Protastúnach Chaisil (1571-1622). Éiríonn leis an údar an dá shnáth a thabhairt le chéile trí imeartas focal a dhéanamh ar ainm baiste nó ainm crábhaidh Mhic Craith, Maolmhuire. Ó thréig sé creidimh a dhúchais, ní dlite mar ainm dó feasta ach Maol gan Mhuire. Leis an gcodarsnacht seo idir Maolmhuire agus Maol gan Mhuire, éiríonn leis an bhfile béim a chur ar dheabhóid do Mhuire mar cheann de shaintréithe an Chaitliceachais. An té a thréigeann an Mhaighdean Mhuire, tréigfidh sé gnéithe riachtanacha eile den Chaitliceachas chomh maith.[4] Níl urraim ar bith ag cléir an chreidimh nua do Mhuire. Ní hamháin sin, ach dá dtabharfadh an Mhaighdean Bheannaithe cuairt ar chaisleán Bhaile Átha Cliath, ní chuirfí d'fháilte roimpi ach dorn sa phus.[5]

Díol spéise na véarsaí thuas sa mhéid go bhfágann an file an feannadh pearsanta ar a iarbhráthair i leataobh chun breithiúntas a thabhairt ar impleachtaí an Reifirméisean in Éirinn i gcoitinne. Trí thagairt a dhéanamh do chaisleán Bhaile Átha Cliath, lárionad na cumhachta gallda chomh maith le lárionad an chreidimh ghallda in Éirinn, déanann an Dubhthach ionannú idir an concas agus an Reifirméisean. Díol suntais freisin úsáid an Bhéarla sna véarsaí thuas agus gur focail iad a bhfuil bríonna diúltacha tarcaisneacha leo. Is léir go dtuigeann an Dubhthach go bhfuil impleachtaí polaitíochta agus cultúrtha ag baint leis an Reifirméisean chomh maith le himpleachtaí reiligiúnda, agus go dteastaíonn uaidh foláireamh dá réir sin a thabhairt dá lucht éisteachta. Má chiallaíonn an Reifirméisean

galldacht agus daoirse, ciallaíonn an Caitliceachas ar an gcuma chéanna Gaelachas agus saoirse. Teachtaireacht ghlé shoiléir atá á craobhscaoileadh ag an bProinsiasach, gan fiacail a chur ann.

Má bhí sainiú ar féiniúlacht Ghaelach ar bun ag na Proinsiasaigh sa cheathrú dheireanach den séú haois déag, creideamh Caitliceach agus cultúr á nascadh le chéile, díol suntais gur bhreathnaigh na húdaráis ar na bráithre bochta mar an freasúra ba threascraí in aghaidh pholasaí reiligiúnda agus concais na corónach in Éirinn. Má tá leagan áirithe de ról agus feidhm na bProinsiasach le feiceáil i scríbhinní Eoghain Uí Dhubthaigh, malairt ghlan agus frithíomhá na feidhme sin a fhaightear i saothar John Derricke, *The image of Irlande with discoverie of woodkarne* (Londain, 1581). Ní gá ach na véarsaí agus na nótaí imeallacha a sholáthraíonn sé i dteannta na ngearrthán adhmaid a léamh chun an fuath agus an imní a spreag na bráithre sna húdaráis a thuiscint:

The fryar he absolves the theefe from all his
former sinne,
And bids plague the princes frendes, if heaven he minde to winne.[6]

Má bhí Proinsiasaigh na hÉireann ag cur go tréan in aghaidh pholasaí pholait-reiligiúnda an stáit, is léir gur bhreathnaigh na húdaráis orthu mar cheann de na bacanna ba dhiongbháilte ar fheidhmiú an pholasaí chéanna sin.

Tháinig cor nua i scéal na bProinsiasach in Éirinn sa bhliain 1601 nuair a loisceadh mainistir na bProinsiasach i nDún na nGall go talamh. Ionad tábhachtach oiliúna do bhráithre óga ab ea an mhainistir seo agus buille trom do thodhchaí an oird in Éirinn ab ea an tubaiste seo. Maidir le deiseanna thar lear, ní raibh mórán measa ag an mbráthair bocht Flaithrí Ó Maoil Chonaire ar na hÍosánaigh a raibh an Coláiste Éireannach i Salamanca faoina stiúir. Sa bhliain 1604 scríobh Flaithrí chuig Francisco de Valdivieso, prócadóir ginearálta na nÍosánach, á mhíniú dó go raibh cosúlachtaí láidre idir cúrsaí teanga sa Spáinn agus cúrsaí teanga in Éirinn. Bhí dhá theanga in Éirinn, Gaeilge agus Béarla díreach faoi mar a bhí dhá theanga sa Spáinn, *castillano* agus *gallego*, iad á labhairt in dhá cheantar dhifriúla faoi seach. Ar an gcuma chéanna bhí Gaeilge á labhairt faoin tuath agus Béarla á labhairt sna bailte. Fiú dá bhféadfaí roinnt Gaeilge a chloisint san bailte, ar éigean a chloisfí Béarla ar bith faoin tuath. Dá gcuirfí sagart ó na bailte ag seanmóireacht faoin tuath, obair in aisce a bheadh ann toisc nach dtuigfeadh an pobal é. Bheadh a chuid seanmóireachta chomh doiléir le tairgreacht, 'tan obscuro como prophesia'.[7]

D'fhreagair na hÍosánaigh go raibh an Ghaeilge ar cheann de na teangacha ba dheacra ar domhan, agus fiú i measc na gcainteoirí ba líofa, nach raibh ach triúr as tríocha míle a raibh léamh agus scríobh na teanga acu. D'áitigh siad freisin gurbh é an Béarla teanga an dlí, teanga na bhforógraí, teanga an dioscúrsa phoiblí i gcoitinne, gur i mBéarla amháin a dhéanfaí rud ar bith a raibh tábhacht ag baint leis.[8] Nuair a chuirtear san áireamh an cháil a bhí ar na hÍosánaigh i gcoitinne maidir le teangacha iasachta a fhoghlaim agus áiseanna foghlama a sholáthar, agus bhreathnaigh siad air seo mar ghné riachtanacha dá straitéis mhisinéireachta sa Domhan Nua, is deacair an drogall a bhí ar Íosánaigh na hÉireann i dtaobh na Gaeilge a thuiscint. B'fhéidir gurbh é an teannas eitneach idir na Sean-Ghaill agus na Gaeil a thug ar Thomas White, reachtaire an Choláiste Éireannaigh i Salamanca, neamhshuim a dhéanamh den Ghaeilge, ach dealraíonn sé gur ghoill an dearcadh seo go mór ar Fhlaithrí Ó Maoil Chonaire. Má bhí an leasúchán creidimh Caitliceach le dul chun cinn a dhéanamh in Éirinn, ní fhéadfaí faillí a dhéanamh sa teanga a bhí á labhairt ag formhór an phobail. Ní raibh ach an teip i ndán do bheartas tréadach a d'fhéachfadh le teachtaireacht Thríonta a chur i bhfeidhm in Éirinn d'uireasa na Gaeilge. Má bhí Proinsiasaigh óga na hÉireann le hoiliúint thar lear, ba léir don iarollamh file nach mbeadh an coláiste Éireannach i Salamanca sásúil ar aon bhealach.

Má bhí cúrsaí oiliúna ag déanamh imní do Fhlaithrí Ó Maoil Chonaire ar an mór-roinn, bhí an saol in Éirinn ag éirí níos déine do Chaitlicigh de bharr an fheachtais a thionscain an stát in aghaidh an chreidimh sa tréimhse 1605-07, sa Pháile ach go háirithe. Tháinig na Proinsiasaigh faoi bhrú chomh maith le cách, mar is léir on litir seo a leanas a scríobh Sir John Davies, Ard-Aighne na hÉireann, chuig Robert Cecil, Viscount Cranbourne, 6 Eanáir 1605:

> In the meantime begs liberty to give his opinion touching the matters of religion, which is that there will be no need of any more laws to make the obstinate gentlemen of the Pale conformable, than such as are in force already, if the bishops will only perform their duties; for if they will excommunicate all such as will not come to church, the common law will imprison them without bail. This is much better than the censure of the High Commission, where there was much abuse and corruption, to the reproach of the Protestant religion and dishonour of the State. As for the priests and Jesuits, the Government desires only a proclamation to banish them, which they themselves expect, and only wait for the publishing of. For within these few weeks one of the friars of Multfernon, in Westmeath, came to the castle of Dublin to visit his fellows imprisoned by the Lord Deputy for boldly erecting a monastery and college of friars, though it was within the Pale; and being stayed by the constable, and asked 'Hoe dare he come to the King's castle?' his answer was, 'That he presumed he might come to any place in the kingdom until the proclamation of their banishment were made, which they expected shortly, and then they would willingly depart the realm.' If, however, they should not depart upon the proclamation, the Government doubts not (as Sir John formerly wrote) but they should make their persons liable to the penal laws of England, which banish them out of England and all other the King's dominions and make them traitors if they return into England or any other of the King's dominions.[9]

D'eisigh Séamas I forógra díbeartha na cléire, 4 Iúil 1605:

> … he declares, publishes and proclaims, that it is his will and commandment that all Jesuits, seminary priests and all other priests whatsoever, made and ordained by any authority derived or pretended to be derived from the See of Rome, shall, before the 10th day of December next, depart out of the kingdom of Ireland. And that no Jesuit, seminary priest, or other priest ordained by foreign authority, shall from and after the 10th of December repair or return into that kingdom upon pain of his high displeasure, and upon such further pain and penalty as may justly be inflicted on them by the laws and statutes of that realm. And upon the like pain, he expressly forbids all his subjects within that kingdom to receive or relieve any such Jesuit, seminary priest, or other priest who, after the said 10th day of December,

shall remain in that realm or return to the same or any part thereof. And if any such Jesuit, seminary priest, or other priest shall continue wilfully to abide in that kingdom after the said day, or shall voluntarily repair or return into the kingdom, or if any subject shall receive or relieve any Jesuits or priests, in contempt of this proclamation, then all governors, sheriffs, justices of peace, sovereigns, portreeves, constables, and all other loyal subjects, are directed to use their best diligence and endeavours to apprehend and imprison all such offenders.[10]

Agus cúinsí na tíre chomh corraithe sin, ní hiontas ar bith é nach raibh Proinsiasaigh na hÉireann in inmhe caibidil an phroibhinse a thionól sa bhliain 1605. Tionóladh caibidil ghinearálta an oird i dToledo na Spáinne mí na Bealtaine an bhliain dár gcionn agus ceapadh Flaithrí Ó Maoil Chonaire mar mhinistir proibhinsil ar bhráithre bochta na hÉireann. Bíodh gur nós an ministir proibhinsil a thoghadh ag caibidlí na bproibhinsí, bheartaigh an ginearál nua, Archangelo Gualterio da Messina, gur mhithid an gnás agus an ceart a shárú i ngeall ar thoscaí urghnácha na hÉireann. Rinne sé amhlaidh d'ainneoin agóidí na dtoscairí Éireannacha a d'áitigh nár chóir a gcearta tofa a bhaint díobh. Ceist phrionsabail seachas col pearsanta le Flaithrí ba bhun leis na hagóidí ach bhí fuar acu. Toisc go raibh toirmeasc curtha ag na Sasanaigh ar Ó Maoil Chonaire filleadh ar Éirinn, d'ainmnigh sé Muiris Ó Duinnshléibhe (Muiris Ultach) mar ionadaí thar a cheann agus sheol ar ais abhaile é. Níorbh fhada i mbun a chúraim nua dó gur scríobh Flaithrí chuig Pilib III na Spáinne agus cead á lorg aige chun coláiste a bhunú i Lobháin d'fhonn Proinsiasaigh óga na hÉireann a oiliúint don tsagartóireacht. Fritheadh an cead agus scríobh an rí ina thaobh chuig Albert, ard-diúca na hÍsiltíre Spáinní, 21 Meán Fómhair 1606. D'eisigh an Pápa Pól V bulla bunaithe 3 Aibreán 1607, agus bhog an chéad chomhluadar isteach an mhí dár gcionn. Leis an gcinneadh seo d'éirigh leis an bproibhinsial an imní a bhí air faoin gcoláiste Éireannach i Salamanca a dhíbirt. Bhí clú agus cáil ar Ollscoil Lobháin mar cheanncheathrú intleachtúil an léasúcháin chreidimh Chaitlicigh i dtuaisceart na hEorpa, agus ina theannta sin bhí pobal Éireannach bunaithe cheana féin thart ar an mBruiséil. Anuas air sin is maith a thuig Ó Maoil Chonaire go raibh an Spáinn le tamall ag breathnú ar lion

'Dochum Glóire Dé agus Onóra na hÉireann', príomhdhoras Choláiste San Antaine, Lobháin.
© Coláiste San Antaine, Lobháin

mór na n-imirceach Éireannach sa tír mar fhadhb phráinneach nár mhór a réiteach gan mhoill. Is ag brú ar an doicheall a bheadh an proibhinsial dá n-iarrfadh sé cead coláiste nua a bhunú i Salamanca féin. Bhí de bhua breise ag Lobháin go raibh sé faoi dhlínse na Spáinne ach fada go maith ó Madrid ag an am céanna.

D'ainneoin an chlú a thabhaigh feachtas foilsitheoireachta Choláiste San Antaine Lobháin i stair litríochta na Gaeilge, díol spéise nach bhfuil tagairt ar bith do thogra dá leithéid sna cáipéisí is túisce a bhaineann leis an gcoláiste.[11] An chéad phíosa lítríochta a d'eascair as Lobháin go bhfios dúinn, níor bhain sé leis na Proinsiasaigh ar chor ar bith, ach is dán é a chum Richard Weston am éigin idir 9 Samhain 1607 agus 28 Feabhra 1608:

Beir mo beanocht go Dún Dalck
Fear rachus go tír Ó Néill
Tabhair tall mo beanocht fós
Do cine mo bean is dó féin.

Má déara Mairgread anois
As olc na rin mé fan,
Dar mo briathar tá breug
Is fearr Í Néill ná mo bean …

Do gheibh mise aig Í Néill
Mass inné is *Mass* inniu,
Ní déara Mineistér liom,
A Ristird Buistiún *Come to Church*.

Ní déara mé gur Pápa
Air eagluis Dé an Rígh,
Ní tiucfa proitestún asteach
In mo theach a gabháil *Priest*.[12]

Údar mór díospóireachta an dán macarónach seo a nascann tacaíocht d'Aodh Mór Ó Néill le dílseacht don chreideamh Caitliceach. D'ainneoin uaignes an fhile i ndiaidh an bhaile agus a mhuintire, is fearr go mór fada leis an deoraíocht féin toisc gur féidir leis a chreideamh a chleachtadh ar a shuaimhneas, gan imní dá laghad air faoi bhagairt na géarleanúna. Ba cheannaí saibhir é ó Dhún Dealgan Weston a d'éirigh chomh cairdiúil sin le hAodh Ó Néill gur chabhraigh sé leis chun an cime Aodh Ruadh Ó Domhnaill a shaoradh ó chaisleán Bhaile Átha Cliath. Fós féin nuair a d'éirigh Ó Néill amach go follasach in aghaidh na banríona sa bhliain 1595, choinnigh Weston an rialtas ar an eolas faoi líon saighdiúirí Uí Néill. Bíodh is go raibh Sir Geoffrey Fenton, an rúnaí stáit, thar a bheith buíoch as faisnéis Weston, bhí riarthóirí eile a cheap nach raibh ann ach 'cunning dissembler'. Má cheap Fenton go raibh Weston ag cur dallamullóg ar Ó Néill, thar-

'Bráthair Proinsiasach', Peter Paul Reubens (1577-1640).

lódh gur ar Fenton féin a bhí sé á dhéanamh. Nuair a bheartaigh sé dul i dteannta na n-iarlaí chuig an mór-roinn sa bhliain 1607, ní féidir bheith lánchinnte faoi na cúiseanna a thug air teacht ar an gcinneadh sin. D'fhéadfaimis glacadh le smaointe an dáin scun scan, gan amhras dá laghad orainn faoi dhílseacht Weston don chreideamh agus d'Ó Néill araon. Má bhí sé ina Thadhg an dá thaobh tráth, áfach, b'fhéidir go raibh sé tar éis filleadh ar a chéad dílseacht. B'fhéidir leis gur mheas sé gurbh fhearr rith maith ná drochsheasamh, agus gurbh eagal leis go n-íocfadh sé go daor as an dílseacht a léirigh sé d'Ó Néill tráth dá bhfanfadh sé sa bhaile, nó nach bhféadfadh sé a chreideamh a chleachtadh gan bhaol. Tharlódh freisin go raibh sé i bpóca an rialtais an t-am ar fad agus gur imigh sé thar lear d'aon ughaim chun leanúint den spiadóireacht ar iarla Thír Eoin. Tharlódh freisin nárbh é Weston údar an dáin chor ar bith, ach gur aor atá ann ar a mhídhílseacht do na Gaeil agus ar an gcur i gcéill a bhí ar bun aige.

Tharla bearna ceithre bliana idir teacht na bProinsiasach go Lobháin agus céadfhoilseachán na mbráithre sa bhliain 1611. Níor mhiste saothar Thaidhg Uí Chianáin, *Turas na nIarladh as Éirinn*

a cheadú más áil linn léargas níos soiléire a fháil ar na céimeanna a spreag na bráithre bochta i dtreo na foilsitheoireachta. 21 Deireadh Fómhair 1607, chuir Flaithrí Ó Maoil Chonaire agus Roibéard Chamberlain (Mac Artúir) fáilte roimh na hiarlaí ag Douai. Ba shagart as deoise Ard Macha é Roibéard Chamberlain, oide faoistine Aodha Uí Néill, duine de na comhairleoirí ba mhó ab ansa leis, an té a scríobhadh litreacha i Spáinnis thar a cheann chuig Pilib III na Spáinne, comhairleoir a thaistil le hAodh Ó Néill agus Ruaidhrí Ó Domhnaill nuair a thug siad cuairt ar an rí i Londain sa bhliain 1603. Is fiú a lua chomh maith gur bhain Chamberlain dochtúireacht sa diagacht amach in Ollscoil Salamanca sular fhill sé ar dheoise Ard Mhacha, rud a mhíníonn a líofa a bhí sé sa Spáinnis. 30 Deireadh Fómhair 1607, bhuail na hiarlaí le hAnraoi, an mac ba shine le hAodh Ó Néill, ag Notre Dame de Hal. B'shin é an chéad teagmháil idir athair agus mac le seacht mbliana. Bhí Anraoi mar choirnéal ar an reismint Éireannach in arm na Spáinne a bunaíodh sa bhliain 1605, agus bhí baint nár bheag ag Ó Maoil Chonaire leis an gceapachán seo.[13]

Díol spéise gurbh é seo an chéad uair go bhfios dúinn a fhaightear an focal *nasión* i dtéacs Gaeilge agus faightear é, dála an scéil, naoi n-uaire ar fad i saothar Uí Chianáin. Díol spéise chomh maith go mbaineann Ó Cianáin leas as an bhfocal *Eirinnach* ar fud an téacs, dosaen uair ar fad, agus nach n-úsáideann sé an focal *Gaedheal* ar chor ar bith. An ní is suntasaí ar fad faoin sliocht thuas an dá fhocal *Éireannach* agus *nasión* a bheith ar fáil ann i dteannta a chéile. Is mór ag an gCianánach ó thus deireadh an *Turais* Éire a léiriú mar náisiún Caitliceach ar chomhchéim leis na Spáinnigh.

Nuair a thug na hiarlaí cuairt ar Antwerp 19 Feabhra 1608, chuaigh daingnithe na cathrach i bhfeidhm go mór orthu, ach thuig Ó Cianáin gur mhór an phribhléid í do na deoraithe gur ligeadh dóibh na hairm chosanta a iniúchadh:

Dá ghunna mhóra práis 's iad ar n-a suidhiughadh go hard, sé troighthe déag ar

fhichid in gach gunna. Ní mór nach gcuirid
trí léige d'athchar a bpeiléir, mar aithrisid
an bhárda. Ní léigid naisión ar bith oile
d'fhéchain nó do bhreathnughadh na hoibre
ach Spáinneach nó Eireannach amháin.[14]

Chuir na hiarlaí chun bóthair i dtreo na Róimhe,
28 Feabhra 1608, Flaithrí Ó Maoil Chonaire agus
Roibéard Chamberlain (Mac Artúir) á dtionlacan.
Breis agus dhá mhí roimhe sin chuir James Loach,
cócaire an Chornéil Anraoi Ó Néill, ceannasaí
reisimint Thír Eoin i bhFlondrás, in iúl d'ionadaí
Shasana sa Bhruiséil: '[that] the Earl of Tyrone was
instantly bound to Rome, accompanied by Father Flarie O'Molconery as his principall guide'.[15]
Cuimhnímis gurbh é Ó Maoil Chonaire an duine
ba mhó taithí ar chúrsaí na hEorpa i measc na dtais-
tealaithe, fear a raibh seal caite aige mar chom-
hairleoir um ghnothaí Éireannacha i gcúirt Philib
III, an duine ba shinsearaí sa ghrúpa. Ní hiontas
ar bith é go dtagrófaí dó mar phríomhthreoraí cé
nár chóir neamhshuim a dhéanamh de thionchar
Chamberlain ach an oiread, nuair a chuirtear san
áireamh go raibh sé ar phríomhchomhairleoirí Uí
Néill in Éirinn.

Nuair a shroich na hiarlaí Milan 23 Márta 1608,
rinne siad iontas den chaisleán agus den trealamh
cosanta ach an oiread le hAntwerp, ach b'fhiú leis
an gCianánach uair amháin eile béim a chur ar an
muinín a bhí ag na Spáinnigh as na hÉireannaigh:

> Caisleán láidir ar daingne an domhain, mile
> saighdiúir Spáinneach go síorraidhe ag a
> bhárdacht d'oidhche agus do ló go n-a n-
> uile chomhgar agus riachtanus i leithimioll
> na cathrach ag a bhfuil a ceannas agus a
> huachtaránacht. Cóig céad gunna mór ar
> n-a gcomhshuidhiughadh ar an gcaisléan.
> Ní líonmhar a léigthear ann ach Spáinnigh
> agus Éireannaigh amháin.[16]

24 Aibreán 1608, rinne díorma beag de na taistealaithe, Ruaidhrí Ó Domhnaill agus Cúchonnacht Mhag Uidhir ina measc, cor bealaigh ag Foligno chun cuairt a thabhairt ar Assisi, áit bhreithe
San Proinsias agus cliabhán an oird a bhunaigh sé.
D'fhan Aodh Ó Néill siar ag Foligno agus chuaigh
ar aghaidh go Montefalco. Tugann an léarscáil le
fios nárbh aon dóichín an cor bealaigh seo agus
dealraíonn sé gurbh é Flaithrí Ó Maoil Chonaire
ba bhun leis an gcuairt ar Assisi. Luaigh Ó Cianáin
go sonrach go raibh ginearál an oird sa bhaile an lá

sin. Ba é seo Archangelo Gualterio da Messina, an
duine céanna a cheap Flaithrí mar phroibhinsial ar
Phroinsiasaigh na hÉireann faoi chúinsí urghnácha
ag caibidil ghinearálta an oird i dToledo dhá bhliain roimhe sin. Is cinnte gur bhreá le Flaithrí an
deis a thapú chun cuairt a thabhairt ar *loci sancti*
an oird. Ach ar éigean ba ghníomh *pietas* amháin
an chuairt seo ar Assisi, ach thug sí caoi don phroibhinsial tuairisc a thabhairt don ghinearáil ar staid
an oird in Éirinn.

Bhain na hiarlaí an Róimh amach, 29 Aibreán
1608. Éiríonn dath Proinsiasach an téacs níos
treise fós le linn na tréimhse a chaith na hiarlaí
i bpríomhchathair na críostaíochta. Thug siad
cuairt ar San Francesco a Ripa lá fhéile San Proinsias 1608, an dáta agus an fhéile araon á lua go
sonrach ag Ó Cianáin. D'fhanadh San Proinsias
féin ag San Francesco a Ripa agus é ar cuairt sa
Róimh. Tá an ceall ina ndéanadh sé guí agus an
charraig a mbaineadh sé leas aisti mar chean-
nadhart fós le feiceáil. Ba chuma nó athAssisi sa
Róimh é an clochar seo. Maidir le Santa Maria
d'Aracoeli, áfach, an teach Proinsiasach Iodálach
ba thábhachtaí sa Róimh, a tógadh d'aon ughaim
ar an Campidoglio, in aithris ar bhaisleac mór San
Proinsias a tógadh ar chnoc Assisi, ní dhearna Ó
Cianáin ach tagairt fhánach dó agus don dealbh
mhíorúilteach den Mhaighdean a bhí sa séipéal
ansin, 29 Méan Fómhair 1608. Díol suntais gur
thagair Ó Cianáin do 'crann iongantach éagsam-
hail oráistidhe' i San Francesco a Ripa.[17] Nuair a
cheadaigh mé an traidisiún sin agus cuairt á tabhairt agam ar San Francesco a Ripa sa bhliain
2007, ba mhór an t-iontas a bhí orm nuair a thug
na bráithre cuireadh dom dul isteach sa gháirdín
agus an crann a fheiceáil le mo dhá shúil féin.
Míníodh dom go raibh an t-eolas faoi thraidisiún seo an chrainn oráiste le fáil i lámhscríbhinn
a scríobh an bráthair bocht Lodovico da Modena
faoi bhúnús na mainistreacha i bproibhinse leas-
aithe na Róimhe, lámhscríbhinn atá ar coimeád i
gcartlann na mainistrech. Bhásaigh da Modena
sa bhliain 1722, áfach, rud a fhágann go bhfuil
fianaise Uí Chianáin ar a laghad ochtó bliain níos
sine ná an fhianaise is sine san Iodáil.

Formhór mór na séipéal ar thug na hiarlaí cuairt
orthu sa Róimh, cuairteanna éarlamhacha a bhí
iontu, sé sin gur ar fhéile éarlamh an tséipéil a tharla
siad, ocáid a mbeadh liotúirge shollúnta ar siúl ann.
Níor nós leis an gCianánach ach an dáta a lua, faoin
léitheoir (nó faoin lucht éisteachta) an nasc a dhéanamh idir an dáta agus an fhéile, rud a thugann le

fios gur ceapadh an téacs do dhaoine a bhí eolach go maith ar fhéilire na naomh. Is fíorannamh ar fad a luaigh Ó Cianáin an dáta agus an fhéile in éineacht, ach rinne sé faoi dhó é i gcás San Proinsias, ní hamháin sa bhliain 1608 ach sa bhliain 1607 chomh maith 'timcheall meadhóin laoi dia Dardaoin, lá S. Proinsias do shonnradh, an ceathramhadh lá Octobris',[18] an lá a tháinig na hiarlaí i dtír ar thalamh na hEorpa don chéad uair i Quilleboeuf na Fraince. Ómós an údair do naomh Assisi faoi dear an t-athrú stíle seo, ach is deacair gan lorg tréan Uí Mhaoil Chonaire ar an téacs a bhraistint freisin.

Léiriú suntasach ar an lorg tréan Proinsiasach atá le sonrú ar fud an *Turais* is ea minicíocht an mhana IHS ar bharr na leathanach. Bhí San Bernardino da Siena (1380-1450) ar dhuine de phríomhbhunaitheoirí an leasúcháin observaintigh i measc na bProinsiasach agus bhain sé leas éifeachtach as an logo IHS chun deabhóid d'ainm naofa Íosa a chraobhscaoileadh ar fud na hIodáile. Tá sé breactha ar bharr bhreis agus dhá thrian de leathanaigh lámhscríbhinn an *Turais*.

Tagann toise Spáinneach agus toise Proinsiasach Uí Chianáin le chéile sa chur síos a rinne sé ar shéipéal San Pietro in Montorio, an séipéal is tábhachtaí leis an gcroiniceoir, déanta na fírinne, agus an mhainistir inar chuir Flaithí Ó Maoil Chonaire faoi le linn a thréimhse sa Róimh. Le linn an chuntais ar oilithreacht na n-iarlaí chuig seacht mbaisleac na Róimhe, 12 Meitheamh 1608, a luaitear an séipéal seo don chéad uair. Sníomhann sé an traidisiún faoi mhairtíreacht Naomh Peadar in Montorio le cuairt na n-iarlaí ar ardeaglais Naomh Peadar sula leanann sé dá chuntas.[19]

Ba ríthábhachtach le Ferdinand bheith mar phátrún ar an séipéal seo, 'rud a bhaineann go dlúth le mo cháil'.[20] Lean Séarlas V, Pilib II, Pilib III agus Pilib IV leis an bpátrúnacht ríoga seo. Threisigh Ferdinand tábhacht agus gradam na Spáinne sa Róimh trí ambasadóir buan a bhunú sa chathair. Chomh maith le cartlanna seasta a bhunú i Seville agus Simancas, bhunaigh Pilib II cartlann sa Róimh chomh maith 'as a tool for staking a claim to this religious and symbolic centre of the Spanish Empire'.[21] Bhí ambasáid na Spáinne buailte ar San Pietro in Montorio, agus is maith a thuig na hiarlaí an oiread a bhí siad ag brath ar dhea-mhéin an ambasadóra, an duine ba thábhachtaí sa Róimh i ndiaidh an phápa féin.

Bunaíodh Comhbhráithreas Spáinneach an Aiséirí Ró-Naofa sa Róimh sa bhliain 1579. Níos

mó ná míle ball aige agus é i mbarr a réime: 'a locus of Spanish power, patronage, religious display and charity'.[22] Is e an comhbhráithreas seo a bhí freagrach as mórshiúl na Cásca sa Róimh agus mórshiúl Corpus Christi. Cé gurbh é an pápa a d'ordaigh gur Éireannaigh a roghnófaí chun an ceannbhrat a iompar thar an Naomh Shacraimint i mórshiúl na bliana 1608, dar leis an gCianánach, pribhléid urghnách amach is amach,[23] is í fírinne an scéil í gurbh é an comhbhráitheas a d'eagraigh, a phleanáil, agus a d'airgeadaigh an mórshiúl seo.

Adhlacadh Ruaidhrí Ó Domhnaill i séipéal San Pietro in Montorio, 29 Iúil 1608, tar éis dó bás a fháil den fhiabhras. Chomh maith le tagairt a dhéanamh do mhórshiúl taibhseach na sochraide a d'ordaigh an pápa, luaigh Ó Cianáin gur gléasadh corpán Ruaidhrí, in aibíd San Proinsias ar a iarratas féin. Ar 15 Meán Fómhair 1608, d'éag dearthair agus adhlacadh é sa séipéal céanna, é gléasta ar nós a dhearthár in aibid San Proinsias.[24]

Cuirtear béim bhreise ar thoise Spáinneach an téacs anseo trí shaintagairt Uí Chianáin do mhiotas bunaidh na nGael (cé go seachnaítear d'aon ughaim an focal sin sna áit is dóchúla a mbeifí ag súil leis) mar dhream a shíolraigh ó Mhíleadh Espáinne. Comhthubaiste d'Éirinn agus don Spáinn araon iad básanna na n-uaisle thar lear i bhfad ó bhaile. An t-aon sólás amháin atá acu gur i séipéal Spáinneach a adhlacadh iad agus gur in aibíd San Proinsias a gléasadh na corpáin. Nuair a chuirtear san áireamh go bhfuil an *Turas* chomh fréamhaithe sin i dtuiscintí an leasúcháin chreidimh Chaitlicigh, tá an tagairt do *fortuna* cineál aisteach, go háirithe le linn searmanais reiligiúnda. Is mó a mbeifí ag súil le tagairt d'fhearg Dé nó d'oirchill Dé ná don bhandia pagánach ina leithéid de chás. Sampla an-luath é seo d'úsáid an fhocail *fortún* sa Ghaeilge, ach níorbh iontas ar bith é ar an ócáid bhrónach seo dá gcuimhneodh Aodh Ó Néill ar an mbronntanas a thug Sir John Harington do 17 Meán Fómhair 1599, cóip dá aistriúchán cáiliúil ar *Orlando Furioso* (1591). Sular thug sé an leabhar dó, d'oscail Harington é trí thaisme, ag tús Canto XLV agus léigh sé amach an sliocht seo a leanas:[25]

Look how much higher Fortune doth erect
The Clyming sight on her unstable wheele,
So much the higher may a man expect
To see his head where late he saw his heele.[26]

Má bhí cloigeann Uí Néill fós slán, is cinnte go raibh an rotha casta ina choinne.

Ní miste sampla eile de dhath Spáinneach an *Turais* a lua. 29 Meitheamh 1608, thug Ó Cianáin tuairisc ar chuairt ambasadóir na Spáinne ar an bpápa. Ba é seo Don Francisco de Moncada, marqués de Aytona, a ceapadh mar ambasadóir sa bhliain 1606. D'éirigh sé cairdiúil le hAodh Ó Néill agus scríobhadh sé litreacha chuig Pilib III thar a cheann. Chuaigh an chuairt seo, cuairt bhliantúil ar fhéile Naomh Peadar, siar chuig conradh a rinneadh idir Pilib II agus an Pápa Pól IV nuair a tháinig deireadh le Cogadh Caraffa sa bhliain 1557. De bharr bhua na Spáinne, bhí an Vatacáin sásta Pilib II a aithint mar rí dlisteanach Napoli. I gcúiteamh an aitheantais seo bhí an rí sásta suim ainmneach 7,000 'ducat' a íoc leis an bpápa mar aon le 'chinea', capall bán Naipleach, a thabhairt dó mar bhronntanas. De bharr na fiacha feodacha seo a íoc leis an bPápa, d'fhéadfadh rí na Spáinne talamh slán a dhéanamh de thacaíocht an phápa agus de phribhléidí airgid chun scéimeana an rí a chur chun cinn i bhFlondrás, i Napoli, sa Chatalóin agus sa Domhan Nua. An mórshiúl bliantúil agus ofráil na mbronntanas 29 Meitheamh, ba léiriú deasghnáthach é ar an gcomhoibriú idir an phápacht agus an Spáinn, léiriú a bhain tús áite de thábhacht na féile féin agus nach raibh ann i ndeireadh na dála ach taispeántas bolscaireachta de chumhacht agus de ghradam na Spáinne sa Róimh.[27] Sa bhliain 1608, an mórshiúl a ndearna Ó Cianáin cur síos air, bhí suas le cúig chéad capall ann, go leor uaisle agus prealáidí, dearthár an phápa san áireamh.[28] Ní hamháin gur thug Ó Cianáin suntas do thaibhseacht an mhórshiúil, ach luaigh sé na sonraí ceananna céanna atá la fáil don bhliain chéanna i gcartlann an Biblioteca Apostolica Vaticana, 'a cóig nó a sé de chéadaibh marcach'. Ina theannta sin luann sé an t-each bán, 'each roidheas bán', agus an sparán mór a bhí ar crochadh ar mhuineál an chapaill, 'gné sparáin nár ba bheag fó a bhrághaid i n-a mbuí cíos na Naples'.[29]

Meastar go raibh 115,000 ina gcónaí sa Róimh ag deireadh an tséú haois déag agus gur Spáinnigh iad tuairim is 25 faoin gcéad acu sin.[30] De réir mar a bhí gradam na Spáinne ag dul i dtreis sa chathair shíoraí, agus tionchar na Spáinne dá réir sin ar choras pátrúnachta na Róimhe, bheartaigh ionadaithe na Spáinne leas a bhaint as an gcomhbhráithris a luadh cheana, agus aontacht náisiúnta a chothú trí aon ainm amháin a thabhairt ar na hIbéirigh go léir a raibh cónaí orthu sa Róimh.[31]

Is féidir an polasaí seo a fheiceáil in alt luath i mbunreacht an chomhbhráithris:

This confraternity being properly of the Spanish nation, it is necessary that he who would be admitted to it should be Spanish and not of another nation; he is understood to have the said quality of being Spanish if he is from the crown of Castile or the crown of Aragon, or from the kingdom of Portugal and the islands of Majorca, Minorca, and Sardinia, or both the islands and mainland of the Indies with no distinction of age, sex or rank … Thus, during the period between 1580 and 1640, the terms Spanish nation and Spaniard served to identify anyone from Iberia, the islands of Sardinia and Majorca, and the Indies.[32]

Má baineadh earraíocht as an bhfriotal *nación española* chun feasacht aontachta a chumadh i measc na *náisiún* Ibéireach beag, ní hiontas ar bith é go mbainfeadh Tadhg Ó Cianáin leas as an téarma *nasión Éireannach* mar fhearas aontachta chun Gaeil agus Sean-Ghaill a thabhairt le chéile, i ngeall ar aon chreideamh amháin, aon chultúr amháin agus aon dílseacht amháin do mhonarc na Spáinne. Díol spéise nach mbaineann sé leas as an téarma *Gaoidheal* oiread is uair amháin sa téacs, rud a thugann le fios gur d'aon ughaim a chinn sé ar an téarma *Éireannach* a úsáid. Ar éigean is comhtharlúint í gur i dtéacs a scríobhadh sa Róimh faoi coimirce rí na Spáinne is túisce a thagann an fheasacht faoi *náisiún Éireannach* chun cinn sa Ghaeilge, an láthair chéanna agus an breogadán intleachtúil céanna inar gaibhníodh coincheap an *nación española*. Má tá a bhuíochas ag dul do Fhlaithrí Ó Maoil Chonaire as an mblas láidir Proinsiasach atá le sonrú ar insint Uí Chianáin, an bhfuil an buíochas céanna ag dul dó as coincheap an náisiúin Éireannaigh a chur chun cinn? Duine mór le rá eile i measc na ndeoraithe Éireannacha sa Róimh ab ea Roibéard Chamberlain, duine de phríomhchomhairleoirí Uí Néill, duine a bhí líofa sa Spáinnis, duine a raibh dochtúireacht sa diagacht aige ó Ollscoil Salamanca. Mar dhuine de shliocht na Sean-Ghall, ba dhóigh leat gurbh fhearr a thuigfeadh seisean buntáiste an ainmneora *Éireannach* ná an Proinsiasach diongbháilte de shliocht na nGael. Tá go leor rúnta fós i bhfolach faoi pheannaireacht néata Thaidhg Uí Chianáin.

Bhí ard-deoise Thuama folamh ón mbliain 1595 agus d'ainmnigh Pól V Flaithrí Ó Maoil Chonaire don fholúntas 30 Márta 1609, tar éis d'Aodh Ó Néill stocaireacht thréan a dhéanamh ar a shon.

Cúig seachtaine ina dhiaidh sin choiscric an Cairdinéal Maffeo Barberini (a cheapfaí mar Phápa Urbanus VIII sa bhliain 1625) é agus d'fhill sé ar an Spáinn go luath ina dhiaidh sin chun cás Uí Néill a chur chun cinn i Madrid. Tháinig Roibéard Chamberlain ar ais go Flondrás agus chuaigh isteach sna Proinsiasaigh i Lobháin 7 Feabhra 1610. Díreach bliain amháin ina dhiaidh sin, rinne sé uacht sular ghlac sé a chuid móideanna rialta agus thug uaidh go foirmeálta a cheart do shealúchas, dílseacht agus maoin shaolta. Díol suntais ar leith an clásal seo a leanas:

> Fágaim an mhéid atá agam ar an rígh re h-aghaidh an Clodh-Gaoidhilge agus neithe do chur a ccló do rachas an onóir do Dhia, a cclú dár násion agus d'Órd San Froinsias …

Seo í an chéad tagairt do thionscadal clódóireachta i Lobháin. Díol suntais freisin an focal *násion* a fheiceáil arís, an dara téacs sa Ghaeilge a bhaineann earraíocht as. Ní cóir neamhaird a dhéanamh den tréimhse a chaith Chamberlain sa Róimh san *ambience* Spáinneach céanna le Flaithrí Ó Maoil Chonaire agus Tadhg Ó Cianáin mar a raibh coincheap an náisiúin Éireannaigh á fhuineadh ar mhúnla *la nación española*.

Bhí an t-iarfhile gairmiúil Giolla Brighde Ó hEodhasa ar na nóibhisigh ba thúisce a chuaigh isteach san ord i Lobháin 1 Samhain 1607, agus thóg sé Bonabhentura mar ainm cráifeach. Mhalartaigh sé a cheird ghairmiúil ar an tsagartóireacht agus chuaigh thar lear go Douai am éigin idir 1600 agus 1604. Tar éis dó MA a ghnóthú i nDouai, scríobh sé chuig cara leis, Robert Nugent, SJ, á thabhairt le fios gur mhaith leis aistriú go Lobháin chun diagacht a dhéanamh toisc, 'gurb ann sin as fearr do-níthear léighionn'. Oirníodh ina shagart i Malines é 4 Aibreán 1609. Agus ardcháilíochtaí idir theanga agus diagacht aige, ní fhéadfaí duine níos fearr a shamhlú chun an leasúchán creidimh Caitliceach a chur chun cinn in Éirinn. Ach dá fheabhas iad na buanna seo, ní fhéadfaí tairbhe ceart a bhaint astu gan tacaíocht airgid, tacaíocht a bhí ar fáil anois de bharr uacht Chamberlain. 17 Meitheamh 1611, thug ardeaspag Malines cead foilsithe do theagasc críostaí Uí Eodhasa d'fhonn iarrachtaí na n-eiriceach chun creideamh mhuintir na hÉireann a shaobhadh trí leabhair a fhoilsiú sa teanga sin cheana féin, a chur ó mhaith.[33] Trí lá ina dhiaidh sin, d'údaraigh Albert agus Isabella, rialtóirí na hÍsiltíre Spáinní an cead foilsithe seo, tar éis dóibh dearbhú an ardeaspaig a léamh.[34]

Mar aon le cead an ardeaspaig, dhearbhaigh Aodh Mac Aingil (Mac Cathmhaoil) agus Roibéard Chamberlain go raibh an teagasc críostaí saor ó earráidí foirceadail. B'fhéidir nár mhiste a aibhsiú anseo go raibh dindiúirí diagachta na beirte thuas i bhfad níos fearr ná cáilíochtaí Uí Eodhasa, dochtúireacht acu araon ó Ollscoil Salamanca, ach mar fhile gairmiúil go raibh tús áite ag Ó hEodhasa i gcúrsaí teanga. Níl ach bearna corradh beag le cois ceithre mhí le fáil idir uacht Chamberlain gona saintagairt do nithe a chur i gcló, agus cead foilsithe an leabhair. Ar éigean a d'fhéadfaí an téacs a scríobh agus a fhoilsiú in achar chomh gairid sin, go háirithe nuair a bhí ar an gclódóir, Jacobius Mesius in Antwerp, foireann litreacha a cheapadh as an bpíosa ar fad, litreacha nach mbeadh aon chur amach aige orthu. Thabharfadh sé sin le fios go raibh sé i gceist ag na bráithre bochta leabhair Ghaeilge a fhoilsiú i bhfad sula bhfuarthas fáltas Chamberlain. Cuimhnímis, áfach, go raibh bliain caite aige leis na Proinsiasaigh i Lobháin sula ndearna sé a uacht agus é ar tí a chuid móideanna a ghlacadh. Sagart tuairim is daichead bliain d'aois a bhí ann nuair a chuaigh sé isteach san ord, agus tharlódh nach raibh san uacht ach réaladh foirmeálta ar chinneadh a bhí tógtha aige le fada an lá. D'fhéadfaí bunús an togra foilsitheoireachta a rianadh siar mar sin go dtí tús na bliana 1610. Ach maidir le cé hé a thionscain an togra, Chamberlain féin, Ó hEodhasa, Mac Aingil nó Ó Maoil Chonaire féin, sin ceist nach féidir a fhreagairt.

I mí na Nollag 1611, chuir Richard Morres ón Teampall Mór, a bhí ag obair mar spiadóir sa Bhruiséil thar ceann rialtas Shasana, an tuairisc seo a leanas chuig Robert Cecil, an Tiarna Salisbury:

> Moreover, he plainly alleged, that after his coming from Prague, he saw one of the books among the Irish soldiers, printed in Irish in Antwerp, and set forth by the friars of Louvaine confirming their own religion, and to the contrary infirming and refusing that of the Protestants, in such sort that infinite readers and hearers of the Irish will presently believe the contents thereof to be true. Finally, the said Richard affirmeth, according to the information of the soldiers in Flanders that know Oge O'Reilly, pensioner of fifty crowns a month, that he went with the King of Spain's letters into Holland, accompanied with a couple of friars in the habit of soldiers, hoping to draw the Irish soldiers from the

English commanders at Denmark and Sweden into Holland, and himself to be colonel bearing dominion over them. But God cut off all their contrary intention herein, and preserve, maintain, exalt, and augment the King and Privy Council of England.[35]

Ní fhéadfadh aon leabhar eile bheith i gceist anseo ach teagasc críostaí Uí Eodhasa. Díol spéise go raibh sé á dháileadh ar shaighdiúirí Éireannacha i reisimint Thír Eoghain chomh maith lena chur ar ais go hÉirinn. Díol spéise freisin an frása 'infinite readers and hearers of the Irish', rud a chuireann béim ar an léitheoireacht phoiblí mar mheán dáilithe eolais san Eoraip nua-aoiseach luath. Mar a dúirt Robert Darnton: 'for most people throughout most of history, books had audiences rather than readers'.[36]

Ní leagan amach 'ceist agus freagra atá ar an teagasc críostaí ach plé ar chúig bhunghné den chreideamh Caitliceach: (1) An Chré, (2) An tÁr nAthair agus an Sé do Bheatha, a Mhuire, (3) na Deich nAitheanta, (4) Na Sacraimintí agus (5) Suáilcí agus Duáilcí. Bunaíodh an leagan amach seo ar shaothar caiticéiseach Peadar Canisius (1555), ar ordaigh Pilib II na Spáinne é a úsáid san scoileanna ar fad san Ísiltír Spáinneach, 6 Nollaig 1557.[37] Dealraíonn sé gur bhain Ó hEodhasa leas as an tiontó Laidine (Cologne, 1609) a rinneadh ar theagasc críostaí cáiliúil Roibéard Bellarminus: 'Dichiarazione più copiosa della dottrina cristiana composta in forma di dialogi'.[38] Is í an ghné is suntasaí den saothar an achoimre véarsaíochta i dtús gach aon rannóige, beartas a chinntigh nach taobh le pobal liteartha amháin a bhí Ó hEodhasa chun a theagasc a chraobhscaoileadh. Díol spéise an dán a chum sé mar réamhrá don saothar ar fad, áit a bhfógraíonn sé go neamhbhalbh nach mór don leasaitheoir Caitliceach tús áite a thabhairt do shoiléireacht na teachtaireachta ar mhaisiúchán friotail. Is beag nach ionann seo agus séanadh iomlán ar phrionsabail stiúrtha na gairme a chleacht sé sula ndeachaigh sé le sagartóireacht, agus nach iontach an rud é go mbaineann sé leas as na prionsabail chéanna sin agus slán á fhágáil aige acu? Tá an dán ar fad bunaithe ar an gcodarsnacht idir solas agus dorchadas agus maíonn an t-údar nach mbíonn de thoradh ar dhealradh agus óradh an bhriathair dhaonna ach briathar geal Dé a dhorchú faoi cheo.

Díol suntais go gcuimsíonn teagasc críostaí Uí Eodhasa trí réim theanga ar fad, ardréim na bh-

'San Proinsias ag fáil créachtaí Chríost', Giotto di Bondone (1266-1337).

filí, réim na filíochta pobail, agus réim phróis atá leathbhealaigh idir an dá réim theanga eile – réim phróis atá feiliúnach do dhioscúrsa na diagachta ar leibhéal na cléire agus leibhéal an tuata thuisceanaigh liteartha araon. Freagra glé é an t-ilréimeachas teanga seo ar dhrogall na nÍosánach an Ghaeilge a úsáid mar ghné dá mbeartas tréadach.

Beagnach trí bliana tar éis don teagasc críostaí a theacht amach, 15 Aibreán 1614, d'iarr Bonabhentura Ó hEodhasa, a bhí faoin am seo ina chaomhnóir ar Choláiste San Antaine, cead ar an arddiúca inneall cló a bheith acu sa choláiste féin.[39] An phríomhschúis leis an gcead seo a iarraidh gur theastaigh ó na bráithre an creideamh a bhí i mbaol i dtír ainnis na hÉireann a chaomhnú ('ad conservandam periclitantem fidem in misera patria'). Gheall an Proinsiasach nach bhfoilseofaí rud ar bith gan údarú a fháil ó ardeaspag Malines nó ó Ollscoil Lobháin, nó ón té a chuirfeadh an t-arddiúca i mbun an chúraim sin. Ach luaigh sé cúis eile i gcorp na litreach.[40]

Rialacha dothrócaireacha an mhargaidh a thagann i gceist anseo. Ní raibh clódóirí na hIsiltíre Spáinní toilteanach carachtair anaithnide a chur i gcló, toisc nach raibh aon dóchas acu go ndéanfaidís brabús ar na leabhair a bheadh i gceist, agus nach bhféadfaidís iad a dhíol in áiteanna eile. Ina theannta sin, ní fhéadfadh na Proinsiasaigh an bhris a chúiteamh leo i ngeall ar a mbochtaineacht féin, gan dóchas ag na clódóirí go gcúiteofaí iad ó

217

fhoinse eile. Is léir uaidh seo go raibh dóthain dá dhua faighte ag Joseph Mesius le teagasc críostaí Uí Eodhasa, agus nach raibh sé sásta tuilleadh stró agus caiteachais a tharraingt air féin le foilseacháin Ghaeilge. Chuaigh an t-ard-diúca i gcomhairle leis an ardeaspag an lá dár gcionn agus fuair freagra dearfach uaidh 7 Bealtaine 1614.[41]

Díol spéise na cúiseanna a thug ar an ardeaspag a bheith chomh báúil sin. Sa chéad áit go mbeadh leabhair Lobháin mar leigheas ar na leabhair a bhí á scaipeadh go laethúil ag na Sasanaigh sa tír, naimhde an fhíorchreidimh Chaitlicigh ('les Anglois ennemys de la vraye foi catholique'). Sa dara háit ba den riachtanas na leabhair seo toisc nach bhféadfadh na Proinsiasaigh dul go hÉirinn d'fhonn an creideamh a chraobhscaoileadh ó bhéal ('puys qu'ils n'y peuvent estre en personne'). Feachtas an stáit in aghaidh na séantachta 1611-19 ba bhun leis an éagumas seo, feachtas a bhí dírithe in aghaidh na cléire don chuid ba mhó.[42] Ach is í an tríú cúis an ceann is spéisiúla, nach raibh Gaeilge ná carachtair na Gaeilge ag na clódóirí san Ísiltír Spáinneach ('que l'on trouve pas imprimeurs en ce pays qui cognoissent leurs langues et charactères'). Is léir go ndeachaigh argóint Uí Eodhasa faoi dhrogall na gclódóirí áitiúla i bhfeidhm ar na húdaráis agus thug an t-ard-diúca an cead 9 Bealtaine 1614.

Ní i ngan fhios do na Sasanaigh a tharla an cor nua seo i dtogra foilsitheoireachta na bProinsiasach i Lobháin, agus ní mó ná sásta a bhí siad ina thaobh. I mí an Mheithimh 1614, scríobh William Trumbull, ambasadóir Shasana sa Bhruiséil, chuig an Ard-Diúca faoi leabhar a scríobh seiplíneach Ridirí Malta dar teideal *Anglorum horror, hereticorum terror*. Toisc go raibh an saothar seo 'stuffed with insults and calumnies' in aghaidh Shéamais I, 'tending to sedition and to incite enemies against the king', theastaigh ó Trumbull go ndéanfaí an leabhar a chosc. Theastaigh uaidh freisin go gcuirfí cosc le foilseacháin religiúnda na bProinsiasach Éireannach i Lobháin.[43]

Níor tugadh aird ar bith ar iarratas rí Shasana agus cuireadh leabhrán beag dar teideal *Suim riaghlachas Phroinsias* amach ar an bhfáisceán cló nua. Ní raibh ach dhá leathanach déag ann agus bhí sé gan dáta. Níor tháinig ach cóip amháin anuas chugainn agus tá an chuma ar an scéal gur le haghaidh úsáid phríobháideach na nóibhíseach i gColáiste San Antaine a réitíodh é. Chomh maith le hachoimre a thabhairt ar riail na bProinsiasach, tá roinnt de na dánta ó theagasc críostaí Uí Eodhasa le fáil sa leabhrán sin.[44]

Ina theannta sin foilsíodh leabhrán eile a bhfuil trí dhán le Bonabhentura Ó hEodhasa le fáil ann. Sa réamhrá a ghabhann leis an gcéad dán acu seo, *Truagh liomsa, a chompáin do choir*,[45] tugtar 'Gáirdian Bhráthar nÉirionnach Lobháin' ar Ó hEodhasa. Nuair a chuirtear san áireamh go raibh sé fós ina chaomhnóir nuair a bhásaigh sé 15 Samhain 1614, is féidir dáta foilsithe an tsaothair a shuíomh am éigin idir Bealtaine agus Samhain na bliana sin. Cumadh an dán fada seo a bhfuil nócha rann ann d'fhonn cara leis an bhfile a mhealladh ar ais ón eiriceacht más fíor, ach b'fhéidir nach raibh sa chúlra seo ach ficsean liteartha a thug deis don údar tráchtas fileata a chumadh faoi shainchomharthaí na heaglaise fíre agus idirdhealú a dhéanamh idir an aon eaglais fhíor amháin agus na heaglaisí a bhunaigh Lúitéar agus Cailbhín. Tharlódh gurbh é an toise poileimiciúil seo a thug ar rí Shasana gearán a dhéanamh faoi na 'seditious libels' a bhí á bhfoilsiú ag na bráithre i Lobháin, ach b'fhéidir gur leor an dearcadh frithPhrotastúnach bhí le sonrú ar eagrán Antwerp den teagasc críostaí chun gradam 'seditious libels' a thabhú dó.

Ar an láimh eile, más d'úsáid phríobháideach amháin a foilsíodh an dá shaothar seo, níor ghá cead oifigiúil a fháil ó na húdaráis chun iad a fhoilsiú. B'fhéidir nach raibh sa dá shaothar tosaigh seo ach píosaí promhaidh a foilsíodh ar inneall cló a cheannaigh na bráithre tamall roimhe sin, na cló-litreacha Gaeilge faighte acu ó Mesius in Antwerp, ach nár iarr siad cead oifigiúil go dtí go raibh siad inniúil ar an trealamh a úsáid go saoráideach.[46] Eagrán eile de theagasc críostaí Uí Eodhasa maille le cóipeanna dá leabhar beag filíochta greamaithe ina lár,[47] an chéad saothar a clóbhualadh ar fháisceán na mbráithre. Ní fios go beacht cathain a cuireadh i gcló é.

Tugadh an cead 9 Bealtaine 1614, agus bhásaigh Ó hEodhasa 15 Samhain 1614. Tá an dáta 1619 breactha ar an gcóip d'eagrán Lobháin atá le fáil i leabharlann Ollscoil Cambridge.[48] Is é an léamh is dealraithí ar an scéal gur bhásaigh Ó hEodhasa go tobann agus an leabhar á réiteach don chló aige, gur thóg ball eile den chomhluadar an cúram air féin ina dhiaidh sin, agus gur tháinig sé amach am éigin sa bhliain 1615.[49] Céim shuntasach i dtogra foilsitheoireachta Lobháin go bhfuair na bráithre inneall cló dá gcuid féin agus níor ghá dóibh feasta brath ar dhrogall agus leisce chlódóirí na hÍsiltíre Spáinní.

Rinne Eoghan Ó Dubhthaigh dlúthnasc ina chuid filíochta idir creideamh agus cultúr, rud a d'fhág go raibh féiniúlacht Éireannach gaibhnithe ag na Proinsiasiagh faoi na cúig déag ochtóidí. Rinneadh tuilleadh beachtaíochta ar an bhféiniúlacht sin i saothar Thaidhg Uí Chianáin, go háirithe san earraíocht a bhain sé as an bhfrása *náisún Éireannach*, na téarmaí eitneacha Gael agus Sean-Ghall á seachaint d'aon ughaim aige, agus é ag áiteamh gur de dhlúth agus d'inneach an náisiúin Éireannaigh sin, Caitliceachas leasaithe Thrionta. I ngeall ar an lorg tréan Proinsiasach atá ar an téacs seo, lorg a d'eascair ó thionchar Fhlaithrí Uí Mhaoil Chonaire, ní mór é a áireamh ar scríbhinní Lobháin. Uacht Roibéard Chamberlain, an chéad téacs eile ina bhfaightear idé an náisiúin Éireannaigh, idir choincheap agus friotal, an chéad téacs freisin a dhéanann saintagairt don togra clódóireachta. Is mór mar shampla idir aidhm Sheáin Uí Chearnaigh, údair an chéad leabhair de chuid na heaglaise státbhunaithe a foilsíodh i mBaile Átha Cliath sa bhliain 1571, 'do chum glóire Dé do chur amach, agus do chum an mhaitheasa phuiblidhe',[50] agus mana Chamberlain, 'an anóir do Dhia, a cclú dár násion agus d'Órd San Froinsias'.[51] Is mór idir náisiun agus maitheas poiblí. Bhainfeadh Aodh Mac Aingil tuilleadh gaisneas as an téarma náisiún, é in úsáid aige seacht n-uaire déag ar fad in *Scáthán Shacramuinte na hAithridhe* (1618), é ag tabhairt le fios gur náisiún Caitliceach í Éire mar 'gach náision Chatoilc eile'.[52] Ní dall a bhí údaráis Shasana ar iarrachtaí seo na bProinsiasach chun Gaeil agus Sean-Ghaill a aontú le chéile in aon náisiún Éireannach amháin a raibh an creideamh Caitliceach agus saíocht na Gaeilge mar tháthchodanna riachtanacha den aontacht sin. Ní fearr rud a léireodh imní seo na Sasanach ná an sliocht seo a leanas ó litir a scríobh William Trumbull chuig Séamas I sa bhliain 1615:

> The perfidious Machiavellian friars of Louvain … seek by all means to reconcile their countrymen in affections and to combine those that are descended of the English race and those that are mere Irish in a league of friendship and concurrence against your majesty and the true religion now professed in your country.[53]

Nótaí

1 *Letters and papers, foreign and domestic, of the reign of Henry VIII*, 1534, pp 366, 957.

2 B. Jennings (ed.), 'Donatus Moneyus, "De Provinciae Hiberniae S. Francisci"', *Analecta Hibernica*, vi (1934), p. 50.

3 C. Mhág Craith (ed.), *Dán na mBráthar Mionúr* (2 vols, Dublin, 1967-80), i, pp 151-3; M. Caball, *Poets and politics: reaction and continuity in Irish poetry, 1558-1625* (Cork, 1998), p. 79; idem, 'Faith, culture and sovereignty: Irish nationality and its development, 1558-1625', in B. Bradshaw and P. Roberts (eds), *British consciousness and identity: the making of Britain, 1533-1707* (Cambridge, 1998), pp 134-5; idem, 'Innovation and tradition: Irish Gaelic responses to early modern conquest and colonization', in H. Morgan (ed.), *Political Ideology in Ireland* (Dublin, 1999), p. 77.

4 Mhág Craith (ed.), *Dán na mBráthar Mionúr*, i, p. 135.

5 Ibid., pp 133-4, 138.

6 John Derricke, *The Image of Irelande with a Discoverie of Woodkarne* (1581), (ed.) J. Small, with the notes of Sir W. Scott (Edinburgh, 1883, p. iv). Féach fosta J. Leerssen, *Mere Irish and fíor-Ghael: Studies in the idea of Irish nationality, its development and literary expression prior to the nineteenth century*, Critical Conditions, Field Day Monographs 3 (Cork, 1996), p. 42.

7 Ó Recio Morales, 'Irish émigré group strategies of survival, adaptation and integration in seventeenth- and eighteenth-century Spain', in T. O'Connor and M. A. Lyons (eag.), *Irish communities in early-modern Europe* (Dublin, 2006), p. 254.

8 Ibid., pp 254-5.

9 *CSPI, 1603-06*, pp 244-5.

10 Ibid., pp 302-3.

11 F. O'Brien, 'Florence Conry, archbishop of Tuam', *Irish Rosary*, xxxvi (1927), p. 901; Pilib III don Ard-Dhiúca Albert, 21 Meán Fómhair 1606, in B. Jennings and C. Giblin (ed), *Louvain Papers, 1606-1827* (Dublin, 1968), pp 1-2; Jennings (ed.), 'Donatus Moneyus, "De Provinciae Hiberniae S. Francisci"', p. 18.

12 T. Ó Fiaich, 'Richard Weston agus *Beir mo Bheannacht go Dundalk*' in D. Ó Doibhlin (eag.), *Ón Chreagán go Ceann Dubhrann Aistí le Tomás Ó Fiaich* (Baile Átha Cliath, 1992), pp 184-6.

13 *Turas*, p. 92.

14 Ibid., p. 124.

15 *CSPI, 1607-08*, p. 359.

16 *Turas*, p. 160.

17 Ibid., p. 384.

18 Ibid., p. 60.

19 Ibid., p. 332.

20 T. J. Dandalet, *Spanish Rome, 1500-1700* (New Haven, 2001), p. 2.

21 Ibid., p. 58.

22 Ibid., p. 10.

23 5 Meitheamh 1608: *Turas*, pp 296-8.

24 *Turas*, p. 374.

25 N. E. McClure (ed.), *The letters and epigrams of Sir John Harington* (Phildelphia, 1930; athchló, 1972), p. 77.

26 D. M. Gardiner, '"These are not the things men live by nowadays": Sir John Harington's visit to the O' Neill in 1599', *Cahiers Élisabéthains*, lv (1999), p. 7.

27 Dandalet, *Spanish Rome*, pp 55-57; féach fosta p. 104.

28 Ibid., p. 104.

29 *Turas*, p. 368.

30 Dandelet, *Spanish Rome*, p. 120.

31 Ibid., pp 113-4.

32 Ibid., pp 116, 118.

33 Bonabhentura Ó hEodhasa, *An Teagasg Críosduidhe*, eag. F. Mac Raghnaill (Baile Átha Cliath, 1976), p. 5.

34 Jennings and Giblin (eds), *Louvain papers, 1606-1827*, pp 32-33.

35 *CSPI, 1611-14*, p. 185.

36 R. Darnton, 'History of reading', in P. Burke (ed.), *New perspectives on historical writing* (2nd ed. Cambridge, 2001), p. 167.

37 P. Begheyn, *Petrus Canisius en zijn catechismus de geschiedenis van een bestseller, Peter Canisius and his catechism: the history of a bestseller* (Nijmegen, 2005), p. 44.

38 Ó hEodhasa, *An Teagasg Críosduidhe*, eag. Mac Raghnaill, p. ix.

39 Jennings and Giblin (eds), *Louvain papers, 1606-1827*, p. 39.

40 Ibid., p. 39.

41 Ibid. p. 40.

42 B. Mac Cuarta, *Catholic revival in the north of Ireland, 1603-41* (Dublin, 2007), pp 167-202.

43 *HMC Downshire, Trumbull Papers, January 1613-August 1614*, iv (London, 1940), p. 213; féach fosta, p. 454.

44 *Rialachas San Proinsias*, eag. P. Ó Súilleabháin, (Baile Átha Cliath, 1953), pp ix-x, 91-96.

45 Mhág Craith, *Dán na mBráthar Miónur*, i, pp 38-51.

46 Ó hEodhasa, *An Teagasg Críosduidhe*, eag. Mac Raghnaill, p. xiv.

47 Ibid., pp xii-xiii.

48 Ibid., p. xii.

49 Ibid., p. xv.

50 B. Ó Cuív, (eag.), *Aibidil Gaoidheilge & Caiticiosma: Seán Ó Cearnaigh's Irish primer of religion published in 1571* (Baile Átha Cliath, 1994), p. 55.

51 C. Ó Lochlainn, *Tobar fíorghlan Gaedhilge* (Baile Átha Cliath, 1939), p. 97.

52 Aodh Mac Aingil, *Scáthán Shacraimuinte na hAithridhe*, eag. C. Ó Maonaigh (Baile Átha Cliath, 1952), p. 4.

53 C. P. Meehan, *The fate and fortunes of Hugh O'Neill, earl of Tyrone and Rory O'Donel, earl of Tyrconnel* (3rd ed., Dublin, 1886), p. 328.

The survival of the Catholic Church in Ulster in the era of the flight of the earls and the Ulster Plantation

Tadhg Ó hAnnracháin

In 1617 a Croatian Jesuit, Marion de Bonis, composed a relation of his missionary activities in the southern parts of what had been the medieval kingdom of Hungary before the sixteenth-century Turkish conquest. The document and other reports composed two years later were filled with a sense of wonder at the thousands of people who flocked to hear mass, receive instruction, and then stood for entire days and nights to have their confessions heard and to take the Eucharist.[1] De Bonis may well have been the first representative of the post-Tridentine Catholic reformation to have made his way to this isolated and largely abandoned Christian population. He noted the manner in which he and his companions refused to look for any material reward for their exertions made a deep impression on their listeners. In addition to the spiritual hunger which he reported, he also encountered shocking ignorance: many were unable to make even the sign of the cross and did not recognise the simplest prayer. The degree of disjunction from the practices of early modern Catholicism which de Bonis discovered was hardly surprising. Following the disastrous battle of Mohács in 1526, this area had fallen under Turkish dominance and had experienced massive demographic shifts and the effective destruction of the structural apparatus of the pre-conquest Catholic Church.[2]

Four years after de Bonis's initial report from Slavonia another Jesuit mission in the Irish diocese of Kilmore encountered a startlingly similar reception. Once again, thousands of people, evidently attracted by the novelty of the practices, flocked to the missionary expedition, to hear mass, to make their confession and to receive Holy Communion. Once again, the Jesuit reported the respect which was evoked by the frugal lifestyle of the missionaries and their evident disinclination to accept gifts or payment for their spiritual work.[3] Similar reports to these certainly existed for other parts of Europe, even areas and jurisdictions such as Italy and France which were securely within the territory of Catholic states. Moreover, a certain commonality of assumption and expectation on the part of the Jesuit compilers probably underscores the similarities between these two reports. Nevertheless, the fact that conditions in Ulster in 1621 bore direct comparison with argu-

ably the most neglected area in Christian Europe is indicative of the degree of damage which Catholic Church structures and sacramental practice had suffered in the province in the preceding decades.

It seems evident that the late sixteenth and early seventeenth centuries were a time of particular crisis for the Catholic Church in Ulster. The conditions which the Jesuits encountered in the 1620s, for instance, differed substantially from those recorded in the visitation report of 1546 in the neighbouring diocese of Armagh *inter hibernicos*. That document had certainly detailed a depressing picture of ruined churches and poverty, but in other respects the behaviour of the clergy was evidently quite impressive, with regular celebration of mass, matins and evensong.[4] Indeed, studies of late medieval Armagh, a diocese which boasts exceptional source material, have tended to emphasise the manner in which an effective Christian ministry had adapted itself to the different ethnic contours of English and Gaelic society.[5] The tenor of the Jesuit account differed substantially to the impressions recorded by the Italian mission which came to Ireland with the papal nuncio, Giovanni Battista Rinuccini, in the 1640s. Dionysio Massari, in particular, who was impressed with the standard of Gaelic Catholicism in general, journeyed on the nuncio's behalf into Ulster and evidently encountered nothing there to alter his conviction of the devout orthodoxy of the native population.[6]

The interval between the Armagh report of 1546, a last snapshot of the late medieval period, and the process of early modern Catholic revival, vanguarded by events such as the Kilmore mission, was a time of extraordinarily rapid change which undoubtedly had severe detrimental effects on both church structures and devotional practice. The second half of the sixteenth century saw the province of Ulster repeatedly devastated by war. In the 1550s and 1560s the chief focus of violence was Shane O'Neill, both in his own campaigns and in the repeated attempts of the English state to destroy him. Shane's fall precipitated a series of failed but bloody colonial endeavours in east Ulster which yielded some of the worst atrocities of sixteenth-century Ireland at Belfast (1574) and Rathlin Island (1575) and which increased the pressure on the lords of central and

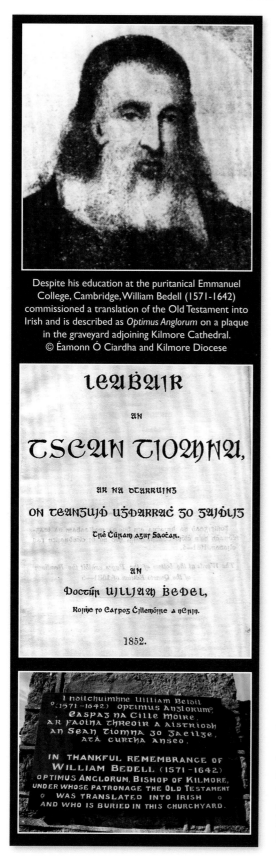

Despite his education at the puritanical Emmanuel College, Cambridge, William Bedell (1571-1642) commissioned a translation of the Old Testament into Irish and is described as *Optimus Anglorum* on a plaque in the graveyard adjoining Kilmore Cathedral.
© Éamonn Ó Ciardha and Kilmore Diocese

LEABAIR

an

TSEAN TIOMNA,

aR na dtaRRuing

ON teangaid ugdaRRac go gaidlig

The Cúnam agur Saoeam.

an

Doctúr UILLIAM Bedel,

Ronne ro Earpog Cillemóine a nepin.

1852.

I noilchuimhne Uilliam Beidil
(1571-1642) optimus Anglorum
easpag na Cille Moire.
ar faoina threoir a aistriodh
an Sean Tiomna go Jaeilge,
atá curtha anseo.

IN THANKFUL REMEMBRANCE OF
WILLIAM BEDELL (1571-1642)
OPTIMUS ANGLORUM, BISHOP OF KILMORE,
UNDER WHOSE PATRONAGE THE OLD TESTAMENT
WAS TRANSLATED INTO IRISH
AND WHO IS BURIED IN THIS CHURCHYARD.

western Ulster to militarise their lordships.[7] Finally, the later years of the Nine Years War exposed the general population of Ulster to a process of ruthless state warfare and scorched-earth tactics which had an unquantifiable but undoubtedly extraordinary demographic impact.[8] Within a decade of the peace of Mellifont a major revolution had occurred; the flight of the earls, Sir Cathair O'Doherty's rebellion and the subsequent plantation of Ulster resulted in the transformation of landownership in the province and the sudden introduction of a substantial settler population of English and Scottish provenance.[9]

The impact of these various events on the Catholic Church was substantial. At the most basic level, enormous damage was done to church buildings and lands, as noted by Sir John Davies in the year preceding the flight.[10] Although approximately three-quarters of the parishes west of the Bann had a priest on the eve of the Ulster plantation, the traditional landholding system which supported the clergy was under pressure. In addition, significant damage had been sustained by the leadership cadres of the Catholic Church. Franciscan convents became the particular target of government forces, and the friars themselves also became the object of attack by state troops. This led to a reduction in the numbers and visibility of one of the most significant obstacles to the spreading of Protestantism in Ireland.[11]

The Catholic episcopate had also been severely weakened. Before the completion of the Tudor conquest the autonomy of the lordships of northwest Ulster had made Protestant appointments to sees such as Derry, Clogher, Dromore, Kilmore and Raphoe impracticable.[12] Equally this factor allowed Rome to continue to make appointments to Ulster dioceses, and as the rebellion developed the Ulster confederates made use of their clerical contacts to lobby continental powers for assistance and to present their struggle in religious terms.[13] Niall O'Boyle of Raphoe, Conor O'Devany of Down and Connor and Richard Brady of Kilmore remained in Ireland after the end of the Nine Years War but by 1612, after O'Devany's execution, all were dead and their sees vacant. The see of Derry also lost its bishop with the execution of Redmond O'Gallagher in 1601.[14] Edmund Magauran, the militant archbishop of Armagh, also suffered a violent death in 1593[15] and was subsequently replaced in 1601, at Hugh O'Neill's behest, by Peter Lombard, the outstanding Irish Catholic intellectual of his generation. As a bishop, however, Lombard, never resided in Ireland, let alone in his diocese. Moreover, as a native of Waterford, he had effectively no personal knowledge of his see and, as the ensuing decades were to indicate, significant cultural differences existed between his own preoccupations and those of even the reforming clergy of Gaelic Ulster.

At the height of the Nine Years War Lombard acted as an influential lobbyist on behalf of the Ulster confederates.[16] Following the flight, however, he opted for a political strategy which stressed accommodation with James VI & I and which emphasised loyalty to the crown as essentially compatible with Catholic belief.[17] Given his exile in Rome, Lombard's chief influence on his see and metropolitan province was exercised through the medium of David Rothe, the vice-primate he appointed in 1609. A native of Kilkenny and bishop of Ossory from 1618, Rothe, like Lombard, was a product of Old English mercantile culture and was equally affected by the significant cultural prejudices and experiences which divided individuals of this background from the Irish of Gaelic Ulster. He did not reside in the ecclesiastical province of Armagh, although he did make visits to it and in 1614 presided over an important synod in Drogheda. Rothe preoccupied himself with firmly embedding a conception of religious reform, which emphasised loyalty to the monarch in all actions which did not interfere with the primacy of fidelity to the Catholic faith.[18] As vice-primate, Rothe was not without achievements in his leadership of religious reform but the level of resistance to direction by Old English clerics became very visible upon Lombard's death in 1625 when concerted and ultimately successful attempts ensured that the vacant primatial see was filled by a Gaelic Ulsterman.[19]

The weakness of the Catholic Church presented a field of opportunity for its state rival, particularly after the implementation of the plantation of Ulster. Even before the flight of the earls, considerable optimism existed in government circles that victory in the Nine Years War offered a unique opportunity to recover the religious losses of the previous century,[20] and this conviction underpinned the coercive Mandates programme of 1605-07.[21] The chief thrust of the Mandates was directed at the Pale and Munster, but a genuine belief also existed that Ulster too could be brought within the fold of the state church, since, in the words of Sir John Davies 'all the people of that province, at least the multitude, are apt to receive any faith'.[22] This perception of the malleability of the Ulster population had been confirmed to some extent by the success of the state church in obtaining conformity from a significant proportion of the ex-

isting clergy of Gaelic Ulster, particularly individuals from among the hereditary ecclesiastical families. A concern to preserve their livelihoods, particularly if they had wives or concubines and offspring, provided a powerful motivation in this respect. Initially the conformity of such clergy did little to prevent the local population from continuing to seek their services at rites of passage such as marriages, christenings and funerals.[23] Gaelic society was certainly not inimical to the Reformation, as the success of Calvinism in neighbouring Gaelic Scotland indicates.[24] Rather than strengthening on the promise of this early beginning, however, the two decades following the Ulster plantation saw a steady alienation of the native population from the state church.

In the first place, the conformist clergy which the state church acquired could hardly be said to constitute a formidable evangelical tool. Economic factors rather than religious conviction seem to have dominated the motivations for entry into the Established Church. In many cases the wives and children of conforming clerics were Catholics, and in the face of death or the drying up of opportunities within the Established Church, many drifted naturally back to their erstwhile religion. Their impact on the general population was extremely limited, where, with the partial exception of east Ulster, there was no sustained pattern of conformity.[25] Moreover, despite efforts by prelates such as the short-lived Brutus Babington in Derry and Andrew Knox in Raphoe to find a place for their conformist clergy, a clear pattern of marginalisation of native Irishmen quickly became visible within the plantation church. Even in Raphoe, where Knox already had extensive experience of dealing with a Gaelic population in the Scottish islands, a process of displacement from the better livings became swiftly evident.[26] From the perspective of the Ulster Protestant bishops, the native Irish clergy were inadequate instruments of reform, lacking both the education and also the commitment to a reformation which integrally linked anglicisation and protestantisation. By the 1630s, settler clergy had been installed in the best livings in nearly all the dioceses of Ulster, with the exception of Kilmore, where the unique influence of William Bedell ensured the survival of a cadre of native ministers.[27]

From the perspective of the bishops who appointed them to benefices, the new clergy of English and Scottish origin were of infinitely higher quality than their native counterparts. However, as an evangelical force the impact of the newcomers on the general population was probably more negative than positive. In terms of pastoral care, the settler clergy largely concentrated on the Protestant population which plantation and private immigration had produced in Ulster.[28] They generally lacked the linguistic skills to attempt to evangelise the Gaelic-speaking population and, in any case, tended to believe that bringing the population to their conception of civility was a necessary precondition of reformation.[29] In addition, they became swiftly resented for their economic impositions. The incoming English and Scottish clergy tended to be over-zealous in exacting dues, often taking not only their entitlements under the remodelled plantation tithe system, but continuing to exact the traditional offerings to the clergy as well. Recusancy fines were also widely imposed in an attempt to extract revenue.[30] As Brian Mac Cuarta has noted, such exactions were particularly resented because even existing ecclesiastical payments had been disrupted during the previous decades, thus heightening the novelty of the newly imposed charges.[31] In the violence which erupted in 1641, it seems clear that much of the hostility directed against Protestant clergymen derived from the economic impact of their activities in the previous decades.[32] Yet, paradoxically, the social effect of such exactions may merely have been to create hardship and antagonism without offering sufficient punitive incentives towards conformity, not least because members of the Protestant laity subverted the activities of their ecclesiastical colleagues in an attempt to maintain cordial relations with the Catholic population, particularly in the context of a shortage of tenants.[33]

Nor did the Established Church manage to make any real impact on the native population by means of education. Astonishingly little evidence exists to indicate that the products of the free schools which were intended for each escheated county in the plantation subsequently made their way to Trinity where they might have been trained as a cadre of native Ulster Protestants. Indeed, startlingly, two of the very few Ulster figures for whom evidence survives within the plantation-era educational system both turned to Catholicism: one going to Salamanca to enter the Society of Jesus, while the other ended up as Catholic dean of Clogher.[34]

While the shortcomings of the Established Church as an evangelical body were undoubtedly manifold, it would nevertheless be unwise to underestimate the degree of antagonism towards the Reformation which already existed in Gaelic Ulster before the great upheaval of the plantation. The interlinking of traditional religious practice with other aspects of Gaelic social experience ensured that resentment of different features of the Tudor conquest impacted on attitudes to Protestantism as well.[35] Significant portions of the Gaelic elite had already evidently internalised a basic hostility towards the new religion by the end of the sixteenth century. This was particularly evident in many families of lordly origin. Even figures as politically motivated and often as violently vengeful as the leaders of the Ulster confederacy, Hugh O'Neill and Red Hugh O'Donnell, may well have been entirely genuine in their commitment to preserving their territories from Protestantism.[36] Indeed, it has been suggested that the initial drift towards conformity on the part of members of the clergy in the early parts of the century may itself be taken as a further indication of the weakening of the traditional power of Gaelic lords.[37] In this regard, it is of particular interest that two of the most hardline of the Catholic bishops of the 1640s, Heber MacMahon and Hugh O'Reilly, sprang from the branches of traditional ruling families. Three others of their contemporaries within the episcopate of the province of Armagh originated from the *lucht tighe* (household) of the Magennis and MacGeoghegan ruling septs.[38]

Yet such attitudes were hardly confined merely to lords. The emphasis on the necessity of coercion articulated by even a figure such as Andrew Knox of Raphoe, who was prepared to accommodate conformist Gaelic clergy, sprang partially from his belief in the 'deadly hatred' which existed towards the new religious dispensation among the native Irish.[39] Such feelings were stoked by the activities of the surviving Franciscan friars whose preaching evidently focused on the diabolic character of the reformed religion,

St Columb's Cathedral, Derry, completed in 1633, was the first purpose-built Protestant cathedral in the three kingdoms.

and the decades before 1641 saw a rapid increase in the numbers of the order throughout Ireland.[40]

It seems very possible that the intrusion of the Protestant Reformation in tandem with the flight and the plantation paradoxically heightened the possibilities of the Catholic revival which began to pick up pace in the period between the early 1610s and 1641. In the face of overwhelming change, native Catholics had redefined all aspects of their identity. If Protestantism represented an unattractive religious choice, the traditional practices of Gaelic Ireland had been exposed to potent criticism on the grounds of barbarism. The individuals who championed reform in Gaelic Ireland claimed to ground their mission on the traditional strengths of their culture, not least the asceticism which they identified as a keystone of Gaelic sainthood,[41] but the overall framework in which they operated was heavily influenced by the contemporary developments in the post-Tridentine Catholic world.

Central to the revival was the leadership of continentally trained clerics. Despite his different cultural background, as vice-primate Rothe neither ignored the needs of Gaelic Ulster for religious leadership nor attempted to create the momentum for reform through Old English delegates. This was of crucial importance, for it ensured that, unlike its Protestant rival, Catholic reform in Ulster could present itself as internal regeneration rather than external imposition. Where possible, Rothe appointed vicars apostolic and vicars general to Ulster dioceses from local products of the continental seminaries, such as Patrick Duffy, Patrick Hanratty and Patrick Matthews.[42] This pattern continued when Rome re-instituted the Irish hierarchy after 1618, appointing native bishops to the sees of the province of Armagh.[43]

In conclusion, Brian Mac Cuarta's recent meticulous depiction of the process of Catholic revival has rightly explored the limits of what the Ulster clerical leadership were able to achieve, given the relative paucity of trained clergy, even when the mission impact of the Franciscans is taken into account.[44] Nevertheless, by the 1620s it seems clear that the Catholic hierarchy had established the outlines of a functional diocesan system which acted as a surprisingly efficient structure for the diffusion of a renewed Catholic identity. Certainly what the reformers identified as abuses continued; but critically in the context of the future evolution of the province, the revived Catholic Church had largely sealed off the native Ulster population from the evangelical reach of the Established Church.

Archbishop Lombard delegated David Rothe (1573-1650), his former secretary, to lead the reconstruction of the Irish Catholic Church. Although unsympathetic to the political interests of the earls and their descendants, Rothe was by no means as hostile to the Gaelic Irish in cultural terms as has been assumed.

ANALECTA
SACRA NOVA
ET MIRA,
DE
REBVS CATHOLICORVM IN
HIBERNIA.
Pro fide & Religione geftis,
Diuifa in tres partes.
Quarum,
I. *Continet femeftrem grauaminum relationem, fe-cundâ bac editione nouis adauctam additamentis, & Notis illuftratam.*
II. *Parænefin ad. Martyres defignatos.*
III. *Proceffum martyrialem quorůdam fidei pugilum.*
Collectore & Relatore T. N. philadelpho.
Colligite quæ fuperauerunt fragmenta ne pereant. IOAN. 6.

COLONIÆ,
Apud Stephanum Rolinum. 1617.
Superiorum permiffu.

Rothe's *Analecta* was a searing indictment of English misgovernment in early seventeenth-century Ireland as well as a vindication of the Irish as a Catholic nation that would choose martyrdom over Protestantism.
© Magee College Library, University of Ulster

Notes

1 M. Balázs *et al* (eds), *Erdélyi és Hódoltsági Jezsuita Missziók 1-2 1617-25* (Szeged, 1990), pp 298-301; T. Ó hAnnracháin, 'A typical anomaly? The success of the Irish Counter-Reformation', in J. Devlin and R. Fanning (eds), *European encounters: essays in honour of Albert Lovett* (Dublin, 2003), pp 78-96.

2 For a brief English language account of post-Mohács Hungary see B. Cartledge, *The will to survive: a history of Hungary* (London, 2006), pp 90-101.

3 B. Mac Cuarta, *Catholic revival in the north of Ireland, 1603-41* (Dublin, 2007), p. 81.

4 H. Jefferies, *Priests and prelates of Armagh in the age of Reformation, 1518-56* (Dublin, 1997), pp 77-81.

5 Ibid.; see also Watt, 'The Church and the Two Nations in Late Medieval Armagh', in W. J. Sheils and D. Wood (eds), *Studies in church history: The churches, Ireland and the Irish*, Studies in Church History, 25 (Oxford, 1989), pp 159-170.

6 T. Ó hAnnracháin, *Catholic Reformation in Ireland: the mission of Rinuccini, 1645-49* (Oxford, 2002), pp 60-65.

7 C. Brady, *The chief governors: the rise and fall of reform government in Tudor Ireland, 1536-88* (Cambridge, 1994), p. 256.

8 V. Carey, '"What pen can paint or tears atone?" Mountjoy's scorched earth campaign', in H. Morgan (ed.), *The Battle of Kinsale* (Bray, 2004), pp 205-16; J. McGurk, 'The pacification of Ulster, 1600-03', in D. Edwards, P. Lenihan and C. Tait (eds), *Age of Atrocity: Violence and Political Conflict in Early Modern Ireland*, ed. (Dublin, 2007), pp 119-29.

9 J. McCavitt, *Sir Arthur Chichester Lord Deputy of Ireland 1605-16* (Belfast, 1998), pp 129-68.

10 A. Ford, *The Protestant Reformation in Ireland, 1590-1641* (2nd ed., Dublin, 1997), p. 132.

11 Mac Cuarta, *Catholic Revival*, pp 18-36.

12 Ford, *Protestant Reformation*, p. 127; Kilmore was filled for four years in the 1580s.

13 G. Henry, *The Irish military community in Spanish Flanders, 1586-1621* (Dublin, 1992), p. 120.

14 D. Conway, 'The Anglican World: problems of coexistence during the pontificates of Urban VIII and Innocent X (1623-55)', in J. Metzler (ed.), *Congregationis de Propaganda Fide Memoria Rerum, 1622-1700* (2 vols, Rome, 1972), i, pt 2, pp 151-2.

15 H. Morgan, *Tyrone's rebellion: The outbreak of the Nine Years War in Tudor Ireland* (Dublin, 1993), p. 145.

16 T. O'Connor, 'Hugh O'Neill: free spirit, religious chameleon or ardent Catholic?', pp 59-72.

17 J. J. Silke, 'Later relations between Primate Peter Lombard and Hugh O'Neill', *Irish Theological Quarterly*, xxii (1955), pp 124-50.

18 A. Forrestal, *Catholic Synods in Ireland, 1600-1690* (Dublin, 1998), pp 42-44.

19 An important survival of this campaign is an undated memorial submitted to Rome on this subject: (Archivio storico della Sacra Congragazione per l'Evangelizzazione dei Popoli o de 'Propaganda Fide', Scritture Originali riferite nelle Congregazioni Generali, 140, ff. 5r-5v).

20 A. Ford, 'Force and Fear of Punishment: Protestants and Religious Coercion in Ireland, 1603-33', in E. Boran and C. Gribben, *Enforcing Reformation in Ireland and Scotland, 1550-1700* (Aldershot, 2006), p. 114.

21 McCavitt, *Chichester* (Belfast, 1998), pp 111-28.

22 Quoted in Ford, *Protestant Reformation*, p. 132.

23 Mac Cuarta, *Catholic revival*, pp 37-70.

24 J. Dawson, 'Calvinism and the Gaidhealtachd in Scotland', in A. Pettegree, A. Duke and G. Lewis (eds), *Calvinism in Europe 1540-1620* (Cambridge, 1994), pp 231-53.

25 Mac Cuarta, *Catholic revival*, pp 51-52.

26 Ford, *Protestant Reformation*, pp 138-44.

27 Ibid., pp 144-7.

28 Ibid., pp 147-8.

29 In this regard see the discussion by P. Palmer, *Language and conquest in early modern Ireland: English Renaissance literature and Elizabethan imperial expansion* (Cambridge, 2001), pp 14-19.

30 Ford, *Protestant Reformation*, pp 148-9.

31 Mac Cuarta, *Catholic Revival*, p. 56.

32 Brian Mac Cuarta, 'Religious violence against settlers in south Ulster, 1641-2', in Edwards *et al* (eds), *Age of Atrocity*, pp 154-75.

33 Mac Cuarta, *Catholic Revival*, pp 60-63.

34 Ford, *Protestant Reformation*, p. 146.

35 M. Caball, 'Innovation and tradition: Irish Gaelic responses to early modern conquest and colonization', in H. Morgan (ed.), *Political Ideology in Ireland* (Dublin, 1999), pp 62-82, there pp 75-76.

36 O'Connor, 'Hugh O'Neill: free spirit, religious chameleon or ardent Catholic?'.

37 Mac Cuarta, *Catholic revival*, p. 44.

38 D. Cregan, 'The social and cultural background of a Counter-Reformation Episcopate, 1618-60', in A. Cosgrove and D. MacCartney (eds), *Studies in Irish history presented to R. Dudley Edwards* (Dublin, 1979), pp 91-93.

39 Ford, *Protestant Reformation*, p. 141.

40 Mac Cuarta, 'Religious violence', pp 168-70; Ó hAnnracháin, *Catholic Reformation*, p. 57.

41 See for instance the discussion of Hugh MacCaughwell in M. O'Riordan, 'The native Ulster mentalité as revealed in Gaelic sources 1600-50', in B. Mac Cuarta (ed.), *Ulster 1641: aspects of the rising* (Belfast, 1993), pp 84-85.

42 Mac Cuarta, *Catholic revival*, pp 77-79.

43 Cregan, 'The Social and Cultural Background'.

44 Mac Cuarta, *Catholic revival*, pp 71-92.

Heroines or victims? The women of the flight of the earls

Jerrold Casway

The flight of the northern earls in September 1607 was a miscalculated stratagem, neither anticipated nor welcomed by Catholic Europe. No post-flight vindications can refute that the earls, intimidated by their failing political circumstances, hoped that their appearance on the continent would incite greater support from their alleged Catholic benefactors. An examination of the various roles of the women caught up in this intemperate exodus provides an insight into a much-neglected side of this controversial gamble.[1] Among the refugees who boarded the eighty-ton vessel at Lough Swilly, seventeen passengers were women, of whom four can be identified by name, three through their marital ties and ten by their service affiliations. Catherine, countess of Tyrone, daughter of Sir Hugh Magennis and sister of Sir Arthur Magennis, first Viscount Iveagh, became Hugh O'Neill's fourth wife in 1598. By the time of the flight she had given birth to three sons: John, Brian and Conn. The second woman was Nuala O'Donnell, immortalised by James Clarence Mangan as the 'woman of the piercing wail', a sister of Red Hugh O'Donnell, and Rory O'Donnell, earl of Tyrconnell. The oldest of the noble women, Nuala had formerly been married to her cousin, Niall Garbh O'Donnell. After ten years of marriage, she left her husband in 1600 after he made a separate peace with the English. Thirdly there was Rosa O'Doherty, daughter of Sir John O'Doherty, lord of Inishowen, and sister to Sir Cathair O'Doherty. She had married Cathbharr, the earl of Tyrconnell's brother, and they had one child, Hugh, after three years of marriage. The final woman who can be identified by name is Caecilia O'Gallagher. She and her husband acted as foster-parents to Rory O'Donnell's son, Hugh. Caecilia served as the child's wet-nurse and looked after the youngster until February 1608 when he was given over to the Convent of the Dames Blanches in Louvain. Other women can be identified by their spouses, including a nurse, the wife of Edward Gruama MacDavitt, Tyrconnell's steward, and also the spouses of Shane O'Hagan, Tyrone's bailiff, and Art Óg O'Neill, Tyrone's nephew, the son of Sir Cormac MacBaron O'Neill.[2] The remaining ten women are unnamed servants who attended the children and noblewomen.

Beside the women on the boat, two others should have been on the flight: Tyrconnell's wife, Brigit Fitzgerald, daughter of Henry, twelfth earl of Kildare, and her unborn daughter. Brigit had been married to Rory O'Donnell for four years, although fifteen years his junior. Pregnant with their third child at the time of the flight, she anticipated being 'brought to bed within 14 days' and only learned of her husband's departure at her paternal grandmother's Maynooth estate.[3] Rory never intended to abandon her; he simply took his wife's condition for granted and expected her to join him after her confinement. Although 'long absent from her husband',[4] nineteen-

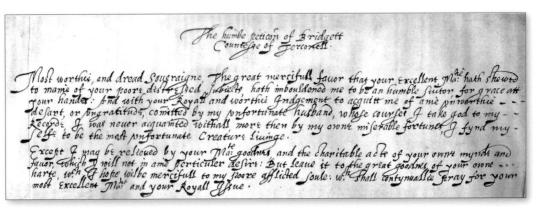

'The humble petition of Bridgett, Countesse of Terconnell', daughter of the twelfth earl of Kildare. She was visiting her mother on the outskirts of the Pale when her husband fled Ulster. Soon after, she gave birth to her daughter Mary, later given the royal name of Stuart by King James. © Hatfield House

year-old Brigit undoubtedly felt distressed at her abandonment. Neither the earl's apologetic letter, nor the gold he sent to pay for her anticipated getaway, pacified her. In testimony taken a few weeks after the flight, Brigit related that Tyrconnell's messenger (a friar, Owen Gruama MacGrath) assured her that her husband's exodus was not 'for want of love … that if Tyrconnell … had known sooner of his going, he would have taken … her with him'.[5] Tyrconnell's haste, Brigit's condition and her inaccessibility had undoubtedly limited their options. Nevertheless, his stealing away with their infant son left his wife to face the expected consequences. Given the gravity of her son-in-law's action, Brigit's mother, the dowager-countess of Kildare, advised her daughter to make the best of a bad situation. Brigit could privately bemoan her abandonment and strive to survive the uncertain political situation created by Tyrconnell's flight. In her defence, Brigit denied any foreknowledge of her spouse's 'unfortunate journey' and prayed that he should have a 'fair death' than 'undergo so wicked an enterprise as to rebel against his prince'.[6]

Brigit O'Donnell never again saw her husband or son. Compelled to dissociate herself from the flight and make a new life for herself, she took the first step to recovery by making a personal appeal at the English court shortly after the birth of her daughter, Mary. With the infant in her arms, Brigit impressed James I with her plight, and he responded sympathetically to her sweet and 'well-favoured face'.[7] Indeed, he confessed that he could not understand how her husband 'left so fair a face behind him' and granted her a pension of £200 from the revenues of her husband's escheated estates.[8] He made Brigit's infant daughter, henceforth known as Mary 'Stuart' O'Donnell, a royal ward.[9] Undoubtedly Brigit benefited from the recuperative powers of her lineage: Charles Howard, the first earl of Nottingham, lord high admiral of England and a privy councillor, was her maternal grandfather.

Allowed to return to her family's Kildare estates, Brigit mourned Rory's death (July 1608) and spent the next decade educating and raising her daughter in the Catholic faith. Sometime around 1617 she married Nicholas Barnewall, some twenty years her senior, a prominent and active Old English lawyer and politician. After her marriage the king increased Brigit's pension to £300 per annum less a £50 deduction for the maintenance of her adolescent daughter Mary.[10] Two years later young Mary was sent over to England to live with her maternal grandmother.[11]

It is not known whether Mary ever saw her mother again, but Brigit would not be without a family. She had nine further children by Nicholas Barnewall, two of whom married into important Old English families. She returned to England around December 1641 after the outbreak of the Irish rebellion. Over the next two turbulent decades her fate was bound to the failing royalist cause, but she and her husband recovered their holdings in the Restoration, and she lived out the rest of her life in quiet anonymity. On her death in 1682 at the age of ninety, Brigit was the oldest surviving person associated with the flight.

The other women of the flight incurred even greater misfortune, their lives stalked by tragedy and loss. Catherine Magennis, countess of Tyrone, reputed to be a lady of 'excellent education and character', was much younger than the earl, and the records show that their relationship was not a placid one.[12] Despite nine years of marriage and three children, Catherine balked at the prospect of leaving her homeland, family and friends. An English account of Tyrone's hurried departure recounted how 'the countess … being exceedingly weary slipped down from her horse, and weeping said she could go no further'. O'Neill responded by threatening her with his sword 'if she would not pass on with him, and put on a more cheerful countenance'.[13] Exhaustion and anxiety aside, Catherine's behaviour could also have been caused by her husband's inability to locate their five-year-old son, Conn, then with his fosterers. Tyrone 'sought him diligently, but … was overtaken with shortness of time'.[14] Once abroad, Catherine's distress did not abate. She was directed by the Spanish court to reside in Rome, where the climate, separation from her children and her diminished lifestyle accentuated her sense of isolation and loss. The countess frequently complained about the 'city's air' and asked to return to Flanders where her young sons, John and Brian, were being raised by the Louvain Franciscans. The Spanish authorities denied all her petitions to relocate near her children. When she pleaded ill-health as a compelling reason for removing from Rome, they suggested that she go instead to Naples or Sicily.[15]

Her fortunes took a dramatic turn in July 1616. After a short illness her husband, Hugh O'Neill, died, leaving her alone with the responsibilities for his family and retainers. A little more than a year after his death Catherine learned that her second son, Brian, had been hanged in his room. Foul play was suspected, but nothing conclusive could ever be proven.[16] These losses magnified her growing isola-

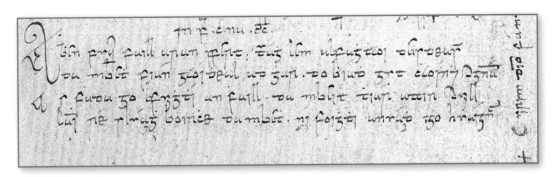

'A bhean fuair faill ar an bhfeart' (Eoghan Rua Mac an Bhaird). In eag., E. Knott *Celtica* 5 (1960), p. 161. Mac an Bhaird's pathos-filled poem to Nuala O'Donnell was rendered as 'The woman of the piercing wail' in the nineteenth century by James Clarence Mangan. © Meamram Páipéar Ríomhaire le caoinchead Clonalis House / Teach Cluain Mhalais

tion. Her youngest son, Conn, the child left behind in Ireland, had been moved from Castlecaulfield to Eton school and eventually to the Tower and oblivion.[17] The oldest child, John, grew to manhood and became estranged from his mother over family finances, specifically Catherine's share of her husband's pension and the maintenance of the late earl's dependants. Her husband's trusted friend, the former Spanish ambassador to Rome, the conde de Castro, asked Philip III to show compassion for Catherine's 'miserable state, alone and without property in a foreign land … with no other protection than that of Your Majesty'.[18] The Spanish council of state debated giving her Tyrone's entire subsidy, a decision predicated upon keeping the late earl's retainers from coming to Spain seeking favours. Phillip III concurred and directed Castro's successor, Cardinal Borja y Velasco, to grant her 'the same allowance' enjoyed by her husband.[19] This decision distressed Tyrone's dependants, who had wanted to divide the pension among themselves.[20]

The problem centred upon her late husband's will. According to the earl's testament, if Catherine maintained 'herself honourably', she would receive 172 crowns a month which fell short of her full monthly Spanish pension of 550 crowns. Controversy ensued when discontented retainers asked Henry O'Hagan, the late earl's secretary, to inform young Colonel John O'Neill that his mother had withheld the money bequeathed them by his late father. They asserted that if the earl's directions were not followed, many 'poor folk' would suffer. They asked for Colonel O'Neill's support and even suggested that Catherine be 'enclosed in a convent of nuns'. They warned him that he should send someone to Rome to deposit the late earl's plate and materials in a bank before the countess seized them. This tension and mistrust exposed the refugees' extreme depend-ency and Catherine's apparent estrangement from her husband and his immediate retainers.[21]

Despite the royal grant of September 1616, Tyrone's widow did not receive any compensation, and without this payment, no dependant could expect relief. Throughout most of 1617 Catherine unsuccessfully petitioned Spain for her monthly stipend.[22] Eventually the suffering countess repaired to Naples to evade her many creditors, find relief for her fragile health, and to be near her protector, the new Spanish Viceroy, the duke of Ossuna.[23] This move, however, did not stem her declining fortunes, and on 22 June 1618, Catherine described herself to Phillip III as 'this afflicted and unprotected widow', who feared 'less to die of hunger than to become the ridicule of the English'.[24] Responding to her alleged neglect, the king ordered her immediate payment. Nonetheless, it remains doubtful whether Catherine ever escaped her difficult situation, for she passed away a mere nine months later in mid-March 1619, to the great distress of her son Colonel John O'Neill. The English ambassador in Flanders reported that the countess died with her pension payments in arrears. Such was the tragic fate of Tyrone's wife, a sad end to a life reduced to loneliness, deprivation and dependence.[25]

Nuala O'Donnell, the earl of Tyrconnell's sister, enjoyed better fortune than Catherine Magennis. Unmarried and without children, she took up residence in Rome with her brother and the O'Donnell dependants, all of whom lived on an inadequate pension of 330 crowns a month.[26] The marqués de Aytona, the conde de Castro's predecessor in Rome, told Phillip III that the pope gave the exiles a house with 'not a stick of furniture' or 'money to buy such bare necessities … so as not to sleep on the floors'.[27] Seeking relief from the tedium and want of their imposed Roman exile, the O'Donnell brothers and

Tyrone's eldest son, Hugh, baron of Dungannon, sought refuge on the sea-coast near Ostia, outside of Rome. After four days, near the mosquito-ridden marshlands, each of the young lords succumbed to a 'hot, fiery, violent fever'. Nursed by Nuala and the other flight women, the earl of Tyrconnell lingered for eleven days before expiring on 28 July 1608. She had no time to grieve as she gave her attention to her failing brother, Cathbarr, who passed away on 15 September. Both brothers were buried in the habit of St Francis in the Church of San Pietro in Montorio in Rome.[28] A growing sense of abandonment magnified her distress at exile, but her responsibilities meant she had little time for self-pity. She alone had the responsibility for her family and their households, which meant consoling Cathbharr's young widow, Rosa O'Doherty, and attending to her two orphaned nephews, the O'Donnell heirs in Louvain.

Ambassador Aytona appreciated her dilemma. He disclosed that the pope was 'exceedingly parsimonious',[29] and since the O'Donnells were 'bereft of all human assistance', he petitioned the Spanish crown that Nuala be granted the late earl's pension.[30] Hugh O'Neill himself wrote on behalf of Nuala and her dependants, asking that the O'Donnell women be permitted to return to Flanders and that their debts and expenses be paid. Tyrone focused his appeal on 'our sister' Nuala by requesting His Majesty to give her 'particular attention'.[31]

Philip III granted the request in order to ensure that the O'Donnells kept to their Roman abode,

a means of placating English fears that the flight refugees would create problems and might use a convenient western port to return to Ireland.[32] This restraint did not dissuade Nuala O'Donnell from soliciting for an exception. Using bad health and the Roman climate as an excuse, she convinced Ambassador Castro and the king to reconsider their former directive. As early as 26 August 1610, Phillip III gave her permission to travel to Flanders on the understanding that 'none of her kinsmen, or any other Irish in Rome go with her', so, as he pointed out to his council, England 'can have no reason for complaint'.[33] Nuala was advanced 300 crowns by Ambassador Castro, and her Roman pension was transferred to the 'secret expenses of army funds' in the Spanish Netherlands.[34] Philip specified these terms in a letter to the Archduke Albert, ordering that he maintain her pension 'as long as she may live or as long as I may wish'.[35]

Once Nuala had organised her finances, she departed for the Low Countries with Dr Eugene Matthews (MacMahon), titular archbishop of Dublin, who had a special commission from the pope to reconcile Flanders's factious Irish Catholic community. After their arrival in mid-December 1611 Matthews headed up the Franciscan-inspired Brussels-Louvain clique that worked to channel the energies and resources of the Irish exiles.[36] Nuala gave her attention to the well-being of her young nephews, who had been left as infants in Louvain. The boys remained with their nurses at the convent until October 1610, when the two Hughs were given over to the care of

Nineteenth-century lithograph which depicts O'Neill threatening his countess as they rode north to Rathmullan. The charge is made in a letter by Sir John Davies, hardly the most objective of commentators. © Inch House Irish Studies Centre

Hugh MacCaughwell, the Franciscan superior of St Anthony's Irish College in Louvain, where they were raised alongside Tyrone's two sons, John and Brian.[37]

Nuala's efforts on behalf of her orphaned nephew, the young claimant to the earldom of Tyrconnell, took an unexpected turn in March 1614. Under the pretext of going on a pilgrimage to the Lady of Hal, she went to Brussels and sent a late-evening message to William Trumbull, the English ambassador, requesting that they confer secretly at her lodgings. According to Trumbull, the young lord's 'tutoress' professed her loyalty to King James and offered to withdraw her nephew from Flanders for the king's 'grace and pardon … together with the restoring of his father's lands'. An astonished Trumbull refused to commit himself, as he could not be sure whether the king would grant her full request because of the late earl's 'ingratitude and offences'. The ambassador did suggest that if Nuala wanted to help her nephew, 'she should only demand his pardon and leave to go to England, and refer the rest to … His Majesty's accustomed bounty and clemency'.[38] Unsurprisingly, her propositions remained stillborn, but the question of her motivation persists. Nuala's appeal was either a desperate O'Donnell move for a separate deal or a Franciscan contrivance to see whether there was any room for negotiation or reconciliation.

Without any hope of relief or restoration, Nuala vigilantly defended her life-sustaining monthly pension in the face of Philip III's attempts to reduce Irish pensions and grants.[39] A list compiled by the archduke at about this time confirmed Nuala's subsidy of 175 crowns, 'through a secret channel'.[40] It also directed her to oversee the major portion of her late brother's grant to her young nephew, for whom she was responsible, though she was not to share in it.[41] After this reference, little is known about Nuala. She continued to live in Louvain where she maintained her relationship with the Irish Franciscan College of St Anthony. When her nephew came of age, he became a court page to the Infanta Isabella and was later was knighted and given a military commission; by 1632 the young Hugh O'Donnell had an Irish regiment of his own.[42] But as he matured, his dependence on his aunt was reversed, and she now required his consent for the distribution of her monthly pension. This was not always forthcoming, and Florence Conry, titular archbishop of Tuam, had to appeal for prompt payment of her allowance when her nephew was not at court.[43] The O'Donnell matriarch, reduced by two decades of exile to a de-

'Owen Roe O'Neill lands at Doe'. © Seán Ó Brógáin

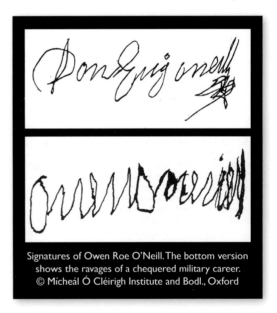

Signatures of Owen Roe O'Neill. The bottom version shows the ravages of a chequered military career. © Mícheál Ó Cléirigh Institute and Bodl., Oxford

pendent pensioner pleading for her monthly allowance, could have hardly anticipated this twist of fate in 1607. Interred in the chapel of St Anthony's College, Louvain, Nuala reposes near her sister-in-law and fellow flight refugee, Rosa O'Doherty.

Rosa, sister of Sir Cathair O'Doherty, lord of Inishowen, the youngest of the aristocratic ladies who accompanied the earls abroad, had married Cathbharr O'Donnell in 1604 and had given birth to a son, Hugh, in June 1605. The boy was born with six toes on one foot, and it was prophesied that such an O'Donnell 'shall drive all the Englishmen out of Ireland'.[44] This prediction appeared to take a setback before the boy's second birthday when he accompanied his parents to the continent. Rosa and Cathbarr had just managed to retrieve him from his foster-parents as the boat readied itself for sailing. The teenage Rosa's world would be turned upside down.[45] The voyage was cramped and beset with turbulent weather during most of the twenty-one days at sea. Ten days after they dropped anchor off the French coast, Rosa and her companions met with relatives and countrymen in Flanders. During the next three and a half months, while Spain decided how to treat these unanticipated guests, the refugees stayed in Louvain. By February 1608 the harsh reality of exile took shape when Spain ordered them to depart for a more secure and insulated haven in Rome. To their dismay, the Spanish authorities ordered that the children should remain in Louvain. The trek to Rome proved arduous, but Rosa's desperation became even more acute when she learned of her brother's disastrous uprising. His death and the confiscations that followed crippled the remaining prospects for Rosa and her fellow refugees. A more immediate tragedy was the death of her husband, carried away by fever.[46] Her sister-in-law Nuala consoled and attended her in her distress. This relationship had a practical side because Rosa's allowance came from Nuala, who administered her late brother's subsidy to the relatives and dependants.[47] Now they were living together in a house provided by the pope, Hugh O'Neill could do little for these unattached O'Donnell women, and he petitioned for their relocation to the Spanish Netherlands in the hope of alleviating their deprivation and placing them in a position to look after the future well-being of the young O'Donnell boys.[48]

Spain's refusals had not deterred Nuala, and Rosa determined to follow her example, and for the next two years she used Nuala's arguments to support her own application to go to Flanders.[49] On 20 June 1612 Castro told King Philip III that he could not dissuade Rosa from this undertaking and that she had already set out for the Low Countries. This daring and desperate step was the result of her powerless condition, and possibly a calculated move on the part of Tyrone to force Spain to accept the *fait accompli*. Ambassador Castro certainly suspected this, as he made clear in his letter transferring Rosa's pension of 80 crowns a month be transferred to Flanders.[50]

Once in the Spanish Netherlands, Rosa took up residence with Nuala in Louvain, and the sisters-in-law oversaw the education and security of the O'Donnell cousins. Her relationship with the Franciscan community also gave the young widow an opportunity to reacquaint herself with Florence Conry's protégé, Owen Roe O'Neill, Tyrone's nephew and the sergeant-major of the Irish regiment serving in Flanders. Rosa had met O'Neill during her original stay in the Low Countries. It is unknown whether their relationship had been affected by personal or political motivations, but these unmarried, well-connected second cousins shared a commitment to the restoration of native Irish power. The couple wed on 18 June 1613.[51]

Within a few years of the marriage, Rosa gave birth to Henry Roe, the only child of this marriage who reached adulthood.[52] Rosa was now the mother of two boys with politically significant lineages, but her oldest son, Cathbharr's child, died at the siege of Breda in 1625 while serving in the Irish regiment. Deaths of this kind were an expected part of a flight refugee's life. Rosa dealt with this grief and went on with her expanded activities and expected duties as the wife of a politically active military leader. Often she seconded and represented her husband during O'Neill's service in the Spanish army. Her best-documented years, the ones immediately preceding the 1641 rebellion, coincide with English surveillance of Owen Roe and his northern Irish cohorts. The purchasing of arms, the assembling of shipments and the gathering of intelligence became some of her identifiable responsibilities. In her only extant letter, of September 1642, she divulged these preoccupations in an inquiry about her spouse's safe return to Ireland. She mainly fretted over the safe transport of Owen's supplies and the need for securing them against the 'Saxons and Scots'.[53] Rosa's whereabouts after her return to Ireland in 1643 often depended on her husband's stationing or the commercial ventures of his supporters and it was not until 1648 that her activities became better known during the time when she was collecting funds and purchasing war materials. One account reported how Rosa lost her cargo, but eluded 'English pirates' by concealing her identity. Most references centred upon her dealings in the western port towns of Limerick and Galway, which compelled one observer to complain that Galway 'will not be quiet, so long as Lady O'Neill and her compatriots live here'.[54]

In Galway, Rosa resided with her daughter-in-law, Eleanor Fitzgerald, and her grandson, Hugh, her only family life at this unsettling stage of the Irish civil war. She was not with Owen Roe when he became mortally ill in November 1649, and he had died before she arrived at Cloughoughter Castle in County Cavan. Six months later she had to endure the execution of her son, Henry Roe, after his capture in the débâcle at Scariffhollis.[55] The twice-widowed survivor of the flight fled from her collapsing homeland, taking her grandson with her. She returned to Flanders, where she resumed her life as a Spanish petitioner and supplicant. After a lapse of forty years, Rosa O'Doherty O'Neill again preoccupied herself with rearing a prominent young Irish claimant. Soon afterwards, assisted by Father Andrea Mangelli, the internuncio in Flanders, young Hugh received papal protection and became a page in the house of Prince Pamfili, Pope Innocent X's family, leaving Rosa alone with only her monthly subsidy and tragic memories. In December 1660, following the death of his kinsman Hugh Dubh O'Neill, Hugh was recognized as earl of Tyrone; soon afterwards he was created a Knight of Calatrava, and rose to the rank of colonel in the Spanish service before his death in 1673. His grandmother, however, never lived to see him receive these honours. She died in November 1660 and lies next to Cathbharr's son and Nuala O'Donnell in Louvain.[56]

The hardships and disappointments suffered by the three noble ladies paled against the vulnerability and suffering of those women of lesser social status who left with the earls. Their difficulties were best exemplified by the plight of Caecilia O'Gallagher, wet-nurse and foster-mother to Tyrconnell's infant son. Caecilia and her husband were O'Donnell clients who 'lost all their possessions in order to come here [Flanders]'.[57] Although they maintained the O'Donnell heir for 'a full year and six months' at their own expense, another nurse, Anna ny Madden, supplanted Caecilia because of the latter's inability to nurse the child. Devastated by this loss, they questioned how a stranger could teach the young O'Donnell 'his mother tongue' and asserted that the child's rightful nurse should remain with him at the convent. In their desperation, the O'Gallaghers bemoaned that they had 'no other consolation except this child, or means of support, or income'. They lamented to the Archduke Albert that they 'had nothing to eat except what your Highness with your wanted kindness is pleased to grant'.[58] The dependence of the O'Gallaghers on reluctant patrons eliminated whatever prospects they anticipated on the continent. Their constant solicitations and pleas only alienated their correspondents. Whereas Irish men found alternative career opportunities in the services of Catholic Europe, their womenfolk had

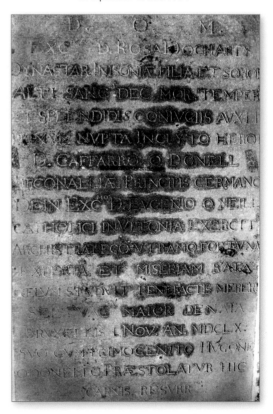

A letter in Irish by Rosa O'Doherty,
16 September 1642. © TNA

Rosa O'Doherty's tomb, St Antony's College Louvain.
© Colm Croker

few options beyond marriage and quickly became reduced to dependency.

In the case of Brigit Fitzgerald's daughter, Mary Stuart O'Donnell, the consequences of the flight touched another generation. Raised as a Catholic in Ireland, Mary, after her mother remarried, was sent in 1619 to England to live with her grandmother, Frances Howard, the dowager countess of Kildare. Within a few years, the strong-willed adolescent estranged her benefactors and family with disputes over her annuities, her Irish Catholic associations and her marital status.[59] Both the Howard family and her grandmother believed a Protestant husband for the attractive and desirable heiress would easily resolve many of Mary's difficulties. But in 1626 the nineteen-year-old Mary got herself involved in a plot to free a number of Irish hostages from the Tower. Summoned to testify before the royal council, Mary, disguised as a young man, escaped to the continent towards the end of the year and made her way to Flanders.[60] In Brussels she met her brother, Hugh, the titular second earl of Tyrconnell for the first time. His influence ensured a good reception at the Infanta's court, and both Archbishop Conry and the papal nuncio recommended her to Cardinal Barberini, the papal secretary of state.[61] Before receiving their dispatches, Pope Urban VIII sent his blessing: 'You, our dear daughter, have given to the world a proof of … what strength and courage are imparted by the true faith'. He praised her 'heroic' nature and noted how she resisted the allurements of court, the menaces of the English king and the 'horrors of an alliance with a Protestant'. Urban praised her defiance and welcomed her tenderly into the bosom of the Roman Church.[62]

These good feelings quickly dissipated when Mary Stuart refused to be used as a marital tool to heal the tensions between the O'Donnell and the O'Neill factions. Florence Conry procured Mary a dowry and the support of the Infanta for a marriage to John O'Neill, styled the third earl of Tyrone. The young woman, anticipating a serious estrangement if she rejected this match, took matters into her own hands. In a machination reminiscent of her

aunt Nuala's actions in 1614, Mary wrote to Lord Conway, the English secretary of state explaining her flight on her 'smallness of means and the fear of losing her reputation' and suggesting that she might 'draw her brother into the king's service' with the right royal guarantees.[63] The futility of her appeal exposed the hopelessness of her position. But true to her flight legacy, the pregnant Mary Stuart fled to Italy with her 'poor Irish captain', Dudley (Dualtach) O'Gallagher.[64] The young couple married, and while living in Genoa Mary gave birth to a boy. With Rome unwilling to support their 'worthy daughter', the young couple survived on a meagre subsidy from the Infanta. As for her brother, Hugh O'Donnell complained that a woman posing as his sister had defamed him and his house.[65] Mary and her husband ultimately found refuge in Austria, where he perished in the Imperial service. The widowed Mary Stuart made her way back to Rome and was last heard from in 1639.[66] As for the titular earls of Tyrone and Tyrconnell, they died fighting for Spain just as rebellion was festering in Ireland.

Of the female fugitives, only Rosa O'Doherty made her way back to Ireland, but this owed to luck and the opportunities afforded by marriage to a well-connected expatriate. As a result, her heroic mantle differed from that of her flight sisters and the thousands of Irish women who later followed their menfolk abroad. For them, survival required an inglorious heroism. Few women had a chance to promote their faith or work towards the restoration of their homeland. The life that awaited them on the continent almost never provided the relief or fulfilled the expectations of their departure. Nothing but the demeaning trials of daily endurance awaited the wives and daughters of Irish lords or the women of undistinguished Irishmen. These vicissitudes made female refugees victims, not romantic heroines. Although their struggle for survival often displayed great fortitude, the plight of the powerless women of the flight became an unfortunate pattern repeated by the struggling multitude of displaced women of the 'wild geese'.[67]

Notes

1 The author would like to thank the *New Hibernia Review* for permission to reprint excerpts of this article. J. Casway, Review of M. Kerney Walsh, *'Destruction by peace': Hugh O'Neill After Kinsale* (Armagh, 1986)', *Irish Literary Supplement* (autumn, 1987), p. 8.

2 Archduke's list, Nov. 1607 (AGS, Negociones de Flandes, leg. 625, frame 24 (Copy in NLI, N. 456, P. 76); M. Kerney Walsh, 'Destruction by peace', pp 184-5; C. Mooney, 'A noble shipload', *Irish Sword*, ii (1955), pp 196, 199-200.

3 Chichester's note on Remington's intelligence, 13 Sept. 1607

(*CSPI, 1606-1608*, p. 571).

4 James Fitzgerald to Salisbury, c. Nov. 1607, HMC, *Salisbury*, (London, 1965), xix, p. 430.

5 Brigit O'Donnell to lord deputy, Sept. 1607 (*CSPI, 1606-08*, pp 296-7); C. Meehan, *The fate and fortunes of Hugh O'Neill, earl of Tyrone and Rory O'Donel, earl of Tyrconnel* (New York, 1868), pp 242-3.

6 Brigit O'Donnell to lord deputy, Sept. 1607 (*CSPI, 1606-08*, p. 297). An interrogated Franciscan, Thomas Fitzgerald, reaffirmed the family's position that Brigit preferred to go to England to resolve her position than accompany Tyrconnell to the continent. Examination of Fr Fitzgerald, 3 Oct. 1607 (ibid., pp 297-8); Chichester to Privy Council, 16 Oct. 1607 (ibid., pp 297-8, 305).

7 Chichester to Privy Council, 16 Oct. 1607 (*CSPI, 1606-08*, pp 305-6).

8 J. Nichols, *The progresses, processions and magnificent festivities of James I* (London, 1828), ii, p. 157; *The Complete Peerage*, xii, pt ii (London, 1910), p. 113; Meehan, *Fate and fortunes*, p. 252; countess of Tyrconnell's petition, 22 Dec. 1608 (*CSPI, 1606-08*, p. 117); petition of Lady Stuart O'Donnell, [c. 1625] (*CSPI, 1615-25*, p. 420. Nicholas Barnewall and countess of Tyrconnell to Lady Stuart O'Donnell, 1617 (10 Dec. 1625 copy) (*CSPI, 1625-32*, pp 55-56); *Complete Peerage*, xii, pt ii, pp 113-4.

9 J. MacGeoghegan, *History* (New York, 1845), p. 564.

10 Petition of Lady Stuart O'Donnell, c. 1625 (*CSPI, 1615-25*, p. 420); Lady Stuart O'Donnell to Lord Conway, 24 Sept. 1625 (*CSPI, 1625-32*, p. 41). Charles I to the lord deputy and lord Treasurer, 10 Oct. 1625 (*CSPI, 1625-32*, pp 43-44); Nicholas Barnewall and Countess Tyrconnell to Lady Stuart O'Donnell, 1617 (10 Dec. 1625 copy) (ibid., pp 55-56). *Complete Peerage*, xii, pt ii, pp 113-4.

11 MacGeoghegan, *History*, p. 564.

12 M. J. Byrne (ed.), *De regno Hibernaie sanctorum insula commentarius* (Dublin, 1930), pp 42-43. M. Walsh, 'Some notes towards a history of the womenfolk of the Wild Geese', *Irish Sword*, v (1961), p. 105.

13 Davies to Salisbury, 12 Sept. 1607 (*CSPI, 1606-08*, p. 270). G. B. Harrison, *A second Jacobean journal* (Ann Arbor, 1958), p. 53; Walsh, 'Womenfolk', pp 104-5.

14 Chichester to Privy Council, 7 Sept. 1607 (TNA, SPI 63/222/126).

15 Castro to Phillip III, 2 Feb. 1615; Phillip III to Castro, 4 Apr. 1615; Castro to Phillip III, 9 Jan. 1616; Phillip III to Castro, 3 Mar. 1616 (all cited in Kerney Walsh, 'Destruction by peace', pp 340, 344-5, 371, 372.

16 For summaries of this incident consult, J. Casway, *Owen Roe O'Neill and the struggle for Catholic Ireland* (Philadelphia, 1984), pp 27, 290 n. 16; Kerney Walsh, 'Destruction by peace', p. 127.

17 Alan Apsley to council, 9 Oct. 1623 (*CSP Dom., 1623-25*), p. 90.

18 Castro to Phillip III, 17 Apr. 1616 (Kerney Walsh, 'Destruction by peace', pp 378-9).

19 Phillip III to Borja y Velasco, 10 Sept. 1616 (ibid., p. 105).

20 Castro to Phillip III, 2 Nov. 1616 (ibid., p. 252). Kerney Walsh, 'Womenfolk', pp 105-6 quotes a similar letter dated 27 Dec. 1616 (AGS, Negoc. De Roma, leg. 1865, f. 19 (copy in NLI, N. 461, p. 81).

21 P. Walsh, *The will and family of Hugh O'Neill, earl of Tyrone* (Dublin, 1930), pp 11-12.

22 Royal orders, 5 Aug., 2 Sept. 1617 (Fondo Santa Sede, leg. 56, ff 253, 250, 251 (copies in NLI); Countess of Tyrone to Phillip III, 22 June 1618 (ibid., f. 253); Kerney Walsh, 'Womenfolk', p. 106.

23 William Trumbull to secretary of state, 21 Mar. 1618/19 (TNA SP, 77/13 I, 201). Initially Phillip III ordered that the earls should be paid from Naples (Royal Directive, 15 July 1608 (Kerney Walsh, 'Destruction by peace', p. 225)).

24 Countess of Tyrone to Phillip III, 22 June 1618 (Kerney Walsh, 'Womenfolk', p. 106).

25 William Trumbull to secretary of state, 21 Mar. 1618-19.

26 Aytona to Phillip III, 22 May 1608 (Kerney Walsh, 'Destruction by peace', p. 217).

27 Aytona to Phillip III, 22 May, 11 Nov. 1608 (ibid., pp 217, 240).

28 P. Walsh (ed.), 'Flight', *Archivium Hibernicum*, iv (1915), pp 239-40.

29 Aytona to Phillip III, 12 Sept. 1608 (Kerney Walsh, 'Destruction by peace', p. 232).

30 Aytona to Phillip III, 4 Aug., 12 Sept., 11 Nov. 1608 (ibid., *Destruction by peace*, pp 230, 232, 239).

31 Tyrone to Phillip III, 13 Sept. 1608 (ibid., p. 234).

32 Council of state to Phillip III (attached to Aytona to Phillip III). 4 Aug. 1608; Phillip III to Aytona, 1 Nov. 1608, 28 Feb. 1609 (ibid., pp 231, 239, 245).

33 Phillip III to Castro, 26 Aug. 1610; Castro to Phillip III, 7 Dec. 1610 (ibid., pp 265, 273).

34 Castro to Phillip III, 11 Sept. 1611 & Phillip III to Castro, 20 Nov. 1611 (ibid., pp 278, 279-80); AGS., Negoc. de Roma, leg. 1863, fr, 15 (copy in NLI, N. 460, 80).

35 Phillip III to Archduke, 20 Nov. 1611 (Kerney Walsh, 'Destruction by peace', p. 280). Her share of her brother's allotment was 175 crowns. The rest (155 crowns) was to be divided among her brother's dependants who remained in Rome (Castro to Phillip III, 31 Jan. 1612 ibid., p. 284).

36 Trumbull to Salisbury, 19 Dec. 1611, 20 Jan. 1612 (TNA, SP 77/10 I, 158v, 165v). Castro to Phillip III, 31 Jan. 1612 (Kerney Walsh, 'Destruction of peace', p. 284); W. Trumbull to J. Digby, 21 Dec. 1611, in HMC, *George Wingfield Digby manuscripts*, 10th Report, p. 550); B. Jennings (ed.), *Wild Geese in Spanish Flanders, 1582-1700* (Dublin, 1964), p. 551. Casway, *Owen Roe*, pp 24-25. For a more detailed discussion of their activities see Casway, 'Gaelic Maccabeanism: the politics of reconciliation', in J. Ohlmeyer (ed), *Seventeenth-century Irish political thought* (Cambridge, 2000), pp 176-88.

37 B. Jennings, 'The career of Hugh, son of Rory O'Donnell, Earl of Tyrconnell, in the Low Countries, 1607-1642', *Studies*, xxx (1941), pp 118, 220-6; idem (ed.), *Wild Geese*, p. 128; Archduke to Phillip III, 1 Nov. 1610 (Kerney Walsh, 'Destruction by peace', p. 273).

38 Trumbull to James I, 7 Apr. 1614; Meehan, *Fate and fortunes*, pp 463-4; Jennings, 'Career of Hugh', pp 118, 226; P. Walsh, *Irish men of learning* (Dublin, 1947), pp 82-83.

39 Archduke to Phillip III, 13 Aug. 1616 (Jennings, *Wild Geese*, p. 149).

40 Archduke to Phillip III, 20 Apr. 1616 (ibid., pp 147-8).

41 Royal order, 29 Jan. 1617 (NLI, Fondo Santa Sede, leg. 56, f. 258).

42 Jennings, 'Career of Hugh', pp 118, 227-32. Casway, *Owen Roe*, p. 38.

43 Abp of Tuam's observations, 30 Jan. 1627 (Jennings, *Wild Geese*, p. 215).

44 Sir John Davies to Salisbury, 12 Sept. 1607 (*CSPI, 1606-08*, pp 270-1).

45 Walsh (ed.), 'Flight', pp 1-9.

46 J. Casway, *Rosa O'Dogherty: a Gaelic woman* (Columbia, Md., 1983), pp 9-10.

47 Aytona to Phillip III. 4 Aug., 12 Sept., 11 Nov. 1608 & 28 Feb. 1609 (Kerney Walsh, '*Destruction by peace*', pp 230, 232, 239, 245.

48 Tyrone to Phillip III, 13 Sept. 1608 (Kerney Walsh, '*Destruction by peace*', p. 234).

49 Castro to Phillip III, 2 Apr. 1612 (AGS, Negoc. de Roma, leg. 997, fr. 9 (Copy in NLI, N. 460, p. 80).

50 Castro to Phillip III, 20 June 1612 (ibid., leg. 998, fr. 13); Castro to Phillip III, 29 Jan. 1614 (Kerney Walsh, '*Destruction by peace*', pp 324-5).

51 Marriage licence, 18 June 1613 (Louvain, City Annals Office). I would like to thank Mr Brian O'Doherty for bringing this document to my attention.

52 For an examination of this contention see Casway, *Rosa O'Dogherty*, pp 15-16; idem, 'The 'illegitimate sons of Owen Roe O'Neill', *Seanchas Ardmhacha*, xii (1986), pp 116-21.

53 Rosa O'Doherty to [Hugh Bourke], 16 Sept. 1642 cited in J. T. Gilbert (ed.), *A contemporary history of affairs in Ireland from 1641 to 1652* (3 vols, Dublin, 1879), ii, pp 523-4; Casway, *Rosa O'Dogherty*, pp 26-27.

54 Andrew Darcy to George Lane, 26 Apr. 1649 (NLI, Ormonde MSS, 2315, Vol. 15, 409). For specific activities see Casway, *Rosa O'Dogherty*, pp 20-21.

55 Casway, *Rosa O'Dogherty*, pp 21-22.

56 Ibid.

57 Petitions of Hugh and Caecilia O'Gallagher, [c. June 1610] Jennings (ed.), *Wild Geese*, p. 126.

58 Ibid.

59 MacGeoghegan, *History*, p. 564; Lady Stuart O'Donnell to Conway, 24 Sept. 1625 (*CSPI, 1625-32*, p. 41). Petition to James I [1623] (ibid., p. 240) Charles I to lord deputy and lord treasurer, 10 Oct. 1625 (ibid., p. 43); lord justice to lord deputy, 10 Oct. 1625 (ibid., p. 44); copy of agreement, 7 July 1617 (10 Dec. 1625, copy) (ibid., pp 55-56).

60 MacGeoghegan, *History*, p. 564; Jennings (ed.), *Wild Geese*, p. 567; J. Casway, 'Mary Stuart O'Donnell', *Donegal Annual*, xxxix (1987), pp 31-32.

61 Abp of Tuam's observations, 30 Jan. 1627 (Jennings (ed.), *Wild Geese*, p. 215).

62 Urban VIII to Lady Stuart O'Donnell, 13 Feb. 1627 (Barb. Lat. MSS, 6140, f. 13r-v, copy in NLI); MacGeoghegan, *History*, p. 565.

63 Lady Stuart O'Donnell to Conway, c. Mar. 1627 (*CSPI, 1625-32*, p. 108).

64 Paulo Philippi to Dorchester, 7 Sept. 1630 (TNA SP 63/251/74); Lady Stuart O'Donnell to Cardinal Barberini, [9] Feb. 1632 (Barb. Lat. MSS, 4994, ff 137r-138v). Andrew Leslie to John Seton, 16 Mar. 1638-39 (*CSP Dom., 1638-39*, p. 569).

65 Hugh O'Donnell to Luke Wadding, 29 July 1630, in B. Jennings (ed.), *Wadding papers, 1614-38* (Dublin, 1953), pp 381-2.

66 Fr Gerald Fitzgerald to Wadding, 26 Apr. 1634, 10 Jan. 1635, in B. Jennings (ed.), 'Irish Franciscan documents, Prague', *Archivium Hibernicum*, ix (1942), pp 275, 280. For full discussion on Mary Stuart O'Donnell's plight see, Casway, 'Mary Stuart O'Donnell', pp 31-32.

67 For a discussion of the 'wild geese' women see J. Casway, 'Irish women overseas, 1500-1800', in M. MacCurtain and M. O'Dowd (eds), *Women in early modern Ireland* (Edinburgh, 1991), pp 112-32.

Irish prisoners in the Tower of London: prerequisites for plantation

John McGurk

Early-modern historians do not underestimate the role of the Tower of London as a high-security state prison during the Irish wars and in the domestic history of the English monarchy. The Tower ever loomed in the background as a threat to anyone who opposed monarchical authority or threatened the succession, or to those who opposed crown territorial ambitions. As a royal palace, it provided secure refuge for the monarch in desperate times – a tradition maintained down to Charles II's restoration in 1660 when that monarch spent the night before his coronation within its stout walls.

The Tower comprises a complex of eighteen towers on the inner and outer wards, each telling its own story. In the period with which this essay is concerned the Tower may be regarded as a monument to the tyrannical behaviour of the Tudor and Stuart monarchies and the English parliament, in mid-seventeenth century.[1] Evidence of its role as a state prison is palpable in the material fabric of the various Tower apartments on lower and upper floors, and in the inscriptions scratched on the walls by its inmates, especially in the Beauchamp and Martin Towers. A few public executions took place both inside the Tower and on Tower Hill and Tower Green, notably those of Queens Anne Boleyn, Catherine Howard and Lady Jane Grey – alongside her husband – as well as Saints Thomas More and John Fisher. Notable sinners, such as Thomas Cromwell, Robert Devereux, the second earl of Essex, Sir Walter Ralegh, Archbishop Laud and the earl of Strafford also met the headsman behind its forbidding walls. Simon Fraser, the unscrupulous Lord Lovat, was the last person to be executed on Tower Hill on 9 April 1747. The block and axe then used are now on display in the Bloody Tower, so named since 1571 but originally called the Garden Tower. Many of the Catholic martyrs, after prolonged torture in the Tower, went to their deaths on Tyburn Hill. Not a few life prisoners such as the Irish aristocrats died of starvation in the Tower or in the overspill prisons of the cities of London and Westminster, including the Fleet, Newgate (now the site of the Old Bailey), the Bridewell, Wood Street Prison, and south of the river, across from the Tower, the Clink, which, along with the Marshalsea, chiefly housed religious offenders. The Gatehouse at Westminster, and the King's Bench Prison, controlled by the Privy Council and the bishop of London, catered mainly for political prisoners and debtors.[2]

Every period of Anglo-Irish relations from the Norman conquest of Ireland to 1916 had a

The Tower of London with Traitor's Gate (inset). © Historic Royal Palaces

representative prisoner: from John de Courcy, lord of Ulster, to Sir Roger Casement. Little more than a catalogue of early modern inhabitants of the Tower can be attempted here for a full account of their lives, careers and trials (whenever conducted) would necessitate an entire volume which would also have to cover the wider history of Anglo-Irish relations in their more gruesome aspects across the sixteenth and seventeenth centuries. Later on, the selected emphasis will be on Irish aristocratic prisoners, for it is argued that their incarceration, together with the transportation of the young Irish swordsmen from Ulster in the years following the flight and O'Doherty's rebellion of 1608, made the resulting planta-tion of Ulster very different from what had been originally intended for the province. Indeed, locking away the Irish political elite, and in many cases taking off their heads, facilitated the confiscation of their lands in Ireland.[3] In view of the continuity of a colonial ideology from the days of Giraldus Cam-brensis, it would be foolhardy to write that the plantation of Ulster would otherwise not have taken place. Nonetheless, the removal of Ulster's leaders by flight, transpor-tation or incarceration in the Tow-er certainly facilitated the entire project. State internment without trial often became a means of po-litical control and regime change in Irish history.

The standard of treatment one endured in the Tower often had much to do with one's ability to bribe the gaolers. Irish prisoners frequently lacked the financial means to ease their confinement. Geffray Mynshul, *Essays and characters of prison and prisoners* (1617).

In the early modern period, for the Fitzgeralds of Kildare, the Tower of London virtually served as a second home, receiving them as guests of the Tudor and Stuart monarchs. At least fifteen mem-bers of the family paid for their own incarceration in the Tower between 1495 and 1608. Henry VII imprisoned Gerald, the eighth and 'Great' earl of Kildare, for supporting Perkin Warbeck, the York-ist pretender, but eventually rehabilitated him, and he returned to Ireland to serve as lord deputy until his death in 1513. His successor, the ninth earl, was less fortunate. Incarcerated by Henry VIII on a charge of treason, he died there in 1534. It is said that his heart was broken by the news of the re-bellion of his son 'Silken' Thomas, the short-lived tenth earl. The ninth earl's name heads the list in-

side the door of St Peter ad Vincula, the Tower's famous chapel in which so many offenders against the English monarchy were laid to rest. Moreover, Silken Thomas's half-finished signature on the wall of his Tower apartment is tangible evidence of his short stay. Thomas and his five uncles, some of whom had played no part in the rebellion, met their end on 3 February 1537, not at Tower Hill, but at Tyburn, and, as was the gruesome custom in London and Dublin, their heads subsequently adorned London Bridge. This state massacre of the Kildare Fitzgeralds left Gerald, Silken Thomas's half-brother, as the only male survivor of a once illustrious house.[4]

Their cousins, the Fitzgeralds of Desmond, also suffered consider-ably in the Tower. After the defeat of the Irish at the battle of Kinsale in 1601 James Fitzthomas Fitzger-ald, earl of Desmond, the *súgán* (or 'straw-rope') earl, languished in the Tower from May 1601 to April 1608. Tower records show that he died insane on 28 April 1608 and lies in the chapel of St Peter's ad Vincula. Citing from the petitions of Sir John Peyton, the lieutenant of the Tower, Brian Harrison shows some of the ex-penses involved in the *súgán* earl's imprisonment: 'for the quarter year from St Michael's Day 1602 till the feast of Our Lord next ... for the said James MacThomas for the said time at £3 the week, physic, surgeon and watcher with him in his lunacy'.[5] In Tudor times, the normal weekly tariff for the better class of prisoner was 6s. 8d. The earl's brother, Sir John FitzGerald and a number of their household serv-ants had also been Tower inmates for years on end. The death of the *súgán* earl in 1608 ended the Fit-zgeralds' long association with the Tower, which spanned the reigns of six English monarchs.

Although clearly not Irish, Sir John Perrot, a former president of Munster (1570-73) and lord deputy (1584-88) and the putative illegitimate son of Henry VIII by Mary Berkley, did have an Irish career. Having fallen foul of his half-sister on a charge of treason, he also died within its forbid-ding walls. In 1605 Guy Fawkes, a Yorkshire-born explosives expert who had plied his trade in Sir

'Silken' Thomas hurls the sword of state onto the council board in Dublin and repudiates Henry VIII as a heretic, in the mistaken belief that his father had been executed in the Tower. This set in chain a sequence of events that altered the manner of English government in Ireland and ultimately led to the flight. © Inch House Irish Studies Centre

William Stanley's Irish regiment in Flanders, masterminded the infamous Gunpowder Plot which radically altered James VI & I's view of his Irish and English Catholic subjects. He faced the executioner with fellow plotters Digby, Wintour, Grant and Bates at the west end of St Paul's Cathedral. Francis Tresham, who could not bear the thought of his own kinsmen being blown up, betrayed the plot to the government, but he too ended up in the Tower for his pains, before making a daring escape.[6] In Edward VI's reign Brian O'Connor, an Offaly chief, is probably the first Irishman on record to have successfully made his escape from the Tower; he was, however, recaptured in Dublin and died there in the Castle in 1560.

The half-finished autograph signature of 'Silken' Thomas Fitzgerald in his cell in the Tower. © Inch House Irish Studies Centre

Given the religious nature of many of the rebellions against the crown in sixteenth-century Ireland, it is no surprise that Irish Catholic clergymen, like their English counterparts, were confined there. Archbishop Richard Creagh of Armagh (1564-85), its most famous Irish ecclesiastical resident and one of the longest-serving Irish prisoners, had three spells in the Tower: 1564, 1567, and, finally in 1572, having spent twenty years as a prisoner of conscience. Like so many Irish and English recusant churchmen, Creagh saw no reason why he could not be both loyal to the queen and also perform his religious duties as a papal archbishop. In this he epitomised the recusants' dilemma in both countries when both the oath of supremacy and the oath of allegiance became tests of loyalty and requirements of all office-holders. Creagh was imprisoned in appalling conditions. His letter of 23 May 1564 to St Francesco Borgia reports how his dungeon had 'little more light than Jonah had in the belly of the whale'. A later letter mentions that his warder had given him a candle.[7] Obviously Creagh did not have what was known as 'the Freedom of the Tower' given to aristocratic prisoners: the right to walk the walls and in the lieutenant's garden, receive and entertain visitors, collect books, and even to make comfortable improvements to their lodgings. Such privileges had been granted, for example, to Sir Walter Ralegh, Lady Arbella Stuart enjoyed similar privileges, as did the 'wizard' earl of Northumberland. The latter had a private still in

The Tower of London as it would have looked in 1615 when it housed Niall Garbh O'Donnell, his son Neachtan and Donal Ballagh O'Cahan. © Historic Royal Palaces

his garden, which was also large enough to contain a bowling green.[8] Creagh's hagiography claims that he had one miraculous escape from the Byward Tower, passing through at least seven doors which should have been locked, and that on asking directions, he was shown to the way out by the sentinel of the Tower, who looked remarkably like the angel who delivered St Peter from jail! Sad to say, this legend is not the reason why the chapel of St Peter ad Vincula is so called, as it was dedicated in 1210.

The archbishop made his way to Louvain and back to Dublin before his final incarceration in the Tower of London, where he died in 1586, allegedly poisoned by his cook, one Robert Poley, who acted at the government's behest. The register of the chapel of St Peter ad Vincula records his burial as occurring on 28 January 1587/8. Regarding burials of the executed, it should be noted that the church of All Hallows by the Tower, also known as 'All Hallows, Barking', founded by the nuns of Barking Abbey (and restored after 'The Blitz') is also the final resting place of many of those executed on Tower Hill. One notable burial was that of Archbishop William Laud, who was interred there in 1645, but was exhumed and re-interred in the chapel of St John's, Oxford, in 1663.

The Gaelic Irish also provided a number of high-profile Tower prisoners especially as English government crept into north Connacht and Ulster

in the 1580s and 1590s. In May 1591 Sir Brian na Múrtha O'Rourke languished in the Tower, attainted on eight charges of treason. Indeed, the first charge covered all the rest – that he sought to depose the queen from her regal power in Ireland, had harboured Spanish refugees from the wrecks of the Armada, hired many gallowglass and 'that he caused her Majesty's name to be set on an image of a woman … and tied to his horse's tail to be drawn through the mire … and getting his gallowglasses to hew, cut and mangle the same with lewd speeches against her Majesty'. King James had had O'Rourke arrested after he had fled to Scotland, and for a price – the preservation of his claim to be Elizabeth's successor – sent him to the queen. Brought under custody to the Tower 9 May 1591, he stood trial in the Great Hall at Westminster on 28 October 1591 and was hanged, drawn and quartered at Tyburn on 3 November of the same year.[9]

O'Rourke's death shocked Gaelic Ireland and contributed in no small part to the emergence of an unusually united Gaelic confederacy to oppose the further advance of English law and administration into Ulster. Headed by Red Hugh O'Donnell and the wily Hugh O'Neill, second earl of Tyrone, the coalition expanded as rebellion spread throughout much of Ireland. It is hardly surprising that some Gaelic leaders would end up in the Tower of London. As the Spanish sought to assist the rebellion the government feared that they would land in the south-western province of Munster. To secure that coastline – nearest to Spain – a number of Munster leaders enjoyed the Tower's Spartan hospitality during the Nine Years War. The Fitzgeralds of Desmond, staunch allies of the Ulster confederates, we have already encountered, but other Munster lords found themselves incarcerated behind its walls. The imprisonment of Florence MacCarthy Reagh (Finghín Mac Cárthaigh Mór) of Desmond and Clancare (d. 1640), is of particular significance in this regard. First sent to the Tower in 1589 for intriguing with Spain, he secured his release, but returned in August 1601. His Gaelic inscription in the Martin Tower attests

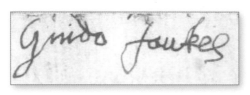

Guy Fawkes's shattered signature revealed the terrifying power of the rack. © TNA

to his residency. At some stage MacCarthy seems to have been transferred to the Marshalsea, and, as part of King James's amnesty in lifting the Mandates, was released again in 1614. However, he was back in custody, though not in the Tower, by 1618 and again in 1624-26. MacCarthy's 'ins and outs' mirror his spells of allegiance during a career which constantly wavered the perimeter of conspiracy. Little wonder O'Neill never quite trusted him, once calling him 'a damned counterfeit Englishman whose only study and practice was to deceive and betray all Irishmen in Ireland'. Strong words, especially considering that O'Neill had inaugurated him as The MacCarthy Mór in 1600. His bouts of imprisonment kept him out of harm's way while the government carved up the MacCarthy Mór lordship in the Munster plantations. Following the example of Ralegh, another more famous literary resident of the Tower, MacCarthy penned 'A concise sketch for antiquarian studies of the earl of Thomond, c. 1610, of Irish history' in the Tower after 1601.[10]

After the Gunpowder Plot (1605), the flight of the earls (1607) and O'Doherty's rebellion (1608) the Tower of London played a key role in ensuring that the leadership of Ulster would find it impossible to regroup, reorganise and renew resistance to English rule in Ireland. It was business as usual for the Tower under the Stuarts, with one important difference, as King James VI & I and Charles I also needed the English Bastille to protect their prerogative from parliamentary interference, as

well as various threats to the succession. The fate of Lady Arbella Stuart (1575-1615) James's first cousin who had married to William Seymour, duke of Somerset (1588-1660) against the royal command, is evidence enough of the general nervousness surrounding James's reign.[11]

James's plans for the plantation of Ulster were greatly facilitated and hastened on by the events of the years 1605-08, and also because the plantation would help to replenish an empty exchequer and reward his favourites and retainers. Lord Deputy Chichester, no friend of the king, summed up the status of Ulster thus: the king became 'now sole proprietor of the most part of the province, as the native lords thereof were formerly accounted and known to be'.[12] Many of the subchiefs (*ur-ríthe*) of the native lords who had neither gone on the flight nor died during the course and aftermath of the O'Doherty rebellion, or were deemed to be a potential hindrance to plantation, found themselves imprisoned in the Tower.

Cormac MacBaron O'Neill, the earl of Tyrone's brother and former *tánaiste* fell under government suspicion when he hurried to Dublin to inform them of the flight and to make his case to take over his brother's lands. Regarded as too ambitious an O'Neill to leave at liberty, he was also suspected of complicity in the flight as O'Neill's brother and brother-in-law of the earl of Tyrconnell. Moreover, Tyrone's patent clearly stated that his lands would be restored for his life with remainders to his sons, Hugh and Henry, and to his brother Cormac.[13] Cormac soon found himself incarcerated in the Tower without trial, where he spent the remaining seventeen years of his recorded life. One of his sons later joined him, another was executed in Derry after the 1615 'conspiracy', a plot allegedly aided and abetted by Hugh O'Neill from Rome in the year before his death.[14] At one stage, in 1618, Cormac received the 'freedom of the Tower'. A poignant lengthy petition from Cormac to the privy council shows laudable concern for the well-being of his wife and children and former tenants:

Whereas your poor petitioner, before the time of his imprisonment, did leave unto his wife and children a competent living … now since his imprisonment, the means being taken from her, whereby she is constrained in lamentable sort to seek help from her friends, far removed from that part of Ireland where the living did lie. And whereas your petitioner did take care with certain of his tenants … to give a good part of his goods and chattels to the value of a thousand pounds … that they should foster and bring up his children in learning … and since your poor petitioner's imprisonment they have not only fraudulently deprived him of the goods and the trust he reposed in them, but do suffer his children to wander up and down the country to seek their relief … and for the tender love and affection he beareth unto his poor wife and children that your lordships will be pleased to commiserate and to issue an order to the Lord Deputy of Ireland that his wife may have some competent sum of money, or so much of the lands restored to her towards her relief and maintenance by those that do withhold the same from her … and that the tenants who have your prisoner's goods and chattels make restitution of them to his wife and children … From the Tower, 11 September 1611.[15]

The petition had little effect. When Lord Justice Winch and Attorney General Davies, visited Augher Castle, Cormac MacBaron's seat in the Clogher Valley, while on the assize circuit, they found his lady so impoverished that she had 'neither bread, drink, meat nor linen to welcome them' and had to scavenge her neighbours for chickens and muttons to entertain them.[16] Cormac MacBaron O'Neill represented a greater danger to government plantation plans than Donal Ballagh O'Cahan, Niall Garbh O'Donnell, his son Neachtan, or Conn O'Neill, the earl's abandoned youngest son – all of whom died in the Tower.[17] All except Conn had been charged with aiding, or at least complicity in, the O'Doherty rebellion.

Niall Garbh's involvement in the attack on Derry in 1608 has been much contested by historians. The jaundiced accusations against him made by his estranged wife Nuala and by her mother, Finola, have been disputed, as has Feidhlimidh Reagh MacDavitt's damning evidence. First imprisoned in Dublin Castle, from whence he made an abortive attempt to escape, he later accompanied his son Neachtan to the Tower. Modern historical judgment indicates that while Niall did not

actively take part in the rebellion, it is likely that he 'calculatedly encouraged Sir Cathair'.[18] Niall's greatest enemies were those of his own household but it is significant that he was included among the Irish prisoners whose escape from the Tower was planned in a daring but abortive plot concocted by his kinswoman, Mary Stuart O'Donnell, the daughter of the earl of Tyrconnell and Brigit Fitzgerald.[19] In common with all the imprisoned Irish leaders, Niall Garbh's status at home had inevitably suffered as a consequence of his long incarceration, and in a joint petition with Donal Ballagh O'Cahan, Niall Garbh echoed Cormac MacBaron's plea to the crown for the means to succour their relatives' needs as they are being deprived of them by 'certain tenants'.[20] The burial register of St Peter ad Vincula records that Niall Garbh died a prisoner in August 1626, having been predeceased by his son Neachtan.[21]

Like the O'Donnells, Sir Donal Ballagh O'Cahan and his son ended up in to the Tower for complicity or 'traitorous juggling', as the charges put it, in the O'Doherty rebellion of 1608. He was yet another victim of broken promises and failed to have his rightful lands restored in a flagrant violation of public faith and private right. As he languished in the Tower O'Cahan may have pondered his folly in saving his father-in-law's life on the field at Clontibret, given their persistent legal wrangling after 1603. It is probable, however, that his mind was more often agitated by his treatment by the government, who, having used him to reduce the earl, cast him aside in the aftermath of the flight as the Jacobean administration seized the opportunity to plant six counties rather than just the lands of the fugitives.[22] While his death in 1617 was not documented in the Tower records, Philip O'Sullivan Beare refers to it is a catalogue of events for 1618.[23]

Like many aristocratic Tower prisoners, the O'Donnells and the O'Cahans were permitted long visits from their womenfolk: Ralegh's wife, the redoubtable Bess Throckmorton, virtually lived with him in the Tower, and the earl of Northumberland has so many carriages visiting that the lieutenant of the Tower instituted traffic controls around its environs. A contemporary report suggested that visiting women kindred had unsettled the Irish knights in the Tower and ought to be sent back to Ireland and maintained there. Honora O'Cahan and Joanne, the sister of Niall Garbh, travelled to London and successfully petitioned for access on

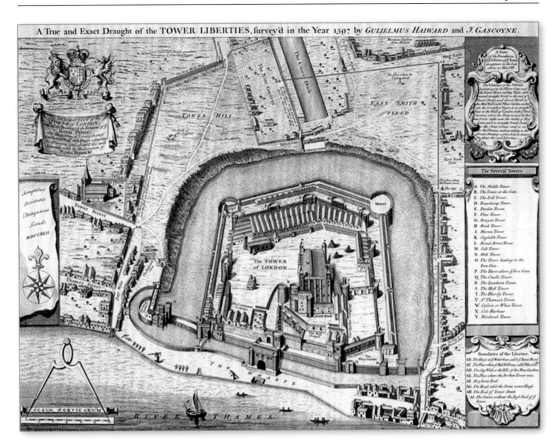

Plan of the Tower from 1597. © Historic Royal Palaces

condition that an interpreter was present.[24] They subsequently procured funds for their return journey to Ireland, a possible consequence of their 'unsettling' effect on their menfolk. Donal Ballagh's petition on behalf of Honora eventually bore fruit after five years as the king authorised Chichester to grant her some land.[25] It is very likely that Donal's second son, Daniel, nicknamed *geimhlach* ('the shackled'), had been conceived by his third wife Honora in the Tower. This son became a valued and trusted officer in Owen Roe O'Neill's regiment in the Spanish service. A very different fate awaited Rory Óg O'Cahan, Donal Ballagh's eldest son with Mary O'Donnell, Red Hugh's sister. Dissatisfied with his small grant of land under the plantation settlement, and deeply resentful of Sir Thomas Phillips' seizure of his father's castles and lands Rory Óg went into rebellion in 1615. Captured, tortured and convicted of treason, he was subsequently executed at Derry.[26] His imprisoned father persisted in his pleas for justice until his dying day – his final petition, made jointly with Niall Garbh, after nine years in the Tower, dates from

30 September 1616. Honora and her son Daniel got the lands in Keenaght formerly held by the executed Rory Óg. A veritable Hector in arms in service with Owen Roe, Daniel died at Clones in May 1643; the death of the last son and heir of Donal Ballagh virtually ended the fortunes of the noble *ur-ríthe* of the O'Neills. The impoverished old lady found in the ruins of O'Cahan's seat at Dungiven by the plantation commissioners, who claimed to 'the wife to The O'Cahan' is likely to have been Honora, his third wife, 'as she alone would have been proud to assert that she was O'Cahan's spouse'.[27]

In the post-plantation political and military climate, any close associate of O'Neill on the loose remained a threat, particularly given the illustrious fugitive's hopes for restoration. The presence of Henry O'Neill's regiment in the service of Spanish Flanders, 'the dark cloud on the horizon' in the words of Geoffrey Fenton, gave teeth to this threat. It is in this fraught climate, especially in the aftermath of the 1615 conspiracy, that young Conn O'Neill found himself transferred from Eton

243

school to the Tower of London. Abandoned at the flight in 1607, Conn had been placed in the care of Sir Toby Caulfield, and it is likely that he paid the school bills to Eton out of the sale of goods and chattels left at Dungannon in 1607. It is certain that Hugh O'Neill did not pay the bills, for his letters to Spain agonised that his son was being raised amongst heretics as well as expressing the hope that Conn would live to avenge the wrongs done to his family. Conn would have been six or seven at the time of the flight and nine or ten when he enrolled in Eton. After his transfer to the Tower he wrote to his father in Rome hinting that his new lodgings were much more congenial than school – an early and damning indictment of the English public-school system. There were plots to rescue him and other Irish prisoners from the Tower, and a folk tradition survives among the O'Neills which claims that Conn did in fact escape to the continent. However, the evidence is rather chimerical, and it is probable that Conn died in the Tower sometime after 1622.[28]

Other Irish prisoners in the Tower remind us that Stuart plantations did not merely concern Ulster – the lands of the O'Rourkes in Leitrim had been affected, not to mention those of other native proprietors in Longford, Wicklow and Wexford.[29] Young Brian O'Rourke, grandson of the executed Brian na Múrtha, a Trinity College and Oxford scholar, spent four years in the Gatehouse and Fleet prisons – the overspill London prisons of the day – for brawling with fellow law students at Middle Inn in 1619. Transferred to the Tower on 12 March 1623 and held without trial, he died there on 16 January 1641, possibly by poisoning. One of his many petitions, that of 1619, to the king requesting his liberty survives in dreadful verse, possibly the reason why it went unheeded:

'To the King's Most Excellent Majesty:
the humble petition of Brian O'Rourke'

O, light thy hart with a sakred fier
Glorious Great King grant my desier
O doe but grant that gracious favor
Now in my misery to prove my savior
Libertie, sweet Sir is that I crave
O grant but that, and then my life you have.
In the meantime, I am bound to pray
For thee my Sovrayne long to beare sway
And from your enemies may you always bee
Garded by heaven's greatest polisie

His last petition, dated 8 January 1641, a week before his death, simply and poignantly reads: 'Petition of Brian O'Rourke Esq., prisoner in the Tower, praying that he may be discharged and have the benefit of the law for the recovery of his estate'. Warrants had also been sent out for the arrest of his brother Hugh, but he escaped to join the wild geese in Spanish Flanders.[30]

Owing to the dubious loyalties and elastic allegiances in religion which characterized the turbulent years 1641-53, it is also not surprising to find descendants of the lost Gaelic leaders of Ulster in the Tower of London well into the seventeenth century. Not all of them ended their days there. Daniel O'Neill, royalist supporter of the Stuart cause and Protestant nephew of Owen Roe, played a dangerous role as double agent, operating between Owen Roe, the marquis of Ormond, the earl of Antrim and King Charles I. He later found himself charged with treason in the Tower in 1640. He escaped by using the tactic of temporary transvestism in 1642, and his steadfast loyalty to the Stuarts was rewarded at the Restoration in 1660 with a good pension and a generous grant of lands.[31]

Other Irish prisoners of the period had less luck. Captured after the abortive plot to capture Dublin Castle in 1641, Hugh MacMahon and Cornelius Maguire were taken to Newgate Prison, and from thence to the Tower in June 1642. They made bold escapes by cutting out the doors of their dungeons and, with the aid of two fellow Jesuit prisoners, swam across the moat into the back streets around the Tower. A 'lady of the town' noted their strange accents and reported them to the warders of the Tower. MacMahon was hanged, drawn and quartered at Tyburn in November 1644, while Maguire delayed his own fate by insisting on his rights to be tried as a lord and, in the likely event of a guilty verdict, reserved the right to choose beheading rather than the noose. The court ignored his pleas, and he was hanged at Tyburn on 20 February 1645. One Hugh Bourke, a Franciscan friar who witnessed the execution, wrote a lurid account of the extreme brutality perpetrated on the unfortunate peer.[32]

In conclusion, the parliament used the Tower as a base for military operations and for the incarceration of royalist prisoners; it did not feature, however, in the imprisonment or execution of England's most famous prisoner, Charles I, king and royalist martyr, who made his celebrated defence in Westminster Hall in January 1649. It is fitting, however, that Hugh Dubh O'Neill, the defender of Limerick and Clonmel against Cromwell's Ironsides, spent a few months confined in the Tower of London until parliament commuted his death sentence as a result of Sir Henry Ireton's representations to Cromwell. After his acquittal on the charge of engaging in military excesses, a further petition to Cromwell from Alonzo de Cardenas, acting on behalf of 'His Most Catholic Majesty' King Philip IV of Spain secured O'Neill's freedom and permission to take a number of disaffected young Irish soldiers to the Spanish service. Hugh Dubh O'Neill asserted his claim to the earldom of Tyrone at the Restoration in 1660, but died within a month.[33] Analogies are dangerous; but it is perhaps not unreasonable to say that in the 'Laboratory of Empire' – namely 'The Plantation of Ulster' – the Tower of London became a catalyst in the interaction of religious, political and economic forces of the sixteenth and seventeenth centuries which helped to shape the subsequent history not only of Ulster but of both islands.

Notes

1 K. Baedeker's *London and its environs* (1898) is just as authoritative for the Tower as its modern virtual tour. See also K. McGillick, *The towers of the Tower of London* (London, 2009) and the still valuable A. L. Rowse, *The Tower of London in the history of the nation* (London, 1974).

2 The list of famous names, men and women, engraved on a brass memorial inside the main door of St Peter ad Vincula are those executed on Tower Hill and on Tower Green. Macaulay called it 'the saddest spot on earth', see his magniloquent passage on it in, Macaulay, *History of England,* (ed.) C. H. Firth (6 vols, London, 1913-15), i, pp 306-7.

3 F. W. Harris, 'The Rebellion of Sir Cahir O'Doherty and its legal aftermath', *Irish Jurist,* xv (1980), p. 320. See Appendix D for a list outlining the landed losses of the leading native Irish families after the events of 1607.

4 L. McCorristine, *The revolt of Silken Thomas: a challenge to Henry VIII* (Dublin, 1987), and see the illustration of his unfinished signature on the wall of his cell in the Tower, p. 153. A contemporary account of his trial is in the 'Act of Attainder for the Earl of Kildare' (28 Henry VIII, c. 1), *Irish Statutes* (1786), i, p. 66.

5 See B. Harrison, *A Tower of London prisoner book* (Leeds, 2004).

6 Guy Fawkes's shaky signature to his confession reminds the reader of the notorious tortures of the Tower – the 'Iron Maiden', the 'Little Ease', 'The Pit' and the 'Scavenger's Daughter', iron gloves and manacles named after Sir Leonard Skeffington, lieutenant of the Tower in Henry VIII's time. Use of the rack in Elizabeth's reign to extract information and incriminations is well documented in the history of the Catholic martyrs: see F. Edwards, *The Gunpowder Plot: the narrative of Oswald Tesimond alias Greenway* (London, 1973) and also the celebrated autobiography of Father John Gerard: P. Caraman (trans.), *John Gerard: an autobiography of an Elizabethan* (London, 1951).

7 See C. Lennon, *An Irish prisoner of conscience of the Tudor era: Archbishop Richard Creagh of Armagh, 1523-1586* (Dublin, 2000).

8 The 'freedom of the Tower' sometimes extended to letting prisoners out altogether to visit relatives but remaining under 'house arrest' with a warden.

9 'The brief of O'Rourke's indictment', HMC, *Salisbury,* iv, pp 170-1. It was treason to deface or clip the coinage of the realm bearing images of the Queen's Majesty. This was the last charge listed by Sir Richard Bingham against O'Rourke. King Philip II sent a personal letter of thanks to O'Rourke for his services to his distressed soldiers and sailors. See also the letter of King James to Queen Elizabeth, 13 April 1594 (HMC, *Salisbury,* iv, pp 509-10).

10 D. M. MacCarthy, *Life and Letters of Florence MacCarthy Reagh* (London, 1867). BL. Add. MSS, 4793 contains MacCarthy's Tower literature, and there is a facsimilie edition in J. T. Gilbert's *Facsimiles of the National Manuscripts of Ireland* (4 vols, Dublin, 1874-84). See also M. MacCarthy-Morrogh, *The Munster plantation* (Oxford, 1986).

11 S. Gristwood, *Arbella, England's lost queen* (New York, 2003). Was her death the result of a hunger-strike? A major charge against Ralegh, that other high-security-risk prisoner, was his plot to have Arbella succeed to the throne. Both have entered the annals of Jacobean tragedy.

12 Chichester to the Privy Council, 14 October (*CSPI, 1608-10,* p. 68).

13 For the re-organisation of Ulster after the Nine Years War see N. P. Canny, 'The Treaty of Mellifont and the re-organisation of Ulster 1603', *Irish Sword,* ix (1969-70), 249-62, and idem, *Making Ireland British* (Oxford, 2001), pp 243-300.

14 R. Gillespie, *Conspiracy, Ulster Plots and Plotters in 1615* (Belfast, 1987); P. J. Corish and B. Millett, *The Irish Martyrs* (Four Courts, 2005).

15 Note that the previously lost correspondence with the Privy Council from 1604-1613 is in BL, Add MSS 11402, which partly supplies the missing years and are now in the Appendices to *Acts of the Privy Council of England,* (ed.) J. R. Dasent (32 vols, London, 1890-1907), pp xxv, xxix, xxxii.

16 Quoted in G. Hill, *The plantation of Ulster* (facsimile repr 1877 ed.; Shannon 1970), p. 179.

17 Captain Hart, of Culmore Castle notoriety in the O'Doherty rebellion of 1608 became one of Cormac's keepers.

18 A. Clarke, 'Pacification, plantation and the Catholic question, 1603-1623', in *NHI,* iii, p. 197 n.1. For Niall's betrayal of Red Hugh and his relations with Sir Henry Docwra see J. McGurk, *Sir Henry Docwra, 1564-1631, Derry's second founder* (Dublin, 2006), ch. 4.

19 Mary first escaped, with considerable difficulty, from her grandmother, the Dowager Countess of Kildare in male attire, purportedly served as a cavalier in the Irish regiments in Flanders and eventually married Don John Edward O'Gallagher. However, all their children died in infancy: see V. O'Donnell (ed), *The O'Donnells of Tyrconnell* (2nd ed., Donegal, 2001) and the reading list in Jerrold Casway's entries on Irish aristocratic women in his entries in The Royal Irish Academy *Dictionary of Irish Biography*. Casway's biography of Rosa O'Dogherty and his essay in this volume highlights the diplomatic importance of Rosa and her circle of Gaelic women in Brussels, Rome and Madrid in maintaining the struggle for Catholic Gaelic Ireland into the seventeenth century.

20 Petition of Sir Neal O'Donell and Sir Donell O'Cahan, Knights, to the King, Mar. 1610 (*CSPI, 1608-10*, p. 414).

21 Harrison, *Tower of London Prisoner Book*, p. 281.

22 R. Hunter, 'The end of O'Donnell power', in *Donegal: History and Society* (Dublin, 1995); see also *History Ireland*, xv: 4 (2007) and the correspondence by Dr John J. Silke in the next edition of the same magazine. O'Cahan neglected to take out a patent for his land, see Canny, *Making Ireland British*, pp 190-1. Few actual parchment Patent Rolls of this time were left in Ireland as most of them were in the Tower's state papers office of record – an ironic coincidence given that some of their Irish owners were also in the Tower; see *Cal. Carew MSS*, vi, pp 106, 279, 313, 365, 456.

23 Cited in M. Kerney Walsh, *'Destruction by Peace'*, p. 109. See also O'Cahan's petition to the Earl of Salisbury of the 30 March 1610, in which he mentions that his wife and children were put out of his house at Limavady by Sir Thomas Phillips; *CSPI, 1608-10*, p. 413.

24 Warrant issued 21 July 1613 (*Acts of the Privy Council, 1613-14*, p. 144).

25 *Cal. Carew MSS*, vi, p. 53 and 'Propositions of Principal Natives', 5 April 1610 (*CSPI, 1608-10*, p. 429), For the Irish women's requests to the government see Privy Council to Chichester 9 Oct. 1613 (*Acts of the Privy Council, 1613-14*, pp 167-8); *CSPI, 1611-14*, p. 390.

26 R. Gillespie, *Conspiracy, Ulster plots and plotters in 1615* (Belfast, 1987), pp 30-32.

27 J. Casway, 'The decline and fate of Donal Ballagh O'Cahan and his family', in M. Ó Siochrú (ed.), *Kingdoms in Crisis: Ireland in the 1640s* (Dublin, 2001), pp 60-62. Also for Lt-Col. Daniel O'Cahan see J. Casway, *Owen Roe O'Neill and the struggle for Catholic Ireland* (Philadelphia, 1984), pp 66, 69-70, 75-76.

28 For Sir Toby Caulfield's exceptionally detailed accounts of the O'Neills' property see some account of them and his disbursements in Hill, *Plantation of Ulster*, esp. pp 239-56.

Conn's school bills for the years 1616-18 survive in Eton College Collections (MSS 272b); Dr R. Hegarty, 'Seán (Juan) Ó Néill and the descendants of the Great Ó Néill', *Dúiche Néill*, xvii (2008), pp 122-31. Likewise M. Lyons, 'The wives of Hugh O'Neill, second earl Tyrone', *Dúiche Néill*, xvi (2007), pp 42-61, sifts through O'Neill's complicated marital relations.

29 K. Nicholls, 'Map no. 45', in *NHI*, ix, p. 45. For Chichester's plantation plans for Wexford see *Cal. Carew MSS*, vi, p. 321; for Leitrim see, ibid., p. 387 and for Longford, ibid., p. 382.

30 For a definitive genealogy of the O'Rourkes see F. J. Byrne, 'The O'Rourkes of Breifne: Kings of Breifne, 1128-1605', 'Succession Lists', *NHI*, ix, p. 228. Betty MacDermot has collected many O'Rourke family records in an affectionate familial work, *O Ruairc of Breifne* (Manorhamiliton, 1990). For his death notice see B. Harrison, *Tower of London Prisoner Book*, p. 291. It is likely that the O'Rourke bard composed the cited verse rather than the prisoner in the Tower.

31 'Daniel O'Neill' (*New Dictionary of National Biography*).

32 A. Clarke, *The Old English in Ireland* (2nd ed., Dublin, 2000), pp 160-1, 183; P. Corish, 'The rising of 1641 and the Catholic confederacy, 1641-45' and 'Ormond, Rinuccini, and the confederates, 1645-49', *NHI*, iii, pp 289-316, 317-35. The brutal account of MacMahon's execution is in *HMC Franciscan MSS*, p. 55.

33 J. Burke, 'Siege Warfare in Seventeenth Century Ireland', in P. Lenihan (ed.) *'Conquest and resistance: war in seventeenth century Ireland* (Brill, 2001); J. Ohlmeyer (ed.), *Ireland from independence to occupation, 1641-1660* (Cambridge, 1995). For a fine general survey of 'The Irish Overseas, 1534-1691' see J. J. Silke's essay in *NHI*, iii, pp 587-632. And for a comprehensive list and account of Tower prisoners see Harrison, *Tower of London Prisoner Book* (Leeds, 2004). For a set of photographs (60 photos and 130 views) of prisoner graffiti in the Tower of London taken in April 2009 see: www.flickr.com/photos

Acknowledgements: For the inspiration to write this essay I am especially indebted to Dr Éamonn Ó Ciardha, of the University of Ulster. Its genesis was a talk he persuaded me to give at the Tower on the occasion of the Plantation of Ulster Conference in London on Friday 26 June 2009. I am also grateful to one of his co-editors, Dr David Finnegan, Visiting Fellow at Goldsmiths, University of London, for his persistent encouragement, as well as Mr Anthony Johnston of Inch House for letting me read his 'The Tower of London and the Nine Years War' (unpublished MA dissertation, Trinity College Dublin, 2007).

After the flight: the impact of plantation on the Ulster landscape[1]

Annaleigh Margey

In his study of the plantation of Ulster, Philip Robinson recognised the significant impact that the flight of the earls had on the cultural and political landscape of the province. This political and military collapse of Gaelic Ulster set in motion a series of events and processes that transformed Ulster from a Gaelic society and landscape into a distinctly British one, not only with the imposition of English political structures but also, and most significantly, with the plantation of British settlers, identity, culture and architecture in the province.

This essay will seek to analyse the transformation of Ulster under the auspices of this plantation from its inception in 1609 to 1622, with reference to maps and surveys. Having explored Ulster's pre-plantation geographical and political structures, it will shift focus to examine its legal aftermath, as British authorities began to gain control of large tracts of lands in the province. The initial proposals, surveys and conditions of the plantation will be discussed in the first instance, while its final section will focus upon the evidence of the transformation of the Ulster landscape by using the major surveys of the plantation undertaken in 1611, 1614, 1618-19 and 1622. Specific reference will be made to the transformation of the Gaelic heartlands of Hugh O'Neill and Rory O'Donnell at Dungannon and Donegal town respectively.

Before the flight a series of Gaelic lordships formed the political geography of Ulster. These lordships comprised significant geographical areas over which a Gaelic lord had power to develop his landscape and govern its inhabitants. Despite significant English incursions in the southern half of the country in the late sixteenth century, the Ulster lordships remained strong and largely inviolate. The rebellions of both Shane O'Neill and Hugh O'Neill against English attempts to gain influence in Ulster in the 1560s and 1590s respectively, focused English minds on the strength of the province's lordship network and the government's poor understanding of its

Donegal Castle, the ancestral seat of the O'Donnells, granted to Sir Basil Brooke, who added the English-style residence in the foreground.
© Marie-Claire Peters

Representation of the new plantation settlement of Bellaghy with new-style English houses and with a bawn – rarely-built in practice – in the background. © Seán Ó Brógáin

geography and politics. This resulted in calls for surveys of Ulster's landscape from the late 1560s onwards.

Queen Elizabeth I issued the first request for a survey in 1567 demanding 'plats of Ulster to be sent' in order to aid in the planting of obedient subjects in the aftermath of Shane's death.[2] Robert Lythe, an Englishman, who had previously surveyed at Calais,[3] received a commission to map Ulster for the purpose of providing administrators with a fundamental and necessary education in the physical and political geography of the province. However, Lythe failed to execute his commission properly, completing instead a regional map of Cooley, Omeath and Mourne, as well as maps of Carrickfergus, between 1567 and 1568.[4] It was not until the late 1590s that government officials required significant provincial surveying and mapping again.

By the 1590s English officials had begun to gain more of a foothold in the heart of Ulster. Hugh O'Neill, baron of Dungannon, had been educated in the Pale, presented at court, and subsequently belted as second earl of Tyrone in 1587. Through Hugh, the crown hoped to increase its influence in the province by setting up 'the Queen's O'Neill' against the wily Turlough Luineach, thereby dividing the powerful and strategically placed O'Neill lordship. However, by the 1590s Hugh had tired of attempts by the English authorities to manipulate him, and having embraced his Gaelic heritage and assumed the title of 'The O'Neill' in 1595, he entered into the Nine Years War with numerous other Ulster lords.[5] The ensuing tumult coincided with increased and widespread English reconnaissance throughout Ulster.

By 1598 Francis Jobson, who had been part of the 1586 commission in Munster, had begun to provide reconnaissance maps of the province which provide a crude outline of its physical geography, the Gaelic lordships and the counties.[6] Further interrogation and decoding provides evidence of a highly contested move from a Gaelic landscape to an English one.[7] Taking both the date of the map – 1598 – and the legend that frames it, it becomes clear that the inclusion on this map of the new English-style county framework is actually an attempt to emphasise proposed English political structures within the province prior to formal plantation.[8] The English claims to Ulster became even more pronounced by Jobson's use of a royal seal as an embellishment.[9] Its location at the top of the map gives symbolic representation to England's view of Ulster as an integral part of the queen's dominion. Thus, almost ten years before the flight of the earls, English authorities and their map-makers began the process of claiming and controlling Ulster's landscape.

At the turn of the seventeenth century new surveys and maps changed to meet military requirements within the province as the authorities grappled with O'Neill and his Irish confederacy. Richard Bartlett, who had arrived in Ulster as part of Lord Mountjoy's entourage, produced numerous military maps which listed key locations and fortifications such as O'Neill's Dungannon Castle and details of the emerging military landscape of the province.[10] These became staples of military reconnaissance in the province, noting both the natural and man-made fortifications that could be both employed against, and utilised by, English soldiers at the height of the war. Following the defeat of Tyrone and his armies at Kinsale (1601), the thoughts of the English turned from reconnaissance to subjugation. While the Treaty of Mellifont (1603) provided a framework to bring O'Neill peacefully back into the English fold, English theorists discussed a more permanent English presence in the province

The Earl of Salisbury explains the project for the settlement to King James I, 1609.
© Derry City Council

through a structured settlement scheme.[11] The flight of the earls facilitated such a settlement.

In the immediate aftermath of the flight, the English government initiated legal proceedings to acquire the lands of the fugitive earls. By late December 1608 a series of juries had been formed at Lifford and Strabane to indict 'the fugitive earls as outlaw traitors' and to confiscate their lands 'through the penalty of forfeiture'.[12] Now the English authorities had control over vast areas of land across the province. By a serendipitous twist, their acquisition of the whole land area of six counties within the province became possible as a result of the rebellion of Sir Cathair O'Doherty, lord of In-

ishowen, in 1608. He had always been a loyal servitor of the English crown having been confirmed as Lord of Inishowen by Lord Deputy Mountjoy at the age of fourteen amidst a struggle for succession. Following his appointment, Sir Henry Docwra, the governor of nearby Derry, mentored the young lord, providing him with an education, and enabling cordial relations between the refounded citadel of Derry and neighbouring Inishowen.[13] However, in 1606 Docwra resigned as governor and was replaced by Sir George Paulet. In the early years of Paulet's governorship, O'Doherty remained in favour with the crown, serving as foreman of the committee that indicted the fugitive earls in December 1607. However, relations between O'Doherty and Paulet soon soured as the latter became increasingly suspicious of the young lord. In early 1608 he accused Sir Cathair of treason and physically assaulted him. Aggrieved at his treatment, O'Doherty seized Culmore, sacked and burned Derry and killed his hated adversary.[14] He himself was eventually killed by English forces at Kilmacrenan, County Donegal on 5 July 1608.[15] His rebellion ultimately paved the way for a plantation in Ulster through the confiscation of his lands at Inishowen and a series of assizes that implicated numerous minor Ulster lords such as Donal Ballagh O'Cahan, Niall Garbh O'Donnell, Feidhlimidh Reagh MacDavitt and Oghy Og O'Hanlon in treasonable activities. The English government confiscated six counties (Donegal, Coleraine, Tyrone, Armagh, Fermanagh and Cavan), and preparations began for a settlement of the province.[16]

Before the authorities decided to proceed with a formal plantation, they commissioned a survey to ascertain the extent of the escheated lands in Ulster. Sir Arthur Chichester, the lord deputy, drove this initiative and set the parameters for its completion. The commission aimed to prosecute those who had

249

The O'Neill stronghold of Dungannon, granted to Sir Arthur Chichester in the plantation. © NLI

taken part in O'Doherty's rebellion, exact 'civil justice' and survey the escheated lands.[17] Key figures in the Dublin administration, including Sir Thomas Ridgeway, treasurer and privy councillor, Attorney General Sir John Davies and Surveyor General Sir William Parsons, participated in the commission. It set out from Dublin on 5 July 1608. The commissioners spent much of their time in Ulster engulfed in post-flight and post-rebellion legal wrangling, thereby ensuring that they spent only five days 'surveying' the escheated lands. They completed these county surveys by inquisition, beginning with Tyrone on the 27 July 1608 and finishing in Cavan on 6 September.[18] Such was the generality of their work that F. W. Harris has noted that 'the findings by inquisition for Armagh and Coleraine, both dated 2 August, were practically the same as for Tyrone'.[19]

The commissioners structured the final survey report – 'A booke of the Kings lands founde upon the last generall survey within the province of Ulster anno le: 1608' – by county.[20] Breaking the landscape down from county to barony level, they examined temporal, ecclesiastical and monastic lands in each barony, before finally commenting on the availability of fishing on the forfeited lands. Taking Dungannon barony, Hugh O'Neill's pre-flight power-base, the very basic level of reconnaissance undertaken by the commissioners in Ulster becomes obvious. Within the Dungannon barony, temporal, ec-

Map of Ulster (c. 1598) by Francis Jobson. © BL

clesiastical and monastic lands are all identified.[21] In terms of the temporal lands, the commissioners provided the name, acreage and valuation of forty-two ballebetaghs. The balliboe of Dungannon, for example, is referred to by 'Dongannon contayning viij [8] balliboes', and is given a value of sixteen shillings sterling per annum.[22]

Similarly, the survey identified twenty-two ballebetaghs comprising ecclesiastical lands, for which it noted annual accrued rent due to the archbishop of Armagh.[23] They recorded only two ballebetaghs of monastic lands 'that wer in his Maiesties hands by force of the Statute of Dissolution' and which only contained one balliboe.[24] It becomes apparent that the very basic and general nature of the reportage would have rendered it of little use to the administration, as it attempted to establish viable plantation estates. It is therefore not surprising that, on receipt of this survey and with the final decision to proceed with plantation being made, the authorities issued a request for a new map survey of the escheated counties to be undertaken.

In 1609 Sir William Parsons received a new commission to undertake a detailed map survey of Ulster:

[so] that readily and by the Eye, the known boundes of every country might be discerned, the Church Land distinguished from the temporall ... the shares for the undertakers [be] laid out with their apparent limits according to certain conceived proportions of different quantity the goodness or badness of the soil to be specified.[25]

He enlisted the help of Sir Josias Bodley, a former military man and a keen fortification surveyor and cartographer, to bring together a team of skilled surveyors, measurers and map-makers.[26] After initial talks in Dublin, the survey began on 29 July 1609, and within a mere two months the commissioners had completed their work.[27]

The survey team mapped the escheated counties on a large-scale barony basis, providing government officials with a more detailed view of Ulster's landscape than they had hitherto received. They mapped each barony separately, eventually producing an estimated forty maps of the province. Only twenty-eight survive for Fermanagh, Armagh, Cavan and Tyrone and are deposited in The (English) National Archives.[28] Original maps for both Counties Donegal and Londonderry are no longer extant, although two contemporary sketches and an engraving of the Bodley maps for County Donegal are housed in Trinity College Dublin.[29]

On examining Bodley's map of 'Parte of the Baronie of Donganon', the level of the detailed analysis of the escheated lands within the map survey becomes obvious. This detail is significantly increased by the use of the barony unit.[30] The map examined three distinct elements of the cultural landscape of the Dungannon barony: land boundaries, landownership and the built environment. In terms of land boundaries, it began the preliminary stages of plantation by implementing the commission's instructions to divide the barony into the new plantation estates or 'proportions'. Using native placenames and a red conventional symbol, Bodley carefully sculpted the lands into plantation estates, thus preparing the barony for plantation.[31] He expanded this study of the land boundaries in the barony of Dungannon by emphasising the differing landownership within its boundaries. For example, he distinguished the church lands that would remain outside the main plantation scheme, using a light green colour to make these areas prominent within the map. He enhanced many of the depictions of these pockets of church land by including small drawings of churches in perspective, such as at 'Plaister' and 'Heskerah' in the south-west of the map.[32]

Bodley also examined the cultural landscape of the barony of Dungannon through an exploration of the built environment. Much of this exploration was selective, emphasising only Gaelic castles and churches that could be utilised by the British settlers and integrated into their new cultural landscape of plantation. His focus on castles is notable within the Dungannon proportion itself, where he provided a detailed representation of the surviving structure of the earl of Tyrone's castle and a nearby church.[33] Perhaps, owing to its prominence as Tyrone's stronghold, he expanded the detail of his normal settlement depictions in his drawing by highlighting numerous architectural features, including two distinct wings, turrets, windows and a large fortified door.[34]

Following the main commission instructions, the maps also examined the physical landscape of the province in great detail, reflecting the authorities' concern to ensure that the new plantation estates would be viable. Each estate would be granted a relatively equal portion of viable lands; furthermore such detailed maps would enable the plantation commissioners to evaluate the potential economic benefits of the Ulster lands. As a result, bogs, forests, islands, lakes, mountains and rivers were all included. Once again, Bodley's second map of the Dungannon barony placed strong emphasis on the physical landscape. Given the concern to create viable estates, he focused on distinguishing profitable and non-profitable lands. With regards to this land quality, Bodley's map represented the drainage pattern of the barony in great detail, with the river network distinguished across the barony by the use of a distinctive blue colour.[35]

The lands of the barony were neatly divided according to profitability by means of a strong colour scheme, as evidenced in the Dungannon barony map and Bodley's representation of the bogland vis-à-vis the rest of the barony's lands. He employed a dark brown colour, for example, to highlight unprofitable bogland, and a light cream colour to distinguish the more profitable land areas for the plantation estates.[36] A similar preoccupation with wood coverage across the barony can also be discerned, with small pockets of trees shown at 'Kilmore' and 'Gortmarren' to the south.[37] These trees could potentially become a key building tool for the new plantation estates, and the location of these woods would facilitate the quick development of new settlements. With this combined exploration of the cultural and physical landscape of Ulster, government officials had a valuable visual and practical tool with which to begin the process of creating viable plantation estates.[38] As a result, these Bodley maps became key instruments in the transformation of Ulster from its Gaelic landscape to that of a model English-structured society.

As surveying of the lands continued, interested parties petitioned the king with plantation schemes. Sir John Davies and Sir James Ley, the chief justice, offered the first project for a settlement scheme in County Tyrone.[39] Their plan envisaged the creation of proportions of different sizes (2,000, 1,500 and 1,000 acres) that would be granted by lottery to Scottish and English servitors and Irish natives.[40] Interim statements such as 'A project for the division for the plantation of the escheated lands' grasped their early plan, expanding it to include the other escheated counties.[41] These schemes did not go unnoticed, and many of their recommendations found their way into the final plantation conditions, announced in April 1610.

These plantation conditions regulated all aspects of the plantation from the size of its estates to the numbers of settlers that had to be introduced.[42] In the first instance, the scheme formerly established the 'precinct' and the 'proportion' (roughly equating to the 'barony' and 'townland') as the two key land units. It provided for proportions of three sizes which would be granted to English and Scottish undertakers and servitors (men who had served in Ireland in a military or administrative capacity) and 'deserving' natives who had remained loyal to the crown in the recent upheavals in Ulster.[43] Grantees would be free to export for seven years without tariff, and would be allowed to utilise local timber for building on their estates. In return, the plantation authorities expected the settlers to fulfil certain conditions.[44] From 1614 an annual rent of £5 6s 6d would be due on every 1,000 acres.[45] In addition, each grantee had to fulfil significant building and settler requirements, dependent on the proportion size. On a 2,000-acre estate the undertaker was expected to build a stone house and bawn; 1,500 and 1,000-acre grantees undertook to build a stone or brick house with a bawn, and a bawn respectively. Finally, all undertakers, or their agent, were expected to reside on their estates for five years.[46]

Grantees also had the responsibility of settling twenty-four English and Scottish men aged eighteen or over on every 1,000 acres, the equivalent of at least ten families.[47] These conditions also had strong provisos for the composition of every 1,000 acres within a grant. Demesne land would make up the largest part, comprising 300 acres. All remaining lands would be divided among two fee farmers on 120 acres, three leaseholders on 100 acres, and four or more families as husbandmen, artificers and cottagers on the remaining 160 acres.[48] The conditions also compelled all settlers to take the Oath of Supremacy.[49] Finally, the plantation scheme set the guidelines for actual settlement. Estates would be let by Midsummer 1610, with the undertakers taking up residence by Michaelmas of the same year. One-third of the settler accommodation had to be built by 1 November 1610, with one-third of the new inhabitants in place by 1 November 1611.[50] All remaining buildings would have to be completed by the following year. To ensure the successful implementation of the scheme, the government would survey the plantation estates at regular intervals. In granting the new estates, the plantation authorities also appear to have used maps to represent the estates and to provide a visual overview of the land allocations to individual grantees at this key juncture.[51]

Outside of the actual estates, the plantation scheme also provided for the granting of the former county of Coleraine ('O'Cahan's country') and part of north Tyrone to 'The Honourable The Irish Society' who enlisted the twelve great livery compa-

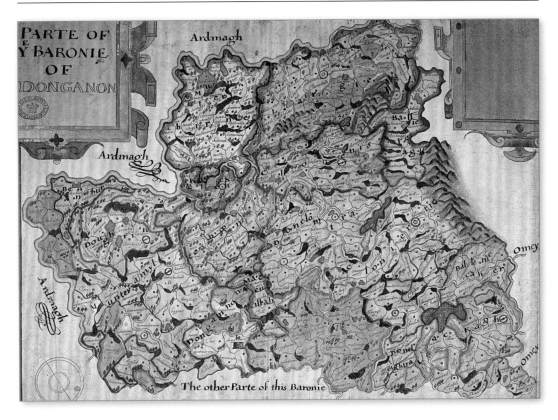

Part of the barony of Dungannon, 1609. © TNA

nies of London to plant the newly escheated county of Londonderry and refound a plantation citadel on the site of Docwra's former settlement at Derry.[52] The plan also envisaged the development of a much larger urban network in Ulster, comprising twenty-five corporate towns including the former Gaelic strongholds of Donegal and Dungannon. This project would be guided by governors or custodians, many of whom undertook estates elsewhere in the planted lands as servitors. Thus the plantation administrators divided the six escheated counties of Ulster into a patchwork of small estates that would finally eradicate much of the strong Gaelic landscape of the province.

Once the plantation estates had been established and the new settlers arrived in Ulster, the plantation authorities aimed to ensure the successful development of the fledgling estates in accordance with the conditions that had been laid down. In order to do so, they commissioned periodical land surveys over the course of the plantation's early years (Sir George Carew, 1611; Sir Josias Bodley, 1614; and Captain Nicholas Pynnar, 1618-19), as well as a specially-formed commission of 1622 which examined all plantations across Ireland. These surveys provided de-

tailed accounts of the individual plantation proportions noting the landholders' names, their building activity, settler numbers, and even recording details of the agricultural and industrial practices on the new estates. Thus, for plantation historians, these surveys hold the key to understanding the radical transformation of Ulster's landscape under the auspices of plantation. Carew, Pynnar and the 1622 Commission, provide detailed accounts of the change wrought at both Dungannon and Donegal, the strongholds of the earls of Tyrone and Tyrconnell respectively, through the early years of the plantation of Ulster.

Sir George Carew commenced the first survey of the new plantation on 29 July 1611, having been charged with a commission to provide 'A Perfect Relation, and Report of the Works, Buildings and fortifications done by the English'.[53] County Donegal became his first port of call. From his report, which now survives in his papers at Lambeth Palace Library, the early plantation development at modern Donegal town can be distinguished. Donegal formed the traditional core of the O'Donnell lordship. As one of the most prominent Ulster lords to flee in 1607, Rory O'Donnell forfeited his lands to the Crown. Under the scheme for plantation, the

253

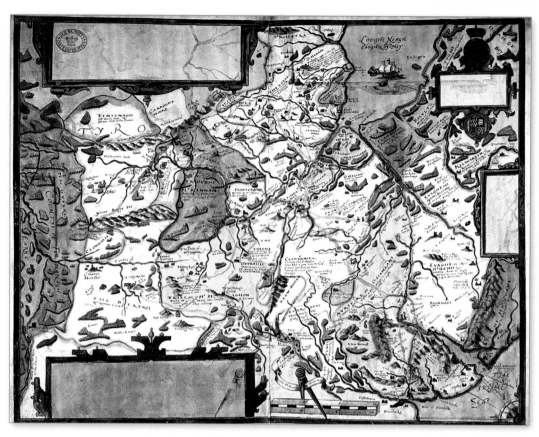

Map of southern Ulster, 1602-03, by Richard Bartlett. © TNA

lordship was broken into numerous proportions, with Donegal earmarked as one of the proposed corporate towns.

Carew's survey provides a stark image of a massive transformation at the heart of the O'Donnell lands, as it distinguished a thriving British plantation settlement. Captain Basil Brooke had been appointed as custodian of the town, and had also received a grant at Edenocarne in the barony of Raphoe, also in County Donegal. Under Brooke's direction, a 'fair bawn … with flankers, a parapet, and a walk on the top of fifteen foot high' had been constructed, with 'a strong house of stone' inside its walls.[54] The settlement had given rise to some spillover development, with houses being built in its environs by English, Scottish and Irish settlers, who had adopted English architectural practices and built 'good copled houses after the manner of the Pale'.[55] A similar fate had befallen the surrounding landscape, where Captain Paul Goare had 'erected a fair stone house out of the ruins of O'Boyle's old castle upon the sea side'.[56] Thus, from a very early stage in the plantation process, English settlements began to transform Donegal's traditional landscape.

In a similar manner to Donegal town, Carew also focused on Dungannon at the heart of Hugh O'Neill's former territory in County Tyrone, where progress had not been as rapid. By 1611 Lord Deputy Chichester, a major grantee, could only report his plans for the site to Carew. He intended 'to build a castle or strong house of lime and stone, and to environ the same with a deep ditch with a counter scarfe of stone to hold up the earth'.[57] The only work that had so far been undertaken was the demolition of O'Neill's iconic castle. Carew detailed how Chichester had enlisted 'masons and workmen to take down such remains of the decayed ruins of the old castle as are yet standing'.[58] In doing so he began the process of anglicisation at the heart of Gaelic Ulster, removing the central component of the O'Neill world and cultural landscape. Chichester intended to further this anglicisation of Dungannon by the development of a distinctly British settlement on the site. Early settlers began to develop the town with houses 'of copels', but Carew stressed that the families 'are bound to build of cage work or stone after the English and make inclosures about the town'.[59] The report thus suggests that Dungannon was bound to become a distinctly British settlement. With the exception of County Cavan, each proportion and plantation grant underwent similar scrutiny throughout Carew's report, which clearly suggests that significant change had taken place within the escheated lands of Ulster at this early stage. Eager settlers had begun to fulfil the conditions of their grants, and Ulster's landscape underwent rapid transformation.

Despite a new survey of the Ulster lands by Josias Bodley in 1614, little additional evidence emerges of the developments at Donegal town and Dungannon until Captain Nicholas Pynnar's survey in 1618-19.[60] Pynnar had been appointed as 'Director General of Fortifications in Ireland' in 1618, receiving his first commission in Ulster on 27 November 1618 which instructed him to complete a report on the progress of the plantation in Ulster and provide details:

> concerning the performance of such things as [were] to be done by the several undertakers, servitors, and natives of and in several counties in the plantations of the Irish granted unto them by his Majesty's letters patents.[61]

Once again, Pynnar's instructions called for a survey that examined each individual proportion in the plantation scheme to ascertain whether the main grantee or undertaker had fulfilled requirements set down by the plantation conditions, including building, population, arms and tillage clauses.[62]

While Donegal town received scant treatment, Pynnar provided a detailed description of Dungannon. By 1619 it appeared that the fledgling town had become an even more integral part of the plantation landscape. It comprised two distinct parts: Chichester's fort on a site of 1,140 acres, adjacent to the site of O'Neill's castle, and the town itself on 500 acres; the former had been built in accordance with English military design which incorporated the favoured early modern European *trace italienne*. Pynnar reported that 'there is built a Fort of Lime and Stone, one hundred and twenty feet square, with four half Bulwarks, and a deep ditch about it twenty foot broad, and counterscarped'.[63] The fort appeared to be a work in progress, with the proposed development of a castle noted by Pynnar, and the emergence of overspill settlement in the outskirts of the fort, where 'three English Houses, being inhabited with English men' had developed.[64]

The adjoining town, which had only emerged in a temporary form at the time of Carew's report, had become a strong and thriving settlement by 1619. Pynnar reported that 'nine fair Stone houses' and 'six strong Timber Houses' had been built at Dungannon, with one of the stone houses having 'a Stone Wall about it'.[65] British societal norms had also emerged, with the religious needs of the new settlement being catered for by the building of a 'large Church with a Steeple, all of Lime and Stone'. Most encouragingly for the authorities, he reported that a large cohort of thirty English families and thirty-six Irish families had been settled, with the latter having 'come to Church, and [had] taken the Oath of Supremacy'. Thus the new settlers, including the Irish had bowed to the required religious and regal allegiances that underpinned the plantation, a development to the rampant anglicisation of the O'Neill heartland in the immediate aftermath of the flight.

By 1622, when the final major report examining the plantation had been commissioned, the transformation of Donegal town and Dungannon into British settlements had almost been completed. King James ordered the establishment of the 1622 commission as he became increasingly 'unhappy with what he learned of his plantation', especially the high rates of retention of native settlers on many Ulster estates.[66] The commission not only examined Ulster, but undertook an examination of all the English and British plantations across Ireland up to 1622. Sixteen commissioners divided the plantation areas between them. Sir Thomas Phillips and Richard Hadsor examined the plantations in Donegal and Londonderry, while Toby, Lord Caulfield, Sir Dudley Digges and Sir Nathaniell Rich, reported for Tyrone and Armagh.[67]

In their final report Phillips and Hadsor provided a detailed description of the plantation settlement that had emerged at Donegal town. They reported significant change to the cultural landscape of the town under the direction of Brooke. By 1622 Brooke had 'voluntarily built a bawn of lime and stone enclosing the raynes [range] of the old castle there', thus enveloping the remnants of O'Donnell's castle in a distinct British development.[68] Within the bawn, the commissioners noted that 'he hath built a house of lime and stone, 2 storeys high, slated, where he, his wife and family inhabit'.[69] Given the significant 'voluntary' improvements that he had made by 1622, it is not surprising that the commissioners reported Brooke's attempts to gain favour and obtain a full grant of the town. The commissioners noted his intention, explaining Brooke's belief that 'if he had the inheritance thereof, he would make it a strong and defensible place for his majesty's service'.[70]

Brooke oversaw the development of a strong corporate town at Donegal. Using his new house and bawn as a development focus, he had encouraged Donegal's expansion. By 1622, the commissioners reported, 'a portreeve and twelve burgesses' had been established, while 'about 30 houses, being for the most part built with stone walls and covered with thatch, inhabited with English' had been constructed. A free school had also been built, thus fulfilling the specific requirements of the plantation conditions for corporate towns. By 1622, then, it appeared that Donegal town had developed as a radically different settlement to that of the original Gaelic site, having both incorporated, and eradicated the Gaelic features through rebuilding and major development of the site.

Caulfield, Digges and Rich's report of the progress at Dungannon town provided even further evidence of the complete transition of the second of these two Gaelic strongholds to a British borough under the auspices of plantation. While the commissioners reported on the fort, the new houses and the church noted by Pynnar three years earlier, the 1622 report outlined major progress in the development of a British society at Dungannon. For example, a system of governance had been put in place by 1622, and the commissioners acknowledged the appointment of 'a provost and twelve burgesses and dwellers and freemen of the said borough'.[71] A basic system of law and order had also emerged, with detailed descriptions of a jailhouse and sessions house in the final survey. The sessions house, an elaborate building with 'a large room for the judges to sit, with two close rooms for the juries and country to attend', had been constructed in an English cagework style.[72] Digges and Rich also noted that a markethouse formed part of the development, an innovation which would enable the regulation of trade within Dungannon. Further evidence of these British societal structures emerged as the commissioners recorded that the houses mentioned in earlier surveys now had gardens and backsides, thus conjuring an image of an English country town.

These reports suggest a widespread transformation of the escheated lands during the decades of plantation, a transformation which nonetheless maintained many of the native Gaelic settlements and buildings and used them to provide the basis from which new plantation settlements could

emerge. This plantation settlement became a significant agent of change within Ulster's cultural landscape, bringing new architectural styles in fortification and house design, and also adopting many of the norms of British society and culture in Ulster.

While the political, social and cultural world of the plantation continued to develop in the years after 1622, the commission of that year marks the final detailed study of the new plantation to take place. What the report suggests is that Ulster had undergone a significant metamorphosis in the fifteen years since the flight of the earls. While the English, and later British authorities had made attempts to gain a foothold and influence in the affairs of Ulster before the flight through reconnaissance surveying and the manipulation of loyal Ulster lords, the Ulster lords had maintained a united offence against the interaction. However, in fleeing their lands in 1607, they left their lands open to confiscation and settlement through forfeiture. Sir Cathair O'Doherty's rebellion expanded the scope and nature of the plantation as his lands, and those of his supporters, also came into the crown's possession.

The dictate of forfeiture enabled widespread surveying and plantation which totally transformed the province, setting in train a process of land division, ownership, settlement and building that dramatically altered the cultural and political landscape of Gaelic Ulster. It continued in the actual developments carried out by the undertakers and settlers themselves. Across Ulster numerous small plantation estates emerged in the style of small contemporary English villages in accordance with the instructions that had been issued. The extent to which this British settlement had a significant effect on the landscape of Ulster was most obvious in Donegal town and Dungannon, the seats of the O'Donnells and the O'Neills respectively.

The surveys commissioned at regular intervals during the early years of plantation in 1611, 1614, 1618-19, and again, in 1622, present much detailed evidence as to how the Ulster landscape changed during the plantation's infancy. In tracing the development of Donegal town and Dungannon within this essay, it becomes apparent just how valuable a resource these surveys are. Both sites underwent the same process of change. In both locations the Gaelic castle became the starting point for the new British settlements. Forts, in the English angular style, emerged as the first element of many of these plantation villages. A fortified house dominated these installations, while numerous houses in the English 'copled' or 'cagework' style were erected outside the forts. In both cases, by 1622, English societal practices and norms had been successfully introduced, with sessions houses, jails, schools and churches all in place. This change was replicated across Ulster, and the surveys record the specifics of the settle-

ment within every proportion. Given the extent of the British plantation and settlement in Ulster during the early years of the project, there can be little doubt that the flight of the earls left the lands open to such change, and that by 1622, the Ulster landscape had been completely and utterly transformed.

Notes

1 I would like to thank Dr Elaine Murphy for her comments on earlier drafts of this essay.

2 *CSPI, 1509-1570*, p. 336.

3 See J. H. Andrews, 'The Irish surveys of Robert Lythe', *Imago Mundi*, 19 (1965), pp 22-31.

4 These maps of Carrickfergus are extant at TCD, MS 1209/26 'Craggfergus'; and TCD, MS 1209/27 'Carigfergus'; and TNA MPF 1/89 (1), Cooley, Mourne and Omeath.

5 For more on the career and life of Hugh O'Neill see H. Morgan, *Tyrone's Rebellion: the outbreak of the Nine Years War in Tudor Ireland* (Woodbridge, 1993); M. D. Finnegan, 'Tyrone's rebellion: Hugh O'Neill and the outbreak of the Nine Years War in Ulster' (MA thesis, NUI, Galway, 2001).

6 BL, Cotton MS Augustus I.ii.19, 'Ulster', Francis Jobson, c. 1598, TCD, MS 1209/17, 'Ulster', TCD, MS 1209/15, 'Ulster', TNA, MPF1/312 (2), 'Ulster'.

7 Ibid.

8 Ibid.

9 Ibid.

10 Bartlett's fortification maps are now housed in the National Library of Ireland (NLI MS 2656). Six provincial and regional maps are located in the National Archives including, TNA, MPF 1/35, 'A Generalle Description of Vlster', MPF1/36, 'South East Ulster', MPF1/37, 'South West Ulster and North Connacht', MPF1/133, 'A description of Lough Eaughe or Lough Sydneye poynting out the fortes latelie erected by Tyrone', TCD MS 2379, 'The descriptione of a parte of Vlster conteining the particular places of the righte Honorable the Lord Montioie now Lord Deputie of Irelande his iorneies, and seruices in the North part of that kingdome, from his entrie therinto vntill this prest August 1601' and BL, Cotton MS Augustus I.ii.37, 'South East Ulster'. Further details of these maps can be found in A. Margey, *Mapping Ireland, c. 1550-1640: an illustrated catalogue of the plantation maps of Ireland* (Dublin, forthcoming). A detailed study of the life and work of Bartlett can be found in J. H. Andrews, *The Queen's Last Map-Maker: Richard Bartlett in Ireland, 1600-03* (Dublin, 2009).

11 Sir Arthur Chichester, the Lord Deputy, proposed a plantation scheme as early as 1605, P. Robinson, *The Plantation of Ulster,* (Dublin, 1984), p. 39.

12 F. W. Harris, 'The Rebellion of Sir Cahir O'Doherty and its legal aftermath', *The Irish Jurist*, xv, 2 (1980), p. 299.

13 'Biography of Sir Cahir O'Doherty' (www.oxforddnb.com).

14 Ibid. For more information on Sir Niall Garbh O'Donnell in the rebellion see: N. G. Ó Domhnaill, 'Sir Niall Garbh O'Donnell and the rebellion of Sir Cahir O'Doherty', *Irish Historical Studies*, iii (1942), pp 34-38.

15 'Biography of Sir Cahir O'Doherty'.

16 Harris, 'The rebellion of Sir Cahir O'Doherty and its legal aftermath', p. 323.

17 Ibid., p. 306.

18 Ibid., pp 316-20.

19 Ibid., p. 316.

20 MS Rawlinson A. 237, The Bodleian Library, Oxford: a booke of the Kinges lands founde upon the last generall survey within the province of Ulster anno le: 1608', *Analecta Hibernica*, iii (1931), pp 151-218.

21 Ibid., ff 151-154.

22 MS Rawlinson A. 237, f. 151.

23 Ibid., ff. 153-154.

24 Ibid., f. 154.

25 Bodley to the earl of Salisbury, 24 Feb. 1609 (TNA SP 64/1/4).

26 Sir Josias Bodley first arrived in Ireland in 1598, when he was sent to Ulster as a captain at the height of the Nine Years War. In 1601 he served as trench-master general to the army at Kinsale, before becoming governor of a number of key locations including Newry and Duncannon. In 1604 he completed a number of fortification plans for coastal locations in Ireland. In 1608 he completed a 'Report on Ulster's fortresses', which is believed to have been the impetus for his selection as map-maker in the 1609 survey. He finished new fortification plans in 1611. By 1613 he had been appointed as Director of Fortifications in Ireland. In the same year, he undertook a written survey of the plantations in Ireland. He died on 22 August 1617 and was buried in Christchurch Cathedral in Dublin. (For further information on Bodley see 'Biography of Sir Josias Bodley', www.oxforddnb.com).

27 J. Andrews, 'The maps of the six escheated counties of Ulster, 1609-10', *Proceedings of the Royal Irish Academy*, lxxiv, C (1974), p. 142.

28 Bodley's maps are located at TNA MPF 1/36 – MPF1/64.

29 F. H. A. Aalen and R. J. Hunter, 'Two early seventeenth century maps of Donegal', *Journal of the Royal Society of Antiquarians in Ireland,* xciv 2 (1964), pp 199-202. Two copies of maps for County Donegal survive in the Muniments Collection in Trinity College, Dublin, see TCD MUN/ME/15, 'A map of the Barony of Tirhugh' and 'The map of the Abby of Kilmacrenan in the Barony of Kilmacrenan'. A further engraved map of barony of Inishowen is also extant in the manuscript collections at Trinity College, Dublin, in

J. H. Andrews, 'An early map of Inishowen', *Long Room*, vii (1973), pp 19-25.

30 'Parte of the Baronie of Donganon', Josias Bodley, 1609-10 (TNA MPF1/45 (2)).

31 Ibid.

32 Ibid.

33 Ibid.

34 Ibid.

35 Ibid.

36 Ibid.

37 Ibid.

38 Salisbury received the Bodley maps on 15 March 1610 (Ridgeway to Salisbury, 15 Mar 1610 TNA SP 64/2).

39 Robinson, *The Plantation of Ulster*, p. 62.

40 Ibid., p. 62.

41 'A proiect for the division and plantacion of the escheated lands in six severall counties of Vlster namelie Tirone, Coleraine, Donegall, ffermanagh, Armagh and Cavan' (BL Harley MS 7009, f. 63).

42 The scheme for plantation has been discussed extensively by other scholars see T. W. Moody (ed.) 'The Revised Articles of the Ulster Plantation, 1610', *Institute of Historical Research Bulletin*, xii (1934-35), pp 178-82 and Robinson, *Plantation of Ulster*, pp 62-64.

43 Ibid., p. 63.

44 Robinson, *Plantation of Ulster*, p. 63.

45 Ibid., p. 63.

46 Ibid., p. 63.

47 Ibid., p. 63.

48 Ibid., pp 63-64.

49 Ibid., p. 64.

50 Ibid., p. 64.

51 'The platt of the six escheated counties of Ulster', 1610 (BL Cotton Ms Augustus I.ii.44). This map, most likely prepared in 1610, represented the estates allocated to individual undertakers after the initial process of granting. While little is known of its history within administration, it is likely that this may have been a derivative of an earlier map used in the initial allocating of lands in 1609. The 1844 British Museum catalogue attributes this map to John Norden. Earlier catalogues failed to identify the map-maker. Edward Lynam argues that while the British Museum appears to have attributed this map to Norden on the basis of the handwriting on the map, the map is unlikely to have been drawn by Norden. Lynam believes that Norden never set foot in Ireland, and therefore never completed his own survey of the country. This, he suggests, is reflected in Norden's Ireland map at TNA MPF1/67, which he argues is an amalgamation of information from a number of contemporary published surveys. If this is the case, he claims that Norden is most unlikely to have compiled the Ulster map. See E. Lynam, 'English maps and mapmakers of the sixteenth century', *Geographical Journal*, lxvi (1950), pp 22-23; A. Margey, 'Representing plantation landscapes: the mapping of Ulster, c. 1560-1630', in *Plantation Ireland: settlement and material culture, c.1550-1700* (Dublin, 2009).

52 For more on the Londonderry plantation see T. W. Moody, *The Londonderry plantation, 1609-41* (Belfast, 1939).

53 *Cal. Carew MSS*, vi, p. 220.

54 Ibid., p. 222.

55 Ibid., p. 222.

56 Ibid., p. 222.

57 Ibid., p. 228.

58 Ibid., p. 228.

59 Ibid., p. 229.

60 Pynnar was a military engineer, who was heavily involved in the mapping of Ireland, surveying areas including Connacht, Londonderry, Leinster and Munster. He mainly produced maps and plans of early fortifications. It was this experience that ensured his joint appointment as Director General of Fortifications in Ireland with Thomas Rotherham in 1618. He was later appointed Surveyor General of Lands, Plantations and Mines: P. Eden and S. Bendall (eds), *Dictionary of land surveyors and local map-makers of Great Britain and Ireland, 1530-1840* (London, 1997), p. 419.

61 Hill, *Plantation of Ulster*, p. 449.

62 'A briefe viewe and survey made at seuerall tymes and in severall places, in the seuerall counties within named betweene the first daie of December 1618 and the 28th of March 1619, by mee Nicholas Pynnar esqr and others'; TCD MS 864, in Hill, *Plantation of Ulster*, pp 449-590.

63 Ibid., p. 552.

64 Ibid.

65 Ibid.

66 Canny, *Making Ireland British, 1580-1640*, p. 209.

67 Canny gives details of the commissioners for the major areas of plantation with 'Sir Adam Loftus (lord chancellor of Ireland), Sir William Jones, and Mr Thomas Crewe [visiting] the plantations in King's and Queen's Counties; Charles, Lord Viscount Wilmot (lord president of Connacht), Sir Dudley Norton, and Sir Francis Blundell [visiting] the plantations in Counties Longford and Leitrim; Sir John Jephson, Sir Thomas Penruddock, Sir Henry Bourchier, and Mr. Theodore Price, DD, [visiting] the plantations in County Wexford in the province of Leinster; Toby, Lord Caulfield (master of the ordinance), Sir Dudley Digges, and Sir Nathaniel Rich [visiting] the plantations in Counties Tyrone and Armagh; Sir Thomas Phillips, and Mr Richard Hadsor [visiting] the Londonderry plantation and that in County Donegal: and Sir Francis Annesley with Sir James Perrott [visiting] the plantation in Counties Cavan and Fermanagh' (*Making Ireland British*, p. 243).

68 V. Treadwell, *The Irish Commission of 1622: an investigation of the Irish administration 1615-22 and its consequences 1623-24* (Dublin, 2006), p. 610.

69 Ibid.

70 Ibid.

71 Treadwell, *The Irish Commission of 1622*, p. 585.

72 Ibid.

The flight of the earls and the origins of modern diasporas

Patrick Fitzgerald

Diaspora is derived from the Greek word for dispersal or scattering, and up until the late twentieth century it was primarily applied to the widespread out-migration of the ancient Israelites and the Jewish people. Thereafter it came to be more liberally used for a variety of groups who had experienced significant dispersal from an identifiable homeland. Almost twenty years ago the term 'Irish diaspora' came to enjoy significant prominence at both popular and academic levels. The publication in 1993 of Donald H. Akenson's *The Irish diaspora: a primer* followed on from Mary Robinson's striking emphasis upon the concept in her inaugural address as President of Ireland in December 1990.[1] The growing currency of the term might be graphically measured by the appearance of the subtitle 'The story of the Irish diaspora' to Tim Pat Coogan's 2000 epic, *Wherever green is worn* or by the fact that 'Diaspora' constitutes one of the most voluminous entries in Brian Lalor's *The Encyclopaedia of Ireland* (2003).[2] Nevertheless, the application of the diaspora model to the 'Irish overseas' has not gone uncontested. In 2006 *Irish Economic and Social History* published a symposium in which three leading historians of modern Irish migration collectively offer a vigorous challenge to the construct.[3] Whether one essentially accepts or rejects the diaspora paradigm in the case of global Irish migration, the issue of periodisation, and particularly origin, remains pertinent. Can any particular significance be ascribed to the events of 4 September 1607 in light of the subsequent transformation in Irish migration patterns? This essay will initially address this question before moving on to consider the subsequent importance of this iconic event for those whose identity and/or allegiance is affiliated with the planter/unionist community.

In turning our attention towards the origins of the modern Irish diaspora, it may be helpful to note that little of the academic debate about diaspora in the context of Irish migration has related to migration at the sub-national level. However, the term need not be exclusively deployed in relation to the nation-state or the island. Indeed, it could be argued that one of the model's key conceptual advantages relates to its protean quality. Individual migrants can be simultaneously viewed as members of family, townland, parish, county and ultimately in the case of trans-oceanic migration, continental diasporas.[4] As innumerable later emigrant letters testify, most migrants and non-migrants in the modern era constructed 'home' at a level well below that of the island or nation-state. Thus arguably Hugh

'Sailing from Rathmullan'.
© Brian Vallely

259

O'Neill and Rory O'Donnell, as they sailed out of Lough Swilly in September 1607, could imagine their departure from the abstract construct or 'imagined community' of Ireland and thus entered an 'Irish' diaspora. At the same time, they would have also related their thoughts of leaving home to the respective specific locations which they knew more intimately and empirically as home. In the case of the earl of Tyrone, he thus proceeded to enter the O'Neill family diaspora, the Drumcart townland diaspora, the Drumglass parish diaspora and the Tyrone lordship diaspora at the same time as he entered an Irish diaspora.

In a literal sense, of course, 4 September 1607 was not the beginning of the Irish diaspora, a tradition of migration from Ireland stretched back for a millennium or more. In the sixth century the early Irish church provided numerous missionaries to the continent, and the iconic figure of Colum Cille may well have entered the mind of O'Donnell, in particular, as he looked back for a precedent during the moment of departure on Portnamurray strand.[5] Much recent work has also enhanced our appreciation of the scale of outward migration from Ireland in the preceding generation; mercantile trade, educational opportunity and military service all served to bolster a significant late Tudor diasporic Irish presence on the near continent.[6] The earls would have been only too conscious of their recent family diasporas. Red Hugh O'Donnell, Rory's older brother, had passed away (allegedly poisoned) in Spain five years previously, while Henry O'Neill, Hugh's eldest son, served as colonel with the Irish regiment in Spanish Flanders since 1605. Furthermore, Cúchonnacht Maguire, who had escaped to the continent earlier in 1607 had been instrumental in acquiring the unnamed vessel which he himself accompanied back to the Swilly in September.[7]

It is thus in the iconic or symbolic sense that the earls' dramatic departure might be presented as a marker denoting the beginning of the modern Irish diaspora. This most poignant, yet enigmatic, leaving came, in time, to occupy a central place in the collective memory of Catholic Ireland and may well have been recalled as an historic precedent by innumerable later emigrants as they caught their last sight of the homeland. However, the role of 1607 as such a marker is far from unambiguous, and a review of the historiography relating to both the flight and later emigration illustrates this point. Casting an eye over a now very voluminous literature relating to historic Irish emigration, one remains struck by the

segmented nature of the corpus. Even considering just what has been published since the early 1990s, when the diaspora model came to prominence, it remains the case that the vast majority of literature retains focus upon Irish migration to one particular and discrete destination. One might also note the relatively limited connectivity between what we might loosely refer to as the early modern and the modern Irish diasporas. Most of the work falls into one of five broad strands: Irish migration to Europe, 1550-1800, to Colonial America, 1607-1782, to North America, 1782-1930, to Britain 1800-1970, to the British Empire or other trans-oceanic destinations, 1750-1960. The task of identifying the connecting strands between Irish migrants across these global destinations and chronological boundaries remains underdeveloped. Dr Thomas O'Connor, one of the historians at the forefront of the rejuvenation in research and publication relating to the Irish in early modern Europe, has revealingly described, following attendance at a major conference in Chicago, the limited recognition many Irish-Americans have of the significant migration stream from Ireland to the continent before 1750.[8] In short, on the far side of the Atlantic the dominating spectre of 'Black '47' overshadows much that went before, and the date 1607 is more likely to conjure thoughts of Jamestown rather than Rathmullan. In this light, it is perhaps worth noting that as part of the commemorative events organised for Rathmullan in September 2007 visitors would have the opportunity to board the Famine-era reconstructed emigrant ship, the *Jeannie Johnston*, in order to re-enact the departure of 1607.

The *Jeannie Johnston*, Ireland's 'Famine Ship', on the open sea. It is ironic that it played a key role in the quatercentenary celebrations of the flight of the earls.
© Donegal County Council

Ironically, O'Neill's flight left his family lands and symbology open to appropriation by the planters and their descendants, as witnessed in these loyalist murals in Belfast. © Bill Rolston

Looking back, more specifically, at literature relating to the flight of the earls, is it possible to find any evidence for the identification of this event as a point of origin for the Irish diaspora? A particularly fascinating reference in this regard is an article by Margaret MacCurtain, published in Liam de Paor's *Milestones in Irish History* (1986).[9] In addressing the flight as such a milestone, she offers the reader the following paragraph:

> We have examined how the flight of the earls merits its place in Irish History. Yet if ever a monument were to be erected to the event in Rathmullan it must surely represent the hulk of the ship with purposeful figures crowding around the prow looking forward. All those who began the Irish diaspora so sorrowfully that September day had no knowledge that they were beginning one of the most splendid pages of Irish history, that of the Irish Abroad.[10]

Apart from explicitly identifying the flight as the start of the Irish diaspora, Mac Curtain's interpretation might be seen as prescient in that it refers to the Irish abroad collectively as the Irish diaspora and because it ascribes an essentially positive depiction to that phenomenon. This capacity to express a positive dimension to historic Irish migration was less developed in the economically depressed era preceding Mary Robinson's presidency. Many of MacCurtain's generation, haunted by the memory of the grim 1950s, might struggle to share the vision of emigration as 'one of the most splendid pages of Irish history'.[11] One might add that figures representing the departing earls should, in truth, look

both forward and backward, capturing the inherent tension in all migrants between the old world which they leave and the new world towards which they journey.

Two of the more recent publications aimed at both a popular and academic audience, John McCavitt's, *The Flight of the Earls* (2002) and Liam Swords's *The Flight of the Earls: A Popular History* (2007),[12] show something of a contrast between the authors on this point. McCavitt suggests in his introduction that 'to a considerable extent the Irish diaspora originated in this period'.[13] Swords makes no reference to a connection of any kind between the flight and later emigration. He stresses, rather, the prelude to the plantation of Ulster which would in turn facilitate significant British immigration in the decades after 1609.[14] Thus, in migration terms, it is fascinating to note that while McCavitt's attention is drawn towards 1607 as a launching-pad for subsequent emigration, Swords views it as a prelude to subsequent immigration. Both perspectives, of course, are entirely valid and may serve, in fact, to prompt us towards thinking of the events of September 1607 as constituting a kind of gateway, facilitating at one and the same time movement both into and out of Ireland. In this way one can argue that while the flight held iconic significance with regard to the evolution of the modern Irish diaspora, it also represented a key moment in the development of another diaspora – the British diaspora in Ireland.

Discussion of the date 1607 within the context of an evolving British diaspora also serves to divert our attention, momentarily, across the Atlantic to Virginia. Here, only months before the earls departure from Rathmullan, a London Company expedition established the settlement of Jamestown in honour of King James.[15] Only a few short years ahead the London Companies would again be drawn into the crown's colonising endeavours on the Foyle and Bann rather than the James River. The connections forged across the nascent trans-oceanic British diaspora remain in our consciousness, for example, through the shared placenames. In August 1612 Captain John Ridgeway, an English undertaker, established the new town of Virginia on the shores of Lough Ramor, in south County Cavan.[16] On the banks of the River Shannon, in the neighbouring county of Leitrim and a decade later, Sir Charles Coote, whose origins lay in Devon, established the walled town of Jamestown.[17] The extent to which this plantation frontier was linked in the minds of the contemporary British migrants with that emerging across the Atlantic has been explored in detail by William J. Smyth.[18]

The very term 'British diaspora' is not likely to be immediately familiar to an Irish audience. The classic conception of diaspora has traditionally been associated with the consequences of human suffering and the role of powerful push factors in shaping the expulsion of involuntary migrants. One tends to think more readily of the Jews, Black Africans, Armenians, Palestinians or Irish Famine emigrants in this light rather than migrants leaving Britain, often but not always to colonies within the emerging

British Empire. However, it is worth reminding ourselves that the Greek word *diaspora* essentially means scattering seed, and this arguably carries a positive connotation in terms of conceptualising dispersal. Furthermore, the original diaspora, the Greek diaspora of the ancient Mediterranean world had been largely shaped through mercantile and colonising activities.[19] In the past two decades, of course, the usage of diaspora across the social sciences and humanities has expanded well beyond the classic definition referred to above, but the application of the diaspora model to an understanding of human dispersal from England, Scotland and Wales over the past centuries is still relatively limited.

In 1998 James Horn explicitly referred to a British diaspora as the product of emigration from Britain during the 'long eighteenth century' and more recently Eric Richards has framed a more wide-ranging consideration of emigration from the British Isles since 1600 as being understandable in the context of a British diaspora.[20] Richards seeks to free 'the silent march of ordinary folk' across the globe from the yoke of Empire.[21] However, his inclusion of Ireland within his frame of reference, particularly in the seventeenth century, arguably raises as many questions as it resolves. One should also note the significant collection edited by Carl Bridge and Kent Fedorowich in 2003 and drawing upon two conferences

The appropriation of the O'Neill legend by the planters and their descendants has not gone uncontested, as evidenced by this flight mural in Ardoyne, West Belfast. © Bill Rolston

held in 1998 and 2002 under the all embracing title 'The British world: diaspora, culture and identity'.[22] Pursuing the application of the diaspora model to British emigration, one may view those leaving the homeland of England, Scotland and Wales and becoming part of the multi-generational British population in Ireland as the British diaspora in Ireland. Like all diasporas, its members sustained, to variable degrees of intensity, a two-way relationship with the British 'homeland' and the remainder of the British global diaspora. Thus, to reiterate, 1607 can be viewed as an iconic point of origin for the British diaspora in Ireland.[23]

It is worth considering how the British diaspora in Ireland came to view this crucial formative moment in its history. Perhaps what is most striking initially is the general absence of 1607 from the unionist or Protestant 'grand narrative' or timeline. If, for example, we look at A. T. Q. Stewart's 1977 work, *The narrow ground: aspects of Ulster, 1609-1969*, the examination commences with the official plantation and the statement that 'Irishmen, whatever their political attitudes, are agreed at least on one point – that the Ulster Question began in 1609'.[24] More recently, Brian Walker, in addressing the unionist sense of history, suggests that 1641, 1689 and 1690 represent the key defining dates rather than either 1607 or 1609.[25] Even more recently, and at a more popular level, it is worth noting that the commemorative programme organised by the Ulster-Scots Agency to mark the four-hundredth anniversary of the Hamilton and Montgomery plantation in north Down labelled this event as 'the dawn of the Ulster-Scots'. Furthermore, the series of articles dealing with this plantation scheme stressed the desolation encountered by Hamilton and Montgomery upon arrival in north Down. Quoting the Montgomery manuscripts compiled at the end of the seventeenth century in relation to 'parishes now more wasted than America', it might be suggested a clear vested interest manifested itself in such a depiction.[26] Of course, it is also hard to escape the realisation that the view of the year 1606 as 'the dawn of the Ulster-Scots' serves to anticipate the departure of Tyrone and Tyrconnell and the consequences which flowed from this.

The present writer's initial interest in the unionist Protestant view on 1607 was stirred by reading a passage in a slim volume authored by Ian Paisley in the US bicentennial year of 1976. In the first chapter of his *America's debt to Ulster* Paisley revisited the 'womb from which the Ulster-Scot was begot-

ten' and quotes a passage from Thomas Hamilton's best-selling *History of the Irish Presbyterian Church* (1886). Describing the flight at some length, Dr Paisley's romantic prose almost suggests a certain sympathy with the departing earls; this might be considered a little surprising.

A return to the immediate post-flight period gives us an appreciation of the very real sense of planter insecurity in contemporary Ulster. Right up until O'Neill's death in Rome in July 1616, there was the ever-present threat of the return of the earls and the possibility of the violent overthrow of the new order. Many opponents, as well as allies, chose to ignore London's depiction of the events of September 1607 as a flight and rather considered it as a strategic withdrawal.[27] There is certainly ample evidence that O'Neill never abandoned the effort to return to Ireland.[28] His menacing presence on the continent supplemented planter fears of possible retaliation by the dispossessed landowners and demobilised kerne, and the perceived threat was real enough for many newcomers seeking to establish settlement in one of the six escheated counties or beyond their bounds. Although the absence of wholesale revolt across Ulster in these years might be taken as a sign that the removal of the earls and their heavy exactions was not universally lamented within native society, one should not exaggerate the smooth transition to peaceful plantation or the swift integration of native and newcomer.[29] As Brian Mac Cuarta points out, issues such as the innovative (and arguably rapacious extension) of tithe to milk, which fell most heavily upon the central staple of native society, could trigger real and violent opposition. Much evidence points to the nervousness of British undertakers and tenants about the ongoing threat posed by the wood-kerne and idle swordsmen whom they perceived to lurk behind almost every tree.[30] Those of the servitor class, in particular, who had come through the experience of the Nine Years War, were not inclined to transform their attitudes rapidly, whatever new dispensation now prevailed. O'Neill's frustration in Rome at the post-1604 transformation in the nature of Anglo-Spanish diplomatic relations would not have been matched by a sense of security among planters on Ulster's lonely frontier.[31]

Before addressing later nineteenth-century unionist perspectives on the events of 1607, it is worth noting that James VI & I was, in a meaningful sense, the first unionist. In spite of all the many other pressing issues competing for the king's attention after March 1603, he spent a large proportion of his time preoccupied with the issue of English-Scottish union and determined to underpin the security of the Stuart dynasty in the two realms, despite limited enthusiasm amongst his new subjects south of the border.[32] It is perhaps worth remembering this particular context in considering the monarch's very personal and direct interest in shaping an Ulster plantation as a joint Anglo-Scottish venture. The north of Ireland, following the departure of the earls, certainly offered both a significant patronage resource, as well as a 'dumping ground' for social problems like the reiving families of the Borders region. However, in establishing continuity with his attempted plantations of Lewis and Harris in the 1590s, James could bind Edinburgh and London together into the civilising mission in Ulster.[33] Shifting forward in time and returning to Ulster itself, let us turn our attention to the writings of Thomas Campbell, graduate of Trinity College Dublin and noted gothicist and antiquarian, born in 1733 at Glack, just to the north east of Aughnacloy in County Tyrone. In his *Strictures on the Ecclesiastical and Literary History of Ireland* (1789), he revealed both his out-of-vogue support for union and strong admiration for his fellow Tyroneman, Hugh O'Neill.[34] Indeed, he had intended to complete a life of the great earl, but abandoned the project for some unknown reason. Nonetheless, it is clear that, viewing the subject from the perspective of one drawn from planter stock, he could openly acknowledge its tragic dimension without compromising his support for constitutional union with Britain. It has been suggested that this may reflect the 'space' created between the fading memory of the rising of 1641 and that still to erupt in 1798.[35]

Moving forward a generation and to the neighbouring county of Armagh, John Donaldson's *An historical and statistical account of the barony of Upper Fews in the county of Armagh,* first published in 1838 but compiled over the course of the preceding two decades, offers an alternative perspective.[36] Donaldson lived at Cloghog, between Crossmaglen and Cullyhanna in south Armagh, and could trace his roots in the area back to the Presbyterian plantation undertaken there during the second quarter of the eighteenth century. Although one should be careful about framing Donaldson's experience at this point in time as being increasingly shaped by sectarian pressures, a Presbyterian minority in a predominantly Catholic district must have vividly recalled the sectarian troubles of the late eighteenth

century and been conscious of the growing cleavage between a resurgent O'Connellite Catholicism and Henry Cooke's fiery brand of popular Presbyterianism.[37] Donaldson offered a short summary of the events which lead to the plantation of 1609 and was in no doubt about the guilt of those from whom the lands were escheated. He suggests:

> Accordingly, we find the Earl of Tyrone, with Lords Tyrconnell and Delvin, and other Irish Catholics, in the beginning of the reign of James I engaged in a conspiracy to stir up the natives again to rebellion; and being impeached therewith they fled to the Continent in 1607.[38]

Although Donaldson went on to acknowledge the role of Sir Cathair O'Doherty's failed rising of 1608 as a spur to the more comprehensive plantation scheme enacted in the following year, he clearly went well beyond the available evidence in ascribing guilt to the earls, thereby reassuring his readers concerning the propriety of the actions leading to confiscation and plantation.

Our next example of 'planter' opinion on the issue of the flight dates from the fevered atmosphere of 1919. Unionists lying under the threat of Home Rule for a generation had just witnessed the sweeping electoral triumph of Sinn Féin in the previous year. In this context, Lord Ernest Hamilton turned his attention to the elusive issue of what the earl's followers actually thought following the Treaty of Mellifont in March 1603. Hamilton (of the Abercorn Hamiltons) was a politician and historian representative of the landed unionist tradition. He is probably best remembered in historical circles for his role in cultivating a popular Protestant culture of victimhood based on the atrocities inflicted upon planters during the rising of 1641.[39] In his *Elizabethan Ulster* (1919) he offered the following account of the reaction of the followers of the earl of Tyrone to the 'new dispensation' which followed in the wake of the Treaty of Mellifont:

> Tyrone, we are told, did his utmost to get his old tenants to return; but these, having once tasted the joys of freedom from 'his extreme exactions, declared that they would sooner be strangled' (Davies to Cecil, April 19, 1604). The peasants, in fact, for the first time in the history of Ireland, were beginning to experience the advantages of being scheduled as hu-

man beings, instead of as mere chattels, and they were by no means eager to revert to the old order of things.[40]

As a conjectural projection of popular attitudes among the tenants and agricultural labourers who populated O'Neill's territory, Hamilton clearly offers a revisionist corrective to the traditional 'native' interpretation. However, one might argue that it equally romanticises and simplifies the collective attitudinal adjustment to a benign, emancipating new regime. Exacting as the wartime regime imposed by O'Neill doubtless may have been, we should recall that 'the peasants' were not prevented from exercising their right to migrate or to choose another overlord.[41]

In the same year Ramsey Colles, a liberal unionist, published his four-volume *History of Ulster from Earliest Times to the Present Day* which addressed the eternally thorny issue of escheated estates or confiscated land (depending upon one's perspective). Colles, whose degree was in law, expresses in suitably legalistic prose style, and in stark contrast to Donaldson, his lack of conviction that the departing earls had been demonstrably engaged in treason at this juncture. He notes that:

The extent of the property confiscated was remarkable. It is to be recollected that there had not been any rising whatsoever, nor even an overt act of treason, nor any evidence to connect either of the Earls with an existing conspiracy. The only evidence against them was the fact of their flight and their subsequent conduct.[42]

Colles then wedges open the cupboard door to reveal a little more of the skeleton as he writes of the consequences of the earls' departure:

But every principle of law required that the forfeiture, which was inevitable, should not extend beyond the beneficial interest of the two Earls themselves. The Government, however, had determined to stretch the confiscation so as to enable the King to deal as absolute owner in fee of Tyrone and Tyrconnell, discharged of every estate and interest whatsoever. For this purpose a theory was invented that the fee of the tribe lands was vested in the chief, and that the members of the tribe held merely as tenants at will. Than this, nothing could have been more false.[43]

Even for the most liberal of unionists this was a courageous interpretation in the context of 1919. However, it should be noted that Colles almost certainly set out this argument before rather than after the Great War, as the conflagration delayed publication of his work. In addition to his legal training, and in contrast to Donaldson, Colles had much less direct connection to the land which had been escheated and then settled after 1607. He was of Sligo extraction, although born in Bengal, India, in 1862, where his father served as a civil engineer. Young Ramsey was educated at Bective and Wesley Colleges and subsequently set up home at Wilton Terrace, Dublin with his wife, Annie Sweeny, the daughter of a Church of Ireland vicar from Kerry.[44]

More than a decade after the Boundary Commission reported in 1926, Cyril Falls published a volume entitled *The birth of Ulster*.[45] Falls had been educated at Portora Royal School in Enniskillen, County Fermanagh and subsequently at the University of London. He was a committed unionist, and a journalist with a strong interest in military history and his book presented Ulster as the post-plantation entity. His cursory treatment of 1607 is hardly surprising. Having stated his belief that Tyrconnell and Maguire, at least, had engaged in treasonable endeavours, he claimed that Tyrone had effectively lost his nerve and bolted.[46] It is arguably the preface to the book which reveals most about Falls's mindset in 1936. Here he very openly lays bare his own subjectivity and explicitly refers to his desire to rebalance the popular unionist focus on the triumph of the Williamite era to take fuller account of the 'stout forbearance of the first generation of Ulster planters'.[47] In pursuing such an agenda, there could be little advantage in delving too deeply into the issues related to the flight and subsequent confiscation.

The American presence in Northern Ireland during the Second World War alerted the Stormont government to the need to sharpen its propagandist effort.[48] In 1946, it commissioned Hugh Shearman to produce a short booklet entitled *Northern Ireland: its history, resources and people*, which strove to highlight the long-standing distinctiveness of north from south.[49] Around the same time, as part of a series on the counties of England, the same author also penned a more voluminous guide to Ulster.[50] In the section which provided historical background to the main text Shearman indulged in a major piece of revisionist editing when he asserted that the entire island 'lay at the disposal' of the London government after the battle of Kinsale![51] In this account the complex twists and turns between the Treaty of Mellifont and the plantation are neatly removed. The author also introduced Englishmen as well as the more traditional Scots as the intrepid planters who secured the Ulster wilderness.

In some respects historical writing in the Republic of Ireland in the post-partition era removed the flight of the earls as a key date in Irish history's traditional timeline, consigning it largely to the northern domain. In 1986 Margaret MacCurtain's paper on the flight, though it appeared in a volume entitled *Milestones in Irish history* located the event to a greater extent within an Ulster framework.[52] For those thinking and writing about the events of 4 September 1607 from a twentieth-century Dublin perspective, the earls were increasingly 'northern' in complexion. While the events of September 1607 may be increasingly corralled within the history of the 'north', the state of Northern Ireland itself struggled to come to terms with historical events associated with the Catholic nationalist minority. This evolved into a long-running problem with the teaching of Irish history in Northern Ireland schools, as evidenced by the political wrangling associated with Shearman's text.[53] Most of those who came through primary and secondary education in the subsequent generation never came into contact with the history of Ireland at all. Even for the minority of students who engaged at some level with Irish history, few in the maintained or voluntary sector engaged with evidence related to the process of plantation, while few in the public sector delved too deeply into the events which paved the way to that process. Elsewhere, evidence exists of the subtle foregrounding of 'planter' history and elision

of 'native' history within Northern Ireland. When this author first visited Tullaghogue, the traditional inauguration site of the O'Neills, about two miles south of Cookstown, in the mid-1990s, he was amazed, not only by the site itself but by the very limited infrastructure or interpretation then on offer. If, for example, one consults a tourist guide such as Ernest Sandford's *Discover Northern Ireland* (1976), Tullaghogue merits just half the explanatory text allotted to Springhill House, the late seventeenth century planter house some five miles to the north.[54]

Perhaps one of the most interesting connections between the flight and plantation eras and the unravelling of the tensions within Northern Ireland in the 1960s was the somewhat tangled identity of the then Northern Ireland prime minister, Sir Terence O'Neill. The surname was occasionally brought to bear in order to establish some connection with the nationalist minority, but the knowledge that his bloodline actually connected him much more directly with Hugh O'Neill's arch-enemy, Sir Arthur Chichester, undoubtedly caused the prime minister a wry smile on such occasions.[55]

Conscious of the recent run of significant historical commemorations and the literature which these have stimulated, it is difficult not to look forward from 2007 and to link the commemoration of the flight of the earls to the subsequent commemoration of the plantation of Ulster.[56] This modest and brief inquiry into planter unionist perspectives upon the events which paved the way for plantation will hopefully remind us that space too should be made in the years ahead for fully exploring and recognising the native reaction to the newcomer as part of the act of commemoration.

Notes

1 D. H. Akenson, *The Irish diaspora: a primer* (Belfast, 1993); J. Horgan, *Mary Robinson: an independent voice* (Dublin, 1997), pp 184-5.

2 T. P. Coogan, *Wherever green is worn: the story of the Irish diaspora* (London, 2000); B. Lalor (ed.), *The encyclopaedia of Ireland* (Dublin, 2003), pp 294-6.

3 'Symposium: perspectives on the Irish diaspora', *Irish Economic and Social History*, xxiii (2006), pp 35-58.

4 For fuller discussion of this see P. Fitzgerald and B. Lambkin, *Migration in Irish history, 1607-2007* (Basingstoke, 2008).

5 The cult of St Colum Cille was particularly developed within O'Donnell's territory, and Rory O'Donnell's grandfather Manus had patronised an Irish-language life of the saint in 1532; see B.

Lacey, *Colum Cille and the Columban tradition* (Dublin, 1997).

6 See for example G. Henry, *The Irish Military Community in Spanish Flanders, 1586-1621* (Dublin, 1992); T. O'Connor (ed.), *The Irish in Europe, 1580-1815* (Dublin, 2001); T. O'Connor and M. A. Lyons (eds), *Irish migrants in Europe after Kinsale, 1602-1820* (Dublin, 2003); M. A. Lyons, *Franco-Irish Relations, 1500-1610: politics, migration and trade* (Bury St. Edmunds, 2003); T. O'Connor and Mary Ann Lyons (eds), *Irish Communities in early modern Europe* (Dublin, 2006).

7 D. McGettigan, *Red Hugh O'Donnell and the Nine Years War* (Dublin, 2005), pp 114-6; G. Henry, 'Ulster exiles in Europe, 1605-41', in B. Mac Cuarta (ed.), *Ulster 1641: aspects of the rising* (Belfast, 1993), pp 46-48; J. McCavitt, *The Flight of the Earls* (Dublin, 2002), p. 84.

8 Thomas O'Connor, personal comment.

9 M. MacCurtain, 'The Flight of the Earls', in L. de Paor (ed.), *Milestones in Irish history* (Cork, 1986), pp 52-61.

10 Ibid, p. 59.

11 Ibid., p. 59; see also D. Keogh, F. O'Shea and C. Quinlan (eds), *Ireland in the 1950s: the lost decade* (Cork, 2004); M. E. Daly, *The slow failure: population decline and independent Ireland, 1920-1973* (Madison, WN, 2006).

12 McCavitt, *The Flight of the Earls*; L. Swords, *The Flight of the Earls: A popular history* (Dublin, 2007).

13 McCavitt, *The Flight of the Earls*, p. 7.

14 Swords, *The Flight*, pp 13, 95-97.

15 B. Wooley, *Savage Kingdom: the true story of Jamestown, 1607 and the settlement of America* (New York, 2007).

16 B. Scott (ed.), *Cavan, 1609-53* (Dublin, 2007), pp 13-14.

17 V. Treadwell, *Buckingham and Ireland, 1616-28: A study in Anglo-Irish politics* (Dublin, 1998), p. 144; A. Thomas, *The walled towns of Ireland* (2 vols, Dublin, 1992), ii, pp 118-20.

18 W. J. Smyth, *Map-making, landscapes and memory: a geography of colonial and early modern Ireland c. 1530-1750* (Cork, 2006), pp 421-51.

19 R. Cohen, *Global diasporas: an introduction* (London, 1997), p. 2; G. Stubos, *The Greek diaspora* (Oxford, 1999).

20 J. Horn, 'British diaspora: emigration from Britain, 1680-1815', in P. J. Marshall (ed.), *The Oxford History of the British Empire: the eighteenth century* (Oxford, 1998), pp 28-53; E. Richards, *Britannia's children: emigration from England, Scotland, Wales and Ireland since 1600* (London, 2004).

21 E. Richards, *Britannia's Children*, p. 12.

22 C. Bridge and K. Fedorowich (eds), *The British World: diaspora, culture and identity* (London, 2003).

23 For further discussion of this idea see P. Fitzgerald and Brian Lambkin, *Migration in Irish history*, pp 257-62.

24 A. T. Q. Stewart, *The narrow ground: aspects of Ulster, 1609-1969* (London, 1977), p. 21.

25 B. Walker, *Dancing to History's tune: history, myth and politics in Ireland* (Belfast, 1996), pp 1-14.

26 See www.hamiltonmontgomery1606.com.

27 I. R. K. Paisley, *America's debt to Ulster: Bicentenary of the United States, 1776-1976* (Belfast, 1976), pp 1-2; T. Hamilton, *History of the Irish Presbyterian church* (Edinburgh, 1886), pp 28-29.

28 Kerney Walsh, *'Destruction by peace'*, pp 3-4; *Irish Times*, 20/8/07.

29 McCavitt, *The Flight of the Earls*, pp 200-22.

30 M. Elliott, *The Catholics of Ulster: a history* (London, 2000), pp 83-97; J. McCavitt, *Sir Arthur Chichester: lord deputy of Ireland, 1605-16* (Belfast, 1998), pp 129-90.

31 B. Mac Cuarta, *Catholic revival in the north of Ireland, 1603-41* (Dublin, 2007), p. 57.

32 P. Croft, 'Rex Pacificus, Robert Cecil and the 1604 Peace with Spain' in G. Burgess, R. Wymer and J. Lawrence (eds), *The accession of James I: historical and cultural consequences* (Basingstoke, 2006), pp 140-54; McCavitt, *Chichester*, pp 149-68.

33 R. Lockyer, *James VI & I* (London, 1998), pp 51-62.

34 M. Perceval-Maxwell, *The Scottish migration to Ulster in the reign of James I* (London, 1973), pp 12, 74-76; J. H. Ohlmeyer, '"Civilizing those rude partes": colonization within Britain and Ireland, 1580s-1640s', in N. P. Canny (ed.), *The Oxford history of the British Empire: the origins of empire* (Oxford, 1998), pp 124-47.

35 T. Campbell, *Strictures on the ecclesiastical and literary history of Ireland* (Dublin, 1789).

36 C. O'Halloran, *Golden ages and barbarous nations: antiquarian debate and cultural politics in Ireland, c. 1750-1800* (Cork, 2004), pp 154-6.

37 J. Donaldson, *A historical & statistical account of the barony of Upper Fews in the county of Armagh, 1838* (Dundalk, 1923).

38 K. Madden, *Forkhill Protestants and Forkhill Catholics, 1787-1858* (Liverpool, 2005); S. R. Jones, 'Presbyterianism in County Armagh', in A. J. Hughes and W. Nolan (eds), *Armagh: history & society* (Dublin, 2001), pp 693-712.

39 Donaldson, *Barony of Upper Fews*, p. 6.

40 Lord E. Hamilton, *Elizabethan Ulster* (London, 1919); see also idem, *The Irish Rebellion of 1641* (London, 1920).

41 Ibid., p. 345.

42 R. Colles, *The history of Ulster from the earliest times to the present day* (4 vols, London, 1919), ii, pp 159-60.

43 Ibid, p. 160.

44 I am grateful to Linde Lunney of the Dictionary of Irish Biography project for providing biographical detail on Colles.

45 C. Falls, *The Birth of Ulster* (London, 1936).

46 Ibid., pp 118-22.

47 Ibid., pp xi-xii.

48 Perhaps the classic example of this is W. F. Marshall, *Ulster sails west* (Omagh, 1943).

49 H. Shearman, *Northern Ireland: its history, resources and people* (London, 1946).

50 H. Shearman, *Ulster* (London, 1949).

51 Ibid., p. 98.

52 MacCurtain, 'Flight of the Earls', pp 52-61.

53 M. E. Smith, *Reckoning with the past: teaching history in Northern Ireland* (Lanham, MD, 2005), pp 115-7.

54 E. Sandford, *Discover Northern Ireland* (Belfast, 1976), pp 106, 129.

55 T. O'Neill, *The autobiography of Terence O'Neill: Prime Minister of Northern Ireland, 1963-69* (London, 1972), pp 1-2, 129.

56 See, for example, J. Leonard, 'The twinge of memory: Armistice day and Remembrance Sunday in Dublin since 1919', in R. English and G. Walker (eds), *Unionism in modern Ireland: new perspectives on politics and culture* (Dublin, 1996), pp 99-114; I. McBride, *History and memory in modern Ireland* (Cambridge, 2001); E. Bort, *Commemorating Ireland: history, politics, culture* (Dublin, 2004); G. Dawson, *Making peace with the past? Memory, trauma and the Irish Troubles* (Manchester, 2007).

HUGH O'NEILL

BRÚ NA NDÉISE

THE FLIGHT OF THE EARLS 1607

Flight of the earls mural,
Bruff, County Limerick.
© Marie-Claire Peters

The Flight of the Earls

COMMEMORATION

The earls in popular memory

Vincent Morley

This essay proposes to examine the way in which the earls were remembered in the eighteenth century. Apart from being the time of greatest interest to the present writer, there are also objective reasons for paying particular attention to the eighteenth-century sources. On the one hand, the period was sufficiently remote from the flight of the earls and from the war which preceded it for all who had experienced these events, and for the great majority of those who may have heard the personal testimony of witnesses, to have passed away. On the other hand, the eighteenth century preceded the emergence of cheap print, mass literacy and nationalist journalism, all of which were nineteenth-century phenomena. As a consequence, references to the earls in the vernacular literature of the period cannot easily be attributed either to the transmission of individual recollections within the Irish-speaking community or to the influence of literary productions originating outside that community. Instead the prominence (or otherwise) of the earls in the Irish literature of the eighteenth century is likely to be a good indicator of their standing in the collective memory of the population.

One must begin by acknowledging that immediately after the flight the earls were extolled, and their departure from Ireland deplored, by members of the *aos dána* in the syllabic metres of *dán díreach* and the classical literary language of a learned élite that had scarcely changed for four hundred years – authors such as Fear Flatha Ó Gnímh (d. 1640), Eoghan Ruadh Mac an Bhaird (†c. 1630) and Eochaidh Ó hEodhasa (d. 1612) come to mind.[1] *Beatha Aodha Ruaidh Uí Dhomhnaill* by Lughaidh Ó Cléirigh (†c. 1630) must also be mentioned in this context.[2] Yet these were professional writers, and their attitudes cannot be assumed to reflect those of the general population. What is much more persuasive and striking is the prominence accorded to the earls in some of the political verse that was composed in modern language and by non-professional authors around the middle of the seventeenth century. If the number of extant manuscripts is any indication, the long historical poem variously entitled 'Aiste Sheáin Uí Chonaill' and 'Tuireamh na hÉireann' has good claims to be

the most popular text ever composed in Irish, and it portrays Aodh Mór Ó Néill and Aodh Rua Ó Domhnaill as defenders of the Gaels against an oppressive English government:

> Dlí beag eile do rinneadh do Ghaelaibh,
> *surrender* ar a gceart do dhéanamh.
> Do chuir sin Leath Cuinn trí na chéile,
> glacaid a n-airm cé cailleadh iad féin leis:
> an t-iarla Ó Néill fuair barr féile
> is an tiarna Ó Domhnaill ba mhór géilleadh.[3]

This is a Munster composition and dates from the 1650s. Likewise, 'An Síogaí Rómhánach', a well-known northern composition from the same decade, opens with the poet grieving at the tomb of the earls in Rome:

> Lá dá rabhas ar maidin im aonar
> ins an Róimh ar órchnoc Céphas,
> lán de ghruaim ar uaigh na nGael san,
> sínte ar lic ag sileadh déara,
> fá bhfuil dias dob fhial fá shéadaibh,
> lenar ghrámhar ábhar m'éagnaigh,
> Iarla mór Thíre Eoghain Néill mhir
> is Ó Domhnaill na n-órlann bhfaobhrach.[4]

From the vantage-point of the mid-seventeenth century, therefore, the earls seemed to be well positioned to secure prominent and honoured places in a national pantheon of heroes. Apart altogether from the intrinsic importance of the Nine Years War and subsequent events – notably the plantation of Ulster – they had been extolled by the last generation of professional poets and by later authors who employed popular literary forms and accessible language.

These early indications were deceptive, however, and the literature of the late seventeenth century onwards contains surprisingly few references to the earls. This is true even when works by Ulster authors alone are considered. My own research has confirmed the accuracy of an observation made by Énrí Ó Muirgheasa in his pioneering anthology of Ulster verse, *Céad de cheoltaibh Uladh*, which appeared in 1915:

No name is more indelibly imprinted on the memory of the Irish people, particularly in Ulster, than Eoghan Ruadh. Eoghan an Chogaidh, "Owen of the War," is another familiar term by which he is known in Ulster ... in their traditionary view of their past history possessed by the native Irish people Hugh O'Neill is nowhere in comparison with Owen Roe.[5]

Having surveyed published anthologies of eighteenth-century verse for a study of the development of historical consciousness in Ireland, I have identified six discrete historical themes that can be said to have acquired iconic status by that time.[6] These themes can be summarised as follows:

1. The mission of St Patrick and the subsequent status of early Christian Ireland as 'oileán na naomh'.
2. The terror and destruction inflicted by the pagan Norse; the overthrow of the tyrant Turgesius by Máel Sechnaill of Meath; and the ultimate Irish victory under Brian Bóruma.
3. The sexual immorality of Diarmait Mac Murchada; his deserved banishment from Ireland; and his treachery in soliciting help from Henry II and procuring the Anglo-Norman invasion.
4. The sexual immorality of Henry VIII, Elizabeth I, Luther, Calvin and lesser heretical reformers who collectively unleashed a wave of persecution against the true church and its adherents.
5. The rising of 1641 on behalf of God, king and country; the military victories of Eoghan Rua Ó Néill; his untimely death which created an opening for Oliver Cromwell to conquer Ireland and intensify religious persecution.
6. The war against William of Orange on behalf of God, king and country – a conflict in which Patrick Sarsfield occupied a position analogous to that held by Eoghan Rua in the war of the 1640s.

The historical episodes which fail to feature in the literature may be as revealing as those that are remembered: Edward Bruce's campaign to win the crown of Ireland, the rebellion of Silken Thomas and the Desmond rebellion are notable examples. But none of these 'sites of amnesia' is more surprising or more obvious than the comparative lack of references to Aodh Ó Néill, Aodh Rua Ó Domhnaill, Ruairí Ó Domhnaill or to the flight of the earls. Indeed, it must also be said that references to the plantation of Ulster are surprisingly scarce.

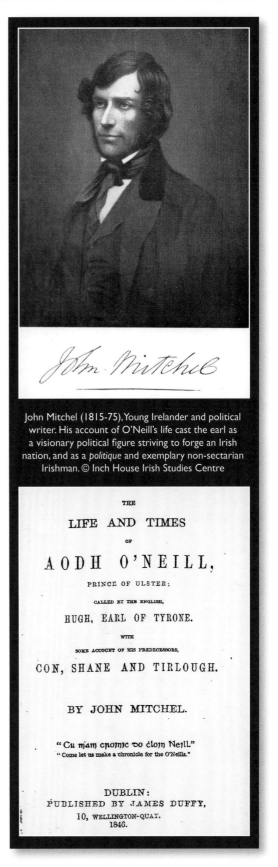

John Mitchel (1815-75), Young Irelander and political writer. His account of O'Neill's life cast the earl as a visionary political figure striving to forge an Irish nation, and as a *politique* and exemplary non-sectarian Irishman. © Inch House Irish Studies Centre

THE
LIFE AND TIMES
OF
AODH O'NEILL,
PRINCE OF ULSTER;
CALLED BY THE ENGLISH,
HUGH, EARL OF TYRONE.
WITH
SOME ACCOUNT OF HIS PREDECESSORS,
CON, SHANE AND TIRLOUGH.

BY JOHN MITCHEL.

"Cu mjaŋ cɲoŋjc ɒo cloŋ Neɪll."
"Come let us make a chronicle for the O'Neills."

DUBLIN:
PUBLISHED BY JAMES DUFFY,
10, WELLINGTON-QUAY.
1846.

I have only found three unambiguous references to either of the earls in the Ulster literature of the eighteenth century. The first of these is an oblique reference occurring in a lament by Séamas Dall Mac Cuarta (c. 1647-1733) for one Niall Óg Mac Murchaidh. The grief of the relatives of the deceased man is compared in its intensity to that experienced by Nuala, sister of Aodh Rua and Ruairí Ó Domhnaill, during her exile in Rome:

> Atá dís leonta ag fraschaoi ar an aiste a mbíodh Nuala
> ins an naomh-Róimh ar feart na nAodh ag
> fadchaoineadh an uaisle.[7]

The second reference occurs in a humorous composition by Peadar Ó Doirnín (c. 1700-69) on the subject of a decrepit horse which was so old that it had been ridden by the sons of Milesius during their war against the Tuatha Dé Danann. This broken-down nag witnessed Cúchulainn killing Feardia; inevitably, Brian Bóruma had ridden him at Clontarf; and he was also present when Aodh Ó Néill defeated Sir Henry Bagenal at Clontibret (1595) and again at the Yellow Ford (1598):

> I gCluain Tiobrad faoin spairní an lá d'imigh
> Bagenal i scaoll,
> nuair a briseadh a ghardaí is básadh a
> cheannfoirt ón Mhí;
> bhí sé in Ard Mhacha is ní áirím i mBéal an
> Átha Buí,
> is faoi Fhéilim go hard ag buansásamh Oileán
> Mhic Aoidh.[8]

Archbishop Giovanni Battista Rinuccini presents Eoghan Rua Ó Néill with his uncle's sword. © Inch House Irish Studies Centre

Interestingly, while Ó Doirnín left his audience to deduce the identity of the victor in these battles, he observed no such reticence when referring to the horse's subsequent presence at the battle of Benburb where he was ridden by Eoghan Rua Ó Néill. The third reference is the only eighteenth-century composition of which I am aware that contains explicit praise for one of the earls. It is found in a lament by Art Mac Cumhaigh (c. 1738-73) for Art Óg Ó Néill, one of the O'Neills of the Fews:

> Bhí Iarla mór Thír Eoghain in éifeacht,
> rí na leon ó Bhóinn go hAontroim,
> is dá bhfaigheadh cuidiú mar chóir ó chóigibh
> Éireann
> Essex 's a shlóite go leonfadh an tréanfhear,
> Elizabeth mhór 's a trón go mbuairfeadh,
> is gheobhadh clann Mháirtín bás go héasca.[9]

This is unquestionably praise of a high order, and it immediately precedes a similarly laudatory verse about Eoghan Rua Ó Néill, but it is exceptional.

On the other hand, there are several compositions in which one might reasonably have expected to find references to Aodh Ó Néill but in which he is passed over in silence. This is particularly obvious in those works which extol Eoghan Rua Ó Néill. What would have been more natural, when praising the military prowess and noble character of the nephew than to have alluded in passing to the achievements of his distinguished uncle? However, the early lament beginning *Do chaill Éire a chéile fíre* by Cathal Mac Ruairí,[10] as well as such later compositions as the anonymous *Pósta feasta ag Gallaibh dar leo féin'*,[11] Muiris Ó Mocháin's *Mar atáid, a Dhé, na Gaedheil gan treoir is truaigh*,[12] and *Níl stáidbhean shéimh de Ghaela beo, monuar* by Pádraig Mac a Liondain (c. 1665-1733),[13] while they are unstinting in their praise of Eoghan Rua, are entirely silent on the subject of Aodh Ó Néill and his allies. Likewise, when Séamas Dall Mac Cuarta envisaged the return of the 'wild geese', he described them as the descendants of Eoghan Rua and failed to mention Aodh Ó Néill:

> Nár thé mé in uaigh-fheart go bhfeicfead
> sluaite
> ag teacht le bua-neart go hÉirinn all;
> sliocht Eoghain Ruaidh 'na longa suadh-cheart
> a chuirfeadh nua-bhroid ar chéadta Gall.[14]

More tellingly still, when Eoghan Ó Donghaile (1649-c. 1724) composed a eulogy in one of the obsolescent syllabic metres some time around 1700, his choice of historical subject fell, not on Aodh Ó Néill, but on his uncle, Seán 'an Díomais' mac Cuinn Bhacaigh (d. 1567).[15] While Ó Donghaile may have needed a suitably antique subject for this exercise in literary pastiche, Aodh Ó Néill would have fitted the bill equally well.

Further evidence of the relative lack of importance attaching to the earls in popular memory is furnished by compositions that survey the history of Ireland but pass over them in silence. This essay will again restrict itself to examples from Ulster. When Pádraig Mac a Liondain of South Armagh engaged the County Meath poet Brian Ó Cuagáin in a debate about the merits of their respective provinces, he cited the treachery of Diarmait Mac Murchada in seeking English assistance, the failure of Máel Sechnaill II of Meath to support Brian Bóruma at Clontarf, the failure of the Confederate Catholics of Leinster to co-operate with Eoghan Rua Ó Néill, and Colonel Henry Luttrell's treachery at Aughrim, as evidence against the Leinstermen. He might equally well have noted the loyalty shown to the crown by the Old English population in towns such as Drogheda, Kilkenny and Wexford during the 1590s, but he chose not to do so:

Agus cé mór a deir tusa ris an taobh thuaidh, ní dóigh liom go dtig leat a rá gur tháinig tuarascáil an mhíghníomha sin a rinne Rí Laighean ón tír thuaidh riamh. Níorbh fhearr an gníomh a rinne rí eile de Laighin darbh ainm Maoileachlainn .i. cliamhain Bhrian Bóraimhe an tan a thionól Lochlannaigh na hÉireann agus Danair na Beirbhe go Maigh Nealta gur fearadh Cath Chluain Tairbh eatarthu leith ar leith áit ar thit rí agus rídhamhna Éireann sa láthair sin ach amháin fir Uladh nár iarr a gcúnamh leis. Bíodh a fhianaise sin ar Eachroim gurb fhearr d'fhir Éireann gurbh fhear den taobh thuaidh a bheadh in áit an Laighnigh .i. an Luitrealach a bhí os a gcionn … Fós mar a dhiúltaigh Cúige Laighean agus an taobh ó dheas ar cheana cuidiú le hEoghan Rua Ó Néill creideamh Chríost a chothú in aghaidh Oilibhéar Cromail agus an Stáit, ní dar tháinig plá, gorta agus léirscrios dár dtír trí mhallacht Nuinteas an Phápa.[16]

Similarly, when Peadar Ó Doirnín enumerated the five great disasters of Irish history, he counted the Norse and English invasions, the violence of Henry VIII and his daughter, the Cromwellian conquest and the defeat of James II:

Is gearr ina dhéidh gur tháinig sin tréanshlua Lochlann dár ndíobhadh
go feadh cheithre mblian déag faoin anfhlaith Turgesius orainn do híocadh.

An dara tromléan a thit ar na Gaeil trí mhírún a ngaolta,
Murchadh ó Laighnibh a mhúscail go hÉirinn Briotanaigh mhaola.

An treas tubaiste d'éirigh dúinne, faraor, Harry is a níonsan,
ler imir go claon a gclaimhthe ar a chéile is ar mhaitheas ár dtíre.

An ceathrú tromléan a tháinig ina dhéidh, slua Chromail ler díthíodh
Ulaidh is Laighin is Connacht go léir, is maitheas na Muimhneach.

An cúigiú maidhm-éacht a tháinig orainn is ar Shéamas an Dara ba rí dúinn,
ler gearradh gach géag dár mhair de shliocht Ghaeil Ghlais againn sa tír-se.[17]

One would think that an Ulster author, in particular, might have found room to include the flight of the earls as a sixth *tromléan* or *tubaist*. Again, when Art Mac Cumhaigh's ruined Catholic church engaged a neighbouring and newly constructed Protestant church in polemics, it mentioned Aughrim and the Boyne, Cromwell and Eoghan Rua's death, Luther and Henry VIII, as occasions of grief but the earls were not referred to:

'Sé mo thuirse gur tréaghdadh maithe na nGael
in Eachroim 's ar thaobh na Bóinne,
's nach maireann i gcéim Eoghan an Chogaidh Ó Néill
'chuirfeadh Cromail i bpéin 's a shlóite;
cha lasfadh *King Harry, Beelsebub* éitheach,
nó Liútar a bhuaradh Fódhla,
New Lights nó *Secéders, Old Presbyterians, Swaddlers* nó *Quakers* leofa.[18]

For nine years, Ó Néill and Ó Domhnaill mounted the most serious challenge to English rule in Ireland since the Bruce invasion. Furthermore, they invoked the defence of Catholicism as a *casus belli*, even appealing for support from the Old English on the basis of a shared religion. Their eventual flight triggered profound changes in the northern province, changes that were felt throughout Ireland in due course. Here, surely, was material ready-made for incorporation in a popular historical narrative – a fact that was recognised, as we have seen, by the authors of 'Tuireamh na hÉireann' and 'An Síogaí Rómhánach' in the seventeenth century. And yet, when the poets of the eighteenth century – even the Ulster poets of the eighteenth century – recalled the salient events of Irish history, the earls were overlooked.

The question must be posed: why did Ó Néill and Ó Domhnaill fail to secure a prominent place in popular historical consciousness? Énrí Ó Muirgheasa, whom I have quoted previously, suggested the following explanation:

> Hugh O'Neill's war was not a national struggle, but was, in fact, carried on in opposition to the sympathies of the bulk of the Irish people, simply because the idea of a unified nation had, during four hundred years of internecine strife, become obliterated from the national mind.[19]

However, Ó Muirgheasa also argued that this position was transformed within a generation:

> But when forty years of confiscations and English penal laws had steam-rolled all of the above classes into one common level of enslavement, the national consciousness began to awaken, and the Confederation of Kilkenny, with all its shortcomings, was the nearest approach to a united national effort which the country had witnessed for many generations. Hence Owen Roe, as the great hero of this era, won a popularity with the northern Irish to which his even greater name-sake, Hugh, never attained.[20]

The style of expression in these passages may shed more light on the political climate of the early twentieth century than on that of the early seventeenth century. Nonetheless, when every allowance is made for his essentialist assumptions about a 'national mind' and the revival of a perennial 'national consciousness', Ó Muirgheasa's core thesis that the post-Kinsale generation witnessed unprecedented levels of popular politicisation is one that cannot easily be dismissed. Crucial developments took place during the thirty years after Kinsale. The accession of James VI of Scotland in 1603 was hailed by the *aos dána*, a learned caste which portrayed the new monarch as a descendant of Milesius and, consequently, as a legitimate king of Ireland – unlike his Tudor predecessors. In 1605 a proclamation abolishing autonomous lordships declared that all Irishmen were 'free, natural, and immediate subjects of His Majesty' and not 'natural followers of any lord or chieftain whatsoever', thereby effectively establishing Ireland as a coherent polity for the first time. From 1610 the New English community was reinforced by the introduction of English and Scottish planters who differed in language, religion, nationality and customs from the indigenous inhabitants, thereby strengthening the sense of identity of the latter. The return from Irish colleges in mainland Europe of increasing numbers of clergy, trained in the doctrines of the Counter-Reformation, secured the position of Catholicism as the faith of the people and facilitated the appointment of bishops throughout the country by the end of the 1620s. The resistance of Catholic parliamentarians to the construction of a Protestant majority in the House of Commons from 1613 onwards, and their campaigns against further threatened plantations and for confirmation of the 'Graces' during the 1620s, helped to fuse the previously antagonistic Old English and Old Irish groups into a new, ethnically composite, Catholic political nation. Any one of these factors would have been significant; occurring within the space of a single generation as they did, they could not fail to have had a profound influence on popular consciousness. It may overstate the case somewhat to describe those who fought under the earls at Kinsale as the combined *slógaí* (mobilised forces) of their chieftains, and to describe those who fought under Eoghan Rua Ó Néill at Benburb as members of a regular army raised by the Irish Catholic nation; but if the contrast is exaggerated, it nevertheless contains a large measure of truth.

Yet this does not explain the popular amnesia in relation to the earls. It is not sufficient to say that the Irish populace had yet to be politicised in 1607 and was well on the way to being so by the 1630s. Many historical episodes which occurred much earlier than the flight of the earls were subsequently

Hugh O'Neill (sitting, third from left) finally takes his place in the pantheon of Ireland's 'illustrious sons' in the nineteenth century. © NLI

incorporated in the national historical narrative that would be elaborated during the course of the seventeenth and eighteenth centuries. Obvious examples include the Reformation, the Anglo-Norman invasion, the Norse wars, and St Patrick – not to mention purely mythological themes such as Fionn mac Cumhail and his Fianna, Cúchulainn and the Craobh Rua, Milesius, the Tuatha Dé Danann and the Fir Bolg. What was it, then, that prevented a similar, retrospective, identification of the earls as heroic fighters for faith and fatherland? After all, the Franciscan annalist Mícheál Ó Cléirigh claimed that Ruairí Ó Domhnaill and Aodh Ó Néill had each distinguished himself 'ag imdhídean/dídean a irsi, agus a athardha' ('defending his faith, and his fatherland') in obituaries written during the 1630s.[21]

It is not possible to give a definitive answer to such a question, but it may lie in the fact that from the mid-seventeenth century onwards the principles of 'faith and fatherland' were no longer sufficient. They continued to be vitally important, but from the period of the Restoration at the very latest a new ideology was embraced as political orthodoxy by all significant sections of Catholic opinion. This was an ideology in which the established principles of faith and fatherland were combined with a more novel third principle: loyalty to the crown. One might say that 'iris agus athardha' was trumped by 'Pro deo, pro rege et pro patria' ('for god, king and fatherland') – the motto of the Confederate Catholics in the 1640s. While the earls could be repre-

sented as heroes who had suffered for church and country, the task of portraying them as sadly misunderstood supporters of royal government would have exceeded the skills of even the most creative myth-makers. Eoghan Rua Ó Néill could plausibly be represented as fighting against the Scottish Covenanters and English Puritans who respectively sold and murdered Charles I; and Patrick Sarsfield could, without the least distortion of fact, be portrayed as fighting to defend the legitimate monarch against a Dutch usurper supported by Protestant traitors, but the earls were embarrassing skeletons in the closet of Catholic Ireland. They could not be rehabilitated until such time as the term 'rebel' became a badge of honour rather than an insult to be hurled at supporters of the Williamite revolution. I will conclude with a final quotation from Énrí Ó Muirgheasa:

> I do not remember meeting with even a single reference to Hugh O'Neill in our modern Irish poetry, except that on page 162 of this volume, which was written in the fifties of [the] last century after 'The Nation' newspaper had been a decade spreading a knowledge of Irish history written from the modern national and patriotic view-point.[22]

There are, as we have seen, a few stray references to the earls in the literature of the eighteenth century, but they are not sufficiently numerous to alter the essential accuracy of Ó Muirgheasa's observation.

Notes

1 For relevant compositions by all of these, see O. Bergin (ed.), *Irish bardic poetry* (Dublin, 1970); for accounts of their lives and work see their respective entries in M. Ní Mhurchú and P. Breatnach, *1560-1781 Beathaisnéis* (Dublin, 2001).

2 Lughaidh Ó Cléirigh, *Beatha Aodha Ruaidh Uí Dhomhnaill*, (ed.) P. Walsh (2 vols, Dublin, 1948-57).

3 'One further law was made for the Irish, that they should surrender their rights. This threw Conn's half [i.e. the north] into turmoil, they took up arms but were lost thereby: earl O'Neill of great generosity and lord O'Donnell of great authority', C. O'Rahilly (ed.), *Five seventeenth-century political poems* (Dublin, 1952), p. 74. I have modernised the spelling of some quotations; all translations are mine.

4 'One day when I was alone at dawn, in Rome on Peter's golden hill [i.e. Montorio], filled with gloom on the grave of those Gaels, stretched on a slab and weeping, beneath which are two who were lavish with valuables, to whom the cause of my distress would have been moving: the great earl of valiant Niall's Tyrone, and O'Donnell of the sharp-edged golden blades', ibid., pp 17-18.

5 É. Ó Muirgheasa (ed.), *Céad de cheoltaibh Uladh* (Dublin, 1915), p. 192.

6 This will be discussed in my forthcoming monograph, *Ó Chéitinn go Raiftearaí*, ch. 3.

7 'There is a grieving pair, weeping copiously the way Nuala used to do in holy Rome on the tomb of the Aodhs, lamenting the nobles at length', S. Ó Gallchóir (ed.), *Séamas Dall Mac Cuarta: Dánta* (Dublin, 1979), p. 42.

8 'In Clontibret [he was] under the warrior on the day Bagenal left in terror, when his guards were crushed and his commanders from Meath died; he was in Armagh not to mention the Yellow Ford, and nobly under Féilim [O'Neill] constantly avenging [the massacre of] Islandmagee', S. de Rís (ed.), *Peadar Ó Doirnín: a bheatha agus a shaothar* (Dublin, 1969), pp 38-39.

9 'The great earl of Tyrone was powerful, king of the lions [i.e. warriors] from the Boyne to Antrim, and had he received due help from the provinces of Ireland the champion would have crushed Essex and his hosts, he'd have shaken great Elizabeth and her throne, and the progeny of Martin [Luther] would have quickly perished', T. Ó Fiaich (ed.), *Art Mac Cumhaigh: Dánta* (Dublin, 1973), p. 122.

10 Ó Muirgheasa, *Céad de cheoltaibh Uladh*, no. 7.

11 Ibid., no. 8.

12 Ibid., no. 9.

13 S. Mag Uidhir (ed.), *Pádraig Mac a Liondain: Dánta* (n. p., 1977), no. 2.

14 'May I not go to the grave until I see armies coming in victorious might to splendid Ireland; the progeny of Owen Roe in their noble excellent ships, who would put hundreds of *Gaill* under a new bondage'. Poem beginning 'Ní maith is léir damh na leabhair Ghaeilig' in S. Ó Gallchóir, 'Filíocht Shéamais Dhaill Mhic Cuarta' (MA thesis, Maynooth, 1967), p. 239.

15 P. de Brún, B. Ó Buachalla and T. Ó Concheanainn (eds), *Nua-Dhuanaire* i (Dublin, 1971), no. 46.

16 'And although you have a lot to say against the north, I don't think you can say that an account of that evil deed done by the king of Leinster [Diarmait Mac Murchada] ever came out of the northern country. No better was the deed performed by another king of Leinster called Máel Sechnaill, i.e. the son-in-law of Brian Bóruma, when the Norse of Ireland and the Danes of the Barrow assembled on Maigh Nealta where the battle of Clontarf was fought between the two sides, a place where the king and royal heir of Ireland fell, except for the men of Ulster whose assistance he had not requested. Let it be said about Aughrim that it were better for the men of Ireland if a man from the northern side had been in the place of the Leinsterman, namely Luttrell, who was in command of them … Also the way in which the province of Leinster and the southern side in general refused to help Owen Roe O'Neill to sustain the religion of Christ against Oliver Cromwell and the state, from which plague, famine and destruction came to our country through the curse of the papal nuncio', Mag Uidhir (ed.), *Mac a Liondain*, pp 19-20.

17 'Shortly thereafter the mighty host of Scandinavia came to destroy us, for fourteen years under the tyrant Turgesius we were ransomed. The second great sorrow befell the Gaels through the malevolence of their relatives – Murchadh from Leinster who enticed the bare-headed Britons to Ireland. The third disaster that befell us, alas, was Harry and his daughter, by whom their swords were used treacherously on his spouse and the welfare of our country. The fourth great sorrow came after – Cromwell's host by which were destroyed all of Ulster and Leinster and Connacht, and the wealth of the Munstermen. The fifth crushing disaster befell us and James II who was our king, by which every surviving branch of the progeny of Gael Glas in this country was cut down', de Rís, *Ó Doirnín*, p. 40.

18 'It is my woe that the Gaelic nobility was pierced at Aughrim and beside the Boyne, and that Owen 'of the war' O'Neill survives not in dignity who would punish Cromwell and his hosts; King Harry, a Beelzebub of lies, wouldn't blaze nor Luther who tormented Ireland, no New Lights or Seceders, Old Presbyterians, Swaddlers or Quakers with them', Ó Fiaich (ed), *Mac Cumhaigh*, p. 86.

19 Ó Muirgheasa, *Céad de cheoltaibh Uladh*, p. 192.

20 Ibid., pp 192-3.

21 *AFM*, vi, pp 2364, 2374.

22 Ó Muirgheasa, *Céad de cheoltaibh Uladh*, p. 192; the poem referred to is one by Art Mac Bionaid.

The flight of the earls in Irish traditional music

Adrian Scahill

One of the key functions of traditional music and song is the role it plays in the construction and maintenance of a collective cultural memory.[1] These acts of remembrancing occur as part of the living tradition, within which a social memory is maintained through performance, repetition, transmission and its accompanying discourse.[2] Indeed, the various festivals and events held in 2007-08 to commemorate the flight of the earls have successfully harnessed these modes of community remembrancing in more formal representations of the tradition in concerts and recordings.[3] These commemorations have also drawn attention to this murky period in the history of Irish music, and to the revitalisation of its music through its performance. However, this essay will focus on sources rather than performance, and in doing so will examine the representation of the flight in Irish traditional music, looking at how the music both preserves its memory and reinterprets its meanings.

There are significant complications in approaching this topic, so a broad, three-stranded approach has been adopted, focusing on, firstly, music that may derive from the general period and has a possible connection with the personalities involved; secondly, music which deliberately romanticises the period; and thirdly, music which contains resonances of the earls and the period. This is by no means an exhaustive survey, but instead highlights specific pieces of note in each area.

The difficulties involved in discussing the music of the seventeenth century are considerable and well documented; notations of music are scarce and were not produced in Ireland until the eighteenth century, while those published in English manuscripts and prints are few in number. Furthermore, those that appear to have some Irish connection are, according to Mícheál Ó Súilleabháin, 'quite unlike those of the succeeding century, and too few tunes have as yet been assembled to allow new stylistic criteria to be established'.[4] In short, most writers concur that what is understood as traditional music overwhelmingly belongs to the eighteenth and nineteenth centuries, and that 'we cannot be sure how much of the old, truly Irish, musical tradition survived the seventeenth century'.[5]

'Two Pipers'. © Brian Vallely

Given this rather barren musical terrain, the location of music with specific associations is difficult, and what could be termed here as remnants may quite well date to a later period. It is not possible to determine with certainty whether these tunes originated in this period, or subsequently gained their ascriptions owing to the almost complete absence of annotations. Apart from the occasional details concerning the music's immediate source, little concrete information concerning its origin is extant. The memorialisation of figures from history through music, while a common practice, is highly problematic: names are often reconfigured to allude to more distant historical events or personalities, so that the memory encapsulated in the music is in fact a construction of the present.[6] And although there may be some validity in distinguishing between a popular, oral, cultural history and an official, literate one,[7] this risks ignoring the weight and potency that such titles carry within (contemporary) traditional discourse.

The march is the tune type with arguably the longest history in Ireland,[8] and is associated in this early period with the bagpipes or warpipes, the chief

277

military instrument of the time.[9] Fynes Moryson's description of an attack made by Hugh O'Neill on a military camp in Armagh in 1601 illustrates the instrument's prominence in this context:

> They came with cries and a sound of Drummes and bagpipes as though if they would attempt the camp and powred into some two or three thousand shot hurting onely two of our men … After these our men had given a volly in their teeth, they drew away and we heard no more of their Drummes or Bagpipes but only mournful cries, for many of their best men were slain.[10]

There are some limited stylistic connections between the marches discussed here, and only one has the 6/8 rhythm which is characteristic of the most widely-known marches from this period, 'O'Sullivan's March'[11] and 'Mairseál Alasdruim'.[12] This is 'O'Donnell's March', which was collected by Edward Bunting from Redmond Stanton, and from the harper Arthur O'Neill.[13] The tune is connected with the period by its subtitle 'Marbhne O Neil', which appears in Bunting's manuscript

notation of the piece. There is no explanation of this apparently contradictory classification of the tune as a lament, and the labelling of similar tunes as death marches for fallen leaders is regarded as being fanciful.[14] Transcribed in 3/8, bars 5-6 seem more natural in 6/8, and this notation (Example 1) is altered to reflect this. The exact repetition of bars 9-10 (as marked) is another point of connection with these other early march tunes.

Two further marches associated with the O'Neills appear in Bunting's manuscripts. The best-known of these marches is 'Marcuis Uí Néill', variously translated as 'O'Neill's cavalcade' or 'O'Neill's riding'.[15] Donal O'Sullivan's commentary on the tune avoids identifying the O'Neill in question,[16] but although no earlier sources exist, it is often associated with Hugh O'Neill, and has been described as 'a tune which can be traced back to the 1600s and possibly one of the oldest piping tunes in existence … [which was] associated with the O'Neill Clan of Ulster, the most powerful family in seventeenth century Ulster'.[17] A connection has been drawn between this and another march named for Owen Roe O'Neill, from the Pigot Collection,[18] and hence it is suggested in

Example 1: 'O'Donnell's March' ('Marbhne O Neil')

Example 2: 'Marcuis Uí Neill'

'March of Owen Roe O'Neill'

'Owen O'Neill's March' (parts 1 & 4 only)

English forces defeat an Irish contingent who leave a dead piper in their wake. From John Derricke's *The Image of Irlande* (London, 1581). © Trinity College Dublin

Fleischmann's *Sources* that the tune in fact refers to him. A second march of this title collected by Bunting is also considered to date from the seventeenth century.[19] What links all of these tunes (with perhaps the exception of 'O'Donnell's March') is their construction from repeated short melodic cells, which reoccur to a greater degree than in later traditional tunes. Another point of commonality shared by these marches is the presence of repeated figures with quicker rhythmic movement than the rest of the tune: semiquavers in the last part of 'O'Donnell's March' and the 'March of Owen Roe O'Neill', and quavers in the second part of 'Marcuis Uí Neill', and the first and final part of 'Owen Roe O'Neill's March'. With the exception of those in 'Marcuis Uí Néill', all of these repeated figures are based around an interval of a third.

One other tune in Bunting's manuscripts may be a march; entitled simply 'O'Neill',[20] it is printed without a time signature and has a similar rhythm to 'O'Donnell's March', though there is no other information on the tune's provenance. A final point about these tunes is that all have quite a narrow range, which indicates that they would be playable by the restricted range of the bagpipes.

Of the three laments discussed here, the first, 'Maguire's Lamentation', or 'The Maguire's Cooach or Cumha', is contained in Bunting's manuscripts and annotated with the comment 'Chieftains of Fermanagh'. The tune was collected from Charles Byrne the harper in 1802, and also

from Catherine Martin at Virginia, County Cavan.[21] The other two laments are perhaps the most fascinating tunes associated with the flight of the earls. The slow airs 'Caoineadh Uí Néill' and 'Caoineadh Uí Dhomhnaill' appear to be independent of any song, but are similar to the 'big songs' of the *sean-nós* tradition in their melodic sweep (see the passages marked 'S' in examples 3 and 4) and intensity. They share a common source, and are notable because of the apparent contradictions between their history and provenance, and how they are popularly perceived by musicians. As both have been frequently recorded recently,[22] the construction of their narrative has been partly achieved and accentuated through the tunes' accompanying discourse, as often revealed in the notes to recordings. The airs' earliest sources are recordings of the Sliabh Luachra fiddle players Pádraig O'Keeffe and Denis Murphy. O'Keeffe appears to be the primary identifiable source, as it is almost certainly the case that Murphy learned these airs from O'Keeffe, who himself learned them from his grandmother.[23] A recording of 'Caoineadh Uí Néill', credited to O'Keeffe and never issued commercially was made during Alan Lomax's recording tours in Ireland in the 1950s.[24] Although the fiddler on this recording is not positively identified, the setting is distinct from Murphy's, and it is a reasonable conjecture to attribute it to O'Keeffe. In the version recorded by Murphy, which was recorded by Ciarán Mac Mathúna, the opening phrase is played with F nat-

urals in place of F sharps.[25] Both recorded 'Caoineadh Uí Dhomhnaill' several times: O'Keeffe for
Séamus Ennis in 1948, and for the BBC in 1952;[26]
Murphy for Mac Mathúna and also Lomax, again
in the 1950s or 1960s.[27] It is somewhat surprising,
given their magnificence, that no earlier printed
sources are found for either tune. They have also
generated very little commentary, with the exception of recent articles on both by Terry Moylan,
which confirms the absence of notated versions
before the tunes' recording.[28] There are several other recent printed notations of this air,[29] but only
in Moylan's article is there one of 'Caoineadh Uí
Néill'. The commentary to O'Keeffe's recordings
note that 'both may be named after the two Ulster
families who led the Irish forces at their downfall at
the Battle of Kinsale',[30] and elsewhere it is claimed
that 'Caoineadh Uí Néill' is 'one of the oldest surviving airs in the Irish tradition written in honour
of the great Irish chieftain O'Neill'.[31] Likewise, the
O'Donnell lament is described as grieving 'for those
slaughtered at Kinsale',[32] being 'named after Red
Hugh O'Donnell, whose departure into exile after
the battle of Kinsale, 1601, heralded the demise
of the clan system in Ireland'.[33] Perhaps the perception of the tunes as ancient additionally stems
from their difference; both are unusual in having
quite irregular phrase structures, and in fact both
also have an affinity with the marches discussed
above in their inclusion of passages with insistently
repeated short phrases (marked 'R' below). If these
are in fact seventeenth-century laments, their survival unnoticed until the twentieth century would
be remarkable, and though their ancientness may
be invented or constructed, it nevertheless remains

'Death of A Piper'. © Brian Vallely

Frontispiece of *O'Neill's Music of Ireland* (Chicago, 1903).
© Inch House Irish Studies Centre

Example 3: Denis Murphy, 'Caoineadh Uí Néill'

Example 4: Denis Murphy, 'Caoineadh Uí Dhomhnaill' (transcription by Terry Moylan)

meaningful and important for contemporary traditional musicians.

Finally, it is worth mentioning the later 'Hugh O'Neill's Lament' here, as by all accounts it caused quite a stir on its publication in Captain Francis O'Neill's *Music of Ireland*,[34] O'Neill writing that it was 'another of those fine melodies from the North of Ireland contributed by Sergeant [James] O'Neill. Judging by the inquiries concerning its origin it has attracted much attention'.[35] Clearly there was excitement at the prospect of a newly discovered lament dating from this period in Irish music, but the name is purely commemorative, as Caoimhín Mac Aoidh has recently confirmed that this tune was in fact composed by James O'Neill, as admitted by Francis O'Neill in a letter to Alfred Perceval Graves.[36]

The events of the period surrounding the flight of the earls remained relatively distant from the consciousness of the people in subsequent centuries, and political songs and ballads almost exclusively concentrated on contemporary issues such as the 1798 rebellion. That is not to say that the figures of this period are totally absent from these songs, and occasionally the names of O'Neill and O'Donnell are evoked, but there appear to be few songs specifically dealing with them or their exploits. It is important to acknowledge their impact, as evidenced in Pádraigín Ní Uallacháin's *A hidden Ulster*, her comprehensive study of the folk culture of Oriel. The

songs compiled and annotated by Ní Uallacháin are laden with allusions to the extended O'Neill clan; in particular, Glasdrumman Castle, the home of the O'Neills of the Fews, is a recurring icon, and both Art Mac Cumhaigh and Séamus Dall Mac Cuarta composed laments bemoaning its destruction. Mac Cumhaigh's lament does not simply accept the passing of the O'Neills and this period as terminal; instead he 'dreamed of the restoration of their power and their patronage'.[37] What emerges from this and his other songs is a construct of tradition with the O'Neills as its foundation, and arguably the potency and durability of his work lay in its ability to represent the past as something recoverable. Thus, Mac Cumhaigh and his fellow poets created 'a matrix of memory which encoded an attainable future enabled by the available past'.[38] The most lasting memorial in song of this area is perhaps the great 'Úirchill a' Chreagáin', an *aisling* in which the poet laments the loss of the O'Neills, and marks their commitment to poetry and music.

For the memorialisation of the events of the seventeenth century, one has to turn to what Georges Zimmermann terms the 'literary imitations of street ballads', products of the romantic and nationalist poeticism of the nineteenth and early twentieth centuries.[39] It could be argued that a discussion of these do not properly belong in a paper on Irish traditional music, but Zimmermann's precedent is followed here in recognising that the authors of these songs perceived that their productions had a continuity with the folk tradition and generally served a similar function.[40] To accept this reading requires a privileging of authorial intention, and it must be qualified by a recognition that these songs would be considered (at best) today to be at the margins of the 'living tradition' or as dormant residues of a now-elapsed period of Irish music. Additionally, to dismiss them from a contemporary perspective would overlook their wide distribution, and ignore the shifting meanings and concepts behind such terms as 'traditional music', 'national music' and 'folk music'. It can also be alleged that, because these were primarily disseminated in printed forms, their status as folk or traditional songs has always been questionable; but such a charge would be blind to the reality that traditional music has never existed as a monolithic entity in complete isolation from a literate dimension.[41] Indeed, the more popular of these romanticisations journeyed from printed collection to ballad sheet and into oral tradition; and if they have subsequently withered in the face of more relevant and popular songs and music, even a passing familiarity with the contemporary tradition alerts us to the continuing retrieval and reanimation of items from a more distant past. As Zofia Lissa has noted, 'Each historical period makes a fresh choice from the available cultural resources of the past, and only this becomes tradition … As cultural layers become deposited in the course of the evolutionary process of a given milieu they gradually develop into that period's history; traditions may become revived and reactivated or the may … disappear to be taken out of the past and become active again in another phase of history'.[42]

Possibly the best-known ballad evoking the period emerged from the 'romantic zeal' of the Young Ireland movement,[43] part of the corpus of songs which reached a vast readership through publication in *The Nation*. These served a dual utilitarian function of informing its readers on matters of history, and through this developing a sense of nationality among them.[44] By presenting idealised and glorified parables from Irish history, the ballads frequently exhibited highly distorted images of the past, with the aim of establishing historical foundations for a nationalist struggle and emphasising a continuity with previous exertions.[45] For Thomas Davis, one of the founders of the paper along with John Blake Dillon and Charles Gavan Duffy, the ballad was 'a

matter of political resource',[46] and the ballads therefore perpetuated a 'cult of violent struggle, sectarian demeanour and Anglophobia', to quote from Harry White's trenchant criticism of this music.[47] All of these are present and correct in 'O'Donnell Abu', first published in *The Nation* in January 1843. The song's gestation illustrates the transformation in meaning that occurs through the construction of such ballads: the melody of 'O'Donnell Abu' was composed as a marching tune early in the nineteenth century by Joseph Haliday, who was bandmaster of the Cavan Militia and inventor of the Royal Kent bugle, an early keyed brass instrument;[48] Michael McCann then added his lyric to this tune, which was initially published as 'The Clan Connell War Song', but in its reprinting in *The Spirit of the Nation* the title was changed to its present form.[49] The song's glorification of Red Hugh O'Donnell and O'Neill is apt for an agenda of patriotic propagandism, but as an intelligencer of history the text is rather vague. Given a date of 1597 in *The Spirit of the Nation*, the battle referred to seems to be the failed attempt of Sir Conyers Clifford to take a castle of O'Donnell's at Ballyshannon, yet the narrative is loose enough to facilitate its transposition to other successful battles of this period; and popular commentaries on the song posit readings which link it to the battle of the Curlews in 1599, among others. These details are anyhow incidental, given that they are in essence a touchstone for inspiring contemporary nationalism: despite the centrality of Ulster to the conflict, the exhortations of the song, 'On for old Erin', and 'Strike! For your Country!', project a nationalist tone, as does the call to 'Make the proud Saxon feel Erin's avenging steel!'.

A second piece from *The Spirit of the Nation* is of more tangential interest, as its status as a song is unclear. Essentially a poem from an earlier date, William Drennan's 'The Battle of Béal-an-Átha-Buidhe' appears without music, although the double jig 'Paddy Whack' is suggested for it in the index.[50] The correspondence between the words and tune are awkward, even if the archetypal concluding refrain of the verses fits nicely into the jig rhythm. Further support for its wider dissemination as a ballad is its publication as a ballad sheet, an example of which is found in P. J. McCall's 'Ballad Sheet Collection'.[51] The text itself narrates a romanticised and account of the battle, depicting the Irish as half-naked, with no guns or armour, instead warring with only pikes, 'rude brambles, sharp furze, and dry fern'.

The final examples of romantic balladry discussed here lie very much at the margins of the contemporary tradition, but are notable for their appropriation of folk tunes, thereby adding another layer of meaning to the original melodies. In the case of 'The Flight of the Earls', although the songs written to the tune in question have faded, the association has persisted, perpetuating the memorialisation of the event. Colm Ó Lochlainn lists two sources for the melody:[52] one of these is an untitled tune in the Petrie collection;[53] the second was a tune called 'The Mattock on My Shoulder', collected between 1890 and 1894 by Dr John Clague on the Isle of Man, and published by Annie Gilchrist in the *Journal of the Folk Song Society*.[54] The tune is also used for 'The Boys of Wexford', another literary ballad written by Robert Dwyer Joyce in the late nineteenth century.[55] The tune's identification as 'The Flight of the Earls' seems to be primarily due to Alfred Perceval Graves's lyric, one of a series of songs entitled 'Songs of Chieftains', all on topics from the seventeenth century, which he claimed were 'written under the influence of the Gaelic Revival'.[56] While the songs were grouped together as poetry in the collection entitled *Songs of the Gael*, they appeared separately in other publications, 'The Flight of the Earls' being first published in *Irish songs and ballads* in 1880.[57] Graves's verse confirms the recent assessment of his work as being a 'curious (and inferior) reanimation of the spirit of Thomas Moore',[58] with none of the vigour of the Young Ireland balladry. Indeed, the poem chiefly forgoes the political and nationalist question and might be read as a ballad of emigration: the central theme is the melancholy of departure and the longing for return:

> To other shores across the sea
> We speed with swelling sail;
> Yet still there lingers on our lee
> A phantom Innisfail.
> O fear, fear not, gentle ghost,
> Your sons shall turn untrue!
> Though fain to fly your lovely coast,
> *They leave their hearts with you.*[59]

This reinterpretation of the flight as a symbol for emigration is completed in an anonymous ballad to this tune, which dispenses with any reference to specific historical figures, places, or nationalism. Instead, the text is loaded with stock images of emigration: the shamrock, St Patrick's Day, 'Sweet

Erin ever blest', 'The lowly cot, the leaping stream – 'The spire upon the hill' – all vague enough to be universally relevant, evoking nostalgia for 'My native land, my home'.[60] This memorialisation of the flight of the earls as symptomatic of the ongoing plight of emigration is also found in a much more recent folk song of the 1980s, 'The Flight of Earls',[61] illustrating how history can be employed as a means of establishing the continuity of emigration as central to the Irish psyche. The reference to 'another bloody Flight of Earls' might seem trivial, yet by (perhaps spuriously) connecting the difficult situation of the 1980s with 1607 the song demonstrates the ability of music to allow history to echo through and add resonance to more contemporary issues.

Returning to the period of the Gaelic Revival, a further lyric to this tune by Percy French seems to take as its point of departure Graves's song: although entitled 'When Erin Wakes', the tune is identified as 'The Flight of the Earls'.[62] With an arrangement by Houston Collison, the song won the 1900 Feis Ceoil award for best arrangement of a folk song. The text does not deal specifically with any one historical event, instead collating disparate figures and moments as a means of exemplifying that 'the Gael has still a heritage that gold can never buy'. Thus Cúchulainn, Owen Roe O'Neill, Sarsfield, Fontenoy are invoked as establishing and representing Ireland's glorious past; they belong to the listener, and French's song contains the promise that, as with the songs of the mid-nineteenth century, their spirit still persists and act as inspiration for others.

Graves wrote three other songs on the subject of the flight of the earls: 'The March of the Maguires', the 'Chieftain of Tyrconnell', and 'O'Donnell's March', but only the last of these seems to have had a lasting impact, although all three were republished frequently during the Gaelic Revival period, reappearing in American publications such as Murphy's *The national songs of Ireland* (1892), and Hyland's *Mammoth Hibernian Songster* (1901). Stanford's arrangements for these bring them into the domain of the art song, although all are based on unrelated folk tunes. 'O'Donnell's March' is interesting because, as with his song 'The Flight of the Earls', the folk song it was based on, 'The Brown Little Mallet', appears to have acquired a new meaning and identity through its new lyrics. This tune was first published in the third edition of John O'Daly's

The poets and poetry of Munster (1888).[63] However-er, a later version of the tune in *Crowley's collection of music for the Highland or Irish bagpipes* invents an entirely new history for it by commenting that it was 'Said to have been played by the pipers of the O'Donnell Clan on their march to the Battle of Kinsale'.[64] A simpler version of this tune was also published in Hardebeck's *Ceol na nGaedheal* in 1937.[65] Both of these seem to have Scottish overtones, with an obvious Scottish snap, and a double-tonic structure in the first part (which is altered in Hardebeck's setting).

This essay has demonstrated how music acts as a conveyor of memory and history, reinforcing our awareness of the events and figures of the flight of the earls, while also serving to recreate and reinterpret this distant episode. As mentioned in the introduction, music has played an important role in marking the anniversary of the flight, from the many concerts held during the flight of the earls / *Imeacht na nIarlaí* Commemorative Festival, to events specifically centred around music, such as the Inishowen Traditional Singers' Circle 18th International Folk Song and Ballad Seminar,[66] and the Musical Journeys with the Flight of the Earls Symposium held at Dublin Institute of Technology.[67] Furthermore, the history of the period has proved to be a generative force for musicians and composers, acting as an inspiration for Michael Holohan's piping piece *The Road to Lough Swilly*;[68] the theatrical extension of this work, *Running Beast*; a work by the American composer Robinson McClellan, *Flight of the Earls: concerto for uilleann pipes* (2007); and a work by Elaine Agnew, *One less petal, one less flame* (2007), which incorporates a prologue with music composed by Tommy Peoples.[69] It seems particularly apt that, given the earls' journey from Ireland to continental Europe, all of these works connect together Irish traditional music and the Western European art music tradition. Thus the marking of the flight of the earls demonstrates that we ourselves are making a return to and a new choice from our available cultural resources, and in the process are helping to reshape the modern tradition through the interweaving of the musical traditions and history of the past.

Notes

1 K. K. Shelemay, 'Music, memory and history', *Ethnomusicology Forum*, xv, no. 1 (2006), p. 32.

2 P. Connerton, *How societies remember* (Cambridge, 1989), p. 4.

3 J. Leerssen, 'Monument and trauma: varieties of remembrance', in I. McBride (ed.), *History and memory in modern Ireland* (Cambridge, 2001), p. 215.

4 M. Ó Súilleabháin, 'Preface', in A. Fleischmann, *Sources of Irish traditional music, c. 1600-1855* (2 vols, New York, 1998), i, p. xviii.

5 J. Rimmer, *The Irish harp: clairseach na hÉireann* (2nd ed., Cork, 1977), p. 54.

6 C. Bithell, 'The past in music: introduction', *Ethnomusicology Forum*, xv, no. 1 (2006), pp 4-6.

7 L. Ó Laoire and S. Williams, 'Singing the famine: Joe Heaney, "Johnny Seoighe" and the poetics of performance', in A. Clune (ed.), *Dear far-voiced veteran: essays in honour of Tom Munnelly* (Miltown Malbay, 2007), p. 233.

8 F. Vallely, 'March', in idem (ed.), *The companion to Irish traditional music* (Cork, 1999), pp 228-9.

9 S. Donnelly, *The early history of piping in Ireland* (Dublin & Glasgow, 2001), pp 13-19.

10 Fynes Moryson, 'Itinerary', quoted in S. Donnelly, 'The warpipes in Ireland, ii', *Ceol*, v, no. 2 (1982), pp 57-58.

11 'O'Sullivan's March', *An Píobaire*, ii, no. 44 (1989), p. 8.

12 S. Donnelly, 'The warpipes in Ireland, iii', *Ceol*, vi, no. 2 (1983), p. 20.

13 Belfast, Queen's University Library, Edward Bunting MS 33(1), fol. 49; E. Bunting, *The ancient music of Ireland* (Dublin, 1840), p. 80.

14 B. Breathnach, 'Mairseál Alasdruim', in S. Potts, T. Moylan and L. McNulty (eds), *The man and his music* (Dublin, 1996), p. 17; W. H. Grattan Flood, *A history of Irish music* (3rd ed., Dublin, 1913; repr., Dublin, 1970), p. 195.

15 E. Bunting, *A general collection of the ancient music of Ireland* (London, 1809), p. 32; C. V. Stanford, *The complete collection of Irish music as noted by George Petrie* (3 vols, London, 1902-5), i, p. 119, no. 472.

16 D. O'Sullivan, 'The Bunting collection of Irish folk music and songs: part v', *The Journal of the Irish Folk Song Society*, xxvii (1936), pp 24-25.

17 'Marcshlua Uí Néill (O'Neill's cavalry)', *The Tartan and Green: official publication of the Irish Pipe Band Association*, xvi (2002), p. 27.

18 P. W. Joyce, *Old Irish folk music and songs* (Dublin, 1909), no. 773.

19 D. O'Sullivan, 'The Bunting collection of Irish folk music and songs: part v', *Journal of the Irish Folk Song Society*, xxvii (1936), p. 26.

20 Bunting MS 5/46.

21 C. Moloney, *The Irish music manuscripts of Edward Bunting (1773-1843): an introduction and catalogue* (Dublin, 2000), pp 250, 322; D. O'Sullivan and M. Ó Súilleabháin,

Bunting's ancient music of Ireland (Cork, 1983), pp 57-58.

22 There are eight commercial recordings of 'Caoineadh Uí Néill' available, and about twenty of 'Caoineadh Uí Dhomhnaill'.

23 A. Ward, 'Music from Sliabh Luachra', *Traditional Music*, v (1976), pp 20-23.

24 Irish Traditional Music Archive: 179-ITMA-Reel, Breandán Breathnach Reel-to-Reel 196, track A3.

25 D. Murphy, *Music from Sliabh Luachra* (RTÉ CD 183, n.d.), track 5. No date or location for the recording is given.

26 *Sliabh Luachra fiddle master Pádraig O'Keeffe* (RTÉ CD 174, 1993), track 14; P. O'Keeffe, D. Murphy, and J. Clifford, *Kerry fiddles* (Topic TSCD 309, 1977), track 5.

27 Murphy, *Music from Sliabh Luachra*, 5; Various, *Traditional music of Ireland: the older traditions of Connemara and Clare*, I (Folkways FW 8781, 1963), B3, as 'The queen of O'Donnell'.

28 T. Moylan, 'Airs and graces: Caoineadh Uí Dhónaill', *An Píobaire*, iv, no. 41 (2007), pp 18-19; idem, Moylan, 'Caoineadh Uí Néill', *An Píobaire*, iv, no. 42 (2007), pp 18-19.

29 See for example T. Ó Canainn, *Traditional music in Ireland* (London, 1978), p. 36.

30 Notes to *Sliabh Luachra fiddle master Pádraig O'Keeffe* (RTÉ CD 174, 1993).

31 Notes to Aoife Granville, *Sráid Eoin shuffle* (Aoife Granville AG001, 2006).

32 Various, *The Seville suite: Kinsale to La Coruna* (Tara CD 3030, 1992).

33 Notes to Kathleen Loughnane, *Harping on* (Kathleen Loughnane, Own Label, 2002).

34 F. O'Neill, *O'Neill's Music of Ireland* (Chicago, 1903), p. 12.

35 F. O'Neill, *Irish folk music: a fascinating hobby* (Chicago, 1910), p. 72.

36 C. Mac Aoidh, *The scribe: the life and works of James O'Neill* (Manorhamilton, 2006), p. 115.

37 P. Ní Uallacháin, *A hidden Ulster* (Dublin, 2006), p. 262.

38 I. McBride, 'Introduction: memory and national identity in modern Ireland', in idem (ed.), *History and memory in modern Ireland*, p. 2.

39 G. D. Zimmermann, *Songs of Irish rebellion: political street ballads and rebel songs, 1780-1900* (Dublin, 1967), p. 75.

40 Zimmermann, *Songs of Irish rebellion*, p. 76.

41 P. V. Bohlman, *The study of folk music in the modern world* (Bloomington and Indianapolis, 1988), pp 28-30.

42 Z. Lissa, 'Prolegomena to the theory of musical tradition', *International Review of Music Aesthetics and Sociology*, i, no. 1 (1970), p. 36.

43 H. White, 'Music, politics, and the Irish imagination', in R. Pine (ed.), *Music in Ireland, 1798-1998* (Cork, 1998), pp 29-37.

44 Zimmermann, *Songs of Irish rebellion*, pp 78, 82.

45 J. Ryan, 'The tone of defiance', in H. White and M. Murphy (ed.), *Musical constructions of nationalism: essays on the*

history and ideology of European musical culture 1800-1945 (Cork, 2001), p. 202; Zimmermann, *Songs of Irish rebellion*, p. 82.

46 H. White, *The keeper's recital: music and cultural history in Ireland, 1770-1970* (Cork, 1998), p. 57.

47 White, *The keeper's recital*, p. 55.

48 F. W. Saunders, 'O Donnell Abú and the Royal Kent bugle', *Irish Book Lover*, xxvi (1939), pp 85-86; R. T. Dudgeon: 'Joseph Haliday, inventor of the keyed bugle', *Journal of the American Music Society*, ix (1983), pp 53-67.

49 *The Spirit of the Nation: ballads and songs by the writers of 'The Nation' with original and ancient music, arranged for the voice and piano-forte* (Dublin, 1845), pp 118-9.

50 *Spirit of the nation*, pp 47-49.

51 P. J. McCall, 'Ballad sheet collection', viii (Irish Traditional Music Archive).

52 C. Ó Lochlainn, *Irish street ballads* (Dublin, 1939), p. 96.

53 Stanford, *The complete collection of Irish music as noted by George Petrie*, I, p. 11.

54 A. G. Gilchrist, 'Songs and tunes from the Clague collection: miscellaneous songs', *Journal of the Folk Song Society*, vii, no. 28 (1924), pp 160-1.

55 T. Moylan, *The age of revolution in the Irish song tradition* (Dublin, 2000), pp 53-55.

56 A. P. Graves, 'Prefatory note', *The Irish poems of Alfred Perceval Graves: songs of the Gael; A Gaelic story-telling* (Dublin & New York, 1908), p. v.

57 A. P. Graves, *Irish songs and ballads* (Manchester, 1880), pp 56-57, 224, 250-1.

58 White, *The keeper's recital*, p. 115.

59 Graves, *Irish songs and ballads*, pp 56-57, 224.

60 W. H. A. Williams, ''Twas only an Irishman's dream: the image of Ireland and the Irish in American popular song lyrics, 1800-1920* (Urbana, 1996), pp 42-46.

61 Written by Liam Reilly, and popularised by the Dublin City Ramblers and Paddy Reilly.

62 J. N. Healy, *Percy French and his songs* (Cork, 1977), pp 73-75.

63 J. O'Daly, *The poets and poetry of Munster* (Dublin, 1888), p. 276.

64 T. O'Crowley (ed.), *Crowley's collection of music for the Highland or Irish bagpipes, Book 1* (Cork, n. d.), p. 48.

65 C. Hardebeck (ed.), *Ceol na nGaedheal* (Dublin, 1937), p. 28.

66 Inishowen Traditional Singers' Circle, 18th International Folk Song and Ballad Seminar. 'Lords, dukes and earls: remembering the Flight of the Earls, 1607', 23-26 March, 2007.

67 'Musical journeys with the Flight of the Earls', DIT Conservatory of Music and Drama, Dublin, 3 February 2007.

68 'New publications: the road to Lough Swilly', *An Píobaire*, iv, no. 14 (2002), pp 7-11.

69 T. Moylan, 'The Flight of the Earls', *An Píobaire*, iv, no. 44 (2008), pp 12-15.

Memorialising Gaelic Ireland: the curious case of the Ballyshannon fragments and the Irish monuments at San Pietro in Montorio, Rome

Elizabeth FitzPatrick

The burial place of the exiled Irish at San Pietro in Montorio, Rome, is perhaps the most iconic Irish diaspora funerary site in Europe, not least because the community interred there (1608-23) are found in the company of Bramante's *Tempietto* (1502) and Bernini's chapel to the Raymondi family (1640) with his *Ecstasy of St Francis Baratta* on the reredos. For all that, the Irish past at the site has received remarkably little scholarly attention since the last record made of the memorials at San Pietro in Montorio by Gasparo Alveri in 1664.[1] The early historiography of the Irish burials is slight, commencing with Tadhg Ó Cianáin's chronicle reference to the funerary rites of Rory O'Donnell in 1608,[2] continuing with a seventeenth-century registry of the parish church of San Pietro in Montorio which records some of the burials up to 1613,[3] and concluding with the most detailed and accurate record of the inscriptions on the Irish memorials in the church floor made by Alveri during his great project to record the modern inscriptions from the churches of Rome in the 1660s. It was the nineteenth century before any further attention was directed to the seventeenth-century exiled Irish buried on Gianicolo.

One of the more significant if not always accurate, and sometimes elusive, commentators on the afterlife of the Irish burials in the nineteenth century was C. P. Meehan. Born in 1812 in the diocese of Dublin, Meehan attended the Irish College in Rome in 1828-35 and later returned to minister in the parish of St Michael and St John, Dublin, in 1835.[4] As a seminarian in Rome, he developed an interest in the memorials of the earls at San Pietro in Montorio, and he included his observations on them in three editions of *The fate and fortunes of Hugh O'Neill, earl of Tyrone and Rory O'Donel, earl of Tyrconnel*, published in 1868, 1870 and 1886. Meehan established the Irish Catholic cleri-

Some Irish Graves in Rome.
© Inch House Irish Studies Centre

cal ownership of the history of the flight of the earls and the monuments in San Pietro in Montorio, and these concerns were subsequently pursued by Patrick Francis Moran, vice-rector of the Irish College in Rome (1856-66),[5] and in publications such as that of John Healy, archbishop of Tuam, on 'Some Irish graves in Rome' (1908).[6] This tradition continued with Tomás Ó Fiaich,[7] whose investigations with Fearghus Ó Fearghail into the memorial inscription to Hugh O'Neill, earl of Tyrone, has been recently documented.[8] The Rome episode of the flight and the use of San Pietro in Montorio as the parish church of the exiled Irish community is, of course, not simply a Catholic Irish or Ulster story, but a political event that has much broader European significance, aspects of which have been portrayed, for instance, by Micheline Kearney Walsh,[9] and more recently by Clare Carroll.[10] San Pietro in Montorio became part of the exilic cultural landscape of Gaelic Ireland, and its interpretation in that context makes it less exotic and better understood in both its contemporary seventeenth-century world and in the nineteenth-century awakening of interest in that past.[11]

A visitor to San Pietro in Montorio today will find two large marble slabs and a commemorative stone in the floor of the nave next to Cappella San Giovanni Battista. The small commemorative plaque, often mistaken for Hugh O'Neill's original memorial stone, marks the approximate position of his burial place (d. 1616) and was commissioned by Tomás Ó Fiaich in 1989 following research into the earl's memorial inscription by Fearghus Ó Fearghail.[12] The original memorial to O'Neill, with its simple Latin inscription, *'D O M HUGONIS PRINCIPIS ONELLI OSSA'* (To God the Best and Greatest, the bones of Prince Hugh

Commemorative plaque, commissioned in 1989 by Tomás Ó Fiaich, Catholic Primate of Armagh, marking the approximate burial place of Hugh O'Neill in San Pietro in Montorio. © Elizabeth FitzPatrick

The new church of San Pietro in Montorio, constructed for the Amadeiti Franciscans (Friars Minor), was consecrated on 9 June 1500. Built on the site of a twelfth-century church, which may have had a ninth-century antecedent, the new church was initially funded by Louis XI of France and subsequently by Ferdinand and Isabella of Spain. © Elizabeth FitzPatrick

Donato Bramante's *Tempietto* was erected between c. 1502 and 1512 in the centre of the first cloister of the convent complex of San Pietro in Montorio. It is a martyrium which, according to a tradition based on the mistaken identification of Mons Aureus with Janiculum, marks the location of St Peter's execution. © Elizabeth FitzPatrick

O'Neill), as recorded by Alveri, has been missing since at least the mid-nineteenth century. It has been suggested that because Meehan – who made frequent visits to San Pietro in Montorio between 1828 and 1835 – does not refer to seeing O'Neill's memorial in the church in that period, and because in an appendix to his first edition of *The fate and fortunes* (1868) he asserts that 'there can be no doubt that the flag-stone has either been reversed or removed in repairing the floor of the church',[13] that it had disappeared before the damage inflicted on the church during the Risorgimento of 1849, perhaps as early as the French occupation of Rome (1798-1814).[14] However, Meehan did not publish the first edition of *The fate and fortunes* until 1868, and therefore he could well have been referring to the fate of the memorial after San Pietro in Montorio had been damaged by the French and Garabaldi's forces during their battle on Gianicolo that continued throughout the month of June 1849. Meehan also provided a reading of O'Neill's epitaph as 'D.O.M. HIC. QUIESCUNT. UGONIS. PRINCIPIS. O'NEILL. OSSA', which is a version not found in Alveri or in any other source, and therefore it could be concluded that it was his attempted reading of a worn inscription before the renewal of the inscriptions on the Irish memorials by Restaldi in 1844.[15] The principal damage to the church in 1849 was to the apse, belfry, roof and floor.[16] With the Irish memorials and burial vault situated just two metres from the apse, it is to be expected that they were also disturbed at that time. The post-Risorgimento restoration work to the church in 1851 apparently involved repaving the church floor with marble slabs,[17] at which time broken memorials would have been discarded or cut up for reuse as paving, as appears to have been the case with the inscribed slab to Eugene Matthews, archbishop of Dublin (d. 1623).

The extant Irish memorials commemorate Hugh O'Neill's son, Hugh, baron of Dungannon (d. 1609) and both Rory O'Donnell, earl of Tyrconnell (d. 1608) and his brother Cathbharr (d. 1608). The slabs lie side by side and share an ornate border. Nearly identical in size at approximately 2.70m by 0.95m, they were probably contrived as a set piece. Their design fits comfortably into the canon of Italian memorials of the period, especially in terms of the use of coloured marble inlay for family arms, crests, *memento mori* and border ornament. It is their inscriptions, however, that establish them as more than just memorials of the dead, and it is because of the inscriptions that such large rectangular slabs of marble were required. The O'Donnell memorial consists of a main slab carrying an inscription and distinguishing arms, two side borders decorated with rhombus, circle, half-circle and cruciform inlays, and top and bottom border strips inlaid with bright yellow *memento mori* in Giallo antico marble. A thirty-seven-line Latin inscription in bold Roman script extols the earl of Tyrconnell and his brother Cathbharr as defenders of the Catholic faith, and openly associates them, the earl of Tyrone and their cause

with Philip III of Spain and Pope Paul V. It also refers to Red Hugh O'Donnell, Rory's and Cathbharr's eldest brother, who died at the castle of Simancas in September 1602 and was buried in the Franciscan church at Valladolid in north-west Spain. Below the inscription there is a jewelled coronet and the arms of O'Donnell: a shield held aloft by a lion and bull rampant, and within it a sleeved right arm, bent at the elbow, the clenched hand holding upright the cross of Colum Cille. The style, detailing and execution of the memorial to Hugh, baron of Dungannon, closely resemble that of Rory O'Donnell. It carries a twenty-three-line Latin inscription, a jewelled coronet and the arms of the baron of Dungannon: a scrolled shield or cartouche decorated with two lions rampant holding aloft the Red Hand of Ulster. A body of water, represented by a blue-grey limestone inlay at the base of shield, is incised with the ichthus or Christian fish symbol.

In 1843 James Molyneux Caulfeild (1820-92), third earl of Charlemont, lord lieutenant of County Tyrone and later MP for Armagh (1847-57), travelled to Rome to inspect the condition of the Irish memorials at San Pietro in Montorio. Finding the

Memorials of Hugh O'Neill, baron of Dungannon, Rory O'Donnell, earl of Tyrconnell, and Rory's brother Cathbharr, with commemorative slab to Hugh O'Neill, earl of Tyrone, bottom left of picture. © Elizabeth FitzPatrick

'inscriptions much defaced, and the precious marbles and inlayings broken and removed', he 'procured copies of the originals from the archives of the convent' and subsequently raised a subscription among the Irish in Rome to pay for their restoration.[18] The wear and tear to the Irish memorials may have been in part inflicted by damage to the fabric of San Pietro in Montorio in 1798 and again in 1809 during the French occupation of Rome (1798-1814),[19] but it should also be noted that the tread of feet on an inscribed marble slab over two centuries would have considerably reduced the quality of the inscriptions and inlays irrespective of one or two episodes of specific damage.

Caulfeild's direct involvement in the project was regarded in some quarters as novel for a member of the Protestant aristocracy and was commented upon in the 20 December 1845 issue of *The Nation*: 'It is still more delightful to find that one of the Protestant aristocracy of the country, in whose veins runs the princely blood of O'Donel [*sic*], feels pride in so noble an ancestry, and cares to preserve the memory of our illustrious dead.' The newspaper referred to the fact that the earl's mother – Elizabeth Browne (d. 1878) the second daughter of Dodwell Browne, of Rahins, County Mayo – was a lineal descendant of the O'Donnell earl of Tyrconnell through her mother's line.[20] The reporter in *The Nation* apologised for having previously attributed the costs of the restoration of the epitaphs on the Irish memorials, 'which had become nearly illegible', to the 'patriotic exertions of Mr Dominick O'Reilly', and duly credited James Molyneux Caulfeild with having defrayed more than half the cost. Dominick O'Reilly, one of the subscribers to the restoration work at San Pietro in Montorio, was a patron of monumental sculpture, subscribing to John Hogan's 1839 marble sculpture at Carlow cathedral of James Warren Doyle (d. 1834), Catholic bishop of Kildare and Leighlin and champion of Catholic Emancipation. In 1843 O'Reilly commissioned his own marble bust from Hogan. He also travelled on the continent in 1844 (the year that the Irish memorials at San Pietro in Montorio were restored) and a letter dated 24 November, from him to the rector of the Irish College in Rome, describes his journey through the Alps that year.[21]

Caulfeild commissioned the neoclassical Irish sculptor, John Hogan (1800-58), who was based in Rome (1824-29) to undertake the work on the Irish memorials.[22] It was executed during Hogan's fourth period in Rome (1843-44) when he was working on his main project, O'Connell's colossal marble figure for City Hall, Dublin.[23] With his full attention on O'Connell, he delegated the project at San Pietro in Montorio to his assistant, Restaldi, whom he describes as *scalpellino* (stone-cutter) in his account book.[24] Restaldi travelled between Ireland and Rome with Hogan – in 1841, for instance, he was 'roughing out' William Beamish's marble bust.[25] When Hogan returned to Ireland for good in August 1849, Restaldi remained with him, and he is again documented in Hogan's account book where he is described in 1852 and 1853 as 'roughing out' new works in Hogan's Dublin studio.

Precise details of the work that Restaldi conducted on the Irish memorials are not given in Hogan's account book but the posthumous report in *The Nation* (20 Dec. 1845) implies that his principal task was to renew the inscriptions and to repair the inlays. According to the same report, Caulfeild had sought out documentation on the epitaphs at San Pietro in Montorio in order to aid Restaldi, which suggests that the inscriptions must have been partly illegible. It is perhaps the case that the memorials after their considerable restoration in 1844 had more the appearance of the nineteenth-century neoclassical style than the work of the early seventeenth-century funerary sculptor who had produced the originals. A close examination of the inscriptions reveals nuances in recutting and in the style of workmanship. Restaldi spent approximately three months on the project. In his account book Hogan notes an initial payment of 10 scudi on 20 April 1844 for the work, eight interim payments, and a final payment on 22 June of that year. In total, Hogan paid Restaldi 70 'scudi' and he praised Restaldi 'for said work which he executed with honour and credit to himself meeting the approbation of all who have seen and examined the Monuments of O'Neill and O'Donnell in San Pietro in Montorio'.[26] Significantly, neither he nor *The Nation* reporting on Caulfeild's involvement, mention that the earl of Tyrone's memorial was missing; it is likely that it was there and that its inscription was renewed by Restaldi.

That the nineteenth-century Catholic interest in the earls bordered on the hagiographical is borne out by an event which took place during the 1880s at St Catherine's Convent, Ballyshannon, County Donegal, which arose as a direct consequence of Meehan's involvement with the Irish memorials at San Pietro in Montorio. In a footnote to his second edition of *The fate and fortunes* (1870) Meehan remarked that discarded marble fragments from the Irish memorials at San Pietro in Montorio were 'in the possession of the

Hon Mrs Caulfeild, Lord Charlemont's mother'.[27] He later added in a footnote to his third edition (1886): 'That lamented and venerable lady directed the writer of this work to send the precious fragments to the nuns of Ballyshannon, and have them inserted in the altar of the convent recently erected in that town.'[28] Construction of the convent, St Catherine's of the Mercy Order, had begun in 1877, a year before Mrs Caulfeild's death, and it officially opened in 1884. Nine letters and a small fragment of Spanish broccatello inlay among the Ballyshannon papers in the provincial archives of the Sisters of Mercy at Bessbrook, County Armagh, uncover the somewhat curious background to the realisation of Mrs Caulfeild's wish. The correspondence is between five parties: Miss Shiel, mother superior of Ballyshannon Convent of Mercy; C. P. Meehan, parish priest in the Dublin parish of St Michael and St John; Daniel Mc-Gettigan, archbishop of Armagh and primate of All Ireland; M. L. Stronge, the sister of James Molyneux Caulfeild, third earl of Charlemont; and Sydney Shiel, sister of the mother superior. Their correspondence, which is sometimes tetchy, spans the period 25 April to 6 December 1880 and concerns the whereabouts of marble fragments from the Irish memorials in Rome and plans to have them incorporated into the Ballyshannon convent's new altar.

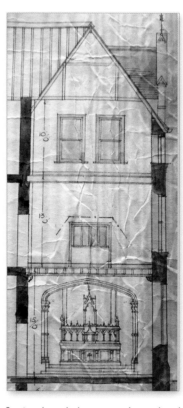

Section through the proposed new chapel of St Catherine's Convent of Mercy, Ballyshannon, showing the 1880 altar *in situ*. The plans were drawn up by W. H. Byrne & Son, Architects, Dublin, in 1929. (MS BN 192 [2]). © Provincial Archives, Sisters of Mercy, Bessbrook

In Meehan's opening letter to Miss Shiel he suggested that 'some one ought to write to Lord Charlemont for the marble fragments which he brought from Rome'. He continued: 'His mother told me that she had them … and that they should be inserted in the altar of the convent of Ballyshannon, and Lord Charlemont should be told this. He will not, I presume, refuse to see his mother's request realised.'[29] A month later Meehan wrote again to Miss Shiel suggesting that the primate might have the fragments, and failing that he urged her again to contact Lord Charlemont. He also vowed to 'take care of the fragments and see them properly inserted in the altar'.[30] That particular letter also reveals that Meehan advised on the design of the altar for the new convent. He suggested that the antependium or altar frontal should carry a motif executed on the entrance to the choir of the Irish Dominican church of San Clemente in Rome. Drawings of the proposed later extension and new chapel at St Catherine's in 1929 show the altar of 1880 *in situ* with a Latin cross on the antependium.[31]

The third letter in the sequence, dated 4 August 1880, is from the primate to Miss Shiel. He explained that Mrs Caulfeild had twice promised that she would send the tomb fragments to him, but that she had not in fact done so, and that she had since died, leaving the family residence, Hockley Hall in Armagh, to her daughter, Mrs Stronge. The primate believed that Mrs Caulfeild's daughter would 'carry out her mother's intentions'.[32] The next two letters, dated 6 and 10 August 1880 are from Mrs Stronge to Miss Shiel, and they are quite strained in tone. Mrs Stronge wrote: 'I remember that the tomb of the Earls was repaired under the direction of my brother Lord Charlemont when he was at Rome by my mother's desire.'[33] She pleaded that there were no marble fragments at Hockley Hall, and furthermore that her brother Lord Charlemont had 'never sent any marbles to Ireland', and that 'if any fragments were ever brought to this country, they never came into my mother's possession. Believe me'.[34]

On 12 August 1880, Meehan wrote to Miss Shiel to tell her that the new altar for the convent was packed and ready to go to Ballyshannon. He regretted that 'the valuable reliques must be lost, as Lord Charlemont seems to know nothing about them'.[35]

It is certain Charlemont considered the project irksome because of his distaste for Roman Catholics at that time, and also because thirty-six years had elapsed since his involvement in the restoration of the Irish memorials at San Pietro in Montorio. It is clear that both he and his sister did not know of their mother's intentions in respect of the 'relics' from the Irish memorials. In the meantime, Miss Shiel's sister, Sydney Shiel, had been doing some research on the Rome fragments. Writing some time in the autumn of 1880, she mentioned that she had sent 'all the documents I have about the relics from Rome'. She adds an important detail to this cat-and-mouse tale – information that Lord Charlemont's brother, Henry Caulfeild, may, before his untimely death in 1867, have delivered the fragments to Meehan.[36]

By November 1880 the marble fragments had materialised. Writing to the primate on the 20 of that month, Meehan briefly informed McGettigan that 'The marble fragments from the tombs of the earls, which the late Hon. Mrs Caulfeild destined for the altar of Ballyshannon Convent, have been for some time in my possession.'[37] Meehan gives no explanation as to how he had acquired the fragments or who had been keeping them. It may be the case that they were recovered among the possessions of the earl's brother Henry. However, it may also be of some interest that Meehan was on the continent in September 1880; it is conceivable, therefore, that the fragments had never been returned to Ireland in 1844, as Lord Charlemont maintained, and that Meehan had acquired them in Rome in September 1880. The primate subsequently wrote to Miss Shiel in early December suggesting that she 'may know some friend going to Dublin, who will call on Father Meehan and bring the Relics to Ballyshannon'.[38] The correspondence about the tomb fragments ends there.

A piece of Spanish broccatello inlay with an accompanying note in the provincial archives at Bessbrook confirm that the 'relics' from the restoration work on the Irish memorials at San Pietro in Montorio had been incorporated into the altar of St Catherine's Convent sometime before it officially opened in 1884. In 1929, during renovations to the convent, the 1880 altar was replaced with the exception of the reredos, which was incorporated into the 1929 altar.[39] One of the inlay fragments from Rome was also transferred to the new altar at that time while a second fragment was placed in the archive of St Catherine's. That piece of Spanish broccatello inlay, now housed in the provincial archives, is in fact a small corner piece (7 cm by 4 cm) of a rhombus inlay from the border of the tomb of Rory O'Donnell in San Pietro in Montorio. It exactly matches the colour of the Spanish broccatello in the border, and if one looks closely at the rhom-

Rhombus marble inlay from the memorial to Rory and Cathbharr O'Donnell in San Pietro in Montorio, Rome. Note the slightly different colour of the marble repair at the right-hand oblique angle of the rhombus. This may have replaced the fragment with the broken edge, which was returned from Rome for incorporation into the altar of St Catherine's convent at Ballyshannon in 1880. The fragment is housed in the Provincial Archives, Sisters of Mercy, Bessbrook.
© Provincial Archives, Sisters of Mercy, Bessbrook

bus inlay, the approximate former position of the broken fragment can be seen where it was replaced by a slightly larger piece of marble.

The seventeenth-century Irish memorials in San Pietro in Montorio enjoyed a renaissance in the nineteenth century, principally because of Elizabeth Caulfeild's concern to maintain her O'Donnell family interests. The restoration of the memorials in 1844, which she directed her son, James Molyneux Caulfeild, third earl of Charlemont, to initiate at Rome, took place at the height of O'Connell's Repeal movement. The commission to restore the memorials was given to John Hogan at the time when the Repeal Association, which 'had taken its proper place as the patron of nationality in art',[40] had also commissioned him to carve a colossal statue of O'Connell for City Hall in Dublin. Hogan became a participant in nationalist politics through the creation of monumental sculpture of Catholic subjects. At O'Connell's monster meeting on the hill of Mullaghmast in 1843, as the apogee of his involvement in nationalism, he placed the green velvet 'Repeal Cap' on O'Connell's head.[41] The restoration of the seventeenth-century Irish memorials at Rome became part of that nationalist landscape. They were the subject of report in national newspapers – such as *The Nation* – in 1844 and 1845, and the subscription list for the work on the monuments included names of those, such as Dominick O'Reilly, who were also subscribers to other sculpture commissions of nationalist Catholic origin.

It was again Elizabeth Caulfeild's reputed concern to have broken fragments from the Irish memorials, and more specifically from the O'Donnell monument (1608-09), in San Pietro in Montorio incorporated into the altar of St Catherine's Convent at Ballyshannon that brought the Irish monuments back into focus in the 1880s. Although McGettigan and Meehan both referred to the Rome fragments as 'relics', it is unclear whether they were regarded as semi-religious or simply as objects of patriotic value because they were associated with O'Donnell. The ambiguity on Meehan's part about the location of the fragments, and Lord Charlemont's denial that they had ever existed, suggests that the Ballyshannon project was problematic.

Notes

1 Thanks to Sister Helena Doherty, Archivist of the Provincial Archives, Bessbrook, for her assistance.
G. Alveri, *Della Roma in ogni stato* (2 vols, Rome, 1664), ii, pp 313-4.

2 Tadhg Ó Cianáin, *The Flight of the Earls, (*ed. & trans.) P. Walsh (Dublin, 1916), p. 241.

3 L. Cipriani, *Memorie istoriche del convento di S. Pietro in Montorio* (Rome, 1986), pp 151-2.

4 Pontifical Irish College, Rome Archives. The entry for Patricius Meehan in the registry of seminarians, Irish College, Rome, notes 'Presbyter 8th Feb. 1835' and 'Discessus 26th Feb. 1835.'

5 P. F. Moran, *History of the Catholic archbishops of Dublin since the Reformation* (Dublin, 1864), p. 466.

6 J. Healy, *Irish essays: literary and historical* (Dublin, 1908), pp 36-51.

7 P. de Barra and T. Ó Fiaich (eds), *Imeacht na nIarlaí* (Dublin, 1972).

8 F. Ó Fearghail, 'The tomb of Hugh O'Neill in San Pietro in Montorio in Rome', *Seanchas Ardmhacha*, xxi-xxii (2007-08), pp 69-85.

9 M. Kearney Walsh, *'Destruction by peace': Hugh O'Neill after Kinsale* (Armagh, 1986).

10 C. Carroll, 'Turas na nIarladh as Éire: international travel and national identity in Ó Cianán's narrative', *History Ireland*, xv, no. 4 (2007), pp 56-61.

11 E. FitzPatrick, *San Pietro in Montorio and the exilic landscape of the Irish in Rome, 1608-23* (forthcoming).

12 Ó Fearghail, 'The tomb of Hugh O'Neill', passim.

13 C. P. Meehan, *The fate and fortunes of Hugh O'Neill, earl of Tyrone and Rory O'Donel, earl of Tyrconnel* (1st ed., Dublin, 1868), p. 477.

14 Ó Fearghail, 'The tomb of Hugh O'Neill', pp 76-77.

15 Meehan, *Fate and fortunes*, 1st ed., p. 446.

16 P. L. Vannicelli, *S. Pietro in Montorio e il tempietto del Bramante* (Rome, 1971), p. 44; L. Cipriani, *Studio storico-giuridico di Luigi Cipriani: S. Pietro in Montorio & il tempietto del Bramante* (Rome, n.d), p. 107.

17 Vannicelli, *S. Pietro in Montorio*, p. 45.

18 *The Nation*, 20 Dec. 1845, p. 152.

19 Vannicelli, *S. Pietro in Montorio*, p. 50.

20 *Burke's peerage and baronetage* (London, 1980), pp 525, 1484.

21 PICR Archives, KIR/ 1844/319.

22 J. Turpin, *John Hogan: Irish neoclassical sculptor in Rome 1800-1858* (Dublin, 1982).

23 Ibid., pp 87-88, 144-5.

24 John Hogan's account book, entries for 26 Nov. 1842 and 21 Jan. 1843 (NLI, MS 4179).

25 Turpin, *John Hogan*, p. 153.

26 John Hogan's account book, entry for Apr. 20, 1844 (NLI, MS 4179).

27 Meehan, *Fate and fortunes* (2nd ed., Dublin, 1870), p. 511. Meehan makes no reference to the existence of the fragments in the first edition, published in 1868.

28 Meehan, *Fate and fortunes* (3rd ed., Dublin, 1886), p. 340.

29 C. P. Meehan to Miss Shiel, 25 Apr. 1880 (Provincial Archives, Bessbrook, MS BN. L. 1A).

30 C. P. Meehan to Miss Shiel, 16 May 1880 (ibid., MS BN. L. 1B).

31 Convent of Mercy Ballyshannon: proposed extension and new chapel, W. H. Byrne & Son Architects, Dublin (ibid., MS BN 192 [2]).

32 Abp McGettigan to Miss Shiel, 4 Aug. 1880 (ibid., MS BN. L.2).

33 Mrs Stronge to Miss Shiel, 6 Aug. 1880 (ibid., MS BN. L.3).

34 Mrs Stronge to Miss Shiel, 10 Aug. 1880 (ibid., MS BN. L.4).

35 C. P. Meehan to Miss Shiel, 12 Aug. 1880 (ibid., MS BN. L.5).

36 Sydney Sheil to Miss Shiel, [Autumn 1880] (ibid., MS BN. L.6).

37 C. P. Meehan to Abp McGettigan 20 Nov. 1880 (ibid., MS BN. L.7).

38 Abp McGettigan to Miss Shiel, 6 Dec. 1880 (ibid., MS BN. L.8).

39 Convent of Mercy Ballyshannon: proposed extension and new chapel, and plan of new altar, 1929 W. H. Byrne & Son Architects, Dublin (ibid., MS BN 192 [2] and [3]). When St Catherine's convent closed, the 1929 altar was transferred to the parish church in Ballyshannon.

40 Turpin, *John Hogan*, p. 81.

41 Ibid., p. 82.

The flight of the earls on-screen[1]

John Gibney

Irish history is often categorised as a story of sorts – with or without a happy ending, depending on one's perspective. Dramatic depictions of its events are comparatively rare on television or in the cinema. This was not always the case in the early years of cinematic production in Ireland, when directors and screen-writers extensively mined Irish history for dramatic material, usually as a deliberate ploy to appeal to an ethnic audience, particularly in the United States. The period between the rebellions of the United Irishmen in 1798 and Robert Emmet in 1803 emerged as the favoured time-frame: a deliberate inclination to avoid more contentious periods in favour of one that could be recast simply, and even then with an emphasis on the personal over the political.[2] But prospective depictions of the events and individuals related to the flight of the earls would be faced with the inevitable problem that it does not seem to present an obvious resolution, let alone a happy ending.

The only cinematic effort even tenuously related to the events of 1607 was the 1966 Disney production *The Fighting Prince of Donegal*, filmed at England's Pinewood Studios and starring the English actor Peter McEnery as Red Hugh O'Donnell.[3] Based on a novel of the same name by Robert T. Reilly, the dramatic core of the film focused on O'Donnell's vexed succession to the lordship of Tír Chonaill against a plausible backdrop of tension related to a potential Spanish invasion, along with his imprisonment and escape from Dublin Castle. Poetic and dramatic licence notwithstanding, the manner in which this was depicted was rather questionable: the costumes, locations and mannerisms – not to mention the accents – mirrored an English Tudor epic. As should probably be expected in any cinematic depiction of the Irish worth its salt, the predominantly English cast spoke in clipped and precise tones amidst much

Red Hugh's dramatic escape from Dublin Castle was given the Hollywood treatment in *The Fighting Prince of Donegal*, a 1966 Disney film starring Peter McEnery in the title role. The film was based on Robert T. Reilly's novel *Red Hugh: Prince of Donegal.* © Inch House Irish Studies Centre

drinking and fighting. Drink enabled the nefarious English to get the better of O'Donnell; the latter got his revenge by attacking, with the unlikely assistance of wheeled artillery, a castle occupied by the English, before driving them out, embarking upon much drinking and feasting, and finally getting the girl on the ramparts of a castle that bears a somehow appropriate resemblance to that at Bunratty Folk Park.

Despite its dubious depiction of the Irish (and their history), *The Fighting Prince of Donegal* ended at some indeterminate point with the rout of an English force and presumably all lived happily ever after. However, the actual events of the Nine Years War and the subsequent flight amply contest that resolution. A dramatic depiction of the career of O'Donnell or Hugh O'Neill would have to grapple with the fact that their careers ended in death or defeat; hence the film ended before it could even begin to depict the events of 1594-1603, let alone those of 1607. This proved an enduring dramatic problem; on the other side of 1607 is the narrative arc of Brian Friel's *Making History*, reliant as it is upon a superficial and clumsy depiction of O'Neill as defeated, exiled, and helplessly at the mercy of Peter Lombard's revisionist posterity. In both cases the facts stood in the way of the story. This may seem an obvious point, but the potential problems of representation inherent in a dramatised version of history cannot be over emphasized. This leaves open the alternative possibility of a broadly factual depiction in the form of a documentary.

Despite the relative dearth of Irish historical dramas, apart from major exceptions such as Neil Jordan's *Michael Collins* (1996) or Ken Loach's *The Wind that Shakes the Barley* (2006), Irish audiences have been reasonably well served in recent years by documentaries. The quality (and, occasionally, the integrity) of some of these productions can easily be questioned, but there has been a conscious effort on the part of public service broadcasters to address a general audience interested in Irish history. This has undoubtedly been true of major commemorative initiatives, such as those related to the Great Famine or the 1798 rebellion, both of which were well served on the small screen.[4] The flight of the earls was no different, as both BBC Northern Ireland and the Irish-language television channel TG4 commissioned major documentaries to be broadcast in the quatercentenary year.

In 2001 RTÉ commemorated the quatercentenary of the battle of Kinsale with a thrifty documentary that seemed to use the same handful of actors running around in slow motion to depict the thousands of English, Irish and Spanish soldiers involved in the battle. *Braveheart* it was not. On the other hand, for the corresponding anniversary of the flight of the earls, BBC Northern Ireland produced a lavish three-part documentary filmed in as many relevant Irish, English and European locations as

Making History by Brian Friel. © Field Day

seemed possible, resplendent with vivid contemporary images, sweeping shots from helicopters, mournful uilleann pipes, sailing ships, and grittily filmed reconstructions of the battles and skirmishes of the Nine Years War. In keeping with the production values of the series, these were far superior to what might usually be expected from such reconstructions: when it came to the ambush at the Ford of the Biscuits, there were no shortage of bodies to be strewn on the shore, or indeed of biscuits to float downstream.

The BBC documentary, entitled *The Flight of the Earls* and produced and presented by Antaine Ó Donnaile, adopted the perfectly sensible narrative form, and was originally broadcast in both English- and Irish-language versions in January-February 2007. The first two episodes covered the events of the Nine Years War and its consequences, with an inevitable emphasis on the enigmatic figure of Hugh O'Neill. The symbolic value of the flight, coming between the war and the plantation of Ulster, easily overshadows the actual event itself; in this case, explaining the context in which it took place assumed paramount importance.

These two episodes dealt with the provocative Elizabethan encroachments upon the Ulster chieftains in

the 1580s and 1590s, through the battles of the Yellow Ford and Kinsale, the subsequent scorched-earth campaign in Ulster, and the eventual Treaty of Mellifont. This set the stage for the subject of the third (and best) episode: the actual departure of O'Neill and O'Donnell in September 1607. This final episode, which could easily have stood alone, dealt with the flight itself and the subsequent wanderings of O'Neill and his cohorts through the courts and cities of Europe. Having landed in northern France, the earls repaired to Louvain in Spanish Flanders, where their presence proved sensitive against the backdrop of negotiations between the Dutch (aligned with England) and Albert, archduke of Austria, who governed the Spanish Netherlands on behalf of Philip III of Spain.

It was from here that their wanderings began, travelling through France, and even risking detours through Protestant regions of Germany on their winding road to Rome, where the exiled earls would find their final resting-places. This is often the most neglected part of the story, but this third documentary ably filled the gap. Philip III viewed O'Neill as a potentially useful asset should hostilities against England recommence, though he did little to reciprocate the latter's fervent hope that the Spanish would provide him with an invasion fleet. The English remained fearful of O'Neill's return to spearhead another war that they would have been hard pressed to deal with, even though the inclination to do so was there: there was no shortage of blood-curdling contemporary English testimonies utilised throughout the series to reveal the extent of their contempt for, and hostility towards, the Irish. The English authorities would have preferred to see O'Neill dead, but were content as he travelled farther and farther from Ireland, towards the final and fruitless Roman exile that lies at the core of Friel's *Making History*.

The flight is a good story, which is well told here. The vivid reconstructions were bolstered by the stunning locations: London, El Escorial, the Irish College at Louvain, Nancy, Lucerne (and Lake Lucerne), rugged Alpine passes, Milan, Florence and finally Rome. While it began at a leisurely pace, as the series got into its stride the quality of the production and the inherent drama of the events made it compelling viewing.

However, the significance of these unfolding events, while often referred to, was not fleshed out in detail; the narrative allowed for only one voice, whereas a few 'talking heads' scattered throughout the series to unpick the meaning of those events would have been useful. The flight came after a war that devastated Ireland and nearly bankrupted the crown and had the potential to destroy English rule in Ireland. The removal of the earls and the confiscation of their lands opened the door to the Ulster plantation. That the rebellion of Sir Cathair O'Doherty (1608), and its ruthless suppression, is depicted in the third episode clearly implies that matters might have been different had O'Neill stayed put.

These are relatively minor quibbles; another way of looking at this issue in the quatercentenary year is that it could whet the appetite to know more. For many of the viewing public, this series may well have been their main encounter with the four-hundredth anniversary of the flight. By telling the story of the events around the flight, this series offered a perfect introduction to this watershed event: a model of public service broadcasting. Even for those familiar with it, the richness of the three episodes made them well worth viewing in order to put flesh on the bones of one of Irish history's more compelling stories.

The other major documentary to be broadcast in the quatercentenary year was another product of public service broadcasting: TG4's award winning *Imeacht na nIarlaí*, originally shown on 16 September 2007. This had a longer gestation than might have been expected: the producer, Bláithín Ní Chatháin, had researched and written the script over the course of the previous three years, having been intrigued by the story after a period of residence in Rome in the 1990s, and the development of the production had been strongly supported by TG4 during that time. Unlike its BBC counterpart, this was a drama-documentary, with dramatisations rather than reconstructions to the fore.

The most noteworthy aspect of this hybrid production was the presence of Stephen Rea, reprising the pivotal role of Hugh O'Neill that he had played in the original Field Day production of *Making History*. Ironically, *Imeacht na nIarlaí* deliberately coun-

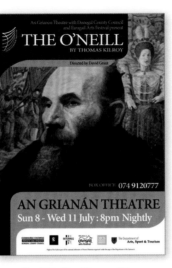

The O'Neill by Thomas Kilroy.
© Seán Ó Brógáin

teracted the impression given by Friel's play (and by Sean O'Faolain's *The Great O'Neill*, the melancholic epilogue of which may have shaped that playwright's vision) of Hugh O'Neill as a broken and disillusioned exile, and to the notion that, as Friel had put it, O'Neill 'ran away'. This impression ran counter to scholarship that actually pre-dated the play; rather that lapsing into morose exile after 1607, O'Neill continued to seek continental assistance with which to return to Ireland and continue his struggle.[5] The dramatisations in *Imeacht na nIarlaí* were evidently intended to reflect this. The dialogue in these scenes is often sourced verbatim from a wide range of contemporary primary accounts, in English, Irish or Spanish, some of which were translated into Irish for the production (indeed, Rea, whose contribution to the production was of vital importance in getting it made, had to learn his Irish lines phonetically).

Imeacht na nIarlaí consciously avoided replicating the BBC series. Obvious parallels existed between the two productions: for example many of the same locations (such as the Irish College at Louvain, and Lake Lucerne), by necessity, appear in both. The third episode of the BBC production provided a much fuller treatment; the TG4 documentary was a far more circumscribed affair than its counterpart. It was thus obliged to deal in broad brush-strokes, as the single production hour was devoted to the flight itself, which had been the subject of only one episode of the BBC series, a luxury that had been exploited to the full. *Imeacht na nIarlaí* compensated for its tighter focus in a number of imaginative ways: using Tadhg Ó Cianáin's narrative as a framing device, while a significant running commentary in the form of a fireside chat between the historians Éamonn Ó Ciardha, Micheál Ó Siochrú and Margaret Mac-Curtain, comprehensively examined the motives for the flight. This was an obvious advantage the TG4 production had over its counterpart; for example, the suggestion contained in the BBC series that the flight was a vital turning-point was challenged in the commentary interspersed through the TG4 production. The BBC series had taken the form of a traditional narrative; TG4's version opted for a more discursive and impressionistic format.

However, this may have been a necessity: tighter budgetary constraints hamstrung the TG4 production. Again, imaginative attempts sought to overcome this, most evidently in the dramatic reconstructions filmed at Ardmore Studios. The director, Paul Larkin (a former European journalist of the year), and the lighting cameraman, Ronan Fox, created a distinctive visual style inspired by both the minimalist sets of Derek Jarman's *Edward II* and the particular contrast between light and shade found in the paintings of Caravaggio. However, without prior knowledge of the inspiration behind them, the reconstructions in themselves could at the very least seem incongruous. The same could be said of the musical soundtrack. While uilleann pipes may almost be a cliché in documentaries and dramas about Irish history, they seem to provide a more appropriate soundtrack to the events of the early seventeenth century than Massive Attack, Portishead, and Bob Dylan's apocalyptic 'A hard rain's a-gonna fall'. These cosmetic issues did not necessarily detract from the substantive content, best reflected in Larkin's award for best director of a foreign documentary for *Imeacht na nIarlaí* at the New York International Independent Film and Video Festival in 2008.

The production of new and often innovative scholarship characterised the anniversaries of both the Famine and the 1798 rebellion; historical episodes

Poster advertising TG4's *Flight of the Earls / Imeacht na nIarlaí* (2007) with Stephen Rea in the role he espoused in Brian Friel's *Making History*.
© Bláithín Ní Chatháin

BBC's *Imeacht na nIarlaí / Flight of the Earls* (2007).
© Antaine Ó Donnaile and BBC NI

that attracted considerable public interest, as reflected (particularly in the case of the 1798 commemoration) by a proliferation of public events. The specialised nature of such new scholarship meant that the conclusions it had reached did not automatically extend beyond a specialised audience. In the case of the flight, the various conferences, symposia, scholarly articles and commemorations provided more specific and detailed versions of the event and its contexts; what was still required was a general account to introduce and outline the bare bones of the subject at hand. BBC Northern Ireland, and to a lesser extent TG4, provided two such accounts.

The strengths and weaknesses of the two respective documentaries cancelled each other out, and given that the BBC presenters also produced and broadcast an Irish version, a case surely existed for a single showcase co-production between the various public broadcasters on the island. It is a remarkable indictment of RTÉ that, for reasons best known to themselves, they did not contribute to either one of these productions, nor did they bring their considerable resources to bear on the quatercentenary of the flight, just as they had done in similar commemorative projects in 1995 and 1998. There will be other opportunities, as there will be other anniversaries. Whether such a collective effort is ever made, however, is a question only time will answer.

Notes

1 This article incorporates material originally published in *History Ireland*, xv, no 4 (2007). I would like to thank Bláithín Ní Chatháin for her assistance in preparing this article.

2 K. Rockett, 'Representations of Irish history in fiction films made prior to the 1916 rising', in L. Geary (ed.), *Rebellion and remembrance in modern Ireland* (Dublin, 2001), pp 214-28.

3 For details of the production see K. Rockett, *The Irish filmography: fiction films, 1896-1996* (Dublin, 1996), pp 175-6.

4 RTÉ produced two major documentary series for each commemoration: Louis Marcus's *Famine*, originally broadcast in November-December 1995; and Kevin Dawson's *Rebellion*, originally broadcast in May 1998.

5 In particular, M. Kerney Walsh, '*Destruction by peace*: Hugh O Neill after Kinsale (Armagh, 1986), pp 69, 85-86, 91-93, 130-7. The issue of the contradiction between the historical O'Neill and Friel's depiction, with particular reference to *Imeacht na nIarlaí* is raised in 'An Irishman's Diary', *Irish Times*, 14 Sept. 2007.

Imeacht na nIarlaí: ó na hAnnála chun an scáileáin

Antaine Ó Donnaile

Ba mhór an phribhléid agam é a bheith ag léiriú agus ag láithriú na sraithe *Imeacht na nIarlaí* don BBC. D'fhás an t-údar aníos i measc dhroimníní thuaisceart Ard Mhacha, áit a bhfuair Ó Néill an bua ba mhó a bhí aige ariamh ar fhórsaí na Banríona Eilís i Lúnasa na bliana 1598. Tharraing Béal an Átha Bhuí clú agus cáil ar Ó Néill mar shaighdiúr agus nuair a d'imigh sé ón tír naoi mbliana ina dhiaidh sin, Méan Fómhair na bliana 1607, bhí se ina laoch go fóill ag Caitlicigh na mór-roinne mar ar gheall ar an bhua sin in Ard Mhacha.

Baineann freagracht mhór le clár teilifíse a dhéanamh ar an tréimhse chinniúnach chorrach sin i stair na tíre. Nuair nach bhfuil na pobail éagsúla in hÉireann aontaithe faoin am i láthair, gan a bheith ag caint ar an am atá thart, is achrannach an mhaise é a bheith ag iarraidh léargas a thabhairt ar an stair do lucht féachana ginearálta.

Ar an dea-uair, bhí mé in ann cuid mhaith den ualach sin a bhaint díom féin trína roinnt le daoine eile. Chun tosaigh orthu sin, bhí an tOllamh John McGurk, iar-cheannasaí ar roinn na staire in Ollscoil Hope, Learpholl. Léigh sé go mionn na leaganacha éagsúla den scriopt a chuir me chuige de réir mar a d'fhorbair an tsraith anuas go dtí an taifeadadh deireannach fuaime. Thug sé comhairle agus moltaí go fial flaithiúil dom agus d'fhoghlaim mé cuid mhór uaidh, ní amháin ar an stair ach ar bhuanna an duine daonna chomh maith agus ar an chríonnacht a thagann le taithí saoil agus le dearcadh dearfach.

Agus mé ag taisteal na mór-roinne, bhí leabhar Thomáis Uí Fhiaich i mo ghlaic i rith an bhealaigh. Eagran de théacs Uí Chianáin é, aistrithe go nua-Ghaeilge ag Pádraig de Barra mar aon le notaí cuimsitheacha Uí Fhiaich. Cé nach dtiocfadh leis a dhéanamh in aon turas amháin, caithfidh gur shiúil Ó Fiaich gach aon choiscéim den bhealach ó Quillboeuf na Fraince go dtí an Róimh agus gur labhair sé le go leor daoine sna ceantair trína ndeachaidh sé. B'iontach an áis againn í mar leabhar; cuntas Uí Chianáin féin mar aon le mion-notaí údarasacha ar na bailte, ar an turas is ar thoscaí polaitiúla na linne. Ba léir dom, fosta, nach mé an chéad duine a bhain leas as an tsaothar áirithe sin, ná baol air;

Imeacht na nIarlaí. © Antaine Ó Donnaile agus BBC NI agus Ionad an Léinn Éireannaigh, Teach Inse

nuair a shiúil mé isteach san Eaglais San Pietro in Montorio, an teampall galánta ornáideach inár adhlacadh Aodh Ó Néill, a mhac Aodh agus Ruairí Ó Domhnaill, bheannaigh seansagart Iodaileach dom i mBéarla, a rá: 'You are from Ireland. You are here for O'Neill'. D'aithin sé gur Éireannach mé ar an leabhar bheag bhuí sin a bhí i mo ghlaic.

Ceann de na rudaí ba mhó a chuaigh i bhfeidhm orm le linn dom a bheith ag déanamh na gclár téil-ifíse, a bheith i mo sheasamh ansin san eaglais sin sa Róimh, an áit a bhfuil cnámha Uí Néill ina luí, na céadta mílte ar shiúil ón áit a dtáinig sé ar an tsaol i nDún Geanainn agus ó Ard Mhacha, áit ar mhian leis a bheith sínte ag taobh a mhuintire. An phian, an crá, an chailliúint daonna, an tábhacht do stair na hÉireann agus do stair na hEorpa, tá na eilimintí sin uilig le mothú ann i gcónaí.

An dara leabhar a bhfuil a lorg go smíor ar an tsraith, ná '*Destruction by peace*: Hugh O'Neill after

Kinsale, de chuid Micheline Kerney Walsh. Is iontach an éacht a rinne sí i gcartlanna idirnáisiúnta ag aimsiú na gcaipéisí sin a bhaineann leis na taoisigh Ghaelacha.

Sula ndeachaidh muid a scannánú sa Chartlann Ghineáralta i Simancas na Spáinne, bhí sé ar ár gcumas cóipeanna de na cáipéisí uilig atá istigh inti a bhaineann le Ó Néill a scrúdú roimh ré i leabhar Kerney Walsh is nuair a bhain muid Simancas amach bhí na cáipéisí sin ina luí romhainn, réidh don scannánú.

Sna cáipéisí sin sa Spáinn gheibh muid aithne eile ar fad ar Ó Néill agus ar na hiarlaí ón aithne a fhaigheann muid sna cáipéisí Béarla. De réir na gcartlanna Sasanacha fuair Ó Néill bás ina photaire gan dóchas, ag cailleadh muiníne chomh maith le radharc na súl de réir mar a chuaigh sé anonn in aois. Ach a bhuíoch sin do scoláirí ar nós Uí Fhiaich agus Kerney Walsh, a d'athraigh an leagan oifigiúil den scéal lena saothar ollmhór i gcartlanna na mórroinne, is féidir linn a fheiceáil gur duine éirimiúil, fuinniúil é nár chaill an tsíoraidhm amháin a bhí aige chun pilleadh ar a dhúiche féin. Míonna beaga sular éag sé i 1616 agus é sé bliana is trí scór d'aois, mar shampla, d'eagraigh Ó Néill iarracht mhór dheireannach amháin le pilleadh chun an bhaile, faoi arm agus eideadh. Scríobh sé:

Is dearbh linn, sinn atá beo, nach bhfanam leis an lá náireach nuair a bheidh Sacsanaigh i gceannas iomlán ár ndúichí, nuair a bheidh ár dteampaill scriosta agus ár gclann meallta acu. Lenár mbeatha féin gheobhaimid an leigheas anois, an scian lenár mbráid, óir ba olc cinnte moill a dhéanamh.

Ach toisc gur dhiúltaigh na Spáinnigh an cuidiú a bhí uaidh a thabhairt, theip ar Ó Néill ina aidhm. Chreid sé go daingean go dtiocfadh athghabháil na hÉireann a chur i gcrích ar bheagán tacaíochta ón Spáinn. Thuig sé sa deireadh nach bhfaighfeadh sé sin.

Maidir le déanamh físiúil na sraithe, bhain go leor dúshlánna leis an obair. Cé gur scéal corrach, corraitheach atá i gceist, lán dóchais, dainséir agus drámaíochta, is beag ábhar físiúil atá ar fáil don léiritheoir teilifíse leis an scéal a léiriú. Tá, ar ndóigh, go leor cáipéisí agus pictiúirí de chuid na haimsire sin atá iontach spéisiúil ar fad ach dá shuimiúla iad ní leor iad amháin le clár spreagúil sultmhar a dhéanamh. Bhí agam agus ag mo chomhghleacaí Gary McCutcheon, a scannánaigh agus a chuir ea-

gar ar an tsraith, le bheith ag smaoineamh ar sheifteanna eile chun an scéal a léiriú. Ar an tseift ba mhó acu sin bhí an t-athchruthú stairiúil.

Bhí an t-ádh linn margadh maith a dhéanamh leis an chomhlacht The Square Sail Company, úinéirí na loinge *The earl of Pembroke* a d'úsáid muid sa chlár. Tá an soitheach céanna le feiceáil in *Apocalypto*, scannán de chuid Mel ('Mellifont Colum Cille') Gibson. Sheol muid an t-aistear uilig ó Bhéal Feirste go deisceart na Breataine agus rinne muid míreanna drámatúla a scannánú ar bord, chomh maith le cuid mhór den tráchtaireacht. Chuir pictiúirí na loinge go mór leis an tsraith.

Lena chois sin bhí sé d'ádh orainn seirbhísí comhlachta athchruthaithe staire, Irish Arms, a bheith againn. Bunús na ndaoine agus na n-uirlísí atá le feiceáil ar an scáileán, ba Irish Arms a sholáthar. Gnáthdhaoine a bhí i mbunús na n-aisteoirí a raibh a gcroí istigh sa stair, agus bhí gach duine acu cóirithe díreach mar ba cheart, idir arm agus éideadh, de réir nósmhaireacht na h-aimsire. Sna tréimhsí ba ghnoithí scannánaíochta, bhí thart ar tríocha fear againn, sé chapall agus púdar á phléascadh go fras. Trí úsáid a bhaint as seatanna teanna agus éifeachtaí fuaime, d'fhéach muid lena chur i gcéill go raibh na mílte i mbun troda. Is dóigh liom gur éirigh linn a bheag nó a mhór.

Agus muid ag iarraidh an oiread físiúlachta agus éagsúlachta a chur isteach sa tsraith, mheas muid go gcuirfeadh ealaíon agus ceol nua-chumtha go mór le heispearas an lucht éisteachta. D'iarr muid ar Brian Vallely, ealaíontóir clúiteach de chuid Ard Mhacha, pictiúir a dhéanamh don tsraith a bhain leis na téamaí agus leis na himeachtaí ann agus d'iarr muid ar a mhac Niall ceol úr a chumadh di. Thaitin go mór liom an plé a bhí agam le Brian agus le Niall faoi na pictiúir, faoin cheol agus faoi na fadbhanna a thugann an stair don ealaíontóir, don chumadóir agus don déantóir cláir. D'fhoghlaim mé go leor óna gcuid físe agus talainne. Tá cruthaithe ag Brian agus ag Niall, trína gcomhbhá tuisceannach leis na téamaí, saothair bheo bhríomhara, lán paisin agus fuinnimh, a chuireann ina luí orainn an costas daonna a bhí le híoc le linn an choncais Éilisigh. Ach saothair dhearfacha dheimhneacha iad ina dhiaidh sin. Freagraí croíúla, cruthaitheacha iad do tharlúintí uafásacha.

Chomh maith le bheith ina scéal epiciúil staire, lena mhórimpleachtaí stairiúla agus comhaimseartha, is scéal daonna é seo thar aon ní eile. Scéal indibhidí ildánacha, a raibh beatha iontu agus dóchas, a d'fhulaing agus a d'éag le linn don stair a bheith á múnlú. Daoine iad a d'iompair na himeachtaí móra staire ar a ndroim.

Éireannaigh a raibh fíorbheagán Béarla acu, nár imigh riamh níb fhaide ná roinnt mílte óna mbailte, fuair siad iad féin mar shaighdiúirí in ollairm ocracha, i gcathanna eachtracha na céadta míle ar shiúil. Buachaillí aimsire, feirmeoirí agus bacaigh as Sasain, baineadh iad de na páirceanna agus de na bealtaí agus seoladh iad anall go hÉirinn le troid i dtír fhuar, fhliuch, chogadh-réabtha in éadán namhad nár aithin siad agus nár thuig siad. B'iomaí tréigeoir ó arm na Sasanach, rud a fhágann an nath cainte againn, 'Is fearr crochadh i mBristó ná bás an mhadaidh in Éirinn'. I measc thuataí na hÉireann, chaoin mná go ciúin le linn dá gcuid páistí a bheith á dtabhairt ar shiúil ag an ghorta ar chuir na fórsaí Sasannacha tús leis d'aon turas.

In amanna, bíonn cuma na nádúrthachta, cuma an chirt, ar an ord ina dtarlaíonn imeachtaí stairiúla, ach rud eile a chuaigh i bhfeidhm orm agus mé ag scrúdú na tréimhse seo don teilifís nach féidir neamhaird a dhéanamh den ról a bhíonn ag taismí sa stair. Maidir leis an choncas Éiliseach is minic a thugtar an cuntas simplí gur tháinig deireadh le Cogadh na Naoi mBlian ag Cath Chionn tSáile agus gurbh é sin a thug ar na taoisigh Ghaelacha teitheadh. Daofa sin a mhair fríd an tréimhse, ní raibh réamhchinniúint ag baint le cinneadh daonna nó le toisc ar bith. Ní raibh a fhios cad é an deireadh a bheadh ar ócáid nó ar imeacht ar bith agus ag pointe ar bith thiocfadh leis an aimsir, leis an tseans nó leis an nádúr daonna cor a chur i stair na hÉireann, agus i stair an domhain fiú. Mar shampla, i ndiaidh Bhéal an Atha Bhuí, bhí réimeas Éilis in Éirinn ar thairseach a scriosta ach níor rug Ó Néill ar a bhuntáiste. Na saighdiúirí gallda a tháinig slán as an ár lig sé daofa imeacht agus níor ionsaí sé Baile Átha Cliath. Ní fios cén fáth.

Corradh agus trí bliana ina dhiaidh sin, ag Léigear Chionn tSáile sa bhliain 1601, bhí saighdiúirí Sasanacha ag fáil bháis den ocras agus den fhuacht i ndúlaíocht an gheimhridh go dtí gur thug Ó Néill isteach d'argóintí Aodha Ruaidh Uí Dhomhnaill ionsaí tobann a dhéanamh ag breacadh lae. Seachrán i measc na nUltach i gceantair neamhaitheanta a thug buntáiste do na Gaill. Rinneadh slad ar na Gaeil agus mairíodh 1,300 díobh. Chaillfí a thuilleadh ach ab é go raibh eachra na nGall stiúgtha leis an ocras.

Scríobhtar go minic gurbh é Cath Chionn tSáile a d'fhógair deireadh an tseansaoil Ghaelaigh agus nach raibh de rogha ag lucht caillte an chatha ach imeacht as Éirinn. Arís, ní raibh cúrsaí chomh néata sin; athcheapadh Ó Néill ina thiarna ar Thír Eoghain ag

Trí íomhanna de 'Chath Bhéal an Átha Bhuí'
© NLI and Brian Vallely

deireadh an chogaidh breis agus bliain ina dhiaidh sin arís i 1603 agus tugadh bunús a chuid tailte ar ais dó. D'imigh ceithre bliana eile thart sular fhág sé slán ag an tír i gcuideachta na n-uaisle eile.

Roinnt factóirí a thug ar Aodh Ó Néill, ar Ruairí Ó Domhnaill agus ar Chúchonnacht Mhag Uidhir imeacht sa bhliain 1607. Chuaigh daorsmacht pholaitiúil, dhlíthiúil agus reiligiúna a d'fhulaing siad faoi lámha an leas-rí, Arthur Chichester, agus a chuid oifigeach, i bhfeidhm go mór orthu. Lena chois, cuireadh ina leith gur ghlac said páirt i gcomhcheilg in éadán na corónach. Gabhadh Mag Uidhir agus cuireadh i bpríosún é i 1606. Ar a scaoileadh saor, d'éalaigh sé chun na mór-roinne, áit ar fhos-

Siniú Uí Néill, 1594 agus 1601.

taigh sé long Bhriotánach, cuireadh cuma soithigh iascaireachta uirthi agus d'fhill sé ar Éirinn lena chomhuaisle a thabhairt chun sábháilteachta. Bhí Ó Néill i gCaisleán Shláine le haghaidh 'comhchainteanna' le Chichester nuair a fuair sé scéal na loinge. Bhí aige le cinneadh gasta a dhéanamh cé acu an imeodh sé nó an bhfanfadh sé. Ba rogha chinniúnach eile í sin i stair na hÉireann agus thiocfadh di gabháil ceachtar den dá bhealach. I ndeireadh na dála, shíl Ó Néill go raibh a bheatha i mbaol. Bhí sé i ndiaidh rabhadh a fháil ó chairde sa chúirt i Londain. Lena chois sin, bhí a fhios aige dá n-imeodh Mag Uidhir agus Ó Domhnaill gan é, go mbeadh tuilleadh amhrais faoi féin, agus ar an ábhar sin, bheartaigh sé a bheith leo ar an long a bhí ar ancaire i Loch Suillí.

Ag mean-oíche ar 4 Meán Fómhair 1607, sheol an long amach as Loch Súillí agus naonúr déag agus ceithre scór ar bord, baill de theaghlaigh uaisle Uladh. Bhí sé ar cheann de na turais ba shuntasaí agus ba thábhachtaí i stair na hÉireann. Réitigh sé an bealach do phlandáil Uladh. Sheasadh sé do dheireadh an tseanoird Ghaelaigh agus do chur i gcrích an choncais Ghallda in Éirinn, idir dhlíthiúil agus mhíleata. Ní raibh sé ariamh i gceist ag na hIarlaí, áfach, imeacht ar fad gan súil le pilleadh. Ba é a mbuanchuspóir teacht ar ais le cuidiú míleata agus airgid ón Spáinn lena gcuid tailte agus cumhachta a bhaint ar ais.

Mheas roinnt d'Uaisle Gaelacha a d'fhán in Éirinn go dtiocfadh leo leas a bhaint as na toscaí úra faoin réimeas úr, ach in aisce. Ar an iomlán, ba thragóid ag na Gaeil é Imeacht na nIarlaí. Ba de theaghlach traidisiúnta fílíochta de chuid Chlann Aodha Bhuidhe Uí Néill é Fear Flatha Ó Gnímh. Go gairidh i ndiaidh na plandála scríobh sé an dán caointeach *Beannacht ar anmain Éireann*:

Beannacht ar anmain Éireann,
inis na gcéimeann gcorrach:

atá Treabh Briain na mbogglór
dom dhóigh ar dhobrón torrach.

Ionann is éag na Fódla
ceilt a córa 's a creidimh,
táire a saormhac 's a saoithe,
más fíor laoithe ná leitir.

Deacair nach bás don Bhanba
d'éis an tréid chalma churadh
do thriall ar toisg don Easbáin
mo thruaighe beangáin Uladh.

Ní leigeann eagla an ghallsmaicht
damh a hanstaid do nochtadh:
atá an chríoch réidhse ríNéill
do chrú fíréin dá folcadh.

Léiríonn Ó Gnímh go sóiléir dearcadh na nGael ar imeacht na dtaoiseach agus ar phlandáil Uladh. Do na Gaeil ba thréimhse scéine agus sceimhle í, ina raibh díbirt na ndúchasaithe, ollmharú cine agus athrú réimis. Ach ina dhiaidh sin agus uile níor chóir a mheas mar olltragóid aontomhaiseach amháin.

Le linn na tréimhse, bhí Éire agus muintir na hÉireann ag croí na polaitíochta idirnáisiúnta le linn don nuaEoraip a bheith á múnlú. Chuir sé síolta an phobail mhóir thábhachtaí sin de bhunadh na hÉireann ar an mhór-roinn a raibh tionchar aige go cionn i bhfad ar chúrsaí míleata, acadúla, polaitiúla agus reiligiúnda in Éirinn. Sa tseachtú céad déag tháinig bláthú ar fhilíocht agus ar litríocht na Gaeilge agus mhéadaigh líon na gcainteoirí Gaeilge, in ainneoin a n-easpa cumhachta agus stadais, suas go dtí na 1840í. Tháinig athbheochan eile ar chúrsaí Gaeilge sa naoú céad déag mar aon le borradh eile faoin litríocht agus faoi na h-ealaíona.

Spreag Imeacht na nIarlaí glúin i ndiaidh glúine de fhilí, scríbhneoirí agus d'ealaíontóirí san il-iomad teangacha agus mean; ón fhile Gaelach Eoghan Ruadh Mac an Bhaird, a bhí ar an long leis na hIarlaí, go James Clarence Mangan, Sean O'Faolain, John Montague, Thomas Ryan, Tomas Kilroy, Brian Friel agus Diarmaid Ó Doibhlin. Ba chóir na pictiúirí agus dealbhanna úra de chuid Sheáin Uí Bhrogáin, Seoirse Uí Dhochartaigh, John Conway, John Behan, Maurice Harron, Brian Vallely, agus saothar ceoil a mhic Niall a áireamh mar chuid luachmhar den chorpus céanna sin. Bhéinn iontach sásta dá n-amharcfaí ar an tsraith BBC mar iarracht mhacánta eile fhreagairt don cheist chéanna.

'Aodh Mór Ó Néill ag fágáil slán ag
Ráth Maoláin'. © Seán Ó Brógáin